The Best Book of:

of:

dBASE IV

RELATED TITLES

Best Book of: Lotus® 1-2-3®, Second Edition
Alan Simpson

Lotus® 1-2-3® Financial Models
Elna Tymes and Tony Dowden with Charles E. Prael

Best Book of: Microsoft® Works for the PC
Ruth Witkin

Best Book of: WordPerfect®, Version 5.0
Vincent Alfieri

WordPerfect 5.0: Expert Techniques
Kate Barnes

Best Book of: WordStar® (Features Release 4)
Vincent Alfieri

Best Book of: WordStar 5.0
Vincent Alfieri

Best Book of: OS/2 Database Manager
Howard Fosdick

dBASE III PLUS™ Programmer's Library
Joseph-David Carrabis

dBASE III PLUS ™ Programmer's Reference Guide
Edward C. Jones

dBASE IV™ Programmer's Reference Guide
Edward Jones

dBASE Mac® Programmer's Reference Guide
Edward C. Jones

Understanding dBASE IV™
Judd Robbins

Understanding dBASE IV™ Programming *(forthcoming)*
Judd Robbins

The Best Book of: DOS. Includes Version 4.0 *(forthcoming)*
Alan Simpson

The Waite Group's Using PC-DOS™ *(forthcoming)*
The Waite Group

For the retailer nearest you, or to order directly from the publisher, call 800-428-SAMS. In Indiana, Alaska, and Hawaii call 317-298-5699.

The Best Book of:

Joseph-David Carrabis

fff

HOWARD W. SAMS & COMPANY

A Division of Macmillan, Inc.
4300 West 62nd Street
Indianapolis, Indiana 46268 USA

International Standard Book Number: 0-672-22652-9
Library of Congress Catalog Card Number: 89-61054

Acquisitions Editor: *Greg Michael*
Developmental Editor: *C. Herbert Feltner*
Manuscript Editor: *Susan Pink, TechRight*
Cover Art: *DGS&D Advertising, Inc.*
Cover Photography: *Cassell Productions, Inc.*
Indexer: *Brown Editorial Services*
Compositor: *Shepard Poorman Communications, Indianapolis*

Printed in the United States of America

Trademarks

To Jim Kreinbring, who treated me with
respect and dignity and offered guidance.

Other Books by the Author

dBASE III Advanced Programming (Que Corporation)

Using Javelin (with Dave Ewing, Que Corporation)

dBASE III PLUS: The Complete Reference
    (Osborne/McGraw-Hill)

dBASE III PLUS Advanced Programming (Que Corporation)

dBASE III PLUS Programmer's Library
    (Howard W. Sams & Company)

Hard Disk Management Techniques for the IBM
    (Howard W. Sams & Company)

dBASE III PLUS Network & Multi-User Systems (MIS books)

The Best Book of: Quattro (with Tom Perkins,
    Howard W. Sams & Company)

Overview

Contents

P   A   R   T

dBASE IV Basics

P   A   R   T

Beginning dBASE IV 61

P   A   R   T

three

Making Things Work Better in dBASE IV   319

P A R T

four

Appendices 497

Preface

For readers familiar with the play, movie, or soundtrack to *Jesus Christ, Superstar,* you may remember the refrain "What's the buzz? Tell me what's happening."

That is pretty much the plague that has followed Ashton-Tate's dBASE IV product for the past year. Much of this is to be expected. The microcomputer database market is turbulent. Ashton-Tate's dBASE III Plus is the king of the hill, with some 80 percent of the microcomputer database market, and there are many usurpers to the throne. I won't pin a qualitative value on any of Ashton-Tate's challengers, but I will tell you what I have experienced in the past: You have to stay hungry to win. When you get comfortable, you get lazy. You don't see threats where you should, and eventually you get ousted from the throne.

That is what has been happening in the microcomputer database market. Now, more than ever, with microcomputers that truly can do what it took a roomful of machinery to do twenty years ago, you have the capability to give users some useful software. I am not saying the existing slurry of microcomputer software isn't useful. I am saying that the current crop of software is exactly what its name implies: microcomputer software. It is designed for one person to sit down at a computer at one time. That was great two years ago. People were going nuts with the power in their hands ("Look, Marge! I can make a spreadsheet with 64,000 active cells!" Sixty-four thousand active cells? Yes, well, the next time I want to calculate a stress analysis of the Golden Gate bridge, that's the product I'll use.) What happened in the microcomputer market had to do with user needs expanding beyond computer capabilities. End users got more power on their desks and therefore wanted more powerful software. More powerful software wasn't a doable option on standard PCs (and even on first string ATs).

Users wanted more power, and computer designers gave it to them. Behold the 386 machine. Wonder of wonders, miracle of miracles. This is an impressive machine for more than the obvious, boy-is-it-fast reason.

It is impressive because it is the first relatively inexpensive machine to bring minicomputer power to the individual user. We must answer, "What is minicomputer power?" The obvious answer has nothing to do with MIPS (millions of instructions per second) or having an eight billion gigabyte drive. The real answer has to do with a computer's capability to share work among several users.

"Networks?" you say. "Networks have been around for a long time. This author doesn't know what he's talking about."

No, no. I don't mean networks as most people know them. Microcomputer networks have been around for several years. They are universally slow, trepidant, and prone to difficulties when you least need difficulties (Murphy designs microcomputer networks, I think.) This isn't due to problems with the software; it is due to the architecture of the machines that the networks run on. Ever hear "You can't squeeze blood from a turnip"? You might instead say "You can't get reasonable response time in a multiuser environment from a machine designed to be used by a single user."

And that is what all previous microcomputers were. They were designed for one user. You asked them to do several things for several users and they did one of three things:

1. They made like they were Lenny talking to George in *Of Mice and Men*: "Tell me about the rabbits, George."

2. They forgot where they put things: things like your balance sheet, your corporate sponsor list, the last chapter of your book.

3. They looked at all the user requests coming at them, put on a trench coat, and pulled a Howard Beale, "I'm mad as hell, and I'm not going to take this anymore!"

Current computer architecture allows none of these problems to occur. Does this mean you can't use dBASE IV, the subject of this book, on anything less than a 386 computer? Yes and no. First, you can use dBASE IV on a non-386 computer. The actual caveats are in both the dBASE IV documentation and in part 1 of this book.

dBASE IV runs quite well on a 386 computer, reasonably well on 286 machines, and not at all well on standard PCs. I don't recommend the product for people with 8088/8086 machines, no matter what size hard disk they have. It will work, but it will work slowly. It will definitely get the job done, but even Ashton-Tate has plans to keep dBASE III Plus on the market specifically to address the needs of 8088/8086 computer users.

How does dBASE IV fit into the competitive marketplace? In dBASE IV, Ashton-Tate has done all the things necessary to keep their share of the market. dBASE IV's commands, functions, and separate modules (SQL, Template, Windowing, financial functions, pseudocompiler, and so on) address products such as Nantucket's Clipper, WordTech's QuickSilver, Wall-Soft's tools, and Fox & Geller's enhancement products. I don't know if

Ashton-Tate is trying to put these worthies out of business, but I think Ashton-Tate has realized that it can't remain king of the hill unless it stays hungry. Ashton-Tate has created a product that gives users the database abilities they will need for the next few years. (No fool, I. I won't say how long dBASE IV will address needs; I'll just say that it will.)

So, what's the buzz about dBASE IV? It's a good product with lots of niceties regarding ease of use, user abilities, forgiveness, and so on. It's an excellent and logical tool for people migrating from dBASE III Plus into larger database applications. It's a good place for users new to database management systems to start their journey.

Acknowledgments

Authors always acknowledge those that helped them finish a book. My list isn't long, but is precious to me. I couldn't get anything done without these people. Thank you.

Michael Kaltschnee and Wendy Greenberg of INSET Systems, for the software that produced the screen shots in this book, and for the standing lunch offer.

Diane Deschenes, who puts up with end user requests like, "I transferred the files from the hard disk to the dumpster. Can I restore them now?"

David Micek and John Montague of Ashton-Tate, who put up with my endless requests for software.

Introduction

*"Genius is nothing but a great aptitude
for patience."*

Georges Louis Leclerc, Comte de Buffon (1707–1788)

The Best Book of: dBASE IV is geared to two user groups. The first user group covers individuals moving from dBASE III Plus to dBASE IV. The second group covers individuals new to database management systems. Although these are two unique groups, their needs are quite similar.

The former group has experience with dBASE technology, knows the terms and expressions in database management systems, and has a working knowledge of how to get things done in dBASE III Plus. But that is about all that marks the first group as distinct from the second group. Both groups will be working with a new software product. True, dBASE III Plus techniques can be used in dBASE IV, but it is similar to using an automatic transmission as if it were a standard transmission. The engine is overworked and used inefficently, and you don't go as far as you could if you let the automatic transmission do its job.

And I know that sometimes you want to use the automatic as if it were a standard: usually when you are stuck in snow (what are you doing out in those conditions anyway?) or soft sand (you wanted to see if your Volvo made an adequate dune buggy? You deserve to be stuck).

This brings us to the opening quotation. "Genius is nothing but a great aptitude for patience," said the Comte de Buffon. Nowhere is that axiom more important than when you explore a new database system. Don't try to do everything at once. You will probably get frustrated and lose confidence in yourself and the product. Be patient. Explore. Investigate.

Both groups need to learn the ins and outs of dBASE IV, its interfaces, work areas, menu system, and so on. This isn't a difficult task, but it can be a long one. How does this book help?

The Best Book of: dBASE IV is a primary guide to the dBASE IV system and documentation. One book cannot tell you everything you need to know, especially about a product as rich as dBASE IV. This book will take you from your first contact with the dBASE IV package, to understanding the product's theory through installation, to database design, to adding and editing data, to reporting and formatting output, up to and including the design of an elementary editing program. You will learn about the dBASE IV menu systems, various interfaces, work surfaces, and areas. dBASE III Plus users may see a few new terms in that list. Don't worry—the dBASE IV product is a rich system with many aspects.

You probably won't make use of all that dBASE IV has to offer for several months. This book will get you to a point where you are comfortable enough with the dBASE IV product to begin exploring on your own. That is the key element of this book, and one that shouldn't be easily discounted. This book is driver's education, and by the time you are done you should be able to drive the car on your own. Will you be able to handle everything that comes up in your work? Probably not, but this book isn't a NASCAR qualifier or a Bondurant Defensive Driving course. Such driving techniques are for intermediate-level books or people with the time to gain the necessary experience. (Remember Buffon's quote?) My job, and the job of this book, is to get you to parallel park, back up, use your mirrors, and so on.

Will you learn how to do power turns—for example, multiple-file indexing? No. But you will learn how to take turns and get a feel for your car—how to design and develop database systems, and how dBASE IV interprets your requests.

So, this book is for beginners from two camps: those who are totally new to database management systems and want to use dBASE IV to develop their system and those who have experience with dBASE III Plus and want a tutorial to bring them up to speed on the new product.

Enjoy.

dBASE IV Basics

Part 1 deals with the basic ideas and concepts necessary for working with dBASE IV. The first chapter explains what a database management system is and how dBASE IV fits the definition of a database management system on minicomputers and microcomputers.

Chapter 2 provides new users with a brief tour of the dBASE IV disks. This might seem frivolous, but it isn't when you consider the size of the full dBASE IV system and all the files that make it up. Specifically, chapter 2 tells you which files are necessary to make dBASE IV do what you want and need. Many users don't need all parts of the dBASE IV system on their computer and can either delete files after they are transferred or tell the dBASE IV installation program, DBSETUP.EXE, which files should not be installed. Some users may run into disk space problems, and knowing which files are not necessary for your needs can save you headaches later.

Chapter 3 finishes the job started in chapter 2, explaining what you need to learn dBASE IV and how to organize the dBASE IV system on your computer to make the best use of your hardware and software.

What Is dBASE IV?

This first chapter is an introduction to the dBASE IV system and is primarily for users new to database management systems. It discusses what a database management system is, how database management systems have been used on various computers, and how dBASE IV can meet various database management system needs.

What Is a Database Management System?

A database management system is something with one purpose and one purpose only. It is designed to tell you where to put "it."

The "it" can be anything. It can be a machine parts inventory, video tape orders, packages to be shipped, service records for the truck fleet, maintenance requests, client records, subscription lists, and on and on and on. All these separate items come under the heading of *data*. The data can be part numbers, payment requests, expense or income ledgers, a general journal . . . the shape of the data is most often irrelevant to the database management system itself.

The database management system is the mechanics—what some call *programming*—that go on behind what you see on the screen. Using dBASE III Plus as an example, figure 1-1 is the data and listing 1-1 is the programming to get the information to the screen in a way that is useful to the user.

Listing 1-1

```
1 -
PROC EDITMENU
    @ 20,0 TO 23,79
    @ 21,1 SAY [ E EDIT   B BACK   S SKIP   G GOTO] +;
         [   K KILL   R RSTR   Q QUIT]
```

Listing 1-1 (cont.)

```
    @ 22,1 SAY [  F FIND   L LOCA   C CONT    D DISP] +;
              [   O COPY   A ADD     U UPDA]
    @ 23,34 SAY " SELECT    "
*
PROC LIBSAY
    CLEA
    @ 3,1 TO 3,78 DOUB
    @ 1,0 TO 18,79 DOUB
    @ 2,PLACE SAY DBF()
    @ 4,3 SAY "TITLE"
    @ 6,3 SAY "AUTHOR"
    @ 7,3 SAY "EDITOR"
    @ 9,3 SAY "CATEGORY"
    @ 10,3 SAY "SUBJECT"
    @ 12,3 SAY "LIBRARY"
    @ 14,3 SAY "ANTHOLOGY"
    @ 14,16 SAY "SERIES"
    @ 14,26 SAY "NUMBER"
    @ 14,39 SAY "TOTAL"
    @ 14,51 SAY "COMPLETE"
    @ 16,3 SAY "REFERENCE"
*
PROC LIBGETS
    @ 2,70 SAY STR(RECNO(),4,0)
    @ 4,12 GET TITLE
    @ 6,12 GET AUTHOR
    @ 7,12 GET EDITOR
    @ 9,12 GET CATEGORY
    @ 10,12 GET SUBJECT
    @ 12,12 GET LIBRARY
    @ 14,13 GET ANTHOLOGY
    @ 14,23 GET SERIES
    @ 14,33 GET NUMBER
    @ 14,45 GET TOTAL
    @ 14,60 GET COMPLETE
    @ 16,13 GET REFERENCE
*
** EOF: PROCEDURES

** LIBEDIT.PRG*
OKAY = .T.
ANSWER = 'X'
DO LIBSAY
DO LIBGETS
CLEA GETS
DO EDITMENU
*
DO WHIL .T.
    @ 0,0 SAY SPAC(80)
    @ 2,60 SAY IIF(DELE(),"DELETED",SPAC(7))
```

```
@ 24,0 CLEA
@ 23,43 GET ANSWER PICT "!"
READ
*
.
.
. (FILE CONTINUES...)
```

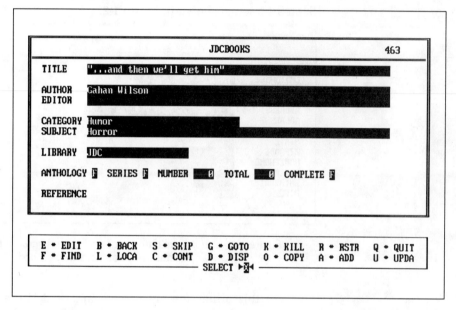

*Figure 1-1 What is on the screen is formatted data. Simple data doesn't
a database management system make, however. Listing 1-1 shows what
is necessary to get the data into a form that people can work with.*

Careful readers should be saying, "Data isn't important? What's
wrong with this guy? That's what I have to work with, so it must be important!"

Yes and no. Yes. Of course data is important. Without data in the form
of credit records none of us would get mail saying we have been prequali-
fied for yet another credit card. No. If you can't get to the data, it is not
worth much. The purpose of this book is to show you how to get to the data
and make it useful. And the first part of that is understanding how a database management system works.

How you manage data is not as individually oriented as most people
think. Certain rules apply no matter what you want done. How your data
looks on the screen can be as individual as your creative urges and screen
size allow. How the data gets there is pretty standard; it is based on the
language used. Before the data gets to the screen, after it is there, and after
it leaves, however, is where the magic takes place.

Consider the following example of the growth of a database management system. This example is from an optical practice. But, aside from the data used, it could be an example of any individual or group with a need to analyze information.

We start with a small office. There are clients. The work group wants to keep track of the clients. Usually, the first database management system is a mailing list. Not so here. This office wants to keep track of information that pertains to the client's health history. This is a straightforward application. All you need to do is put the data on the screen so that it can be edited. Such a screen is shown in figure 1-2.

Figure 1-2 A first-level data input and output screen. It shows the user what information is in a record.

For this office, the most important field is the memo field. This is where most of the relevant client information will be entered. There is no attempt to place this screen under program control. It is strictly for data input and output and is not part of a larger database management system. Indeed, this screen is displayed by getting to either the Control Center (figure 1-3) and pressing the [F2] (Data) key or by entering either APPEND, EDIT, or CHANGE at the dBASE prompt. The operation is not sophisticated.

Time marches on and so do the database management needs of this office. The office personnel decide they want to keep track of who owes what and when. Not a bad idea. The first attempt is to place all relevant data on the same screen as shown in figure 1-2. This generates the screen shown in figure 1-4. This screen is acceptable, but it tends to be fatiguing due to the layout of the data. It is not neatly broken up. Even after seeing this screen a thousand times, your eyes won't quickly delineate where data is located. It can get worse. Many clients are repeat customers, and the office does not want to repeat all client data for each repeat visit.

The time has come to manage the data. We want to see the data on the screen, but we want it organized. In particular, we want to separate customer data from sales data. This is not entirely accurate because sometimes we will want to see both data sets at the same time. This involves some

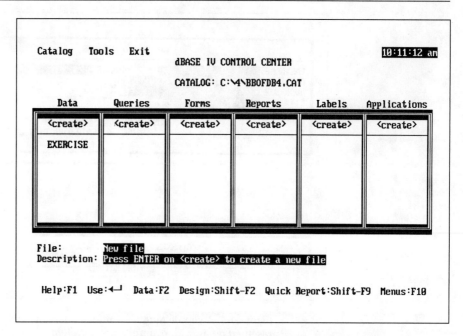

Figure 1-3 The dBASE IV Control Center provides many of the database management system services necessary for new users.

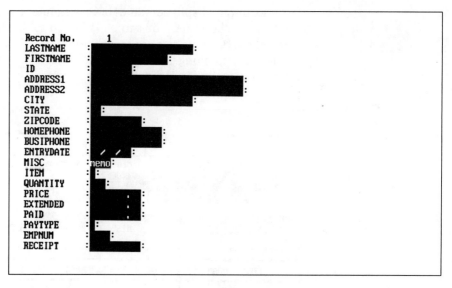

Figure 1-4 Too much unmanaged data on a screen causes confusion and fatigue after continuous use.

simple programming and should not frighten anyone. After data is on the screen, you want to develop a simple program that allows you to access and manipulate the data (which is what we do in this book). See figure 1-5.

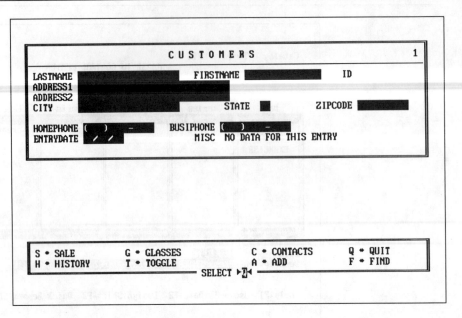

Figure 1-5 *A simple database management system. The data is presented along with a simple menu system. This puts the user in control of the data, rather than at its whim.*

An example of split-screen data management is shown in figure 1-6. The data on the bottom of the screen is linked to the data on the top of the screen, but the two data sets are in individual files. There are advantages to splitting the data along these lines. For example, you can now create a mailing list directly from the customer database without having to work

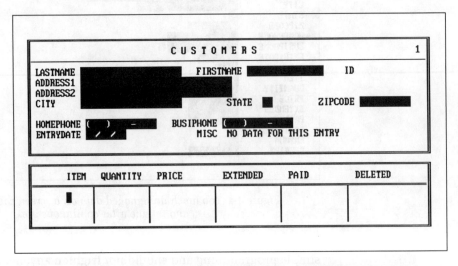

Figure 1-6 *A split-screen, two-database entry screen. This is another example of managed data.*

through sales data. There is a one-to-one correspondence between customers and mailing list entries. If customer information was linked directly to sales information, there would be a one-to-many correspondence between customers and their appearance on the mailing list. For example, suppose somebody purchased five items over five days. If each sale entry forced a new customer entry, that customer's name would appear five times on the mailing list. Experienced dBASE III Plus users take note: Ways around this—such as using INDEX UNIQUE—are unsatisfactory solutions in this example.

From here, the needs of the database system grow. It becomes necessary to squirrel away more information on each client. That means more databases. That means more management. More databases also mean better methods of linking data in the separate databases (account number, client name, chart number, demographic data, and so on).

And what about getting clients to pay accounts in a timely manner? We need to develop a program or at least know the interactive command to list which clients should receive dunning letters.

What if the bills are paid? We need to update our existing payments database. We also need to have the updated payments database report to the ledger and journal files.

Lots and lots of data coming at us. We have two choices. We can either be overwhelmed, like Howard Beale, or we can manage it. What are we constantly asking the database management system?

What clients need to come in for a consult, exam, or meeting?

Where did we put the list of clients we need to see?

Who hasn't paid yet?

Where did we put the dunning list?

Who hasn't picked up products from the warehouse?

Where did we put unclaimed items?

Which trucks are due for maintenance?

Where did we put the service schedule?

Who needs to be invoiced?

Where did we put the receivables?

We are constantly asking, "Where did we put *it*?"

The last things to note about database management systems are how quickly they can grow and the ensuing danger. The growth described in the previous example took place in less than a month. It is a typical example of starting a project with no real knowledge of what the end product should look like. This is in part due to not knowing from the beginning what the end product should do. So, what is the first step in database management system work? Know what you want to do, then plan to do more. There is a corollary to this, one taught to me during a game of pool: If you shoot at nothing, you will usually hit it.

Always have a goal in mind. For example, suppose you start with a mailing list. Think ahead. At some point, not necessarily soon, you might want that mailing list to generate selective mailings. The following command generates a label for every record in the database:

```
LABEL FORM mail TO PRINT
```

Now you need to put conditions on the database. Suppose you want to send mail only to people in New England. You need something like

```
SET FILTER TO ZIPCODE = [0]
LABEL FORM mail TO PRINT
```

This is not difficult in interactive mode, but it can be difficult if you haven't coded for the eventuality in program mode. An example of a full mailing list system is in Appendix A.

What you need to know, at the beginning of anything involving data, is how to *prototype* it. Prototyping does not deal with determining which amoeba belongs in which phylum. Prototyping deals with establishing rules or criteria at the outset of any database project. I will take a few minutes to describe this because the best place to start with the basics is in a book that starts with the basics.

You need a working idea of where your database needs are going before you can start building your database system.

Before you tell dBASE IV what you want the database to look like, before you create reports to output your data, before you use the Control Center or the template language, before you do anything, sit back and relax. You must ask yourself one question before you start doing anything else: Where is your database management system going?

This one simple question, however, has many involved parts. Are you starting with a simple client list and planning on something you can market in two years? How do you want the data presented on the screen? On paper? Who do you want to have access to the data? Do you want to develop modules that handle certain data tasks, then link all these modules? Are you going to fully develop programs that each do a complete job, then use these complete programs as separate parts of the whole? How many users do you plan on developing for? Are their needs identical?

All these questions and more are answered during the database management system prototyping stage. This information does not apply only to consultants or developers. It applies to anyone who wants to work with a database management system.

Six things are important in prototyping:

1. You must start by doing the impossible. This means you have to start the project knowing, in detail, everything you plan on being able to do with the data. You must sit back, relax, and plan in detail, defining everything that will be needed today, tomorrow, next year, and after you have left your current position. This is not

easy, but you would be surprised how quickly projects become developed beyond control when there is no prototyping. So think about what you are going to do before you start to do it. Remember Buffon's quote at the beginning of this book.

2. Before you start designing the database management system, talk to anyone who will be using it. Get everybody's input. And I mean everybody. A data entry operator who gets lost and does not understand dBASE IV's help messages can ruin a project. Find out what people will be looking for before you start. Save any surprises for birthday parties.

3. Know what you can do and what you can't do. Some people will say this piece of advice is from a consultant and is therefore jaded. Not so! A consultant is an out-of-work person with a briefcase. This is from somebody with experience. When you take care of the first two steps, look at what is in store for you. Determine how long you think it will take you to do what has been asked (this advice is especially for people who need to get up to speed with dBASE IV to finish some project). Determine which parts of the database management system you feel comfortable doing and which parts you are shaky about. Do you have the time to do them while learning how to use dBASE IV? If you can't subcontract parts of the database management system, ask for help from your coworkers.

4. Based on step 3, determine which parts of the project can be completed in chunks of two weeks or less. Those are the parts to do first. When something looks like it will take more than two weeks to complete, divide it into separate parts that will take two weeks or less to complete. This keeps things manageable and keeps goals in sight.

5. Know ahead of time how to handle "impossible" problems. An impossible problem occurs when you have planned something in steps 1 and 2 that you know is undoable. No problem is totally impossible, although some are intractable. Design around problems. If that doesn't work, let everybody involved with the database management system, both administrators and users, know about changes and how they will affect the work. Chances are your coworkers will come up with a way around the problem.

6. Let users and administrators see how things are going during the database management system development process. This goes along with steps 4 and 5. Step 4 tells you to break the development of the database management system into two-week projects. Let people know how things are after those two weeks. Step 5 lets everyone know that things are snafu, but not fubar. Anyone with naval experience will tell you that you can work your way out of snafu problems. With fubar problems, you have to start from scratch.

You should be getting the idea by now that data doesn't a database management system make. Good. With this in mind, we can proceed to the next section, where I explain how database management systems work on various computer architectures.

Database Management Systems on Micros, Minis, and Mainframes

This section is for users who have experience with other database management systems. It concentrates on database management systems on microcomputers because my suspicion is that the majority of dBASE IV users are in this category. The second part of this section deals with database management systems on minicomputers and mainframes.

We know that data doesn't a database management system make. The corollary is that the type of data you plan on working with dictates how it is managed. If the data is in the form of six-digit numbers that represent satellite telemetric data (my first programming job), your database management system can be based on FORTRAN (which mine was—yech).

The type of database management system plays a role in the machine on which you place your data. Ideally, you won't use a PC to handle a database with more than two million records. This information goes back to the discussions in the preface. The 386 architectures make large data manipulation possible for single users in nonnetwork system configurations. You can use several types of database tools, depending on the data. For example, dBASE IV is not the best tool if the data is text based (such as research notes or diagnostic records). If all the data is numerical, you could get by more easily by coding in C, Pascal, or BASIC. Buildable data, such as that found in inference and knowledge systems, is best handled by Smalltalk, Prolog, LISP, or similar language systems.

Most often, data is a mix of numerical and text data. Consider the following address label:

Marc Kral, Clarion Swine

185 S. York Rd.

Chicago, IL 60126

It contains numbers and characters. None of the data is recorded as numbers, however. All of it is recorded as characters, including the zipcode (see figure 1-7). This serves two functions. First, it allows better management because all the data is the same. Second, it allows easier coding because fewer error checks have to be designed to validate the data when it is entered.

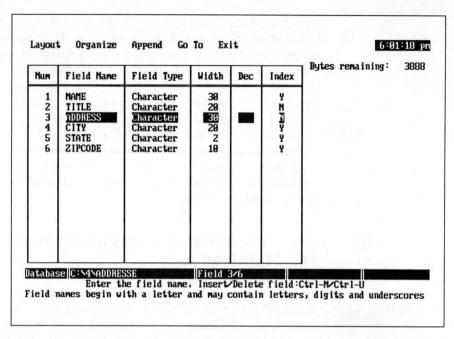

Figure 1-7 All fields in this database are of type character, even though
some data is numeric.

Database Management Systems on Microcomputers

There are a variety of database tools in the microcomputer world. These
range from simple, flat-file managers to complex, entity-relational models.
All systems can work with similar data. Indeed, you can use dBASE IV as a
flat-file manager by using only a single file at a time in a work session. Flat-
file managers are hierarchical in structure. This means the currently active
database points only to itself. One step up from hierarchical databases are
relational databases. A relational database system allows a user to have one
database point to, look at, link with, and otherwise make use of databases
other than the currently active one.

New users need some terms explained, no doubt. A database is
termed *currently active* or *in use* if it contains data that is the immediate and
primary source of information for the immediate task. In the first section,
for example, you saw how a simple database need turns into a complicated
system in a short time. When all you want to do with the information is
generate mailing labels, all you need is the customer database. During the
time you are only generating labels, dBASE IV is a flat-file manager. The
data in one record might point to data in another record, but only because
you have ordered the records in a certain fashion (by zipcode, for example).

What about entering sales data? That is when dBASE IV demonstrates relational properties. Each customer record points at one to many

sales records. Similarly, one or many sales records point to a single customer record. The data in the two distinct databases is related. When you are entering sales information, the sales database is the currently active database. The sales database can get information from the customer database (for example, the account number or customer data), but not much else. The sales database may then send information to the receivables database and the journal database (more relations).

In all of this, note that all work is done in a database environment. Microcomputer users don't expect a spreadsheet to pop up in the middle of their work session. This has to do with limitations of the computers and the software that runs them. It is also something being overcome in the current crop of database systems.

Database Management Systems on Minicomputers and Mainframes

By and large, people with microcomputer experience have a limited experience due to the limits of microcomputers and their software. For example, do you know there is no such thing as a spreadsheet on a mainframe? There are things that look like a spreadsheet, but they aren't. In the minicomputer and mainframe worlds, there are only databases. The difference in the minicomputer and mainframe computer worlds is based on how the data is presented at any given time. Databases are so intimately linked to the workings of large computers that it is often difficult to see where the operating system ends and the database begins. An example of this is IBM's OS/2 Extended Edition. This product includes SQL commands (which are database commands) as part of the operating system. You can query files from the system prompt and get results without entering any specific database environment.

Or did you enter a database environment and not know it? After all, with large computer systems, the operating system is often the database environment.

In large computer systems, how the data is represented and how the data is stored are vastly different. The best example of this in the microcomputer world is the Javelin financial modeling tool. How the information is presented on the screen is independent of how the data is stored in the file. The file remembers the last display type, but data on a given variable can be displayed as a table, a flat-file database, a word-processible file, a graph, a chart, in spreadsheet format, and so on.

This is a microcomputer analog to how data is stored and displayed on mainframe and minicomputer systems. There are exceptions to the rule, in a way. Some supercomputers and neural networks reconfigure themselves as different data is stored, but such leading edge technology is not viable until it is usable. It is impressive, but so are quintuplets. You know you should congratulate somebody, but you want to leave before feeding time.

With current, mainstream technology, computer systems store information in rigid, set formats. These formats give a computer system the ability to present data in a variety of displays. What the architect puts on the screen as a building is stored as a set of volumes, shapes, textures, angles, and so on. This is retrieved by the contractor as a set of numbers detailing amounts of concrete, board feet, landscaping needs, and plumbing, electrical, and heating requirements. It is also retrieved by the financiers as spreadsheet data determining initial costs versus payback time. Then there are the letters sent to various subcontractors based on the contractor's needs.

So, there is a great difference between how data is stored and used in a microcomputer and how it is stored and used in a mainframe or minicomputer. The next section explains how, why, and where dBASE IV fits into this schema.

How Does dBASE IV Fit the Bill?

We have described the steps necessary to designing a database management system before you touch the keyboard. Then we saw how database systems differ on microcomputers and in the minicomputer and mainframe world. This section explains how, where, and why dBASE IV fits into the database management system field.

If you read the first section carefully, you may have realized that expanding database needs translate into additional lead time during the system development cycle. Designing a mailing list is not an involved process after you have done it sixty times. It gets pretty boring around the forty-fifth time you have to do it. But a mailing list manager is a flat-file system and is ideally suited to PC technology.

That is exactly what the first personal computer databases were, and it is still a powerful analog. HyperCard, the Apple Macintosh database system, for all that it is, is patterned on a file card system. It's an impressive file card system, but it's still a file card system.

We also saw how system needs usually grow faster than programming skills and development time allow. There are two ways to solve this problem. The first method is to get a job that doesn't entail this problem. The other solution is to get more powerful computers and software. Ideally, you would like a computer system that is fast (I still remember when 1.8 MHz was a fast machine, whoosh!) and software that is as forgiving and helpful as possible.

How fast does fast need to be? That depends on your needs. For example, I wrote a program that depended heavily on an involved text search algorithm. No matter what I did, the algorithm took from twenty to thirty seconds to do its stuff. This was painfully slow to me, and I thought it would be so for the client. The time came for me to demonstrate the program and the search algorithm. The clock ticked off the seconds and I ticked off the sweat. It was an inexorably long wait. Eons later, the computer alerted us to a match between the desired text and the search text. The client looked at me and said, "Boy, that was fast!"

I looked him right in the eye and said, "And I coded it to be just that."

How fast does fast need to be? You decide. dBASE IV is faster than its predecessor, dBASE III Plus, in many ways. The increase in speed comes from dBASE IV's ability to pseudocompile programs during runtime. This has some significance to everyone, including those who don't plan to program. Consider the following two-line program, mentioned previously:

```
SET FILTER TO ZIPCODE = [0]
LABEL FORM mail TO PRINT
```

These two simple commands can be entered easily through the Control Center or from the dBASE prompt. They take a few moments to execute, however, because dBASE IV is an interpreted language when used at the dBASE prompt.

What does that mean, "interpreted language?"

Sit in on a UN General Session. Listen to the ambassadors. You probably can't tell what many of them are saying because many of them don't speak English. Now put on the headphones, preferably the ones marked for translation into a language you are comfortable with. Now you can understand what the ambassadors are saying, right?

Wrong. You can now understand what an interpreter thinks the various ambassadors are saying. You are counting on the interpreter's experience and training to make sure what you hear is what the various ambassadors said. (I know you heard what you think I said, but I don't think what you heard is what I meant to say.) You should also notice that interpreters don't translate words as they are being spoken. You won't hear something like

Je ne parle pas français très bien.

I

don't speak

French

very

well.

or:

Ich nicht sprech Deutsch zehr gut.

I

don't

speak

German

very

well.

You won't hear the previous for a number of reasons. First, it is written. You can't hear things that are written. Second, ambassadors from France and Germany speak their native languages quite well. Third and most important, an interpreter waits until the entire sentence is spoken before interpreting it. The standard exception is prepared speeches, wherein the interpreter reads from standardized notes.

The principal element in this discussion is that interpreters wait until a complete sentence is spoken before they do their thing. In other words, they wait. Entering a command at the dBASE prompt forces dBASE IV to wait until your command is completed and you have pressed the [ENTER] key before it acts. Entering commands at the Control Center is equally time-consuming because dBASE IV needs to get information from the Control Center interface, then build the command prior to execution.

dBASE IV's pseudocompiler allows more complex applications to run in less time than in previous versions of dBASE.

Fortunately, dBASE IV has a built-in pseudocompiler. A pseudocompiler is a software device that looks at command lines in programs as if they are prepared speeches by ambassadors. Everything, from first to last, is set out for them. There is no waiting during code execution. How does this help the nonprogrammer? Basically, you can use the Applications Window (from the Control Center), use the Editor Interface, or simply use the MODIFY FILE command from the dBASE prompt to enter a single command as if it were a line of code in a program. When you exit to the dBASE IV system, you have done just that: you have written a one-line program. You DO (the dBASE IV command to execute a program file) once. The one line of code runs perceptibly faster than your having to type it each time. You can even tell dBASE IV to assign the one-line program to a macro key, in which case executing your one line of code becomes a two-keystroke operation. The difference in this method is that dBASE IV no longer has to wait for the interpretation before executing your command. Now dBASE IV bypasses interpretation and goes directly to execution. Nice.

All this can be summed up by saying that dBASE IV is a powerful package on a microcomputer. Note that dBASE IV can also be used on supermicros, also known as 386 machines. A 386 computer is really a minicomputer in disguise. It is traveling incognito, sitting on your desk or towered beside it. The 386 architecture can easily support more than a single user with standard PC/AT applications, such as database management. Several parts of dBASE IV directly address the niceties of the fuller 386 architecture. One of these niceties is transaction processing.

dBASE IV allows transaction processing through its SQL environment. With this new tool, you can recover from yesterday's mistakes.

Transaction processing is familiar to people with minicomputer and mainframe experience, but may be new to microcomputer users. Think of it this way: You work all day and close your files when it is time to go home. You even shut off the computer. You come back the next day and somebody says, "We have to undo everything we did yesterday. We can't keep anything." At this point, microcomputer users see themselves in Gehenna, weeping and wailing. Minicomputer and mainframe users shrug and tell the computer system to ROLLBACK. It may take anywhere from a few minutes to an hour, depending on the complexity of yesterday's work. But when the computer is finished, the system and its files appear as if yesterday never occurred.

It gets better. What do you do if the power goes out and you don't have an uninterruptible power supply? No problem. You tell the computer system to ROLLFORWARD. The system finds the last program run, finds the last executed instruction in that program, and continues working. Whoosh!

So, how does dBASE IV fit in the current computer world? It is, simply, a minicomputer-based product that works on the microcomputer and minicomputer level. This means people with complex, multifile database management system needs but without enough shekels to purchase $50K systems can get by with smaller computer systems. More powerful software is here.

Summary

This opening chapter should give you a feel for how to begin working with dBASE IV and where dBASE IV fits into your database management system needs. It is intended to get you comfortable with what is involved in learning to do useful dBASE work.

Chapter 2 explains what each dBASE IV file does and how relevant it is. Although it is not necessary reading, it can be helpful if you need to get things done fast.

A Tour of the dBASE IV Disks

Chapter 2 is useful for people who need to know where specific items are located on the dBASE IV disks and which files perform what functions in the dBASE IV system. Chapter 3 shows how the dBASE IV system should be organized on various computer configurations. This chapter doesn't cover installation of the dBASE IV system because that is handled in the dBASE IV documentation.

The full dBASE IV system can come on as many as twenty-two disks. Depending on the dBASE IV flavor you have purchased, you may not have or need all twenty-two disks. This chapter lists what pieces of the dBASE IV system are on each disk. This information is useful for determining if the package you have purchased will do the job you want it to do.

For example, suppose you eventually want to compile and distribute dBASE IV applications. You will need the nine system disks, the four run-time disks, and the Developer's Utility disk supplied in the dBASE IV Developer's Edition. If you want to develop a system, you will need the menu system disks plus the two template language disks, also in the Developer's Edition. Or perhaps you want to use dBASE IV as the front end to an SQL installation on a minicomputer network. You will need only the nine system disks, as explained later in this chapter.

Also note that the numbering of the disks is not as important as what is on the disks. That being the case, disks are referenced by their information as well as their disk number. Last, this section is written for 360K disks. This was done because all files on the 720K disks are on the 360K disks, and using the 360K disks as examples ensures using all the dBASE IV files, no matter what hardware you are using.

The Installation Disk

The first disk in the dBASE IV disk set is labeled Installation. The disk's files are

```
ADDUSER4  COM     17120
DBSETUP   EXE     80784
DBSETUP   RES     27246
DBSETUP   OVL    147968
DBSETUP   PRD      5893
INSTALL   BAT        23
```

Depending on your computer system, you will use this disk either frequently or once in a great while. People with hard disk systems will be using this disk once in a while to both establish the dBASE IV environment and make modifications—such as installing new printers or monitors—after installation is complete. Chances are that users with floppy disk systems will be using this disk more often as their database management system needs grow.

Five files (DBSETUP.EXE, DBSETUP.RES, DBSETUP.OVL, DBSETUP.PRD, and INSTALL.BAT) are necessary only when you are installing dBASE IV or modifying your current installation. One file, DBSETUP.RES, is important for more than simply transferring files during installation. This file produces the screen shown in figure 2-1. It is also the part of the setup system that remains in memory no matter what else you do during the installation or modification procedure.

The Installation disk is the mastermind of the installation process. Unlike previous versions of dBASE, dBASE IV requires a great deal of information about your computer system. This is based on the improved help, printing, and graphics capabilities of dBASE IV. The next important screen you will encounter during installation is shown in figure 2-2.

If you type DBSETUP instead of INSTALL, the screen shown in figure 2-3 is displayed. From this screen, type *I* and press [ENTER]. The software registration screen shown in figure 2-1 is displayed if you are performing a first-time installation. Entering the serial number of your disk is the most important part of this screen because dBASE IV won't work without it. Your dBASE IV serial number is located on System disk 1.

After you have entered the correct serial number, you are led through all the disks in your package, selecting files for your hardware setup and so on.

The first file in the list, ADDUSER4.COM, is necessary when using either dBASE IV in network mode or the Protect module for a single-user installation in which several people may use the same software package during the day. ADDUSER4.COM tells dBASE IV that more than one person will be on the computer and lets the database administrator enter information regarding the different users. If you are not using dBASE IV in

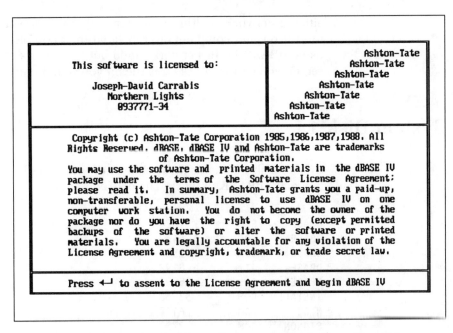

```
 Install  Config.db  Tools  DOS  Exit                          8:47:24 am
┌─ Software Registration ────────────────────────────────────────────┐
│                                                                     │
│  User Name  ...................    ████████████████████████         │
│                                                                     │
│  Company Name  .................   ████████████████████████         │
│                                                                     │
│  Serial Number  ................   ██████████  -                    │
│                                                                     │
└─────────────────────────────────────────────────────────────────────┘

        ┌──────────────────────────────────────────────┐
        │   Before using this product for the first time, │
        │   you must fill in this registration form.  Once │
        │   you save the form, it cannot be changed.    │
        │                                               │
        │   Use Ctrl-End to save this form once you have │
        │   provided the requested information.         │
        └──────────────────────────────────────────────┘

 DBSETUP  A:\                                      360K Floppy
      Enter registration information.  Save - CTRL-END.  Cancel - ESC.
              Install dBASE IV to a specified harddisk
```

Figure 2-1 This screen is produced by the DBSETUP.RES file and must be filled out before you can begin to either install or work with the dBASE IV system.

```
┌──────────────────────────────────────┬──────────────────────┐
│                                      │        Ashton-Tate   │
│   This software is licensed to:      │       Ashton-Tate    │
│                                      │      Ashton-Tate     │
│      Joseph-David Carrabis           │     Ashton-Tate      │
│         Northern Lights              │     Ashton-Tate      │
│          0937771-34                  │      Ashton-Tate     │
│                                      │       Ashton-Tate    │
├──────────────────────────────────────┴──────────────────────┤
│   Copyright (c) Ashton-Tate Corporation 1985,1986,1987,1988. All │
│   Rights Reserved. dBASE, dBASE IV and Ashton-Tate are trademarks │
│                  of Ashton-Tate Corporation.                │
│   You may use the software and  printed materials in  the dBASE IV │
│   package  under  the  terms  of  the  Software  License  Agreement; │
│   please  read it.   In summary,  Ashton-Tate grants you a paid-up, │
│   non-transferable,  personal  license  to use  dBASE  IV on one │
│   computer work station.   You do not become  the owner of the │
│   package nor do you have  the  right  to  copy  (except permitted │
│   backups  of  the  software)  or alter  the  software or printed │
│   materials.   You are legally accountable for any violation of the │
│   License Agreement and copyright, trademark, or trade secret law. │
├──────────────────────────────────────────────────────────────┤
│   Press ↵ to assent to the License Agreement and begin dBASE IV │
└──────────────────────────────────────────────────────────────┘
```

Figure 2-2 The dBASE IV installation procedure's first screen. This screen is displayed when you begin installing dBASE IV with the INSTALL command. You can also install or modify a current dBASE IV installation by using the DBSETUP file, shown in figure 2-3.

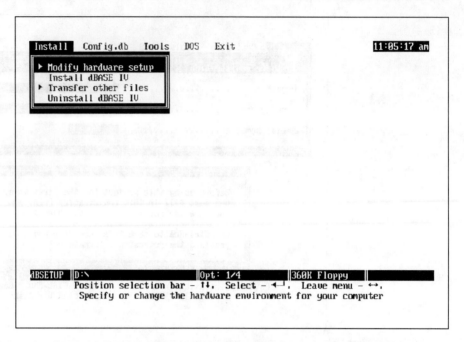

Figure 2-3 The dBASE IV DBSETUP screen. You will see this screen if you don't use the INSTALL.BAT file located on the Install/Setup disk.

either a network, multiuser, or many-separate-users mode, you won't see this file on your computer after installation is complete. Further, if you are using dBASE IV in network mode but your workstation is not the file server, you still won't see this file on your computer.

System Disk 1

System disk 1 contains the first layer of files that dBASE IV needs to actually make dBASE IV work. The disk contents are

```
DBASE      SER        1024
DBASE      LOD      146432
DBASE      COM        2304
DBASE      AT         8192
DBASE3     OVL       85024
INSTALLH   COM       38960
NLOD       COM        6112
SIGNON     COM        2752
```

It would be nice if dBASE IV was the DBASE.COM file, that slightly over 2K file, but such is not the case. The DBASE.COM file merely does the housekeeping chores necessary to get dBASE IV up and running on a floppy disk system. It more or less turns on the clock radio, turns on the coffee, and gets the shower going: "Come on, dBASE, time to go to work." You won't see this file in a completed hard disk installation because the DBASE.COM file becomes part of the larger DBASE.EXE file.

DBASE.SER is for network installation, DBASE.LOD looks for and loads necessary parts of the dBASE IV system when you first start it on a network, and DBASE.AT tells the dBASE IV system certain things about a once popular computer architecture.

DBASE3.OVL is one of several dBASE IV overlay files. I offer the following explanation for readers not familiar with overlay (OVL) files.

Computer applications are developed in stages. All too often, individual parts of the computer application are developed by different groups. Each group is in charge of one aspect of the completed project. This is the equivalent of an accounting supervisor telling the accounting department, "Employee #1, from now on you will only be doing Accounts Receivable. Employee #2, from now on you will only be doing Accounts Payable. Employee #3, from now on you will only be handling the Journal . . . " In other words, individual employees have responsibility for a select part of the entire general accounting picture.

You can also use house construction and general contracting as an analogy. A general contractor hires excavators, framers, masons, plumbers, electricians, finish carpenters, landscapers, and so on. Each subcontractor is responsible for his or her individual specialty.

So it is with software development. There is a great difference between building a house or running an accounting department and software design, however. In accounting, everybody knows that the books have to zero out at the end of an accounting period. Everybody knows they are working with two basic structures: credit and debit. With construction, everybody knows rock lath will be going up over the 2x6 interiors, everybody knows the frame must sit squarely on the foundation, everybody knows jack studs, cripples, and headers will be needed around windows and doors.

In both accounting and construction, each person knows—or at least has a solid concept of—how his or her part of the books or building fits in with everybody else's. Do you think software development is like that?

Noooo.

More often than not, software development takes the form of "I need this here, now." A cauldron of individuals who cackle like Macbeth's witches and look like deep cave newts, then march into the subterranean depths and produce some code that places "this" "here" "now." Usually, all they know about "this" is that it is supposed to be some type of number. All they know about "here" is that it is a memory register in the computer. All they know about "now" is that they won't get any more Cokes or Twinkies until the problem is solved.

Usually, several groups like the one described work on a single software product simultaneously. The result is lots of blocks of code that do what has been asked, but don't communicate effectively with anything else. What these blocks of code most often don't communicate with well is other parts of the finished software product.

All these separate parts of the finished software product are called overlay, or OVL, files. Each time you want a large, complex software product to do something different from what it is already doing—such as first entering data, then generating a report on that data—the software has to load in a new OVL file to handle the new task. (How many uniquely separate aspects are there to dBASE IV? How many overlay files are in the complete product?) This means somebody has to orchestrate the passing of information from one OVL file to the next. Whose job is that? Depending on your installation, either DBASE.EXE or DBASE.COM has the job of conducting the orchestra.

Back to DBASE3.OVL. As you might guess, this file contains some of what the dBASE IV system needs to do some tasks.

A new fellow on the block is INSTALLH.COM. This file is necessary for hard disk installation. It is not a copy protection file. INSTALLH.COM determines available disk space, how much of the dBASE IV system should be optimized for your system configuration, and so on. It should not appear in your finished installation's file directory.

The last two files in the listing, NLOD.COM and SIGNON.COM, are used for network installations. NLOD.COM handles the job of letting more people access the dBASE IV system. SIGNON.COM does what its name suggests, letting people sign on to an up-and-running dBASE IV network installation.

System Disk 2

System disk 2 comes with a vast array of files, divided into a root directory and subdirectory (SQLHOME). The root directory files are:

AMT	PR2	808
ANA6000	PR2	808
ANA9625B	PR2	808
ASCII	PR2	680
CANA2_15	PR2	680
CGP220	PR2	808
CI1550A	PR2	808
CI1550S	PR2	808
CI3520	PR2	808
CI715_2	PR2	680
CI815	PR2	808
CI8510A	PR2	808
CI8510S	PR2	808
DBASE1	RES	74594

DBASE6	OVL	114832
DIAB630A	PR2	808
DP_8050	PR2	808
DP_P80	PR2	808
DS180	PR2	808
DS220	PR2	808
DX10	PR2	680
EPSN8177	PR2	808
FAC4512	PR2	808
FUJ24C	PR2	808
FUJ24I	PR2	808
FX80_1	PR2	808
FX85_1	PR2	808
FX86E_1	PR2	680
GEM10	PR2	680
GENERIC	PR2	680
GQ35_150	PR2	680
HPDSK150	PR2	808
HPJET	PR2	808
HPLAS100	PR2	808
HPLAS2I	PR2	808
HPLAS2ID	PR2	808
HPLASL	PR2	808
HPQJET1	PR2	680
HR15	PR2	808
IBMCJET2	PR2	808
IBMGP	PR2	808
IBMPRO_1	PR2	808
IBMQ2_1	PR2	808
IBMQ3_1	PR2	808
IBMQUIET	PR2	808
IBMWHEEL	PR2	808
JX80_2	PR2	808
LQ1500_1	PR2	808
LQ800_2	PR2	808
LX80	PR2	808
MX80G	PR2	808
NEC3550	PR2	808
NEC7710	PR2	808
NEC8850	PR2	808
NECP5	PR2	808
OKI182	PR2	808
OKI182PN	PR2	808
OKI192_2	PR2	680
OKI2410	PR2	808
OKI82AGR	PR2	808
OKI84	PR2	808
OKI92PNP	PR2	680
OKI92_2	PR2	808
P1340	PR2	808

P351	PR2	808
QUME11	PR2	808
RIC6K10	PR2	808
RIC6K10L	PR2	680
TI855	PR2	808
TOSLAS15	PR2	680

The majority of these files have the PR2 extension, which marks them as printer driver files. These files contain the information dBASE IV needs to take what you want printed from the computer and send it to the printer. When you select the printers for dBASE IV to work with (figure 2-4), dBASE IV needs to get the appropriate printer driver file from this list.

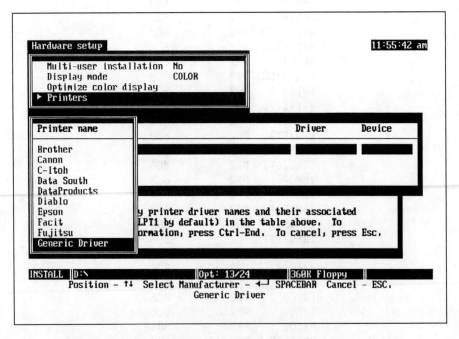

Figure 2-4 This screen allows you to install various printers for your dBASE IV system. The files necessary for this operation are the PR2 files found in the root directory of System disk 2.

The first non-PR2 file is DBASE1.RES. DBASE1.RES is the part of the primary dBASE IV system that remains active no matter what part of the dBASE IV system you are using. The best way to describe what DBASE1.RES does is to say "it becomes what goes where and why."

The next non-PR2 file is DBASE6.OVL. Now, class, who has been paying attention to this lecture? What is an OVL file?

The subdirectory on System disk 2 holds the following files:

SQLDBASE	STR	194
SYSAUTH	DBF	1156
SYSCOLAU	DBF	226
SYSCOLS	DBF	5586
SYSDBS	DBF	162
SYSIDXS	DBF	418
SYSKEYS	DBF	226
SYSSYNS	DBF	163
SYSTABLS	DBF	1094
SYSTIME	MEM	41
SYSTIMES	DBF	427
SYSVDEPS	DBF	270
SYSVIEWS	DBF	258

These files are necessary for individuals wishing to use dBASE IV as either an SQL system or a front end to a mini or mainframe SQL system. They contain the necessary information for dBASE IV to swap information to and from the SQL format, determine authorization levels, SQL index files, and security, and date and time stamp SQL records and files.

System Disk 3

The next disk, System disk 3, doesn't hold a significant number of files. But the files it holds are highly significant. The file list is

DBASE1	OVL	349120
DBASE3	RES	7642

The most important file on this disk is the first one, DBASE1.OVL. Overlay files were described previously. It is enough to say that this file contains much of what dBASE IV needs to porform most common requests. The other file is the DBASE3.RES module. RES files were also discussed previously.

System Disk 4

System disk 4 picks up where disk 3 lets off, which is what you might expect. The disk contains the following file:

DBASE2	OVL	361616

The DBASE2.OVL file contains some of what DBASE1.OVL contains, plus lots of other good things.

System Disk 5

System disk 5 contains the following file:

```
DBASE1    HLP     247155
```

The DBASE1.HLP file is the primary help file that the dBASE IV system calls when you press the [F1] (Help) key or when you want general help. The dBASE IV system can run without this file, but most people like to keep it handy even after they have mastered the intricacies of the system.

System Disk 6

Another simple disk in the dBASE IV system is System disk 6. Often, this disk is not required by dBASE IV systems. The file is

```
DBASE5    OVL     321904
```

When dBASE IV starts working (for example, when you first start it from the DOS prompt or from your AUTOEXEC.BAT file), the first thing it does is check for all the necessary overlay files. It does this even if you have never used the product before and don't plan on using for the rest of your life all of what dBASE IV considers is a necessary portion of the product.

So, dBASE IV starts checking around for necessary overlay files when you first start it. What happens when dBASE IV can't find a file it considers necessary? It asks for the appropriate disk:

```
Overlay loader can't find file DBASE4.OVL,
Insert System Disk 2 and press ENTER, or press Ctrl-C to abort.
```

The DBASE5.OVL file is necessary for users wanting to take advantage of the SQL interface. As a matter of fact, and in keeping with the previous discussion, you can start dBASE IV without having DBASE5.OVL on the disk. Obviously, that file is not too important, right?

Quite true for much dBASE IV work. Try to get the SQL server started without DBASE5.OVL, however, and you get the message shown in figure 2-5.

Before using the SQL server, the most memory hungry aspect of dBASE IV, you will probably need to clear all TSRs.

Not all users will want to make use of SQL (explained in more detail in this chapter and Appendix B). Any user with an interest in the SQL aspects of dBASE IV should be aware that you need to clear out many or all of your TSR (terminate and stay resident) programs when using dBASE IV SQL on a 640K DOS 2.x or 3.x computer. TSR programs are also called *desktop utilities* and include things like SuperKey, SideKick, and ProKey.

```
                    Press the F1 key for HELP
              Type a command (or ASSIST) and press the ENTER key (◄─┘)
    *DIR DBASE?.OV?
    DBASE1.OVL        DBASE2.OVL        DBASE3.OVL        DBASE4.OVL
    DBASE6.OVL        DBASE5.OVR


    1465768 bytes in      6 files
    15355904 bytes remaining on drive


    *SET SQL ON
    Overlay loader can't find file DBASE5.OVL.
    Insert System Disk 2 and press ENTER, or press Ctrl-C to abort.
```

Figure 2-5 DBASE5.OVL is not necessary for the dBASE IV system
unless you plan on using the SQL server. This figure shows the dBASE
IV system working, but unable to SET SQL ON because the necessary
OVL file has been renamed DBASE5.OVR.

If you plan on using SQL and get the message

Insufficient memory

unload your TSRs from memory, starting with the least important and
working up to the most important. See if you can activate dBASE IV's SQL
server after each TSR has been unloaded. For example, I use a memory
organizer program, screen capture program, and caching utility. When
writing a book, the screen capture program is a priority (it is the program
that generates the figures for the book). I have to unload the caching utility
and the memory organizer in order to load the SQL server OVL file,
DBASE5.OVL.

System Disk 7

Another simple dBASE IV system disk is System disk 7. It contains the
dBASE4.OVL file.

System Disk 8

System disk 8 contains the following files:

DBASE2	RES	101545
DBASE2	HLP	79971
DBLINK	EXE	55024
LABEL	GEN	15481

RES files were discussed previously. The DBLINK.EXE file is used by the dBASE IV system after you have developed a program. The DBLINK.EXE file is used by the BUILD routines (described later) and performs part of the linking of pseudocompiled applications with the necessary library routines and information. This is important for developers and nondevelopers. Developers obviously need the ability to link their finished applications into a single package. Nondevelopers still need to have their PRG file (a PRG file is a dBASE program file) pulled together so that the applications will run faster.

The LABEL.GEN file is necessary for the actual layout and design of labels. You might think of files with the GEN extension as generator files. This means the LABEL.GEN file is really the LABEL GENERATOR file.

System Disk 9

System disk 9 contains a wide variety of files:

CHRTMSTR	DBO	38996
DBLINK	RES	1993
DCONVERT	EXE	60928
DOCUMENT	GEN	27271
FORM	GEN	8349
LABEL	PRF	698
MENU	GEN	50927
PROTECT	OVL	19232
REPORT	GEN	32487
REPORT	PRF	698

All files with the PRF extension are print form files. These PRF files should not be confused with FRM (form) or LBL (label) files, which are forms generated when you ask dBASE IV to design a label or a report. PRF files contain information used by dBASE IV when you want to send a label or report to your printer.

The CHRTMSTR.DBO file is used to send and receive files in the CHARTMASTER format. DCONVERT.EXE converts existing dBASE II and dBASE III Plus files into the more compressed dBASE IV formats. DBLINK.RES is used by DBLINK.EXE, discussed in the last section. DBLINK.RES is one of the files that aids DBLINK.EXE as it pulls together and chains separate but necessary PRG files.

The other two files, FORM.GEN and REPORT.GEN, are necessary for the actual layout and design of I/O screens and reports. The one radically new file is PROTECT.OVL. This overlay contains the information necessary to encrypt and decrypt your files.

Encryption and decryption are security issues that usually have more importance on networks and multiuser systems than on single-user systems. They can also be important for single users who work in secure or risk-based situations. dBASE IV's encryption and decryption follow the DES standards. This means that after you protect delicate data, it is hard for somebody to figure out how you protected it. If this is a concern to you, be aware that it is impossible to build a better mousetrap because mice spend most of their time making better mice. You protect your file, and somebody will come along, somebody determined enough and with enough time, and that somebody will undo your protection.

Still, if securing your work is a concern, this is a logical alternative. The PROTECT.OVL file is automatically copied to your computer system during installation, regardless of the environment (networking, multiuser, or single user). After installation, you can access dBASE IV's protection system by typing PROTECT at the dBASE prompt. You will be walked through a standard protection session, starting with the prompt

```
dBASE IV Password Security System
Enter password
```

Be sure to remember your passwords into the system. (This should not be done by writing them on your desk blotter.) dBASE IV asks for confirmation of the first-level password:

```
dBASE IV Password Security System
Please reenter password to confirm
```

After this is done, the program is inside the dBASE IV Protect system, as shown in figure 2-6.

At this point, your computer system will have all the files necessary for interactive, standard dBASE IV work as well as the files necessary for programming, generating various forms, and doing SQL work. It will not contain any sample or tutorial files, nor will it contain many of the files found in the dBASE IV Developer's Edition. The actual file list is shown at the top of figure 2-7. You will note that the SQL system files are located in the SQLHOME subdirectory. Those files are shown in the second listing in figure 2-7.

Sample Disk 1

Sample disk 1 will probably be the most interesting disk to both minicomputer users and those who like the latest googah on their computer because this disk contains dBASE IV SQL sample files. The root directory contains a single subdirectory listing, SQLSAMP. SQLSAMP contains the following files:

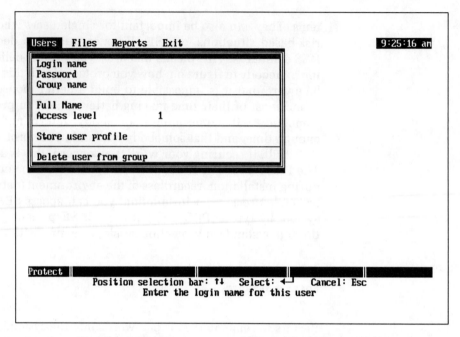

Figure 2-6 The first screen you will see after you are inside
the Protect system.

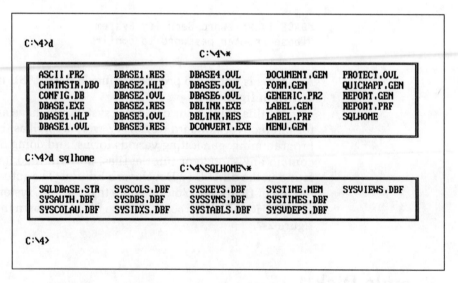

Figure 2-7 This file list contains all the files necessary to perform all
interactive, standard dBASE IV work.

ACCT_REC	FRG	5994
ASSEMBLY	DBF	354
CHRTMSTR	PRG	40056
CODES	FRG	4640

```
CUST      FRG      7041
CUSTOMER  DBF      2666
EMPLOYEE  FRG      6302
FORMBROW  GEN     29384
FORMBROW  COD     39009
GOODS     FRG      7384
INVENTRY  DBF      2371
INVOICE2  DOC      4619
INVOICE2  SCX       598
INVOICE2  KEY       137
ITEMS     DBF       893
ORDERS    FRG      6738
SALES     DBF       894
STAFF     DBF      1142
SYSAUTH   DBF      1156
SYSCOLAU  DBF       226
SYSCOLS   DBF      7831
SYSIDXS   DBF       418
SYSKEYS   DBF       226
SYSSYNS   DBF       163
SYSTABLS  DBF      1539
SYSTIME   MEM        41
SYSTIMES  DBF       427
SYSVDEPS  DBF       270
SYSVIEWS  DBF       258
VENDORS   FRG      5660
```

These files can be divided as follows:

```
ASSEMBLY  DBF       354
CUSTOMER  DBF      2666
INVENTRY  DBF      2371
ITEMS     DBF       893
SALES     DBF       894
STAFF     DBF      1142

SYSAUTH   DBF      1156
SYSCOLAU  DBF       226
SYSCOLS   DBF      7831
SYSIDXS   DBF       418
SYSKEYS   DBF       226
SYSSYNS   DBF       163
SYSTABLS  DBF      1539
SYSTIME   MEM        41
SYSTIMES  DBF       427
SYSVDEPS  DBF       270
SYSVIEWS  DBF       258
```

The first set of files is standard dBASE IV database files. The second set is files necessary for SQL to perform its varied tasks. The

SYSTIME.MEM file is a dBASE IV memory-variable file that contains information necessary when time-stamping records or databases, such as you might do during reporting or auditing. Time-stamping is a key function to SQL systems.

Sample Disks 2 and 3

Sample disks 2 and 3 are considered as a single unit because both send files to the SAMPLES subdirectory of the dBASE IV directory.

Experienced dBASE users will recognize many of the files in the SAMPLES subdirectory. For example, the file list contains the following PRG files:

```
ACCT_REC   PRG      8192
AREACODE   PRG      4864
BACK_RES   PRG      4096
BUSINESS   PRG      4037
CUST       PRG      8576
EMPLOYEE   PRG     10112
EMP_REPT   PRG      7552
GOODS      PRG      7040
INVOICE2   PRG     17920
INVOICES   PRG     12288
LIBRARY    PRG     40832
ORDERS     PRG      9344
VENDORS    PRG      7552
```

All files with PRG extensions are dBASE IV program files. These are the files you write to automate a dBASE IV process. A new file type is ADDCODES.UPD. This is actually a query-by-example file put to the specific purpose of updating by a query.

What does that mean, updating by a query? An example is this:

```
Find every record where the ACCOUNT = "1025L" and
COMPANY = "BOOMBATZ, INC." and increase all credits by 10%
```

This is a query-by-example (QBE) because you are querying dBASE IV for all records that match the example

```
ACCOUNT = "1025L" .AND. COMPANY = "BOOMBATZ, INC."
```

You are updating the records that match the query because you are increasing all credits by 10 percent.

The next file type is FRM, or report form file. These files contain the instructions dBASE IV needs to present data according to some specified output format. The FRM files are

```
ACCT_REC    FRM         4224
ALLNAMES    FRM         2482
CARDREC     FRM         2048
CODES       FRM         1664
CUST        FRM         4736
EMPLOYEE    FRM         5888
GOODS       FRM         4608
INVENTRY    FRM         2656
ORDERS      FRM         3712
REGIONAL    FRM         4070
VENDORS     FRM         3968
```

Similar to FRM files are dBASE IV's LBL, or label, files. These files contain instructions dBASE IV uses when sending data to a label type of specified output. The LBL files are

```
CARDONLY    LBL         1457
CUST        LBL         1536
EMPLOYEE    LBL         1792
INVITES     LBL         1394
MAILALL     LBL         1428
NAMETAGS    LBL         1400
VENDORS     LBL         1536
```

dBASE IV makes use of its own file directory system. This file directory system is located in the CAT, or *catalog*, files. dBASE IV's catalog files can be thought of as application-specific file directories. For example, suppose you are developing an application that has twenty PRG files, eight DBFs, eight MDXs, twelve NDXs, three FRMs, three LBLs, and twenty FMTs. You can go looking for them all over the disk when you need them, you can include the file names as lines of code and hope dBASE IV will be able to isolate them when necessary, or you can tell dBASE IV to keep track of all these files in a CAT file. The end result of using such a CAT file is that you only need to tell dBASE IV

```
SET CATALOG TO filename
```

From that moment on, dBASE IV acts as if no other files exist. Sample disk 2 contains the two CAT files CATALOG.CAT and SAMPLES.CAT, which in turn contain information on which files work with which other files in the SAMPLES directory.

The next file to consider is the MEMO field file. MEMO field files have the DBT (database text file) extension. The reason for a separate file to hold the contents of memo fields has to do with what memo fields are.

Memo field data is located in the DBT file, not in the memo field.

First, a memo field is not a normal database field. When you look at a database record that contains a memo field (figure 2-8), you won't see any information in that memo field. Instead, you will see the word *memo*. There is information in the memo field, but nothing you would recognize as what you placed there. The word *memo* actually covers a bit of information that dBASE IV uses to determine where in the DBT file the real memo has been placed. When you want to look at the contents of a memo field, dBASE IV gets the memo's address from the memo field in the DBF (database file), goes to the location in the DBT file that is specified in the DBF memo field, and begins reading the text from the DBT file.

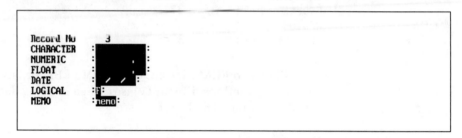

Figure 2-8 *An example of a database record with a memo field.*

Why all the shenanigans? It has to do with dBASE working with fixed-length records. Figure 2-9 gives an example of a database record's length. Every time you create a record or append a record onto a database, dBASE IV reserves the full length of the record (50 characters in this example) regardless of whether you put information into the record or not. Why so? dBASE IV does not know when or if you will put information into a particular field, but it does know that you might. Rather than reshuffle an entire database just because you entered information into a field that was previously blank, it is easier to reserve the space by "fixing" the amount of space to be used by any single record. This is like building a house and "fixing" the floor plans to have six bedrooms even though it is only you and your partner. Nothing is going in those extra bedrooms at present, but you plan for the future.

So what happens with memo fields? The data has to go somewhere, and the data is probably going to be more than ten characters wide. Further, the purpose of the memo field is to hold text. The size of the text can change from record to record and even in a single record as information in that record changes. How do you handle this? You create a separate file, a DBT file, that contains all text information in a "floating" format. The floating format means dBASE IV shuffles the file as things are changed. It is easier to shuffle a file of single text-type fields than to shuffle a file of various field types. The DBT files on Sample disk 2 are CLIENT.DBT, CONTENTS.DBT, and ORDERS.DBT.

The next set of files to consider is not dBASE IV specific, other than their intended use by the dBASE IV sample system. The files are GET-

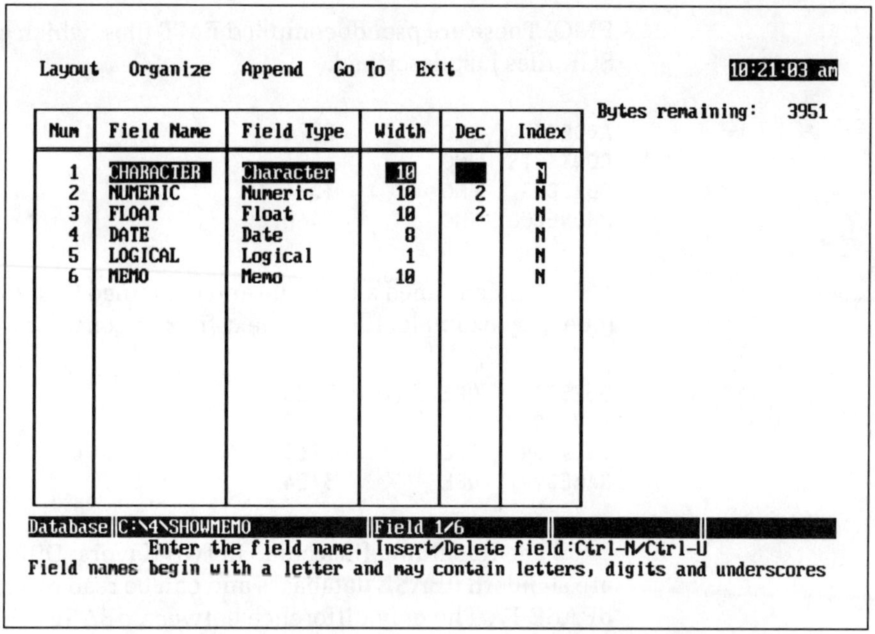

```
  Layout   Organize   Append   Go To   Exit                      10:21:03 am
                                                        Bytes remaining:    3951
 ┌─────┬───────────────┬──────────────┬───────┬─────┬───────┐
 │ Num │  Field Name   │  Field Type  │ Width │ Dec │ Index │
 ├─────┼───────────────┼──────────────┼───────┼─────┼───────┤
 │  1  │ CHARACTER     │ Character    │  10   │     │   N   │
 │  2  │ NUMERIC       │ Numeric      │  10   │  2  │   N   │
 │  3  │ FLOAT         │ Float        │  10   │  2  │   N   │
 │  4  │ DATE          │ Date         │   8   │     │   N   │
 │  5  │ LOGICAL       │ Logical      │   1   │     │   N   │
 │  6  │ MEMO          │ Memo         │  10   │     │   N   │
 │     │               │              │       │     │       │
 └─────┴───────────────┴──────────────┴───────┴─────┴───────┘
 Database C:\4\SHOWMEMO                 Field 1/6
            Enter the field name. Insert/Delete field:Ctrl-N/Ctrl-U
   Field names begin with a letter and may contain letters, digits and underscores
```

*Figure 2-9 Each field in the database has a fixed length. dBASE IV
reserves the length of each field in each record on disk even if there is
no data to put in the record.*

DRIVE.ASM and GETDRIVE.BIN. Some readers may be familiar with the
ASM extension and recognize it as assembler. After they recognize ASM
as signifying an assembly language program, they get out crucifixes and
strings of garlic and prepare to put stakes through the computer's heart.
The BIN file is the machine language version of the ASM file. These files
contain instructions to help dBASE IV determine which disk drive to look
on for certain information. They should not concern you as files you need
to understand.

The rest of the files discussed in this section are on Sample disk 3. The
simplest type of file on this disk is the SCR, or screen, file. This file is
created when you design a screen-based input/output form. The SCR file is
written in a coded form that dBASE IV interprets and uses to generate an
FMT, or screen format, file. The FMT file contains the actual PRG file-type
statements. The SCR files are

```
ADDBOOK    SCR       2649
CONTACTS   SCR       2445
INVOICE2   SCR       3226
OBJECTS    SCR       2438
PHONELOG   SCR       4232
```

The next set of files to consider has a distinctly dBASE IV extension:

FMO. These are pseudocompiled FMT files, which are generated from the SCR files just described.

```
ADDBOOK    FMO       2076
CONTACTS   FMO       1504
OBJECTS    FMO       1884
PHONELOG   FMO       2460
```

We mentioned a UPD file and explained that it was a specialized QBE (query-by-example) file. The next files to consider are true QBE files:

```
GUESTS     QBE       3428
INVOICE2   QBE       4048
LOCATOR    QBE       4763
NAMESQRY   QBE       3124
```

The remaining files come in two flavors: DBFs and MDXs. DBF files are standard dBASE databases and can be read by either dBASE III Plus or dBASE IV. The only difference between dBASE III Plus and dBASE IV is the amount of information dBASE IV gives you regarding the database file itself. This is shown in the following two listings. The first listing is made with dBASE III Plus, and the second is the dBASE IV listing.

dBASE III Plus Listing

```
Structure for database: a:sysviews.dbf
Number of data records:        0
Date of last update   : 03/21/88
Field  Field Name  Type        Width   Dec
    1  VIEWNAME    Character      10
    2  CREATOR     Character      10
    3  SEQNO       Numeric         1
    4  CHECK       Character        1
    5  READONLY    Character        1
    6  JOIN        Character        1
    7  SQLTEXT     Character      200
** Total **                          225
```

dBASE IV Listing

```
Structure for database: A:\SYSVIEWS.DBF
Number of data records:        0
Date of last update   : 03/21/88
Field  Field Name  Type        Width   Dec   Index
    1  VIEWNAME    Character      10             N
    2  CREATOR     Character      10             N
    3  SEQNO       Numeric         1             N
    4  CHECK       Character        1             N
    5  READONLY    Character        1             N
    6  JOIN        Character        1             N
```

```
     7  SQLTEXT      Character     200              N
** Total **                                  225
```

The other files have the MDX extension. These are dBASE IV's new multiple key index files. Prior to the release of dBASE IV, all dBASE index files had an NDX extension. This was because each separate NDX file could only contain a single index key, such as shown in the following listing:

```
Currently Selected Database:
Select area:  1, Database in Use: w:expense.dbf   Alias: EXPENSE
    Master index file: w:expto.ndx  Key: EXPTO
          Index file: w:expfor.ndx  Key: EXPFOR
          Index file: w:expamnt.ndx  Key: AMOUNT
          Index file: w:expdate.ndx  Key: EXPDATE
          Index file: w:check.ndx  Key: CHECK
```

The dBASE IV equivalent is

```
Currently Selected Database:
Select area: 1, Database in Use: C:\4\EXPENSES.DBF Alias:
EXPENSES
Production   MDX file:  C:\4\EXPENSES.MDX
          Index TAG:    EXPTO  Key: EXPTO
          Index TAG:    EXPFOR  Key: EXPFOR
          Index TAG:    CHECK  Key: CHECK
          Index TAG:    AMOUNT  Key: AMOUNT
          Index TAG:    EXPDATE  Key: EXPDATE
```

dBASE III Plus has to open a separate file for each index key. Thus, one to seven separate NDX files are in use for each separate DBF file. But this creates problems due to the working file limits of both dBASE III Plus and DOS. The solution is to put more than one index key in a single file, then just tell the system which of the several index keys in the multiple-key file should be given priority. The DBF and MDX files are

```
ACCT_REC   DBF      1280
ACCT_REC   MDX      8192
CLIENT     DBF      1664
CLIENT     MDX      6144
CODES      DBF      1152
CODES      MDX      6144
CONTENTS   DBF      2304
CONTENTS   MDX      4096
CUST       DBF      2048
CUST       MDX      6144
EMPLOYEE   DBF     12288
EMPLOYEE   MDX     23552
```

GOODS	DBF	5120
GOODS	MDX	6144
NAMES	DBF	4096
NAMES	MDX	14336
ORDERS	DBF	1280
ORDERS	MDX	4096
PEOPLBAK	DBF	2048
PEOPLE	DBF	2048
PEOPLE	MDX	4096
STOCK	DBF	1664
STOCK	MDX	6144
STOKNAME	DBF	640
STOKNAME	MDX	4096
STOKPRIC	DBF	896
STOKPRIC	MDX	4096
TRANSACT	DBF	640
TRANSACT	MDX	6144
VENDORS	DBF	1920
VENDORS	MDX	4096

The placing of several key fields in a single file is also the means by which SQL software thinks of key field information, by the way. For those with an interest, I offer the following section.

What Is SQL?

SQL (Structured Query Language) has become the de facto industry standard relational database management system on minicomputers and mainframes since its introduction in the mid 1960's. Recently, thanks to the increasing power of microcomputers, SQL has become a viable problem-solving tool for the small office network and, in some cases, the single user.

SQL did not appear on microcomputers until recent years for several reasons. First, SQL creates a tremendous amount of files for even the simplest application. Figure 2-10 shows all the SQL files necessary for a single library management system. The same work is done in dBASE III Plus with the files shown in figure 2-11. Quite a difference! This is an example of a simpler database management system fitting needs more easily than SQL. It also shows why SQL has only recently infiltrated the microcomputer market. As a further reference, figure 2-12 shows the files necessary to handle this system in dBASE IV.

First, SQL requires lots of disk space. You need lots of room on hard disks, and you really don't want to run an SQL application on floppies (unless you are using dual 1.2M 5.25" or 1.44M 3.5" floppies). Second, SQL requires lots of processing power due to its file management system. All the files in figure 2-10 are necessary and, when compared with the file list in figure 2-11, give you an idea of what kind of file processing problems

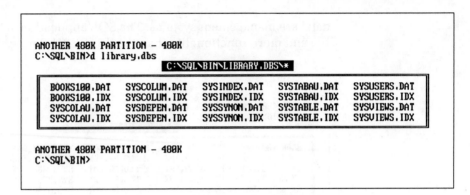

Figure 2-10 *All the files necessary for SQL to handle a simple library management system.*

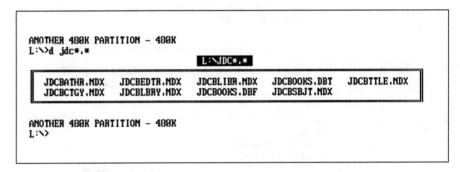

Figure 2-11 *By contrast with figure 2-10, this figure shows all the dBASE III Plus files necessary to handle a simple library management system.*

Figure 2-12 *All the files necessary for dBASE IV to handle the application shown in figures 2-10 and 2-11.*

SQL might encounter. This does not mean SQL won't work on an XT or AT style computer. It does mean it will work slowly. The final word? There are better single-user database management systems if you have a simple application and a slow computer. (Slow? Remember when we thought the 1.8 MHz Apple IIe was fast?) For a better contrast, look at figures 2-13 and 2-14. This is an example of an SQL application that can fly over most PC-based database management systems. The SQL application actually has one less file and more functionality than the dBASE III Plus system.

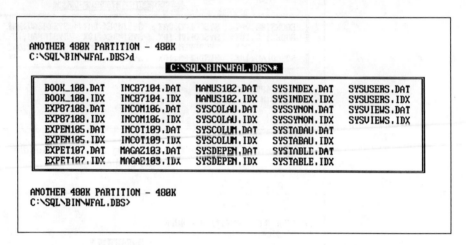

```
ANOTHER 480K PARTITION - 480K
C:\SQL\BIN\WFAL.DBS>d
                        ┌───── C:\SQL\BIN\WFAL.DBS\* ─────┐
┌──────────────────────────────────────────────────────────────────────────┐
│  BOOK_100.DAT    INC87104.DAT   MANUS102.DAT   SYSINDEX.DAT   SYSUSERS.DAT │
│  BOOK_100.IDX    INC87104.IDX   MANUS102.IDX   SYSINDEX.IDX   SYSUSERS.IDX │
│  EXP87108.DAT    INCOM106.DAT   SYSCOLAU.DAT   SYSSYNON.DAT   SYSVIEWS.DAT │
│  EXP87108.IDX    INCOM106.IDX   SYSCOLAU.IDX   SYSSYNON.IDX   SYSVIEWS.IDX │
│  EXPEN105.DAT    INCOT109.DAT   SYSCOLUM.DAT   SYSTADAU.DAT                │
│  EXPEN105.IDX    INCOT109.IDX   SYSCOLUM.IDX   SYSTABAU.IDX                │
│  EXPET107.DAT    MAGAZ103.DAT   SYSDEPEN.DAT   SYSTABLE.DAT                │
│  EXPET107.IDX    MAGAZ103.IDX   SYSDEPEN.IDX   SYSTABLE.IDX                │
└──────────────────────────────────────────────────────────────────────────┘

ANOTHER 480K PARTITION - 480K
C:\SQL\BIN\WFAL.DBS>
```

Figure 2-13 A file list of a useful SQL application. It contains one file less than is necessary to do the same type of work in dBASE III Plus.

```
ANOTHER 480K PARTITION - 480K
C:\WFAL\TEMP>d
                        ┌───── C:\WFAL\TEMP\* ─────┐
┌──────────────────────────────────────────────────────────────────────────┐
│  87EXP.DBF      87INCFOR.NDX   EXPDATE.NDX    INCFOR.NDX     MANUSCRI.DBF  │
│  87EXPAMN.NDX   87INCFRO.NDX   EXPENSE.DBF    INCFROM.NDX    MAUDS.NDX     │
│  87EXPDAT.NDX   BAUDS.NDX      EXPETTLS.DBF   INCOME.DBF     RECEIVED.NDX  │
│  87EXPFOR.NDX   BOOK.DBF       EXPETTLS.NDX   INCOTTLS.DBF   SUBWHEN.NDX   │
│  87EXPTO.NDX    BOOK.DBT       EXPFOR.NDX     INCOTTLS.NDX   TITLE.NDX     │
│  87INC.DBF      BOOK.NDX       EXPTO.NDX      MAGAZINE.DBF                 │
│  87INCAMN.NDX   CHECK.NDX      INCAMNT.NDX    MAGAZINE.DBT                 │
│  87INCDUE.NDX   EXPAMNT.NDX    INCDUE.NDX     MAGAZINE.NDX                 │
└──────────────────────────────────────────────────────────────────────────┘

ANOTHER 480K PARTITION - 480K
C:\WFAL\TEMP>
```

Figure 2-14 This file list is necessary to do the same work as the files shown in figure 2-13 It demonstrates SQL's ability to handle complex applications with fewer files than standard PC database management systems.

SQL is a language specifically designed for accessing structured data. Each individual SQL application is called a *database*. This is an important difference between SQL and most popular PC-based database management systems. A whole SQL application is called a database. Each database stores data in individual *tables*. Figure 2-14 shows a group of dBASE III Plus database (*.DBF) files and index (*.NDX) files necessary for a single application. Figure 2-13 shows a group of tables, all of which are necessary for a functionally equivalent SQL application.

If you look at the full name, Structured Query Language, you will note that the language is specifically designed to ask questions of databases. It is not intended to update, edit, or add to an existing database (although it does do those things). The raison d'être of SQL is to extract data from one or more tables (what dBASE users usually call a database) easily and quickly. SQL is not a general-purpose programming language. Again, SQL is designed to ask questions. This and the limited number of commands and attributes mean SQL is best used from within one of the following types of work situations:

- An interactive SQL facility, such as dBASE IV SQL, INFORMIX SQL, Lotus DBMS SQL, Microsoft SQL, or Oracle SQL
- A report writer or generator, such as those usually included in each SQL installation
- A fourth-generation programming language (4GL), such as INFORMIX-4GL
- A traditional third-generation programming language (3GL), such as dBASE III Plus, Paradox PAL, RBASE, or the Lotus Command Language

This should rightly and wrongly give you an idea of SQL's power and lack thereof. It is an idiot savant: There are few systems better when it comes to asking questions, but it does nothing else. The Thebian Sphinx would have starved or jumped earlier if mealsome wanderers had an SQL machine at their side.

Another important aspect of SQL systems is the demanding structure the data must be in. This rigid structure contributes to SQL's power and multiplicity of necessary files. All SQL databases have the same basic components. The major component is the table. Each table has a uniform structure and is designed to hold data of a similar type. A table consists of *rows* and *columns*. Each column (or field) is of a defined type such as character or number, similar to the data types of traditional computer languages.

More information on SQL can be found in Appendix B, which presents a single exercise in using an SQL database to solve a typical business problem.

Tutorial Disk

The dBASE IV Tutorial disk holds files that are analyzed in more detail in chapter 3. What is emphasized in chapter 3 is that the files on this disk can be removed from your computer system after you feel comfortable with the dBASE IV system. The files are shown in figure 2-15.

```
C:\4>d dbtutor
                        C:\4\DBTUTOR\*
    D000      D209      D312      D501      D604
    D001      D210      D313      D502      D605
    D002      D211      D314      D503      D606
    D101      D212      D3SU      D504      D607
    D102      D213      D401      D505      D608
    D103      D2SU      D402      D506      D609
    D104      D301      D403      D507      D6SU
    D105      D302      D404      D508      DS00
    D1SU      D303      D405      D509      DS01
    D201      D304      D406      D510      DS02
    D202      D305      D407      D511      DS03
    D203      D306      D408      D512      DS04
    D204      D307      D409      D513      DS05
    D205      D308      D410      D5SU      DS06
    D206      D309      D411      D601      INTRO.COM
    D207      D310      D412      D602      TA.DAT
    D208      D311      D4SU      D603      TAQUES.DAT

C:\4>
C:\4>
```

Figure 2-15 *The files on the dBASE IV Tutorial disk.*

Template Disks 1 and 2

Template disks 1 and 2 are only available in the dBASE IV Developer's Edition. A discussion of the disks' contents is included for people with an interest in seeing if the grass is necessarily greener. The files are shown in figure 2-16.

Template disk 2 contains all the COD extension files, template source files. New users may find the concept of templates intimidating. But most people have used templates throughout their lives and not known it. A "boilerplate" letter, for example, is a template. The boilerplate letter has some standard text and blanks for the word processor to include the name, company, title, and so on. Another example of templates comes from the machine production business. Presses and cutters use templates of machine parts to cut raw material into standard, interchangeable parts (all bow down to the assembly line, thank you). This is why you can get a new fender in a day or two and why all cars have similar headlights. A template is used to ensure similarity.

This is also true with dBASE IV's template system. Suppose you design input, output, report, label, and documentation programs for one system. Then you need to code another system. You find a duplication of types of work from one system to the other—for example, both involve browsing and selected editing. You use the template language to design one system, then just change the name of the variables in the first system so that the template language designs the second system for you.

In some areas, this is called CASE, or computer-aided software engineering. To a certain degree it is; to a certain degree it is not. True, the template language is used to create software. That is computer aided soft-

```
Changing to C:\4

C:\4>d dtl
                              C:\4\DTL\*

 ┌──────────────────────────────────────────────────────────────────┐
 │ AD_APND.COD   AD_RECL.COD   AS_MENU.COD   DD_APND.COD   DS_BOX.COD  │
 │ AD_BROW.COD   AD_REPL.COD   AS_MENUB.COD  DD_BROW.COD   DS_DOC.COD  │
 │ AD_CALL.COD   AD_REPT.COD   AS_MULTI.COD  DD_COPY.COD   DS_ORDER.COD│
 │ AD_COPY.COD   AD_RNDX.COD   AS_MUSER.COD  DD_DELE.COD   DS_TPOST.COD│
 │ AD_DELE.COD   AD_SORT.COD   AS_ORDER.COD  DD_EDIT.COD   DS_UDF.COD  │
 │ AD_EDIT.COD   AD_XDOS.COD   AS_PAUSE.COD  DD_EXPT.COD   DTC.EXE     │
 │ AD_EXP.COD    APPLCTN.DEF   AS_POSIT.COD  DD_FCOPY.COD  FORM.COD    │
 │ AD_FCOPY.COD  AS_ACTN.COD   AS_PRIN.COD   DD_IMPT.COD   FORM.DEF    │
 │ AD_IMP.COD    AS_AFTAK.COD  AS_PROC.COD   DD_LABL.COD   LABEL.COD   │
 │ AD_INLN.COD   AS_CHKD.COD   AS_SCSET.COD  DD_LIST.COD   LABEL.DEF   │
 │ AD_LABL.COD   AS_CLNUP.COD  AS_SETUP.COD  DD_PACK.COD   QUICKAPP.COD│
 │ AD_LIST.COD   AS_COLR.COD   AS_TIMEX.COD  DD_RECL.COD   REPORT.COD  │
 │ AD_NDX.COD    AS_ERROR.COD  AS_TPOST.COD  DD_REPL.COD   REPORT.DEF  │
 │ AD_PACK.COD   AS_FLCHK.COD  AS_TRCE.COD   DD_REPT.COD               │
 │ AD_PROG.COD   AS_HEADR.COD  AS_UDF.COD    DD_SORT.COD               │
 │ AD_QUIT.COD   AS_HELP.COD   BUILTIN.DEF   DGEN.EXE                  │
 └──────────────────────────────────────────────────────────────────┘

C:\4>
```

Figure 2-16 The files on both Template disks, which come in the dBASE IV Developer's Edition.

ware engineering. However, you still have to learn how dBASE IV works and how the template language works. This can be an involved process and is probably not worth the time investment unless you plan on developing a set of standard software tools.

Template disk 1 contains two file types, DEF and EXE. The two EXE files, DGEN.EXE and DTC.EXE, are used to create the template source file from the COD file (DTC's job) and then generate the finished object file (DGEN's job). The DEF files tell the template system how to interpret template language directives for the various object types (report, label, and so on).

Runtime Disks

This section discusses the files on the four dBASE IV Runtime disks. These disks are only available in the dBASE IV Developer's Edition.

Runtime disk 1 contains two important files, RUNTIME.EXE and RUNTIME.RES. The EXE file converts your PRG files into a third-level format. The first-level format is the PRG file that you type directly into the computer. The second-level format occurs when you DO your PRG file and dBASE IV pseudoptimizes the PRG file into a DBO file. The third-level format occurs when you send your DBO or PRG/PRS file through Runtime. This creates a pseudocoded file that can be marketed, if you wish, because the buyer does not need a full dBASE IV system to run your program. The RES file is what is necessary for your pseudocoded file to behave properly outside the full dBASE IV environment. INSTALL.BAT is also on disk 1 with the other two files mentioned here.

Runtime disk 2 contains two Runtime OVL files, 1 and 3. Runtime disk 3 contains RUNTIME2.OVL and RPROTECT.OVL. RUNTIME2 is a standard Runtime OVL file. The RPROTECT.OVL file is necessary if your marketed application uses dBASE IV's protection, encryption, and decryption features. Runtime disk 4 contains the fourth Runtime OVL file.

Developer's Utilities Disk

The next disk to consider in this set is the Developer's Utilities disk. This disk contains the three BUILD files, BUILD.COM, BUILDX.EXE, and BUILDX.RES. These three files are used by dBASE IV to put the separate parts of your applications into a single, pseudocompilable file.

One last disk in the dBASE IV Developer's Edition is the LAN key disk. This disk contains the files necessary for developers to check their applications on multiuser systems without having to purchase a complete dBASE IV LAN pack.

Summary

This chapter presented an overview of what you will find on your dBASE IV disks, including disks found only in the Developer's Edition. Chapter 3 describes the files relevant for learning and using the dBASE IV system.

Understanding the dBASE IV System

What You Need to Learn dBASE IV

Learning dBASE IV is relatively easy. There are three ways to go about it, none of them long or involved.

The first method is to go through the tutorials provided in the dBASE IV package. The files are placed in a subdirectory of the dBASE IV directory and are shown in figure 2-15. These tutorials take the new user from a lack of knowledge to a degree of comfort with the dBASE IV system.

The second method is for people with previous dBASE experience or familiarity with another database management system. This method involves knowing what you want to do, knowing how you did it in your previous database management system, and simply finding the new commands that perform the functions. Again, this method is best used by people with prior experience in a database system.

The last method is the one I strongly recommend and the one for which this book is written. It is the empirical method of knowing what you want done—the project or end product for which you purchased dBASE IV—and sitting down with dBASE IV until you get it done. When you use this method without help, it is called *hunt and peck*. I should emphasize that no one does a complete hunt and peck. Some theory is always involved, and theory and empiricism must go hand in hand. The theory of dBASE IV problem solving begins with the knowledge that you need to start with a database and that the database can have a design that contributes to or detracts from the problem's solution. After a database is designed, theory tells you the most important aspects of managing that database (for example, what fields should be indexed). Next, you develop a program to solve the problem.

The good thing about theory is that it can apply to anything. The theory is *force equals mass times acceleration*. This equation holds true for everything in the Newtonian universe, except for the places where it doesn't hold true. Do you junk the theory? No, you rearrange the information to fit it.

Sorry, just kidding. What you do is modify the theory. To modify the theory, you experiment with the system to find out where the theory breaks down, then modify the theory to fit the new information.

This book helps you avoid the hunt and peck method by giving you a solid grounding in the parts of the theory that directly apply to the dBASE IV system. You will learn the parts of the Control System that are necessary to perform the basic database management system functions. This book uses some standard examples, but I strongly recommend that you have some kind of database in mind before starting the next section. This book provides all the information necessary to create applications from the Control Center, but it also shows you how to leave the Control Center behind and work directly with dBASE IV.

For the purposes of this book, you only need the basic dBASE IV installation. You can work your way through the DBTUTOR system, shown in figure 3-1, if you wish.

```
┌──────────────────────────────────────────────────────────────────┐
│                                                                    │
│  ─ Introduction to dBASE IV  ·  Main Menu ──────────────────────   │
│                                                                    │
│                                                                    │
│     1   What is a database?        4   Forms                       │
│                                                                    │
│     2   dBASE IV basics            5   Queries                     │
│                                                                    │
│     3   Database files             6   Reports                     │
│                                                                    │
│         ──────────────────────────────────────────                 │
│                                                                    │
│     S   Summaries                  Q   Quit the Introduction       │
│                                                                    │
│        Type the number or letter of your choice  _   and press ◄─┘ │
│                                                                    │
└──────────────────────────────────────────────────────────────────┘
```

Figure 3-1 dBASE IV's training tutorial is useful for
the first time database user.

People with no prior database management system experience should start with option 1 in figure 3-1. People without the time to go through the tutorial can get information from the following description.

A dBASE IV database is comprised of two major elements, *fields* and *records*. Working from the smallest element to the largest, we will start with the database field.

A database system is like a vessel. The vessel can contain a nuclear reactor on the way to meltdown or a two-layer white chocolate cheesecake—it all depends on what you put into the database.

Simply put, a database field is an individual's incoming and outgoing mailbox. The larger element of a database is a record. If a field is an individual's mailbox, a record is a department in a company. The end of the analogy is to say that the database is the company itself.

How does all this come together? I want to send a letter to my friend, FIRSTNAME, who works in department 121 of the company. The first thing I must do is make sure I am delivering mail to the correct company. This means I have to make sure I am currently using the desired database. You can tell dBASE IV which database you want to use in two basic ways. One method is through the Control Center, shown in figure 3-2. The other method is through the dBASE prompt command:

USE *database*

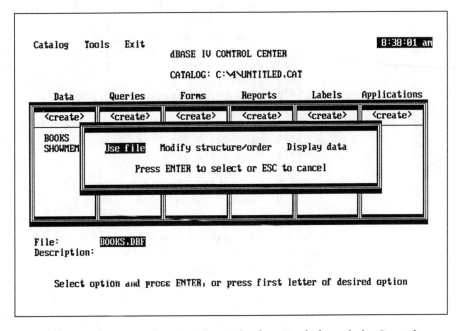

Figure 3-2 You can do most of your database work through the Control Center, shown here placing a database in current use.

The next trick is to make sure I am at department 121. Each department corresponds to a record number in the database. So we have gone from the largest attribute, the company or database itself, and now we are working on the department or record level. Databases, like companies, can have one department to thousands. The following is a listing of a simple dBASE IV database:

```
Record#  left(title,30)                    trim(author)
   1150  4th Dimension toward A Geometr     Rudy Rucker
```

1151	Algorithms	Robert Sedgewick
1152	Computer Solutions of Linear P	J.L. Nazareth
1153	Islands	H.W. Menard
1154	Devil In The Shape Of A Woman,	Carol F. Karlsen
1155	Mind From Matter?	Max Delbruck
1156	Manchurian Candidate, The	Richard Condon
1157	Quahog Walks Among Us, The	Don Bousquet
1158	Perfume	Patrick Suskind
1159	1988 Annual World's Best SF, T	
1160	Spin Glasses And Other Frustra	Debashish Chowdhury
1161	What's What	David Fisher
1162	Facts On File Dictionary of Ma	
1163	Facts On File Dictionary Of Bi	
1164	Facts On File Dictionary Of As	
1165	Facts On File Dictionary Of Bo	
1166	Facts On File Dictionary Of Ph	
1167	Ancient Of Days	Michael Bishop
1168	Wide Awake At 3:00 A.M. By Cho	Richard M. Coleman
1169	Blood And Water And Other Tale	Patrick McGrath
1170	Weave-World	Clive Barker
1171	Fractals	Jens Feder
1172	Symmetries, Asymmetries, and t	T.D. Lee
1173	Equal Rites	Terry Pratchett
1174	QED The Strange Theory of Ligh	Richard P. Feynman
1175	Mind Tools The Five Levels of	Rudy Rucker
1176	Mind's New Science, The	Howard Gardner
1177	On Knots	Louis H. Kauffman
1178	Ecological Imperialism The Bio	Alfred W. Crosby
1179	Chaos	James Gleick

But these individual mailboxes (the individual fields) can only hold one letter at a time. They are that small! I can check if there is something in FIRSTNAME's mailbox before I put my letter there, then I can decide if I want to put my new letter in FIRSTNAME's mailbox. Fortunately, FIRSTNAME and I are on such good terms that reading his mail isn't a problem. What the heck, I'm the only person that writes to him anyway.

So I can see if there is any existing mail in FIRSTNAME's mailbox, read it if there is some mail, then either edit the letter (remember, I sent it) or put in a completely new letter. And I can do this with everyone in department 121. Heck, I can do this with everyone in every department in the company. So much for what a database is.

After you know what a database is, you need to understand how the different parts of dBASE IV work together and how to utilize these different parts for your benefit.

The basic part of dBASE IV is the database, which we have described. You also need to know about queries, I/O forms (also known as screen format files), reports, labels, and applications.

A query is a question put into a form dBASE IV can work with easily. You ask a question about the database and get an answer. Sometimes the answer is that there are no answers, and that is valid, too. A query takes the form of the command set

```
SET FILTER TO condition(s)
reporting command
```

You can also create queries through the Command Center, as shown in figure 3-3. This method allows you to build a question by looking at the data in the database itself. For example, using a book library database, we can create a question such as

```
Show us all books on physics written by Arthur somebody.
```

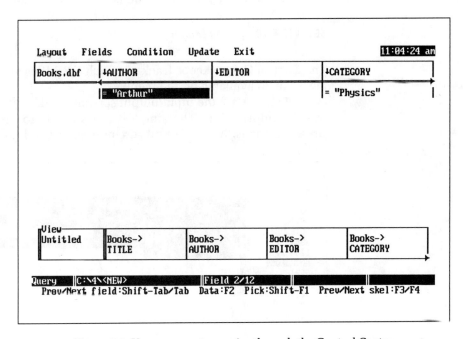

Figure 3-3 *You can create queries through the Control Center.*

dBASE III Plus put asking questions of the database on the next level of ease with the query, or QRY, file. You basically created a question in a near English form and let dBASE III Plus translate your question into a QRY file. This stored your question but not the answers. You could then use the QRY file to repeat your question each time the database changed, either through adding, deleting, or editing data.

How did you repeatedly ask the same question? Back in the days of dBASE III Plus, you did it with the command

```
SET FILTER TO FILE qry filename
```

This told dBASE III Plus to find the named FILE and place a FILTER on the database based on the question in the named FILE. This same command works in dBASE IV, but only when you want to use a dBASE III Plus QRY query file. dBASE IV query files are QBE files. You can't use the SET FILTER TO FILE command to call up a QBE file. You can use the QBE file in the dBASE IV SET VIEW TO command, as follows:

```
SET VIEW TO qbe filename
```

Much like the dBASE III Plus SET FILTER TO qry filename command, dBASE IV can take the question you create through the Control Center and place it in a reusable file. Next time you want to ask the same question of a given database, all you need to do is enter the command

```
SET VIEW TO qbe filename
```

The Control Center keeps track of which QBE files you have created and makes them available on the menu.

I/O forms are the input/output screens used by you and dBASE IV to transfer information. The simplest types of I/O forms are the Edit and Browse screens. A simple Edit screen is shown in figure 3-4.

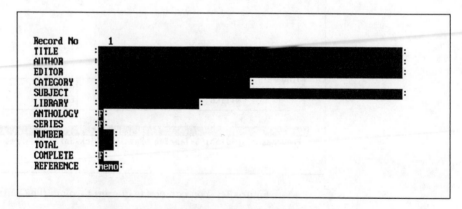

Figure 3-4 A simple Edit/Change screen for data input and output.

The Edit screen displays information a single record at a time. It displays information in a rather bland format: first field to last field, top to bottom. The other alternative is the Browse screen, shown in figure 3-5.

The Browse screen is displayed in a multiple-record (left to right) screen format. The Browse screen shows all the information in the database, but the information is displayed with each separate record on a separate line of the screen. The display might need to be scrolled up or down (to display other records in the database) or left or right (to display other fields in an individual record).

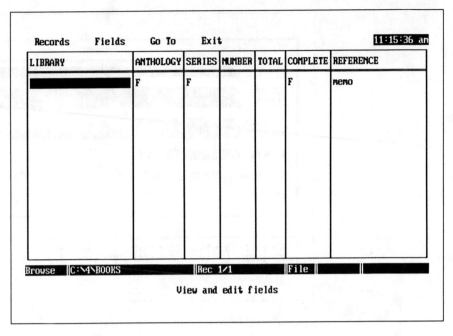

Figure 3-5 A simple Browse screen for data input and output.

These two screens perform input and output. This means you can add data to the database or edit data with these screens. It also means you can display data and perform rudimentary reporting of data already in the database.

Another possibility is a customized data I/O form, such as the one shown in figure 3-6. This screen form is created by dBASE IV based on instructions you give it with the screen painter, shown in figure 3-7.

The next part of the dBASE IV system is the report. You can easily send database information to the screen. That is all well and good, but a screen 24 rows by 80 columns does not allow much of a data display. dBASE IV makes up for this by presenting data in a written report format. You might think of a report as an intelligent data listing. You tell dBASE IV how, where, and when you want the information to appear on the report. Then dBASE IV generates an FMT file. Labels are tied closely to reports. You can think of labels as reports containing nothing more than address information.

The last item necessary to understanding dBASE IV is the application file, which has an APP extension. An application file is something that contains a collection of information, all of which is relevant to a particular database management system.

For example, suppose your database management system is a library management system. The application file will contain information on the databases, index expressions and files, report formats, input and output screens, and any programs which string all these separate objects together.

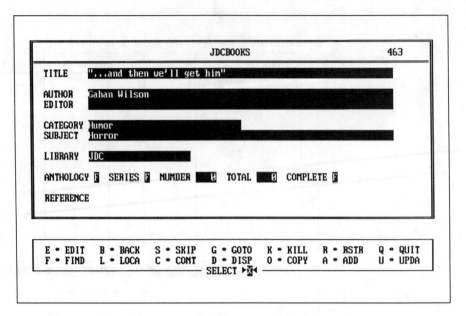

Figure 3-6 A customized input/output screen for use with the database
shown in figures 3-4 and 3-5.

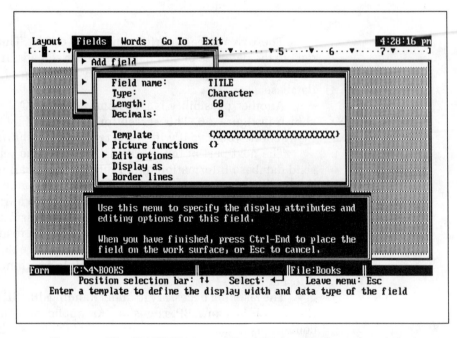

Figure 3-7 The dBASE IV screen painter lets you design custom input/
output forms such as that shown in figure 3-6.

Of all the things in an application file, usually the most important are
the programs that string the other files together. When I say string together,

I mean "make everything else easier to use." The application file contains information on menus, relations between menus, which programs lead to which other programs (the main menu leading to the data editor, for example), and what to do if there is an error.

Many novices to dBASE IV and database management systems spend much of their energy having the dBASE IV application generator create code for them. This is good if you are using what the application generator creates as a study tool for how individual commands and objects should be designed and entered, but not good if you plan on using the finished product. Code created by the application generator works about 80% of the time. The rest of the time, the code has problems. This is where it is better to read a good book and write your own code.

Also note that the dBASE IV application generator writes more code than is usually necessary because it attempts to write code to cover every possibility in the hopes of covering the one possibility you throw at it. This goes along with using a tactical nuclear weapon to fumigate a house. There are no more mice in the house after the tactical nuclear device is detonated, and getting rid of the mice is what you wanted to do. There is also no more house.

The next section is for those who want to learn the minimum configuration for making dBASE IV work. People who want to keep the installed configuration of dBASE IV can go directly to chapter 4 to begin learning how to use the product.

Organizing the dBASE IV System on Your Computer

If you were to add every file on all the dBASE IV disks, you would be working with some 220 files! Are they all necessary? Certainly not. The working number is a bit less, about 17 (for a typical single-user installation). These files are

DBASE	EXE	172032
CATALOG	CAT	607
CONFIG	DB	316
DBASE1	RES	77548
DBASE1	OVL	344560
DBASE1	HLP	278529
DBASE2	OVL	303264
DBASE2	RES	95449
DBASE2	HLP	79689
DBASE3	OVL	66756
DBASE3	RES	7449
DBASE4	OVL	289760
DBASE6	OVL	139456
LABEL	PRF	103
PROTECT	OVL	18848

```
REPORT    PRF      103
UNTITLED  CAT      607
```

If security is not an issue, you can even do away with the PRO-
TECT.OVL file. You should be aware that many higher aspects of dBASE
IV work, especially those of importance to developers and people wanting
to learn to program, won't be available. The preceding file list is for people
who are running short on disk space and can't install the full dBASE IV
system or those who don't want confusion when looking for files.

A more typical installation is

```
DBASE     EXE    172032
BUILD     RES       790
BUILD     EXE      9569
BUILDX    RES      5088
BUILDX    EXE    124301
CATALOG   CAT       607
CHRTMSTR  DBO     38976
CONFIG    DB        316
DBASE1    RES     77548
DBASE1    OVL    344560
DBASE1    HLP    278529
DBASE2    OVL    303264
DBASE2    RES     95449
DBASE2    HLP     79689
DBASE3    OVL     66736
DBASE3    RES      7449
DBASE4    OVL    289760
DBASE6    OVL    139456
DBLINK    RES      1767
DBLINK    EXE     52944
DCONVERT  EXE     60928
LABEL     PRF       103
MKPRINT   EXE     45760
PROTECT   OVL     18848
REPORT    PRF       103
UNTITLED  CAT       607
_DBTEMP            34
```

This provides all the files necessary for using everything except the
SQL server part of dBASE IV. Asking dBASE IV to install the SQL server
forces it to create a subdirectory, SQLHOME, in the dBASE IV directory.
All the files in that directory are necessary for SQL to function, as explained in chapter 2. That file list is identical to the file list shown for the
dBASE IV SQL disk, with the exception of the INSTALL.BAT file. Note also
that dBASE IV's installation routine creates a subdirectory called DBDATA
for tutorials based on your responses to certain prompts.

So, then, what are all those files for and what do they mean? Many of them were listed and explained in chapter 2. Some of the ones not discussed are files dBASE IV creates either during installation or during the first time you start dBASE. Examples of the latter are UNTITLED.CAT and _DBTEMP. UNTITLED.CAT shows up on the first Control Center screen. A CAT file is used by dBASE III Plus and dBASE IV to hold information about which files are linked to other files.

For example, suppose you create a database, an MDX multiple-index file, perhaps a dBASE III Plus standard single-key index file (you would do this if you needed to send data to a dBASE III Plus environment), a label file, and a format file. As long as you have a Catalog file active and SET ON, dBASE IV captures all file generation and modifications to the active CAT file. This information is used to tell dBASE IV which files to open automatically. Consider the following listing:

```
USE NEW.CAT
DISP ALL
Record#  PATH              FILE_NAME      ALIAS     TYPE TITLE  CODE TAG
1   C:\4\TEMPDATA.mdx      TEMPDATA.mdx   TEMPDATA  mdx           0
2   C:\4\TEMPDATA.DBF      TEMPDATA.DBF   TEMPDATA  dbf           2
3   C:\4\tempdata.ndx      tempdata.ndx   tempdata  ndx  field2  2
4   C:\4\TEMPDATA.SCR      TEMPDATA.SCR   TEMPDATA  scr           2
5   C:\4\TEMPDATA.fmt      TEMPDATA.fmt   TEMPDATA  fmt           2
6   C:\4\TEMPDATA.lbl      TEMPDATA.LBL   TEMPDATA  lbl           2
7   C:\4\TEMPDATA.lbg      TEMPDATA.lbg   TEMPDATA  lbg           2
8   C:\4\NEWDATA.DBF       NEWDATA.DBF    NEWDATA   dbf           3
9   C:\4\TEMPDAT2.mdx      TEMPDAT2.mdx   TEMPDAT2  mdx           0
10  C:\4\TEMPDAT2.DBF      TEMPDAT2.DBF   TEMPDAT2  dbf           4
11  C:\4\tempdat2.ndx      tempdat2.ndx   tempdat2  ndx  field2  4
12  C:\4\CONFIG.DB         CONFIG.DB      CONFIG                  0
```

We have created a simple database, TEMPDATA.DBF, and related files as described in the previous paragraphs. Note that all files, except the MDX file (explained later), are linked by the Code field. When a CAT file is active, dBASE IV knows which ancillary files (such as FRM, LBL, and FMT) belong with which database by matching these code numbers among the files. It can tell which files are databases by analyzing the file type. An example of this is shown in figure 3-8.

Figure 3-8 shows how a CAT file lists databases. Figure 3-9 shows how the CAT file remembers linked files. Not sure which LABELs can be used with the current database? You can ask with the command

```
LABEL FORM ?
```

MDX files are created by dBASE IV at your request. dBASE IV does not ask you for a file name when it creates an MDX file. Instead, it assigns the MDX file the same file name as the current database. This is done even though a single database can have several MDX files, each with a different

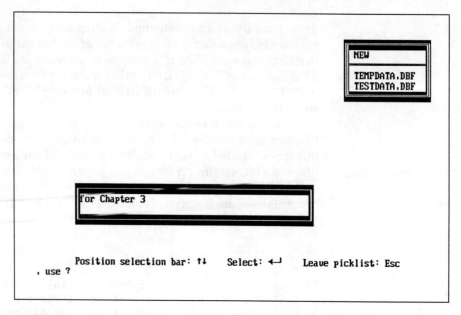

Figure 3-8 A Catalog file listing available databases.

name. Because dBASE IV links MDX files to databases by name or an explicit command, there is no need to ask for an MDX file name except when you expressly create one. You set MDX files with the following command:

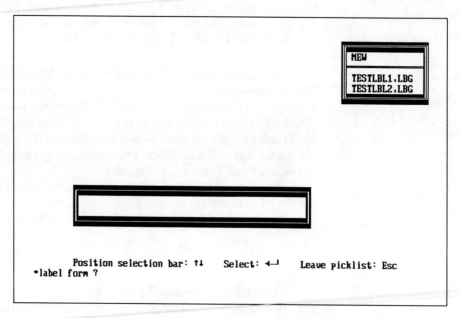

Figure 3-9 A Catalog file listing available LABEL files for the current database.

```
SET INDEX TO mdx file list TAG mdxtag OF mdxfilename
```

You create MDX files with

```
INDEX ON fieldname TAG tagname OF mdxfilename
```

The only other file to discuss here is the _DBTEMP file. This is a dBASE memory variable file. You create memory variable files with the command

```
SAVE TO memory file
```

This instructs dBASE IV to save all variables to a disk file for later use. It does not save field values, database values, record values, or anything related to actual databases. It saves only the values and names of the variables you have created in a given work session. It is a good idea to save these variables if you plan to use them during your next work session. You save them to disk, end the work session, come back for the next work session, then call up the variables to start where you left off. Good idea, no?

The _DBTEMP file contains memory variables dBASE IV uses for its own housekeeping. The variables include values for printer offsets, print colors, margins, and memo field widths.

Summary

Okay, you have learned enough to be ready for the big plunge. This chapter gave you the basic knowledge you need to start working with dBASE IV. You have been given a common language and some concepts to start your explorations. The rest of this book provides the explorations.

Beginning
dBASE IV

*Here we are, where the real meat of this book begins. No
doubt some of you skipped here immediately and missed all
my great puns and anecdotes. Well, maybe they weren't so
great.*

*Part 2 starts with a tour of the dBASE IV menu system.
The complexity of the dBASE IV product doesn't make the
menu system mandatory, but does make it a useful tool for
understanding how and why dBASE IV does things. The rest
of Part 2 begins the actual work of getting information into
and out of dBASE IV.*

Understanding the dBASE IV Menu System

When you first start dBASE IV, straight out of the box, you are greeted by the screen shown in figure 4-1. The reason for this is a single command in a file called CONFIG.DB. The CONFIG.DB file holds information dBASE IV uses to make you and itself comfortable during your work session. It's like getting into your own car before driving. The mirrors are set, the seat is set, the steering wheel is set. The CONFIG.DB file sets the mirrors, seat, and steering wheel so you can safely and comfortably drive dBASE IV down the database management system highway.

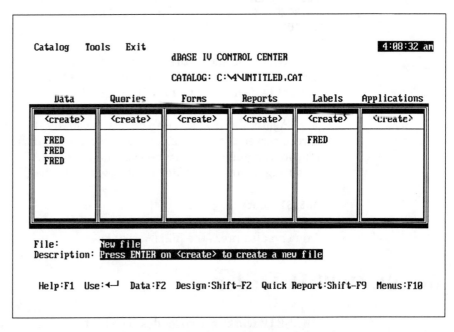

Figure 4-1 The dBASE IV Control Center.

The single command in the CONFIG.DB file that tells dBASE IV to call up the Control Center is

```
COMMAND = ASSIST
```

This command is automatically installed on your computer system because the CONFIG.DB file is copied onto your computer system during the installation procedure. That file looks like this:

```
*
*       dBASE IV Configuration File
*       Thursday September 29, 1988
*

COLOR OF NORMAL      = W+/B
COLOR OF HIGHLIGHT   = GR+/BG
COLOR OF MESSAGES    = W/N
COLOR OF TITLES      = W/B
COLOR OF BOX         = GR+/BG
COLOR OF INFORMATION = B/W
COLOR OF FIELDS      = N/BG
COMMAND              = ASSIST
DISPLAY              = COLOR
PDRIVER              = GENERIC.PR2
PRINTER 1            = GENERIC.PR2 NAME "Generic Driver Any
                       printer not listed" DEVICE LPT1
SQLDATABASE          = SAMPLES
SQLHOME              = C:\4\SQLHOME
STATUS               = ON
```

When you start working, one of the first things dBASE IV does is look for the CONFIG.DB file. You can tell dBASE IV to start at the dBASE prompt by using any text editor or the dBASE IV editor (figure 4-2) to remove the COMMAND =ASSIST line from the CONFIG.DB file.

Again, the first screen you see is usually the one in figure 4-1. That screen serves as the focus point of this chapter. If the Control Center is not on your computer screen when you are using dBASE IV, and you happen to be sitting at your computer right now, get to the dBASE prompt and type

```
ASSIST [Enter]
```

You can also press the [F2] (Assist) key.

dBASE IV Work Modes

dBASE IV works in two modes. The first mode is menu laden and designed to make work easy for novices. The other mode is devoid of menus and designed for intermediate to advanced users. There are also levels in between these two extremes. These intermediate levels occur when the help system is successively shut off. This is similar to being able to have dBASE IV selectively offer help.

At the lowest level, dBASE IV offers help through prompts at the bottom of the screen (no pun intended). The next level occurs when you type an erroneous command (figure 4-3). dBASE IV responds by letting you know it does not understand what you want to do. It either offers help or asks you whether you want to edit or cancel your command.

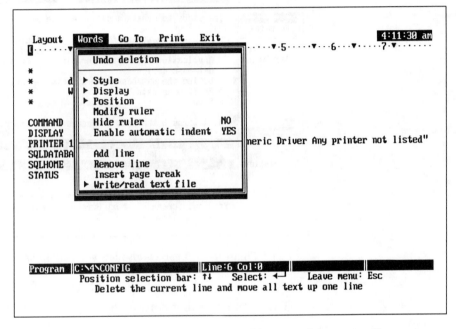

Figure 4-2 dBASE IV has a serviceable, menu-driven text editor.

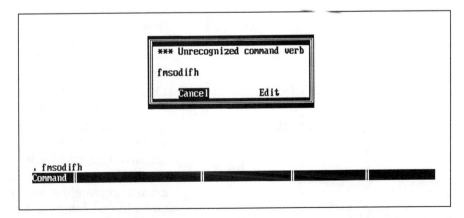

Figure 4-3 dBASE IV lets you know when you enter a command it
does not understand.

The last level is when you specifically request help from the system by pressing the [F1] key (figure 4-4). The more help you want, the slower the response from dBASE IV. Although dBASE IV works fastest with the help systems shut off, this is not recommended for new users.

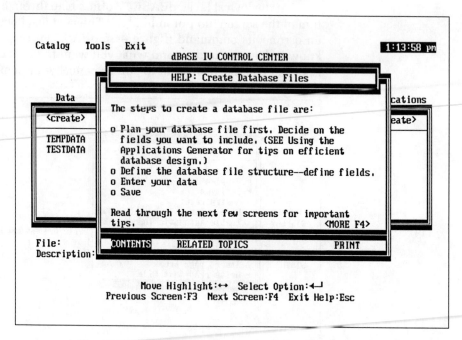

Figure 4-4 *dBASE IV also lets you call up help by pressing the [F1] (Help) key.*

The commands that control the help functions follow:

SET HELP ON/off   This command modifies the screen in figure 4-3 so that the Help option is the default choice. The modification is shown in figure 4-5. Selecting the Help option from the menu in figure 4-5 causes dBASE IV to offer any help relating to the command in question.

SET INSTRUCT ON/off   This command tells dBASE IV to display or not display help boxes.

SET MENUS ON/off   Users unfamiliar with dBASE III Plus will wonder why dBASE IV has a nonfunctioning command. SET MENUS ON/off is included in the dBASE IV syntax merely to provide program compatibility with III Plus. This command has no function in the dBASE IV system; it has been replaced with the SET INSTRUCT ON/off command.

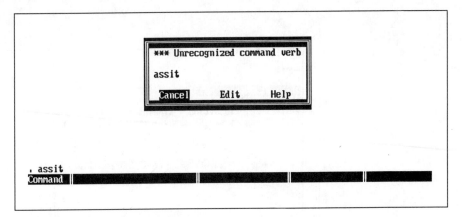

Figure 4-5 *The SET HELP ON command creates a new option on the error menu. Selecting the Help option causes dBASE IV to offer any help relating to the command in question.*

SET TRAP OFF/on

This dBASE IV command will be of great interest to users wanting to learn programming. First, you should know that you can force dBASE IV to stop executing a program in a number of ways. The most common method is to press the [Esc] key. Normally, dBASE IV responds with the screen shown in figure 4-6. This is with SET TRAP OFF, dBASE IV's standard mode of operation. With SET TRAP ON, however, pressing [Esc] forces dBASE IV's interactive debugging environment into operation (figure 4-7).

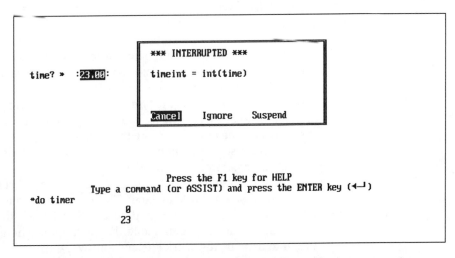

Figure 4-6 *The standard response from dBASE IV when you press the [Esc] key during program execution.*

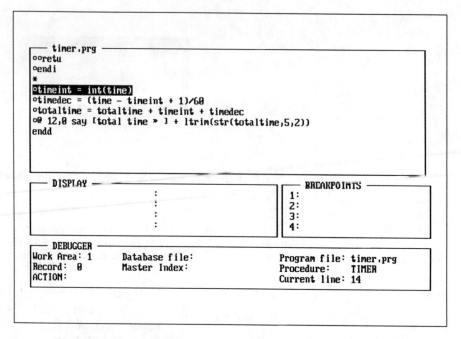

```
    ┌── timer.prg ────────────────────────────────────────────
    ○○retu
    ○endi
    *
    ┌─────────────────────────────┐
    │○timeint = int(time)         │
    ○timedec = (time - timeint + 1)/60
    ○totaltime = totaltime + timeint + timedec
    ○@ 12,0 say [total time » ] + ltrim(str(totaltime,5,2))
    endd


    ┌── DISPLAY ──────────────────────────┐  ┌── BREAKPOINTS ──────
    │                          :           │  │ 1:
    │                          :           │  │ 2:
    │                          :           │  │ 3:
    │                          :           │  │ 4:
    ┌── DEBUGGER ──────────────────────────────────────────────
    │Work Area: 1    Database file:        Program file: timer.prg
    │Record:  0      Master Index:         Procedure:    TIMER
    │ACTION:                               Current line: 14
```

Figure 4-7 *The screen dBASE IV responds with when you press the*
[Esc] key during program execution and SET TRAP is ON.

Work Space and Work Surface

Your work space is your office; your work surface is your desktop.

A principal feature of dBASE IV's new technology is the work space and its extension, the work surface. The dBASE IV documentation does not directly address work spaces except to say that certain aspects of the design routines are based on WYSIWYG (what you see is what you get). A better analogy might be to a painter, a canvas, and a palette.

You, the painter, stand before a scene and want to take what your eye sees and translate it onto the canvas. You have natural talent, perhaps some schooling, perhaps the numbers on the canvas, and your palette as your resources. Now suppose that you are not standing in front of something but are looking at or imagining a business form. You are still a painter, but now the canvas is the computer screen. You are going to "paint" the form onto the computer screen, much like a painter puts a landscape, figure, or face onto a canvas. After you paint your form, you take it from the work space and put it onto one of the many dBASE IV work surfaces.

So what is a work surface? The work surface is where you enter or edit data, get information, and so on. Sometimes the work surface and work space are interchangeable. For example, when you first put paint-brush to canvas, the work surface and work space are the same. How so? Because you are, in a sense, giving dBASE IV data to work with. The data is not part of a database management system, however. It is data on how to put information on a screen, in a report, and so on. After the design phase is completed and you are using your screens for data entry and editing, you are relying on a work surface and its related editing commands. The work space is again in the background, where dBASE IV rests while waiting to interpret your commands.

dBASE IV Menus

As mentioned, the first dBASE IV menu you are likely to see is the Control Center, shown in figure 4-1 and elsewhere in this book. All dBASE IV menus have some features in common but, like grammar, there are more exceptions to rules than there are rules. The Control Center menu is a good example of this. We start by analyzing the Control Center, then show common menu features, then describe variations from the standard.

This section uses the files in the SAMPLES subdirectory. This subdirectory may or may not have been installed when you set up your dBASE IV system. Don't let the possible lack of this subdirectory bother you. If you made the conscious decision not to set it up, you probably can learn all you need by simply following along in this book. We start with the screen shown in figure 4-8.

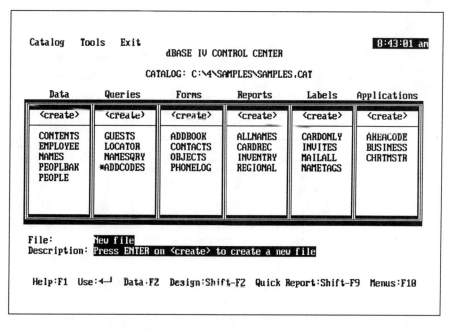

Figure 4-8 The Control Center screen in the dBASE IV
SAMPLES subdirectory.

The top of the screen contains a menu (Catalog, Tools, and Exit) and a time stamp. The next line is the screen title. Below the screen title is some information unique to the Control Center: a description of the current file catalog (CAT file). Because we are working in the SAMPLES subdirectory of the dBASE IV directory, we are told that we are working in

```
C:\4\SAMPLES\SAMPLES.CAT
```

Note that I have installed dBASE IV to the 4 directory, not a dBASE directory.

Below the catalog line is the menu system itself. Think of the Control Center as a master menu that leads to all other menus. For example, when you start working in the Control Center, the highlight is on ⟨create⟩ in the Data column. This means dBASE IV starts the Control Center with the assumption that you want to work with a database and most likely will create a new one.

Looking across the columns on the menu, you will see that all aspects of dBASE IV are available. You can create or use a database, create or perform queries on existing databases, create or use I/O displays (with the Forms option), create or use reports, create or use labels, and, finally, create or run applications. Remember, because we are working with a CAT file, selecting any file from any part of the list causes dBASE IV to place all related files in use. This is shown in figure 4-9.

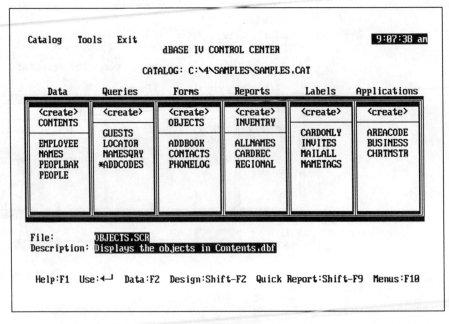

Figure 4-9 *The OBJECTS form is selected from the Forms option list; dBASE IV places all related files into use.*

You should know about the potential danger in selecting files in this manner. Normally, CAT files check to make sure all their listed files can be found by looking for them along the path information contained in the CAT file itself. The SAMPLES.CAT file contains the following path information:

```
Record#   Path
      1   CONTENTS.DBF
      2   EMPLOYEE.DBF
      3   NAMES.DBF
      4   PEOPLBAK.DBF
      5   PEOPLE.DBF
      6   ALLNAMES.FRM
      7   CARDREC.FRM
      8   INVENTRY.FRM
      9   REGIONAL.FRM
     10   CARDONLY.LBL
     11   INVITES.LBL
     12   MAILALL.LBL
     13   NAMETAGS.LBL
     14   AREACODE.PRG
     15   BUSINESS.PRG
     16   CHRTMSTR.PRG
     17   GUESTS.QBE
     18   LOCATOR.QBE
     19   NAMESQRY.QBE
     20   ADDBOOK.SCR
     21   CONTACTS.SCR
     22   OBJECTS.SCR
     23   PHONELOG.SCR
     24   ADDCODES.UPD
```

This listing tells dBASE IV that all listed files can be found on the current drive and in the current directory. A more complicated path listing might look like the following:

```
Record#   PATH                      FILE_NAME
      1   C:\DATA\CONTENTS.DBF      CONTENTS.DBF
      2   C:\DATA\EMPLOYEE.DBF      EMPLOYEE.DBF
      3   C:\DATA\NAMES.DBF         NAMES.DBF
      4   C:\DATA\PEOPLBAK.DBF      PEOPLBAK.DBF
      5   C:\DATA\PEOPLE.DBF        PEOPLE.DBF
      6   C:\FRMS\ALLNAMES.FRM      ALLNAMES.FRM
      7   C:\FRMS\CARDREC.FRM       CARDREC.FRM
      8   C:\FRMS\INVENTRY.FRM      INVENTRY.FRM
      9   C:\FRMS\REGIONAL.FRM      REGIONAL.FRM
     10   C:\LBLS\CARDONLY.LBL      CARDONLY.LBL
     11   C:\LBLS\INVITES.LBL       INVITES.LBL
     12   C:\LBLS\MAILALL.LBL       MAILALL.LBL
```

```
13   C:\LBLS\NAMETAGS.LBL      NAMETAGS.LBL
14   C:\PRGS\AREACODE.PRG      AREACODE.PRG
15   C:\PRGS\BUSINESS.PRG      BUSINESS.PRG
16   C:\PRGS\CHRTMSTR.PRG      CHRTMSTR.PRG
17   C:\QBES\GUESTS.QBE        GUESTS.QBE
18   C:\QBES\LOCATOR.QBE       LOCATOR.QBE
19   C:\QBES\NAMESQRY.QBE      NAMESQRY.QBE
20   C:\SCRS\ADDBOOK.SCR       ADDBOOK.SCR
21   C:\SCRS\CONTACTS.SCR      CONTACTS.SCR
22   C:\SCRS\OBJECTS.SCR       OBJECTS.SCR
23   C:\SCRS\PHONELOG.SCR      PHONELOG.SCR
24   C:\UPDS\ADDCODES.UPD      ADDCODES.UPD
```

Note that I have included the file name in this listing to demonstrate the difference between dBASE IV acknowledging a file's name versus a file's path. The danger mentioned previously happens when a file is requested but not found. When this happens, dBASE IV tells you it can't find the file. A more serious problem occurs when dBASE IV starts deleting entries from the CAT file because it can't find listed files. An example of this is shown in the following listing:

```
SET CATA TO C:\4\SAMPLES\SAMPLES
CONTENTS.DBF does not exist.  Deleted from catalog
EMPLOYEE.DBF does not exist.  Deleted from catalog
NAMES.DBF does not exist.  Deleted from catalog
PEOPLBAK.DBF does not exist.  Deleted from catalog
PEOPLE.DBF does not exist.  Deleted from catalog
ALLNAMES.FRM does not exist.  Deleted from catalog
CARDREC.FRM does not exist.  Deleted from catalog
INVENTRY.FRM does not exist.  Deleted from catalog
REGIONAL.FRM does not exist.  Deleted from catalog
CARDONLY.LBL does not exist.  Deleted from catalog
INVITES.LBL does not exist.  Deleted from catalog
MAILALL.LBL does not exist.  Deleted from catalog
NAMETAGS.LBL does not exist.  Deleted from catalog
AREACODE.PRG does not exist.  Deleted from catalog
BUSINESS.PRG does not exist.  Deleted from catalog
CHRTMSTR.PRG does not exist.  Deleted from catalog
GUESTS.QBE does not exist.  Deleted from catalog
LOCATOR.QBE does not exist.  Deleted from catalog
NAMESQRY.QBE does not exist.  Deleted from catalog
ADDBOOK.SCR does not exist.  Deleted from catalog
CONTACTS.SCR does not exist.  Deleted from catalog
OBJECTS.SCR does not exist.  Deleted from catalog
PHONELOG.SCR does not exist.  Deleted from catalog
ADDCODES.UPD does not exist.  Deleted from catalog
```

All these files were deleted because I opened the CAT file from a different drive (drive D in this case). Because dBASE IV assumed I was referring to the current path and drive, it could not find any of the files (note that the CAT file is located on drive C in the \4\SAMPLES\ subdirectory).

Does the Control Center give you any information on the file you have chosen? Yes. Below the Control Center main menu is the File line. This line contains the full file name of the file you have cursored to on the menu. When you place the cursor on any of the ⟨create⟩ options, *New file* appears in the File window. When you move to any file, the file name appears. For example, if you cursor to INVENTRY under Reports, *INVENTRY.FRM* appears in the File window.

Under the File line is the Description line. This line is similar to the File line because its contents depend on where the cursor is on the main menu. When the cursor is on a ⟨create⟩ option, the Description line contains *Press ENTER on ⟨create⟩ to create a new file.* When the cursor is on a file, the Description line contains information about that file. Where does this information come from? From the CAT file. In particular, it comes from the Title field in the CAT file. Following is the contents of the SAMPLES.CAT Title field:

```
Record#  trim(title)
    1  Personal inventory listing
    2  A file of company workers
    3  A name and address file
    4  Used by "Using the dBASE IV Applications Generator" for
       backups.
    5  A second name and address file
    6  A report of all people in People.dbf
    7  A report of people in People.dbf receiving cards
    8  What is in the personal inventory
    9  People in Guests organized by state
   10  Labels for the names in People.dbf marked to receive cards
   11  Invitation labels for people in the Guests view
   12  Labels for everyone in People.dbf
   13  Name tags for award winners in Employee.dbf
   14  A program to show cities and area codes
   15  A small business application
   16  This file prepares data for use with Chart Master.
   17  People to invite to party
   18  Query Employee database file on partial information
   19  Find out who lives in Washington, D.C.
   20  Address book of friends
   21  People in Employee to call
   22  Displays the objects in Contents.dbf
   23  Provides overview of employee information
   24  Finds area codes and cities from Employee and adds to
       Codes
```

How this information gets into the CAT file is described later.

The bottom line of the Control Center screen contains another menu of sorts. You might think of this as an immediate menu because these items give you immediate access to several dBASE IV features.

The standard is the [F1] (Help) key. No matter where you are in dBASE IV, the [F1] key always calls up the dBASE IV Help system. Figure 4-10 shows a context-sensitive Help screen. *Context sensitive* means the help system is aware of what you are trying to do and gives you information directly useful to what is going on.

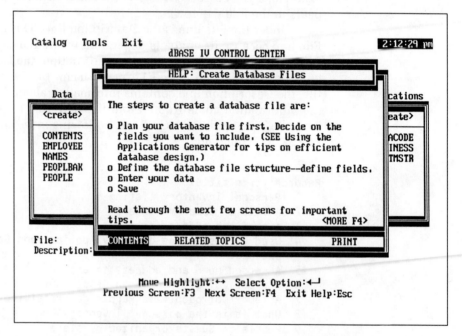

Figure 4-10 The [F1] (Help) key accesses a context-sensitive Help system throughout the dBASE IV product.

Next to the Help:F1 prompt is Use. This can be somewhat confusing unless you know that you are being prompted to press the [Enter] key in order to either use a file currently under the cursor or create a file type based on the current column in the main menu.

The [F2] (Data) key causes the Control Center to change to the Browse mode of the current database, no matter where the cursor is on the menu itself. Browse mode has been mentioned before. It is a full-screen data editing/entry mode complete with its own menu system (explained in more detail in chapter 6). It is worth noting that the Browse menu is an excellent example of the dBASE IV work surfaces concept.

The [Shift-F2] (Design) key is used to create new files based on the current column. If the cursor is in the Queries column and you press [Shift-F2], the query design work surface appears (figure 4-11). Note the similarities between this work surface and the Control Center surface (top line, description lines, and so on).

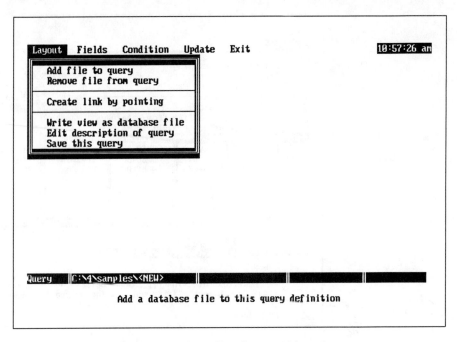

Figure 4-11 The Query design work surface.

The next immediate menu item is Quick Report:Shift-F9. This is an option only if a database is currently in use or the cursor is on an unopened database. When a database is in current use, the cursor can be anywhere on the screen, except on another database. Press [Shift-F9] and you are prompted for information regarding how you want the report to appear. (This makes the menu title a bit of a misnomer; the report is not too quick if you are asked questions you have no idea how to answer. As always, experiment. Reports are covered in chapter 8.) If the cursor is on a database but that database is not in current use, dBASE IV first opens the database, then prompts you for information regarding the report format.

The last option on the immediate menu, Menus:F10, brings us back to the top of the screen. Press the [F10] key from the Control Center and the top line of menu items is made available, beginning with the leftmost menu item. If no item is highlighted, dBASE IV defaults to the first menu item. Note that accessing top line menu items changes the prompts at the bottom of the screen (figure 4-12). These prompts are for moving through and selecting menu item options. The bottom of the screen changes back to the original work surface setting when you exit any top line menu option.

Use the [Esc] key to move through menu levels.

A few things are not so obvious about the Control Center (or any work surface for that matter). First, you can stop what you are doing by pressing the [Esc] key. Pressing [Esc] from a top line menu item returns you to the work surface. Pressing [Esc] from the work surface causes dBASE IV to prompt you for confirmation that you want to quit what you are doing (figure 4-13) and exit to the dBASE prompt.

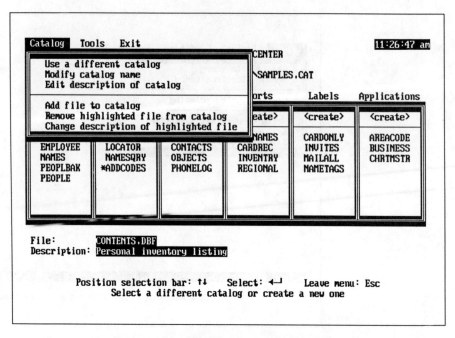

Figure 4-12 *Accessing a top line menu item changes the prompts at the bottom of the screen. Usually, the information has to do with movement through the menu options rather than the complete work surface itself.*

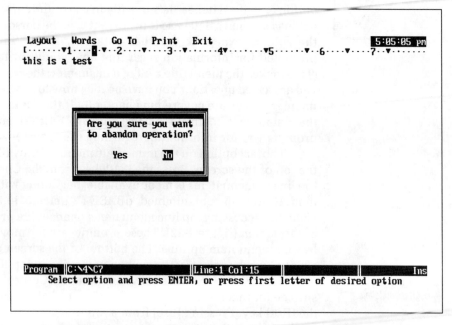

Figure 4-13 *Pressing the [Esc] key from any work surface causes dBASE IV to prompt for confirmation that you want to abandon the current operation.*

Use the [Alt] key to quickly call up a specific menu.

Another equally unobvious item is the ability to call up any top line menu item by pressing the first letter of the menu item and the [Alt] key simultaneously. For example, you can call up the Tools top line menu by pressing the [Alt-T] keystroke combination.

Basic Work Surface Features

The previous section provided a tour of the Control Center and the basics of menu use. This section looks specifically at how things are done on work surfaces. dBASE IV work surfaces are primarily the Create screens and dBASE IV Edit screens (as opposed to I/O screens you create). Work surfaces and their operations are covered in more detail in later parts of this book. Here they are only used for demonstration.

Figure 4-14 is a typical Create Database work surface. Figure 4-15 is an example of a Modify File work surface. First note the features on these work surfaces that have not changed from the Control Center: the top menu line starting at the left and extending towards the center, the clock tucked into the top right of the screen, and the central work area.

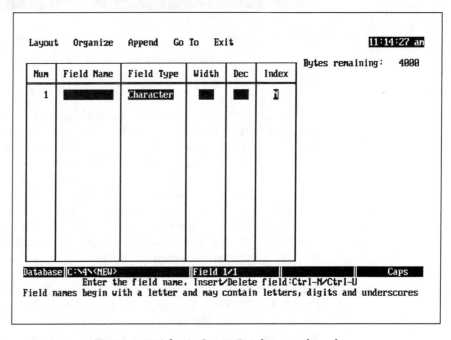

Figure 4-14 A basic Create Database work surface.

What is different? Look at figure 4-14 and you will see that the bottom of the screen differs from the Control Center screen. First, what is an immediate menu on the Control Center is replaced by some keystroke combination information and information immediately useful to the creation of databases. This is common on all work surfaces.

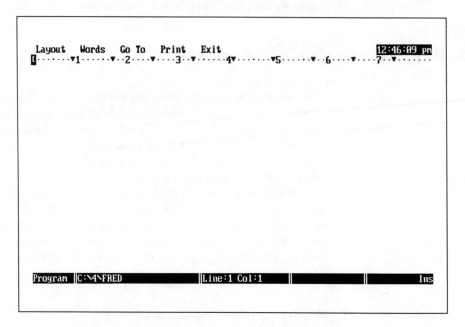

Figure 4-15 A basic Modify File work surface.

Want to see the rule broken? Look at figure 4-15. There is no information regarding immediate keystroke combinations or help at the bottom of the screen. This is because figure 4-15 is a Modify File screen, as opposed to a "structured" information work screen (such as figure 4-14).

What is the difference? When you CREATE or MODIFY a database, you are working with something—a database—that has a definite structure. The database structure is records and fields and information about individual fields that is necessary for a given database to hold the necessary data. The MODIFY FILE command essentially tells dBASE IV to start working in a word processing environment. Note the menu line at the top of figure 4-15. The entire work space is intended for free use of the full screen. You can put the cursor anywhere on the screen and type information. You can use the MODIFY FILE command to write a letter, enter a program, design a menu, and so on. The fact that the Modify File screen is unstructured is what makes it different from the Create Database screen.

Despite differences in what each work surface is doing, note the similarities in structure. This is the important element to leave this chapter with. This chapter has provided only the basic screen layouts. The following chapters cover each screen in more depth, with particular emphasis on how to quickly and accurately get each screen's specific task done.

Understanding and Designing Databases

This chapter starts the actual process of using dBASE IV to do relevant work. We begin with a database designed on paper, then transfer that design to the dBASE IV system. We use two methods that are really one in the same, as you will see. The first method is through the Control Center; the second method is from the dBASE prompt. Note that I use the > > symbol as my dBASE prompt. Most people use a period. There is nothing wrong with using either of these or any other symbol as your prompt. Originally, I used < > as my dBASE prompt because I was having an intimate relationship with Janus. Then I started seeing Justice and used no visible prompts at all. Not being able to see the prompts posed a problem, so I went out with Juno, but she insisted on yoking me to the computer like some dumb ox.

Hey, this can be fun. Give it a try.

Understanding Databases

What is there to understand about a database? You put information in, you get information out, right? Oh, that it were that easy.

The database is the fundamental part of your database management system.

The database is the central method of passing information from one person to another. The key word in the preceding sentence is *passing*. It does some but not much good when only one person ever uses the database. You can put information in and get it back out, but you probably know what information is in there because you put it in there to begin with. You can correlate the information differently than how you first entered it into the database, but that implies you have an idea of what you are looking for. Often, this isn't the case. Usually people associated with certain data already know which correlations they want and plan their systems accordingly. But when the data is looked at by an outside person, someone not intimately associated with the data, wheels turn, gears mesh, things click, and new correlations are hypothesized. This is why some people are expert at designing database management systems and other people are expert at data analysis.

So, what must be understood about databases? The rules can be broken down as follows:

1. Databases should be simple. You don't want to create a database with more than twenty fields. Never design a database with more than twenty-five fields.

2. Remember what is important and make that information easily accessible to both the user and the database system itself.

3. Don't go wild with power. The more you build into a database or a database management system, the more things can go wrong. Only put in what is relevant to getting the job done. (In the early sixties, everybody could learn how to do basic automotive repair. Now engines are so complex it takes a registered mechanic just to open the hood. Keep your databases as simple as cars were in the early sixties.)

4. Databases are something you communicate with. Think of how difficult some interpersonal communications are and realize you have to speak clearly, directly, and without ambiguity.

5. The database, not the database management system, is your principal tool. From it, you build all your other tools. This is an important concept. You create a database, add data, begin seeing relationships among the data, then create other relationships to see how they work. All of the work you do, however, is based on the database. This means you must look ahead to determine what types of relationships you and others will want to work with. Good luck!

There you go. There are probably lots more rules to understanding databases, but these make a good start and I suspect all the other rules are permutations of these. Much of these rules apply directly to the design of databases and are covered in the next section in a practical manner. Direct design applications cover rules 1, 2 and 3.

What about rules 4 and 5? When I say "databases are something you communicate with" I am asking you to recognize that you will tell your database management system something and then ask it questions. You will tell it data and then ask questions about that data. If you don't tell your database management system the initial information clearly, it will become muddled and confused when you ask it a question about that data. Similarly, you can't ask your database management system a question if you are not sure what you want to know.

Not being sure what you want to know is often a problem for database users. Someone says, "That information has got to be in the database somewhere. All we have to do is find it." I love it when someone says that.

"We never designed the system to look for that type of information."

A database is a GIGO device. You put garbage in, you get garbage out.

"Does that mean it's not there?"

"I don't know. It might be, but not in its present form."

Then comes the big statement you will always hear: "Then fix it."

This is all well and good for me to hear because I make part of my living by fixing things. But you may not make part of your living doing so, and not being able to fix things may cost you your job. The solution? Tell everyone up front what they can expect based on the designs you have been given. Tell everyone they have to be clear, concise, and direct in what they want to know and how they want to know it.

What about rule 5, "the database is your principal tool"? That it is. I strongly suggest that you start with a basic database design (as shown in the next section) and add layers of complexity as time goes on. The layers of complexity can be report forms, QBEs, applications built around the database, linking different databases, and so on. But the key element is the database itself. Your first step is to create a simple database, then build on it. You start with simple bread, then go on to more complicated recipes such as Challah and sourdough. You don't start with Winter Rye bread as your first baking experience.

Database Design Techniques and Concepts

Rules 1 through 3 in the preceding section have to do with actual database design, in particular, dBASE IV databases and their design. Rule 1 says you should not design a database with more than twenty fields and never design a database with more than twenty-five fields.

Let's consider a basic accounting system as an example. What types of information should a basic accounting system be able to give you?

Account number

Account title

Account description

Credit/Debit

Balance

Entry date

Account address

Account name

Account contact

Account city

Account state

Account zip

Account phone

This is an extremely simplified accounting system. It does contain much of the information you would want, however, to do basic work.

Note that the information is divided into two parts. The first part contains the actual numbers for the account. The second part contains the contact information for the account. The two parts make up a total of thirteen fields. Now think for a moment; is there ever a time when you want to see all thirteen fields on the screen at one time?

Of course there is. You want to see all thirteen fields on the screen at one time when you first enter the account into the system. After that, you want only one set of fields or the other, but usually not both. You may want a few fields from each set for reporting, but that adds a level of complexity to the system that we should avoid right now. The point is to make two simple databases instead of one. This example uses thirteen fields, but the point is valid for larger databases in a number of ways.

Using databases with large numbers of fields means filling the computer's memory with lots of dead space. When you create a database with lots of fields, you have lots of records in which not every field is used. This means the computer's memory is filled with empty space. Although this may be the usual status of people in your office, it should not be the case with your computer. You want to use the computer's memory in tight little chunks. In this way, you can keep more useful information in the computer's memory—hence speeding up operations—than if you used databases with many fields that were relatively empty.

When does the problem begin occurring? When you have about twenty to twenty-five fields.

Another reason to keep databases to twenty-five or fewer fields has to do with human engineering considerations. Despite what software companies may tell you, people don't process information the way computers do. Humans aren't designed to think in rows and columns, but spreadsheets do and now we have learned to as well. Humans definitely don't think in binary or assembler. Some people find it odd when I say I'm fluent in about six languages and twenty or so dialects. "Which ones?" they ask. English, French, Spanish... is what they wish to hear. Instead, I say, "dBASE, C, Prolog, Smalltalk..." Okay, so maybe I do know some English.

The point of this isn't an exercise in vanity. It is to let you know that people don't think the way computers do. In the case of database management systems, this means people can't easily handle more than a screenful of information at a time. Does this mean you can create systems with several screens of information, provided you present the information to the user a single screen at a time?

Come on, now. How else can you present it except a single screen at a time? No, I mean you can't design a system where data input or editing has to cover more than a single screen. If you design a database that requires two data I/O screens for proper handling, you need to include a means of toggling from one screen to the other. Ideally, you should design the screens so that information from the noncurrent screen is viewable. This makes things complicated and confusing. Complications are the programmer's source of income. Confusion is the programmer's source of unemployment. And this scenario is simply using a two-screen data I/O system. Imagine if the database required three or more I/O screens to be functional? Not only would you need a method of toggling from one screen to another, you would need a means of calling any of the available screens from the system. Whoosh!

This all comes down to human engineering. Remember that your database designs will be used by humans. The computer can handle databases with lots more than twenty-five fields. People can't. Engineer for humans, not for machines. You will keep your job longer.

Rule 2 says to remember what is important and make that information easily accessible to both you and your database. Don't be disheartened by what I say next: Your database is more important than you are. If you don't make the important fields easily accessible to the database management system, the whole system will become sluggish and wasteful. In my dBASE III Plus books, I emphasized that key fields—the fields you index your database on—should always be the first fields in the database, regardless of how many fields are in the database as a whole. The reason for this emphasis with dBASE III Plus was that product's use of separate index files for each key field. You had a total of seven index files per database, so the ability to create multiple-field search keys demanded that key fields be quickly accessible to the system. You didn't want the database management system to be looking all over the database for key fields; you wanted them to be darn handy so things could move quickly.

How does this translate into dBASE IV? dBASE IV doesn't use key fields and index files in the same way as dBASE III Plus. dBASE IV can use standard dBASE III Plus NDX files, but it is happier using MDX (multiple key field index) files. Each individual MDX file can contain up to forty-seven index keys. These individual index keys must be single fields in the database if the MDX file is created using only the database design work space (described in this chapter and shown in figures 5-1 and 5-2).

Be careful about this. dBASE IV automatically creates a production MDX file when you create a new database and request an index on any field. But production MDX indices are best thought of as vanilla ice cream compared to what dBASE IV's nonproduction MDX files can do.

Production MDX index expressions must be based on a single field from the current database. You can have as many index expressions as you want, but each expression must be a single field. Pretty vanilla, huh?

A key to understanding this is knowing what an *index expression* is. Index expressions are the pieces of information dBASE IV copies from the database file when it creates the index file, whether the index file is a dBASE IV MDX file or a III Plus compatible NDX single-index file. The pieces of information dBASE IV copies are all based on data in the fields in the database and can be parts of separate fields, collections of parts of different fields, or complex programmatic expressions based on parts or all of the different fields in the database.

This is where an example conveys the idea better than anything else.

Index expressions can be as simple as a single field or as complex as the following sentence:

Index on the two-digit code for the month the person was born, the first and last characters of the person's last name, the first character of the person's first name, the last two digits of the year in which the person was born, the two-digit code for the day on which the person was born, and a single digit to ensure that this index expression is unique in case everything that came before was duplicated somewhere.

Suppose you have a database with FIRSTNAME, LASTNAME, and DOB (date of birth) fields and a memory variable, UNIQUER. The sentence becomes the dBASE IV index expression

```
IIF(LEN(LTRIM(STR(MONTH(DOB)))) = 1, [0] + ;
    LTRIM(STR(MONTH(DOB))), LTRIM(STR(MONTH(DOB)))) + ;
    LEFT(LASTNAME,1) + RIGHT(LASTNAME,1) + ;
    LEFT(FIRSTNAME,1) + LTRIM(STR(YEAR(DOB))) + ;
    IIF(LEN(LTRIM(STR(DAY(DOB)))) = 1, [0] + ;
    LTRIM(STR(DAY(DOB))), LTRIM(STR(DAY(DOB)))) + ;
    LTRIM(STR(UNIQUER))
```

This is the algorithm New Hampshire uses to issue licenses, by the way. And they let us remain first in the nation primary?

The point here is that dBASE IV won't let you enter anything more complicated than FIRSTNAME or LASTNAME or DOB as index expressions when you create a production MDX file. You can enter the preceding, highly complex index expression when you create an MDX file outside the database design work surface. Simply put, the possibilities for index expressions are endless when you design an MDX outside the database design work surface, but not endless while you are inside it. Inside the database design work surface, you are strictly limited to using single fields from the database when you create a production MDX file.

Back to the basics. Figure 5-1 shows the first set of fields from our basic accounting system, described previously in this chapter. Note that we index on the account number (ACCTNUM), the account title (ACCT-TITLE), and the entry date (ENTRYDATE). Note also that I haven't placed every key field at the top of the database, which is what you would expect me to do based on our previous discussion.

Before going further, one little mystery needs to be cleared up: I created the Credit/Debit field as CR and made it a logical field. In other words, the CR field is either true—the account is a credit account—or false—the account is a debit account. This is useful for people who don't use standard accounting procedures.

Back to why the key fields are not all at the top of the file. When you create a database and instruct dBASE IV to index some fields in that data-

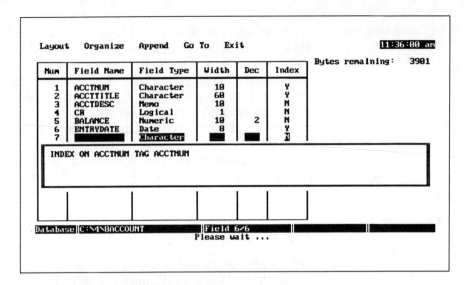

Figure 5-1 With single-field indices, you can tell dBASE IV which
fields are to be indexed when you design the database. To use multiple
key field indices, you have to design the MDX file separately.

base, dBASE does something uncommon among microcomputer-based
database management systems. It creates something similar to an SQL indexing scheme on the marked fields in the database. This means dBASE IV
looks at the fields you want indexed and creates a separate file that contains the field names and the record numbers corresponding to those field
values in the desired indexing scheme, but in a tightly organized form that
allows the system to do some fast searching. It works like this: when you
ask dBASE IV to create an MDX file, it creates that file with a special purpose. The MDX file is called a production file and is automatically opened
each time you open the corresponding DBF file.

Unlike dBASE III Plus, where you had to specifically mention which
NDX files you wanted opened with each database, dBASE IV opens production files when you first open a database. Because the database is linked
to the production multiple-index file, you do not have to place all key fields
at the top of the database during the design phase.

But what if you want to use your database with an existing dBASE III
Plus system? Your best bet is to place the key fields at the top of the database, then index them. This allows dBASE IV and III Plus to access the key
field information quickly, speeding editing and reorganizing of data.

Be aware that you can create multiple-index key files with calculated
key fields, but not during the database design phase.

Rule 3 is the most important rule for new users and the most difficult
one to deal with. Basically, don't try to build a house if you have never held
a hammer. As a matter of fact, don't attempt to hang a picture if you think a
hammer is any object that is heavy on one end and has a handle. I have seen
too many pictures covering holes left by frying pans to know that people
use what is handy rather than get the right tool.

Let the database do its job for a while before modifying it.

After you have designed the basic database, you will find either yourself or other people asking for more and more things from the database. Don't listen to yourself or them. At least not for a while. Wait and see what happens to the existing database before you attempt to put anything else into it or get anything else from it. Don't attempt to design something that answers everybody's questions because everybody's questions are not always worth answering and certain questions may come up so rarely they are not worth answering at all. Understand?

Okay. You're ready. Go sit at the computer and get the Control Center up on the screen. We are going to design a database.

Designing Fields

The first question you ask might be this: How do I get to the Control Center? You may be looking at the Control Center if that is how your dBASE IV is set to start up. There are two other options for getting the Control Center on the screen. The first method is to press the [F2] (Assist) key. The second method is to type the following at the dBASE prompt:

```
ASSIST [Enter]
```

Both these methods will get you to a screen similar to the first figure in chapter 4 (figure 4-1). The highlight is on ⟨create⟩ underneath the Data column, so press [Enter]. You are now at the database design screen, shown in figure 5-2.

Six columns are on the database design screen. These columns are Num, Field Name, Field Type, Width, Dec, and Index. The first column, Num, contains the number of the particular field in the database. The topmost field in the database is the first field. Remember that in dBASE II, dBASE III, and dBASE III Plus the first field should be the most referenced field, primarily for indexing. This is because dBASE II, III, and III Plus need to maintain a separate NDX file for each key field or key field combination. dBASE IV can maintain up to forty-seven key fields or key field combinations in a single MDX file. Thus, key field placement in dBASE IV is not as important as it is in dBASE IV's predecessors (unless you are designing a dBASE IV database for use with dBASE III or III Plus).

The Num column header tells you the field number of a given field in the current database. This is useful when you need to do quick editing of a large database structure. Suppose you have a database of twenty to twenty-five fields and you want to edit field 20 of the entire structure, but no others. You could use the cursor control keys to move the highlight to field 20. An easier method is to use the [Alt-G] keystroke combination, shown in figure 5-3. This keystroke combination gets you to a menu which lets you enter the field number directly, saving time and keystrokes.

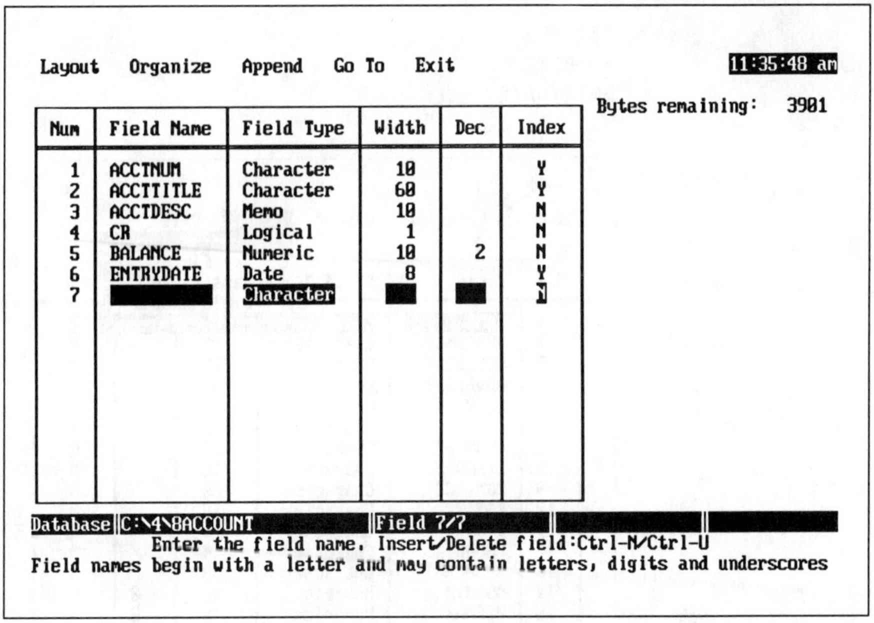

```
 Layout   Organize   Append   Go To   Exit                    11:35:48 am
                                                  Bytes remaining:   3901
 ┌─────┬────────────┬─────────────┬───────┬─────┬────────┐
 │ Num │ Field Name │ Field Type  │ Width │ Dec │ Index  │
 ├─────┼────────────┼─────────────┼───────┼─────┼────────┤
 │  1  │ ACCTNUM    │ Character   │  10   │     │   Y    │
 │  2  │ ACCTTITLE  │ Character   │  60   │     │   Y    │
 │  3  │ ACCTDESC   │ Memo        │  10   │     │   N    │
 │  4  │ CR         │ Logical     │   1   │     │   N    │
 │  5  │ BALANCE    │ Numeric     │  10   │  2  │   N    │
 │  6  │ ENTRYDATE  │ Date        │   8   │     │   Y    │
 │  7  │ ███████    │ Character   │  ██   │ ██  │   N    │
 └─────┴────────────┴─────────────┴───────┴─────┴────────┘
 Database C:\4\8ACCOUNT          Field 7/7
         Enter the field name.  Insert/Delete field:Ctrl-N/Ctrl-U
 Field names begin with a letter and may contain letters, digits and underscores
```

Figure 5-2 *The database design screen. This is the principal software tool for putting the database together in the best way possible. The best tool for database design is paper and pencil because the actual design of the database and its fields should be done before the computer is even turned on.*

In the Field Name column, the actual field name is entered, edited, and listed. Field names can be as expressive and explicit as you wish, provided they follow the following rules. All database field names must begin with a letter. You can't use a number, a math symbol, brackets, underscores, hyphens, graphic characters, and so on as the first character in the field name. After you have used a letter as the first character in the field name, however, you can use any letter, any number, or the underscore character as part of the field name. Further, database field names can't exceed ten characters. They can be a single character, but you can't have more than ten characters in any field name. Note that you can be extremely descriptive with ten characters but not usefully descriptive with a single character. It is better to use all ten characters and be verbose when naming a field rather than use one or two characters and hope everybody knows what you meant when it comes time to redesign the system.

The following are valid database field names:

```
MELVIN
SERIALNUM
SNUM
ADDRESS1
ADDRESS2
```

CAT_NUM
YO_BOY
ENTRYDATE

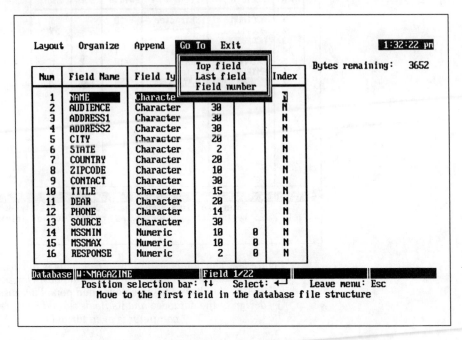

Figure 5-3 *The field number can be useful when modifying the structure of a database. Here, the [Alt-G] keystroke combination is used to activate the Go To menu.*

The next column is Field Type. dBASE IV supports several data types. These data types have different uses and are significant for more than just data entry. The data types are

character

numeric

float

date

logical

memo

Figures 5-4 through 5-9 show how the database design screen changes depending on which data type you are placing in the database. You can run through the possible field data types by pressing the [Spacebar]. You can also simply enter the first letter of the desired data type. This latter method forces dBASE IV to put the cursor in the Width column, described next in this section.

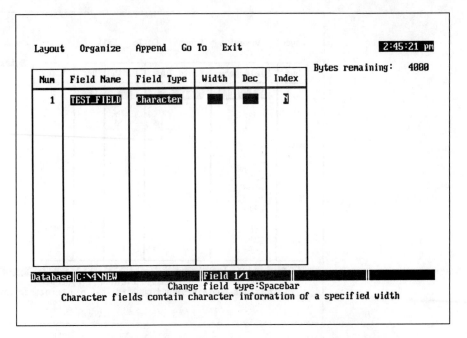

Figure 5-4 A character field type is entered in the database structure.
Note that dBASE IV wants you to determine the field width for a
character field. This is not the case with some of the other field types.

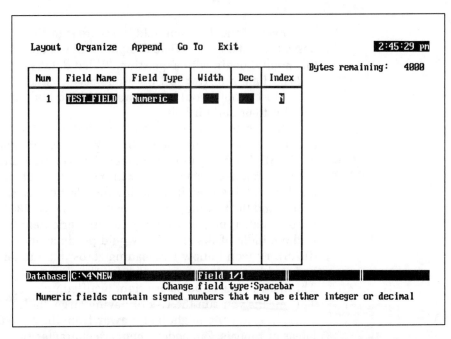

Figure 5-5 A numeric field type is entered in the database structure.
Note that dBASE IV wants you to determine the field width and field
decimal width for a numeric field (necessary only for numeric
and float data types).

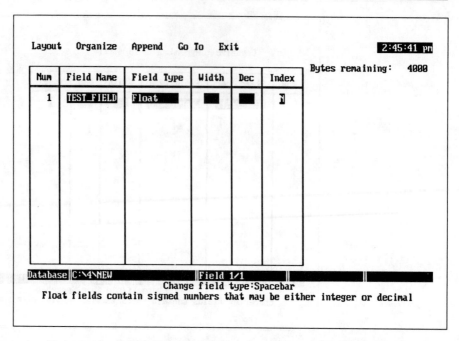

```
   Layout   Organize   Append   Go To   Exit              2:45:41 pm

                                                  Bytes remaining:   4000
   ┌─────┬────────────┬────────────┬───────┬─────┬───────┐
   │ Num │ Field Name │ Field Type │ Width │ Dec │ Index │
   ├─────┼────────────┼────────────┼───────┼─────┼───────┤
   │  1  │ TEST_FIELD │ Float      │   █   │  █  │   ▌   │
   │     │            │            │       │     │       │
   │     │            │            │       │     │       │
   │     │            │            │       │     │       │
   │     │            │            │       │     │       │
   │     │            │            │       │     │       │
   │     │            │            │       │     │       │
   │     │            │            │       │     │       │
   │     │            │            │       │     │       │
   └─────┴────────────┴────────────┴───────┴─────┴───────┘
 Database C:\4\NEW                      Field 1/1
                    Change field type:Spacebar
      Float fields contain signed numbers that may be either integer or decimal
```

*Figure 5-6 A float field type is entered in the database structure. Note
that dBASE IV wants you to determine the field width and field
decimal width for a float field (necessary only for numeric
and float data types).*

Each of the different field types are significant and have unique purposes when it comes to field design. I will use an anecdote to demonstrate
this point. I begin with a question, "What data type would you use for zip
codes?" I am referring to US Postal Service zip codes (this is a hint).

Most people would say "Numeric." I'd nod my head knowingly and
wait for their call for help.

No, zip codes aren't numeric, even though the US Postal Service uses
only numbers in its zip code listings. Zip codes are character data because
of dBASE IV's thoughts on character data versus numeric data. Begin with
the idea that a zip code entry will be ten characters (03061-3861, for example, contains the zip code for the Nashua, NH, central Post Office,
03061, and the box number for Northern Lights, 3861). First, numbers are
the only data type you can place in a numeric field type. Thus, the hyphen
in the middle of the zip code would produce an error message. Second,
dBASE IV won't allow any leading zeros in a numeric field. That means
you could not enter any zip codes for New England in a numeric field type.
Third, all numeric fields are right justified unless you specify otherwise.
This means you run the risk of having large "holes" in your printout because the zip code might be far away from the state field when you print
labels or reports. Zip codes, then, are character fields.

Character fields can be from 1 to 254 characters wide. Think about
this for a minute before you go wild creating character fields that are 254

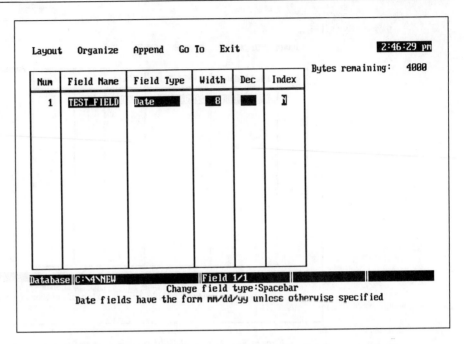

Figure 5-7 A date field type is entered in the database structure.
dBASE IV automatically enters a field width of eight characters
because all date field types are displayed in the form nn/nn/nn or
nn-nn-nn. Note that the delimiter between digits may vary depending
on which date convention (American or French) you are using. dBASE
IV stores dates and hours internally as serialized numbers.

characters wide. Your computer screen is only 80 characters wide. Unless
you have a fancy as heck printer, you can probably get printouts only 180
characters wide, at best. Trying to enter 254 characters into a database field
means wrapping the entry across the screen at least four times, not a pretty
sight. One option for using 254 characters in a single field is through
dBASE IV's @ SAY...GET PICTURE "@Sn" function. This line can bo used
to place a field on the screen in a variety of ways. All of the different ways
come down to this simple method: Place a smaller field window on the
screen and scroll the field's information through the window. In general,
however, you don't want a single-character field to hold more than a single
screen line of information (about 70 characters).

Fixed-length character fields should be used for data that seldom changes.

The best way to think of character fields is as sources of immediate
text-based information. Address1, for example, contains some immediate
text-based information. So does Company, Title, Contact, and so on. This
information also bears the mark of being somewhat static—it isn't going to
change often, if at all. After this type of data is entered, it is probably going
to stay around for a while. These fields are also much less than 254 characters wide. So, back to my original lecture of designing on paper before you
sit at the computer. Why would you want to enter, for example, 100 to 254
characters of text data into a field?

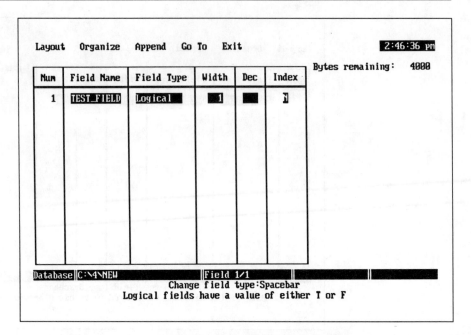

Figure 5-8 A logical field type is entered into the database structure. dBASE IV automatically enters a field width of one character because all logical fields are viewed as up or down, 0 or 1, on or off— literally a single bit of data.

You would want to do that if the text data was an explanation regarding the rest of the record or at least the part of the record currently on the screen. For example, suppose you are tracking past due accounts. Maybe you would like to include a brief note in the record that the individual whose record you are using has been in the hospital for six months and therefore has not been able to pay this particular bill. This brief explanatory piece of text will change as the information regarding this record changes. Such a field might include special shipping instructions or emergency contact personnel. The data is dynamic and is more often an explanation or elaboration of data in another field or fields rather than actual information such as the data in Contact, Address1, or Company. Note that character fields can be indexed.

What do you do if you want lots of text data, regardless of the data being static or dynamic? You might want to consider a memo field. As mentioned, memo fields have two very different components in the dBASE IV system. Remember that creating a memo field in a database causes dBASE IV to create an auxiliary text file. This auxiliary file has the same name as the current database, but the file extension is DBT (database text).

The first component of the memo field is the marker in the DBF file. This is the ten-character field with the four-character placeholder, as shown in figures 5-10 and 5-11. Information in a memo field may not be truly dynamic. After something is in there, it may stay there forever, which

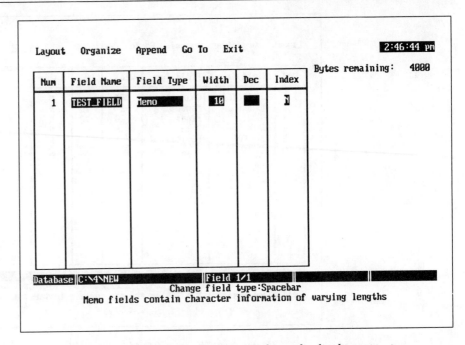

Figure 5-9 A memo field type is entered into the database structure. dBASE IV automatically enters a field width of ten characters for this field type. As described earlier, entering a memo field type tells dBASE IV to create an auxiliary DBT file where the actual memos are stored. The ten-character field created in the DBF file is used to store the location of a particular record's memo in the DBT file.

is a long time. What might happen, however, is that new information might be added to the existing data. This is often the case in medical and dental record keeping, maintenance records, and the like.

Figure 5-10 The memo field shows up in a full-screen edit as a four-character field.

There are some things you should know about memo fields and how dBASE IV works with the DBT files that hold them. First, dBASE IV gives

```
  Layout   Organize   Append   Go To   Exit                    4:10:14 pm

                                                 Bytes remaining:    3687
  ┌─────┬─────────────┬─────────────┬───────┬──────┬───────┐
  │ Num │ Field Name  │ Field Type  │ Width │ Dec  │ Index │
  ├─────┼─────────────┼─────────────┼───────┼──────┼───────┤
  │  1  │ CHARACTER   │ Character   │  254  │      │   N   │
  │  2  │ NUMERIC     │ Numeric     │   20  │  18  │   N   │
  │  3  │ FLOAT       │ Float       │   20  │  18  │   N   │
  │  4  │ DATE        │ Date        │    8  │      │   N   │
  │  5  │ LOGICAL     │ Logical     │    1  │      │   N   │
  │  6  │ MEMO        │ Memo        │   10  │      │   N   │
  │     │             │             │       │      │       │
  └─────┴─────────────┴─────────────┴───────┴──────┴───────┘

  Database C:\4\C8-2                     Field 6/6
            Enter the field name.  Insert/Delete field:Ctrl-N/Ctrl-U
  Field names begin with a letter and may contain letters, digits and underscores
```

Figure 5-11 *The memo field is entered into the database as a ten-character field. It appears as only four characters wide in a full-screen edit because dBASE IV uses the ten-character field to mark the current record's memo position in the DBT file with a number corresponding to the number of 512-byte blocks that mark the beginning of the desired memo.*

you a nice visual clue as to whether or not data exists in the memo field. Look at figures 5-12 and 5-10. The memo field indicator in figure 5-12 is in uppercase (MEMO) because I entered some text in record 1's memo field. The memo field indicator in figure 5-10 is in lowercase (memo) because no text has been entered.

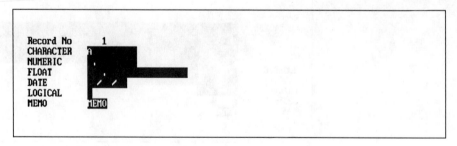

```
  Record No       1
  CHARACTER    A
  NUMERIC
  FLOAT
  DATE
  LOGICAL
  MEMO        MEMO
```

Figure 5-12 *The memo field indicator in this figure is in uppercase (MEMO), which indicates the existence of data in the memo field.*

The second thing to know about memo fields and DBT files has to do with what happens when you remove records from the DBF file. The removal of records from a database is usually a two-step operation. First you DELETE the records from the database. This does not actually remove the records from the database; it simply marks the records for physical removal. The physical removal of records is done with the PACK command. This two-step operation is the best and safest way to remove records from the database. Why? Because you can always RECALL the DELETEd records, at least up until you physically PACK the database. You can be adventurous and ZAP your database. This single command is equivalent to DELETEing all the records in your database, then PACKing the database.

What happens when you remove records from the DBF file and some of the records have corresponding memo field data in the DBT file? Consider the following two directory listings. In the first directory listing, all four records in the database contain data. Wait, there is more. There is also data in the DBT file. Specifically, there is a string of text in the memo field of each of the four DBF files. Where did these text strings go? Into the DBT file, of course. Note the size of these files. Remember that the DBT file has text data, and the text data is stored in 512-byte blocks. This means that even writing the text string, "This is the data for the first record's MEMO field," consumes 512 bytes of room both in memory and on the disk, when saved to a file, even though the text string is only 48 bytes long.

```
C8-2       DBF         466    11-17-88    4:51p
C8-2       DBT        2560    11-17-88    4:51p

        2 Files        3026 Char. 11927552 Free
```

The next directory listing was made after we DELETEd and PACKed the DBF file. You will notice that the size of the database is reduced some 240 bytes. Is the DBT file size reduced? No! Trust me, we did DELETE ALL the records and then PACK the database. A peculiarity of dBASE III, dBASE III Plus, and dBASE IV is that they don't do good housekeeping when it comes to purging DBT files of unwanted information.

```
C8-2       DBF         226    11-17-88    7:43p
C8-2       DBT        2560    11-17-88    7:43p

        2 Files        2786 Char. 11923456 Free
```

A memo field should be your field of last resort due to its use of a secondary file and problems with removing data from it.

What does this have to do with you and database field design? It means don't use memo fields unless you really have to. Using memo fields and their related DBT files can cause you to lose disk space when you work with a large file. Note that third-party packages are available to collapse and PACK DBT files, without losing the memos for records you want to keep in the DBF file.

It gets scarier. Just because you PACK or ZAP the database and records are no longer in the DBF file, information is still in the DBT file. You can't get to it because you can't get to a record number that correctly accesses the file block containing information in the DBT file. Why? Even though the data in the DBT file still exists, it is essentially hidden to most dBASE IV users. When you PACK or ZAP the database, you remove DBF file information of where things exist in the DBT file. When you add new records to the DBF file and get to a point where your new data is hitting the old, hidden DBT file data, the old DBT file data is erased to make room for the new data. But there are giants in the woods, children, and all should beware. People with either lots of patience and no computer skill or no patience and lots of computer skill can still access, read, print, and generally publish the hidden DBT file data, the very data you thought was either PACKed or ZAPped. As mentioned, third-party software products remove hidden data from the DBT file. If you don't want to go this route, you may want to consider the bigger hammer method of removing hidden data from the DBT file:

1. Use a word processor and the CONFIG.DB WP command to transfer valuable DBT file data into word processing files.

2. MODIFY the STRUCTURE of the database to completely remove the memo field. This tells dBASE IV to erase the existing associated DBT file from the disk.

3. MODIFY the STRUCTURE a second time to create a new DBT file.

4. Use the word processor to bring the saved data into the DBT file.

I recognize that this is not the best method for solving the stated problem. It is a matter of time and money. If your time is cheap, this method is fine. If your time is valuable, it is probably more worthwhile to invest in a third-party software package that does a more elegant job.

This last warning regarding DBT files is for people bringing DBT files into dBASE IV from dBASE III Plus. dBASE III Plus allowed memo field data to exceed 64K of space. That is a lot of text! Unfortunately, dBASE IV does not allow such verbosity. You are limited to 64K of text per memo field. This means you should not take a working dBASE III Plus DBT file and use it in dBASE IV if you know or even suspect you have some memo fields that exceed 64K in length. dBASE IV will truncate the field size and you will lose information. Which information will you lose? The most important information, of course. Your best bet is to make a copy of the dBASE III Plus DBT file and its matching DBF file and store them where dBASE IV will never find them, the land of Goshen, for example. Note that memo fields can't be indexed in the dBASE IV system.

So much for character data. How about digits that are numbers and not characters, such as posted income instead of zip codes?

dBASE IV has two methods of handling numeric data in a database. The first method, which should be familiar to anyone who has used dBASE II, III, or III Plus, is the standard numeric field format. Standard numeric format means each number is fixed in length. Fixed in length? Yes, as in each number will be, for example, five digits before the decimal point and three after, for a total of nine characters wide (5 before + 3 after + 1 decimal point = 9 characters total).

This is a powerful data format for accounting and similar applications because accounting is one member of the family of "fixed digit applications." Accounting is a fixed digit application because usually only two digits are after the decimal point. In some cases the numeric values may be rounded off to the nearest dollar. Accounting systems that routinely deal with million dollar amounts may round off to the nearest thousand. No matter what the size of the entry, fixed digit applications require a high degree of accuracy, depending on the degree of roundoff. Construction is another fixed digit application. You want the estimate to be as close as possible to the actual figures before you begin construction. Clever readers will recognize this as accounting in another guise. So, then, anything that has to do with money transfers can safely be thought of as a fixed digit application. All such applications are best handled with dBASE IV's numeric data format. Numeric fields can be indexed.

The other number format is floating. This is new with dBASE IV and brings the dBASE product line into the realm of engineering and similar disciplines. The important thing to realize about floating numbers is that *floating* means the accuracy is in question. Note the following: The accuracy of the value, not the number of digits in the value, is in question. This occurs most often in engineering and scientific notation calculations, especially in multiplication and division.

For example, you can add 345.678 and 9182.38445 and retain a high degree of accuracy in the sum in both numeric and floating data formats. The sum is 9528.06245, but you can have accuracy only to three places to the right of the decimal point because that is all the accuracy your numbers have. Sure, you may see 345.678 as 345.67800, but you don't know what those last two digits really are and you are guessing at best that the fourth and fifth digits to the right of the decimal point are both 0. So, the true answer to our summation is 9528.062. This is the same value as we got before, with the fourth and fifth digits to the right of the decimal point removed.

Now we will multiply our two numbers, 345.678 and 9182.38445. The value is 3174148.50. Heck of a number, huh? The answer to this multiplication could also be 3174148.29190710 or 3155481.68, depending on whose accuracy you want to believe. The real answer is not important because a numeric data type will only give you the number of decimal places you allow it to. The best answer will give you eight digits to the right of the decimal point and let you know that the accuracy is good only to six places. Why six? Because the least number of digits to the right of the decimal place is three, and that is in 345.678. You can only be accurate to twice the number of digits as the least number of digits you have when you multiply two numbers together. You might as well throw the 45 of 9182.38445 away for all the accuracy those two digits will give you. Further, a floating numeric format recognizes this and shifts the decimal point up or down—to the right or left—depending on where the most significant digits are found.

This means dBASE IV automatically creates an exponential notation format for any calculations used to place data in a float field. Note that you are still limited to the number of digits and decimal places you designed for the field if you directly enter data. You can use floating fields for indexing.

The date format is an eight-character field filled with three sets of two-character data sections, with each data section separated by a marker of your choice. The date format is nn/nn/nn and can be in any of several international formats. The formats are set with the SET DATE command. Date representations for 20 November 1988 in the different formats follow:

SET DATE AMERICAN	11/20/88
SET DATE ANSI	88.11.20
SET DATE BRITISH	20/11/88
SET DATE FRENCH	20/11/88
SET DATE ITALIAN	20-11-88
SET DATE JAPAN	88/11/20
SET DATE USA	11-20-88
SET DATE MDY	11/20/88
SET DATE DMY	20/11/88
SET DATE YMD	88/11/20

After you have chosen a date format, you should decide on a date separator, also known as a date delimiter. The delimiters used in this listing are the slash, the period, and the hyphen. You can set the date delimiter in two ways. The direct method is with the SET MARK command. This command lets you use any keyboard or graphics character as the date delimiter. The command form, shown in figure 5-13, is either

```
SET MARK TO "character"
```

or

```
SET MARK TO CHR(n)
```

Note that the *n* in the second SET MARK TO command form is any number from 0 to 255, which covers the extended ASCII character set. (Entering 0 results in no change in the date delimiter.)

The other method of entering a date delimiter is through the SET command. At the dBASE prompt, type SET and press [Enter]. You will see a screen similar to that shown in figure 5-14. One of the SET options is Date separator. You can toggle through only three separators with this method, however. The three options are those shown in the preceding SET DATE listing (slash, period, and hyphen). Note that Date fields can be indexed.

The next format is logical. The logical field format is a one-bit field

```
•use c8-2
Default alias is A
•? date()
11/21/88
•disp
Record#   CHARACTER        NUMERIC      FLOAT DATE     LOGICAL MEMO
     1                      0.00   .1219E+14 11/20/88  .F.    memo
•set mark to "x"
•? date()
11x21x88
•disp
Record#   CHARACTER        NUMERIC      FLOAT DATE     LOGICAL MEMO
     1                      0.00   .1219E+14 11x20x88  .F.    memo
•set mark to chr(1)
•? date()
11◙21◙88
•disp
Record#   CHARACTER        NUMERIC      FLOAT DATE     LOGICAL MEMO
     1                      0.00   .1219E+14 11◙20◙88  .F.    memo
•
```

Figure 5-13 You can use any ASCII character as the date delimiter
when you enter the delimiter with the SET MARK TO command. The
date delimiter will appear in date functions, in commands, and as the
delimiter in database fields and records.

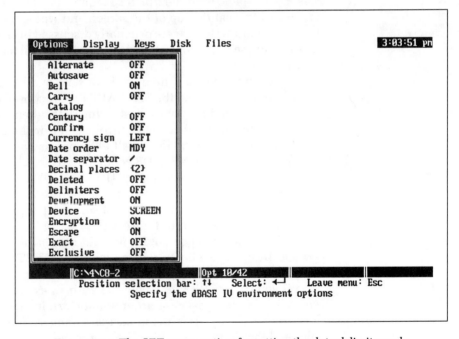

Figure 5-14 The SET menu option for setting the date delimiter only
offers the standard three options: slash, period, and hyphen.

that takes up one character width. One character width is necessary because dBASE IV automatically translates the logical single bit value into
the single characters Y, N, T, or F. These characters represent yes, no, true,
and false, respectively. You can enter data in a logical field in either upper-

case or lowercase (for example, *T* or *t*). Logical data fields can't be indexed in either an NDX or MDX file.

What good can such a slight little bit of data do in a database file? Do you remember the CR field described previously in this chapter? That field was a logical field that indicated if the amount in the record was a credit or a debit. The value of the logical CR field can even be calculated based on values in the amount field. So what? Eventually, you can write your applications so that they scan the CR field and send out dunning letters only for those whose CR value is .F., which implies that the entry is a debit. This is a much faster method than using an INDEXed amount field (even if the field is numeric) because dBASE IV scans only a single bit instead of an entire field.

Using the Database Design Menu System

Now that you have some idea of the uses for the different fields, it is time to place your design into the dBASE IV system. You should be familiar or at least comfortable with the dBASE IV database design menu system. This menu system is at the top of the screen and was shown in figure 5-2. The basics of menu systems were originally discussed in chapter 4. This section takes a more in-depth look at navigation and special techniques in the database design system.

The first important item for both new and experienced users is to make sure you have used the SET SAFETY ON command. You run the risk of overwriting and otherwise destroying data when you use the CREATE command, through either the Control Center or the dBASE prompt. The SET SAFETY command defaults to ON unless you or someone else has changed it with the CONFIG.DB commands. Check before starting any keyboard design work either by typing DISPLAY STATUS and pressing [Enter] or by pressing the [F6] key. You will get a great deal of information on the current status of dBASE IV. The first screenful of information is the most important and is shown in figure 5-15.

What is most important for us right now is the status of the SAFETY switch. In figure 5-15, you will notice that SAFETY is OFF. This means dBASE IV will automatically write over and destroy any existing database files if you try to CREATE a new file with an existing DBF's file name. It won't ask for permission or attempt to determine if you want to preserve any existing files. This is an unnecessary danger. You can avoid the loss of files and their data by entering the command

```
SET SAFETY ON
```

dBASE IV then responds to possible file overwriting with a *File already exists* prompt.

```
Currently Selected Database:
Select area:  1, Database in Use: C:\4\EXERCISE.DBF    Alias: EXERCISE
Production   MDX file:  C:\4\EXERCISE.MDX
      Master Index TAG:      EXERCISE  Key: EXERCISE

File search path:
Default disk drive: C:
Print destination: PRN:
Margin =      0
Refresh count =      0
Reprocess count =      0
Number of files open =      5
Current work area =     1

ALTERNATE  - OFF   DELIMITERS - OFF   FULLPATH   - OFF   SAFETY      - OFF
AUTOSAVE   - OFF   DESIGN     - ON    HEADING    - ON    SCOREBOARD  - OFF
BELL       - ON    DEVELOP    - ON    HELP       - OFF   SPACE       - ON
CARRY      - OFF   DEVICE     - SCRN  HISTORY    - ON    SQL         - OFF
CATALOG    - OFF   ECHO       - OFF   INSTRUCT   - ON    STATUS      - OFF
CENTURY    - OFF   ENCRYPTION - ON    INTENSITY  - ON    STEP        - OFF
CONFIRM    - OFF   ESCAPE     - ON    LOCK       - ON    TALK        - ON
CONSOLE    - ON    EXACT      - OFF   NEAR       - OFF   TITLE       - ON
DEBUG      - OFF   EXCLUSIVE  - OFF   PAUSE      - OFF   TRAP        - OFF
Press any key to continue...
```

Figure 5-15 The results of asking dBASE IV to DISPLAY STATUS.
Note that SAFETY is OFF. You usually don't want that and should
issue the SET SAFETY ON command.

Now, with that caveat, let's go through the design screen menu. The top row of the database design work surface contains a menu with the following options: Layout, Organize, Append, Go To, and Exit. The top right corner of the screen has the time stamp. Just below that is the *Bytes remaining* status. This is where dBASE IV tells you how much room is left in your database design for more fields. Remember that the total record size is limited to 4000 bytes, which can be thought of as 400 memo fields. Don't go wild with that information. You are limited to 255 fields per database record. Remember what I said earlier in this chapter? You don't want to design a database with more than twenty-five fields per record. Still, you may see a need to go nuts, and you will. Go nuts, that is. You will do that whether or not you see the need.

The left center of the screen is filled with the field design chart, which was described already. Across the bottom of the screen and directly below the field chart is the status line. The status line, from left to right, tells you that you are in the database design system, the path and name of the database you are working with, the current field position of the cursor, and the current settings of various keyboard toggles (Caps, Num, and Ins, for example). Below the status line is help information regarding the current cursor position on the screen.

We will learn about the database design menu by using it in the next section to design a database.

Designing a Database

The previous sections gave you an understanding of how databases work, how fields should be placed in them, and a basic concept of the database design menu and workspace. This section helps you get familiar with the actual design system by having you create a database.

Note that the following is intended to provide an understanding of how the dBASE IV database design system works. You can use the tools, talents, skills, and knowledge you gain here to design similar and more complex systems of your own.

Everyone's a little health conscious these days, so we will use a basic weight lifting exercise maintenance system as an example. We start by designing our database on paper.

What do we want to know about our exercise regimen? We probably want to know the day we are working out. We probably also want to know the time, which will give us a clue as to our energy level at different times during the day. We need the names of the exercises and a way of entering how much work we do at each one. At this point it might be worthwhile to explain a little bit about exercises and how they work.

You can be a body builder or someone interested in general toning. People interested in general toning do lots of repetitions of an exercise, do several sets of repetitions, and use low weights. People interested in body building do a low number of repetitions and a low number of sets of repetitions, but use much heavier weights. This has to do with what is called slow twitch and fast twitch muscle tissue—a fascinating subject, but well beyond the scope of this book.

The point to be made is that your database needs some way to keep track of the total weight used for an exercise, the number of repetitions, the number of sets, and the weight used for each set. For those unfamiliar with weight lifting regimens, each time you repeat a particular movement you are doing a rep, or repetition, of the movement. Each time you repeat a group of repetitions of a movement you are doing a set. Therefore, you can repeat a particular movement ten times at one weight and you have done ten reps. You then do the same movement another ten times, regardless of an increase or decrease in weight, and you have done another ten reps, but you have also done two sets, each of ten reps. A typical body building regimen will consist of six sets, each set consisting of four to fifteen reps.

Whoosh! Good thing we didn't choose something difficult for our first database, huh?

We will design the database for someone interested in body building simply because demonstrating this uses less room on paper. The actual design techniques are the same no matter which exercise path we take and apply to any type of database design work.

So far, our wish list looks something like this:

FIELD	TYPE	WIDTH	CALCULATED?	INDEXED?
Exercise Date	DATE	8	No	Yes
Exercise Time	CHAR	8	No	Yes
Exercise Name	CHAR	20	No	Yes
Set 1 Reps	NUM	3	No	Yes
Set 1 Weight	NUM	4	No	Yes
Set 2 Reps	NUM	3	No	Yes
Set 2 Weight	NUM	4	No	Yes
Set 3 Reps	NUM	3	No	Yes
Set 3 Weight	NUM	4	No	Yes
Set 4 Reps	NUM	3	No	Yes
Set 4 Weight	NUM	4	No	Yes
Set 5 Reps	NUM	3	No	Yes
Set 5 Weight	NUM	4	No	Yes
Set 6 Reps	NUM	3	No	Yes
Set 6 Weight	NUM	4	No	Yes
Total Weight	NUM	5	Yes	Yes
Comment	MEMO	10	No	No

What do you notice about this design before anything else? How about the facts that I didn't include a decimal column and I did include a Calculated column? We won't be working with fractions of weights, so decimal values are needless. However, we will need to calculate the total weight used during an exercise. You should also notice that I included a memo field, Comment, in case you want to write in something like, "Had a good time, thanks," or "Barely able to breathe when done. Why am I doing this to myself?" to describe an exercise.

Before going any further, I want you to realize that this design is *not* an optimal design. It is, however, an excellent place to start. We will make refinements to this system throughout the book. This will help you grow comfortable with the database design system, the programming interface, the report generator, the form and screen generator, and so on.

Now that we have our database designed on paper, let's create it in dBASE IV. First, fight your way through the field form, moving only with the cursor keys, until the information is filled in. Fighting your way through the database design form will give you a deep appreciation of what I will tell you next.

```
USE EXERCISE
DISP STRUC
Structure for database: C:\4\EXERCISE.DBF
Number of data records:       0
Date of last update  : 11/23/88
```

Field	Field Name	Type	Width	Dec	Index
1	DATE	Date	8		Y
2	TIME	Character	8		Y
3	EXERCISE	Character	20		Y
4	SET_1_REPS	Numeric	3		Y
5	SET_1_WGT	Numeric	4		Y
6	SET_2_REPS	Numeric	3		Y

```
 7   SET_2_WGT    Numeric      4              Y
 8   SET_3_REPS   Numeric      3              Y
 9   SET_3_WGT    Numeric      4              Y
10   SET_4_REPS   Numeric      3              Y
11   SET_4_WGT    Numeric      4              Y
12   SET_5_REPS   Numeric      3              Y
13   SET_5_WGT    Numeric      4              Y
14   SET_6_REPS   Numeric      3              Y
15   SET_6_WGT    Numeric      4              Y
16   TOTAL_WGT    Numeric      5              Y
17   COMMENT      Memo        10              N
** Total **                   94
```

The database design menu is not really helpful when you are first designing your database. It can help you after the fact because it contains powerful organizational, display, and editing functions. Other keys, however, can be of help.

The [Enter] and [Tab] keys move the cursor from one column entry to the next. For example, if the cursor is currently in the Field Name column and a field name exists, pressing either [Enter] or [Tab] moves the cursor to the Type column. Again, if the cursor is currently in the Type column and a field type exists (note that dBASE IV defaults to a character field type), pressing either [Enter] or [Tab] moves the cursor to the Width column. Also note that dBASE IV moves the cursor from the Type to Width columns only for character, numeric, and floating data types. dBASE IV automatically fills in field widths for date, logical, and memo fields. Further, dBASE IV lets you enter decimal values only for numeric and floating data types and will not allow you to index memo or logical data types.

The [Shift-Tab] keystroke combination moves the cursor from the current column to the preceding column. For example, if the cursor is currently in the Type column, pressing [Shift-Tab] moves the cursor to the Field Name column.

The [Up-Arrow] and [Down-Arrow] cursor control keys move the cursor up or down, respectively, in the current column. If the cursor is in the Type column in the first field definition row on the design tablet and you press the [Down-Arrow] key, the cursor will still be in the Type column but one field definition row lower. You can't [Up-Arrow] past the topmost field definition, nor can you [Down-Arrow] past the first blank field definition. Attempting the latter causes dBASE IV to erase the bottom help lines and prompt you with *Field name required. Press any key to continue.*

During the design process, you may decide that you want to change something before you even start entering data. For example, you may want to put the Total_Wgt field under the Exercise field instead of at field definition row 16. First you cursor to field definition row 16 and press [Ctrl-U], which tells the dBASE IV database design system to delete the current row from the database design. Next cursor to field definition row 4 and press [Ctrl-N], which tells the dBASE IV database design system to insert a blank row into the current database design. Why did you have to delete the row before inserting it elsewhere? dBASE IV does not allow two fields in a database to have the same name. It does not matter if the two fields have different field types, widths, or number of decimal places or if they are indexed or not. You can use a given field name only once per database.

Now, if you have made the change I have just described, change the database design back to the way I originally described it. This is good exercise for you and gives me a chance to tell you a little more about good database design.

The Total_Wgt field will be a calculated field. We will calculate the number of reps times the amount of weight per set over all six sets to determine the total weight per exercise per day. In equation form, the preceding sentence would look like this:

```
TOTAL_WGT = (SET_1_REPS x SET_1_WGT) +;
(SET_2_REPS x SET_2_WGT) +;
(SET_3_REPS x SET_3_WGT) +;
(SET_3_REPS x SET_4_WGT) +;
(SET_5_REPS x SET_5_WGT) +;
(SET_6_REPS x SET_6_WGT)
```

Calculated fields should be the last fields in the database structure.

You can perform this calculation just as easily if the Total_Wgt field is located before the Set_n_Reps and Set_n_Wgt fields. But placing the Total_Wgt field before the other fields means you then have to get data into the latter fields, perform the calculation, go back to the top of the record and enter the calculated result, and jump back to the bottom of the record to finish entering data into any remaining fields. This is not an aesthetically pleasing way to get data from you to the computer.

Other cursor control keys make moving through the design table easier. These keys are the [PgUp], [PgDn], [Home], and [End] keys. The [PgUp] and [PgDn] keys move one screen of field definition information up or down the screen, respectively. If the cursor is currently on the first field definition row and you press [PgDn], the cursor moves down to the 17th field definition row (on a standard 25 row PC monitor). Repeatedly pressing the [PgDn] key eventually moves the cursor to the first blank field definition row. The [PgUp] key moves towards the first field definition row. You can't [PgUp] past the first field definition.

The [Home] key moves the cursor to the Field Name column of the current field definition row. The [End] key moves the cursor to either the Index column of the current field definition row or, if the field type is an unindexable one, the Field Name column in the next field definition row.

Telling dBASE IV to Save Your Design

There are four methods of telling the dBASE IV database design system that you have finished designing the database and want to get back whence you came. Whence you came can be the Control Center or the dBASE prompt. The first method is to press [Enter] when the cursor is on a blank record. dBASE IV puts a *Press ENTER key to confirm. Press any other key to resume* prompt on the help line (see figure 5-16).

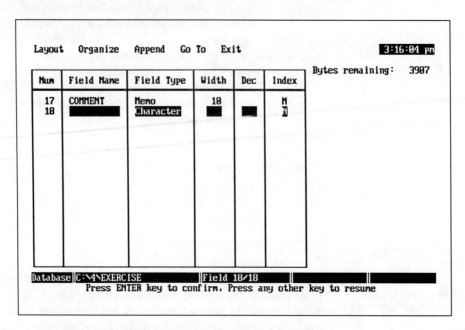

Figure 5-16 *One method of telling dBASE IV you have completed a database design is to press the [Enter] key. dBASE IV asks for confirmation with this prompt.*

The second and third methods of telling dBASE IV you have completed a database design are the [Ctrl-W] and [Ctrl-End] keystroke combinations. These methods also pertain when you have made changes to the database design that you want to keep. dBASE IV prompts you for confirmation differently depending on what you have done to the database design. Figure 5-16 shows dBASE IV prompting for confirmation after the initial design of a database is completed. Figure 5-17 shows dBASE IV prompting for confirmation after a previously designed database has been modified.

The last method of returning from the database design system whence you came is by pressing the [Esc] key. dBASE IV prompts you as shown in figure 5-18. No matter what changes you have made to the database design, pressing [Esc] tells dBASE IV you want to return to the original, unmodified database design and structure.

Other dBASE IV Design Keys

Be advised that two keys act as you would expect, but only when you would least expect them to. These two keys are [Ins] and [Del]. The [Ins] key toggles

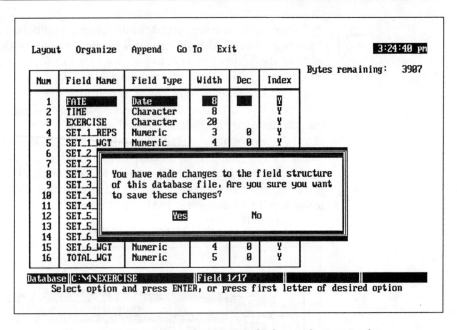

Figure 5-17 This is how dBASE IV asks for confirmation after a database's design has been modified.

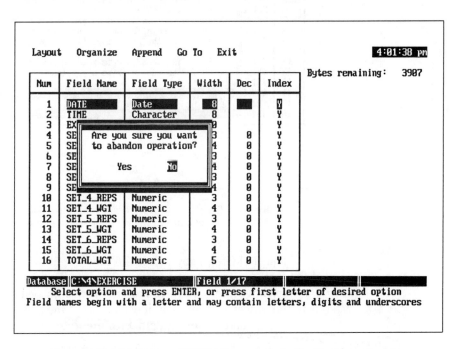

Figure 5-18 This is how dBASE IV responds to the [Esc] key. Pressing the [Esc] key tells dBASE IV to abandon any and all changes you have made and return to the original, unmodified database design and structure.

between overwrite and insert mode, as you would expect. However, insert mode—which dBASE IV indicates by placing the Ins flag on the rightmost side of the status bar—pushes characters to the right of the cursor. This means you might push wanted characters right out the system. Similarly, the [Del] key deletes only characters under the cursor; it does not delete characters to the left of the cursor. Characters are pulled from right to left as you delete them. Be careful that you don't delete something you want.

Anyone who has used any of the PC/MS-DOS based dBASE products should know that [F1] is the Help key. In database design, pressing the [F1] key calls up a context-sensitive help screen, such as shown in figure 5-19. You can press the [F1] key anytime during design work, and dBASE IV will return with information based on the position of the cursor when you pressed the [F1] key.

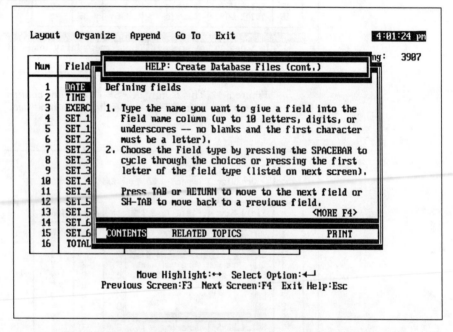

Figure 5-19 *The [F1] key produces a context-sensitive help screen when you are in the database design system.*

The [F1] (Help) key is not the only function key that is used by the dBASE IV database design system. The [F2] (Data) key opens the dBASE IV Browse/Edit system when you are in the design system. After the database is initially designed and you have accepted the structure, you are asked if you want to start entering data with the following prompt:

```
Input data records now? (Y/N)
```

Answering Y places the program in Edit mode (see figure 5-20). This is a basic data entry and editing mode, but not a particularly pleasing one. dBASE IV uses Edit mode when there is no data in the database, which is exactly the way things are immediately after you have designed the database. You can press [F2] a second time for Browse mode (figure 5-21). The [F2] key lets you toggle between Edit and Browse modes.

What if some data is in the database, such as when you are modifying the database design and structure and press the [F2] key? This is covered in

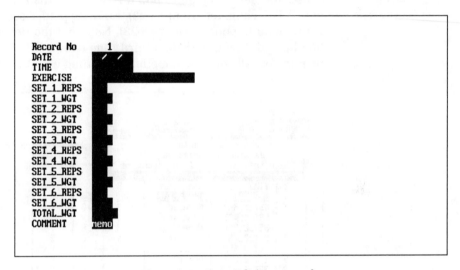

Figure 5-20 Data Edit/Entry mode.

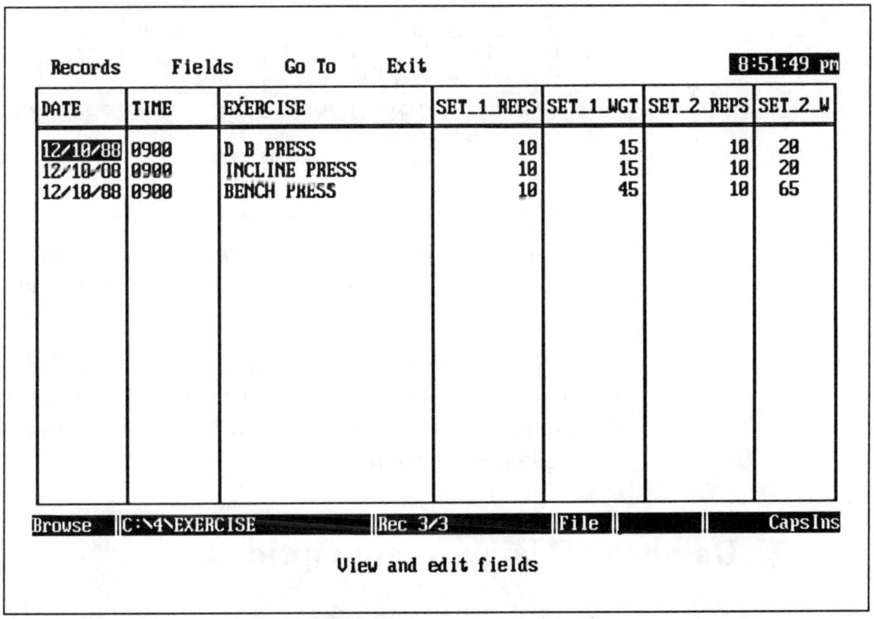

Figure 5-21 Browse mode.

this chapter in "Modifying Your Design," but I will give you an idea here. Pressing [F2] during design modification causes dBASE IV to drop into Browse mode, shown in figure 5-21.

The [F4] key functions exactly like the [Tab] key. It moves from one column to the next during database modification and design.

A key of major interest is the [F10] (Menu) key. This key activates the top row menu options. For example, pressing [F10] during database design causes the Layout menu to pop up. Note that the *Print database structure* option is highlighted (figure 5-22). Pressing [F10] a second time causes the Print menu to pop up (figure 5-23). Note that the *Begin Printing* option is highlighted. Pressing [F10] a third time causes dBASE IV to either begin printing or tell you that something is wrong with the printer (figure 5-24).

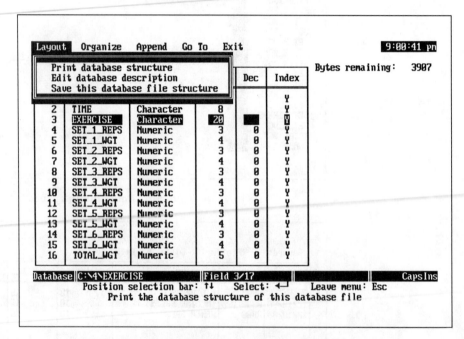

Figure 5-22 *Pressing the [F10] (Menu) key once during database design causes the Layout menu to pop up.*

[F10] does not necessarily default to the leftmost menu option. In other words, it won't always cause the Layout menu to pop up when you are in the database design system. The [F10] (Menu) key defaults to popping up the last used menu.

Database Design Menu Options

This brings us to calling up menu options with the [Alt-key] keystroke combination. You might ask which keys have to be pressed with the [Alt] key.

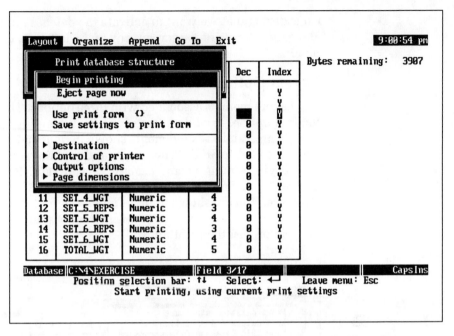

Figure 5-23 Pressing the [F10] (Menu) key twice during database design
causes the Layout Print menu to pop up.

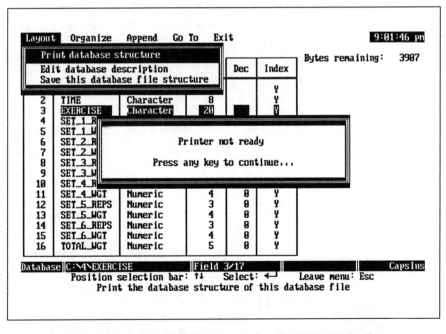

Figure 5-24 Pressing the [F10] (Menu) key thrice during database
design causes dBASE IV to either start printing or tell you there is
something wrong with the printer.

Considering that we want to activate the database design menu, which is along the top row of the screen, any of the letters *L, O, A, G,* or *E* are good options.

Layout Option

The Layout menu is associated with three options. There is a lot to do with the first option, *Print database structure.* When this option is highlighted, press [Enter] and a second menu, shown in figure 5-23, is presented. This is similar to all dBASE IV Print menus and contains some important options.

Begin *printing* means exactly what it says. Press [Enter] or *B* and dBASE IV begins printing. In this case, dBASE IV prints the database structure. You are shown another menu (figure 5-25) that tells you how to control the printing. Note that this menu does not tell you how to control the printer, just the printing.

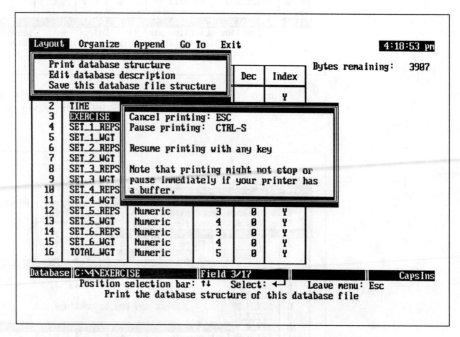

Figure 5-25 dBASE IV gives you the option of either stopping printing completely or momentarily pausing output.

The next option in figure 5-23 is *Eject page now.* This option is used if you are printing and want to start the database structure printout on a clean sheet of paper. This option also serves to clear the print buffer of anything stored there.

The *Use print form* option requires a bit of explaining. If you have set up your system according to the Ashton-Tate DBSETUP routine, the LABEL.PRF and REPORT.PRF printer form files should be in your dBASE directory. These files contain information on how you want things printed.

You can select any PRF file by typing the first letter of the file's name. (If there is more than a single file with the desired first letter, the cursor is positioned at the first file in the list with the desired first letter.) After you have highlighted the desired file, press [Enter] and the PRF file's name is placed in the braces beside *Use print form*.

So what are these print form settings, anyway? Skipping over *Save settings to print form*, you will see four options: *Destination*, *Control of printer*, *Output options*, and *Page dimensions*. Each of these opens another menu that covers a variety of print form settings. For example, the Destination menu lets you switch between the printer and a DOS file, as well as the printer driver installed during the DBSETUP procedure or straight ASCII text. Of all the menu options, the one most likely to cause confusion is at the bottom of the Control of printer menu. *Starting control codes* and *Ending control codes* have to do with special instructions sent by the computer to the printer for such print features as compressed print, expanded print, and optional print colors or fonts.

The other two options on the Layout menu, *Edit database description* and *Save this database file structure*, are relevant to the creation and modification of databases in specific ways. You will notice that you can't access the *Edit database description* option. This is because you are editing the database structure and description when you are either creating or modifying it. You can, of course, save a database's file structure. When you select *Save this database file structure*, dBASE IV confirms the file's name before saving it to disk. This gives you the chance to save similar file structures under different names.

Organize Option

The Organize menu is not an ideal topic for the first-time creation of a database. Parts of that menu that are relevant to these operations are discussed in the next section of this chapter.

Append Option

You may remember that dBASE IV asks if you want to enter information into the database when you instruct it that you are through with the design phase. Another method is through the Append menu. The three options on this menu are *Enter records from keyboard*, *Append records from dBASE file*, and *Copy records from a non-dBASE file*. Selecting the first option puts the program in standard Edit mode. The second option causes dBASE IV to open a menu that shows DBF files. You can select a file as described in the paragraph on PRF files.

But what does *appending* mean? It means all the records in the file you have selected are copied to the current file. None of the existing file's records are overwritten, and the records from the selected database appear as new records at the end of the current database's data. The *Copy records from a non-dBASE file* option opens another menu that displays all the file types dBASE IV knows about. When you select a file type from those listed, dBASE IV attempts to find that file type in the current directory or in the search path you have specified.

Go To Option

One menu that is useful is the Go To menu. The three options on this menu are *Top field*, *Last field*, and *Field number*. The first two are obvious; they go from wherever you are currently positioned to either the first field or the last field in the database structure. The last option, *Field number*, is a way of quickly moving to a specific field in the database structure. This is useful if you have made the mistake of designing large database structures.

Accessing the Query Design System During Database Design

So much for enumerating the usefulness of the menu. One other keystroke combination is useful, although not directly in the design phase. [Shift-F2] causes dBASE IV to open a query design menu, shown in figure 5-26. Designing query forms is covered in detail in chapter 8.

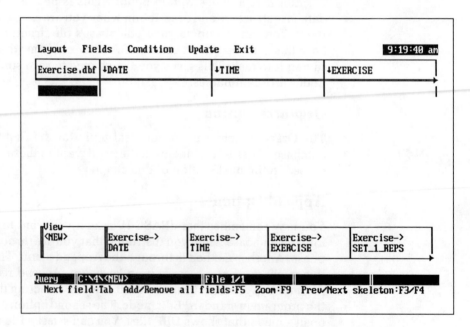

Figure 5-26 You can get to the query design system by pressing [Shift-F2] while in the database design system.

You wouldn't often want to design a query form simultaneously with designing a database. The obvious exception is when you design a database to provide specialized reports on certain aspects of the data. This goes back to discussions on database design and is worth bringing up again.

If you are creating a database and are interested in only one aspect of the data, you can design the database so that a simple DISPLAY or LIST command provides the report you need. But if you are creating a complex database design and are interested in several aspects of the data, it might be better to design query forms. These forms place filters on the database so that only specific information is reported. A query form can be thought of as a coffee filter.

The coffee filter keeps residue and sediment from getting into the drinkable coffee. Good. What the coffee filter lets pass are the various constituent chemicals that give coffee its characteristic taste, which is what you want in your cup. You don't want some floating detritus; you want some good taste. This is what query forms do for database reports, labels, and the like.

The query form keeps all the detritus—the reams of data that are not relevant to the current question—from getting into your cup—your report or whatever. Instead of getting residue, the query form only passes the data you have specifically requested. Sometimes nothing in the database matches your request. That is useful information, too. Knowing you know nothing is better than thinking you know something when you don't.

Deciding Which Fields to Index

How do you know which fields should be indexed when you design your database? That question carries a lot of baggage and is not the easiest one to answer. Look at the Exercise database and you will see that the only field not indexed is the memo field, Comment. That was not a tough decision to make because dBASE IV can't index memo fields, anyway.

Part of the decision is made easier for you thanks to dBASE IV's MDX files. Now you can create a single file that holds up to 47 separate index keys. Before, you had to create a separate file for each index key, which meant you were limited to seven different indices (seven open index files was the limit of dBASE III and III Plus). dBASE IV's limit of 47 index keys per MDX file does not mean you can create indices for any reason. There is still a method to what we do.

We start by looking at the worst example of indexing available, the EXERCISE.DBF file. Why are we indexing on individual weights and repetitions? Do we want to see how many leg lifts we can do versus how many bench presses? That does not tell us much. The problem is that the data contained in a weight varies greatly from exercise to exercise. In other words, there is no congruity to the data. Knowing that we can do more sit-ups than push-ups is not something we necessarily want to report on and therefore is not necessarily something we would want to index.

Create indices only for fields or field expressions that you want to search repeatedly.

Did you catch that last part? We would not want to *report* on it; therefore we would not want to index it. Generally speaking, you only want to create an index for something that is important enough to be analyzed. How do we analyze things in dBASE IV? By reporting on them.

So, going back to the Exercise database, we probably want to index on the Date field so we can see the progression in our exercise routine. We may want to index the Time field, but so many variables relate time to exercise (Did we sleep well? Did we eat today? Was it a stressful day?) that analyzing our workout against time might be self-defeating. We definitely want to compare the exercises themselves, so we want to index the Exercise field.

What is this telling you? I hope it is giving you an idea of what makes relevant data. The Date field is relevant because it is the key to seeing changes over time. The Exercise field is relevant because it is the key to seeing changes in a particular item. For example, indexing the Date field allows us to produce reports of exercises by date. Indexing the Exercise field allows us to produce reports of changes in a particular exercise.

This brings us to an important feature. What do you do if you want to create an index on more than a single field? With the database design system's field descriptions, you can only key single fields at a time. You may want to combine fields for a multiple key, such as EXERCISE + SET_1_ WGT. Note that Set_1_Wgt is a numeric field and must be converted to a character expression before it can be combined with the Exercise field as an index key expression.

All of this is easy to do with the Organize menu. The Organize menu lets us create new MDX and NDX files, create index keys for those files, SORT a database, RECALL records marked for deletion with the *Unmark all records* option, and PACK the database with the *Erase marked records* option.

First, we want to remove a lot of MDX file index tags. This is done with the *Remove unwanted index tag* option (figure 5-27). You work this menu as you do all dBASE IV's pull-down and point-and-shoot menus: highlight the desired selection and press [Enter]. This is perhaps the quickest way dBASE IV offers to remove unwanted single-field keys from an MDX file, remembering that we want to keep the Date and Exercise fields as key fields.

The next thing we want to do is create some useful index keys. Those index keys are the expressions of Date and Exercise, Date and Exercise and Total_Wgt, Exercise and the Set_n fields, and perhaps Date and Exercise and the Set_n fields. We create key field expressions with the *Create new index* option at the top of the Organize menu. Remember that what you enter here is going into the production MDX file.

The first thing to enter is the name of the new index tag (figure 5-28). You can be as brief or as expressive with the tag name as you want. In this case, the index expression is

```
EXERCISE + STR(SET_1_WGT)
```

The index name WGT_1 is good enough for this expression.

dBASE IV also offers a useful, if time consuming, tool to help build index expressions. Move the highlight to the *Index expression* line, press

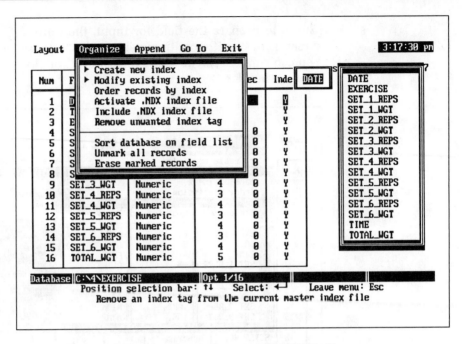

Figure 5-27 Perhaps the quickest way dBASE IV offers to remove unwanted single-field keys from an MDX file is with the Organize menu's Remove unwanted index tag option.

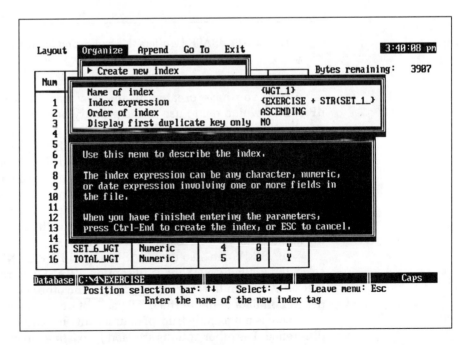

Figure 5-28 The Create new index menu.

[Enter] to prepare the field for input, then press [Shift-F1]. Part of the screen is overwritten with panels similar to those shown in figure 5-29. You can simply type in your expression if you do not want to use the expression builder.

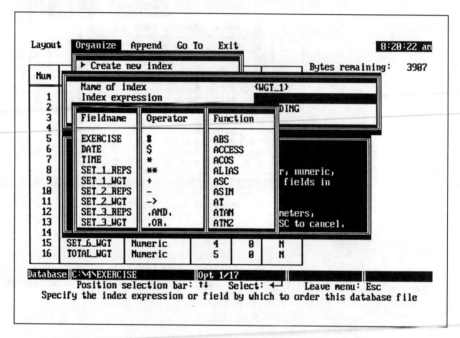

Figure 5-29 *dBASE IV offers this expression builder to help you build index expressions involving more than a single field.*

After you have created all the necessary index tags, you can tell dBASE IV which tag to use as the primary one. In other words, of the 47 possible index tags you can have, which tag do you want to pay the most attention to? That is the one you tell dBASE IV to place in front of the others, and that is done with the *Order records by index* option. When you select this option, dBASE IV presents the tag names available in the current MDX file. As you cursor through the available tag names, you are presented with each tag name's respective index expression. This lets you make sure that the index you are looking for is the one you get, in case the tag name is not as expressive as it should be.

dBASE IV can also use dBASE III and III Plus NDX files. When you select the *Activate .NDX index file* option, dBASE IV presents a list of available NDX files in the current directory. The other Organize menu options depend on data being in the database, not on any aspect of design work.

That is not exactly true, of course, but only Oliver North could tell the difference. The other options are *Modify existing index, Include .NDX index file,* and *Sort database on field list.*

The last option, *Sort database on field list,* is based on the dBASE SORT command. You SORT a database in much the same way you INDEX one. The only difference is that indexing creates a secondary file that dBASE IV uses to place some logical order on the database. Sorting a database does not create a secondary file. Instead, it creates a new database in which the logical ordering is physically imposed on the records themselves. Consider the following ten record examples:

```
DATABASE            INDEXING        SORTING
Record    Data      Data Record     Record    Data
1         E         A    3          1         A
2         I         B    10         2         B
3         A         C    9          3         C
4         D         D    4          4         D
5         F         E    1          5         E
6         G         F    5          6         F
7         H         G    6          7         G
8         J         H    7          8         H
9         C         I    2          9         I
10        B         J    8          10        J
```

The first major column, DATABASE, represents a database of ten records. The data in these records was entered in a random order. With indexing, shown in the second major column, dBASE IV places some kind of logical order on the database (alphabetic sorting, in this case). However, this logical order is only accessible when the index file is active. No active index file, no logical order. dBASE IV looks at the index file first when an index file is active. It gets the record number from the index file, and the record number is found by first looking for the data.

Sorting is shown in the third column. Information is taken from the database and placed in a new database with the desired logical order imposed on the data. This is important. Sorting does not create any ancillary files; it creates a new database using the data from the old database. You are not designing anything new; you are merely rearranging data into a more logical order.

The *Include .NDX index file* option is useful when you plan on passing information from your dBASE IV environment to a dBASE III or III Plus environment. As mentioned, dBASE III and III Plus can't use dBASE IV's multiple-index files. You might want to create or use a single-index NDX file if you plan on using this database in a dBASE III or III Plus office and want to maintain compatibility with that product.

Modify existing index can be thought of as some kind of design work, but only because it allows you to make modifications to your NDX key expressions and your MDX tags. You are not modifying the layout or design of your database, only the logical order that you want on your database.

Modifying Your Design

Your database is together and you have played with it a bit—enough to know there are some problems with it. It is time to modify the design. This can be done through the Control Center or with the MODIFY STRUCTURE command. Either method gets you to the database design system.

Modifying a database is similar to designing one. The only difference is that the database is designed in the computer and not on paper, although some of your changes to the database design may be on paper.

You may want to modify your database structure to make key field placement more logical.

The primary reason for modifying a database design has to do with rearranging field placement for indexing considerations. This is a dBASE III and III Plus problem, but not so much of a problem with dBASE IV. Consider dBASE III and III Plus DBF files and their associated NDX files. Each NDX file is built on either a field or field expression in the DBF file. The fastest way for NDX files to work is to have the field they use as close to the top of the field list as possible. The reason for this is the same reason you keep your favorite clothes easily accessible in the closet and not in mothballs in the attic. You wear them often and want to be able to get to them quickly; you don't want to look for them. dBASE III and III Plus are the same as you with your favorite clothes; place the necessary key fields somewhere near the middle or bottom of the database and III and III Plus have to look for the fields whenever the NDX file is created, modified, or REINDEXed. Place the key fields near the top of the database and III and III Plus can get to them quickly and easily and everything moves along real smooth.

But what about dBASE IV and the MDX index file? Do you need to place key fields at the top of the database when you can put 47 keys into the index file? Not necessarily.

The joy of the MDX file is the way it handles key fields and key field expressions. As mentioned, instead of keeping a sorted list of field values and their associated record numbers (which is how NDX files kept track of what data was where), the MDX file keeps only the title of the field expression, the field expression itself or the name of the field being indexed, and a list of the record numbers in the requested order (ascending or descending) for that individual index key. Modifying the design of a database simply to accommodate the needs of the MDX file is not worth the trouble. If you are designing a system that will be used on both a dBASE IV system and either a dBASE III or III Plus system, however, you should design for the needs of those systems, which means designing the fields for high-speed NDX file use.

So what changes would we make to the Exercise database? We have noted that we won't index on the Time field, but we will index on most of the others. Even though we don't need to rearrange the database design for MDX file use, we should be aware that most users will enter data by exercise, not by date. Remember how the basic Edit screen looks? It was shown in figure 5-20. Using this as our example, we should design the database so that data entry is as clean and error free as possible. This means placing the Exercise field at the top of the database structure so that it is presented first to data entry workers.

Our example database has the Exercise field in the third field description line. To move this field from line 3 to line 1, first place the highlight on the third row and press [Ctrl-U]. dBASE IV erases the entire line. (Remember that you can abandon any changes to the database structure by simply pressing the [Esc] key and then typing Y at the prompt, as shown in figure 5-18.) Next, move the highlight to row 1 and press [Ctrl-N]. This tells dBASE IV to place an empty line in the first field description line. Now enter the name of the field, field type, width, decimals, and whether or not the field will be indexed.

Voila, you have modified a database structure!

Wait a minute. What about all the data you had in the erased field? This can be a problem, depending on how you have restructured the database. First, if all you did was move a field from one place to the other, as was done in this exercise, dBASE IV will copy data from the old field's position to the new field's position with no problem. You may get a message that dBASE IV is reindexing on one or more of the MDX file's key fields, depending on how complicated your modifications are.

What happens if you change the name of one or more fields? You are asked if data should be copied to those fields from the original database: *Should data be COPIED from backup for all fields? (Y/N).* What dBASE IV is asking can be anthropomorphized as "Should I copy the data from field #1 in the original file structure to field #1 in the new file structure? Should I copy the data from field #2 in the old file structure to field #2 in the new file structure?" and so on.

Summary

Well, now you are an expert at database design, indexing theory, and modification. Now that your database is designed, it is time to learn about getting data into your database with dBASE IV's standard data entry methods. Then you can see how you would like to improve dBASE IV's standard methods. This is all the province of chapter 6, along with learning how to debug, or error check, the validity of the entered data.

Designing and Using Screen Forms

Chapter 5 showed you much of the concepts of databases and database design and how to determine whether a field should be indexed.

All well and good. But how do you get data into the darn thing? This was initially discussed in chapter 5 when we mentioned using the [F2] key in design mode to toggle between the Edit and Browse data screens. We also mentioned that these data entry and editing forms are serviceable but not what we would expect to make eagle scout with. The Edit/Browse screen is more like our first offering to mother, when we said, "Here, I made this for you in shop."

This chapter will get you into designing data entry and editing screens. As with all aspects of dBASE IV, this can be done in two ways. The first way is through the Control Center; the second way is with the CRE-ATE SCREEN and MODIFY SCREEN commands. These two methods are the focus of this chapter. A third method, through dBASE IV's template language, is covered later in this book.

Understanding Data Screens

Take a look at figures 5-20 and 5-21. Figure 5-20 is a standard dBASE IV Edit screen. You can add data to the database with that screen. You can also edit data already in the database with that screen. But that screen is not pleasing to the eye; it has no life; it is a straight up-and-down visual nightmare. Figure 5-21 is the Browse screen. This screen can also be used for both data entry and editing. It is aesthetically more pleasing than the Edit screen, but it is difficult to move through. Look at figure 5-21 and you will notice that not all the fields in the database are on the screen at the same time. You see more of the data because more records are shown; but you see less of the data in each record because the fields scroll off the screen to the left and right.

You can move the cursor through the records and fields, but this is not the best method for adding or editing data in a single record at a single time. Adding and editing individual records is best done with a visual tool that clearly shows the user where the data is and what the data is, offers help, and prompts when the user gets confused. This is all done with a data screen.

Some of the psychology of data screens was mentioned previously. For example, you do not want the user to have to move through too many screens for any single record. This has to do with keeping the number of fields in a database structure to a minimum. If there are more fields in a database structure than can comfortably fit on a single screen, consider using more than one database.

Another part of the psychology of data screens has to do with making sure each data item is clearly labeled and that labels point to their data items. Does this sound as if I said the same thing twice? Consider figures 6-1 and 6-2.

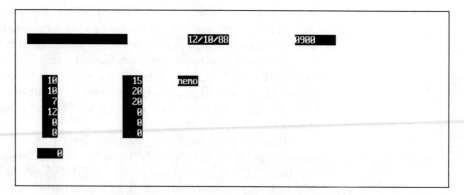

Figure 6-1 A data entry screen with utterly no information for the user. It is worthless for real work because the names of the fields are secret.

Figures 6-1 and 6-2 are both data entry screens. Which one helps you determine what data goes where and why? I hope you picked figure 6-2. Those of you who chose figure 6-1 will find gainful employment in the government.

Figure 6-2 is a better screen because it tells you a great deal about the database you are working with and gives information about the data that should go into the individual fields in the records of the database. For example, the cursor is in the Exercise field. How do I know that? Because the label, *Exercise*, is directly in front of the field and I trust that the system designer—myself, in this case—would not mislabel something. What if I do not know what is meant by *Exercise*? At the bottom of the screen is the prompt: *Enter the name of the exercise in this field.*

"Aha! This data field must be where I put the name of the exercise."

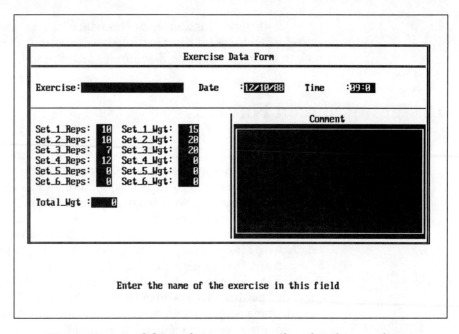

Figure 6-2 A much better data entry screen than that shown in figure
6-1 for several reasons. First, data fields are clearly marked. Second,
there are prompts for the user. Third, default values are automatically
entered into the fields.

Users who do not experience that "Aha!" should not tie their shoelaces too
tight because there is obviously a problem with blood flow to the cerebrum.

Note that neither figure 6-1 nor 6-2 can do much in the way of reporting the data to you. Both can display one record's worth of data at a time.
Some might consider this a problem. But remember that we are currently
interested in getting data into the database. The screen shown in figure 6-2
is fine for data input. What about editing data? You can edit individual
records with the screen shown in figure 6-2, but you would still be working
with information from a single record at a time. This is acceptable, but
might be too restrictive if you need to compare the data in several records
while editing.

This last does go against the basic theory of databases stated previously. You don't want too much data on the screen at a single time because you can confuse the user. Further, having the data from several
records on the screen and being able to edit any of those records simultaneously can cause problems. First, you have to make sure the user knows
which record they are in (as in, "I know what record you wanted to edit, but
is the record you are in the one you wanted to edit?"). Second, you need to
verify and validate data as it is entered. Third, you have to provide users
with an escape if they know they have made a bigger mess of things than
what the database was like before they started. All of this is covered in this
chapter. Editing data is shown in chapter 7.

This brief discussion should convince you that there is more to working with databases than just getting data in and out. The next section shows how to design screens for data input and editing.

Designing Screen Forms

This book would be remiss if it did not provide an understanding of how the screen form design system's menus work. I hope to demonstrate those menus in a more useful way than just "This does this and this does that." We will use the menus as we design our screen form. This method is a little different from that used in previous chapters and with good reason. Designing screen forms is not difficult, nor is it obvious. Teaching you didactically will, I hope, help you retain more than simple pontification would.

Because I have taught college, I know that you will probably skip the following theory section. You will probably go straight into sitting at the computer and putting the form on the screen. That means I have to tell you how to get out of the screen design menu system before I tell you anything else.

There are several methods of exiting the screen form design system. Each does something a little different as it exits back to wherever you were when you entered the screen form design system. The first method, [Alt-L] S, does not actually drop you back whence you came. This method tells dBASE IV to open the Layout menu and Save the screen form. dBASE IV creates the FMT file based on the current screen image but does not exit the screen form design system.

The next method is [Alt-E] S. This method tells dBASE IV to Save the current screen image as an SCR file only (don't generate either an FMT or FMO file) and Exit back whence you came. Next is [Alt-E] A, which is Abandon all work done and get out of the screen form design system.

Pressing [Ctrl-W] or [Ctrl-End] from the top level of the screen design system tells dBASE IV to save the SCR file and create both FMT and FMO files. The FMO file is simply the pseudocompiled FMT file. You can also press [Ctrl-End] from within any level of menu on the screen form design system. Doing so tells dBASE IV to accept whatever changes or edits may have been made. You tell dBASE IV to ignore any edits or changes to any level menu by pressing [Esc]. dBASE IV will prompt for confirmation that you want to abandon any work that may have been done. Also note that pressing [Esc] from the top level of the screen form design system causes dBASE IV to prompt for confirmation that you want to abandon any work done to the form as a whole.

Last, pressing [Ctrl-Enter] instructs dBASE IV to generate the screen form without leaving the screen form design system. It is equivalent to the [Alt-L] S command.

There are two ways to get into the screen design workspace, shown in figure 6-3. The first method is through the Control Center. You start by placing the highlight in the Forms column, on the word ⟨create⟩, and pressing either [Enter] or [Shift-F2]. See figure 6-4. The second method is by entering the CREATE SCREEN or MODIFY SCREEN command at the dBASE prompt.

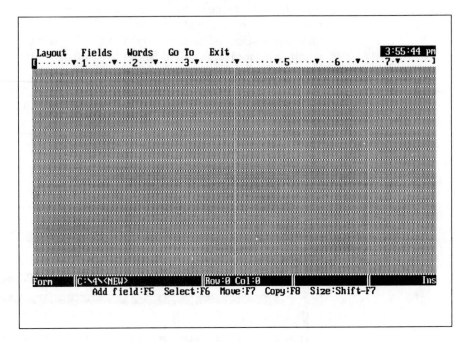

Figure 6-3 *The design screen workspace.*

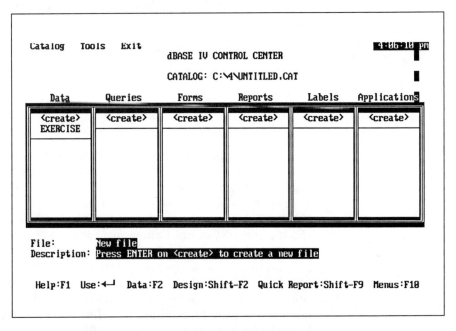

Figure 6-4 *You can get to the design screen workspace through the Control Center.*

Entering the screen design system through the Control Center might offer you more options than simply using the CREATE SCREEN or MODIFY SCREEN command. For example, using the Control Center tells dBASE IV to place any newly created file in the current Catalog. This means any file you create through the Control Center can have an explanatory line associated with it (figure 6-5). The screen design system senses whether or not it was called from the Control Center or the dBASE prompt and offers you the ability to edit the current screen file's explanatory line (figure 6-6). This Layout menu option is not available if you use the CREATE SCREEN or MODIFY SCREEN command from the dBASE prompt.

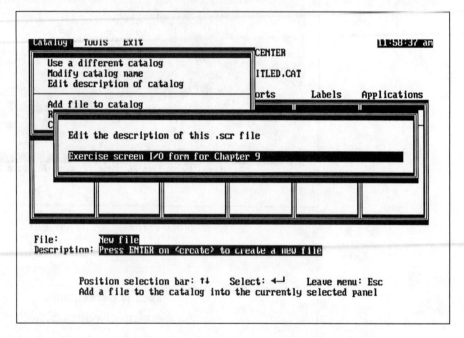

Figure 6-5 The Control Center system is prompting for an explanatory line regarding a newly created file.

At this point I will ask you to remember what we are doing. We are designing a data entry and editing screen form for a particular database. That being the case, none of these methods are satisfactory unless you have already placed a database in use or intend to design a screen form with nothing but memory variables and calculated fields. In fact, dBASE IV responds to your Control Center request to design forms differently if you have already placed a database in use. Let me show you something to prove my point.

Place a database in use by highlighting it on the Control Center and pressing [Enter]. You will be shown a screen like that in figure 6-7. The cursor is already highlighting *Use file,* so press [Enter] again. The database's name moves above the active file line.

Now highlight ⟨create⟩ under Forms and press [Enter]. The design

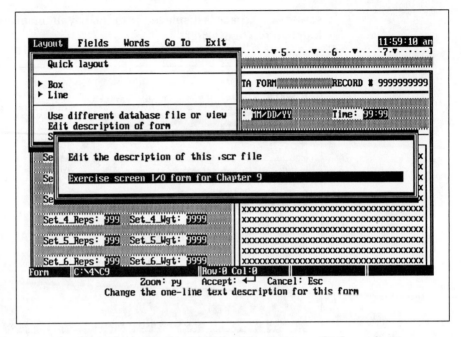

Figure 6-6 The screen form design system lets you edit the explanatory line created in figure 6-5. This option is not available if you enter the design system with the CREATE SCREEN or MODIFY SCREEN command and no Catalog file is active.

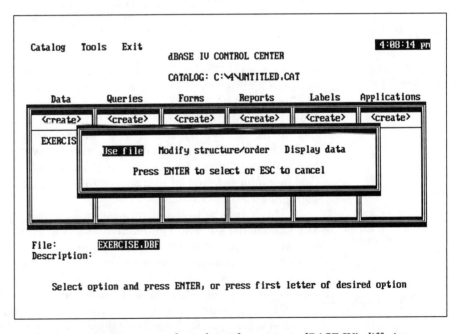

Figure 6-7 Figures 6-5 through 6-8 demonstrate dBASE IV's differing responses to the Control Center's ⟨create⟩ Forms command depending on whether or not a database is currently in use. This figure shows how to activate a database file from the Control Center.

screen workspace is displayed with the Layout menu's *Quick layout* option highlighted (figure 6-8).

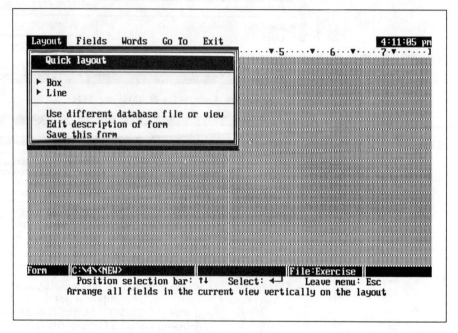

Figure 6-8 dBASE IV starts the screen form design process by offering the Quick layout *option from the Layout menu when a database has been placed in use.*

Now press [Esc] twice and Y once. You are back at the Control Center with the highlight on 〈create〉 under Forms. Cursor over to the database and press [Enter]. You are presented with another series of options, with *Close file* highlighted (figure 6-9). The database name drops under the active file line. Cursor back to 〈create〉 under Forms and press [Enter]. You are back at the design screen workspace, but now the suggested menu item is *Use different database file or view* (figure 6-10). It should be. You can't design a data entry or editing screen unless you know what data you are going to be working with.

This brings us to the next question in the design process. Do you really know what you want your screen form to look like? I'll bet you do. If you are a beginner to database management systems, you probably designed your database on paper as you wanted it to appear on your computer screen. You probably did not design it by defining the size of fields, whether or not the fields would be indexed, and so on. No problem. You probably know more than an expert (who doesn't know your needs) about how you want your database to function even if you did not use the "right" words to describe things.

So let's look at your screen form. All that is important for the screen

You can design your database I/O screen first; this gives new users a good example of how the database itself should be designed.

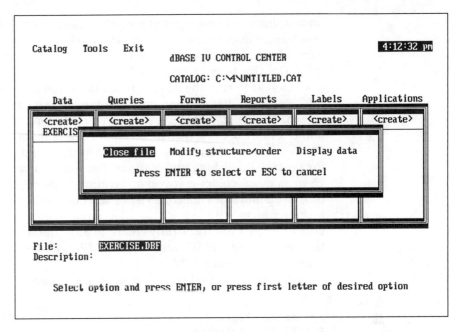

Figure 6-9 You can take a database out of use by selecting the Close file option from this Control Center menu.

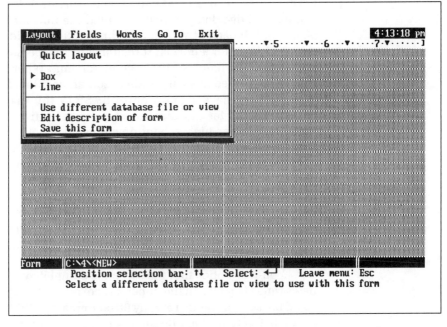

Figure 6-10 dBASE IV starts the screen form design process by offering Use different database file or view from the Layout menu when no database is in use.

form is that you know what you want on the screen. It does not have to be exact, and it does not have to be pretty. I will introduce a new term for your vocabulary: *paint.* You are painting the screen when you design a screen form. How the term came about I don't know, but it seems to have ingratiated itself as part of the lingua franca of designing screen forms.

Be aware that you can only paint on 25 rows and 80 columns of the screen. This is not exactly true; every rule has exceptions. First, you can paint on more of the screen if you have a computer monitor with more than 25 rows or more than 80 columns, such as the monitors specially designed for desktop publishing applications. Second, you can paint on more than 25 rows by 80 columns if you are willing to have your data entry screen broken up into more than one visible screen. In other words, you can create a screen form with something like "hello there!" at screen coordinate 28,38. dBASE IV will dutifully create an FMT file with the desired information. But will dBASE IV create the FMT file with the desired information at screen coordinates 28,38?

No. You will find the following lines in your FMT file:

```
*-- Format Page: 2
@ 3,38 SAY "hello there!"
```

What happened? Well, you asked dBASE IV to place information where the normal screen coordinates can't reach. dBASE IV thought about what you wanted and decided you really wanted the information to be on the next page. So, it looked at screen coordinate 28 and said, "Screen position 28 minus 25 lines for a normal screen means this person wants this information placed on line 3 of the second screen." What happens if you want something placed at a truly radical screen position, for example, 101,200?

First you have to know how dBASE IV thinks of screen coordinates. Screen and printer coordinates are given by a cartesian pair. Readers who remember either high school or college geometry may remember Renè Descartes, who thought, therefore he was. Well, Renè is dead now, so chances are he neither thinks nor is. What has lived beyond Descartes is his way of looking at plane geometry, which we call the cartesian coordinate system. This coordinate system merely means that any point on a surface can be identified by a pair of numbers. The first number is the X axis, the second number is the Y axis, and the two numbers are separated by a comma. Figure 6-11 shows how these X,Y coordinate pairs map out the screen surface.

You will notice that the screen is completely filled when the coordinates range from 0,0 in the upper left corner to 24,79 in the lower right. But I said the screen was 25 rows by 80 columns. No, this is not a case of author as idiot. Top to bottom, the number of rows on the screen is 25, counting from 0 through 24. Think of it according to the following schema:

Screen row 0 is the first screen row.

Screen row 1 is the second screen row.

Screen row 2 is the third screen row.

.

.

.

Screen row 24 is the twenty-fifth screen row.

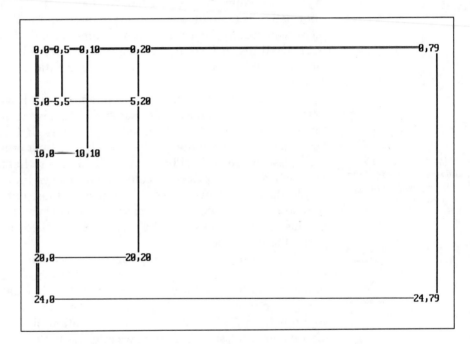

Figure 6-11 This figure shows how an X and Y coordinate pair can map out the screen surface.

How does dBASE IV handle outlandish column arguments? The computer monitor is 25 rows long and 80 columns across, with a big "period" after the latter. The screen will not wrap around several times to get you to a Y coordinate of, for example, 200. So how does dBASE IV interpret a request to place information at position 101,200? It looks at the X coordinate, 101, and skips down to the second row of the fifth screen (101st row divided by 25 rows per screen equals the 5th screen, 1st row). Then it looks at the Y coordinate, 200, and becomes gravely ill. The moral? Make your screen forms as long as you like, but not as wide as you like.

Putting the Database on the Screen

Back to your screen form. You can't put more than 80 columns of information across the form. This means you have to be careful how wide you make your data fields, or at least how wide you make their representations on the screen. (There are ways to cheat, such as the scrolling character field described in the last chapter, and some of those methods are covered here.) I want to emphasize that you should not create a screen form longer than one screen. Creating an entry and editing form longer than a single screen necessitates repeating key fields from screen to screen and giving the user the ability to jump from one screen to another, not necessarily from preceding to succeeding screens. Further, you have to make sure that the repeated information is not editable after it is entered on the first screen of a multiple screen record. These suggestions come from designing a variety of input and editing surfaces for an even wider variety of users. Experience has taught me that people work best when information is clearly laid out on a single screen.

With all this knowledge and experience at our fingertips, let's map our exercise database on the screen. Remember that we want to design a screen for input and, considered later, editing. This is slightly unfair, of course, because we have seen the final screen already (in a previous chapter).

First, we must decide if any of the database fields are so important that we want them placed to catch the user's eye immediately. In our example, the three primary fields of interest are those containing the name of the exercise itself, the date the exercise was performed, and the time of the exercise session. These are the primary input fields and should go at the top of the input screen form.

Something important was said in the last paragraph, so let's investigate it further. You want the important fields—the fields of high interest—at the top of the data form. Why? Because that is where people's eyes are going to go first. We are trained to read written material from left to right, top to bottom. This is also true of information on a computer screen. In written material, such as fiction, we might read half, even three quarters of the way through a paragraph before we get to the key sentence that gives the entire paragraph meaning. But we do not think of information on a computer screen in this way, so we expect to find the most important information at the top. This lets us know if we want to go through the rest of the information on the screen or go to the next screen.

After the most important information, place the fields for repetitive information, unkeyed information, or fields that won't necessarily be filled in for each record in the database. The first two options (repetitive and unkeyed information) are the Set_n information in our EXERCISE database. The field that won't necessarily be filled in for each record in the database is the Comment field. It is a good idea to place any fields that might be skipped towards the end of the input screen and to place fields that will be seldom used at the end of the input screen.

The less important a field is, the more likely it should be placed near the end of the input screen. Nothing is worse than having to cursor or press [Enter] through several fields until you get to the field you want to enter information into. In our EXERCISE database, the Comment field is at the end of the database with good reason. The database won't use that field in every record. Also, we are more likely to put information in the Set_1_ Reps and Set_1_Wgt fields than we are to put information into the Set_6 _Reps and Set_6_Wgt fields. Further, it is more likely that we will put information in the Set_n fields starting at the lower numbers and less likely that we will put information into the fields corresponding to the higher numbers. In other words, it is more likely that we will do the first set of an exercise than that we will do the last set of an exercise.

We can use the data entry form already shown in this book as if it were the form we designed on paper. Get at the computer, get dBASE IV into the screen form design system, and let's get our form into the system.

Design philosophy 301: Always leave room for a menu.

Design philosophy 401: dBASE IV supports pop-up menus, so you don't have to leave room for a menu on the screen. You can pop them in and out as you need them.

Isn't progress great? Yes!

What's all this about design philosophy? dBASE II, III, and III Plus placed a tough constraint on any screen form design. The user had to have information regarding what went where and why. This usually took the form of a menu, and many applications placed the menu at either the top or bottom of the screen. An example is shown in figure 6-12.

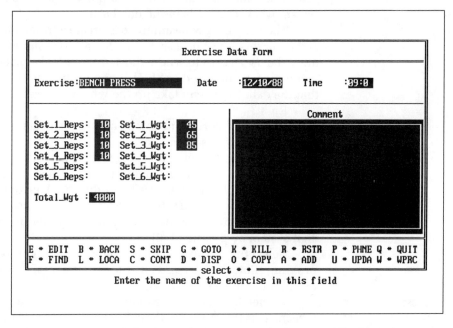

Figure 6-12 A database editing menu at the bottom of the Exercise entry screen. dBASE II, III, and III Plus needed space on the screen for menus, which sometimes posed a design problem when creating a screen entry form. Because dBASE IV's pop-up menus do not require screen space, you can make full use of the screen surface for your design form.

The menu shown at the bottom of figure 6-12 contains commands for the majority of database work. It is useful and designed to take up as little room as possible so that field spacing and placement can be both prioritized and placed properly. The problem is that it does take up space and is static. The space part could not be solved in dBASE II, III, and III Plus, but it can be solved in dBASE IV. The static problem goes back to user psychology.

Most people use menus for the first few days or weeks of work. When I say the menus are "used," I mean people need to see the options available each time they sit down to do work. This is true whether the software is a word processor, a database management system, a spreadsheet, graphics software, and so on. After a short time, the user stops looking at the menus because the necessary keystroke sequences are learned. The fingers press the necessary keys automatically; the user stops thinking about which keys to press and begins thinking of what needs to be done.

The menu shown in figure 6-12 is static. It stays on the screen no matter how many times it is used. This means part of the screen is forfeit, even though the users have learned the necessary keystroke sequences for their work. An ideal solution would be a menu that appears either on request or if no keys are typed after a certain period of time. You could do this with dBASE III and III Plus, but dBASE IV gives you the advantage of being able to design a true pop-up or pull-down menu, thus freeing up screen surface for what is most important about database management system work, the fields in the database.

The first thing we want to do is create a frame for our database fields. Although this is not necessary, it adds a professional touch and does help draw the user's eyes to where the action will take place. The discussion of menu placement and dBASE IV's pop-up menus should be an indication that the data frame can take up the whole screen.

Right?

Close, and correct in some cases. Let's design the form, then worry about modifications for all cases.

Starting with the screen form design system shown in figure 6-3, press [Alt-L] to call up the Layout menu. dBASE IV automatically selects the *Quick layout* option. Guess what the Quick layout option creates for a screen input form? It creates the Edit screen as shown in the last chapter, the same screen you get from the Control Center or from the database design system by pressing [F2].

Select the *Box* option by typing *B* or highlighting the *Box* option and pressing [Enter]. A second-level menu appears, as shown in figure 6-13. Select the *Double line* option.

Remember that we are going to create a frame for our data entry screen. This frame can be thought of as a picture frame. The frame should draw attention to the picture without drawing attention to itself. The picture we want to frame is the data fields we will place on the screen. Can we use the whole screen? Yes and no.

dBASE IV uses two lines for its own purposes, but only at specific times. The two lines used are the 0th and 24th lines. The times these lines

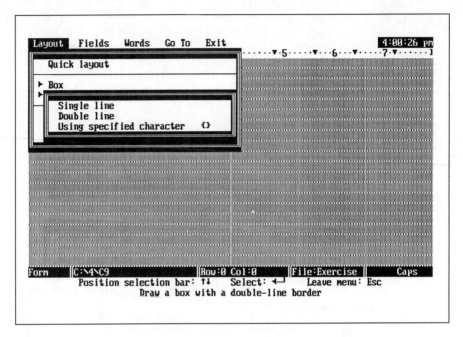

Figure 6-13 *The* Box, Double line *option from one of the second-level Layout menus.*

are used have to do with how two SET commands, SET SCOREBOARD and SET STATUS, are toggled in the dBASE IV environment. The status line, described elsewhere in this book, is the line at the bottom of the screen. The scoreboard is similar to the status line, but is placed on the 0th line of the screen. If STATUS is OFF and SCOREBOARD is ON, the keyboard toggles *Ins*, *Num*, and *Caps* appear in the 0th line of the screen (figure 6-14). If STATUS is ON, these three keyboard toggles appear in the status line regardless of the scoreboard setting (figure 6-15). You should also note that setting STATUS ON ties up more than just the 24th line; you basically lose from line 21 down.

We also know that we might have to communicate information regarding data, fields, and so on to the user. We should reserve some of the screen for this. Good choices are either or both of the lines dBASE IV uses for the scoreboard and status: lines 0 or 24. When someone gives you a good idea, you should go with it.

After you have selected the *Double line* option from the second-level Layout menu, you are back to the design form workspace. At the bottom of the screen, in the middle of the status line, you will see that the cursor is at screen position 0,0. Under the status line is the prompt, *Position start of line with cursor keys. Complete with ENTER.* We know that the 0th line is forfeit, so cursor to screen position 1,0 and press [Enter]. Now use the cursor control keys to stretch the box from position 1,0 to 24,79.

Careful readers will note that I did not want to use the 0th screen line, but I am willing to use the 24th screen line. Why is this?

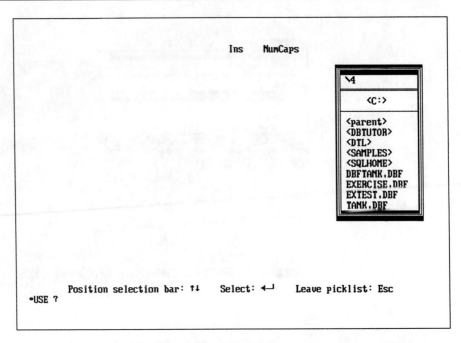

Figure 6-14 Keyboard toggles appear in the screen's 0th line when
SCOREBOARD is SET ON but STATUS is SET OFF.

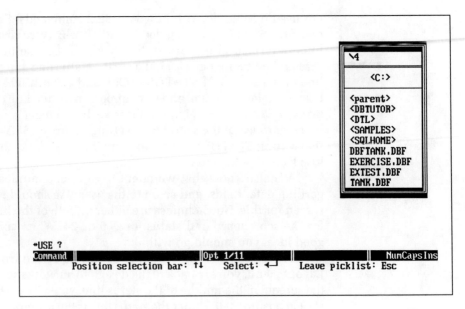

Figure 6-15 Keyboard toggles appear in the status line when STATUS
is SET ON, regardless of the scoreboard setting.

As you create format files, you will notice that dBASE IV gives you
the ability to create helpful messages at the bottom of the screen. Normally,

this can be done only with the status line SET ON. Not so when you are using programming mode. In other words, you can use the bottom of the screen in some imaginative ways, as I will show you momentarily.

Adding Class to Your Screen Forms

It is nice to title your screen forms, and the best time to do this is after you have drawn the frame for your data. Move the cursor to the second screen line and type the title for your data screen. In our example, we are going to use Exercise Data Form. Don't worry about positioning your title. dBASE IV will do that for us in a moment.

Press [Alt-W] to call up the screen design Words menu (figure 6-16). Type P to call up the Position submenu, then type C to instruct dBASE IV to center the text on screen line 2.

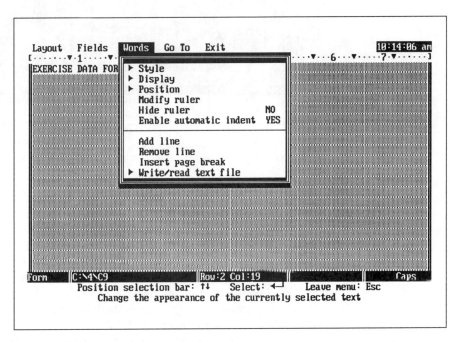

Figure 6-16 You can call up the screen design workspace's Words menu either by pressing [Alt-W] or by using the [F10] (Menu) key to call up the last referenced menu, then typing W for the Words menu or cursoring to the Words menu itself.

It is aesthetically pleasing—a major part of screen forms—to separate the screen title from the data itself. That can be accomplished with a double line directly under the screen form's title. Use the [Down-Arrow] key to move the cursor to screen line 3, then press the [Home] key. This moves the cursor to the left side of the screen. Move the cursor off the box, to screen position 3,1, and press [Alt-L]. Next type *L* for *Line* and *D* for *Double*. The cursor is already on the starting position for your line, so press [Enter] as instructed at the bottom of the screen (figure 6-17). Move the cursor to position 3,78 and press [Enter] a second time. Voila, you have a double line.

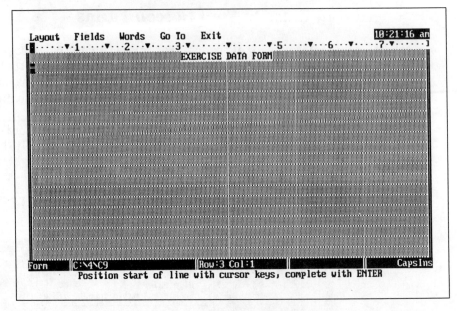

Figure 6-17 *You can start your double line anywhere on the screen by placing the cursor at the starting screen position and pressing [Enter].*

Before placing the data fields on the screen, take a moment to think about what dBASE IV will do for you and what you have to do yourself. For example, dBASE IV provides the status line to give the interactive user a great deal of information that may or may not be useful. If Ashton-Tate did not think that the status line is a useful feature, they would not have included it as a default in the product. What does the status line tell you? It tells you which part of the dBASE IV system you are working with (form design, command design, report design, and so on) and the location on a given drive and path (figure 6-17, for example, tells us that we are working on drive C in the 4 directory with the C9 file). The center of the status line gives information relevant to the immediate operation (such as screen position), and the far right has the keyboard toggle indicators.

Other things the status line can tell the user have not been covered yet. The information just presented is nice, but not relevant to the general data entry and editing operator. Much of what the status line tells the user is not helpful and can be neglected when working in a program mode. What the status line can tell you, and what is useful no matter what mode you are working in, is whether or not an individual record has been deleted and what the current record number is. We will not use the status line for our screen form. You can if you want, but doing so causes you to lose the bottom four lines of the screen (21, 22, 23, and 24). You can give the same useful information as that already on the status line and not lose any screen lines.

Here is how you do it. Move the cursor to screen position 2,2 by pressing [Home] [Up-Arrow] [Right-Arrow] [Right-Arrow]. Make sure you are in overwrite mode by looking at the right side of the status line and making sure the Ins (Insert) indicator is off. You can turn it off by pressing the [Ins] key. Now type the following

`!RECORD DELETED!`

You can be more imaginative than I by using graphics characters in place of the exclamation points.

To get to the graphics characters, press [Alt-L] to call up the Layout menu, then type L for *Line*, then U for *Using specified character*. After a moment, dBASE IV presents the full ASCII character set (figure 6-18). To select a character, highlight it and press [Enter]. You can quickly move through the selections by using the [PgDn], [PgUp], [Home], and [End] keys. You can also select any ASCII character except 0, 7, and 255 by typing the desired ASCII character's value. ASCII character 0 is the null character, which is darn difficult to show on most computer monitors. You can't use ASCII 7 because that is the keyboard bell/beep/whistle/whine/generally annoying noise. ASCII character 255 is unavailable for graphics display.

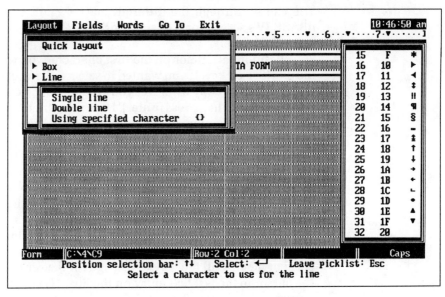

Figure 6-18 *You can use graphics characters in your screen form by selecting the* Using specified character *option from the* Line *or* Box Layout *submenus.*

There is a slight problem when simply entering the ASCII value of a desired character. The first time you use the graphics menu to select a character, the cursor automatically highlights ASCII character 1, which is the white happy face. Suppose you want the spade, which is character 6. You can type 6 and the spade will appear at the current cursor position. Now suppose you want to use ASCII character 2, the black happy face, somewhere else on the screen. You press [Alt-L] *L U* for Layout menu, Line submenu, *Using specified character* and type 2 for the second ASCII character. dBASE IV gives you the 20th ASCII character, which is the paragraph symbol. Do this repeatedly and you get ASCII characters 21, 22, 23, 24, 25, 26, 27, 28, 29, then you skip to ASCII character 200, then you proceed through ASCII characters 200 to 254. This is a flaw to be aware of, unless you want to pull your hair out as I often do.

One other note regarding the use of graphics characters for lines and boxes: You place the cursor at the starting position, press [Enter], and the graphics character goes away. This does not mean you have lost it. It means dBASE IV is building the screen and hasn't had time to refresh itself. Just go ahead and make your line. dBASE IV is doing its job and you should not worry.

You have used a graphics character and now you type in your RECORD DELETED message. My RECORD DELETED message uses an exclamation point before the first *R* and after the last *D*. What if you want to use a graphics character at the end of your RECORD DELETED message? You know how to select a graphics character using [Alt-L] *L U*. What if you want to use the same character that you placed in front of your message? You can go through the different menus again or you can use some of dBASE IV's screen form design workspace's other features, which is what we will do here.

Position the cursor on the first character you want to copy and press the [F6] (Select) key. If you wanted to select a string of characters or an area of the screen to copy or move, you would use the cursor keys to highlight the entire area, then press [Enter]. Here we want to copy only a single character, so we leave the cursor on the desired character and press [Enter]. Now move the cursor to the screen position where you want the copied or moved information to be placed and press the [F8] (Copy) key. (You would use the [F7] (Move) key if you wanted to erase some screen information from where it was and move it to a new position.) The cursor is already placed where we want it to go, so press [Enter]. Voila, we have copied some display information.

The next thing we want to do is put something on our form to let people know what record they are working on. Press [End]. Note that instead of moving all the way to the right of the screen, the [End] key moves the cursor to the last text entry on the line. Use the cursor keys to move to screen position 2,60. Type

```
RECORD # 9999999999
```

Another master stroke. You have made a method of telling the world where they are in the database. Now we can start placing the database fields on the screen.

At this point, a caveat: Some versions of dBASE IV are a little ditsy. This is not to say the product should not be used; it is merely letting you know that the first shipment of the product has some high-end memory management problems. That's a longhand way of saying, "Save your work repeatedly and often." Those of you who are working along with the example in this book should press [Alt-L] S to open the Layout menu and choose the *Save this form* option. You will see a screen such as the one in figure 6-19. You can simply press [Enter] to save the screen form with the name listed or, even better, give the screen form a new name, and I don't mean Fred, Wilma, Barnie, or Betty. A better naming method is to use something like C9-1, C9-2, C9-3, and so on to give your work a history. This allows you to go back through different stages should you want to make changes.

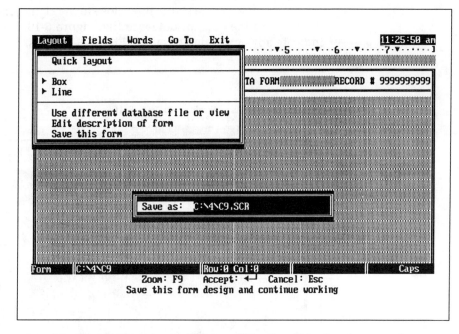

Figure 6-19 *You can save a screen form during the design process by typing [Alt-L] S. Press [Enter] to accept the file name provided by dBASE IV or enter another name. Note that you should change the file name for each save when designing a screen form in stages.*

The key to keeping your sanity with dBASE IV is to save your work often.

Suppose you have created a screen form in five stages and have files labeled INVEST1.SCR, INVEST2.SCR, INVEST3.SCR, INVEST4.SCR, and INVEST5.SCR. A time comes when you want to make changes to the form, but you don't want to destroy the form you have already created. You can go as far back in the creation cycle as necessary to design the new form.

There is another, more relevant reason for saving your design work in stages. Someone might trip over the power cord, usually just as you finish your screen form and always right before you save it.

Laying Out Fields on the Screen Form

Now comes the time to lay out the data fields on the form. As mentioned, I will use the EXERCISE database for the example. You can use whatever database you'd like. I will explain the logic to my layout decisions at each step; the logic and the decisions based on the logic are applicable to all design work you do.

We want the most important fields at the top of the input/edit screen. We have already decided that these fields are Exercise, Date, and Time. Before we put them on the form, however, we have to make sure we have the correct database in use.

If you look at the status line, close to the right-hand side, you will see the name of the current database file. Figure 6-19, for example, does not indicate any active database file. Figure 6-20 does.

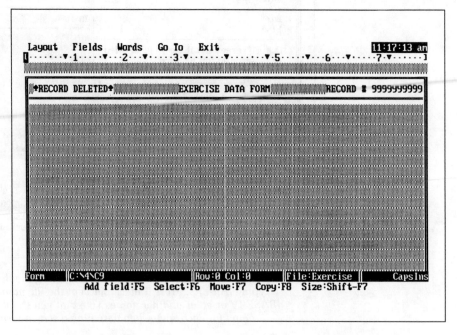

Figure 6-20 The status line now indicates which database file is active. The EXERCISE file is listed close to the right-hand side of the screen, directly on the status line, with File:Exercise.

There are a number of ways to make a database active. You can do so through the Control Center, as shown in the last chapter. You can enter the USE command at the dBASE prompt, such as

USE EXERCISE [Enter]

You can also activate a database through the screen design form menus. Press [Alt-L] *U* to open the Layout menu's *Use different database file or view* list, as shown in figure 6-21. You can point to and shoot the file of your choice with the cursor control keys or type the first letter of the file of interest. You can also move from the current directory to a subdirectory on the same disk by selecting one of the names enclosed in ⟨ ⟩. Figure 6-21 shows DBTUTOR, DTL, SAMPLES, and SQLHOME as subdirectories of the current directory, 4, which is at the top of the pick list. You can also move from the current directory to other directories by selecting the ⟨parent⟩ option. This option moves you from the current directory to the immediately preceding entry in the directory tree structure. Figure 6-22 is an example of a DOS disk directory tree structure.

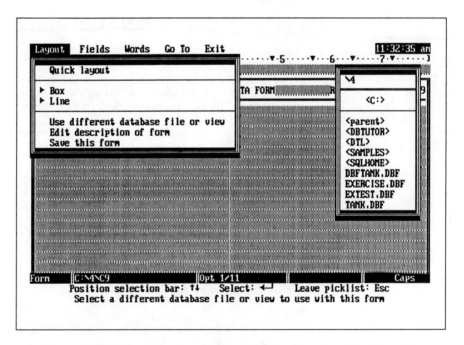

Figure 6-21 You can use the point-and-shoot options from the files pick list to select a database file, select a view file, move to a different directory, or move to another drive.

Figure 6-23 shows how you can move from the current disk to another disk using the point-and-shoot options. You initiate this process by highlighting the listed drive, C, then pressing [Enter]. dBASE IV opens another menu listing the available drives. This system makes use of all 26 available drives, although only 18 are shown on the screen at one time.

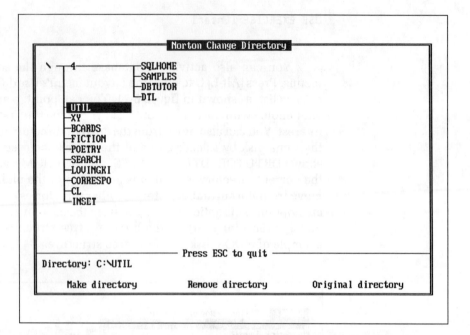

Figure 6-22 A simple directory tree structure for a 20M hard disk.
Using this tree and the menu selections shown in figures 6-19 and 6-21,
you can tell that the parent directory to 4 is the root directory, 4 is the
parent to DBTUTOR, DTL, SAMPLES, and SQLHOME, and the root
directory can lead to several other directories on this hard disk.

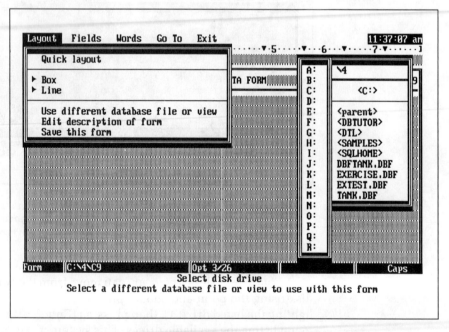

Figure 6-23 You can also move from the current disk to another disk
with these options.

Field Description Menu

Okay, we've got a database in use and we know what fields we want at the top of the form. Now it is time to put them there. Remember, we don't want things too clustered. That would make reading difficult and the screen too busy. Move the cursor to position 5,3, type *Exercise:* and a space, then press [F5]. This opens a different menu than what you would get if you pressed [Alt-F] to open the Fields menu. At this point, we don't want to modify any fields; we only want to place them on the screen. The [F5] (Add field) key does this nicely.

The first menu is an alphabetized listing of the available database fields on the left and a list of any existing calculated fields on the right. Calculated fields should only go at the end of an input screen, unless you are working on an advanced application (this is covered later in the chapter). Select the most important field and press [Enter]. A screen such as that shown in figure 6-24 is displayed.

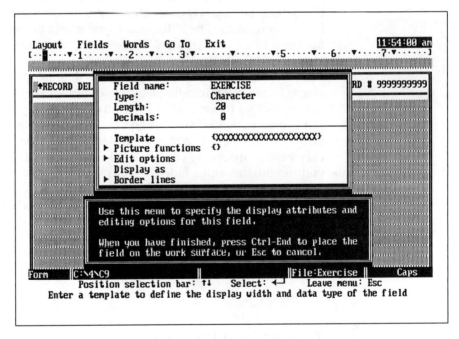

Figure 6-24 This menu lets you customize how data appears, is entered, and is edited on your screen form.

Template Symbols

Template symbols can be used to force the correct data types into specific fields.

Look at the screen in figure 6-24 and recognize everything it is telling you and offering you. The top of the menu tells you which database field you are working with. The immediate option is *Template*. A template can best be thought of as a blueprint for how you want things to look. A template

147

goes one better than a blueprint, however, because a template is a blueprint carved in stone. You want only numbers to appear in the database field, even though the field contains character data? No problem. You specify that here and dBASE IV won't let anything but numeric characters into the field. You want only uppercase? No problem, you can tell dBASE IV to convert every lowercase character placed in the field into an uppercase character.

With the cursor on *Template,* press [Enter]. You are provided with a list of available Template symbols. dBASE IV uses these symbols to determine what information to allow into the selected field. The default is the X character, which means "Take anything they give you and be happy with it." You will notice that some Template symbols are specific; others are general (like the X character). For example, you can use the 0 to specify only digits and signs (such as −1029), but only for numeric, floating, and character input.

The # symbol is another example of this restriction on which Template symbols can be used with which field types. A only accepts alpha characters, not digits, punctuation, or signs, and hence can be used only for character data. The N Template symbol can be used to allow digits but not signs in a character field. Both the Y and L Template symbols are for logical fields.

The ! symbol converts all character data to uppercase. This function places information into the database in uppercase only, even if you want information to be entered in lowercase but displayed in uppercase. This can cause problems if you design a screen form with an indexed field enabled to accept both uppercase and lowercase, then redesign the form to only accept uppercase. You have to either tell dBASE IV to perform an undifferentiated alpha index (not case sensitive) on the field or REPLACE the given field's data with uppercase data.

The last Template symbol, *other,* is one with which you can have lots of fun. You can place any character not previously listed into the field template. That character will appear exactly where you place it in the template each time data is entered, edited, or displayed. An example of this is the ten-character zip code field. A ten-character US zip code takes the form

03063-3861

This can be placed into the template as

99999-9999

Note that I have used two Template symbols here. The 9 character tells dBASE IV that numeric characters should be used; the hyphen is an *other* symbol and always appears in the field. When data is entered or edited, the cursor skips over the hyphen completely. You won't be able to edit the hyphen out of any data field.

For our purposes, we want to use the ! Template symbol to force all Exercise data to be uppercase. You can backspace over the Xs and enter twenty !'s.

But what if the data field is more than twenty characters long? What if the field is longer than can be shown on the menu? Press the [F9] (Zoom) key. The cursor is placed directly above the status line and an 80-character template entry display is shown. You actually have 254 characters available, if that is the size of your field, but only 80 characters show at a given time.

Following are other Template symbols not presented on the Template menu:

$ Display the current currency character instead of leading zeros in a numeric or floating field. There are two things you have to know before you can understand the use of this Template symbol. These two things are explained immediately following this Template symbol listing.

*   Display asterisks instead of leading zeros, should any exist in a numeric value.

,   Display a comma in a numeric field if there are any digits to the left of the comma. Consider the following:

        123.45 $$$,$$$.99   123.45

        123123.45 $$$,$$$.99   123,123.45

    The top line shows that the comma Template symbol is not used, even though it is placed in the template, because there are not enough digits in the number being displayed to warrant its use. In the second line, the comma Template symbol is used because there are enough digits to warrant its use.

.   The period Tomplate symbol tells dBASE IV where to place the decimal point in a numeric field. This gives you the opportunity to force decimal point positioning on reports and displays.

What are the two things you need to know before you can use the $ Template symbol? First, the current currency character is whatever dBASE IV has been told it is with the SET CURRENCY TO command. You can tell dBASE IV to use the bar symbol (¦) with

SET CURRENCY TO "¦"

This forces currency displays to appear as ¦123.45 instead of $123.45. Real useful, huh? Yes, actually, because you can use up to nine characters to display currency. You could, therefore, tell dBASE IV to mark Japanese values with

```
SET CURRENCY TO "YEN"
```

The amount would appear as YEN123.45.

Oh, come on now, nothing is ever that easy. You're right. You have to have enough space in the data field to display the selected currency marker. dBASE IV truncates the currency marker when there is not enough room to display it completely. The truncation occurs from left to right. The YEN example would progressively become *EN*, then *N*.

How does this work with the $ Template symbol? You tell dBASE IV to use the current currency character or characters by specifying the $ Template symbol as many times as you want the currency character or characters to appear.

Suppose we have a ten-character number field and we use the following command somewhere early in our work:

```
SET CURRENCY TO "HI,KID"
```

Then we set the Template symbol to $$$$$$$.99. Suppose the field value is 1.89. It is displayed as

```
HI,KID1.89
```

What if the field width was 18 characters and we used $$$$$$$$$$$$$$$$.99 as the Template symbol? We would get

```
KIDHI,KIDHI,KID1.89
```

Inventive, huh? You should know about three other SET commands when using the $ Template symbol. The first is SET CURRENCY LEFT/right. This command tells dBASE IV whether or not to show the currency character to the left or the right of the numeric value. dBASE IV defaults to showing the currency character to the left of the value. The next SET command is SET POINT TO. The POINT is the decimal point in a numeric display. You can set the point to any single character except digits or spaces. dBASE IV defaults to the period. The last SET command is SET SEPARATOR TO. This command tells dBASE IV which single character to use to separate hundreds from thousands, hundred thousands from millions (we all use that one, don't we?), and hundred millions from billions (common enough for me). These two command forms are

```
SET POINT TO ","
SET SEPARATOR TO ":"
```

Now comes the tricky part. No matter what you SET the CURRENCY, POINT, and SEPARATOR TO, you must write the Template symbol as if it were good old English. You tell dBASE IV you want currency, point, and separator as !, ?, and ¦ with SET commands. You tell dBASE IV how you want a ten-character number to be displayed with

`$$$,$$$.99`

Now, the other thing you need to know about is the concept of leading zeros. A partially filled ten-digit numeric field can be represented in two basic ways. Suppose the ten-digit field contains the value 123.45. This is a six-character value. The first way it can be represented is

`____123.45`

The underscores (_) in the above indicate blank spaces that appear before the digits which represent the value. These blanks lead the digits. These are automatically put in by dBASE IV because dBASE IV normally right justifies all numeric fields and variables. The other way the number can be displayed is

`0000123.45`

This method of display is also useful because it guarantees that there are no missing digits, due to a blown monitor pixel for example. And do you know what the four zeros that lead off the numeric value are called? Bonus points for readers that stood up and said, "Leading zeros, sir."

So then, the other use for the $ Template symbol is to supress leading zeros.

Picture Functions

Back to the Field description menu. The next option is *Picture functions*, and this option leads to a menu that might seem to duplicate the Template selections (figure 6-25).

The first three options on the Picture functions menu mimic the template *A*, *!*, and *other* symbols. The difference is in how the Picture functions and Template symbols are interpreted by dBASE IV. For example, by typing the *!* symbol twenty times, we told dBASE IV to perform an uppercase conversion on all alpha characters typed into the Exercise field. We can perform the same function using the following:

`PICTURE "@!"`

I demonstrated how a literal character can be placed in the data field using a Template symbol. There is a difference between the *other* Template symbol and the @R Picture function. The *other* Template symbol appears in the database field as it appears on the edit/entry screen. The @R Picture

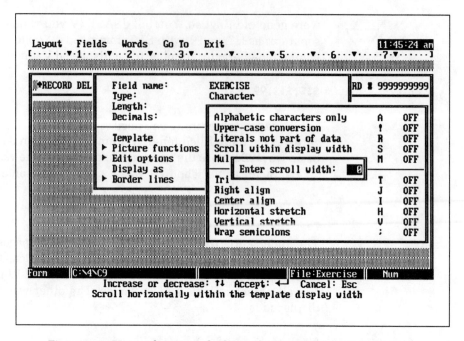

Figure 6-25 Picture functions duplicate the Template symbols in many
ways, but also offer more options on how the data is placed in a
displayed field and, something new with dBASE IV, a Multiple choice
option. This figure also shows the scroll width prompt.

function does not appear in the database field; it only appears on the edit/
entry screen. This can be useful but also confusing. When some users see a
dollar sign in a numeric field, they assume they must enter that dollar sign
character when they want to search the field. If data was entered or edited
with the dollar symbol used as an *other* Template symbol, there is no problem. If the data was entered or edited with the dollar symbol as part of an
@R Picture function, it won't be in the database field.

Another nicety of the Picture functions is the scroll feature, referenced with *Scroll within display width* on the Picture functions menu. This
option does not usually apply to a 20-character-wide field, but can be useful
when you have a character field wider than 60 characters. You can tell
dBASE IV to display only 60 characters but to scroll left and right through
the entire field with the Picture function

PICTURE "@S60"

This is accomplished on the Picture functions menu by typing S, then entering the width of the scroll window at the prompt (figure 6-25).

A new feature with dBASE IV is the *Multiple choice* Picture function.
The Exercise field we are using does not need a multiple choice entry, but
we will create one for the field to demonstrate how it works.

First, what if you want to create a multiple choice list that has single character values (the choices must be *character* values). You select the *Multiple choice* option and enter your choices separated by commas. It's as simple as that. Figure 6-26 shows a multiple choice list comprised of the lowercase alphabet in the [F9] Zoom window.

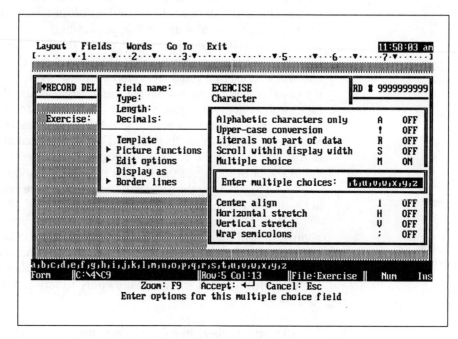

Figure 6-26 *Creating multiple choice Picture functions is as easy as listing your choices in the multiple choice window, separating each choice by a comma.*

Multiple-choice Picture functions must contain entries that have a unique first character.

It's that easy. It's also that dangerous. The Exercise field is a twenty-character field. Creating a multiple choice, single-character response forces dBASE IV to only allow single-character entries in that field. You can't type in something like *bench press* because dBASE IV will think you are going through the separate selections of *b, e, n, c, h, i* (typing a blank space causes dBASE IV to cycle to the next option in the choice list. This means it would offer *i* after it reached *h*), *p, r, e, s,* and *s* again. And it gets worse. Note that we have already told dBASE IV that we want the Exercise field to be forced uppercase with the ! Template symbol. The lowercase multiple choice options override the Template symbols and force lowercase entries into the field. The moral? Be careful!

The end result of a multiple choice Picture function is that dBASE IV places the first listed multiple choice option in the field when the field is displayed in edit/entry mode. You can press the [SPACEBAR] to cycle through the options, type the first letter of the desired selection (which means selections with the same first letter become part of the cycling—for

153

example, selections a0, a1, and a2 are retrieved by typing *a* three times), or simply type in your choice. Be advised, however, that you can't type in something not on the choice list. Doing so causes dBASE IV to replace your entry with the first option on the multiple choice list.

If you are creating the same screen form as the one described in this book, you will notice another set of Picture functions that are not available to you. These functions are listed under the ones we have just described but are not accessible. Why aren't they accessible?

The dBASE IV designers did a clever thing. I know it's clever because I do it myself, have suggested that others do it in my many dBASE books, and will suggest that you do it in later sections of this book. The clever thing is to use kernel coding. Kernel coding means you use the same code for as much and as many things as you can. This applies to the dBASE IV system because the form design screen and the report design screen are almost identical. They're so similar that you can use almost all the same code for one as you can for the other. Just about the only part of the code you can't use is the bottom half of the Picture functions' options menu.

And that is why the bottom half of the Picture functions menu is not accessible through the form design menu.

Other Picture functions aren't on the menu but are worth knowing about. Some of these Picture functions are used for other parts of our form, and we will reference them during those discussions as well. Seven Picture functions apply only to numeric fields. Many of these Picture functions aren't useful for data entry and may only function during data editing or display.

^ Display numbers in a field in scientific notation. This data form is helpful when working with floating fields, although you may want to use it for large numeric fields.

The term *scientific notation* merely indicates a way to show numbers. (You might think of dollar amounts with no cents as *accountant notation*.) For example, the number 1234567.89 in scientific notation is 1.23456789×10^6. You can specify scientific notation of only three decimal places, which changes the number to 1.234×10^6. Notice that the number of decimal places only applies to the numbers before the multiplication symbol. Numbers in scientific notation are sometimes written without the *x 10*; for example, the preceding number would be 1.234E6.

$ Display the numeric data as currency. Remember that all currency displays are subject to the SET POINT TO, SET SEPARATOR TO, and SET CURRENCY TO settings.

(Enclose negative numeric values in parentheses, a common bookkeeping practice. A −1000 field value would appear as (1000).

C Display CR after a positive numeric value. A field value of 1000, for example, would show up as 1000CR.

L Display leading zeros in a field.

X   The *X* Picture function is an example of how a Picture function can be different from a Template symbol. The *X* Template symbol told dBASE IV to accept anything in the field. The *X* Picture function tells dBASE IV to show *DB* (debit) after a negative numeric value. For example, −1000 appears as 1000DB.

Z   Display numeric values of 0 as blank entries. This can be helpful when you don't want to use a seed value in a numeric field and don't want to show a zero just because the field is blank.

The following Picture functions apply only to character fields:

B   Left justify text in a field.

I   Center text in a field.

J   Right justify text in a field.

T   Trim all blanks, both leading and trailing, from a field. This Picture function is fairly useless for data entry or editing and is best used for report generation.

Two other Picture functions, *D* and *E,* are for Date fields. The *D* Picture function tells dBASE IV to use the current SET DATE format for Date field representations. The *E* tells dBASE IV to use the European date format (dd/mm/yy).

Edit Options

Okay, so much for Template symbols and Picture functions. These two items control how the data looks. We also need to have power over the data itself, not just how pretty it is. We can design a foolproof system and some fool will come along and prove us wrong. These things are taken care of on the Edit options menu (figure 6-27).

The following are options on the Edit menu:

Editing allowed
: I ask you, where will you get more power over data entry and editing than here? The default is yes. You can toggle to No by pressing [Enter]. You probably want to set the Editing allowed toggle to No if you want certain fields displayed and not edited.

The Permit edit if *function gives you decision-making ability regarding whether or not a user will have access to a field in a database.*

Permit edit if
: Do you remember what I said about programmers and why certain parts of programs don't fit together as seamlessly as one might like? I mentioned that programmers get their orders and retire to deep subterranean passages, chuckling and chortling like Macbeth's witches. When you get menu options like *Editing allowed* and *Permit editing if,* you begin to

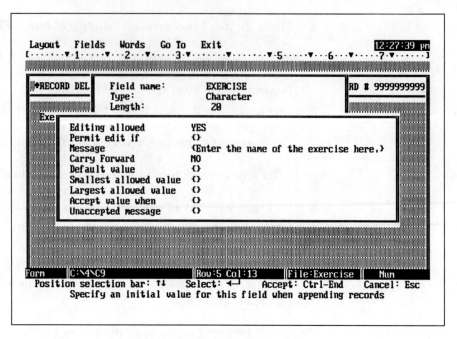

Figure 6-27 *The Edit options submenu is where you get real power
over data entry and editing.*

believe these people have been throwing too many role-playing dice. You can almost see the words Ultimate Charisma and Ultimate Power leeching off the screen.

This field lets you decide if and when a user has the right to edit data in a field. This is a buildable editing function, which means you can make editing of this field dependent on data in other fields, values of memory variables, and so on. This is one method of making the first field in a record a calculated field. Usually, if no data is entered in the first field of a blank record during data entry, dBASE IV exits back whence it came (the dBASE prompt, the calling routine, and so on). You can force dBASE IV to not exit back whence it came and allow editing of fields other than the first data field with the *Permit edit if* editing function if you allow for some other method of exiting the data entry screen. This is demonstrated later in this chapter.

Message

This is excellent. Now we can tell the user exactly what we want them to enter. This will provide hours of entertainment when you watch people read your prompt message and still not know what they are supposed to do. The message for the Exercise field is *Enter the name of the exercise here.* Remember that you can always use the [F9] (Zoom) key to open a screen-wide line to enter your message. After I explain the rest of the edit option, I will demonstrate how to use the bottom of the screen with the *Message* option.

Carry Forward

This option won't have much use in the Exercise field, but can be useful if you want a value entered in one field of a record to be repeated in the same field in succeeding records.

Default value

Useful when you want an entry to be in a field, regardless of whether or not the user enters information. There are some countries, I'm told, where this option is used heavily during elections.

Smallest allowed value

This can be thought of as the minimum value you want entered in the field. Enter a value here and dBASE IV allows no numbers lower than that specified to be entered. You can force the user to enter data into a numeric field by specifying a default value of 0 and a smallest allowed value of 10, for example. dBASE IV won't let the user leave the field until a value of 10 or higher is entered.

Largest allowed value

This works exactly like the *Smallest allowed value* editing function, except this is the maximum value you want to allow the user to enter in a field.

Accept value when

Another example of software designers throwing role-playing dice. I have mentioned a few ways you can frustrate users by tweaking the default value, the smallest allowed value, and the largest allowed value editing functions. Here is the bigger hammer method of doing the same thing. Like *Permit edit if*, this editing function is buildable and can be useful when you want a calculated expression evaluated and met before letting the user out of the data field.

Unaccepted message

What do you do when you have laid some rules for dBASE IV regarding when to accept data in a field and the user refuses to obey those rules? You tell them they are doing something wrong. Then you kill them. This is where you do it— the telling, not the killing—and this editing function works identically to the previously mentioned *Message* function.

I mentioned that we don't need to place a menu at the bottom of the screen anymore, thanks to dBASE IV's pop-up menus. I further stated that this gives us a chance to use screen lines 21 through 24. There can be a conflict if you wantonly use screen lines 21 through 24 *and* tell dBASE IV to place messages on the screen with the *Unaccepted message* Edit option. The *Message* takes over the bottom of the screen and obliterates anything you might have placed there.

I also said that we could use the bottom of the screen for our own messages and such. Here I will demonstrate how to get away with it.

Open the *Message* option in the Edit Options menu as described. Press the [F9] (Zoom) key to expand the Message window to the entire width of the screen. Now hold down the [Alt] and [Ctrl] keys and use the numeric keypad to enter the number 200. The lower-left corner character appears in the [F9] Zoom window. Now hold down the [Alt] and [Ctrl] keys and enter 205 on the numeric keypad. You will see the little double line character. Repeat this until the cursor has gone across the screen. When you get to the right corner, hold down the [Alt] and [Ctrl] keys and enter 188 on the numeric keypad. Make sure the Ins toggle is off, go back to some- where left of center in the Zoom window, and start to type in your message. After a while, you will center things without even trying (see figure 6-28 for an example).

This method is easy to use because the screen box acts as a guide and sizing your message isn't a problem. You can also enter a string such as the following:

```
CHR(200) + REPLICATE(CHR(205), 21) +;
    [Enter the name of the exercise here] +;
    REPLICATE(CHR(205), 22) + CHR(188)
```

Be careful counting spaces before you use this method, however. The one last caveat regarding these methods of utilizing the Edit option Message line for your own purposes is to remember to SET COLOR OF MESSAGES TO the same color as the rest of the screen.

Again, if you have been building a screen using the database designed so far in this book, you will see two other field options not highlighted and therefore inaccessible to you. These options, *Display as* and *Border lines*, come into play when we place the Comment memo field onto our screen form.

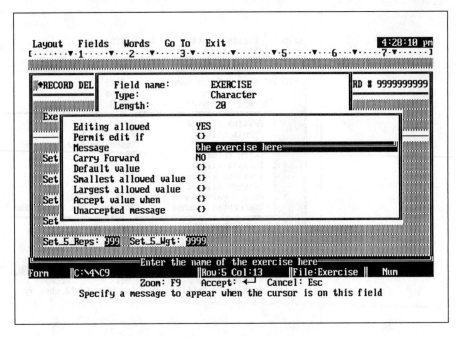

Figure 6-28 *You can use the [F9] (Zoom) key to create full screen width messages that utilize the bottom of the screen without affecting your display. Remember to SET COLOR OF MESSAGES TO the same color as the rest of the screen.*

Finishing the Screen Form

We have explored much of the [F5] (Add fields) submenus just by placing one field on the screen. Now let's finish with the rest of our fields. Move the cursor to screen position 5,38, type *Date:*, type a space, then press [F5] again. Highlight the Date field and press [Enter]. The Fields submenu is displayed again, but this time only the *Edit* options are highlighted. We allow editing; the Message reads *Enter the date you exercised here*; we carry forward (just type *C* after you exit the Message line); the default value can be 01/01/89 (note that dBASE IV expects date values to be entered in braces); we accept the value if the date that the data is entered is at least the same day the exercise was done (we don't want people entering data on future exercise sessions); and we specify a message for those few times the data will be unacceptable (such as *You can't enter data for future workouts!*) because we are specifying when data should be accepted. This can all be seen in figure 6-29.

Move to screen position 5,60 and type *Time:*, type a space, then press [F5]. Type *T* for *Time*. Select Template symbols from the Fields submenu, backspace over the Xs, and enter 99:99.

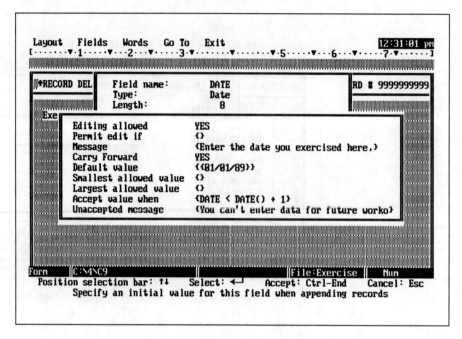

Figure 6-29 *All the options necessary for our Exercise
screen form's Date field.*

Wait a minute, Joseph. You told us to make the field eight characters wide so we could enter the correct time.

Yes, I did, but I don't think too many people keep track of their workout times by the seconds. I wanted to give us something to consider editing out of the database. We will get back to this after the screen form is completed.

Back to the Fields submenus. Skip the Picture functions and open the Edit options menu. Editing is allowed, the Message should be *Enter your workout starting time here,* carry it forward, and put in a default value of 00:00.

By the way, you are remembering to save your work as we go along, aren't you?

The next step is a "prettifier." Press [Home] [Down-Arrow] [Down-Arrow] [Right-Arrow]. The cursor should be at screen position 7,1. If not, get there. Press [Alt-L] *L S.* This tells dBASE IV to display the Layout menu, go to the Lines submenu, and prepare to draw a single line on the screen form. Press [Enter], then move the cursor to screen position 7,78 and press [Enter] again. Now your primary interest fields are separated from your general interest fields. Nice.

Move the cursor to screen position 9,3. We will start entering the Set_ n fields. Much of this is repetitive, so I will demonstrate only the first two Set_n fields, Set_1_Reps and Set_1_Wgt.

Type *Set_1_Reps:,* type a space, then press [F5] *S* [Enter]. You can do this because we want the first Set_n offering, which is what dBASE IV gives us when we type S, when the database fields are displayed.

The Template symbol is fine so we can proceed to the Picture functions (figure 6-30). Remember that I said dBASE IV offers some different Picture function options when you work with a numeric field? Here they are.

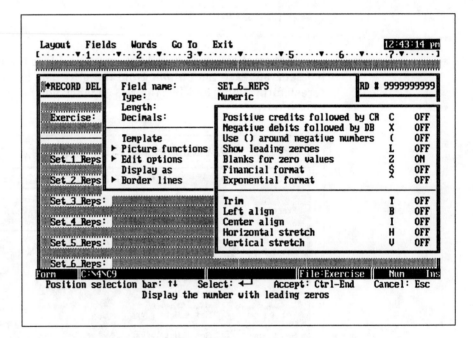

Figure 6-30 dBASE IV offers different Picture functions when you work with a numeric field versus a character field. Character field offerings are shown in figure 6-23.

Despite what we may think of ourselves and our strengths, we don't want exponential format. We also know we don't need financial format. We don't want to show leading zeros, necessarily, but it might be nice to show blanks for zero values. Type B to toggle the *Blanks for zero values* option.

Onto the *Edit* options. Editing is allowed; the Message should be *Enter the number of repetitions you performed for your first set here;* we know that the number of repetitions throughout a workout is fairly standard so we want to carry the data forward to other added records; and we can make the default value 0.

Move the cursor to screen position 9,20 and type *Set_1_Wgt:* and a space, then press [F5] S [Down-Arrow] [Enter]. This tells dBASE IV to use the Set_1_Wgt field. We can accept the Template symbol and move directly to Picture functions, where we simply type B to use blank spaces for zero values.

Our *Edit* options, however, are a little different. Yes, we do want to allow editing; the Message is *Enter the amount of weight used for your first set here;* and set the default to 0.

The new item is *Permit edit if.* We want someone to edit or enter data in this field only if they have already entered data into the corresponding Set_n_Reps field. This means our *Permit edit if* option should contain the following formula:

```
SET_1_REPS # 0
```

Repeat these steps for all Set_n fields. Place them under each other, but separate each Set_n pair from the next pair by one blank line. Your screen form should look like figure 6-31 when you have finished this part of the exercise.

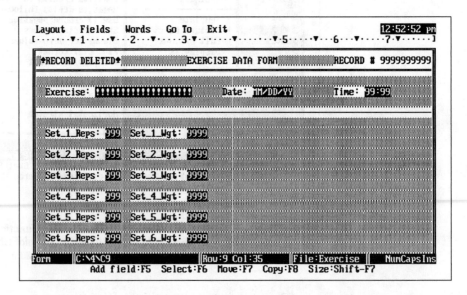

Figure 6-31 The Exercise screen form with all the Set_n pairs entered.

Hello again. Entering those first fields took some work, right? By the time you were entering the Set_5 and Set_6 fields you were flying right along, right? Good.

Move the cursor to screen position 21,10 and type *Total_Wgt:* and a space, then press [F5] *T* [Down-Arrow] [Enter]. We are entering the Total_Wgt field here. The Template symbol is fine. Our Picture function uses blanks for zeros so toggle this option with *B*.

Now we come to an interesting part of our screen form project. We said that the Total_Wgt field is actually the sum of the Set_n pairs in a given record. This means Total_Wgt is a calculated field, correct?

Yes, but not in the way dBASE IV wants to calculate a field. When you tell dBASE IV to ⟨create⟩ a calculated field on the [F5] (Add field) menu, dBASE IV just creates a command that basically says, "Go get the information and figure out what they want to know and show it here."

Calculated fields can only work with the present record's data if that data already exists in a usable form.

Sounds good, doesn't it? Oh, were it only so! The flaw is that a screen form doesn't have any information to get; therefore, the calculated field in a screen form also won't have any information to process. In data entry mode, information is not in the database until the screen form has been completely used at least once. Therefore, there is nothing to use in calculations. After data has been entered in the screen form, you can get the information, use it for calculations, and display it. Of course, you have gone on to the next data entry record by this time. There is no problem with editing or simply displaying data, but data entry can be a problem.

There are four solutions. Make sure the user has a TSR calculator utility, make sure the user has a real calculator, remove all calculated fields, or do some simple programming, which is demonstrated at the end of this chapter. Believe me, the programming is simple and you will be all the more a wizard for having tried it.

In any case, the Total_Wgt field will be calculated and never edited. Therefore, we toggle *Editing allowed* OFF by typing E.

There is only one more field to place on our data entry form. The Comment memo field is a word-processable field, but we don't want people writing tomes about their exercises in it. It is also the least important field in the database, so we will isolate it with a vertical bar. Move the cursor to screen position 23,40 and press [Alt-L] *L S* [Enter]. Now move the cursor to screen position 8,40 and press [Enter] again.

And now for some magic. Place the cursor at screen position 7,40. Hold down the [Alt] and [Ctrl] keys, and enter 194 on the numeric keypad. Presto, a smoothly integrated line. Let's repeat the trick at the bottom. Go to screen position 24,40, then hold down the [Alt] and [Ctrl] keys and enter 207 on the numeric keypad.

Okay, we have marked an area for our Comment field. Now all we need to do is title the box and place the Comment field there. Place the cursor on screen position 7,56 and type *Comment*. Don't worry that this is on a line. Move the cursor to screen position 9,42 and press [F5]. The first thing you will notice is that all Field options are not available. We only want to add the *Message Edit* option—*Enter any comments you have about this exercise set here.*

Back to the Fields options. We can choose to display the Comment field as a marker or a window. Because we have the room on the screen, we will go with an editable window. Remember that a marker is just the word *memo* in the field. You can toggle the *Display as* mode from marker to window by typing D.

We might also want to have dBASE IV place a box around our memo field, even if we later edit out the box. Our example won't use the dBASE IV box because we have already drawn our own. However, we would normally use the dBASE IV box because dBASE IV can place the memo field in our target area far more easily than we can. When you [Ctrl-End] out of the Fields options menu, you are prompted to place the memo field box on the screen. Place the cursor at screen position 8,41, press [Enter], then move the cursor to 23,78 and press [Enter] again.

Oh, what the heck, move to screen position 7,7 and type *Repetitions and Weights.*

At this point, you are ready to have dBASE IV generate the screen form for you. Some users will have difficulty when it comes time to do this, depending on how their computer's memory is set up. If there is a problem, dBASE IV displays an *Insufficient memory* message.

The problem is not with dBASE IV, per se, but with how much memory it needs to do certain things. The *Insufficient memory* message means dBASE IV could not load and run the files it needs to process your screen form into an FMT file, then into a compiled FMO file. No problem. You have not lost your work yet, nor are you going to. Press [Alt-E] S. dBASE IV saves the SCR file without generating anything else and drops you back whence you came. Exit dBASE IV completely, unload some of the memory resident software, and go back into dBASE IV to have it generate your screen form files. Sometimes, you only have to exit from the screen form design system to the dBASE prompt and go back into the design system.

Modifying a Database After the Screen Form Is Designed

When we were laying out the screen form, we changed the screen representation of the Time field from what we designed in the database. Yes, it's true, it can happen to you, when you botch your design (to be sung to the tune "When you're young at heart"). The big question is, "Is there a way to modify the structure of the database from inside the screen form design system?"

The big answer is, "No, there isn't." The reason for this section is to point out something originally stated in chapter 5, repeated there quite often, reinforced in this chapter, and hammered into you here.

After you complete your screen form, you will notice things you want to change in your database structure

Nothing is engraved in stone, especially database structures. First, you designed the form according to someone else's instructions. Granted, that someone else was me and I of all people should know what's coming. Second, I want you to be sensitive to the fact that all you can count on in life, more than the surety of death and taxes, is change. People change, relationships change, and database structures and demands change. What you have to decide is what is more important, representation or literal structure.

The literal structure of a database is what it really looks like. The literal structure of the EXERCISE database can be seen in chapter 5. The representation of the database is what we have created in this chapter with the screen form design system. The two are not mutually exclusive. You can elect to design forms that show all aspects of your database to the user. You don't have to, of course. You can elect to design forms that only reveal data conditionally. An example of this is a screen form that is sensitive to the security level of the current user. Low priority users can't see too much data. High priority users can see more data. Highest priority users can see anything they want. We created a screen form that shows data slightly differently than how the data appears in the actual database. dBASE IV represents the data with the screen form as we have told it to, not how the data is actually represented in the database. Is it worth making the change to the database structure if dBASE IV will handle representation for us without a hitch?

Another big yes and no. Yes, it is worth making the change to the database structure when there is a radical difference from the representation and the structure *and you don't want any differences to exist*. This is important. If you want a difference between representation and structure, don't make the change. If you want a one-to-one correspondence between representation and structure, make the change.

Note also that your database design should not be restricted by your representation's limitations. It is easier to change a screen form than it is to change a database structure. Further, changing a database structure after data has been entered can be dangerous. Always make a backup copy of a filled database before modifying anything. True, dBASE IV makes a backup copy for you, but don't rely on anything that is automatic. Like the old saying, "The strongest memory is nothing compared to a note on paper," so "The best automatic safeguard is nothing compared to manually safeguarding something yourself."

Change the database structure only when you are sure the change will benefit the system as a whole, not just one small part of the system.

No, you should not make changes to the database if you are only making those changes for aesthetic reasons. Aesthetics have a way of catching up to you after a while. You finish a painting and continue to add little touches over time. The next thing you know you've covered the original masterpiece with lots of little drops of paint. DaVinci carried the Mona Lisa with him for years after "finishing" it. He would always do little things to it. Sure, it's one of the world's great art treasures now, but DaVinci's dead, didn't get any real money for it, and the guy in the picture looks like a woman.

You can change the EXERCISE database structure if you want. Note that you will make the database slightly smaller simply because you are changing a field from eight characters to five. Over a thousand records, this saves roughly 3K of disk space. Saving disk space usually is the best reason to modify a database structure to match a representation.

More on Picture Functions

Template symbols are fairly straightforward operators on the data they represent. You use a template to make a drawing of how you want the data to appear on a screen. You want three digits before the decimal point and two digits after? Make the drawing 999.99 and you are done. You want five uppercase characters, a hyphen, then four numeric characters? You make the drawing !!!!!-9999 and you've got it.

Picture functions are not quite like that. In the first place, there are pictures and there are functions. The difference is subtle and can cause lots of confusion. I will demonstrate by creating a picture and a function, both of which do the same thing.

I want to read something into a character database field. I want whatever is read to be only alpha characters (no numerics allowed) and I want everything to be uppercase. I can do that with the Picture function @A!. I can also do it with the Function A!. There is a subtle difference between the two.

The Picture function uses the at sign (@) to introduce the actions I want to perform on any data being entered into or being displayed from the field. The straight Function doesn't use the ampersand. Why? Because of Template symbols.

If you let dBASE IV generate a screen form from the screen image we created in the section titled "Designing Screen Forms" and then read the resulting FMT file, you'd notice that dBASE IV's concept of Template symbols and Picture functions is closely linked. You might think you would see some code differences such as the following:

Template symbol   @ 10,10 GET var TEMPLATE "AAAAA"

Picture function   @ 10,10 GET var PICTURE "AAAAA"

Can you guess which of these two lines of code results in the Template symbol allowing only alpha characters in a five-character database field? Yes, this is a trick question because the answer is the second line of code, the one containing *PICTURE "AAAAA."* There is no dBASE IV command or function called TEMPLATE. There is one called PICTURE, however.

A Template symbol is nothing more than an extended Picture function. It is useful if you have only one kind of qualifier on the database field, for example, ! or A. To combine Template symbols, you have to use a Picture function. This allows you to gang operators, such as @!A. The ! and *A* Template symbols tell dBASE IV to force all uppercase or only allow alpha characters. The Picture function tells dBASE IV to force uppercase and accept only alpha characters.

Next quiz. Which of the following two lines tells dBASE IV to accept only alpha characters and force uppercase?

Function   @ 10,10 GET var FUNCTION "A!"

Picture   @ 10,10 GET var PICTURE "@A!"

Answer? Both. Which one you use is up to you, although you can't use the at sign as a string literal (you can't force dBASE IV to accept it as a character to be placed into the database field) unless you work with the FUNCTION argument. Other than that, Functions work identically to Picture functions.

Calculated Fields and Advanced Screen Forms

I mentioned that the concept of a calculated field in dBASE IV is not quite the same as in the rest of the database management system world. To clarify, let me explain what a truly calculated field is.

You are working with your database system. You are putting data in some fields, either adding or editing information, generally having a good time with the system. Somewhere in the screen form is a field that you never truly enter, yet information gets in there and you can see it change as you add or edit data in other fields in the database or the immediate record.

This field has two things that mark it as a calculated field. First, you never enter or edit any information in the field. Second, the field's value changes based on information in other fields. In other words, the calculated field's value is determined by what goes on elsewhere. Several database management systems keep information on how to determine the value in a calculated field in the database, but don't keep the calculated values themselves. This is good because the values are subject to change more often than other fields. (If any one field necessary to determine the calculated field's value changes, the calculated field changes. However, the reverse is not true. A change in the calculated field does not predicate a change in all the fields that affect it.) It is good also because disk space is not used to hold volatile data. The calculated field's value is kept only in memory and only when that particular database is active. Some database management systems call this type of calculated field a *virtual field*.

dBASE IV's idea of a calculated field is similar, but not identical. In some other database management systems, the calculated field is updated as soon as changes are made to the fields that the calculated field is dependent upon. dBASE IV requires that the information in the other fields be READ into the database before the value of the calculated field can be determined. This is not a problem when you have already put information in a record, such as when you are editing or updating existing information. It is not useful when you are adding data because the newly added data must be READ before dBASE IV can use it to calculate a field's value. This implies that you want an actual database field that takes up real space in the database and holds real data; not something that only exists in memory.

This brings us to the next topic. You can have a part of your screen form which holds calculated information, but is not necessarily a real database field. You can have something as simple as displayed data, a memory variable, or a real field.

There are pros and cons to each. First, displayed data is nothing more than what dBASE IV currently gives you when you ask for a calculated field. You ask for a calculated field and dBASE IV writes in a command such as

```
@ x,y SAY field1 * field2
```

It does not matter that I use a simple multiplication of two fields. You might want another arithmetic combination, or a function acting on database fields, or an expression involving memory variables and database fields. The displayed data type of a calculated field must have data already available to perform its calculations.

A calculated field using a memory variable can behave in different ways. A calculated field based merely on memory variables always shows a value, even if other fields in the record are blank. The value shown is the memory variable's value. If the calculated field is dependent on a memory variable and a field in the current record, nonzero values depend on the arithmetic expression involving the variable and field. There is a good use for this type of calculated field. You can use a memory variable that is entered or updated by the user for a default value. This means you don't have to create your screen form with default values installed. Instead, you can prompt the user for a seed value, place the seed value in a memory variable, then create a calculated field that is an arithmetic expression of the seed value and the field itself.

The last option is to use a true database field as a calculated field. There are lots of restrictions on this, based on what I have mentioned earlier in this section. You can't expect to have information pop into a calculated field until information has been accepted into the record elsewhere, unless you are basing your calculation on data in other records.

As always, there are ways around this. You can create a calculated field as the first field in your record. This calculated field is not dependent on other fields in the same record; it is dependent on fields in the previously added record, as mentioned. Note the implied caveat: This method works only with records that are being added to the database. Why is this so?

If data already exists in a record and the record's data is placed on the screen, the calculated field will have information. If the record is being added to the database, there is no information in the other records to use in calculations. But there is data in previous records. You can use data from fields in the preceding record to calculate a field in the current record. You can't count on using data in the preceding record to calculate a field in the current record when data already exists in the current record.

Analyzing and Modifying the dBASE IV Generated FMT File

Listing 6-1 is what dBASE IV creates when you have finished designing your screen form and press [Ctrl-W], [Ctrl-End], or [Ctrl-Enter]. (Some lines are wrapped to fit within the margins.) Note that the last option, [Ctrl-Enter], instructs dBASE IV to generate the screen form without leaving the screen form design system. Remember that the actual @ SAY GET commands are based on the fields in the EXERCISE database. Your FMT file might look different if you used a different database. This won't be a problem because we will be analyzing how a screen form is transformed into an FMT file, then determining how we might change the dBASE IV generated FMT file to better suit our purposes.

Listing 6-1

```
01 : ****************************************************************
02 : *-- Name....: C9.FMT
03 : *-- Date....: 12-24-88
04 : *-- Version.: dBASE IV, Format 1.0
05 : *-- Notes...: Format files use " " as delimiters!
06 : ****************************************************************
07 :
08 : *-- Format file initialization code -----------------------
09 :
10 : IF SET("TALK")="ON"
11 :    SET TALK OFF
12 :    lc_talk="ON"
13 : ELSE
14 :    lc_talk="OFF"
15 : ENDIF
16 :
17 : *-- This form was created in EGA25 mode
18 : SET DISPLAY TO EGA25
19 :
20 : lc_status=SET("STATUS")
21 : *-- SET STATUS was OFF when you went into the Forms Designer.
22 : IF lc_status = "ON"
23 :    SET STATUS OFF
24 : ENDIF
25 :
26 : *-- Window for memo field comment.
27 : DEFINE WINDOW Wndow1 FROM 8,41 TO 23,78
28 :
29 : lc_carry = SET("CARRY")
30 : *-- Fields to carry forward during APPEND.
31 : SET CARRY TO date,time,set_1_reps,set_2_reps,set_3_reps,set_4_
     reps;
32 :    ,set_5_reps,set_6_reps ADDITIVE
33 :
34 : *-- @ SAY GETS Processing. ---------------------------------
35 :
36 : *--   Format Page: 1
37 :
38 : @ 1,0 TO 24,79 DOUBLE
39 : @ 2,2 SAY CHR(6)
40 : @ 2,3 SAY "RECORD DELETED"
41 : @ 2,17 SAY CHR(6)
42 : @ 2,31 SAY "EXERCISE DATA FORM"
```

Listing 6-1 (cont.)

```
43 : a 2,60 SAY "RECORD # 9999999999"
44 : a 3,1 SAY "═══════════════════════════
         ════════════════════════════════"
45 : a 5,3 SAY "Exercise: "
46 : a 5,13 GET exercise PICTURE "!!!!!!!!!!!!!!!!!!!!!" ;
47 :     MESSAGE "╚═══════════════════════Enter the name of the exercise
         here═══════════════════════╝"
48 : a 5,38 SAY "Date: "
49 : a 5,44 GET date ;
50 :    VALID DATE < DATE() + 1 ;
51 :    ERROR "You can't enter data for future workouts!" ;
52 :    DEFAULT {01/01/89} ;
53 :    MESSAGE "╚═══════════════════════Enter the date you exercised
         here═══════════════════════╝"
54 : a 5,60 SAY "Time: "
55 : a 5,66 GET time PICTURE "99:99" ;
56 :    DEFAULT "00:00" ;
57 :    MESSAGE "╚═══════════════════════Enter your workout starting
         time here═══════════════════╝"
58 : a 7,1 SAY "═══════Repetitions and Weights═══════════════╤
         ═Comment═══════════════════════"
59 : a 8,40 SAY "|"
60 : a 8,41 GET comment OPEN WINDOW Wndow1 ;
61 :    MESSAGE "╚═══════════════════Enter any comments about this
         exercise or set here═══════════════╝"
62 : a 9,3 SAY "Set_1_Reps: "
63 : a 9,15 GET set_1_reps PICTURE "@Z 999" ;
64 :    DEFAULT 0 ;
65 :    MESSAGE "╚═══Enter the number of repetitions you performed
         for your first set here═══════╝"
66 : a 9,20 SAY "Set_1_Wgt: "
67 : a 9,31 GET set_1_wgt PICTURE "@Z 9999" ;
68 :    WHEN SET_1_REPS # 0 ;
69 :    DEFAULT 0 ;
70 :    MESSAGE "╚═══════════Enter the amount of weight used for your
         first set here═══════════╝"
71 : a 9,40 SAY "|"
72 : a 10,40 SAY "|"
73 : a 11,3 SAY "Set_2_Reps: "
74 : a 11,15 GET set_2_reps PICTURE "@Z 999" ;
75 :    DEFAULT 0 ;
76 :    MESSAGE "╚═══Enter the number of repetitions you performed
         for your second set here═══════╝"
77 : a 11,20 SAY "Set_2_Wgt: "
78 : a 11,31 GET set_2_wgt PICTURE "@Z 9999" ;
79 :    WHEN SET_2_REPS # 0 ;
80 :    DEFAULT 0 ;
81 :    MESSAGE "╚═══════════Enter the amount of weight you used for
         your second set here═══════════╝"
```

```
 82 : @ 11,40 SAY "|"
 83 : @ 12,40 SAY "|"
 84 : @ 13,3 SAY "Set_3_Reps: "
 85 : @ 13,15 GET set_3_reps PICTURE "@Z 999" ;
 86 :    DEFAULT 0 ;
 87 :    MESSAGE "╚════Enter the number of repetitions you performed
          for your third set here═════╝"
 88 : @ 13,20 SAY "Set_3_Wgt: "
 89 : @ 13,31 GET set_3_wgt PICTURE "@Z 9999" ;
 90 :    WHEN SET_3_REPS # 0 ;
 91 :    DEFAULT 0 ;
 92 :    MESSAGE "╚═══════Enter the amount of weight used for your
          third set here═════════╝"
 93 : @ 13,40 SAY "|"
 94 : @ 14,40 SAY "|"
 95 : @ 15,3 SAY "Set_4_Reps: "
 96 : @ 15,15 GET set_4_reps PICTURE "@Z 999" ;
 97 :    DEFAULT 0 ;
 98 :    MESSAGE "╚═══Enter the number of repetitions you performed
          for your fourth set here═════╝"
 99 : @ 15,20 SAY "Set_4_Wgt: "
100 : @ 15,31 GET set_4_wgt PICTURE "@Z 9999" ;
101 :    WHEN SET_4_REPS # 0 ;
102 :    DEFAULT 0 ;
103 :    MESSAGE "╚═══════Enter the amount of weight you used for
          your fourth set here═════════╝"
104 : @ 15,40 SAY "|"
105 : @ 16,40 SAY "|"
106 : @ 17,3 SAY "Set_5_Reps: "
107 : @ 17,15 GET set_5_reps PICTURE "@Z 999" ;
108 :    DEFAULT 0 ;
109 :    MESSAGE "╚═══════Enter the number of repetitions you performed
          for your fifth set here═════╝"
110 : @ 17,20 SAY "Set_5_Wgt: "
111 : @ 17,31 GET set_5_wgt PICTURE "@Z 9999" ;
112 :    WHEN SET_5_REPS # 0 ;
113 :    DEFAULT 0 ;
114 :    MESSAGE "╚═══════Enter the amount of weight you used for
          your fifth set here═════════╝"
115 : @ 17,40 SAY "|"
116 : @ 18,40 SAY "|"
117 : @ 19,3 SAY "Set_6_Reps: "
118 : @ 19,15 GET set_6_reps PICTURE "@Z 999" ;
119 :    DEFAULT 0 ;
120 :    MESSAGE "╚═══Enter the number of repetitions you performed
          for your sixth set here═════╝"
121 : @ 19,20 SAY "Set_6_Wgt: "
122 : @ 19,31 GET set_6_wgt PICTURE "@Z 9999" ;
123 :    WHEN SET_6_REPS # 0 ;
124 :    DEFAULT 0 ;
```

Listing 6-1 (cont.)

```
125 :    MESSAGE "┕═══════════Enter the amount of weight used for your
         sixth set here═══════════┙"
126 : @ 19,40 SAY "|"
127 : @ 20,40 SAY "|"
128 : @ 21,10 SAY "Total_Wgt: "
129 : @ 21,21 SAY total_wgt PICTURE "@Z 99999"
130 : @ 21,40 SAY "|"
131 : @ 22,40 SAY "|"
132 : @ 23,40 SAY "|"
133 : @ 24,40 SAY "±"
134 :
135 : *-- Format file exit code ----------------------------------------
       ----------------
136 :
137 : *-- SET STATUS was OFF when you went into the Forms Designer.
138 : IF lc_status = "ON"  && Entered form with status on
139 :    SET STATUS ON   && Turn STATUS "ON" on the way out
140 : ENDIF
141 :
142 : IF lc_carry = "OFF"
143 :    SET CARRY OFF
144 : ENDIF
145 :
146 : RELEASE WINDOWS Wndow1
147 :
148 : IF lc_talk="ON"
149 :    SET TALK ON
150 : ENDIF
151 :
152 : RELEASE lc_carry,lc_talk,lc_fields,lc_status
153 : *-- EOP: C9.FMT
```

This is what dBASE IV makes of your pretty picture. Some of the edits we will make to this file are necessary; others depend on how you want your FMT file to work.

Normally, an FMT file becomes active when you use the SET FORMAT TO command. This FMT file's name is C9.FMT, so we would activate it with

```
SET FORMAT TO C9
```

After the FMT file is SET, the full-screen editing commands EDIT, CHANGE, APPEND, INSERT, and READ make use of the FMT file. Note that you can tell dBASE IV to use a file other than an FMT file to SET the FORMAT by including the non-FMT file extension in the command (such as SET FORMAT TO C9.PRG). However, if the file you select to replace the standard FMT file has some nonimmediate commands or functions, dBASE IV can't use it properly.

The first advantage of the SET FORMAT TO command is that it places the FMT file into memory. Second, all the @ SAY, @ GET, and screen-handling commands are in one file. This frees the programmer from having to do much work. Other than that, I don't think there is much use for FMT files. A significant problem with FMT files is that each READ, EDIT, CHANGE, APPEND, or INSERT causes the entire screen to be rewritten. This means each new record causes lines 34 to 135 to be rerun, essentially repainting the screen. This takes time and can be a hindrance, especially if you are working on a network. There is also no reason to repaint the entire screen just to fill a record with data or edit existing data in a record. And remember, that is all you really want to do. If you simply view the data, that is just editing without touching the keys. What we will do first is analyze the form and make some minor changes, then we will see how to use the FMT file as part of a more sophisticated program.

Lines 1 to 6 are called the header, a series of notes about the file. You will note lots of blank lines (7, 9, 16, and so on). These lines separate blocks of code and have no effect on processing because dBASE IV pseudocompiles the FMT file into a faster running FMO file and ignores the blank lines during this process. Also note that dBASE IV ignores lines starting with an asterisk. These are comment lines and are not used during processing.

Lines 8 through 33 tell dBASE IV how the computer and dBASE IV itself were set up before the FMT file was made active. In particular, was TALK SET ON or OFF, how was the DISPLAY SET, was STATUS ON or OFF, and how was CARRY SET? The particular computer used to generate this code uses an EGA25 display. Line 27 is where dBASE IV creates a screen variable, Wndow1, to hold the Comment field. Note that the screen variable is defined to cover the area we mapped out when we drew the Comment field on our screen form.

In lines 31 and 32, dBASE IV transforms the Edit options' CARRY toggle into the list of fields we want carried from one record to the next. The names of the fields we want carried forward are the only ones listed. The ADDITIVE clause at the end of the SET CARRY TO command tells dBASE IV to add these fields to any other fields that might have been previously listed as CARRY forward fields. Removing the ADDITIVE clause would cause dBASE IV to CARRY only the listed fields forward.

So much for what happens in the background. What happens on the screen when you SET a FORMAT TO something? This begins on line 34 and continues to line 135. As line 34 says, the FORMAT file is really a bunch of dBASE IV @ SAY GET commands. And as line 36 says, our entire screen fits on one (screen) page. Line 38 creates our picture frame; lines 39 and 41 create the special characters we use around our RECORD DELETED message (line 42). Lines 42 and 43 finish the rest of our top-of-form labels. Line 44 is the double line we use to separate our top-of-form labels from the data fields. The rest of the file, up to line 135, can be divided into a series of @ SAY commands and @ GET commands.

The @ SAY commands tell dBASE IV where to put the field names that we type onto the screen. The @ GET commands tell dBASE IV where to retrieve field data that the user types in. Note that the @ GET commands also contain our Edit options, Template symbols, and Picture functions. Line 50, for example, is really our Date field *Accept value when* argument. Line 52 is the *Default value* for the Date field, and lines 51 and 53 are the *Unaccepted message* and *Message* Edit options, respectively. Line 55 shows the Picture function for the Time field, which we entered on the Picture function menu.

An interesting @ GET command is on line 60. This is how dBASE IV GETs a memo field through a screen window. Remember that dBASE IV DEFINEd a WINDOW on line 27? The DEFINEd WINDOW is used in line 60.

The next interesting item is the way dBASE IV processes the blanked numeric fields. Remember that we told dBASE IV to show 0 entries with blanks? Look at any of lines 63, 67, 74, 78, and so on and you will see how a Picture function differs from a Function. Picture function arguments are separated by spaces, with the first argument introduced with an at sign (@). Also note that the @ GET SET_n_WGT commands (any of the lines listed in this paragraph) make use of the WHEN clause. This is how dBASE IV translates our request not to open a field for data entry or editing if the related Set_n_Reps field has a zero entry.

Also note the doubled @ SAY lines, such as 71 and 72, 82 and 83, and 93 and 94. These are the commands used to generate the single line that separates our Comment field on the right of the screen from the Set_n pairs on the left of the screen.

Lines 137 to 152 return dBASE IV to the status it had before we SET the FMT file. Line 153 merely says, "End Of Program: C9.FMT."

This code works well. But remember the programmer's motto: If it works, fix it!

The code dBASE IV generates is serviceable, but not the best for what we want our screen form to do. We need to make changes, but let's analyze our needs before we begin putting in our desires.

Actually, there are some minor problems with the code dBASE IV produces for us. First, we want to get to the Comment field last, not fourth. We also want the screen to remain the same color throughout. As written, the Message lines are a different color than the rest of the screen. Last, many status tests will be done by other programs, not necessarily just the block of code that should only be displaying, editing, or adding data to the database.

In short, we can add a few lines here, remove a few lines there, and rearrange the rest to produce listing 6-2.

Listing 6-2

```
1 : ** EXPROC.PRG PROCEDURE FILE FOR EXERCISE PROGRAM
2 : *
3 : PROCEDURE GETSTATS
4 : IF SET("TALK")="ON"
5 :    SET TALK OFF
6 :       lc_talk="ON"
7 : ELSE
8 :       lc_talk="OFF"
```

```
 9 : ENDIF
10 : *
11 : SET DISPLAY TO EGA25
12 : *
13 : lc_status=SET("STATUS")
14 : *
15 : IF lc_status = "ON"
16 :     SET STATUS OFF
17 : ENDIF
18 : *END OF PROCEDURE GETSTATS
19 : *
20 : PROCEDURE EXERSAY
21 : SET COLOR OF MESSAGES TO color codes
22 : DEFINE WINDOW Wndow1 FROM 8,41 TO 23,78
23 : *
24 : lc_carry = SET("CARRY")
25 : SET CARRY TO date,time,set_1_reps,set_2_reps,; set_3_reps,set_4_
     reps;
26 :    ,set_5_reps,set_6_reps ADDITIVE
27 : @ 1,0 TO 24,79 DOUBLE
28 : @ 2,31 SAY "EXERCISE DATA FORM"
29 : @ 3,1 SAY "══════════════════════════════════════
     ════════════════════"
30 : @ 5,3 SAY "Exercise: "
31 : @ 5,38 SAY "Date: "
32 : @ 5,60 SAY "Time: "
33 : @ 7,1 SAY "───────Repetitions and Weights──────────┬──────
     ─Comment─────────"
34 : @ 8,40 SAY "|"
35 : @ 9,20 SAY "Set_1_Wgt: "
36 : @ 9,3 SAY "Set_1_Reps: "
37 : @ 9,40 SAY "|"
38 : @ 10,40 SAY "|"
39 : @ 11,3 SAY "Set_2_Reps: "
40 : @ 11,20 SAY "Set_2_Wgt: "
41 : @ 11,40 SAY "|"
42 : @ 12,40 SAY "|"
43 : @ 13,3 SAY "Set_3_Reps: "
44 : @ 13,20 SAY "Set_3_Wgt: "
45 : @ 13,40 SAY "|"
46 : @ 14,40 SAY "|"
47 : @ 15,3 SAY "Set_4_Reps: "
48 : @ 15,20 SAY "Set_4_Wgt: "
49 : @ 15,40 SAY "|"
50 : @ 16,40 SAY "|"
51 : @ 17,3 SAY "Set_5_Reps: "
52 : @ 17,20 SAY "Set_5_Wgt: "
53 : @ 17,40 SAY "|"
54 : @ 18,40 SAY "|"
55 : @ 19,3 SAY "Set_6_Reps: "
56 : @ 19,20 SAY "Set_6_Wgt: "
```

Listing 6-2 (cont.)

```
57 : a 19,40 SAY "|"
58 : a 20,40 SAY "|"
59 : a 21,10 SAY "Total_Wgt: "
60 : a 21,40 SAY "|"
61 : a 22,40 SAY "|"
62 : a 23,40 SAY "|"
63 : a 24,40 SAY "±"
64 : * END OF PROCEDURE EXERSAY
65 : *
66 : PROCEDURE EXERGET
67 : a 2,3 SAY IIF(DELETED(), CHR(6) + "RECORD DELETED" + CHR(6),
       SPACE(17)
68 : a 2,60 SAY "RECORD # " + STR(RECNO(),7)
69 : a 5,13 GET exercise PICTURE "!!!!!!!!!!!!!!!!!!!!!" ;
70 :    MESSAGE "⌐                    Enter the name of the exercise
       here                    ¬"
71 : a 5,44 GET date ;
72 :    VALID DATE < DATE() + 1 ;
73 :    ERROR "You can't enter data for future workouts!" ;
74 :    DEFAULT {01/01/89} ;
75 :    MESSAGE "⌐                    Enter the date you exercised
       here                    ¬"
76 : a 5,66 GET time PICTURE "99:99" ;
77 :    DEFAULT "00:00" ;
78 :    MESSAGE "⌐                    Enter your workout starting
       time here                    ¬"
79 : a 9,15 GET set_1_reps PICTURE "aZ 999" ;
80 :    DEFAULT 0 ;
81 :    MESSAGE "⌐    ter the number of repetitions you performed for
       your first set here            ¬"
82 : a 9,31 GET set_1_wgt PICTURE "aZ 9999" ;
83 :    WHEN SET_1_REPS # 0 ;
84 :    DEFAULT 0 ;
85 :    MESSAGE "⌐            Enter the amount of weight used for your
       first set here            ¬"
86 : a 11,15 GET set_2_reps PICTURE "aZ 999" ;
87 :    DEFAULT 0 ;
88 :    MESSAGE "⌐    Enter the number of repetitions you performed
       for your second set here            ¬"
89 : a 11,31 GET set_2_wgt PICTURE "aZ 9999" ;
90 :    WHEN SET_2_REPS # 0 ;
91 :    DEFAULT 0 ;
92 :    MESSAGE "⌐            Enter the amount of weight you used for
       your second set here            ¬"
93 : a 13,15 GET set_3_reps PICTURE "aZ 999" ;
94 :    DEFAULT 0 ;
95 :    MESSAGE "⌐    Enter the number of repetitions you performed
       for your third set here            ¬"
96 : a 13,31 GET set_3_wgt PICTURE "aZ 9999" ;
```

```
 97 :     WHEN SET_3_REPS # 0 ;
 98 :     DEFAULT 0 ;
 99 :     MESSAGE "╚═══════════Enter the amount of weight used for your
          third set here═══════════╝"
100 : @ 15,15 GET set_4_reps PICTURE "@Z 999" ;
101 :     DEFAULT 0 ;
102 :     MESSAGE "╚═══════Enter the number of repetitions you performed
          for your fourth set here═══════╝"
103 : @ 15,31 GET set_4_wgt PICTURE "@Z 9999" ;
104 :     WHEN SET_4_REPS # 0 ;
105 :     DEFAULT 0 ;
106 :     MESSAGE "╚═══════════Enter the amount of weight you used for
          your fourth set here═══════════╝"
107 : @ 17,15 GET set_5_reps PICTURE "@Z 999" ;
108 :     DEFAULT 0 ;
109 :     MESSAGE "╚═══════Enter the number of repetitions you performed
          for your fifth set here═══════╝"
110 : @ 17,31 GET set_5_wgt PICTURE "@Z 9999" ;
111 :     WHEN SET_5_REPS # 0 ;
112 :     DEFAULT 0 ;
113 :     MESSAGE "╚═══════════Enter the amount of weight you used for
          your fifth set here═══════════╝"
114 : @ 19,15 GET set_6_reps PICTURE "@Z 999" ;
115 :     DEFAULT 0 ;
116 :     MESSAGE "╚═══════Enter the number of repetitions you performed
          for your sixth set here═══════╝"
117 : @ 19,31 GET set_6_wgt PICTURE "@Z 9999" ;
118 :     WHEN SET_6_REPS # 0 ;
119 :     DEFAULT 0 ;
120 :     MESSAGE "╚═══════════Enter the amount of weight used for your
          sixth set here═══════════╝"
121 :     READ
122 : REPLACE TOTAL_WGT WITH SET_1_REPS*SET_1_WGT +; SET_2_REPS*SET_2_
       WGT +;
123 :        SET_3_REPS*SET_3_WGT + SET_4_REPS*SET_4_WGT +; SET_5_
       REPS*SET_5_WGT + SET_6_REPS*SET_6_WGT
124 : @ 21,21 SAY total_wgt PICTURE "@Z 99999"
125 : @ 8,41 GET comment OPEN WINDOW Wndow1 ;
126 :     MESSAGE "╚═══════════Enter any comments about this
          exercise or set here═══════════╝"
127 : * END OF PROCEDURE EXERGET
128 : *
129 : PROCEDURE SETSTATS
130 : *
131 : IF lc_status = "ON"  && Entered form with status on
132 :    SET STATUS ON   && Turn STATUS "ON" on the way out
133 : ENDIF
134 : *
135 : IF lc_carry = "OFF"
136 :    SET CARRY OFF
137 : ENDIF
```

Listing 6-2 (cont.)

```
138 : *
139 : IF lc_talk="ON"
140 :     SET TALK ON
141 : ENDIF
142 : *
143 : * END OF PROCEDURE SETSTATS
144 : ** END OF PROCEDURE FILE
```

The code listing is simply a rearrangement of what dBASE IV created for us. The significant difference has to do with all the commands being grouped into series of PROCEDUREs, then placed in one PROCEDURE file, EXPROC.PRG. This file is then utilized by the following program, EX-ERADD.PRG (listing 6-3).

Listing 6-3

```
 1 : ** EXERCISE DATA ADDITION MODULE
 2 : *
 3 : SET PROCEDURE TO EXPROC
 4 : DO GETSTATS
 5 : DO EXERSAY
 6 : *
 7 : DO WHILE .T.
 8 :    APPEND BLANK
 9 :    DO EXERGET
10 :    READ
11 : *
12 :    IF LEN(TRIM(EXERCISE)) = 0
13 :        RELEASE WINDOWS Wndow1
14 :        RELEASE lc_carry,lc_talk,lc_fields,lc_status
15 :        EXIT
16 :    ENDIF
17 : *
18 : ENDDO
19 : *
20 : DO SETSTATS
21 : *
22 : ** END OF EXERADD.PRG
```

There are advantages and disadvantages to performing this recoding. Most of the disadvantages arise from going through the trouble of this recoding when all the code you have is the previously displayed FMT file. Doing so wastes memory. The next best method—if all you have to work with is a single FMT file—is to separate all the PROCEDURES listed in the EXPROC.PRG file into individual PRG files. These files would be broken out as GETSTATS.PRG, EXERSAY.PRG, EXERGETS.PRG, and SET-STATS.PRG. The recoding just shown is best used when you have several routines calling the same set of programs. For example, several groups of

@ SAY and @ GET commands might need to know the same information as provided in the GETSTATS and SETSTATS PROCEDURES.

The point to be made by the recoding is that it is your first chance to program and start working towards a fully integrated and extendible system. It is also somewhat easier to edit a system that has been broken down into its separate components (get the computer/dBASE IV system status, paint the screen, enter/edit the data, reset the computer/dBASE IV system status) than when all the components are lumped together.

For example, I mentioned editing the screen form so that it could detect the priority level of users and therefore deny access to certain individuals. This is akin to the dBASE IV PROTECT system, but you can take direct control. All changes need to be made only to the short EXER-ADD.PRG file in listing 6-3.

Directly after line 2 in EXERADD.PRG, you could enter the following code:

```
USERLEVEL = [AO]
CLEAR
a 10,0 SAY [What is your user level? -> ] GET USERLEVEL PICT [XX]
READ
*
IF USERLEVEL # {your option here}
    QUIT
ENDIF
*
```

This is an elementary form of protection, but it illustrates the concept. You can use a database instead of a memory variable to hold user levels, then check the entered user level against the database to determine access levels.

Previously in this chapter, I mentioned checking a field other than the first field for input and exiting data addition mode based on input to that other field. This goes back to how FMT files work.

Basically, full-screen editing commands that work with an FMT file during data addition check to see if the first field on the screen form has any input. If no data is added to the first field and the [Enter] key is pressed, the full-screen editing commands exit back to whatever called them (the dBASE prompt or some dBASE IV program). This is fine except when you don't care if the first field on the screen form gets filled in each record or when you need to make sure that fields in addition to the first field get filled to validate a record as being worth keeping.

There are some ways around this. First, however, you should be saying to yourself, "You spent most of the chapter telling us to put the most important fields at the top of the screen form. Now you tell us we may not want to test the first field on the form? Too much brandy in the coffee, Joseph?" No, I'm simply acknowledging that you may not take my advice.

You can override dBASE IV's urge to exit from full-screen editing

FMT mode by not pressing [Enter]. Instead, use the [Down-Arrow] key to move from the first screen form field to the one you want to use. When you have moved to the next record, dBASE IV dutifully saves the last record's information regardless of whether or not there is data in the first screen form field.

Another solution to getting past the first field problem comes from a little recoding of the EXERADD.PRG file. Line 12 of EXERADD.PRG reads

```
IF LEN(TRIM(EXERCISE)) = 0
```

This line of code tests to see if the first screen form field, Exercise, has any data. IF the LENgth of the TRIMmed (blank spaces) Exercise field is 0, exit the data entry loop. You can tell dBASE IV to test any other field in the database or to test any combination of fields with this method. For example, you can tell dBASE IV to test for data in two character fields with

```
IF LEN(TRIM(field1) + TRIM(field2)) = 0
```

The next topic is how to handle calculated fields, especially if the first field in the database is a calculated one. First, we consider a calculated field at the end of the screen form.

Go back to EXERADD.PRG. Adding the following code directly after line 17 tells dBASE IV to perform a calculation and enter the data into the calculated field and prompts the user to confirm that the result is what was expected.

```
        ANSWER = .F.
*
        DO WHILE .NOT. ANSWER
            REPLACE calculated field WITH expression
            @ x,y SAY calculated field
            @ 0,0 SAY [Okay to continue? (Y/N) -> ];
            GET ANSWER PICTURE "Y"
            READ
*
            IF .NOT. ANSWER
                @ 0,0 CLEAR TO 0,79
                DO EXERGET
                READ
            ENDIF
*
        ENDDO
*
```

This code initializes a memory variable, ANSWER, to FALSE each time you add a record to the database. As long as ANSWER remains FALSE, dBASE IV will REPLACE the calculated field WITH whatever the expression is. It will then SAY the calculated field at the assigned screen position (x,y). Remember that I said we might want to use the 0th line of the screen sometime? Here we do just that, to ask the user if everything is okay. IF NOT, CLEAR the 0th line prompt, execute the EXERGET commands again, and READ them. It's as simple as that.

What if you want to start your new record with a calculated field? This is a little different, as the following code demonstrates. We start by adding the following lines immediately following line 8:

```
REPLACE calculated field WITH memory variable or expression
@ x,y SAY calculated field
```

The rest of the code is comprised of a single line that goes after line 17 of EXERADD.PRG:

```
memory variable = expression based on current record's fields
```

The REPLACE and @ SAY commands act as they do in the previous example. The only difference is that the REPLACE command can use either a calculated expression *not based on the current record's fields* or a memory variable based on the previous record's data. The reason for the apparent discrepancy has to do with the position of the commands in the EXER-ADD.PRG file. The *memory variable =* line comes before a new record is added to the data. Note that you would have to initialize a memory variable to some value before you executed this code; otherwise, dBASE IV would give you an error message. The variable only needs to be initialized the first time the code is called. You don't need to initialize a memory variable if the REPLACE command uses an expression not involving the current record's data. Remember, when the REPLACE command is issued, no data has been added to the record.

Summary

This chapter has provided the second part of what you need to do serious database management system work with dBASE IV. Chapter 5 showed you how to design, develop, and modify a database. This chapter showed you how to design, develop, and modify a data entry and edit form. Chapter 7 continues by showing you how to scan your database for information and by taking up the quest of developing a menu driven system for your database management system needs.

Inputting and Editing Data

You created a database in chapter 5 and created a screen form in chapter 6. In this chapter, we learn more about putting data in the database and editing the data after it is in there. In particular, we will learn how to use the screens we have designed and the visual tools dBASE IV gives us.

We start with data input and the various dBASE IV full-screen editing commands. These commands, mentioned in chapter 6, include APPEND, BROWSE, CHANGE, EDIT, INSERT, and READ. There are other full-screen editing commands, but this list pertains to the commands used when actually working with data in the database.

Adding Data to the Database

You have designed a database and screen form. Because you have to put data into the database before you can edit it, we will start this chapter by discussing ways to add new data to the database. We will work with an empty database and add records as we go, but you can add information to a database that already contains records in the same manner. You start the process of adding data to the database from the Control Center, the dBASE prompt, or a dBASE IV program. As always, choosing the Control Center or the dBASE prompt as entry points to add data will produce similar results. Adding data with a program opens a multitude of possibilities, only a few of which are covered in this chapter.

We start by showing how to add data through the Control Center. Your Control Center screen may or may not look like the one shown in figure 7-1. Don't worry if yours doesn't look like mine. All that is shown in figure 7-1 is the EXERCISE database and the C9.FMT format file created in chapter 6. This keeps the screen as clear as possible for the work to be done in this chapter. When there are fewer options, there is less chance of choosing the wrong one.

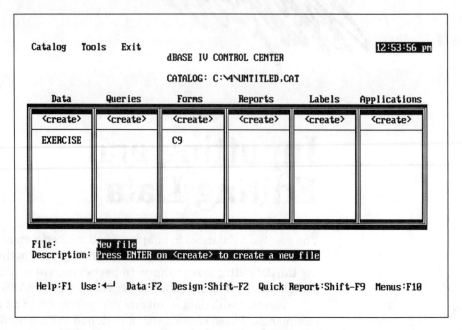

Figure 7-1 *The Control Center is one place to start the process of adding data to the database.*

The Control Center begins with the prompt on ⟨create⟩ in the Data column. Because we want to use the EXERCISE database, highlight it but don't do anything else yet. Remember from chapter 5 that the [F2] key is the Browse/Edit toggle? Without pressing any other key since you highlighted Exercise, press [F2]. dBASE IV changes to Edit mode, shown in figure 7-2. dBASE IV selects Edit mode because the database is empty. dBASE IV would have chosen Browse mode if data already existed in some of the records.

Edit mode is the first and perhaps easiest method of adding a single record to the database. Note that none of the features (carry data forward, permit edit if, templates, Picture functions, and so on) we designed in the format file in the last chapter are available through this data entry mode.

What problems are inherent when adding data using Edit mode? First, you have to add information to the first field on the display. Simply pressing [Enter] causes dBASE IV to exit the data entry mode and go back to the Control Center. (Should you do so, you will notice that the EXERCISE database is now above the active line on the Control Center.) You can use the cursor control keys to move through the display without dropping back to the Control Center, however. For example, the [Up-Arrow] and [Down-Arrow] keys move up and down a field, respectively. You can't cur-

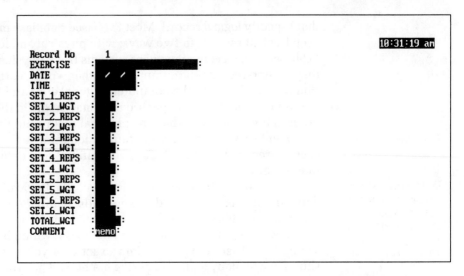

```
                                                              10:31:19 am
Record No      1
EXERCISE     :                              :
DATE         :  /   /   :
TIME         :        :
SET_1_REPS   :   :
SET_1_WGT    :       :
SET_2_REPS   :   :
SET_2_WGT    :       :
SET_3_REPS   :   :
SET_3_WGT    :       :
SET_4_REPS   :   :
SET_4_WGT    :       :
SET_5_REPS   :   :
SET_5_WGT    :       :
SET_6_REPS   :   :
SET_6_WGT    :       :
TOTAL_WGT    :         :
COMMENT      :memo:
```

Figure 7-2 dBASE IV switches to Edit mode when you highlight a
database in the Control Center and press [F2].

sor above the first field in the first record, but pressing [Up-Arrow] in the
first field of any other record causes dBASE IV to back up one record in the
database (from 5 to 4, 4 to 3, and so on). Pressing [Down-Arrow] on the last
field in a record causes dBASE IV to go to the next record in the database. If
no record exists, a new record is added to the file. The [Left-Arrow] and
[Right-Arrow] keys move one character left or right in each field, respectively. The [Home] and [End] keys move to the first and last character in a
filled field, respectively. [PgUp] and [PgDn] move to the preceding or succeeding record, respectively. Note that dBASE IV displays an *Add new records?* prompt to ensure that you want to enter new records if the database
wasn't empty when you entered data entry mode. You won't see this
prompt if there are no records in the database and data is being added for
the first time.

One last thing before we move on. Before any data is entered in a
database, you can press [F2] all you want and you will only get to the Edit
screen. Why? Because there is no data to Browse. After you have entered as
little as one field in one record, however, you can press [F2] and Browse all
you want or continue pressing [F2] and see how fast your computer and
dBASE IV can toggle from Browse to Edit mode. Further, after data is in
the database, highlighting the database on the Control Center and pressing
[F2] automatically drops the program into Browse mode (not Edit mode),
although you can toggle to Edit mode with the [F2] key.

More time is spent on the intricacies of dBASE IV's Browse mode
later in this chapter. It is mentioned here because it can be quite useful for
adding data to the database *after* some data already exists. With data currently in your database, press [F2] to call up Browse mode. The cursor is
positioned at the first field in the first logical record in the database. Note

that I specify *logical* record. Most PC-based database management systems keep track of records in two ways: with physical and logical records. Most PC-based database management systems track physical records exactly as they are entered into the computer, in other words, garbage in, garbage out. You put the data into the computer helter-skelter and that is what you get out. It makes looking for specific information difficult because there is no order to the data, other than the physical record numbers. Thus, you have to remember which records contain which information and then get to the specific record you want before you can use any data in that record. Not much fun.

The best way to start a new database is with an active index file. Then data is ordered from the beginning of work and remains so until the work is complete.

The other option is with logical records. Logical records have a user-defined order, usually based on key fields. Figures 7-3 and 7-4 demonstrate the difference between physical and logical ordering of a database. Figure 7-3 shows the physical order of the database, which is dBASE IV's way of saying "I will show you the data exactly as you entered it." Figure 7-4 shows one of many logical ordering methods. The ordering method used in figure 7-4 is based on the information in the Exercise field in each record. Physical and logical records coincide when no ordering method is imposed on the database.

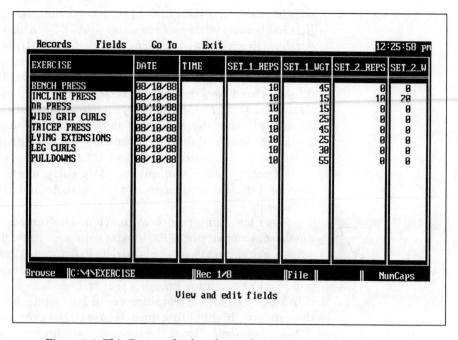

Figure 7-3 This Browse display shows the physical ordering of records in the database. Figure 7-4 shows the same database ordered logically by the information in each Exercise field.

We want to add new records to the database, and that is easy to do in Browse mode. Press [Alt-R] to open the Records menu. Our choice is A for

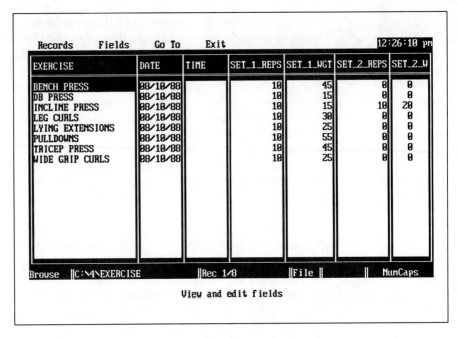

| Records | Fields | Go To | Exit | | | | 12:26:10 pm |

EXERCISE	DATE	TIME	SET_1_REPS	SET_1_WGT	SET_2_REPS	SET_2_W
BENCH PRESS	08/10/88		10	45	0	0
DB PRESS	08/10/88		10	15	0	0
INCLINE PRESS	08/10/88		10	15	10	20
LEG CURLS	08/10/88		10	30	0	0
LYING EXTENSIONS	08/10/88		10	25	0	0
PULLDOWNS	08/10/88		10	55	0	0
TRICEP PRESS	08/10/88		10	45	0	0
WIDE GRIP CURLS	08/10/88		10	25	0	0

Browse ‖C:\4\EXERCISE ‖Rec 1/8 ‖File ‖ ‖ NumCaps

View and edit fields

Figure 7-4 *This Browse display shows the logical ordering of records in the database. These records are ordered by the information in the Exercise field. Figure 7-3 shows the same database with physical ordering.*

Add new records. Add a few records and you will notice that dBASE IV does not update the order of the database as the records are entered; dBASE updates only after you have entered the last new record.

As mentioned, Browse mode provides more data per screen than Edit mode. There is a price, of course, and the price is having to learn cursor control navigation keys again. Some keys work as you would expect and are identical to the Edit cursor control keys. These are [Up-Arrow], [Down-Arrow], [Right-Arrow], and [Left-Arrow]. The [Up-Arrow] and [Down-Arrow] keys move up and down the Browse display and hence up and down though the records in the database. You can't [Up-Arrow] from the first displayed record in the database. Pressing [Down-Arrow] at the last displayed record causes dBASE IV to ask if you want to enter new records, as it did in Edit mode.

The [Home] key moves the highlight to the first displayed field in a record. The [End] key moves the highlight to the last displayed field in a record. This is unlike the Edit mode [Home] and [End] keys, which only move to the first and last character in a given field. Last, the [PgUp] and [PgDn] keys move one screenful of information backward or forward through the database. Usually, this is seventeen records at a shot, but can be changed to nineteen records per keystroke as explained later in this chapter. You can't [PgUp] beyond the first displayed record, and you can't [PgDn] beyond the last displayed record.

One last thing to know about Browse mode is how it interprets a blank entry. You may remember that pressing [Enter] at the first field in Edit mode told dBASE IV to exit Edit mode. This doesn't happen in Browse mode. Instead of automatically exiting Browse mode, dBASE IV lets you [Enter] through the entire record before assuming you don't want to enter any information. The blank new record is ignored and doesn't appear on the Browse screen, although you do have to [Enter] through all the fields to convince dBASE IV you don't want the record to appear in the database.

Enough on the simplest method of adding data to the database. Now we look at other methods of adding data to the database using the Control Center.

In the preceding discussion, we started by simply highlighting the desired database. What happens if you highlight a database and press [Enter] instead of [F2]? You are prompted to either *Use the file*, *Modify structure/order*, or *Display data*. Type *D* for *Display data* and the program is in Edit mode if no data exists in the database or Browse mode if data does exist. dBASE IV does not apply any particular order to the database when you enter it using the *Display data* option on the Control Center because dBASE IV does not apply any MDX or NDX file order to the database, even though these other files may exist.

What if you want some kind of order on the file, especially if that is how you designed the database from the beginning? You can use the Control Center to check if an MDX file, an NDX file, or both are active with the current database. With the highlight on the database of interest, press [Enter]. You are presented with one of two displays. If the database is not currently active, you are offered *Use file*, *Modify structure/order*, and *Display data*. Pressing [Enter] on an active database (one that is shown above the active line on the Control Center) displays *Close file*, *Modify structure/order*, and *Display data*. In either case, you want *Modify structure/order*, so type *M*. This drops back to the database design system, discussed in chapter 5. You can also get to the database design system by highlighting any database listed on the Control Center and pressing [Shift-F2].

The cursor is automatically positioned on *Create new index* in the Organize menu. Type *O* for *Order records by index*. dBASE IV pops up a set of available MDX file tags if they exist (figure 7-5). You won't be able to use this option if no production MDX file exists for the current database.

dBASE IV automatically creates production MDX files unless you specify not to do so. This can be handy for the beginner but can cause problems for more experienced users who are only interested in working with temporary files.

Because the last sentence in the last paragraph may have slipped past you, I will emphasize it with an explanation. dBASE IV creates a production MDX file each time you create a database and specify some fields to be indexed. It does this automatically. Further, dBASE IV gives the production MDX file the same file name as you give the database. You call the database FRED and dBASE IV creates a production MDX file called FRED; create a database called LOUIE and dBASE IV creates a production MDX file called LOUIE. dBASE IV even does a little bit more than just creating MDX files with the same name as that given the database. It places a gremlin in the database file. This gremlin has one job. Whenever a database

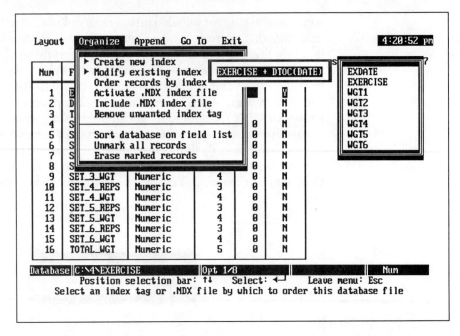

Figure 7-5 *When you select* Order records by index *on the database design system's Organize menu, dBASE IV lists any available MDX file tags.*

becomes active, the gremlin jumps up and down and screams, "There is a production MDX file out there!"

For readers who don't like metaphor, the gremlin is a *flag* in the database header. dBASE IV reads the database file header when it opens a database. From the file header, a great deal of information is extracted about the version of dBASE IV under which the database was created, whether the file is SQL compatible, whether the database has a related DBT MEMO file, the date the file was last updated, the number of records in the database, the total number of bytes in each record (remember the flag in the upper right corner of the database design screen that told you the number of bytes remaining in the design? This is where that information is stored), a flag for SQL work sessions indicating if the file is currently being worked upon, a flag indicating whether the file is encrypted, a flag to inform dBASE IV whether the file is being used on a network, a flag indicating the presence of a production MDX file, and last, the name, type, width, and decimal count of the fields in the database. Of all these, dBASE IV checks the production MDX file flag to see if a production MDX file exists and should be opened when the database is opened. This flag does not tell dBASE IV if a nonproduction MDX file exists. (A nonproduction MDX file is one you create with the INDEX ON command.)

Catch your breath; I'm going to tell you an anecdote. In my high school biology class, there was an idiot savant who one day asked the teacher how X rays could go through things. This particular student was constantly asking for detailed answers he did not have the sophistication to understand. This time the teacher apologized to the class before answering, told this particular student to copy everything the teacher said, and went on for a two-hour lecture on how X rays worked, starting with the hydrogen atom and going through electron shells through decaying orbits and photon release and so on. The preceding paragraph on how dBASE IV knows an MDX file should exist can be considered in much the same way as my biology teacher's explanation of how X rays work.

The database design system only knows about these production MDX files because it reads the name of the currently active database and hears the gremlin screaming. Figure 7-6 shows what happens if the gremlin is a liar.

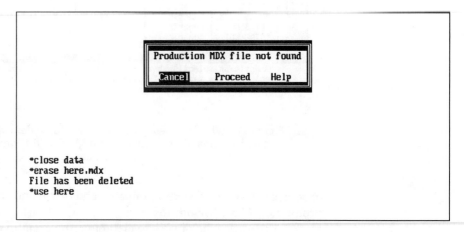

```
                    ┌─────────────────────────────┐
                    │ Production MDX file not found │
                    │ Cancel    Proceed    Help     │
                    └─────────────────────────────┘




*close data
*erase here.mdx
File has been deleted
*use here
```

Figure 7-6 dBASE IV automatically looks for a production MDX file
when a database is opened and that database has a flag telling
dBASE IV that a production MDX file exists.

Back to ordering your database. dBASE IV shows you what tags are available in the production MDX file. Remember that the tags represent the different ways you want dBASE IV to index the file in the multiple index file. Highlight the tag you want and press [Enter]. You won't notice anything different, but dBASE IV will have ordered the database by the desired tag.

And here is the rub. Ordering the database by a particular MDX file tag or NDX file using the Assist menu's *Modify structure/order* option tells dBASE IV to make your chosen ordering the prioritized method of working with the database. In other words, after you have selected an ordering method through the menu system, dBASE IV always calls up the database with that particular ordering method in place. This continues until you select another ordering method through the menus or through the SET INDEX TO and SET ORDER TO dBASE prompt commands.

Back to work. You have accessed the database through the Assist menu and added data with Browse or Edit mode. Remember that you can toggle from one mode to the other with the [F2] key. What other methods are there for adding data to the database?

Well, we spent a lot of time designing a screen form in chapter 6. Why don't we use it now?

Before we access the format file designed in chapter 6, take a minute to look at the Assist menu system as shown in figure 7-1. Remember that we have as few files as possible on the menu to keep things simple. We know that the EXERCISE database and the C9 format file are meant to be used together. The problem that may occur for some of you is a simple one and is based on having designed the C9.FMT file outside the Assist menu system.

Designing a format file outside the Assist menu system can have the aggravating side effect of not alerting the dBASE IV system to the linkage between the format file and its associated database. This goes back to the discussions of Catalog files and how dBASE IV keeps track of which files are meant to work with which other files. Catalog files were mentioned in previous chapters and, because we are finally in a position to do something useful with them, they are mentioned again here.

Figure 7-1 shows the Catalog as C:\4\UNTITLED.CAT. This is the standard name dBASE IV assigns to any new working catalog. dBASE IV creates new catalogs when you request or when it feels a need to. Generally, it feels the need to create a new catalog only once, at your first Assist menu work session. If you have been working through the Assist menu while going through this book, you are working with UNTITLED.CAT. Let's assume you want to change the name of the Catalog to something more easily recognized as a collection of work files. This will also give you more experience using the Assist menu's command sequences.

Press [Alt-C] M for the Catalog menu's *Modify catalog name* option. You will see a screen similar to that shown in figure 7-7. Backspace over UNTITLED.CAT and type in whatever name you like. I will use BBOFDB4.CAT. Press [Enter] after you have completed your entry and you will see the new name on the Catalog line at the top of the Assist screen.

Remember that Catalog files keep track of which files will be used with which other files. Remember also that I said creating a file outside the Assist menu system might result in dBASE IV not knowing which files are supposed to work with which other files. It is possible that your Catalog file might not know that the format file you designed in chapter 6 should work with the database you designed in chapter 5. How can you tell if dBASE IV knows that your format file is linked to your DBF file? First, I will assume that no database is active, which means no database is above the active line on the Assist menu. If a database is listed above the active line, just highlight the database, press [Enter], and type C. This tells dBASE IV to CLOSE the database, which means to take it out of current use.

Now highlight either the format file (under the Forms column) or the DBF file (under the Data column) and press [Enter]. Type U if you highlighted the database. This tells dBASE IV you want to make the database active but you don't want to go into any particular mode. If both the database and the format file appear above the active line now, dBASE IV knows

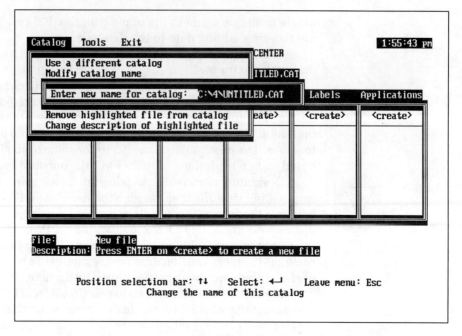

Figure 7-7 You can use [Alt-C] M to change the name of a Catalog file.

the two files are linked. Type D if you highlighted the format file. This tells dBASE IV you want to use the format file with its associated database to display the data in the database. If dBASE IV shows you the screen form you designed in chapter 6, it knows the files are linked.

What if it does not know the files are linked? You will get a screen such as shown in figure 7-8.

This is not a problem, however. All you need to do is give dBASE IV what it wants. It wants to know which file the format file is linked to. Cursor to the Data column, highlight the database that the format file is linked to, press [Enter], then type U to place the database in USE. Cursor back to the Forms column, highlight the format file, press [Enter], and type D.

This method has a drawback. You can use the format file with the current database if the two were designed to be used together, but dBASE IV still won't know to automatically open one when the other is opened, and that is the point of the Catalog file. How do we permanently link a format—or any other file—with a DBF file? Go to the dBASE prompt (press [Alt-E] E), and I will show you how it is done.

Type the following command at the dBASE prompt:

```
SET CATALOG TO ?
```

This command tells dBASE IV to open a Catalog file. Why did I use ? instead of giving dBASE IV the exact name I wanted to use? To demonstrate something, of course. Figure 7-9 shows dBASE IV providing a list of avail-

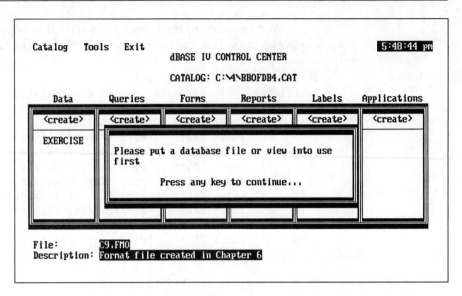

Figure 7-8 You can place an FMT file in use through the Assist system, but dBASE IV must know which files it is linked to before you can use it for data editing or addition.

able Catalog files. Just highlight the desired Catalog file and press [Enter]. You can, of course, just type in the name of the Catalog file you want when you enter the SET CATALOG TO command provided you remember the name of the file.

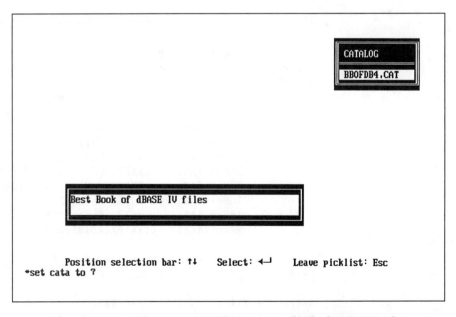

Figure 7-9 The SET CATALOG TO ? command tells dBASE IV to list all the currently available Catalog files.

What becomes of the Catalog file after it is active? Consider the following listings. The first listing was made before the Catalog file was SET.

```
Currently Selected Database:
Select area:  1, Database in Use: C:\4\EXERCISE.DBF   Alias:
EXERCISE
Production   MDX file:  C:\4\EXERCISE.MDX
            Index TAG:     WGT6  Key: EXERCISE + STR(SET_6_WGT)
            Index TAG:     WGT3  Key: EXERCISE + STR(SET_3_WGT)
            Index TAG:     WGT5  Key: EXERCISE + STR(SET_5_WGT)
            Index TAG:     WGT4  Key: EXERCISE + STR(SET_4_WGT)
            Index TAG:     EXERCISE  Key: EXERCISE
            Index TAG:     EXDATE  Key: EXERCISE + DTOC(DATE)
            Index TAG:     WGT1  Key: EXERCISE + STR(SET_1_WGT)
            Index TAG:     WGT2  Key: EXERCISE + STR(SET_2_WGT)
            Memo file:     C:\4\EXERCISE.DBT

Alternate file: C:\4\15-10-14.TXT
File search path:
Default disk drive: C:
Print destination:  PRN:
Margin =      0
Refresh count =    0
Reprocess count =    0
Number of files open =    7
Current work area =    1
   Delimiters are ':' and ':'
```

The following listing was made with the Catalog file SET:

```
Currently Selected Database:
Select area:  1, Database in Use: C:\4\EXERCISE.DBF    Alias:
EXERCISE
Production   MDX file:  C:\4\EXERCISE.MDX
            Index TAG:     WGT6  Key: EXERCISE + STR(SET_6_WGT)
            Index TAG:     WGT3  Key: EXERCISE + STR(SET_3_WGT)
            Index TAG:     WGT5  Key: EXERCISE + STR(SET_5_WGT)
            Index TAG:     WGT4  Key: EXERCISE + STR(SET_4_WGT)
            Index TAG:     EXERCISE  Key: EXERCISE
            Index TAG:     EXDATE  Key: EXERCISE + DTOC(DATE)
            Index TAG:     WGT1  Key: EXERCISE + STR(SET_1_WGT)
            Index TAG:     WGT2  Key: EXERCISE + STR(SET_2_WGT)
            Memo file:     C:\4\EXERCISE.DBT

Select area: 10, Database in Use: C:\4\BBOFDB4.CAT   Alias:
CATALOG

Alternate file: C:\4\15-10-14.TXT
File search path:
Default disk drive: C:
```

```
Print destination:  PRN:
Margin =      0
Refresh count =     0
Reprocess count =     0
Number of files open =     8
```

The underline in the listing is mine, although the listing is pure dBASE IV. The important difference is where dBASE IV places the Catalog file: in work area 10. dBASE IV does this because the Catalog file is a specialized database file, as mentioned. Because it is a specialized database file, you can do all sorts of database-type things to it. And one of those database-type things you can do to the Catalog file is BROWSE it.

Are you beginning to see how everything is linked when you learn a database system?

You can make modifications to the Catalog file with the following commands:

```
SELECT 10
BROWSE FIELDS FILE_NAME, TAG
```

The SELECT 10 command tells dBASE IV to go to the 10th work area, the location of the Catalog file. The BROWSE FIELDS FILE_NAME, TAG command is necessary so that dBASE IV shows only the fields of interest on the screen. Your display should look basically like figure 7-10.

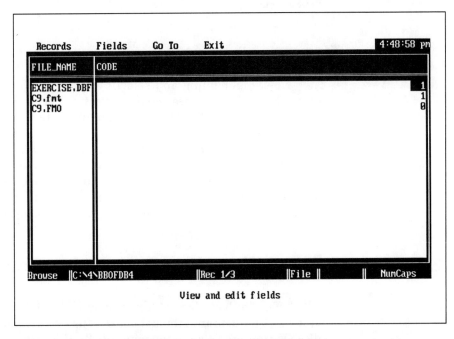

Figure 7-10 BROWSEing the Catalog file is useful when you want to make links between files.

Just find the EXERCISE.DBF file under FILE_NAME and look for the related Code value. Figure 7-10 shows EXERCISE.DBF with a Code value of 1. Code values are how dBASE IV keeps track of what files are linked with what other files. Now, notice in figure 7-10 that C9.FMT also has a Code value of 1. How come dBASE IV did not automatically link C9.FMT and EXERCISE.DBF when they were used simultaneously on the Assist menu?

Look back at figure 7-8 for a moment. Notice that the name of the file is C9.FMO, not C9.FMT. The FMT file is the source code dBASE IV produced when we exited the screen form generator. The FMO file is the pseudocompiled screen form dBASE IV uses in place of the FMT file. The Catalog knows the FMT file and the DBF file are linked. But it does not know the FMO file and the DBF file are linked, and the FMO file is the one it wants to use when you select C9 under the Assist menu Forms column.

Highlight the Code value corresponding to the file you want linked to your database and enter the exact Code value as it is listed for your database. Press [Ctrl-W]. This is equivalent to [Alt-E] E, but much quicker.

You can custom link files by editing the Catalog file.

Note that we just did a simple edit of the Catalog file using the Browse mode. Extend this concept a bit and you will realize that you can quickly link a group of files by editing a Catalog file. Slick.

One last thing. After you have made the changes to your Catalog file, type in the following commands:

```
SELECT 1
CLOSE ALL
[F2]
```

SELECT 1 tells dBASE IV to go back to the first work area, CLOSE ALL tells it to deactivate all files, and [F2] starts up the Assist system.

Now, highlighting and selecting either the format or database file causes both files to appear above the active line. It gets a little better, too. Highlight the activated format file and press [F2] again. Now dBASE IV uses the activated format file instead of Edit mode as one of the [F2] (Data) toggle options. The [F2] modes become the format file or a highly modified Browse mode. In fact, the Browse mode makes use of all the Template symbols, Picture functions, Edit options, and so on that were designed into the format file. dBASE IV does not use the activated format file as one of the Data screen options if you press [F2] while highlighting the database file.

Editing and Appending With Interactive Commands

All of what has been demonstrated so far is based on using the Assist menu system to get data into the database. What if you want to work from the dBASE prompt? This is done with dBASE IV's interactive full-screen editing commands: APPEND, BROWSE, CHANGE, EDIT, INSERT, and

READ. Each of these commands functions slightly differently, although each can be used to enter and edit data in the database. This section covers these commands and lists the pros and cons of each.

All interactive editing commands are directly affected by the AUTOSAVE status. AUTOSAVE can be set in the CONFIG.DB file or through the SET AUTOSAVE command. dBASE IV defaults to AUTOSAVE OFF.

AUTOSAVE is a directive that tells dBASE IV whether or not to write the last edited record to disk (sometimes called *commit*) each time a record is changed. You can change a single field or several—all that matters to dBASE IV is that you have changed a record and told it to either exit the editing mode you are in or go to another record. When you SET AUTO-SAVE ON, dBASE IV blinks the disk drive light, letting you know it has written the record to disk.

Think about that. You are using a 2MB file and change a single re-cord. dBASE IV writes the record to disk. This is possible without lots of work because dBASE IV uses fixed-length fields, as described previously. It can write changed records to disk without rewriting the entire file be-cause each record, whether all the fields are used or not, contains all the space necessary to save any and all data that might be stored in that record. It does not have to go looking for room. Things are slightly more compli-cated when you use MDX and NDX files. The MDX and NDX files might get shuffled a bit, but the time loss is not worth thinking about.

What do you gain by SETting AUTOSAVE ON? You get peace of mind. No, you don't. You just think you do. When you SET AUTOSAVE ON, dBASE IV writes a given record to disk after each edit or after each new record is added to the file. This means the database file, the one you have been maintaining all these months and your job depends on, is, in computer terms, constantly open.

This means the database file, the one you have been maintaining all these months and your job depends on, is, in human terms, constantly vul-nerable. What is it vulnerable to? Anything that would mung it up. What would mung it up? Anything. In short, your database is not safe.

It is better to use dBASE IV in AUTOSAVE OFF mode because there is less chance of accidents destroying all or part of your database.

What about SET AUTOSAVE OFF, which is the way dBASE IV wants it to be? dBASE IV then stores changes to existing records and newly added records only when the file buffer gets full. File buffer? Think of a school bus going down the street. It picks up kids at every stop. It does not let any of the kids out until it gets to school. The school bus is adding information to the buffer at each stop and does not release any information until the bus is full, which happens to be at school. How many kids can the bus hold before it has to let them all off? (This is a key element: all the children get off at the same place.) That depends on your computer system and how it is set up. This also is not the best method for saving changes to a file.

Unfortunately, there are no safer methods when all you need to do is edit or add a single record. What if you know you will be making changes to several records? You can make your life much safer with a little program-ming.

The following program uses production MDX files and key field searches, but can be easily modified to handle a wider variety of situations.

```
USE masterbase
SEEK keyfield value
COPY TO TEMP WHILE keyfield = keyfield value
USE
SELECT 2
USE TEMP
INDEX ON keyfield TAG tag name OF TEMP
full-screen or other editing command
SELECT 1
USE masterbase
UPDATE ON keyfield FROM TEMP ;
     REPLACE edited field1 WITH TEMP->edited field1,;
     edited field2 WITH TEMP->edited field2, ...
CLOSE DATA
```

I would be lying if I said this code saves time. What it does save is the chance of corrupting the master database, or masterbase, by leaving it open too long. Instead of the masterbase being open and vulnerable during the entire editing or record addition process, it is only open for updating. The updating takes place at machine speed, not human speed. The code works as follows.

Open the master database in work area 1. dBASE IV chooses work area 1 by default. There is no magic involved. We SEEK a key expression. The SEEK command performs a high speed search of key field values in the MDX or NDX file. Next, we COPY TO a TEMPorary file all the records with a key field value that matches our SEEKed key field value. The USE command closes the masterbase so that nothing can happen to it.

SELECT work area 2 because I know what is coming up next. USE the TEMP file created with the earlier COPY command. Now BROWSE, EDIT, INSERT, whatever (anything but APPEND) the TEMP file. SELECT work area 1 again. Open the masterbase a second time. UPDATE the masterbase with the edited information FROM the TEMP file. Finally, CLOSE the DATAbases and you are done. This code is only slightly modified if your interest is in adding data to the database and not editing existing data:

```
USE masterbase
COPY STRUC TO TEMP
USE TEMP
APPEND or other record addition command
USE masterbase
APPEND FROM TEMP
CLOSE DATA
```

The active ingredient in this code is the APPEND FROM command, which tells dBASE IV to add the records in TEMP to the masterbase.

APPEND Command

The APPEND command does the following things to an active database. First, it positions the record pointer to just past the physical end of the file. Second, it creates a totally new, naked-as-a-jaybird record at that position. Third, it opens either the SET format file or an Edit style screen for data input.

The APPEND command is the dBASE IV interactive full-screen command you will probably use most if you want to simply add data to an active database. The command does everything for you, from getting records tacked onto the database to presenting a screen input form. APPEND also does more, depending on what other files are active and associated with the current database file.

You can exit Append mode by either pressing [Enter] in the first field of a blank record or pressing [Ctrl-End], [Ctrl-W], or [Esc] anywhere in a filled record. The first two options save the data in the current record. The [Esc] option tells dBASE IV to remove the current record from the file.

I have already mentioned that APPEND will make use of any SET format file. APPEND also automatically updates any MDX or NDX files that may be active with the current database. Because it is worth knowing what happens when MDX and NDX files are active, I will take a minute to describe how APPEND works with them.

As mentioned, APPEND positions the record pointer to just after the last physical record in the database. I also mentioned that there is a difference between the physical record order and the logical record order. Physical records are ordered from 1 to whatever and are counted as 1, 2, 3, and so on until the end of the file. Logical records are ordered according to the contents of some key field, mixture of key fields, functions of key fields, and so on. Logical records can be ordered from the first record in the key field pattern to whatever and can be counted as wildly as 53, 54, 55, 56, 3, 113, 114, 115, 1, 28, 43, 246, 168, 169, 12, and so on until the end of the file.

Even though APPEND adds a record at the physical end of the database, it also alerts any MDX and NDX files that a new record is being added to the database and that they should be prepared to shuffle their information accordingly. In other words, if you APPEND a record that logically should be placed between physical records 53 and 54, dBASE IV will do so. Note that it does not change the physical ordering of the records, only the logical ordering.

There are several variations on the APPEND command, but only one—APPEND BLANK—has any use for interactive data entry. APPEND BLANK works differently than a simple APPEND command. Like a simple APPEND, APPEND BLANK positions the record pointer to just past the physical end of file and creates a new, naked-as-a-jaybird record there. Unlike APPEND, APPEND BLANK does not drop into any data entry mode.

The code in chapter 6 uses the APPEND BLANK command instead of APPEND because the code splits the format file into its constituent parts and places the parts in a PROCEDURE file. The format file's @ GET commands are grouped for use in the EXERGET PROCEDURE, which is activated by a READ command.

BROWSE Command

The BROWSE command is extensive. In this section, we look at the subtleties and nuances involved in the dBASE IV BROWSE command. First, we list all the qualifiers available to the BROWSE command. Then we give examples of how to use them. The qualifiers are listed alphabetically for easy reference. This alphabetic listing is not necessary when using the command, nor do you need to use all the qualifiers available to BROWSE.

COMPRESS

Look at figures 7-3, 7-4, or 7-10 and you will see a non-COMPRESSed Browse display. Figure 7-11 shows a COMPRESSed Browse display. Entering BROWSE COMPRESS tells dBASE IV to show two more records on the screen.

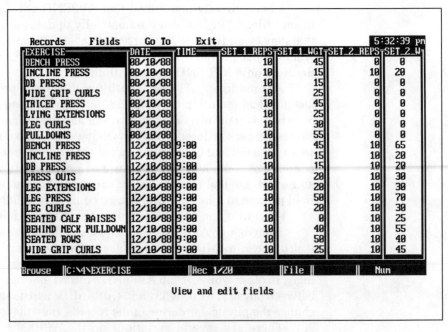

*Figure 7-11 With BROWSE COMPRESS, dBASE IV displays two more
records on the screen by compressing the field titles at the top
of the display.*

FIELDS

The FIELDS qualifier tells dBASE IV which database fields to show on the screen. This means not which fields to show on a single screen, but which database fields to show the user even when the cursor control keys are used to move left and right through the display. The FIELDS qualifier is useful because it allows you to control what the user sees, especially when you use the BROWSE FIELDS command in program mode. You can also control what the user sees in a nonprogram mode by assigning a BROWSE FIELDS command to a function key and instructing the user to activate the command from there. Such a function key substitution might have the following form:

```
SET FUNCTION 2 TO "BROWSE FIELDS EXERCISE, TOTAL_WGT;"
```

This command tells dBASE IV to put up a Browse display showing only the Exercise and Total_Wgt fields each time the [F2] key is pressed. Note that this overrides the [F2] (Assist) setting provided by dBASE IV upon startup. Also, this example assumes the EXERCISE database has been placed in USE.

FIELDS *calculated field name* = *expression*

The FIELDS qualifier has several qualifiers of its own, and you can mix these qualifiers in a single FIELDS statement. This version of the FIELDS command, FIELDS *calculated field name* = *expression*, can be used as an example of how the BROWSE command might be used to automatically enter the Total_Wgt data into the database. Remember that Total_Wgt is a calculated field based on information entered in the Set_n fields. That being the case, we would create the following FIELDS statement:

```
FIELDS TOTAL_WGT = SET_1_REPS * SET_1_WGT +;
    SET_2_REPS * SET_2_WGT + SET_3_REPS * SET_3_WGT +;
    SET_4_REPS * SET_4_WGT + SET_5_REPS * SET_5_WGT +;
    SET_6_REPS * SET_6_WGT
```

This command tells dBASE IV that the Total_Wgt field should be filled with the arithmetic expression. Note that this form only shows the Total_Wgt field on the Browse screen. Using the FIELDS qualifier to enter data into a calculated field causes dBASE IV to make the calculated field read only. This means you can see the data in the field but you can't edit it on the Browse screen.

It gets worse. I mentioned that dBASE IV views calculated fields as nothing more than an @ SAY expression command. In other words, no data is placed into the database when you tell dBASE IV to create a calculated field. This is also the case when you tell dBASE IV to use a FIELDS calculated field name in a BROWSE command. Suppose you tell dBASE IV that the Total_Wgt data is the result of a calculation involving several other fields and memory variables. dBASE IV places data on the screen where you would expect that data to go. But be advised that the data will not appear in the database unless you, the user, or some program specifically place the data in the field. This is no problem if you only want a calculated field to show on the screen and you don't even have the field in the database (a true virtual field). If you want a field which is calculated by dBASE IV

and has the calculated data in the database without going through a calculation each time you want to see that data, however, be prepared to find
other avenues of getting the calculated data into the field.

FIELDS *field name list*

FIELDS *field name list* is the standard form of the FIELDS qualifier, as described previously. You simply type in the field names you want dBASE IV
to show in the Browse table. Note that you must include at least one valid
field name in the command if you use the FIELDS qualifier. The field name
can be a calculated field or an existing database field, but you must put one
in the command. You can list any or all the fields in the database with the
FIELDS qualifier. dBASE IV defaults to showing all the fields in the order
they appear in the database when you simply enter BROWSE. Also note that
you can vary the order of the fields on the screen from the order of the fields
in the database simply by entering the field names in an order different from
that in the database. Examples of this are figures 7-12 and 7-13. Figure 7-12
shows the fields in the order they appear in the database; figure 7-13 shows
the fields in an order other than how they appear in the database.

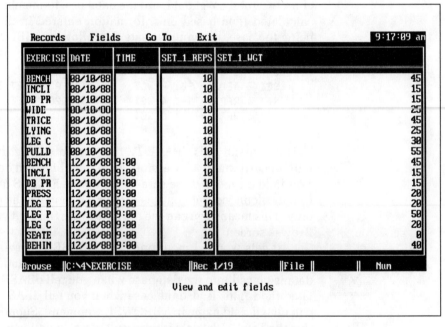

Figure 7-12 *This screen is generated by dBASE IV based on the*
command BROWSE FIELDS EXERCISE /5, DATE, TIME,
SET_1_REPS, SET_1_WGT.

The ability to BROWSE fields in an order other than how they appear
in the database is useful when you work with a database that has several

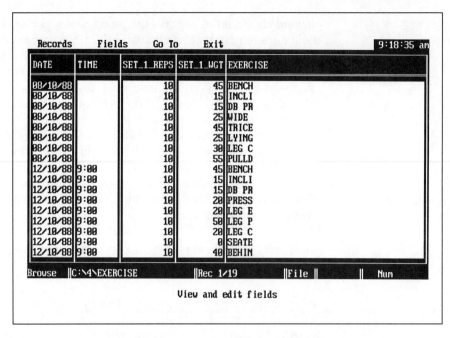

Figure 7-13 This screen is generated by dBASE IV based on the command BROWSE FIELDS DATE, TIME, SET _ 1 _ REPS, SET _ 1 _ WGT, EXERCISE /5.

indexing schemes applied to it. You can tell dBASE IV which MDX tag file or NDX file to use as the master indexing method, then tell it to BROWSE with the key field as the first displayed field on the screen.

FIELDS *field name /n*

The FIELDS *field name /n* qualifier is an amplification of the FIELDS *field name* qualifier. The /n tells dBASE IV how wide to make this one field in the display. Because some interesting things happen when you use this form of the FIELDS qualifier, we will explore them before we go on.

dBASE IV determines the default width of a Browse column in two ways. The first way is by determining how much space is available on the screen. A simple BROWSE command (figures 7-3 and 7-4) determines how much of each field appears on the screen by giving each field a portion of the screen equal to the width of the field.

The Exercise field is twenty characters wide, so that is how wide the field appears on the screen. Likewise with the Date field (the field is eight characters wide, so that is what dBASE IV allows it on the screen) and the Time field (eight by eight). Funny things happen with the Set_n fields. The Set_n_Reps fields are three characters wide, and the Set_n_Wgt fields are four characters wide. Notice that dBASE IV gives them a great deal more space than three and four characters, respectively. This is because dBASE IV's first choice for assigning field width is the width of the field. Its second choice is the width of the field's name. Notice that the Set_n_Reps fields are ten characters wide and the field names (such as Set_1_Reps and Set_2_Reps) are also ten characters wide. Notice that the Set_n_Wgt fields are nine characters wide and the field names (such as Set_1_Wgt and Set_2_Wgt) are also nine characters wide. The last field displayed in figure 7-3, Set_2_Wgt, is truncated because the field is scrolled off the right edge of the screen.

So, dBASE IV assigns field widths in Browse mode first by the width of the field, then by the width of the field name. Whichever is larger determines how wide the field is displayed on the screen. Now we want to tell dBASE IV how wide to display certain fields. We will do it with the FIELDS *field name* /n qualifier. Using the EXERCISE database as an example, you could enter the command

```
BROWSE FIELDS EXERCISE /5, DATE, TIME, SET_1_REPS,;
        SET_1_WGT
```

(Note that putting a semicolon at the end of a command line tells dBASE IV that the command is continued on the next line.) How would you expect dBASE IV to display information based on this command? Would you expect it to look like figure 7-12?

First, this command tells dBASE IV to prepare the Browse display for five fields: Exercise, Date, Time, Set_1_Reps, and Set_1_Wgt. Second, it tells dBASE IV to present the fields in the order listed. You could tell dBASE IV to present the fields in another order by entering a different field ordering on the screen. For example, you could BROWSE FIELDS DATE, TIME, SET_1_REPS, SET_1_WGT, EXERCISE /5 (figure 7-13) and see the fields on the screen in that order.

Back to figure 7-12. Remember that dBASE IV has a full screen to fill even if you have not requested a full screen's worth of information. Figure 7-12 is a demonstration of how it goes about this task. We asked dBASE IV to limit the Exercise field to five characters with the /5 qualifier. Note that the data in the column is truncated to five characters even though the column is displayed eight characters wide (the width of the field name, Exercise). Also note that the four-character wide field, Set_1_Wgt, is expanded to fill the rest of the screen. Now look at figure 7-13. We changed the placement of EXERCISE /5 and dBASE IV dutifully truncates *the data* to five characters, but leaves the displayed field width as large as necessary to fill the screen.

There are strict limits to what you can do in BROWSE mode. Don't overdue the BROWSE mode qualifiers; you might use so many qualifiers that they cancel each other out.

The moral is to make sure you don't waste keystrokes when you use the /n qualifier. Don't tell dBASE IV to BROWSE a field at two characters wide when the field name is five characters wide because dBASE IV will use a five-character wide screen column to show that field.

FIELDS *field name* /R

The FIELDS *field name* /R qualifier tells dBASE IV to make the listed field read only. dBASE IV highlights the field but you can't edit or enter it, much like a calculated field.

FORMAT

I mentioned that the [F2] (Data) key toggles between a Browse mode and an Edit mode except when you press [F2] from the Forms column on the Assist menu. Pressing [F2] from a highlighted format file or an active format file in the Forms column on the Assist menu causes dBASE IV to toggle between the selected format file and a Browse mode that makes use of all the logic (the Template symbols, Picture functions, Edit options, and so on) in the format file. The FORMAT qualifier does the same thing, but from the dBASE prompt. The command form is

```
BROWSE FORMAT
```

Note that you don't specify the format file by name in the command. The command assumes you have either already used the SET FORMAT TO file name command before the BROWSE command or you made a format file active through the Assist menu. Remember my earlier admonition that you might not want all the logic of the format file to be active in Browse mode. You can be selective and still use a format file's logic by mixing the FIELDS qualifier with the FORMAT qualifier so that only certain fields are displayed, but those fields use the FORMAT file's logic.

FREEZE *field name*

The FREEZE qualifier is sometimes confused with the next listed qualifier, LOCK. The two qualifiers do something similar; both hold a certain position of the Browse mode as sacrosanct. FREEZE tells dBASE IV to allow changes to only one field. In particular, it tells dBASE IV to only let the cursor into a single field and make all cursor control key moves apply to that single field. dBASE IV still displays all the fields requested, but you can edit or enter only the single frozen field. Further, dBASE IV allows you to FREEZE only a single field at a time.

LOCK *n*

Like FREEZE, LOCK tells dBASE IV to make some part of the screen inviolate. Unlike FREEZE, LOCK tells dBASE IV how many fields to fix on the left side of the screen. For example, you can tell dBASE IV to always show Exercise, Date, and Time on the left of the screen but allow scrolling through all the other fields in a record with the following command:

```
BROWSE LOCK 3
```

dBASE IV knows to fix Exercise, Date, and Time on the left of the screen because those are the first three fields in each record and I didn't include a different ordering with the FIELDS qualifier. I could fix different fields on the left of the screen with a command such as

```
BROWSE FIELDS TOTAL_WGT, COMMENT, EXERCISE, DATE,;
    TIME, SET_1_REPS, SET_2_REPS, SET_3_REPS, LOCK 2
```

There is a subtle danger in the LOCK qualifier. You can LOCK more than you can chew. More exactly, you can LOCK more than the screen can chew, as shown in figure 7-14. The error message at the bottom of the screen says we can't scroll to the right because we have LOCKed too many fields on the display. How many fields did we LOCK? Ten. This is too many for the EXERCISE database's structure. The number of locked fields that cause a locked Browse display depends on the structure of the database being BROWSEd.

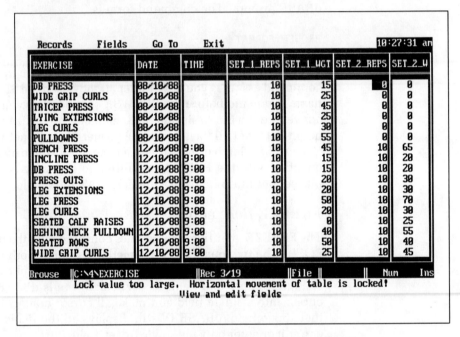

Figure 7-14 dBASE IV tells you when you have LOCKed too many fields for BROWSEing.

NOAPPEND

You can add, or APPEND, records to a database through Browse mode. Using the NOAPPEND qualifier tells dBASE IV that no records are to be added to the file. You can cursor down to the last available record in the file and no further. Also, dBASE IV will not prompt you to see if you want to add records to the database.

NOCLEAR

NOCLEAR can result in confusing displays unless your code handles leaving the uncleared Browse table on the screen.

The NOCLEAR qualifier tells dBASE IV to leave the Browse table—not the entire Browse display—on the screen after exiting Browse mode. This is shown in figure 7-15. Compare figure 7-15 with any of the previous Browse displays in this chapter and you will notice that figure 7-15 does not have the Browse menu, the STATUS bar, the prompt line, or the help line.

EXERCISE	DATE	TIME	SET_1_REPS	SET_1_WGT	SET_2_REPS	SET_2_W
BENCH PRESS	08/10/88		10	45	0	0
INCLINE PRESS	08/10/88		10	15	10	20
DB PRESS	08/10/88		10	15	0	0
WIDE GRIP CURLS	08/10/88		10	25	0	0
TRICEP PRESS	08/10/88		10	45	0	0
LYING EXTENSIONS	08/10/88		10	25	0	0
LEG CURLS	08/10/88		10	30	0	0
PULLDOWNS	08/10/88		10	55	0	0
BENCH PRESS	12/10/88	9:00	10	45	10	65
INCLINE PRESS	12/10/88	9:00	10	15	10	20
DB PRESS	12/10/88	9:00	10	15	10	20
PRESS OUTS	12/10/88	9:00	10	20	10	30
LEG EXTENSIONS	12/10/88	9:00	10	20	10	30
LEG PRESS	12/10/88	9:00	10	50	10	70
LEG CURLS	12/10/88	9:00	10	20	10	30
SEATED CALF RAISES	12/10/88	9:00	10	0	10	25
BEHIND NECK PULLDOWN	12/10/88	9:00	10	40	10	55

Figure 7-15 The NOCLEAR qualifier tells dBASE IV to leave the
Browse table—not the entire Browse display—on the screen after
exiting Browse mode.

NODELETE

The NODELETE qualifier tells dBASE IV to ignore any requests to DE-
LETE records from the database. Normally, you can DELETE records
while BROWSEing by highlighting any field in a record and pressing [Ctrl-
U] or [Alt-R] M. This last method tells dBASE IV to open the Records menu
and Mark the currently highlighted record for deletion.

DELETEing a record and physically removing it from the database
are two separate actions. You tell dBASE IV you want a record removed
from the database with [Ctrl-U] or [Alt-R] M in Browse mode. You remove
the record from the database with either the PACK command from the
dBASE prompt or with the database design system's Organize *Erase
marked records* menu option.

Back to DELETEing records. Adding the NODELETE qualifier to the
BROWSE command causes dBASE IV to ignore the [Ctrl-U] keystroke combination and to remove *Mark record for deletion* as an available option on
the Records menu.

NOEDIT

NOEDIT tells dBASE IV to make the entire Browse table read only. You can
cursor through the table in any direction and highlight any field you want,
but you can't edit any of the fields. You can enter new records, however, as
described previously in this chapter.

NOFOLLOW

The NOFOLLOW qualifier has to do with how dBASE IV keeps track of the record pointer when you change the contents of the key field using an indexed database. Yes, I know that was confusing. I'm going to try again.

When you use a database and either an MDX or NDX file, you tell dBASE IV to impose some kind of logical ordering on the database. This has been described before and won't be rehashed here except to mention that the logical ordering is based on one or more fields in the database and these fields are then called key fields. NOFOLLOW comes into play when you make a change to one of these key fields.

Suppose you edit a key field in a record. Normally, dBASE IV repositions the edited key field in logical order. If you start with a logical ordering of 22, 25, 56, 67, 10 and edit record 56's key field, you end up with a logical ordering of 56, 22, 25, 67, 10. dBASE IV continues to use the logical ordering unless you tell it otherwise. Record 56 went from third on the totem pole to first. dBASE IV makes note of that, then places the cursor in record 22 because that is the next logical record after reshuffling. Record 67 was next on the hit list before you edited record 56's key field data. This is an example of dBASE IV shuffling the record order to move the edited information around the database.

What if you don't want dBASE IV to follow the edited information? What if you want to make changes to the database according to the old logical order, even though dBASE IV is making note of where the edited records should go? Use the command

```
BROWSE NOFOLLOW
```

This tells dBASE IV to shuffle the database according to the edited information, but do not take the record pointer along for the shuffle. In our example, the database would be reshuffled to 56, 22, 25, 67, 10 but the cursor would be placed on record 67 after you finished with record 56. In other words, dBASE IV is *not following* the changes to the key field, even though it acknowledges that changes have been made.

NOINIT

The NOINIT qualifier translates to: do *not initialize* Browse mode. It is useful if you enter a long BROWSE command from the dBASE prompt, exit Browse mode to do some other work, then want to get back into Browse mode with the same qualifiers you used in the previous command. An example follows:

```
BROWSE COMPRESS FIELDS EXERCISE, DATE, TIME, SET_1_REPS,;
       SET_1_WGT, SET_2_REPS, SET_2_WGT, SET_3_REPS,;
       SET_3_WGT, SET_4_REPS, SET_4_WGT, SET_5_REPS,;
```

```
SET_5_WGT, SET_6_REPS, SET_6_WGT,;
TOTAL_WGT = SET_1_REPS * SET_1_WGT +;
SET_2_REPS * SET_2_WGT + SET_3_REPS * SET_3_WGT +;
SET_4_REPS * SET_4_WGT + SET_5_REPS * SET_5_WGT +;
SET_6_REPS * SET_6_WGT, COMMENT LOCK 2 NOMENU FORMAT
```

That is one long BROWSE command. It contains five qualifiers (COM-PRESS, FIELDS, LOCK, NOMENU, and FORMAT) and an unfortunately long but necessary field list. You don't want to type this in at the dBASE prompt each time you want to start using Browse mode. Instead, you can type

```
BROWSE NOINIT
```

dBASE IV acts as if you retyped the complete BROWSE command.

NOMENU

Notice the menu line at the top of the Browse screen? The offerings are Records, Fields, Go To, and Exit. Including the NOMENU qualifier in the BROWSE command tells dBASE IV to put a Browse table on the screen without that top line menu. You won't be able to access any of those menu options. This is useful when the Browse table is only a single screen of information or you want to limit the user's abilities to modify the data.

WINDOW *window name*

To display your own messages on the screen, limit the size of the Browse table.

The standard Browse display takes up the entire screen. You can tell dBASE IV to limit the Browse display to a selected portion of the screen with the WINDOW qualifier. Note that you must first define a window before you can include the WINDOW qualifier in the BROWSE command. An example of this is shown in figure 7-16, where the NOCLEAR qualifier is also used to show both the window location and the commands that created it.

WIDTH n

The WIDTH qualifier acts as a global version of the FIELDS *field name* /n qualifier. The FIELDS *field name* /n qualifier told dBASE IV how wide to display the named field in the Browse display. The WIDTH qualifier tells dBASE IV how wide to display all fields in the Browse display. An example of this is shown in figure 7-17. Note that dBASE IV selects either the WIDTH argument or the actual size of the field, whichever is smaller, as the display width of a field. The command that creates figure 7-17 is BROWSE WIDTH 9. The Date field, which is only eight characters wide, is displayed as only eight characters wide.

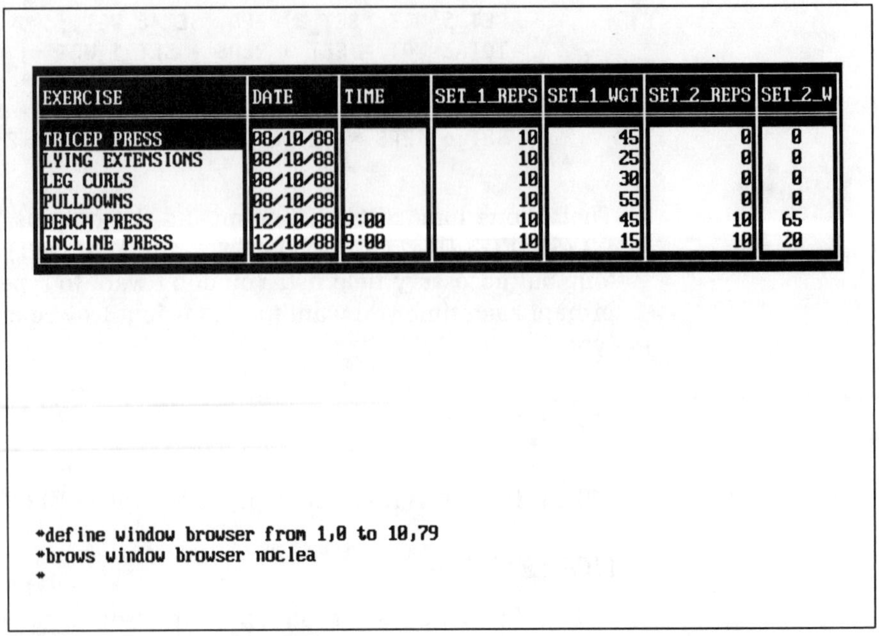

EXERCISE	DATE	TIME	SET_1_REPS	SET_1_WGT	SET_2_REPS	SET_2_W
TRICEP PRESS	08/10/88		10	45	0	0
LYING EXTENSIONS	08/10/88		10	25	0	0
LEG CURLS	08/10/88		10	30	0	0
PULLDOWNS	08/10/88		10	55	0	0
BENCH PRESS	12/10/88	9:00	10	45	10	65
INCLINE PRESS	12/10/88	9:00	10	15	10	20

```
•define window browser from 1,0 to 10,79
•brows window browser noclea
•
```

Figure 7-16 *You can specify a selected area of the screen for the Browse table by including the WINDOW qualifier in the command. You must first DEFINE a WINDOW before using the WINDOW qualifier, however.*

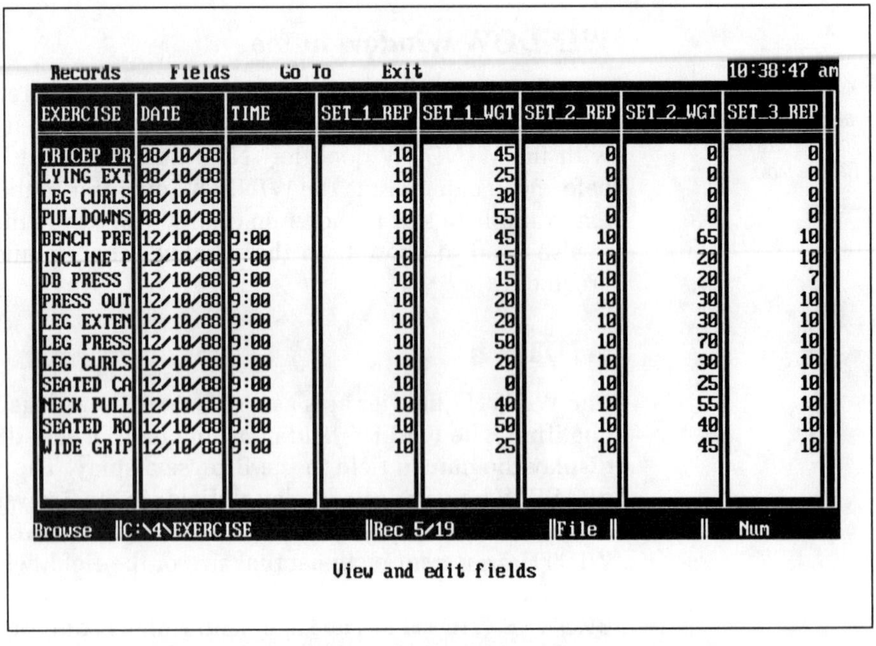

Records	Fields	Go To	Exit				10:38:47 am
EXERCISE	DATE	TIME	SET_1_REP	SET_1_WGT	SET_2_REP	SET_2_WGT	SET_3_REP
TRICEP PR	08/10/88		10	45	0	0	0
LYING EXT	08/10/88		10	25	0	0	0
LEG CURLS	08/10/88		10	30	0	0	0
PULLDOWNS	08/10/88		10	55	0	0	0
BENCH PRE	12/10/88	9:00	10	45	10	65	10
INCLINE P	12/10/88	9:00	10	15	10	20	10
DB PRESS	12/10/88	9:00	10	15	10	20	7
PRESS OUT	12/10/88	9:00	10	20	10	30	10
LEG EXTEN	12/10/88	9:00	10	20	10	30	10
LEG PRESS	12/10/88	9:00	10	50	10	70	10
LEG CURLS	12/10/88	9:00	10	20	10	30	10
SEATED CA	12/10/88	9:00	10	0	10	25	10
NECK PULL	12/10/88	9:00	10	40	10	55	10
SEATED RO	12/10/88	9:00	10	50	10	40	10
WIDE GRIP	12/10/88	9:00	10	25	10	45	10

Browse	C:\4\EXERCISE	Rec 5/19	File		Num

View and edit fields

Figure 7-17 *The WIDTH qualifier tells dBASE IV the maximum width for each displayed field in the Browse table.*

An Example of BROWSE in a Program

The BROWSE command has lots of options, as you might have guessed from the listing of qualifiers. How these commands can be useful can be shown with some simple programming.

Suppose you want to produce listings based on data entered in the Browse table. You could create a database with a field, REPORT, which is only seen on Browse displays. (You can hide a single field from data entry by removing the field's @ SAY GET lines from the format file.) Now suppose you want to create a list of weights and repetitions for certain exercises. You can create a Browse display as shown in figure 7-18 with the following commands:

Listing 7-1

```
** BROWDISP.PRG
* This program uses a format file and BROWSE command to create a
*    toggle field, REPORT, which is used to mark records for
*    reporting.
*
SET FORMAT TO C10
BROWSE FIELDS EXERCISE, DATE, TIME FREEZE REPORT FORMAT NOAPPEND
SET FORMAT TO
DISPLAY TO PRINT FOR REPORT
REPLACE ALL REPORT WITH .N.
*
** EOP: BROWDISP.PRG
```

The contents of the C10.FMT file, listing 7-2, follow:

Listing 7-2

```
** C10.FMT
* This format file is used by BROWDISP.PRG to place a message
*    at the bottom of the screen instructing the user on how to
*    select records for listing.
*
@ 10,0 GET EXERCISE
@ 11,0 GET DATE
@ 12,0 GET TIME
@ 13,0 GET REPORT PICTURE "Y" MESSAGE [MARK THE RECORDS TO LIST
WITH A "Y"]
*
** EOF: C10.FMT
```

These two bits of code are quite simple, and you should not be concerned if they include dBASE IV commands you have not seen before.

The first five lines of BROWDISP.PRG are comments. Every time you see an asterisk as the first character on a line in a dBASE IV program, you are looking at a comment of one kind or another. Sometimes the asterisk is used to separate one logical block from another; other times it contains

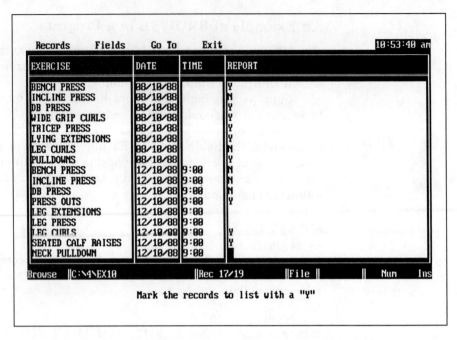

Figure 7-18 This Browse display is created with the BROWDISP.PRG
program. It uses a logical Report field to produce listings without
allowing editing or input to any fields.

messages concerning the program itself. These five comment lines explain
the code. The next line, SET FORMAT TO C10, is necessary because we
use the FORMAT qualifier in the BROWSE command. What we say in the
format file is discussed in a moment.

The next line in BROWDISP.PRG is the actual BROWSE command.
We use the FIELDS, FREEZE, FORMAT, and NOAPPEND qualifiers to
make dBASE IV do what we want. In this case, we only want four fields
shown. Three of the fields— Exercise, Date, and Time—are listed with the
FIELDS qualifier. Because the fourth field, Report, is the only one we want
the user to be able to edit, we use the FREEZE qualifier. We include the
FORMAT qualifier because we want to use some formatting features. Last,
we don't want the user to add any new records to the database, hence
NOAPPEND is added at the end of the BROWSE command.

After we have BROWSEd the database and marked the records we
want to report, we SET FORMAT TO. This tells dBASE IV to take
C10.FMT out of memory. This line is not truly necessary unless you are
having memory management problems on your computer.

The next line, DISPLAY TO PRINT FOR REPORT, tells dBASE IV to
print all the fields except Comment and to print only records that have a
Report field value of Y. The Comment field is not printed because dBASE
IV only DISPLAYs memo fields if they are specifically requested in the
DISPLAY command. TO PRINT is a qualifier on the DISPLAY command

instructing dBASE IV to send the information to the printer. FOR REPORT
is a qualifier that translates to "for each record where the Report field is set
to true."

The last command line, REPLACE ALL REPORT WITH .N., tells
dBASE IV to change the Report field in each record back to a False, or No,
value. The last two lines are comment lines.

Now we must investigate the format file, which is also simple. The
FORMAT qualifier tells dBASE IV to use the currently active format file's
Template symbols, Picture functions, and Edit options on the Browse display. dBASE IV defaults to the standard Browse display when there is no
currently active format file and the FORMAT qualifier is used on the command line. However, dBASE IV can be confused by a bogus format file.

Consider the following bogus format file:

```
** C10DUMMY.FMT
* This is a blank format file used in this chapter as
*    an example. There are absolutely no processable
*    commands in this file.
*
** EOF: C10DUMMY.FMT
```

The comments in the file tell you there are no processable commands
in C10DUMMY.FMT. What happens when you enter the following command sequence?

```
SET FORMAT TO C10DUMMY
BROWSE FORMAT
```

dBASE IV tells you something is wrong, as shown in figure 7-19.

Figure 7-19 dBASE IV tells you there is a problem when you SET a
bogus format file, then issue the BROWSE FORMAT command.

You don't need something as obviously bogus as C10DUMMY.FMT
for dBASE IV to tell you an error has occurred. Suppose that you create a
format file called C10-1FIELD.FMT that contains information on a single
field:

```
** C10-1FIELD.FMT
*
@ 13,0 GET REPORT PICTURE "Y" MESSAGE [MARK THE RECORDS TO LIST
WITH A "Y"]
*
** EOF: C10.FMT
```

If you enter the following command sequence:

```
SET FORMAT TO C10-1FIELD
BROWSE FIELDS EXERCISE, DATE, TIME FREEZE REPORT FORMAT
```

dBASE IV would set up the Browse display with a single field, Report, on the table because only one field is used in the format file.

It doesn't matter what database fields you list with the FIELDS qualifier after a format file is SET. The FORMAT qualifier takes precedence and only offers the fields you have defined in the format file itself. dBASE IV won't tell you there is a problem when you do this—you can go nuts trying to figure it out.

CHANGE and EDIT Commands

The two dBASE IV commands CHANGE and EDIT are like identical twins. They do the same thing; the only difference is their names. They are also siblings of BROWSE in that they allow full-screen editing of records in a database, although both CHANGE and EDIT are limited to presenting a single record at a time.

Like BROWSE, CHANGE and EDIT have qualifiers. The CHANGE and EDIT qualifiers are

FIELDS *field name list*

FOR *expression*

n

NEXT *n*

NOAPPEND

NOCLEAR

NODELETE

NOEDIT

NOFOLLOW

NOINIT

NOMENU

WHILE *expression*

The FIELDS, NOAPPEND, NOCLEAR, NODELETE, NOEDIT, NOFOL-
LOW, NOINIT, and NOMENU qualifiers are identical to their BROWSE
counterparts. You might consider the oddity of a command such as EDIT
NOEDIT, but remember that you are telling dBASE IV to allow the user to
read the records, add new records, mark records for deletion, but not alter
any existing information in any record.

Before describing the CHANGE/EDIT specific qualifiers, it is worth
looking at how CHANGE/EDIT behaves when called from Browse mode.
First, you can toggle to CHANGE/EDIT with the [F2] (Data) key. dBASE IV
displays the Change/Edit screen with the record that was last highlighted
in Browse mode or highlights in Browse mode the record that was on the
Change/Edit screen. Note that dBASE IV places the current record at the
top of the Browse display when entering Browse from Change/Edit mode.

CHANGE/EDIT accepts and uses any of the BROWSE compatible
qualifiers. It ignores COMPRESS (there is no horizontal title bar to compress), FREEZE (it won't restrict you to a single record for editing), LOCK
(because there is no right/left scrolling, LOCKing a single field is unnecessary), WIDTH (because fields are listed vertically, there is no need to define
a global WIDTH qualifier), and WINDOW (the Change/Edit table is designed from the database structure, not to conform to a tabular screen
form). For its part, BROWSE uses only those CHANGE/EDIT qualifiers
that it has as part of its own repertoire.

So what about qualifiers peculiar to CHANGE/EDIT? Explanations
are listed in the following sections.

FOR *condition*

The FOR qualifier is excellent when you need to do things based on nonkey field data. It lets you specify a logical condition for the records you
want to CHANGE/EDIT. For example, we might want to EDIT only those
records that meet the condition TOTAL_WGT > 1000. That goes into the
command line as

```
CHANGE FOR TOTAL_WGT > 1000
```

or

```
EDIT FOR TOTAL_WGT > 1000
```

Another example of a logical condition is DATE = {10/12/89}. dBASE IV
only displays records that meet the logical condition. For example, if you
have a database with 1000 records, only 13 of which meet the stipulated
condition, dBASE IV would give you access only to those 13 records.

n

The n signifies a record number that you want to CHANGE/EDIT. You
enter a command such as

```
CHANGE 103
```

dBASE IV reads the command and places the record pointer at record number 103. This also works with the EDIT command. This command form doesn't stop you from CHANGEing or EDITing other records in the database; it merely starts you at the entered record number.

NEXT n

The NEXT n qualifier is similar to the n qualifier. This command tells dBASE IV how many records, starting at the current record position, can be CHANGEd or EDITed. For example, the following command tells dBASE IV to only allow editing to the next five records, starting at the current record position:

```
EDIT NEXT 5
```

You can mix the n and NEXT n qualifiers to tell dBASE IV where to start editing and how many succeeding records to allow in the edit. An example of this is

```
EDIT 103 NEXT 5
```

WHILE condition

The WHILE condition qualifier is similar to the FOR qualifier but is usually used with either SORTed or INDEXed files. You have to understand what SORTed and INDEXed files are like to understand how WHILE works.

NDX and MDX files force a logical ordering on a database file. I know I have said that ad nauseam, but it can't be emphasized enough. SORTing a database works similarly, only you don't need an MDX or NDX file to SORT the database. For example, you can INDEX the EXERCISE database on the Set_1_Wgt field with the command

```
INDEX ON SET_1_WGT TAG WGT1 OF EXERCISE
```

This tells dBASE IV to place a logical order on the Set_1_Wgt field of the current database, to call the logical order WGT1, and to place information about this logical ordering in the EXERCISE.MDX file. This command form is peculiar to dBASE IV. The dBASE III and III Plus equivalent is

```
INDEX ON SET_1_WGT TO WGT1
```

This command could also be used in dBASE IV to make a dBASE III and III Plus compatible NDX file.

In any case, the INDEX command creates a situation where equivalent expressions are grouped together. All Set_1_Wgts of 100 are grouped, all 200s are grouped together, and so on. Further, the order of groupings is based on the information in the key field. You wouldn't have groupings of 100 followed by 200 followed by 150 followed by 125. The groupings would be 100, 125, 150, 200. A SORTed database is much the same, except the logical order is directly in the database. No MDX or NDX files are necessary for the logical order to exist.

The WHILE qualifier makes use of this logical ordering by allowing a command pair such as the following:

```
SEEK keyfield value
EDIT WHILE keyfield = keyfield value
```

There may be twenty-five records that meet the condition *keyfield =keyfield value*. The SEEK command tells dBASE IV to find the first record that meets the condition. The EDIT command tells dBASE IV to allow editing to the database records WHILE the *keyfield* equals *keyfield value*. This means you might end up CHANGEing or EDITing one record or several hundred.

You should be aware of one thing when using the WHILE command. You might know the database has, for example, two hundred records that meet the *keyfield* = *keyfield value* condition. EDITing or CHANGEing the key field value moves it from its current position in an INDEXed database and probably throws off the record pointer. The way to alleviate this problem is to use the NOFOLLOW qualifier with the CHANGE/EDIT command.

INSERT Command

INSERT is similar to APPEND. It creates a new blank record in the database. The difference is that INSERT places the record at some point in the database and APPEND places the new record at the end of the database.

INSERT has three forms: INSERT, INSERT BEFORE, and INSERT BLANK. INSERT places a blank record directly after the current record in the database. Suppose the record pointer is at record number 349. INSERT creates a new blank record at location 350 and pushes all following records up one in the database. What was record 350 becomes record 351. What was 351 becomes 352, and so on. INSERT also causes the program to go into the full-screen editor, which may mean you go to Edit mode or a Format mode, if an FMT file is in memory.

INSERT BEFORE is similar to INSERT, except it places the new record directly before the current record position. Suppose you are at record position 349. INSERT BEFORE creates a new record 349, then pushes all succeeding records up one in the database. What was 349 becomes 350, 350 becomes 351, and so on. INSERT BEFORE also drops the program into full-screen editing mode.

INSERT BLANK, like INSERT, creates a new record at the current record position. The only difference is that INSERT BLANK doesn't drop the program into full-screen editing mode.

READ Command

READ is a command you most often find used in programs, not used interactively. It is included in this section because it does make use of the availabe full-screen editing formats.

READ works with @ GET commands. Take a look at the FMT files in this book or the ones you have created and you will see lots of @ GET commands. The READ command tells dBASE IV to GET whatever is in the @ GET command and enter it into either memory—in the case of a memory variable—or the currently active database. You can appreciate how clumsy this command would be in interactive mode. What would be the point, for example, of entering the following commands interactively when EDIT NEXT 1 FIELDS EXERCISE, DATE, TIME would do the exact same job?

```
@ 1,0 SAY [EXERCISE] GET EXERCISE
@ 2,0 SAY [DATE] GET DATE
@ 3,0 SAY [TIME] GET TIME
READ
```

READ can cause problems if you don't know what is in the BUCKET memory. (BUCKET memory is where dBASE IV keeps track of format files.) READ looks in the BUCKET before doing anything else, and that may not be what you want.

READ does reveal its power, however, when you have previously SET a FORMAT file in memory. If you SET a FORMAT file, you can have full screen editing of the current record just by typing the READ command either at the dBASE prompt or through a program file.

The READ command has one qualifier, SAVE. READ by itself tells dBASE IV to gather information from the current @ GETs and place the data accordingly. Further, dBASE IV essentially blanks out the @ GETs after their values have been READ. READ SAVE tells dBASE IV to get information from the current @ GETs but leave their value available for the next READ command. Thus, you could READ them a second time and have the same information in the various @ GET expressions as you entered during the first READ command. You could think of it as READ SAVE not clearing the information last placed in the @ GETs but leaving that information for the next READ command.

Editing and Debugging Input

This section might appear to be too advanced for first time users of dBASE, but it isn't. Because more coding techniques are shown in this section, you may want to skip over it until you are more familiar with dBASE IV when working from the dBASE prompt and from the Assist menu.

This section shows small code segments that can be run on any database. This code will save you time checking for data entry errors in certain situations.

Placing Information in the Database Before Interactive Entry

The first case we look at occurs when the contents of one or more fields will contain repetitive data. We could CARRY the data from one record to another with the SET CARRY ON command mentioned previously, but SET CARRY ON means a field could still be edited by the user. We want to make something where the field or fields don't even have to appear on the screen during entry. They might be necessary for editing, but not for entry.

Using the EXERCISE database as an example, we notice that we CARRY the Date and Time fields from one record to the next. It would be quicker if the user was asked what values should go in these records, then let dBASE IV do the data entry automatically each time a new record is added to the database. Further, the Date and Time fields can be either made read only during data entry or removed from the screen form completely.

So how is all this done?

With smoke and mirrors, of course. Actually, the following modifications to the code written in chapter 6 do the trick. The first block of code is EXPROC.PRG with some modifications. The modifications are clearly marked and make the code run cleaner.

Listing 7-3

```
00001 : ** EXPROC.PRG PROCEDURE FILE FOR EXERCISE PROGRAM
00002 : *
00003 : PROCEDURE GETSTATS
00004 : PUBLIC lc_talk, lc_status, lc_carry
00005 : *
00006 : IF SET("TALK")="ON"
00007 :    SET TALK OFF
00008 :       lc_talk="ON"
00009 : ELSE
00010 :       lc_talk="OFF"
00011 : ENDIF
00012 : *
00013 : SET DISPLAY TO EGA25
00014 : *
00015 : lc_carry = SET("CARRY")
00016 : lc_status=SET("STATUS")
00017 : *
00018 : IF lc_status = "ON"
00019 :    SET STATUS OFF
00020 : ENDIF
00021 : *
```

Listing 7-3 (cont.)

```
00022 : *END OF PROCEDURE GETSTATS
00023 : *
00024 : PROCEDURE EXERSAY
00025 : CLEAR
00026 : SET COLOR OF MESSAGES TO r/w
00027 : DEFINE WINDOW Wndow1 FROM 8,41 TO 23,78
00028 : *
00029 : SET CARRY TO set_1_reps,set_2_reps,set_3_reps,set_4_reps;
00030 :    ,set_5_reps,set_6_reps ADDITIVE
00031 : @ 1,0 TO 24,79 DOUBLE
00032 : @ 2,31 SAY "EXERCISE DATA FORM"
00033 : @ 3,1 SAY "═══════════════════════════════════
         ══════════════════════════"
00034 : @ 5,3 SAY "Exercise: "
00035 : @ 5,38 SAY "Date: "
00036 : @ 5,60 SAY "Time: "
00037 : @ 7,1 SAY "─────────Repetitions and Weights───────────┐
         ──Comment──────────────────"
00038 : @ 8,40 SAY "|"
00039 : @ 9,20 SAY "Set_1_Wgt: "
00040 : @ 9,3 SAY "Set_1_Reps: "
00041 : @ 9,40 SAY "|"
00042 : @ 10,40 SAY "|"
00043 : @ 11,3 SAY "Set_2_Reps: "
00044 : @ 11,20 SAY "Set_2_Wgt: "
00045 : @ 11,40 SAY "|"
00046 : @ 12,40 SAY "|"
00047 : @ 13,3 SAY "Set_3_Reps: "
00048 : @ 13,20 SAY "Set_3_Wgt: "
00049 : @ 13,40 SAY "|"
00050 : @ 14,40 SAY "|"
00051 : @ 15,3 SAY "Set_4_Reps: "
00052 : @ 15,20 SAY "Set_4_Wgt: "
00053 : @ 15,40 SAY "|"
00054 : @ 16,40 SAY "|"
00055 : @ 17,3 SAY "Set_5_Reps: "
00056 : @ 17,20 SAY "Set_5_Wgt: "
00057 : @ 17,40 SAY "|"
00058 : @ 18,40 SAY "|"
00059 : @ 19,3 SAY "Set_6_Reps: "
00060 : @ 19,20 SAY "Set_6_Wgt: "
00061 : @ 19,40 SAY "|"
00062 : @ 20,40 SAY "|"
00063 : @ 21,10 SAY "TOTAL_WGT: "
00064 : @ 21,40 SAY "|"
00065 : @ 22,40 SAY "|"
00066 : @ 23,40 SAY "|"
00067 : @ 24,40 SAY "±"
00068 : * END OF PROCEDURE EXERSAY
```

```
00069 : *
00070 : PROCEDURE EXERGET
00071 : @ 2,3 SAY IIF(DELETED(), CHR(6) + "RECORD DELETED" + CHR(6),
         SPAC(17))
00072 : @ 2,60 SAY "RECORD # " + STR(RECNO(),7)
00073 : @ 5,13 GET exercise PICTURE "!!!!!!!!!!!!!!!!!!!!!" ;
00074 :    MESSAGE "╚═══════════════════Enter the name of the exercise
         here═══════════════╝"
00075 : *
00076 : ***** THE FOLLOWING BLOCK HAS BEEN ADDED TO THE CODE
00077 : IF PROCNAME = [DATETIME]
00078 :   @ 5,44 SAY date
00079 :   @ 5,66 SAY time
00080 : ELSE
00081 :   @ 5,44 GET date ;
00082 :       VALID DATE < DATE() + 1 ;
00083 :       ERROR "You can't enter data for future workouts!" ;
00084 :       DEFAULT {01/01/89} ;
00085 :       MESSAGE "╚═══════════════Enter the date you
         exercised here═══════════╝"
00086 :   @ 5,66 GET time PICTURE "99:99" ;
00087 :       DEFAULT "00:00" ;
00088 :       MESSAGE "╚═══════════════Enter your workout starting
         time here═══════════╝"
00089 : ENDIF
00090 : ***** END OF NEW CODE BLOCK
00091 : *
00092 : @ 9,15 GET set_1_reps PICTURE "@Z 999" ;
00093 :    DEFAULT 0 ;
00094 :    MESSAGE "╚════Enter the number of repetitions you performed
         for your first set here═════╝"
00095 : @ 9,31 GET set_1_wgt PICTURE "@Z 9999" ;
00096 :    WHEN SET_1_REPS # 0 ;
00097 :    DEFAULT 0 ;
00098 :    MESSAGE "╚═════════════Enter the amount of weight used for your
          first set here═══════════╝"
00099 : @ 11,15 GET set_2_reps PICTURE "@Z 999" ;
00100 :    DEFAULT 0 ;
00101 :    MESSAGE "╚════Enter the number of repetitions you performed
         for your second set here═══════╝"
00102 : @ 11,31 GET set_2_wgt PICTURE "@Z 9999" ;
00103 :    WHEN SET_2_REPS # 0 ;
00104 :    DEFAULT 0 ;
00105 :    MESSAGE "╚═════════Enter the amount of weight you used for
         your second set here═══════╝"
00106 : @ 13,15 GET set_3_reps PICTURE "@Z 999" ;
00107 :    DEFAULT 0 ;
00108 :    MESSAGE "╚════Enter the number of repetitions you performed
         for your third set here═══════╝"
00109 : @ 13,31 GET set_3_wgt PICTURE "@Z 9999" ;
00110 :    WHEN SET_3_REPS # 0 ;
```

Listing 7-3 (cont.)

```
00111 :     DEFAULT 0 ;
00112 :     MESSAGE "⌐════════════Enter the amount of weight used for your
            third set here════════╝"
00113 : @ 15,15 GET set_4_reps PICTURE "@Z 999" ;
00114 :     DEFAULT 0 ;
00115 :     MESSAGE "⌐═══Enter the number of repetitions you performed
            for your fourth set here════╝"
00116 : @ 15,31 GET set_4_wgt PICTURE "@Z 9999" ;
00117 :     WHEN SET_4_REPS # 0 ;
00118 :     DEFAULT 0 ;
00119 :     MESSAGE "⌐════════Enter the amount of weight you used for
            your fourth set here════╝"
00120 : @ 17,15 GET set_5_reps PICTURE "@Z 999" ;
00121 :     DEFAULT 0 ;
00122 :     MESSAGE "⌐═══Enter the number of repetitions you performed
            for your fifth set here════╝"
00123 : @ 17,31 GET set_5_wgt PICTURE "@Z 9999" ;
00124 :     WHEN SET_5_REPS # 0 ;
00125 :     DEFAULT 0 ;
00126 :     MESSAGE "⌐════════Enter the amount of weight you used for
            your fifth set here════════╝"
00127 : @ 19,15 GET set_6_reps PICTURE "@Z 999" ;
00128 :     DEFAULT 0 ;
00129 :     MESSAGE "⌐═══Enter the number of repetitions you performed
            for your sixth set here═══╝"
00130 : @ 19,31 GET set_6_wgt PICTURE "@Z 9999" ;
00131 :     WHEN SET_6_REPS # 0 ;
00132 :     DEFAULT 0 ;
00133 :     MESSAGE "⌐════════════Enter the amount of weight used for your
            sixth set here════════╝"
00134 :    READ
00135 : REPLACE TOTAL_WGT WITH SET_1_REPS*SET_1_WGT + SET_2_REPS*SET_2_
         WGT +;
00136 :    SET_3_REPS*SET_3_WGT + SET_4_REPS*SET_4_WGT + SET_5_REPS*SET_
         5_WGT + SET_6_REPS*SET_6_WGT
00137 : @ 21,21 SAY total_wgt PICTURE "@Z 99999"
00138 : @ 8,41 GET comment OPEN WINDOW Wndow1 ;
00139 :     MESSAGE "⌐═══════════════Enter any comments about this
            exercise or set here════════╝"
00140 : * END OF PROCEDURE EXERGET
00141 : *
00142 : PROCEDURE SETSTATS
00143 : *
00144 : IF lc_status = "ON"   && Entered form with status on
00145 :     SET STATUS ON      && Turn STATUS "ON" on the way out
00146 : ENDIF
00147 : *
00148 : IF lc_carry = "OFF"
00149 :    SET CARRY OFF
```

```
00150 : ENDIF
00151 : *
00152 : IF lc_talk="ON"
00153 :    SET TALK ON
00154 : ENDIF
00155 : *
00156 : * END OF PROCEDURE SETSTATS
00157 : ** END OF PROCEDURE FILE
```

Changes in the code from the original listing range from lines 76 to 90 and are marked by lines beginning with five asterisks. These subtle changes give you the ability to have dBASE IV decide if the data is being edited or added. What is PROCNAME? This is shown in the DATE-TIME.PRG file, listing 7-4.

Listing 7-4

```
00001 : ** DATETIME.PRG
00002 : * THIS PROGRAM GETS CARRYied FIELD DATA FROM THE USER AND
00003 : * AUTOMATICALLY PLACES THE DATA IN THE FIELDS.
00004 : *
00005 : MDATE = {00/00/00}
00006 : MTIME = SPACE(5)
00007 : PROCNAME = [DATETIME]
00008 : CLEAR
00009 : @ 10,10 SAY [ON WHAT DATE DID YOU DO THESE EXERCISES (dd/mm/yy)?
         -> ] GET MDATE
00010 : @ 12,10 SAY [AT WHAT TIME DID YOU DO THESE EXERCISES (nn:nn)? ->
         ] GET MTIME
00011 : READ
00012 : SET PROCEDURE TO EXPROC
00013 : DO GETSTATS
00014 : DO EXERSAY
00015 : *
00016 : DO WHILE .T.
00017 :    APPEND BLANK
00018 :    REPLACE DATE WITH MDATE, TIME WITH MTIME
00019 :    DO EXERGET
00020 :    READ
00021 : *
00022 :    IF LEN(TRIM(EXERCISE)) = 0
00023 :         EXIT
00024 :    ENDIF
00025 : *
00026 : ENDDO
00027 : *
00028 : DO SETSTATS
00029 : RELEASE WINDOWS Wndow1
00030 : RELEASE lc_carry,lc_talk,lc_fields,lc_status
00031 : *
00032 : ** END OF DATETIME.PRG
```

The core of this program begins with line 12, SET PROCEDURE TO EXPROC. From there down, DATETIME.PRG is quite similar to EXEREDIT.PRG, shown in the last chapter. What is new and interesting?

Three variables (MDATE, MTIME, and PROCNAME) are "initialized" on lines 5, 6, and 7, respectively. This is because dBASE IV is a procedural programming language and one of the parts of being a procedural programming language is needing to know what will be necessary to solve a problem. This program needs to know that we will be storing a date, a five-character time variable, and another character string to memory. We tell dBASE IV we need these things at the start of the program because these variables are carried all the way through DATETIME.PRG and into EXPROC.PRG, where a test is made to see which fields should be masked.

We need to do this test because we don't want to mask the Date and Time fields if EXEREDIT.PRG calls EXPROC.PRG; we only want to mask those fields if DATETIME.PRG calls EXPROC.PRG. Note that having EXPROC.PRG check for PROCNAME means EXEREDIT.PRG would need to include a line, PROCNAME =[EXEREDIT], before accessing the EXERGET PROCEDURE.

The next change from EXEREDIT.PRG to DATETIME.PRG is in the DO WHILE...ENDDO loop running from line 16 to line 26. We add REPLACE DATE WITH MDATE, TIME WITH MTIME (line 18) after APPEND BLANK (line 17). This command tells dBASE IV to enter the memory variable values of MDATE and MTIME into the database record's Date and Time fields.

Masking Fields During Data Entry

The relatively small changes to our original code shown in the last section provided us with a great deal more power over how data goes into the database. This section shows how to prevent users from accessing fields in a database. We start by making a list:

1. Which fields do we want masked?
2. If these fields change at each work session, how do we get dBASE IV to know what we want to do?
3. How do we get dBASE IV to look for this masked field information when someone else is doing the data entry?

These are all good questions. We go from the questions to a program outline such as the following:

1. Ask which fields should be masked.
2. Store the fields in memory.
3. Ask if the program should proceed to data entry or exit. If exit, save the masked field information to disk.

4. Retrieve the masked field information.

5. Proceed with data entry.

None of this is involved or tedious. In fact, most of it can be coded by using what we have coded already as our starting point. Items 1 and 3 in this scheme become FIELDMSK.PRG. Item 2 is handled by SET-FIELD.PRG. Items 4 and 5 become GETDATA.PRG. FIELDMSK.PRG is new, but GETDATA.PRG is EXEREDIT.PRG again. We also make modifications to the EXPROC.PRG file, but nothing that isn't obvious. We start with FIELDMSK.PRG, listing 7-5.

Listing 7-5

```
00001 : ** FIELDMaSK.PRG
00002 : * THIS PROGRAM GETS INFORMATION REGARDING WHICH FIELDS SHOULD BE
00003 : * MASKED IN THE DATABASE
00004 : *
00005 : SET TALK OFF
00006 : SET PROCEDURE TO EXPROC
00007 : SET MESSAGE TO
00008 : M = 1
00009 : TRUTH = .F.
00010 : FIELDNAMES = []
00011 : CLEAR
00012 : a 10,0 SAY [DO YOU WISH TO MASK ANY FIELDS IN THE DATABASE (Y/
        N)? -> ] GET TRUTH
00013 : READ
00014 : CLEAR
00015 : *
00016 : IF .NOT. TRUTH
00017 :    a 10,0 SAY [DO YOU WANT TO DO DATA ENTRY (Y/N)? -> ] GET TRUTH
00018 :    READ
00019 : *
00020 :    IF TRUTH
00021 :        DO GETDATA
00022 :    ENDI
00023 : *
00024 :    SAVE TO FIELDMSK ALL LIKE FIELDNAMES
00025 :    RETURN
00026 : ENDIF
00027 : *
00028 : USE database
00029 : COPY STRUCTURE EXTENDED TO TEMP
00030 : SELECT 2
00031 : USE TEMP
00032 : DECLARE TEMP[RECCO(),1]
00033 : COPY TO ARRAY TEMP FIELDS FIELD_NAME
00034 : DEFINE POPUP GETFIELD FROM 1,30
00035 : *
00036 : SCAN
```

Listing 7-5 (cont.)

```
00037 :    DEFINE BAR M OF GETFIELD PROMPT TEMP[M,1]
00038 :    M = M + 1
00039 : ENDSCAN
00040 : *
00041 : ON SELECTION POPUP GETFIELD DO SETFIELD WITH BAR()
00042 : CLEAR
00043 : SET MESSAGE TO "SELECT THE FIELDS TO MASK FROM THIS LIST. TYPE
         [ESC] TO EXIT"
00044 : USE
00045 : ERASE TEMP.DBF
00046 : SELECT 1
00047 : SHOW POPUP GETFIELD
00048 : *
00049 : DO WHILE .T.
00050 :    ACTIVATE POPUP GETFIELD
00051 : *
00052 :    IF BAR() = 0
00053 :        EXIT
00054 :    ENDIF
00055 : *
00056 : ENDDO
00057 : *
00058 : IF [] = FIELDNAMES
00059 :    RETURN
00060 : ENDIF
00061 : *
00062 : SET MESS TO
00063 : CLEAR
00064 : @ 10,0 SAY [DO YOU WANT TO DO DATA ENTRY (Y/N)? -> ] GET TRUTH
00065 : READ
00066 : *
00067 : IF TRUTH
00068 :    DO GETDATA
00069 : ELSE
00070 :    SAVE TO FIELDMSK ALL LIKE FIELDNAMES
00071 : ENDIF
00072 : *
00073 : ** EOP: FIELDMSK.PRG
```

The first four lines are comments. I should point out that comment lines are a nuisance in dBASE II, III, and III Plus, but not so in dBASE IV. Comment lines are a nuisance in those earlier dBASE languages not to the user, but to the computer. Previous incarnations of dBASE are interpreted languages. This means dBASE goes through the program files line by line, inch by inch, as it works. It usually takes just as long to recognize something as a comment and therefore ignore it as it takes to recognize something as a processable command and execute it. dBASE IV looks at the program as a whole before it executes any commands in it. This first look reads the original program and turns it into something the computer can work with more easily. Part of this process is stripping out comment lines. Hence, comment lines aren't such a nuisance to the computer and can be useful to people trying to debug your code.

Line 5 is SET TALK OFF. The various versions of dBASE can work in one of two ways. They can be chatterboxes or they can be mutes. You don't mind a chatterbox when you are trying to figure out what is going on and need all the information you can get; you prefer a mute when you don't want to hear anything and just want to get things done. SET TALK OFF turns dBASE IV into a mute. You want a mute now because you don't know who is going to be using the code and you don't want them inundated by unnecessary messages.

Line 6 tells dBASE IV that this file will need code in the EX-PROC.PRG file. Line 7 shuts off any MESSAGE that might appear at the bottom of the screen.

Lines 8 through 10 initialize variables that are used later in the program. M is a counter, TRUTH isn't, and FIELDNAMES is a character variable that holds the names of the masked fields.

Line 11 is where the program begins doing recognizable work. CLEAR the screen and ask if any fields should be masked (lines 12 and 13). Lines 16 through 26 handle the possibility that no fields will be masked. Perhaps the user wants to go directly to data entry (lines 17 and 18)? If so, DO GETDATA (lines 20 through 22). If not, or if we have already done GETDATA, SAVE any FIELDNAMES information to a special type of dBASE IV file called a memory-variable file. Memory-variable files are simply files that contain all or specified memory variables currently defined in the program or work session. Line 24 saves the FIELDNAMES variable to the memory-variable file FIELDMSK.MEM. Line 25 RETURNs processing control back to the dBASE prompt, in this case. It could return processing control back to whatever program called FIELDMSK.PRG.

Line 28 opens a database. The word *database* is used in place of an actual name that you would provide for your own code. Line 29 makes a special type of COPY of the database USED in line 28. This special type of copy provides a definition of the structure without recreating the actual structure. This structure definition is placed in a TEMPorary database. Following is a listing of the information provided in the TEMP.DBF file:

Record#	FIELD_NAME	FIELD_TYPE	FIELD_LEN	FIELD_DEC	FIELD_IDX
1	EXERCISE	C	20	0	N
2	DATE	D	8	0	N
3	TIME	C	8	0	N
4	SET_1_REPS	N	3	0	N
5	SET_1_WGT	N	4	0	N
6	SET_2_REPS	N	3	0	N
7	SET_2_WGT	N	4	0	N
8	SET_3_REPS	N	3	0	N
9	SET_3_WGT	N	4	0	N
10	SET_4_REPS	N	3	0	N

11	SET_4_WGT	N	4	0 N
12	SET_5_REPS	N	3	0 N
13	SET_5_WGT	N	4	0 N
14	SET_6_REPS	N	3	0 N
15	SET_6_WGT	N	4	0 N
16	TOTAL_WGT	N	5	0 N
17	COMMENT	M	10	0 N

We go to work area 2 (line 30) and USE the TEMPorary database file (line 31).

So far, everything we have done is similar to dBASE III and III Plus coding. Line 32, where we create a two-dimensional array, begins to show the power available through dBASE IV. The array, also called TEMP, is one element wide and as long as there are records in the TEMPorary database—17 records, through the dBASE IV RECCO( ) function. After the TEMP array is declared, the FIELD_NAMEs are copied from TEMP.DBF into the TEMP array.

Line 34 is also dBASE IV specific. We create a pop-up window, GETFIELD, anchored at screen position 1,30. This pop-up is shown in figure 7-20.

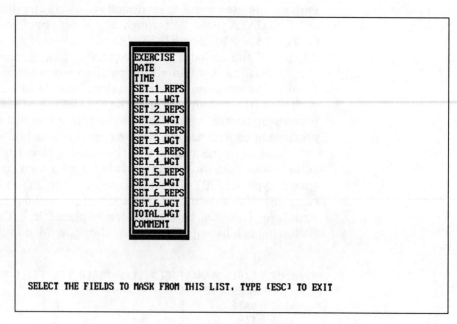

SELECT THE FIELDS TO MASK FROM THIS LIST. TYPE [ESC] TO EXIT

Figure 7-20 An example of the FIELDMSK.PRG display using the EXERCISE database.

Lines 36 through 39 are also dBASE IV specific. We are DEFINEing items for the pop-up menu based on the field names we have stored in the

TEMP array. The SCAN...ENDSCAN loop tells dBASE IV to start at the beginning of the current database, TEMP.DBF, and move the record pointer through from first to last until no more records are left to SCAN. Advanced readers may guess where this is going and already realize a way to shorten the code. The shortened code is shown at the end of this section.

Line 41 is translated as follows: When a choice is made on the GETFIELD pop-up menu, DO the SETFIELD routine. Specifically, tell SETFIELD which line was SELECTED on the pop-up menu with the BAR( ) function. Line 43 SETs a new MESSAGE to help the user during the field selection process. Close TEMP.DBF in line 44, ERASE it from the disk in line 45, and go back to the first work area in line 46. Last, before the actual selection process begins, SHOW the POPUP menu GETFIELD (line 47).

Lines 49 through 56 transfer dBASE IV's attention to the pop-up menu (line 50) and check to see if no selections were made from the menu (lines 52 through 54). EXIT the DO WHILE...ENDDO loop if the BAR( ) function returns a 0 value because 0 indicates no selections were made (line 53). Otherwise, continue to transfer attention to the pop-up menu until no more selections are made.

At this point, you have to remember what line 41 told dBASE IV to do. It said, "When a selection is made on the GETFIELD pop-up menu, transfer control to the SETFIELD routine." We will look at the SETFIELD.PRG file in a moment, but first let's finish FIELDMSK.PRG.

Lines 58 through 60 are merely a way out of the program if no fields are entered. One exit from the program was given earlier. This block is merely a second method of exiting from the program. If you don't select any fields to mask, this program assumes you really don't want to do anything. Magnanimous, don't you think?

Line 62 clears the previously entered MESSAGE. Line 63 CLEARs the screen. Lines 64 through 71 determine if the user wants to go directly to entering data or simply quit from the program. These lines behave identically to lines 20 through 26. The only difference is that you don't need a RETURN command. dBASE IV will automatically return control from wherever it came because it has nowhere else to go; it has reached the end of the FIELDMSK.PRG file.

What is the trick advanced readers might have guessed? FIELDMSK.PRG doesn't need lines 8, 32, 33, or 38 to work. Delete those lines and rewrite line 37 as

```
DEFINE BAR RECNO() OF GETFIELD PROMPT FIELD_NAME
```

This line makes direct use of the database during the SCAN...ENDSCAN process—and much more elegantly than did the previous code. The record number, RECNO( ), is used to define each line on the pop-up menu, and the data in the Field_Name field is used to create the pop-up menu PROMPTs.

Now we look at SETFIELD.PRG, listing 7-6.

Listing 7-6

```
00001 : ** SETFIELD.PRG
00002 : * THIS PROGRAM GETS FIELDNAMES FROM FIELDMSK.PRG AND BUILDS A
00003 : * LIST OF FIELDS TO MASK
00004 : *
00005 :    PARAMETER BAR
00006 : *
00007 :    IF BAR # 0
00008 :        FIELDNAMES = FIELDNAMES + [ ] + FIELD(BAR)
00009 :    ENDIF
00010 : *
00011 : ** EOP: SETFIELD.PRG
```

SETFIELD.PRG starts with four lines of comments. The first executable command is line 5, PARAMETER BAR. This isn't a truly necessary command, and more advanced users might be able to determine why. An explanation comes later.

Line 5 is necessary in the code's present form because FIELD-MSK.PRG's line 41 specifically sends the value of the BAR( ) function to SETFIELD.PRG. SETFIELD.PRG will be looking for this information and needs someplace specific to store it. That specific storage spot is the variable BAR; the PARAMETER command does the looking.

Lines 7 through 9 do the actual work of SETFIELD.PRG. If the BAR( ) function sends a nonzero value to SETFIELD, BAR is nonzero. This means a field was selected from the GETFIELD pop-up menu and we need to place the name of the selected field into the FIELDNAMES variable. That is done in line 8, where the current value of FIELDNAMES has a blank space added to it followed by the name of the FIELD( ), based on the line selected on the GETFIELD menu.

The field name is added to FIELDNAMES with the FIELD( ) function. Remember that we already made our original database current back in FIELDMSK.PRG's line 46 but didn't activate the pop-up menu until line 50. We got the selected line on the pop-up menu with the BAR( ) function. BAR( ) is actually telling us which field was selected, because the fields are listed on the pop-up menu in the same order they appear in the database. Therefore, FIELD( ) can use the BAR value to determine which field is being selected in the database for masking.

How can you make the code a little cleaner? You can rewrite FIELDMSK.PRG's line 41 as

```
ON SELECTION POPUP GETFIELD DO SETFIELD
```

This eliminates the need to contain a PARAMETER command in SETFIELD.PRG because nothing is specifically being passed to that routine. You don't have to specifically pass anything to SETFIELD.PRG because any variables created in program A are available to program B unless you tell dBASE IV otherwise. In other words, information from A can be used by B can be used by C and so on unless you tell dBASE IV not to do such. However, information created in B won't be available to A, but will be available to C, D, and so on. Likewise, information created in C won't be available to A or B, but will be available to D, E, and so on. This applies only to newly generated information, not to information that already existed in the calling program and is updated in the called program.

Thus, we don't have to pass any specific information to SETFIELD.PRG. This means you can delete line 5 and replace each occurrence of BAR with BAR( ). SETFIELD.PRG will still work perfectly.

Next we look at GETDATA.PRG, listing 7-7.

Listing 7-7

```
00001 : ** GETDATA.PRG
00002 : *   THIS PROGRAM GETS DATA INTO A DATABASE WITH MASKED FIELDS
00003 : *
00004 : DO CASE
00005 :   CASE TYPE([FIELDNAMES]) = "U" .AND. .NOT.;
        FILE([FIELDMSK.MEM])
00006 :       FIELDNAMES = [ ]
00007 :   CASE TYPE([FIELDNAMES]) = "U"
00008 :       RESTORE FROM FIELDMSK
00009 : ENDCASE
00010 : *
00011 : SET PROCEDURE TO EXPROC.PRG
00012 : TRUTH = .T.
00013 : DO GETSTATS
00014 : DO EXERSAY
00015 : *
00016 : DO WHILE TRUTH
00017 :   APPEND BLANK
00018 :   DO EXERGET
00019 :   READ
00020 :   @ 0,0 SAY [ADD ANOTHER RECORD (Y/N)? -> ] GET TRUTH
00021 :   READ
00022 :   @ 0,0 SAY SPACE(40)
00023 : ENDDO
00024 : *
00025 : CLEAR
00026 : DO SETSTATS
00027 : RELEASE WINDOWS Wndow1
00028 : RELEASE lc_carry,lc_talk,lc_fields,lc_status
00029 : *
00030 : ** END OF GETDATA.PRG
```

GETDATA.PRG is EXEREDIT.PRG with some minor changes. The first change is in lines 4 through 9. We need to see if GETDATA.PRG is being called from FIELDMSK.PRG or being started on its own. How can we tell? If dBASE IV thinks FIELDNAMES are unknown (U), GETDATA.PRG was started on its own. How come? If GETDATA.PRG was called from FIELDMSK.PRG, FIELDMSK.PRG would have passed the FIELDNAMES variable to GETDATA.PRG. Line 5 checks to see if both FIELDNAMES are unknown and no FIELDMSK.MEM file exists on the disk. We check for the FIELDMSK.MEM file because we stored FIELDNAMES information to that file back in FIELDMSK.PRG. Therefore, even if GETDATA.PRG is being started on its own, it can retrieve the necessary field-masking data.

What if dBASE IV doesn't know about FIELDNAMES but FIELDMSK.MEM does exist? Then go get it on line 8.

How come there is no case for dBASE IV specifically knowing about FIELDNAMES? You don't need one. If dBASE IV knows about FIELDNAMES and GETDATA.PRG is running, GETDATA.PRG was called from FIELDMSK.PRG.

Line 11 is necessary just in case GETDATA.PRG is started on its own and the PROCEDURE file hasn't been SET by a calling program.

The next change from EXEREDIT.PRG is lines 16 through 22. We don't know if the first field in the database is masked, so we can't test to see if any information is being entered in that field. Instead, we have to specifically ask (lines 20 through 22) if more records will be added to the database. If so, go through the DO WHILE...ENDDO loop again. If not, exit it. Note that line 12 initializes TRUTH so that we go through the DO WHILE...ENDDO loop at least once.

Last, we take a look at changes to EXPROC.PRG, listing 7-8.

Listing 7-8

```
00001 : ** EXPROC.PRG PROCEDURE FILE FOR EXERCISE PROGRAM
00002 : *
00003 : PROCEDURE GETSTATS
00004 : PUBLIC lc_talk, lc_status, lc_carry
00005 : *
00006 : IF SET("TALK")="ON"
00007 :    SET TALK OFF
00008 :    lc_talk="ON"
00009 : ELSE
00010 :    lc_talk="OFF"
00011 : ENDIF
00012 : *
00013 : SET DISPLAY TO EGA25
00014 : *
00015 : lc_carry = SET("CARRY")
00016 : lc_status=SET("STATUS")
00017 : *
00018 : IF lc_status = "ON"
00019 :    SET STATUS OFF
00020 : ENDIF
00021 : *
00022 : *END OF PROCEDURE GETSTATS
00023 : *
```

```
00024 : PROCEDURE EXERSAY
00025 : CLEAR
00026 : SET COLOR OF MESSAGES TO r/w
00027 : DEFINE WINDOW Wndow1 FROM 8,41 TO 23,78
00028 : *
00029 : SET CARRY TO set_1_reps,set_2_reps,set_3_reps,set_4_reps;
00030 :   ,set_5_reps,set_6_reps ADDITIVE
00031 : @ 1,0 TO 24,79 DOUBLE
00032 : @ 2,31 SAY "EXERCISE DATA FORM"
00033 : @ 3,1 SAY "═══════════════════════════════════════
            ═══════════════════════"
00034 : @ 5,3 SAY "Exercise: "
00035 : @ 5,38 SAY "Date: "
00036 : @ 5,60 SAY "Time: "
00037 : @ 7,1 SAY "────────Repetitions and Weights────────────┐
            ─Comment────────────────"
00038 : @ 8,40 SAY "|"
00039 : @ 9,20 SAY "Set_1_Wgt: "
00040 : @ 9,3 SAY "Set_1_Reps: "
00041 : @ 9,40 SAY "|"
00042 : @ 10,40 SAY "|"
00043 : @ 11,3 SAY "Set_2_Reps: "
00044 : @ 11,20 SAY "Set_2_Wgt: "
00045 : @ 11,40 SAY "|"
00046 : @ 12,40 SAY "|"
00047 : @ 13,3 SAY "Set_3_Reps: "
00048 : @ 13,20 SAY "Set_3_Wgt: "
00049 : @ 13,40 SAY "|"
00050 : @ 14,40 SAY "|"
00051 : @ 15,3 SAY "Set_4_Reps: "
00052 : @ 15,20 SAY "Set_4_Wgt: "
00053 : @ 15,40 SAY "|"
00054 : @ 16,40 SAY "|"
00055 : @ 17,3 SAY "Set_5_Reps: "
00056 : @ 17,20 SAY "Set_5_Wgt: "
00057 : @ 17,40 SAY "|"
00058 : @ 18,40 SAY "|"
00059 : @ 19,3 SAY "Set_6_Reps: "
00060 : @ 19,20 SAY "Set_6_Wgt: "
00061 : @ 19,40 SAY "|"
00062 : @ 20,40 SAY "|"
00063 : @ 21,10 SAY "TOTAL_WGT: "
00064 : @ 21,40 SAY "|"
00065 : @ 22,40 SAY "|"
00066 : @ 23,40 SAY "|"
00067 : @ 24,40 SAY "±"
00068 : * END OF PROCEDURE EXERSAY
00069 : *
00070 : PROCEDURE EXERGET
00071 : @ 2,3 SAY IIF(DELETED(), CHR(6) + "RECORD DELETED" + CHR(6),
         SPAC(17))
```

Listing 7-8 (cont.)

```
00072 : @ 2,60 SAY "RECORD # " + STR(RECNO(),7)
00073 : *
00074 : IF [EXERCISE] $ FIELDNAMES
00075 :    @ 5,13 SAY exercise
00076 : ELSE
00077 : @ 5,13 GET exercise PICTURE "!!!!!!!!!!!!!!!!!!!!" ;
00078 :      MESSAGE "╚═══════════════════Enter the name of the exercise
         here═══════════════════╝"
00079 : ENDIF
00080 : *
00081 : IF [DATE] $ FIELDNAMES
00082 :    @ 5,44 SAY date
00083 : ELSE
00084 :    @ 5,44 GET date ;
00085 :         VALID DATE < DATE() + 1 ;
00086 :         ERROR "You can't enter data for future workouts!" ;
00087 :         DEFAULT {01/01/89} ;
00088 :         MESSAGE "╚═══════════════════Enter the date you
         exercised here═══════════════╝"
00089 : ENDIF
00090 : *
00091 : IF [TIME] $ FIELDNAMES
00092 :    @ 5,66 SAY time
00093 : ELSE
00094 :    @ 5,66 GET time PICTURE "99:99" ;
00095 :         DEFAULT "00:00" ;
00096 :         MESSAGE "╚═══════════════════Enter your workout starting
         time here═══════════════╝"
00097 : ENDIF
00098 : *
00099 : IF [SET_1_REPS] $ FIELDNAMES
00100 :    @ 9,15 SAY set_1_reps
00101 : ELSE
00102 :    @ 9,15 GET set_1_reps PICTURE "@Z 999" ;
00103 :      DEFAULT 0 ;
00104 :      MESSAGE "╚═══Enter the number of repetitions you performed
         for your first set here═══╝"
00105 : ENDIF
00106 : *
00107 : IF [SET_1_WGT] $ FIELDNAMES
00108 :    @ 9,31 SAY set_1_wgt
00109 : ELSE
00110 :    @ 9,31 GET set_1_wgt PICTURE "@Z 9999" ;
00111 :      WHEN SET_1_REPS # 0 ;
00112 :      DEFAULT 0 ;
00113 :      MESSAGE "╚═══════════════Enter the amount of weight used for
         your first set here═══════════╝"
00114 : ENDIF
00115 : *
```

```
00116 : IF [SET_2_REPS] $ FIELDNAMES
00117 :    @ 11,15 SAY set_2_reps
00118 : ELSE
00119 :    @ 11,15 GET set_2_reps PICTURE "@Z 999" ;
00120 :         DEFAULT 0 ;
00121 :           MESSAGE "╚════Enter the number of repetitions you
         performed for your second set here════╝"
00122 : ENDIF
00123 : *
00124 : IF [SET_1_WGT] $ FIELDNAMES
00125 :    @ 11,31 SAY set_2_wgt
00126 : ELSE
00127 :    @ 11,31 GET set_2_wgt PICTURE "@Z 9999" ;
00128 :       WHEN SET_2_REPS # 0 ;
00129 :         DEFAULT 0 ;
00130 :           MESSAGE "╚════════Enter the amount of weight you used for
         your second set here════╝"
00131 : ENDIF
00132 : *
00133 : IF [SET_3_REPS] $ FIELDNAMES
00134 :    @ 13,15 SAY set_3_reps
00135 : ELSE
00136 :    @ 13,15 GET set_3_reps PICTURE "@Z 999" ;
00137 :         DEFAULT 0 ;
00138 :           MESSAGE "╚═══Enter the number of repetitions you performed
            for your third set here═════╝"
00139 : ENDIF
00140 : *
00141 : IF [SET_3_WGT] $ FIELDNAMES
00142 :    @ 13,31 SAY set_3_wgt
00143 : ELSE
00144 :    @ 13,31 GET set_3_wgt PICTURE "@Z 9999" ;
00145 :       WHEN SET_3_REPS # 0 ;
00146 :         DEFAULT 0 ;
00147 :           MESSAGE "╚════════════Enter the amount of weight used for
         your third set here═══════════╝"
00148 : ENDIF
00149 : *
00150 : IF [SET_4_REPS] $ FIELDNAMES
00151 :    @ 15,15 SAY set_4_reps
00152 : ELSE
00153 :    @ 15,15 GET set_4_reps PICTURE "@Z 999" ;
00154 :         DEFAULT 0 ;
00155 :           MESSAGE "╚═══Enter the number of repetitions you performed
            for your fourth set here════╝"
00156 : ENDIF
00157 : *
00158 : IF [SET_4_WGT] $ FIELDNAMES
00159 :    @ 15,31 SAY set_4_wgt
00160 : ELSE
00161 :    @ 15,31 GET set_4_wgt PICTURE "@Z 9999" ;
```

Listing 7-8 (cont.)

```
00162 :        WHEN SET_4_REPS # 0 ;
00163 :        DEFAULT 0 ;
00164 :        MESSAGE "└═══════Enter the amount of weight you used for
         your fourth set here═══════┘"
00165 : ENDIF
00166 : *
00167 : IF [SET_5_REPS] $ FIELDNAMES
00168 :    @ 17,15 SAY set_5_reps
00169 : ELSE
00170 :    @ 17,15 GET set_5_reps PICTURE "@Z 999" ;
00171 :        DEFAULT 0 ;
00172 :        MESSAGE "└═══Enter the number of repetitions you performed
          for your fifth set here═══════┘"
00173 : ENDIF
00174 : *
00175 : IF [SET_5_WGT] $ FIELDNAMES
00176 :    @ 17,31 SAY set_5_wgt
00177 : ELSE
00178 :    @ 17,31 GET set_5_wgt PICTURE "@Z 9999" ;
00179 :        WHEN SET_5_REPS # 0 ;
00180 :        DEFAULT 0 ;
00181 :        MESSAGE "└═══════Enter the amount of weight you used for
         your fifth set here═══════┘"
00182 : ENDIF
00183 : *
00184 : IF [SET_6_REPS] $ FIELDNAMES
00185 :    @ 19,15 SAY set_6_reps
00186 : ELSE
00187 :    @ 19,15 GET set_6_reps PICTURE "@Z 999" ;
00188 :        DEFAULT 0 ;
00189 :        MESSAGE "└═══Enter the number of repetitions you performed
          for your sixth set here═══════┘"
00190 : ENDIF
00191 : *
00192 : IF [SET_1_WGT] $ FIELDNAMES
00193 :    @ 19,31 SAY set_6_wgt
00194 : ELSE
00195 :    @ 19,31 GET set_6_wgt PICTURE "@Z 9999" ;
00196 :        WHEN SET_6_REPS # 0 ;
00197 :        DEFAULT 0 ;
00198 :        MESSAGE "└═══════Enter the amount of weight used for
         your sixth set here═══════┘"
00199 : ENDIF
00200 : *
00201 : READ
00202 : REPLACE TOTAL_WGT WITH SET_1_REPS*SET_1_WGT + SET_2_REPS*SET_2_
         WGT +;
00203 :    SET_3_REPS*SET_3_WGT + SET_4_REPS*SET_4_WGT + SET_5_REPS*SET_
         5_WGT + SET_6_REPS*SET_6_WGT
```

```
00204 : @ 21,21 SAY total_wgt PICTURE "@Z 99999"
00205 : *
00206 : IF [COMMENT] $ FIELDNAMES
00207 :    @ 8,41 GET comment OPEN WINDOW Wndow1
00208 :    CLEAR GETS
00209 : ELSE
00210 :    @ 8,41 GET comment OPEN WINDOW Wndow1 ;
00211 :       MESSAGE "└═══════════════Enter any comments about this
          exercise or set here═══════════┘"
00212 : ENDIF
00213 : *
00214 : * END OF PROCEDURE EXERGET
00215 : *
00216 : PROCEDURE SETSTATS
00217 : *
00218 : IF lc_status = "ON"  && Entered form with status on
00219 :    SET STATUS ON     && Turn STATUS "ON" on the way out
00220 : ENDIF
00221 : *
00222 : IF lc_carry = "OFF"
00223 :    SET CARRY OFF
00224 : ENDIF
00225 : *
00226 : IF lc_talk="ON"
00227 :    SET TALK ON
00228 : ENDIF
00229 : *
00230 : * END OF PROCEDURE SETSTATS
00231 : ** END OF PROCEDURE FILE
```

The big change to EXPROC.PRG is the IF...ELSE...ENDIF test placed around each @ GET field command in PROCEDURE EXERGET. We test to see if each field is listed in FIELDNAMES. If a particular field is listed, just SAY whatever information is in the file. If a particular field isn't listed, perform the normal GET. The function that does this is $. The function takes the form "A $ B" and returns a logical True or False. $ returns True if expression A can be found in expression B and False if expression A can't be found in B.

The fact that the $ function tests for the existence of one expression in another is why we placed a blank space in FIELDNAMES before we added new field names to it. Suppose expression A is [TODAY] and expression B is [TO DAY]. A$B returns False, which is correct thanks to the space between TO and DAY. What if expression B contains the two words TO and DAY but no space? A$B would return True, which is incorrect. Note that this recoding of EXPROC.PRG means it needs to know what FIELDNAMES is before EXERGET can be called by another routine. An undefined FIELDNAMES would cause dBASE IV to give you an error, as shown in figure 7-21.

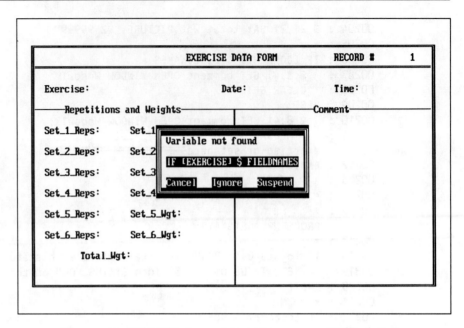

Figure 7-21 dBASE IV gives you an error message if it can't find a
necessary variable when programs are executed.

Summary

We are making lots of headway here. You have learned how to design and
modify a database, how to design and modify data entry forms, and how to
input, edit, and program data entry systems. The next chapter follows this
logical progression of database management system use by showing how to
get information from the database in useful forms.

Reporting Your Data

Do you have any idea of how far you have come in so short a time? You have learned how to design and modify a database, how to design and modify screen forms, and how to input and edit data in the database.

You have covered the first three things necessary to database management system work. The next thing you have to learn is how to report what is in the database to yourself and others.

Why do we need to create reports?

Reports are the method of getting more power from the database than even the most gifted analysts could perform from simply looking at the data. Do you remember hearing that a picture is worth a thousand words? Reports are the pictures and the database is the thousand words. Reports are where we learn to make comparisons and investigate patterns which would otherwise not be obvious to us. Have you heard about something being intuitively obvious to the casual observer? Reports are where we make things intuitively obvious.

This chapter starts by showing how reports are designed. From there it shows how to design labels. Label forms can be thought of as highly specialized reports. The last section demonstrates a programmatic method of getting a quick report out of dBASE IV.

Designing Report Forms

A correctly laid out report is the surest way to determine how your data is shaping up, the location of erroneous data, and what corrections need to be made to your system as a whole.

What are reports and why would you want to use them? Reports are a means of collecting and ordering your data, performing specialized work with the data, and quickly seeing if what you thought happened is what really happened. For example, as I write this book it is close to IRS megadeath time. How can I handle that? I can print a report form of last year's expenses broken down by what each taxable expense was for, as shown in the following:

EXPENSES LISTED BY WHAT FOR

TO	CHECK NUMBER	DATE	AMOUNT
** FOR -> Books			
B. Dalton Bookseller	cash	02/20/88	13.45
B. Dalton Bookseller	cash	02/06/88	13.97
Book Store	cash	04/10/88	3.95
Book Store	cash	02/29/88	14.95
Book Store	cash	02/13/88	25.90
Booksmith	cash	02/13/88	29.95
Citibank Visa	1962	05/16/88	86.54
Diane Deschenes	2224	12/16/88	7.75
Library of Science	2061	08/15/88	31.42
Library of Science	2093	09/06/88	53.33
Macmillan Book Club	1915	04/16/88	26.42
Macmillan Book Club	1974	05/24/88	55.19
Macmillan Book Club	1977	05/31/88	117.10
Macmillan Book Club	1854	02/23/88	7.84
MasterCard	1852	02/20/88	36.65
Paperback BookSmith	cash	04/10/88	3.96
Provident Visa	2042	07/28/88	30.20
Quality Paperback Book Club	1961	05/16/88	11.73
Quality Paperback Book Club	1858	02/24/88	15.92
Quality Paperback Book Club	1887	03/20/88	51.37
Quality Paperback Book Club	1920	04/16/88	9.58
Quality Paperback Book Club	2062	08/15/88	20.17
Quality Paperback Book Club	2098	09/10/88	18.99
Quality Paperback Book Club	2147	10/24/88	22.39
Quality Paperback Book Club	2164	11/04/88	98.00
Quality Paperback Book Club	2202	01/12/88	85.41
Quality Paperback Book Club	2224	12/16/88	7.75
Science Fiction Book Club	1936	04/29/88	96.20
Science Fiction Book Club	1892	01/28/88	43.45
Science Fiction Book Club	2096	09/10/88	15.19
Science Fiction Book Club	2166	11/05/88	19.07
Scientific American Library	1825	01/25/88	28.26
Scientific American Library	1986	06/13/88	28.26
Scientific American Library	2005	06/27/88	79.08
Scientific American Library	2046	07/29/88	28.26
Scientific American Library	2128	10/05/88	28.26
The Library Of Science	2141	10/18/88	117.53
Time Life Books	1819	01/20/88	17.97
Time Life Books	1830	02/01/88	17.39
Time Life Books	1885	03/18/88	17.97
Time Life Books	1921	04/16/88	17.97
Time Life Books	2022	07/10/88	18.22
WDBC	2080	08/26/88	29.35
WDBC	2104	09/14/88	18.35
WDBC	2220	12/12/88	17.50

```
Writer's Digest Book Club    1810    01/18/88      16.85
Writer's Digest Book Club    1971    05/20/88      15.95
** Subtotal **

                                                 1570.96


** FOR -> Charitable Contribution
Appalachian Projects         cash    06/05/88      10.00
Appalachian Projects         cash    09/24/88       5.00
Child & Family Services      1999    06/17/88      30.00
WBUR Radio Station                   03/08/88     120.00
WBUR Radio Station                   03/03/88     200.00
WENH Channel 11              2041    07/26/88     240.00
WGBH                        1912    11/04/88     500.00
** Subtotal **

                                                 1105.00


** FOR -> Cleaning
Peggy Hormy                 2180    11/15/88      60.00
Peggy Hormy                 2197    11/29/88      60.00
Peggy Hormy                 2217    12/12/88      60.00
Peggy Hormy                 2249    01/10/89      30.00
Peggy Hormy                 2242    01/03/89      60.00
** Subtotal **

                                                  270.00


** FOR -> Coffee
Provident Visa              1976    05/31/88      38.99
Provident Visa              2003    06/26/88      41.99
** Subtotal **

                                                   80.98
```

All nice and neat and ready to enter on my tax forms. Yes, this information had been entered as the year went on, but correlating it as shown definitely makes filling out IRS forms easier. And this is a III Plus report! Imagine how much more elegant a dBASE IV report would be!

Designing the Report

Broken record time. Sketch your report on paper before you start laying it out on the computer. This is what I have said regarding the database itself, the indexing system, the screen form, just about everything regarding your database management system. I say it again here.

Design your report form on paper before you put the report form in the computer.

Our example reports some information in the EXERCISE database. We want two reports. One is an exercise by date report. This tells us how our weight training is progressing. The other is a date by exercise report.

This tells us how our exercise regimen is progressing. Although lots of other reports can be pulled from the data, these two are simple, elegant, and display much of what you need to create a wider variety of custom reports in dBASE IV.

Start by laying out your report as explained here. The first concept you need to work with is the dBASE IV report *band* concept.

Bands are not new, although some of the terminology may be oblique to you. Think of the dBASE IV report form as a book. The book has a cover with some catchy phrases on it. These catchy phrases are designed to get you to part with some money. (The publishers don't care if you read the book; they just want you to buy it.) Inside the cover are a few pages of quotes from other people who read the book or an excerpt of the book. Again, these are intended to tease you or tickle you into spending some money for the book. After you get past the insignificant, you get to the part of the book that you can read and learn from, profit by, enjoy. You finish the book and there are some notes on the author, maybe a bibliography, perhaps a glossary—some text to wind up and explain what you read or why you read it.

Think of these different facets of a book as bands and you have a good handle on how dBASE IV report form bands work. The Page Header band (figure 8-16) contains the name of the report, perhaps your name, perhaps page numbers, basically whatever information you want gently and quietly repeated to people as they read the report. Much of what is available on the dBASE IV report form design system was discussed when we laid out our screen form in chapter 6. Here, we design a report to help us see how our exercises are going.

Our exercise by date report will have a header that contains a brief title of the report, our name (so everyone knows who to either blame or applaud), the page number, and the date of the report. This header should be repeated on each page of the report.

Next, we want a brief introductory statement explaining what the report is about. The report will be broken down by exercise by date. We want the Set_n information after that. Next should come some closing comments. We could place some information at the bottom of each page, but this is not necessary.

With this as a guide, the report should look like the following:

```
                                        Exercise by Date
                                    Carrabis, Page - #
                                        <report date>

Introductory material

<A paragraph or two of verbiage for those who need it. This is
    the cover page. The actual data starts on a new page.>

<Name of exercises, according to index>
        Date      Set_1_Reps    Set_2_Reps   ...   Set_6_Reps
```

```
          Set_1_Wgt     Set_2_Wgt     ...     Set_6_Wgt
     Total_Wgt
```

```
<The above italicized block is repeated for each exercise. Note
that the words are not entered in italicized print; the italics
merely indicate which block is repeated for each exercise.>
```

```
<A new page containing the closing comments of the report.>
```

This is what the exercise by date report should look like. Next, we lay out the date by exercise report. Much of what we did in the previous report can be directly carried into this exercise by date report.

```
                              Date by Exercise
                              Carrabis, Page - #
                                 <report date>
```

```
Introductory material
```

```
<A paragraph or two of verbiage for those who need it. This is
    the cover page. The actual data starts on a new page.>
```

```
<Date of exercises, according to index>
    Exercise            Total_Wgt
    Comment about exercises. (On new page if comment exists.)
```

```
<The above italicized block is repeated for each exercise. Note
that the words are not entered in italicized print; the italics
merely indicate which block is repeated for each exercise.>
```

```
<A new page containing the closing comments of the report.>
```

Very good. Our reports are designed. Now we must lay them out on the dBASE IV report form design system.

Laying Out the Report

There are two basic ways of getting into the report form design system (figure 8-1). The standard method for newcomers to dBASE IV is through the Assist system. You can also get to the report form design system with either the CREATE REPORT or MODIFY REPORT commands.

You have to place a database in USE before you can get into the report form design system, no matter which method you use. dBASE IV prompts for a database when you call the report form design system from the dBASE prompt or the Assist system.

Remember that you only want to place a database in USE. This means you can either use the USE database command from the dBASE prompt or select the *Use file* option on the Assist menu. Note that dBASE IV opens the

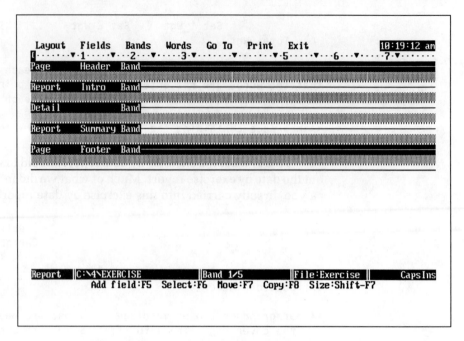

Figure 8-1 *The report form design system.*

report form design system with the Layout menu's *Quick layouts* option
highlighted. What is a quick layout?

There are three of them: Column, Form, and Mailmerge. What do
these three quick report forms offer? First we will look at the Column form.
The screen layout of the Column form is shown in figure 8-2. The EXER-
CISE database is used in all cases.

There is more information in the report than is shown on the screen.
You can scroll right, left, up, and down on the screen to show more of the
report form (figure 8-3).

The following listing is the quick layout report form. It is also an example that quick is not necessarily pretty.

```
Page No.    1
01/27/89

EXERCISE              DATE      TIME        SET_1_REPS   SET_1_WGT
SET_2_REPS   SET_2_WGT   SET_3_REPS   SET_3_WGT
SET_4_REPS   SET_4_WGT   SET_5_REPS   SET_5_WGT
SET_6_REPS   SET_6_WGT   TOTAL_WGT   COMMENT

BENCH PRESS           08/10/88                  10          45
0            0          0         0         0          0
0            0          0         0       450
INCLINE PRESS         08/10/88                  10          15
10          20          0         0         0          0
```

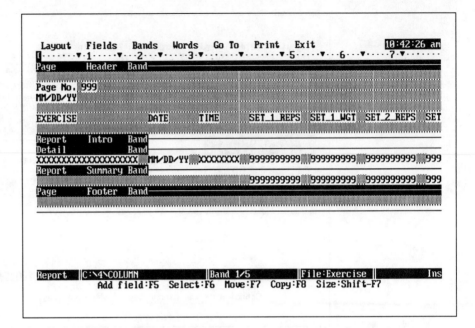

Figure 8-2 *This is how dBASE IV translates the request for a quick Column report form to an editable report screen form. The EXERCISE database is used in this example.*

0	0	0	0	350		
DB PRESS		08/10/88			10	15
0	0	0	0	0	0	
0	0	0	0	150		
WIDE GRIP CURLS		08/10/88			10	25
0	0	0	0	0	0	
0	0	0	0	250		
TRICEP PRESS		08/10/88			10	45
0	0	0	0	0	0	
0	0	0	0	450		
LYING EXTENSIONS		08/10/88			10	25
0	0	0	0	0	0	
0	0	0	0	250		
LEG CURLS		08/10/88			10	30
0	0	0	0	0	0	
0	0	0	0	300		
PULLDOWNS		08/10/88			10	55
0	0	0	0	0	0	
0	0	0	0	550		
BENCH PRESS		12/10/88	9:00		10	45
10	65	10	85	10	95	
10	65	10	45	4000		
INCLINE PRESS		12/10/88	9:00		10	15
10	20	10	25	10	25	
10	25	10	15	13		

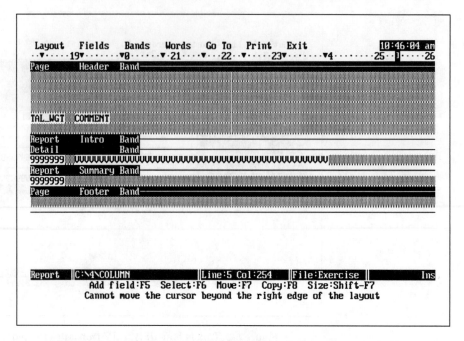

Figure 8-3 *Use the cursor control keys to move through any report or dBASE IV generated quick report. Because this report extends to 254 columns, it is not a very attractive report unless you use a special printer and special printer control codes and don't show it on the screen.*

DB PRESS		12/10/88	9:00	10	15
10	20	7	20	12	15
0	0	0	0	670	
PRESS OUTS		12/10/88	9:00	10	20
10	30	10	30	10	40
10	30	10	20	1700	
LEG EXTENSIONS		12/10/88	9:00	10	20
10	30	10	40	10	50
10	50	10	30	2200	
LEG PRESS		12/10/88	9:00	10	50
10	70	10	90	10	110
10	0	10	0	3200	
LEG CURLS		12/10/88	9:00	10	20
10	30	10	40	10	50
10	40	0	0	1800	
SEATED CALF RAISES		12/10/88	9:00	10	0
10	25	10	45	10	35
10	35	0	0	1400	
NECK PULLDOWN		12/10/88	9:00	10	40
10	55	10	70	10	85
10	100	10	55	4050	
SEATED ROWS		12/10/88	9:00	10	50
10	40	10	40	10	40

10	40	0	0	2100	
WIDE GRIP CURLS		12/10/88	9:00	10	25
10	45	10	45	10	45
10	45	10	25	2300	
				190	555
120	450	107	530	112	590
100	430	70	190	26183	

The Column and Form quick report formats are basically unformatted data dumps. They are good for quick information fixes, but you probably would not want to use them for door prizes at the board of directors meeting.

I have removed a good deal of dead space from this file. I told you it would look like a mess. Essentially, the Column quick report form provides the same output as a blind LIST command does. This is also the report form dBASE IV generates if you use the [Shift-F9] (Quick Report) option from the Assist menu. This keystroke combination works when any file except an application is highlighted, and it is also available in Browse and Edit modes.

The Form quick report, shown in figure 8-4, creates a report in which each record in the database is displayed in the Edit format. Each page of the report holds as many records as can neatly fit, which means records with more than 54 fields are divided across more than one page. An example of that output follows:

```
Page No.      1
01/27/89

EXERCISE      BENCH PRESS
DATE          08/10/88
TIME
SET_1_REPS    10
SET_1_WGT     45
SET_2_REPS    0
SET_2_WGT      0
SET_3_REPS    0
SET_3_WGT      0
SET_4_REPS    0
SET_4_WGT      0
SET_5_REPS    0
SET_5_WGT      0
SET_6_REPS    0
SET_6_WGT      0
TOTAL_WGT     450
COMMENT

EXERCISE      INCLINE PRESS
DATE          08/10/88
TIME
SET_1_REPS    10
SET_1_WGT     15
SET_2_REPS    10
SET_2_WGT     20
SET_3_REPS    0
SET_3_WGT      0
```

```
SET_4_REPS      0
SET_4_WGT       0
SET_5_REPS      0
SET_5_WGT       0
SET_6_REPS      0
SET_6_WGT       0
TOTAL_WGT       350
COMMENT

EXERCISE        DB PRESS
DATE            08/10/88
TIME
SET_1_REPS      10
SET_1_WGT       15
SET_2_REPS      0
SET_2_WGT       0
SET_3_REPS      0
SET_3_WGT       0
SET_4_REPS      0
SET_4_WGT       0
SET_5_REPS      0
SET_5_WGT       0
SET_6_REPS      0
SET_6_WGT       0
TOTAL_WGT       150
COMMENT
```

This report goes on for several pages, but that is unimportant. What is important is that the Form quick report layout produces this moderately useless report. If this were your interest, you could tell dBASE IV to print each record's Edit screen.

The last quick report form is Mailmerge (figure 8-5). This is a special report form intended as a template for boilerplate letters.

Yes, dBASE IV does a nice job of generating these simple report forms. But what is the cost? Each time you ask dBASE IV to create a report form, it creates an entire program around that report form. The report form used to start this section is a dBASE III Plus REPORT FORM, a special file that dBASE III Plus and not too many others understand. It appears in a directory as

```
EXPFOR    FRM      1990   13-03-88   11:26a
```

The dBASE III Plus REPORT FORM takes up 1990 bytes, a little less than 2K of disk space. Ask dBASE IV to use this form and the first thing it does is convert the III Plus FRM file into a dBASE IV FRG file. Is there a difference? The directory information on the dBASE IV files follows:

```
EXPFOR    FRG      6289   27-01-89   3:30p
EXPFOR    FRO      6660   27-01-89   3:30p
```

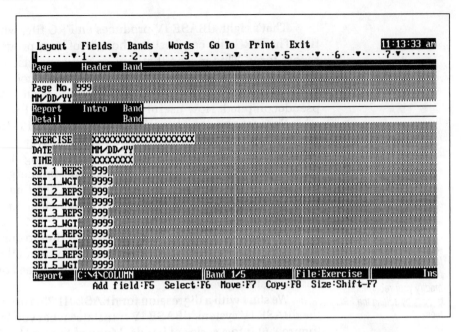

Figure 8-4 *The Form quick report layout screen. This report produces a listing similar to repeated Edit screens of each record in the database.*

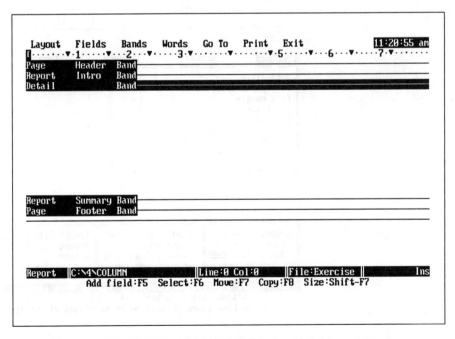

Figure 8-5 *The Mailmerge quick report form. No fields are placed on the design because the Mailmerge quick report form is intended as a template for boilerplate letters.*

That's right. dBASE IV produces an FRG file, which is an ASCII text file. This FRG file can best be thought of as a program that creates the report form. This means that you or someone else can edit, modify, or mung up the FRG file at will. dBASE IV also produces an FRO file, which is a report form object file. An object form file is an FRG file that has been pseudocompiled. How useful are these FRG and FRO files?

Because you don't have much control over FRO files, there is no point in discussing them. You have ultimate control over the FRG files, however, because that is where your eventual programming skill will come in quite handy. Remember the Column, Form, and Mailmerge reports? dBASE IV took the quick Column layout and created a 291 line FRG program file to generate that report. The Form quick layout came in at 256 lines of code, and Mailmerge was just short of midway with 269 lines of code. Whoosh!

After you are comfortable with dBASE IV commands, functions, and programming, you can modify your report forms directly by editing the FRG files.

But you can edit these dBASE IV FRG files to customize your reports even beyond what the report form design system allows. This is impressive. First we explore the design system, then we see how to tweak what the design system gives us.

We start with a digression for dBASE III Plus users making the shift to the dBASE IV system. dBASE IV translates what you knew as report forms (figure 8-6) into a series of bands. Many of the dBASE III Plus report form design system menu items are located on different and sometime difficult to find dBASE IV report form design system menus. The following explains the location of the old menu items.

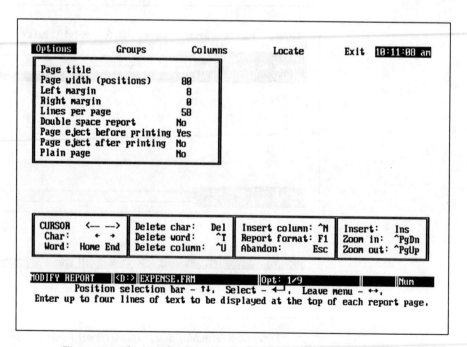

Figure 8-6 *The standard screen for a dBASE III Plus MODIFY or CREATE REPORT FORM command.*

dBASE III Plus **Options menu**	**dBASE IV**
Page title	Now located in either the Page Header band or the Report Intro band, depending on the setting of *Page heading in report intro* on the Bands menu (figure 8-7).
Page width	No longer necessary because dBASE IV lets you design forms up to 254 characters wide. You can also set the page width through the *Modify ruler* option in the Words menu.
Left margin	Located on Print Page dimensions menu as the *Offset from left* option (figure 8-8).
Right margin	No longer necessary because dBASE IV lets you design forms up to 254 characters wide. This can also be set through the *Modify ruler* option in the Words menu.
Lines per page	Replaced by Print Page dimensions *Length of page* option (figure 8-8).
Double space report	Replaced by Print Page dimensions *Spacing of lines* option (figure 8-8).

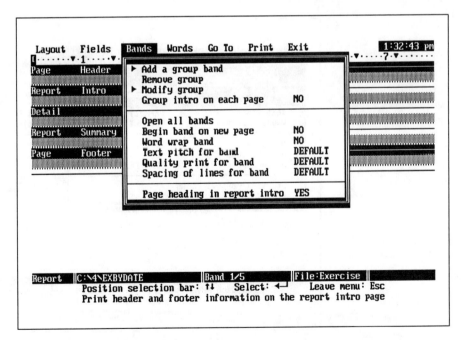

Figure 8-7 The dBASE IV report form design system's Bands Page heading in report intro *option takes the place of dBASE III Plus's* Options Page title *command.*

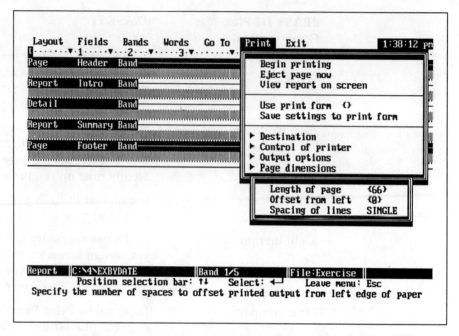

Figure 8-8 The dBASE III Plus Left margin report form *command*
has been replaced by dBASE IV's Print Page dimensions
Offset from left *option.*

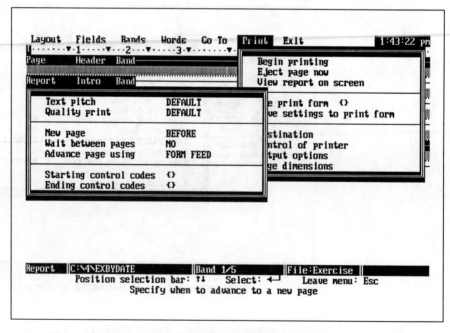

Figure 8-9 The dBASE III Plus Page eject before printing *command*
has been replaced by the dBASE IV Print Control of printer
New page BEFORE *command.*

dBASE III Plus	dBASE IV
Page eject before printing	Replaced by Print Control of printer *New page BEFORE* option (figure 8-9).
Page eject after printing	Replaced by Print Control of printer *New page AFTER* option. The Print Control of printer *New page* option toggles through *BEFORE, BOTH, NONE,* and *AFTER.* dBASE III Plus's *Page eject after printing* option is dBASE IV's *New page AFTER* option.
Plain page	Done by designing the report to be plain.

Groups menu

Group on expression	Done through the Bands menu.
Group heading	Now handled by a variety of Bands options.
Summary report only	Now handled by a variety of options available through the *Summary* options in the Fields Add field menu (figure 8-10).
Page eject after group	Replaced with Bands *Begin band on new page* option.
Subgroup on expression	Replaced with a variety of Bands menu options.
Subgroup heading	Replaced with a variety of Bands menu options.

Columns menu, Field menu options

Contents	Available through direct entry of column heading to report surface.
Heading	Available through direct entry of column heading to report surface.
Width	Available through the Picture function and Template options.
Decimal Places	Available through the Picture function and Template options.
Total this column	Now handled by a variety of options available through the *Summary* menu options in the Fields Add field menu.
Locate menu	Replaced with the Go To menu.
Exit menu	Exit menu.

Back to dBASE IV's report form bands. The report we will design uses the EXERCISE database. It also shows the majority of dBASE IV report form features.

With the cursor positioned in the Page Header band, type

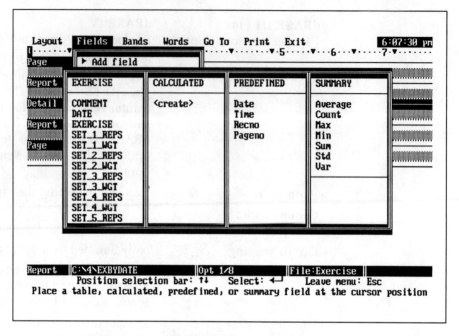

*Figure 8-10 Many of the dBASE III Plus Summary report abilities
are now available through the dBASE IV Fields Add field
Summary options.*

```
Exercise Progress Report [Enter] <your name>, Page -
```

Remember that [Enter] means to press the [Enter] key to place a new line on
the screen, and 〈your name〉 means to type in your name on the new line.
Next, press [Alt-F] *A* [Right-Arrow] [Right-Arrow] *P* [Enter]. This keystroke
sequence tells dBASE IV to open the Fields menu, open the Add field submenu, move to the Predefined fields column, then highlight and select the
Pageno (page number) predefined field. See figure 8-10. Note that these
predefined fields are how you place the system date, the system time, page
numbers, and record numbers onto the report forms.

These keystrokes will cause another menu to pop up. This menu (figure 8-11) is a modified Picture function and Template menu for this
predefined field.

Press [Ctrl-End] to tell dBASE IV that everything is okay with the
Pageno field. Now press [Enter] [F10] *A* [Right-Arrow] [Right-Arrow]
[Enter] [Ctrl-End]. This places the predefined Date field directly under your
name. By the way, you can toggle between Date, Time, Recno, and Pageno
on the modified Picture function and Template menu by pressing [Enter].
You can get to the Fields menu by pressing [F10] instead of [Alt-F] because
the [F10] (Menu) key always opens the last opened menu.

We have defined the information we want in our page header, but not
the location. We want it on the right of each page, not the left. Move the
cursor to the first of the three lines, on the *E* of *Exercise*, and press [F6].

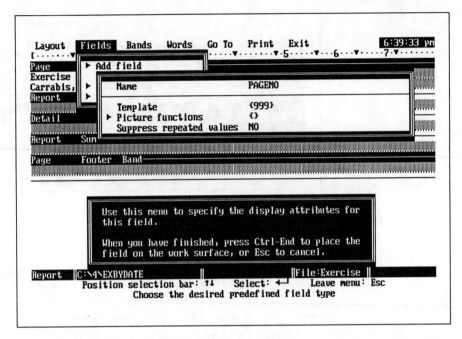

Figure 8-11 Predefined fields use a modified Picture function and Template menu to show these fields on the report form.

Press [End] [Down-Arrow] [Down-Arrow] [Enter]. You have blocked off the information in the page header. Now press [Alt-W] M to open the Words menu and select the *Modify ruler* option. The cursor goes to the ruler line of the report design system, directly below the top row of menu options. Move the cursor to column 65 and press [Enter]. This tells dBASE IV that the right margin of the report is at the 65th column. Now press [F10] P R. This tells dBASE IV to move the highlighted text to the right margin of the report. Slick.

Remember that your report should have a good appearance. You can generate the report once or twice to get an idea of how it looks, but then you should take the time to make it look good.

Remember that we want things to look good? Add a few blank lines under your Page Header band by pressing [Enter] a few times. This leaves some room between the page header we just defined and the text of the report, which we define next.

Move the cursor to the Report Intro band. This is where you place the opening lines of text that help explain your report: what readers are going to see, what they should be looking for, what your report does. As you move the cursor to the Report Intro band, notice that the report form design work surface changes slightly from figure 8-8 to figure 8-12. The bands no longer define the entire report form from Page Header band to Page Footer band. They now define the report form from Report Intro band to Report Summary band. Recognize that you are working through different levels of the report, just as if you were reading deeper into a book.

Place the cursor directly on the Report Intro band, not above nor below. Press [Alt-W] M to change the margins for this band. The left margin should be on column 0, which is fine. Make sure the right margin is on

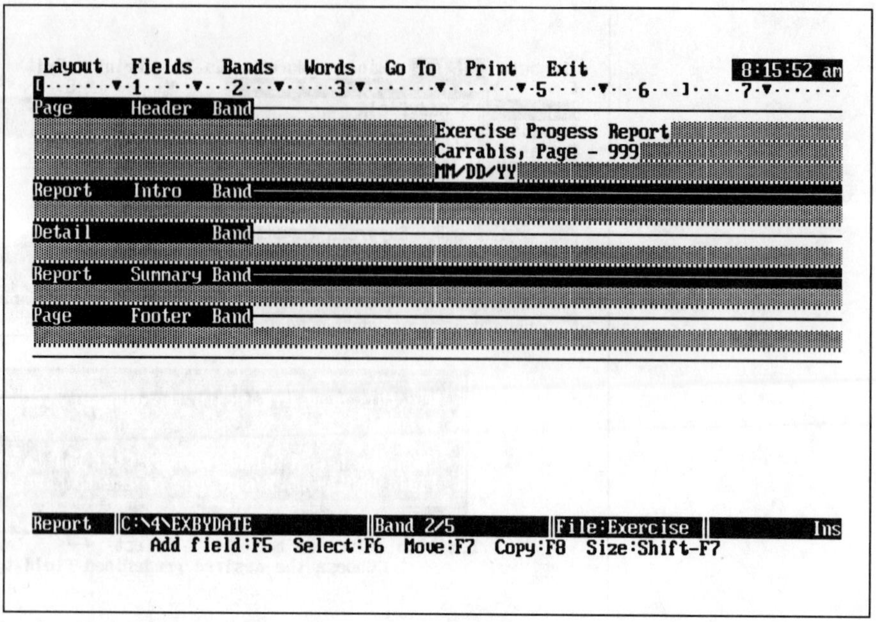

Figure 8-12 *The area of the report which is affected changes as you move the cursor deeper into the heart of the report. This figure shows the defined area of the report as Report Intro band to Report Summary band. Figure 8-8 shows the defined area of the report as Page Header band to Page Footer band.*

column 65. Press [Enter] to lock those margin settings into dBASE IV for this band. Now press [Alt-B] W to open the Bands menu and turn word wrap on for this band.

Move the cursor directly under the Report Intro band and type in a few lines of mirth and merriment. The following is what I typed in my report form Report Intro band:

```
This report is based on an exercise format designed by Denise
Dargie. The style of the workout and intensity are changed over
time, according to Ms. Dargie's instructions; therefore, this
report is broken down as Exercise by Date, listing repetitions
and weights. The goal of this report format is to show the
individual's progression over time.

Ms. Dargie is holder of several weight lifting and body building
titles in the Northeast and Eastern United States.
```

People who know me know I'm not going to type something in twice unless I really really really have to, and here I don't. I copied these paragraphs to a file, transferred the file to my dBASE IV system, then used the [Alt-W] W R (Words menu *Write/Read file Read* command) to copy the file directly into the Report Intro band. Nice.

Now is the time to save the work you have done so far. You don't have to save the unfinished file to disk, but there is a chance you will encounter memory problems somewhere along the way if you don't save the file periodically as you work. As a matter of fact, you might encounter memory problems simply trying to save the file at this point. Play it safe and press [Ctrl-End]. This saves the file without going through the menu system and sends you back whence you came, either the dBASE prompt, the Assist menu system, or some calling program. You might then want to copy the unfinished report form to a working file, for example, TEMP.FRM, with the command

```
COPY FILE original.FRM TO TEMP.FRM
```

Braver readers might want to try using the [Alt-L] S command on the dBASE IV report form design system. This command tells dBASE IV to open the Layout menu and save the report (figure 8-13). Save the report under a different file name.

I say this is the braver option because there is a chance that dBASE IV will lock up, argue with you, or simply not do what you ask it to do. The purpose of the [Alt-L] S command is to save the current file and continue working. This is not always what happens. As mentioned, some early ver-

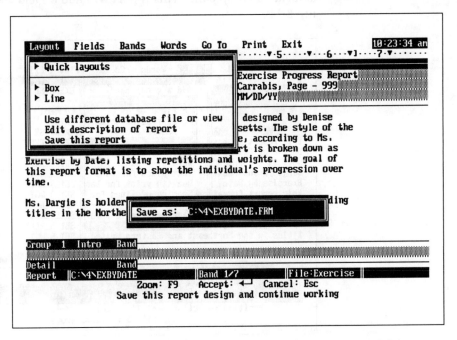

Figure 8-13 *You can use the [Alt-L] S command to save your work in progress on a report form file, but be aware that dBASE IV can experience memory management problems that might cause you to lose your file.*

sions of dBASE IV have severe memory management problems, and saving work in progress is where these necessary management problems most often show up. Be careful!

Now we must place the actual report information into the report. This is the part of dBASE IV report form design that is closest to dBASE III Plus report form design.

Now you must understand what a dBASE IV group is. A dBASE IV group is a chapter in a book. The dBASE IV REPORT FORM is a textbook, not a work of fiction (this depends on your data, of course). As a textbook, each chapter should be a self-contained unit. All information that belongs to a given group or group band should be located in that band. Don't leave items for summary bands or other bands unless you are sure that they don't belong in the current grouping.

Because the band is comprised of exercises broken down by date, we want to create groups based on exercises, and have information on date, sets, and so on within each of these groups. Where do we put the groups?

Contrary to most people's first thought, we don't put groups in the Detail band area. We must add the first one above the first Detail band. Then succeeding ones can be added below the first Detail band, and dBASE IV will expand the report form as necessary.

Place the cursor a few lines under your Report Intro paragraphs by pressing [Enter] once or twice. Now press [Alt-B] *A* to open the Bands menu and *Add a group band*. This report will add a *Field value*, EXERCISE (figure 8-14).

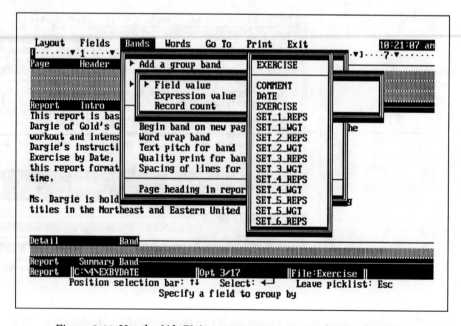

Figure 8-14 *Use the [Alt-B] A menu option to open the Bands menu and select the Add a group band option. The first group band goes directly under the information you enter into the Report Intro band.*

Move the cursor into the newly created band. This new band will be called *Group 1 Intro band*. This is where you enter any information that might help the reader understand the reason for this grouping. This report will have *Exercise ->* followed by the Exercise name. Type *Exercise ->*, enter a space, then press [F5] and the Fields menu appears on your screen. Select EXERCISE if you are working along with this example, or select the field you want for your own Machiavellian purposes. The Picture function and Template menu is shown next. This is identical to what we worked with in chapter 6 and won't be discussed here.

You can add most fields through the [F5] (Add Fields) key. When you want to access fields through the Fields menu, press [Alt-F]. The reasons for going through the Fields menu include modifying fields already on the report form and adding a hidden field.

A hidden field is a calculated field that is concealed from the user. Most often, the hidden field contains summary information, such as the average or total value for a given field. One reason this type of information may be hidden is the need to know the status of the individual who reads the report. Ollie North turned his hidden fields off when he sent his report to Congress, but turned them on when he sent the reports to Secourt. Obviously, Secourt needed to know but Congress didn't. Leave it to Obfuscating Ollie to anticipate some dBASE IV features in pre-release.

Take a moment to save the file using any method you choose; just remember the memory management problems dBASE IV sometimes has. Also at this time, you might want to see how your report is taking shape. This might be necessary because you are new to the report form design system or simply to make sure what you are creating is what you want.

It is a good idea to view your report periodically during the design phase.

Use [Alt-P] V to view the report on the screen. This will give you an idea if the report is coming out the way you intended. You will notice that dBASE IV stops the display from scrolling when the screen fills with report information. You can continue to view the report by typing a space, or you can go back to the report form design system by pressing [Esc].

Another slight digression might be necessary here. This [Alt-P] V technique to quickly view the report in progress is nice, but can be time consuming when you are creating a long and involved report form. When all you want to see is how one band is shaping up, close the other bands by positioning the cursor on the actual band line—not the contents of a band—and pressing [Enter]. dBASE IV alternately closes and opens the band for viewing (figure 8-15). Any closed bands won't appear during output. You can open all the bands when you are ready to view or print the finished report with [Alt-B] O (Bands menu *Open all bands* option).

Next we put our Detail band in place. The Detail band contains the actual fields we want to report from the database. Our Detail band for this report contains the Date and Set_n fields from the EXERCISE database.

Place the cursor in column 0, directly beneath the Detail band line, and press [F5] to call up the Fields menu. Press D to select the Date field, then [Ctrl-End] to accept the dBASE IV default Picture function and Template settings. Press [Tab] [F5] to move to the first tab setting and call up the

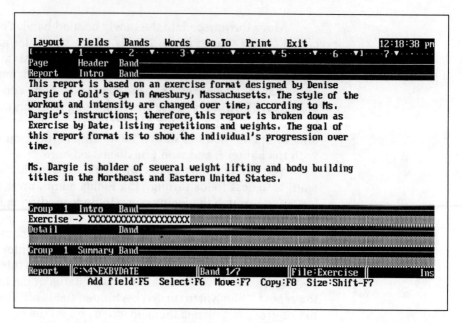

Figure 8-15 *You can stop dBASE IV's report form design system's [Alt-P] V command from displaying certain bands by placing the cursor on the band's name line and pressing [Enter]. This closes the band from viewing, printing, and so on. This figure shows the Page Header band closed.*

Fields menu again. Now highlight Set_1_Reps and press [Enter] [Ctrl-End] to place the default Sct_1_Reps settings on the report. Repeat this procedure until the six Set_n_Reps are located at the remaining tab settings.

Now press [Enter] to open a new line on the Detail band and press [Tab] [Tab] to position the cursor under the Set_1_Reps entry. Press [Backspace] [F5] and highlight the Set_1_Wgt field. Press [Enter] [Ctrl-End] and the Set_1_Wgt field is entered on the report form. Why do we go to the tab position of the Set_n_Reps field, then back up one space? The Set_n_Wgt fields are one digit longer than their Set_n_Reps counterparts. Because we want the fields to be right justified, not left justified, we must make sure the ends of each field pair are aligned on the report. Repeat this until all the Set_n_Wgt fields are under their respective Set_n_Reps fields. Press [Enter] a few times to place some space between this date's information and the next date's data. Readers following my examples should have a screen that looks like figure 8-16.

It is time to both save the report's present form (under a different file name) and view our work in progress. Press [Alt-L] S and give the file some name according to our previous examples, and remember the caveats about dBASE IV'S memory management problems! Now press [Alt-P] V to see what your handiwork looks like on the screen (figure 8-17).

Not too bad, don't you think? This report goes a lot further than what

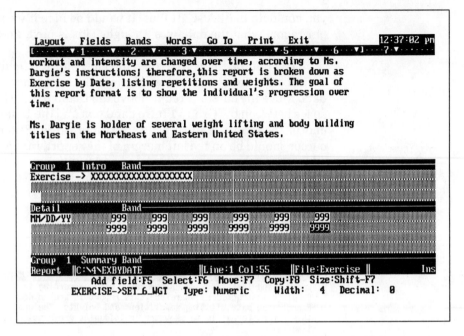

Figure 8-16 This figure shows how to lay out database fields for a
multiple-line listing report.

	45	0	0	0	0	0
12/18/88	10	10	10	10	10	10
	45	65	85	95	65	45
Exercise -> DB PRESS						
08/18/88	10	0	0	0	0	0
	15	0	0	0	0	0
12/18/88	10	10	7	12	0	0
	15	20	20	15	0	0
Exercise -> INCLINE PRESS						
08/18/88	10	10	0	0	0	0

Cancel viewing: ESC, Continue viewing: SPACEBAR

Figure 8-17 This figure shows how the report designed
in figure 8-16 looks.

you could do in dBASE III Plus. It would be nice if we told people reading our report what the data was, though. This is next, and it is an important part of laying out a report.

Lay out the fields first, then the labels for the fields. It is much easier to find out where your data will be located, then place your labels near the data. Move the cursor directly above the Detail band. If you don't have any space between the Group 1 Intro band text and the Detail band, move to the end of the Group 1 Intro band's text and press [Enter] three times. The cursor should be on the left margin of the report, in the Group 1 Intro band space. Keep the cursor in this band and position it above the middle of the first field located in the Detail band. Type in the field name or something else that explains the field contents to your readers. Our example uses *Date* above the Date field (figure 8-18).

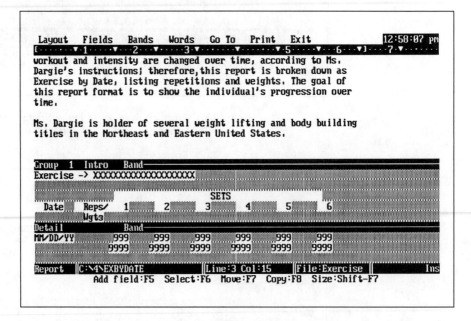

Figure 8-18 One way to lay out labels for a multiple-line listing report.

We also place other text in the Group 1 Intro band, as shown in figure 8-16. The dBASE IV report form design system lets you do lots of things with text. For example, we can add an underline from 1 to 6 beneath SETS. Remember, you are not entering field information here, you are entering text. Everything you enter is a label and can be keyed in directly. You can look at the report again with the [Alt-P] V command (figure 8-19).

Now it is time to be creative and go beyond our original design. This example's report is modified slightly by going back to the Detail band and adding *Total_Wgt ->* as text, typing a space, then pressing [F5], highlighting the Total_Wgt field, and pressing [Enter] [Ctrl-End]. The Total_Wgt field is also aligned with the first set of Set_n fields, as shown in figure

8-20, and a few blank lines are added under it to separate this entry from the next one when the report is printed out.

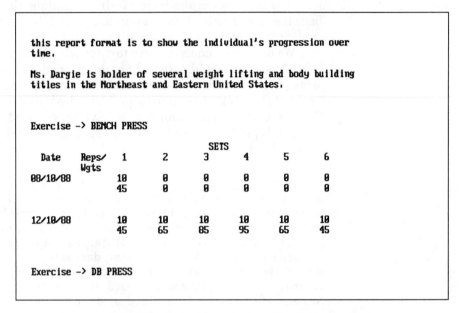

Figure 8-19 *How the report designed in figure 8-18 looks.*

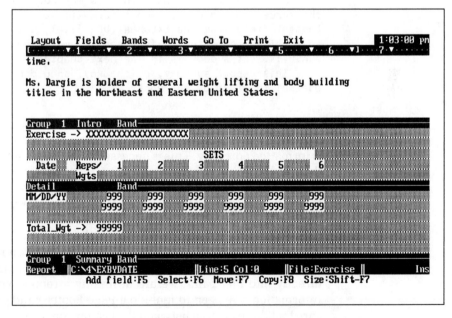

Figure 8-20 *After the necessary data and labels are laid out on the report form, you can be creative. This form includes the Total_Wgt field, which is informative but not part of our original design.*

When you add a group band, you automatically add a group summary band. You can choose to add information here—fields, or text, or both—as you wish. Because this report doesn't require any group summary information, it is time to use the band closing technique described previously. Place the cursor on the Group 1 Summary band line and press [Enter]. The band closes and won't show up on reports.

We do want some summary text for the report as a whole, however, and that is entered in the Report Summary band. Remember that this will be text, not data, and the margins should be set and word wrap should be on for this band. Both operations were described previously in this section. The text for the report summary, which follows, is entered into the report with [Alt-W] *W R filename* (Words menu *Write/Read file Read filename* option).

Designing and laying out a report form can show previously unnoticed flaws in the logic and flow of a database system. Designing this report shows that we rarely use the Comment field, but we do know that field is useful.

It would be useful to separate the EXERCISE database into two separate databases. The first database, called EXERCISE, should include the Date, Time, and Set_n fields. The second database, called EXCOMMNT, should include the Date, Time, and Comment fields. The Time field might prove unnecessary in both cases, but we can keep it for now. The Date field is necessary as a way to link the two databases.

Modifying the database in this way would mean reworking the screen form and the report form (if we want to include the Comment field from the EXCOMMNT.DBF file), but would also provide an excellent opportunity for learning more about the workings of dBASE IV. Let's do this in the next chapter.

This report summary, by the way, should be considered as part of the text of the book.

Whenever you use the [Alt-W] *W R filename* command to pull text into a report form—or any work surface—cursor through the text to make sure it is formatted correctly. This is necessary even if you set the margins and use the word wrap commands. Forcing correct alignment is not difficult, but it can be tedious. Use the [F6] (Select) key to highlight either all the entered text or the part of the text that did not format properly, then use the margin setting and word wrap commands on the selected text.

Back to the report. We don't need the Page Footer band, do we? After all, we are not going to put any information in that band, are we? You lose if you say no, we don't need it. Even though we won't place any text or data directly into that band, we are designing a report with several pages of information. We need to include a Page Footer band of blank space to insure that there is room between the last text on a page and the physical end of the page. Just press [Enter] a few times in that band and you are done.

You tell dBASE IV the report is completed by pressing [Alt-E] S for the

Exit menu *Save* option. Remember that you can also try [Ctrl-End], [Ctrl-Enter], and [Ctrl-W] if you get memory problems. A last resort might be trying [Alt-L] S. This saves the file image (what dBASE III Plus people remember as the actual report FRM file) to disk, if possible. This FRM file can be compiled into FRG and FRO files later, as necessary.

What does the finished report look like? Like the following:

```
                                      Exercise Progress Report
                                      Carrabis, Page -   1
                                      02/01/89
```

This report is based on an exercise format designed by Denise Dargie. The style of the workout and intensity are changed over time, according to Ms. Dargie's instructions; therefore, this report is broken down as Exercise by Date, listing repetitions and weights. The goal of this report format is to show the individual's progression over time.

Ms. Dargie is holder of several weight lifting and body building titles in the Northeast and Eastern United States.

Exercise -> BENCH PRESS

				SETS			
Date	Reps/ Wgts	1	2	3	4	5	6
10/08/88		10	0	0	0	0	0
		45	0	0	0	0	0
Total_Wgt ->		450					
10/12/88		10	10	10	10	10	10
		45	65	85	95	65	45
Total_Wgt ->		4000					
11/03/88		10	10	7	7	7	10
		45	85	105	95	95	65
Total_Wgt ->		4015					

Exercise -> DB PRESS

Date	Reps/ Wgts	SETS					
		1	2	3	4	5	6
10/08/88		10	0	0	0	0	0
		15	0	0	0	0	0
Total_Wgt ->	150						
10/12/88		10	10	7	12	0	0
		15	20	20	15	0	0
Total_Wgt ->	670						

```
                            Exercise Progress Report
                              Carrabis, Page -   2
                                02/01/89
```

Exercise -> INCLINE PRESS

Date	Reps/ Wgts	SETS					
		1	2	3	4	5	6
10/08/88		10	10	0	0	0	0
		15	20	0	0	0	0
Total_Wgt ->	350						
10/12/88		10	10	10	10	10	10
		15	20	25	25	25	15
Total_Wgt ->	1250						
11/03/88		10	10	10	10	7	10
		20	25	25	25	30	25
Total_Wgt ->	1410						
11/04/88		7	7	7	7	6	7
		25	30	35	35	40	25
Total_Wgt ->	1290						

```
Exercise -> LEG CURLS
```

		SETS					
Date	Reps/ Wgts	1	2	3	4	5	6
10/08/88		10	0	0	0	0	0
		30	0	0	0	0	0

```
Total_Wgt ->   300
```

		SETS					
10/12/88		10	10	10	10	10	0
		20	30	40	50	40	0

```
Total_Wgt ->   1800
```

		SETS					
11/03/88		10	10	10	10	10	0
		20	30	40	50	20	0

```
Total_Wgt ->   1600
```

```
                              Exercise Progress Report
                                 Carrabis, Page -   3
                                 02/01/89
```

```
Exercise -> LEG EXTENSIONS
```

		SETS					
Date	Reps/ Wgts	1	2	3	4	5	6
10/08/88		10	0	0	0	0	0
		25	0	0	0	0	0

```
Total_Wgt ->   250
```

		SETS					
10/12/88		10	10	10	10	10	10
		20	30	40	50	50	30

```
Total_Wgt ->   2200
```

		SETS					
11/03/88		10	10	10	10	10	10
		30	50	70	90	100	50

```
Total_Wgt ->   3900
```

Exercise -> LEG PRESS

Date	Reps/ Wgts	SETS					
		1	2	3	4	5	6
10/12/88		10	10	10	10	10	10
		50	70	90	110	0	0

Total_Wgt ->   3200

11/03/88		10	10	8	10	10	10
		50	140	140	110	50	0

Total_Wgt ->   4620

Exercise -> PRESS

Date	Reps/ Wgts	SETS					
		1	2	3	4	5	6
11/03/88		10	10	7	7	7	10
		30	30	30	20	20	10

Total_Wgt ->   1190

Exercise Progress Report
Carrabis, Page -   4
02/01/89

11/04/88		7	7	7	7	7	7
		10	20	20	20	30	40

Total_Wgt ->   980

Exercise -> PRESS OUTS

Date	Reps/ Wgts	SETS					
		1	2	3	4	5	6
10/08/88		10	0	0	0	0	0
		45	0	0	0	0	0

Total_Wgt ->   450

10/12/88	10	10	10	10	10	10
	20	30	30	40	30	20

Total_Wgt -> 1700

11/03/88	10	10	10	10	7	10
	10	20	30	30	40	20

Total_Wgt -> 1380

11/04/88	7	7	7	7	7	7
	20	30	30	20	20	10

Total_Wgt -> 910

Exercise -> PRESS SEVENTH SET

Date	Reps/ Wgts	SETS					
		1	2	3	4	5	6
11/04/88		7	7	7	7	4	4
		65	85	105	115	135	145

Total_Wgt -> 3710

Exercise Progress Report
Carrabis, Page -   5
02/01/89

Exercise -> PULLDOWNS

Date	Reps/ Wgts	SETS					
		1	2	3	4	5	6
10/08/88		10	0	0	0	0	0
		55	0	0	0	0	0

Total_Wgt -> 550

10/12/88	10	10	10	10	10	10
	40	55	70	85	100	55

Total_Wgt -> 4050

11/03/88	10	10	10	10	0	0
	40	70	115	70	0	0

Total_Wgt ->   0

11/04/88	7	7	7	7	4	7
	60	80	120	130	140	120

Total_Wgt ->   4130

Exercise -> SEATED CALF RAISES

				SETS			
Date	Reps/	1	2	3	4	5	6
	Wgts						
10/12/88		10	10	10	10	10	0
		0	25	45	35	35	0

Total_Wgt ->   1400

Exercise -> SEATED ROWS

				SETS			
Date	Reps/	1	2	3	4	5	6
	Wgts						
10/12/88		10	10	10	10	10	0
		50	40	40	40	40	0

Total_Wgt ->   2100

Exercise Progress Report
Carrabis, Page -   6
02/01/89

11/04/88	7	7	6	7	7	7
	70	90	90	80	80	70

Total_Wgt ->   3270

Exercise -> UPRIGHT ROWS

SETS

Date	Reps/ Wgts	1	2	3	4	5	6
11/03/88		10	10	10	8	10	10
		25	35	45	55	55	45

Total_Wgt -> 2490

Date	Reps/ Wgts	1	2	3	4	5	6
11/04/88		7	7	7	7	7	7
		25	45	65	65	65	45

Total_Wgt -> 2170

Exercise -> WIDE GRIP CURLS

				SETS			
Date	Reps/ Wgts	1	2	3	4	5	6
10/08/88		10	0	0	0	0	0
		25	0	0	0	0	0

Total_Wgt -> 250

10/12/88		10	10	10	10	10	10
		25	45	45	45	45	25

Total_Wgt -> 2300

11/04/88		7	7	7	7	6	7
		25	35	35	65	65	25

Total_Wgt -> 1685

    Designing and laying out a report form can show previously unnoticed flaws in the logic and flow of a database system. Designing this report shows that we rarely use the Comment field, but we do know that field is useful.

    It would be useful to separate the EXERCISE database into two separate databases. The first database, called EXERCISE, should include the Date, Time, and Set_n fields. The second database, called EXCOMMNT, should include the Date, Time, and Comment fields. The Time field might prove unnecessary in both

Exercise Progress Report

cases, but we can keep it for now. The Date field is necessary as
a way to link the two databases.

Modifying the database in this way would mean reworking
the screen form and the report form (if we want to include the
Comment field from the EXCOMMNT.DBF file), but would also provide
an excellent opportunity for learning more about the workings of
dBASE IV. Let's do this in the next chapter.

This report summary, by the way, should be considered as
part of the text of the book.

Note that I have removed a great deal of extra space from the report.
This was necessary because the report was sent to a file with the REPORT
FORM exbydate TO *filename* command, which means dBASE IV generated the report for later printing. As such, the report contained lots of room
for page breaks and so on.

Readers who have been following along with this example, especially
those who have been generating report forms at the rate I have been sug-
gesting, have probably begun to notice something.

Repeatedly generating reports takes lots of time on slower machines.
What is a slower machine? Any computer running at less than 12 MHz is
slow for dBASE IV, and that covers a lot of machines. You can run dBASE
IV on just about any XT or AT style computer. The strongest suggestion is
that you get a 386, unless you want to wait a long time. What is a long time?
When I can go get a cup of coffee—two flights downstairs and two flights
back up—and the computer is still working, it takes too long. This is part of
the price for the increased functionality of dBASE IV.

Fortunately, there are some things you can do to increase the speed of
laying out and running reports. First, simply save the file during your work
session, don't save it *and* compile it. You do this with the [Alt-L] S command
by not renaming the file. Of course, you might encounter a memory management problem and destroy all your work. The solution? Save the file,
then rename it outside the dBASE IV report form design system.

Next, don't put calculated fields into a report unless you are working
with a 386 screamer. You may have noticed that I included the Total_Wgt
field in the EXBYDATE.FRM. And you may remember that the Total_Wgt
field is a calculated field. Total_Wgt is calculated each time a record is
added to the database—when the record is added through the PROCE-
DURE file we designed or through the FMT file designed in chapter 6. Here
we have the option of including a calculated field in the report. Why do we
create the field as a real field in the database when dBASE IV is willing to
calculate it each time we need it? Asking dBASE IV to calculate the field
each time we need it slows things, and this shows up more in the report
forms, so don't.

dBASE IV may be seeing FRG and FRO files that stop it from compiling a new FRM file.

The next bit of advice does not have anything to do with getting dBASE IV to save time during report form generation. It has to do with saving you lots of aggravation and gnashing of teeth. Sometimes dBASE IV won't recompile a new version of an FRM file if an FRG or FRO file already exists on the disk. This means you can have EXBYDATE.FRM, EXBY-DATE.FRG, and EXBYDATE.FRO on the same disk and copy a new EXBY-DATE.FRM from another disk or across a network. Even with SET DEVELOPMENT ON—the SET toggle that instructs dBASE IV to check the creation times and dates of files to determine if things should be recompiled—dBASE IV will sometimes use the old FRG and FRO files. This means all the changes you made to the FRM don't show up and you go nuts trying to figure out why. You call up the new report FRM file with MODIFY REPORT and see clearly on the screen the changes you made. You generate the report form with REPORT FORM *filename* and don't see your changes in the report. Grrr! If you know you have created a new report form and the report form that dBASE IV is using does not include those changes, delete the report form's associated FRG and FRO files.

It is time to create our next screen form. This one will go much faster for two reasons. First, the report contains less information. Second, you are a pro at designing report forms.

We start by calling in our existing report form because it can serve as a useful template:

```
MODIFY REPORT filename [Enter]
```

Using the EXBYDATE.FRM file designed previously in this section, cursor to *Exercise Progress Report* on the first line of the Page Header band, make sure the Ins toggle is off, and type *Date by Exercise Report*. Cursor down to the Report Intro band and edit the text to read as follows:

```
This report is based on an exercise format designed by Denise
Dargie. The style of the workout and intensity are changed over
time, according to Ms. Dargie's instructions; therefore, this
report is broken down as Date by Exercise, listing exercises
and total weights. The goal of this report format is to show
the individual's daily regimen and the progress in that
regimen.

Ms. Dargie is holder of several weight lifting and body building
titles in the Northeast and Eastern United States.
```

The new text is italicized. Move the cursor to directly on the Group 1 Intro band and press [Alt-B] *M F* [Enter] *D* [Enter] for Bands menu, *Modify group*, *Field value*, *Date field*. Cursor to the first row in the Group 1 Intro band and press [Alt-W] *R* (for Words menu), *Remove line* until none of the previous report's information is in the band. Now type *Date ->*, type a

273

space, and press [F5] *D* [Enter] [Ctrl-End] to place a label and the Date field on the first line of this group.

Go to the Detail band, delete everything there with the [Alt-W] *R* command or use the [F6] key to highlight the entire band, then press [Enter] [Del] *Y*. Move to the second tab stop and press [F5] *E* [Enter] [Ctrl-End] to place the Exercise field at the second tab stop. Move to the end of the Exercise field, press [Tab] twice, then [F5] *T* [Down-Arrow] [Enter] [Ctrl-End] to place the Total_Wgt field at that tab stop.

Move the cursor back up to the Group 1 Intro band, position it about midway over the Exercise field, and type *Exercise*. Move the cursor to a few columns before the Total_Wgt field and type *Total_Wgt*.

See how fast this is going?

Now something a little different. We want to use the Group 1 Summary band. Open the band by placing the cursor on the Group 1 Summary band line and pressing [Enter]. Go to the first line in this band and type *Total number of exercises performed on,* type a space, then press [F5] *D* [Enter] [Ctrl-End] -> [F5] [Left-Arrow] [Down-Arrow] [Enter]. This translates to the following:

Total number of exercises performed on	entered text
[F5]	open the Fields menu
D [Enter]	highlight and select the Date field
[Ctrl-End]	accept the default Picture functions and Templates
>	more entered text
[F5]	open the Fields menu again
[Left-Arrow]	move to the Summary fields column
[Down-Arrow] [Enter]	highlight and select the COUNT function

You are now at something similar to the Picture function and Template screen, except you are working with an operation and not a true field. This is a calculated field, and I have already told you how I feel about them. This, however, is a calculated field that we can't truly place inside the database. This calculated field is a true virtual field, as mentioned previously, and must be calculated as the report is generated. Why? This calculated field counts the number of records that meet some condition. This is not the type of information you can easily and neatly place in a record. We don't need to give the calculated field a name or description. All we need to do is change the Template to 99. If we plan on doing more than 99 exercises in a day, we need more help than this book can provide.

Make the necessary change and press [Ctrl-End] to tell dBASE IV you have completed this operation. Put a few blank lines in the Group 1 Summary band as we did before. Close up the Report Summary band, and we are ready to save the new report. We do that with the [Alt-S] command, this time giving the report a new name. How does this one look?

                                        Date by Exercise Report
                                        Carrabis, Page -   1
                                        02/01/89

This report is based on an exercise format designed by Denise
Dargie. The style of the workout and intensity are changed over
time, according to Ms. Dargie's instructions; therefore, this
report is broken down as Date by Exercise, listing exercises
and total weights. The goal of this report format is to show the
individual's daily regimen and the progress in that regimen.

Ms. Dargie is holder of several weight lifting and body building
titles in the Northeast and Eastern United States.

Date -> 10/08/88

Exercise	Total_Wgt
BENCH PRESS	450
INCLINE PRESS	350
DB PRESS	150
WIDE GRIP CURLS	250
PRESS OUTS	450
LEG EXTENSIONS	250
LEG CURLS	300
PULLDOWNS	550

Total number of exercises performed on 10/08/88 ->   8

Date -> 10/12/88

Exercise	Total_Wgt
BENCH PRESS	4000
INCLINE PRESS	1250
DB PRESS	670
PRESS OUTS	1700
LEG EXTENSIONS	2200
LEG PRESS	3200
LEG CURLS	1800
SEATED CALF RAISES	1400

```
                    PULLDOWNS                      4050
                    SEATED ROWS                    2100
                    WIDE GRIP CURLS                2300

          Total number of exercises performed on 10/12/88 -> 11



          Date -> 11/03/88

                         Exercise               Total_Wgt
                         BENCH PRESS              4015
                         INCLINE PRESS            1410
                         PRESS                    1190
                         UPRIGHT ROWS             2490



                                            Date by Exercise Report
                                            Carrabis, Page -   2
                                            02/01/89



                         PRESS OUTS               1380
                         LEG EXTENSIONS           3900
                         LEG PRESS                4620
                         LEG CURLS                1600
                         PULLDOWNS                   0

          Total number of exercises performed on 11/03/88 ->  9



          Date -> 11/04/88

                         Exercise               Total_Wgt
                         PRESS SEVENTH SET        3710
                         INCLINE PRESS            1290
                         PULLDOWNS                4130
                         SEATED ROWS              3270
                         PRESS                     980
                         UPRIGHT ROWS             2170
                         PRESS OUTS                910
                         WIDE GRIP CURLS          1685

          Total number of exercises performed on 11/04/88 ->  8
```

Again, I have removed a lot of blank space from this report.

There has been a lot in this section, but you have learned a lot about the dBASE IV report form design system and how reports should be designed, then laid out. The next section shows how to design mailing and other types of labels. You will be amazed at the similarities between the two systems.

Designing Label Forms

You know that you have to first design a report, then lay it out in the report form design system. What about labels?

Labels are specialized reports. The design interface between the two is similar, although it might not readily appear so. Compare figures 8-21 and 8-7.

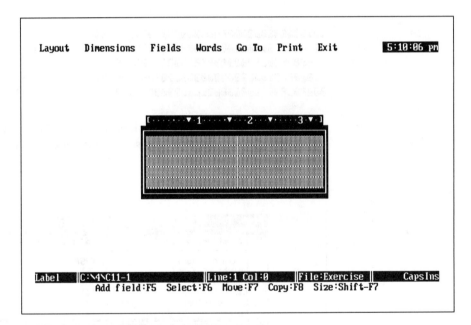

Figure 8-21 The label form design system.

What is so similar about the two? Nothing, until you start using them. You might think of a label form as a tiny report form without the detail or complexity of reporting styles. Both the report design system and the label design system have the Layout menu options. The label system's Layout menu doesn't offer any quick label options, nor does it allow for boxes or lines. This doesn't mean you can't create boxes or lines in your labels, it simply means dBASE IV doesn't provide an easy way to do it.

The Fields menu option is similar to the report design system's menu, with the exception of no *Hidden field* option. There is no need to hide any fields on a label because you probably won't use a label to hold summary information. If you are, you have the wrong design system. It would be easier to design a very small report than to design a label with hidden fields.

The Words and Go To menus are identical in the label and report design systems. The Print menu contains one option not found in the report system's menu. The *Generate sample labels* option lets you send a series of asterisks to the printer for the sole purpose of seeing if the label size you have defined on your screen fits the label you have placed in your printer. An example of the label sample is shown in the following listing.

```
aaaaaaaaaaaaaaaaaaaaaaaaaaaaaaaaaaaaaaaaaa
aaaaaaaaaaaaaaaaaaaaaaaaaaaaaaaaaaaaaaaaaa
aaaaaaaaaaaaaaaaaaaaaaaaaaaaaaaaaaaaaaaaaa
aaaaaaaaaaaaaaaaaaaaaaaaaaaaaaaaaaaaaaaaaa
aaaaaaaaaaaaaaaaaaaaaaaaaaaaaaaaaaaaaaaaaa


aaaaaaaaaaaaaaaaaaaaaaaaaaaaaaaaaaaaaaaaaa
aaaaaaaaaaaaaaaaaaaaaaaaaaaaaaaaaaaaaaaaaa
aaaaaaaaaaaaaaaaaaaaaaaaaaaaaaaaaaaaaaaaaa
aaaaaaaaaaaaaaaaaaaaaaaaaaaaaaaaaaaaaaaaaa
aaaaaaaaaaaaaaaaaaaaaaaaaaaaaaaaaaaaaaaaaa
```

These samples are for the default $15/16$-by-$3\frac{1}{2}$-by-1 inch label. You can use any of the predefined labels or create your own through the Dimensions menu (figure 8-22).

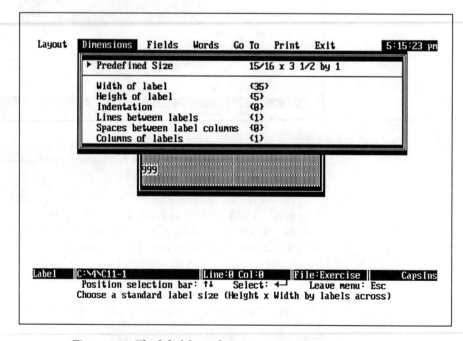

Figure 8-22 The label form design system's Dimensions menu.

Note that any custom entries in the *Width of label, Height of label, Indentation, Lines between labels, Spaces between label columns,* and *Columns of labels* options take precedence over any predefined label form on the screen.

Reporting by Programming the LIST and DISPLAY Commands

You put data in, you get information out. The information you get out of your database is usually in the form of reports, but there are other methods of getting information from your system. You probably already know that BROWSE, EDIT, and CHANGE can be used to get information from the database, but these commands are limited to a single record or a single screen of information. We want something that will give us a printout to look at or a file to scan with nondatabase techniques, either in or out of the dBASE IV environment.

The LIST and DISPLAY commands allow rudimentary reporting on the database. We will investigate these two commands because they afford quick and dirty reporting abilities.

LIST and DISPLAY are to reports what EDIT and CHANGE are to BROWSE. LIST and DISPLAY do pretty much the same thing, with only two differences.

The first difference is that DISPLAY works on the record level, but LIST works on the file level. In other words, when you enter DISPLAY at the dBASE prompt, dBASE IV shows the data in the current record only (figure 8-23). When you enter LIST at the dBASE prompt, dBASE IV shows all the data in all the records, starting at the current record and continuing until the end of the file is reached.

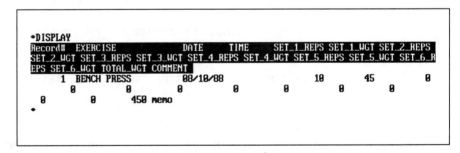

Figure 8-23 The DISPLAY command shows all the data in the current record only.

The second difference is that even when you tell dBASE IV to DISPLAY ALL the records, it stops when a screen is filled and asks you to *Press* any key to continue (figure 8-24). LIST just keeps on running on, dumping information to the screen indiscriminately.

```
*DISPLAY ALL
Record#  EXERCISE               DATE      TIME      SET_1_REPS SET_1_WGT SET_2_REPS
SET_2_WGT SET_3_REPS SET_3_WGT SET_4_REPS SET_4_WGT SET_5_REPS SET_5_WGT SET_6_R
EPS SET_6_WGT TOTAL_WGT COMMENT
         1  BENCH PRESS         08/10/88            10         45        0
         0         0       450 memo          0        0         0        0
    0         0       450 memo
         2  INCLINE PRESS       08/10/88            10         15        10
        20         0       350 memo          0        0         0        0
    0         0       350 memo
         3  DB PRESS            08/10/88            10         15        0
         0         0       150 memo          0        0         0        0
    0         0       150 memo
         4  WIDE GRIP CURLS     08/10/88            10         25        0
         0         0       250 memo          0        0         0        0
    0         0       250 memo
         5  TRICEP PRESS        08/10/88            10         45        0
         0         0                          0        0         0        0
Press any key to continue...
```

Figure 8-24 *The DISPLAY ALL command shows all the data in all the records in the database, but stops when a screen is full.*

LIST and DISPLAY share the same qualifiers, some of which were described for BROWSE, EDIT, and CHANGE. The FIELDS *field list*, FOR *expression*, *n*, NEXT *n*, and WHILE expression qualifiers work identically to the BROWSE/EDIT/CHANGE qualifiers of the same name and won't be discussed again here. The new qualifiers are OFF, TO FILE, and TO PRINTER.

We start by showing a slightly cleaned up display. Figures 8-23 and 8-24 scramble information across the screen. You can't get a good idea of what is going on because everything is thrown at you. Figure 8-25 is better, and we will work with it for now.

First, consider the command that produces figure 8-25. The command, at the top of the screen, is

```
LIST EXERCISE, DATE, TIME, SET_1_REPS, SET_1_WGT ;
     FOR SET_1_REPS = 10
```

Notice that there is a field list but no FIELDS qualifier. Rightly so. You don't need the FIELDS qualifier for either LIST or DISPLAY. The FIELDS qualifier is useful for clarity when you work with database fields with names that are also the names of memory variables.

Figure 8-25 is a useful and informative list of what is in the database. The listing can be made more useful by changing the controlling index tag or NDX file, by setting other conditions on the LIST command with FOR and WHILE, and so on.

```
•LIST EXERCISE, DATE, TIME, SET_1_REPS, SET_1_WGT FOR SET_1_REPS = 10
Record#  EXERCISE              DATE      TIME    SET_1_REPS SET_1_WGT
    1    BENCH PRESS          08/10/88                  10        45
    2    INCLINE PRESS        08/10/88                  10        15
    3    DB PRESS             08/10/88                  10        15
    4    WIDE GRIP CURLS      08/10/88                  10        25
    5    TRICEP PRESS         08/10/88                  10        45
    6    LYING EXTENSIONS     08/10/88                  10        25
    7    LEG CURLS            08/10/88                  10        30
    8    PULLDOWNS            08/10/88                  10        55
    9    BENCH PRESS          12/10/88  9:00            10        45
   10    INCLINE PRESS        12/10/88  9:00            10        15
   11    DB PRESS             12/10/88  9:00            10        15
   12    PRESS OUTS           12/10/88  9:00            10        20
   13    LEG EXTENSIONS       12/10/88  9:00            10        20
   14    LEG PRESS            12/10/88  9:00            10        50
   15    LEG CURLS            12/10/88  9:00            10        20
   16    SEATED CALF RAISES   12/10/88  9:00            10         0
   17    NECK PULLDOWN        12/10/88  9:00            10        40
   18    SEATED ROWS          12/10/88  9:00            10        50
   19    WIDE GRIP CURLS      12/10/88  9:00            10        25
```

Figure 8-25 *This listing is used for the discussion of LIST and DISPLAY commands as reporting tools.*

But we are more interested in getting things printed out so we can peruse them at our leisure. Easy enough to do. Modify the command to the following:

```
LIST EXERCISE, DATE, TIME, SET_1_REPS, SET_1_WGT ;
     FOR SET_1_REPS = 10 TO PRINT
```

What does this modification give you? It gives you a printout of the screen shown in figure 8-25. This is useful. The next modification to the command could be even more useful, depending on your point of view. You can change the command and get a word-processable file of figure 8-25 as follows:

```
LIST EXERCISE, DATE, TIME, SET_1_REPS, SET_1_WGT ;
     FOR SET_1_REPS = 10 TO FILE filename
```

The *filename* part of the command can be any conventional eight letter file name you want to use. dBASE IV automatically adds the TXT extension to the file unless you specify otherwise. This command creates the following listing:

```
Record#  exercise            date      time      set_1_reps set_1_
wgt
    1  BENCH PRESS          08/10/88                  10
45
```

	2	INCLINE PRESS	08/10/88	10
15				
	3	DB PRESS	08/10/88	10
15				
	4	WIDE GRIP CURLS	08/10/88	10
25				
	5	TRICEP PRESS	08/10/88	10
45				
	6	LYING EXTENSIONS	08/10/88	10
25				
	7	LEG CURLS	08/10/88	10
30				
	8	PULLDOWNS	08/10/88	10
55				
	9	BENCH PRESS	12/10/88 9:00	10
45				
	10	INCLINE PRESS	12/10/88 9:00	10
15				
	11	DB PRESS	12/10/88 9:00	10
15				
	12	PRESS OUTS	12/10/88 9:00	10
20				
	13	LEG EXTENSIONS	12/10/88 9:00	10
20				
	14	LEG PRESS	12/10/88 9:00	10
50				
	15	LEG CURLS	12/10/88 9:00	10
20				
	16	SEATED CALF RAISES	12/10/88 9:00	10
0				
	17	NECK PULLDOWN	12/10/88 9:00	10
40				
	18	SEATED ROWS	12/10/88 9:00	10
50				
	19	WIDE GRIP CURLS	12/10/88 9:00	10
25				

What is the elegant beauty of this listing? It came directly from dBASE IV into the word-processing file as ASCII text. This means any word processor that can read an ASCII text file can read information from a dBASE IV database with the LIST command.

I mentioned that the DISPLAY command is almost identical to the LIST command. You could use the DISPLAY command to get the preceding listing. The DISPLAY command pauses when the screen is full of information, but lists the information to a file without any pauses in the file.

Next, we need to know if we can do a little programming to automate the process of getting information to the printer or a file. Of course we can. Listing 8-1 does it for you easily enough. Unlike previous programs in this book, it is not built from existing code. But much of the following program is made from bits and pieces of other programs we have developed. Fore-warning: You can solve the coding problem in ways easier than the first way I show you. Don't skip ahead to the easiest solution, however, because you will learn a lot about dBASE IV by seeing the differences in coding methodologies.

Listing 8-1

```
00001 : ** LISTER.PRG
00002 : * THIS PROGRAM QUERIES THE USER ON WHAT INFORMATION SHOULD BE
00003 : * INCLUDED IN A LISTING, THEN ASKS WHETHER OR NOT THE
00004 : * LISTING SHOULD GO TO EITHER A PRINTER, THE SCREEN, OR
00005 : * A FILE.
00006 : *
00007 : SET PROCEDURE TO GETFILES
00008 : SET TALK OFF
00009 : INEXACT = SET("EXACT")
00010 : *****
00011 : SET CONSOLE OFF
00012 : SET MESSAGE TO [SELECT THE DATABASE FROM THE ABOVE LIST. ] + ;
              [TYPE "ESC" TO QUIT]
00013 : DISPLAY FILES TO FILE HERE
00014 : USE DIRTANK
00015 : ZAP
00016 : APPEND FROM HERE SDF
00017 : DEFINE POPUP TANK FROM 1,10
00018 : 1
00019 : *
00020 : *****
00021 : DO WHILE .NOT. EOF()
00022 : *
00023 :    IF RECNO() < 3 .OR. RECNO() > RECCOUNT() - 3
00024 :         DEFINE BAR RECNO() OF TANK PROMPT TRIM(ENTRY) SKIP
00025 :    ELSE
00026 :         DEFINE BAR RECNO() OF TANK PROMPT TRIM(ENTRY)
00027 :    ENDIF
00028 : *
00029 :    SKIP
00030 : ENDDO
00031 : *****
00032 : *
00033 : ON SELECTION POPUP TANK DO GETDBF
00034 : CLEAR
00035 : ACTIVATE POPUP TANK
00036 : TRUTH = .F.
00037 : FIELDNAMES = []
00038 : CLEAR
00039 : @ 10,0 SAY ;
              [DO YOU WANT TO LIST ALL THE FIELDS IN THE DATABASE (Y/N)? -> ] ;
              GET TRUTH
```

Listing 8-1 (cont.)

```
00040 : READ
00041 : CLEAR
00042 : *
00043 : IF .NOT. TRUTH
00044 :    COPY STRUC EXTE TO TEMP
00045 :    SELECT 2
00046 :    USE TEMP
00047 :    DEFINE POPUP TANK FROM 1,30
00048 : *
00049 :    SCAN
00050 :          DEFINE BAR RECNO() OF TANK PROMPT FIELD_NAME
00051 :    ENDSCAN
00052 : *
00053 :    ON SELECTION POPUP TANK DO GETFIELD
00054 :    CLEAR
00055 :    SET MESSAGE TO "SELECT THE FIELDS TO LIST FROM THE " + ;
00056 :                "ABOVE OPTIONS. TYPE [Esc] TO EXIT"
00056 :    USE
00057 :    ERASE TEMP.DBF
00058 :    SELECT 1
00059 :    SHOW POPUP TANK
00060 : *
00061 :    DO WHILE .T.
00062 :          ACTIVATE POPUP TANK
00063 : *
00064 :          IF BAR() = 0
00065 :                EXIT
00066 :          ENDIF
00067 : *
00068 :    ENDDO
00069 : *
00070 : ENDIF
00071 : *
00072 : TARGET = []
00073 : DEFINE POPUP TANK FROM 1,30
00074 : DEFINE BAR 1 OF TANK PROMPT [SCREEN]
00075 : DEFINE BAR 2 OF TANK PROMPT [FILE]
00076 : DEFINE BAR 3 OF TANK PROMPT [PRINTER]
00077 : SET MESS TO [SELECT A LIST TARGET FROM THE ABOVE OPTIONS]
00078 : CLEAR
00079 : ON SELECTION POPUP TANK DO GETTARGET
00080 : ACTIVATE POPUP TANK
00081 : SET MESSAGE TO
00082 : CLEAR
00083 : @ 10,0 SAY ;
           [ARE THERE ANY CONDITIONS TO PLACE ON THE LISTING? (Y/N) ];
           GET TRUTH PICT "Y"
00084 : READ
00085 : *
```

```
00086 :  IF TRUTH
00087 :    CLEAR
00088 :    SET MESSAGE TO
00089 :    ON ERROR DO NOTHING
00090 :    SET VIEW TO ?
00091 :    COUNT TO ALLRECS
00092 :  *
00093 :    IF ALLRECS = RECCOUNT()
00094 :        CLEAR
00095 :        @ 10,0 SAY [YOU EITHER CHOSE NO QUERY FILE OR ] + ;
                   [THE QUERY FILE YOU CHOSE HAS NO EFFECT.]
00096 :        SET MESSAGE TO [TYPE "ESC" TO EXIT PROGRAM]
00097 :        DEFINE POPUP TANK FROM 1,30
00098 :        DEFINE BAR 1 OF TANK PROMPT [DESIGN A QUERY FORM]
00099 :        DEFINE BAR 2 OF TANK PROMPT [ENTER A CONDITION]
00100 :        ON SELECTION POPUP TANK DO GETQUERY
00101 :        ACTIVATE POPUP TANK
00102 :        CLEAR
00103 :    ENDIF
00104 :  *
00105 :  ENDIF
00106 :  *
00107 :  SET CONSOLE ON
00108 :  CLEAR
00109 :  LIST &FIELDNAMES &TARGET
00110 :  SET FILTER TO
00111 :  SET EXACT &INEXACT
00112 :  ON ERROR
00113 :  *
00114 :  ** EOF: LISTER.PRG
```

Hellish amount of code just to produce a list, don't you think? Yes and no. Yes, it is a lot of code if all you want to do is produce a list. No, when you consider that the code will work with any database and any fields in a given database, send output wherever you want, and can either use existing query files or create them as needed.

So how does it work? Passing by the first six comment lines, we SET TALK OFF in line 8. This prevents the screen from being cluttered with dBASE IV telling us what it is doing. Being told what dBASE IV is doing can be entertaining or confusing, depending on the user's point of view, and it is best if you don't risk confusing the user.

Line 9 gets the status of the EXACT flag. dBASE IV can search for things in two ways; it can look for exactly what you ask for or it can look for a close approximation. What is exact by dBASE IV's definition?

[John] = [John] is exact. [J] = [John] is not exact. If EXACT is SET ON and you ask dBASE IV to find [J] in a first name field, dBASE IV shows you only records where the first name field contains the single letter J. If, on the other hand, you SET EXACT OFF and make the same request, dBASE IV shows you all the records that start with the letter J. This is a significant difference. Line 9 finds out the EXACT flag status because we SET EXACT OFF later and then SET it back to its original status before we exit.

Lines 11 through 30 show some clever but useless programming. We want to let the user select a database to list. Starting at line 11, SET the CONSOLE OFF. This tells dBASE IV not to send information to the screen. Why? Again, it addresses the confusion and clutter problem. Line 12 SETS a MESSAGE for the user regarding how to select a database from the list.

Line 13 uses a variation of the DISPLAY command. We DISPLAY FILES TO an ASCII FILE, HERE.TXT. The DISPLAY FILES command is equivalent to the DIR command, showing only dBASE IV recognizable DBF files. Consider the following listings:

```
DIR
Database Files      # Records    Last Update      Size
EXOLD.DBF                 12      01/25/89         1706
EXERCISE.DBF             19      01/25/89         2364
DISKSALE.DBF            701      01/25/89       168690
DIRTANK.DBF              13      01/26/89          859
XYWORDS.DBF               0      01/26/89           66
EX10.DBF                 19      01/12/89         2415
EXPENSE.DBF             809      01/13/89       110251
INCOME.DBF               97      01/13/89        14453

 300804 bytes in     8 files
44595200 bytes remaining on drive

DISPLAY FILES
Database Files      # Records    Last Update      Size
EXOLD.DBF                 12      01/25/89         1706
EXERCISE.DBF             19      01/25/89         2364
DISKSALE.DBF            701      01/25/89       168690
DIRTANK.DBF              13      01/26/89          859
XYWORDS.DBF               0      01/26/89           66
EX10.DBF                 19      01/12/89         2415
EXPENSE.DBF             809      01/13/89       110251
INCOME.DBF               97      01/13/89        14453

 300804 bytes in     8 files
44595200 bytes remaining on drive
```

The two commands produce identical information. But there are differences in where you can direct the output of the commands. The DIR command can send information directly to the printer only if you have toggled the printer on with [Ctrl-P]. Press [Ctrl-P], then type DIR and you get a listing of DBF files on the screen and at the printer. (The printer toggle key is [Ctrl-P]. Pressing [Ctrl-P] once tells dBASE IV to echo screen output at the printer; pressing it a second time tells dBASE IV to stop echoing screen output at the printer.) You can achieve the same result with the DISPLAY

FILES command by using the [Ctrl-P] toggle or by including the TO PRINT qualifier as follows:

```
DISPLAY FILES TO PRINT
```

One thing you can do with DISPLAY FILES that you can't do with DIR is send the output to a file, which is what is done in line 13 of LISTER.PRG. Before going on, note that both commands can directly take file skeletons as arguments. For example, both DIR *.NDX and DISPLAY FILES *.NDX produce a listing of all NDX files on the currently selected drive and path.

Line 14 is where the inelegance of this program is blatant. We need to use a temporary database file, DIRTANK.DBF, to hold the directory information. This means the disk always has this file on it, unless you don't plan on ever using this version of LISTER.PRG.

Line 15 ZAPs the database. I warn people about this command in each of my books, in my columns, in my lectures, and in my sleep. ZAP is a single command equivalent to DELETE ALL followed by PACK. In other words, ZAP physically and permanently removes all the records in the current database. There are third-party software products which can find ZAPped information. This is a dangerous command. dBASE IV offers some protection against accidentally ZAPping databases, but only if SAFETY is ON. This is demonstrated in the following listing:

```
SET SAFETY ON
USE DIRTANK
ZAP
ZAP C:\4\DIRTANK.DBF? (Y/N) No
SET SAFETY OFF
USE DIRTANK
ZAP
```

As you can see, dBASE IV does not prompt you for confirmation before it ZAPs the database when SAFETY is OFF. User beware.

We can use ZAP on line 15 because we want to get rid of any old information in DIRTANK.DBF before we add new directory information to it with line 16. This is how the APPEND command is used to get information from a system data file that is not a standard dBASE III Plus or dBASE IV database file. An SDF is often called a fixed-length file. This means each line in the file contains one record's worth of information, each line is terminated by a CR-LF pair (carriage return-linefeed, also ASCII 13 and 10), and all the data on any given line is made up of fixed-length fields.

Remember when I described how dBASE IV could AUTOSAVE edits to records without having to run the disk continually? This had to do with dBASE IV's use of fixed-length records. Every record in a dBASE IV database is the same size as any other record in the same database, whether there is information in the record or not. An SDF file uses this concept and places data at fixed intervals on a line, even if there is no data to go in a certain field. Normally, you send information to an SDF file for use in another application. Our EXERCISE database would create an SDF file as follows:

```
BENCH PRESS         19880810      10 45  0   0  0   0  0
0  0   0  0    0 450
INCLINE PRESS       19880810      10 15 10  20  0   0  0
0  0   0  0    0 350
DB PRESS            19880810      10 15  0   0  0   0  0
0  0   0  0    0 150
WIDE GRIP CURLS     19880810      10 25  0   0  0   0  0
0  0   0  0    0 250
TRICEP PRESS        19880810      10 45  0   0  0   0  0
0  0   0  0    0 450
LYING EXTENSIONS    19880810      10 25  0   0  0   0  0
0  0   0  0    0 250
LEG CURLS           19880810      10 30  0   0  0   0  0
0  0   0  0    0 300
PULLDOWNS           19880810      10 55  0   0  0   0  0
0  0   0  0    0 550
BENCH PRESS         198812109:00  10 45 10  65 10  85 10
95 10  65 10   45 4000
INCLINE PRESS       198812109:00  10 15 10  20 10  25 10
25 10  25 10   15   13
DB PRESS            198812109:00  10 15 10  20  7  20 12
15            670
PRESS OUTS          198812109:00  10 20 10  30 10  30 10
40 10  30 10   20 1700
LEG EXTENSIONS      198812109:00  10 20 10  30 10  40 10
50 10  50 10   30 2200
LEG PRESS           198812109:00  10 50 10  70 10  90 10
110 10   0 10    0 3200
LEG CURLS           198812109:00  10 20 10  30 10  40 10
50 10  40      1800
SEATED CALF RAISES  198812109:00  10  0 10  25 10  45 10
35 10  35      1400
NECK PULLDOWN       198812109:00  10 40 10  55 10  70 10
85 10 100 10   55 4050
SEATED ROWS         198812109:00  10 50 10  40 10  40 10
40 10  40      2100
WIDE GRIP CURLS     198812109:00  10 25 10  45 10  45 10
45 10  45 10   25 2300
```

Note that each field sends information to the SDF in fixed-length intervals.

We can make use of this SDF concept in reverse by using a database specifically designed to accept information from the SDF file. The DIRTANK.DBF structure is a single field, Entry, that is TYPE character and sixty characters wide. There is no indexing on the database. Not included in this program is a way to produce an alphabetized listing of the database files placed in DIRTANK.DBF. This is possible, but it requires a lot more programming than we can go into here.

By the time we get to line 16, we have taken the listing produced in line 13 and put it in the DIRTANK.DBF file. The contents of DIR-TANK.DBF now look like the following:

Record#	ENTRY			
1				
2	Database Files	# Records	Last Update	Size
3	EXOLD.DBF	12	01/25/89	1706
4	EXERCISE.DBF	19	01/25/89	2364
5	DISKSALE.DBF	701	01/25/89	168690
6	DIRTANK.DBF	0	01/26/89	66
7	XYWORDS.DBF	0	01/26/89	66
8	EX10.DBF	19	01/12/89	2415
9	EXPENSE.DBF	809	01/13/89	110251
10	INCOME.DBF	97	01/13/89	14453
11				
12	300011 bytes in	8 files		
13	44707840 bytes remaining on drive			

Our next task is to define a menu from which the desired database is selected. We define the pop-up menu in line 17. Then we must load the pop-up menu with the information in DIRTANK.DBF. That is handled in lines 18 through 30. Line 18 positions the record pointer to the first record in the database. (Remember, DIRTANK.DBF is not indexed. We would use the GO TOP command if the database were indexed.) The DO WHILE...ENDDO loop from line 21 through line 30 does the actual loading. What is the IF...ELSE...ENDIF code block doing in there?

Look at the listing and you will see that we don't want to use some records as menu options. In particular, we don't want to use the first two records and the last three records in the database. Record #1 is blank, record #2 is a header containing information on the rest of the display, the last record is free disk space information, the next to the last record is information on the size of the files in the list, and the third to the last record is blank.

We can be sure that the first two records are worthless no matter how large the DISPLAY FILES listing is. We don't know how large it will be, however, so we use the RECCOUNT( ) (record COUNT) function to find out how many records are in the database. Line 23 reads "If the current record is one of the first two or if the current record is one of the last three..."

What if the current record is one of the first two or one of the last three? Line 24 tells dBASE IV to DEFINE a menu BAR corresponding to the current RECNO( ) in the database and place the menu BAR information on the TANK pop-up menu. Further, use whatever is in the ENTRY database field as the PROMPT for that menu BAR. Last, SKIP over this BAR when you display the menu. The last part of the command, SKIP, is why we test for the record number being one of the first two records or one of the last three records in the database.

What if the current record is not one of the first two or one of the last three records in the database? Use the information it contains to DEFINE a menu BAR as you normally would. This is done by ELSE on line 25 and the DEFINE BAR command on line 26.

We need to move through DIRTANK.DBF's records sequentially, so we SKIP to the next record on line 29 and close the DO WHILE...ENDDO loop on line 30.

This shows you some interesting ways to use dBASE IV's commands and functions. Careful readers will see that much of the listing comes from FIELDMSK.PRG with minor modifications. Can you see a much easier way to code this? I will explain at the end of this section.

Lines 33 through 35 tell dBASE IV what to do when the TANK pop-up becomes active, CLEAR the screen, and activate TANK. At this point you should note something. We created a pop-up in chapter 6, but the user was expected to make several selections from that menu. The user is expected to make a single selection from this menu. dBASE IV does not like to give up pop-up menu control easily. Our last use of pop-ups used the BAR( ) function returning a 0 value when the user finished making selections. GETDBF.PRG, the program dBASE IV executes when a selection is made on TANK, has some changes to make sure dBASE IV does not want to give the user more than one try at selecting a database. The menu created in this way is shown in figure 8-26.

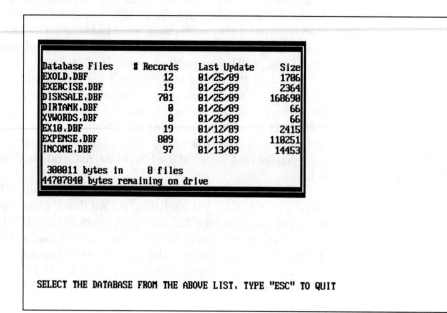

```
Database Files    # Records    Last Update      Size
EXOLD.DBF             12        01/25/89         1706
EXERCISE.DBF          19        01/25/89         2364
DISKSALE.DBF         701        01/25/89       168690
DIRTANK.DBF            0        01/26/89           66
XYWORDS.DBF            0        01/26/89           66
EX10.DBF              19        01/12/89         2415
EXPENSE.DBF          809        01/13/89       110251
INCOME.DBF            97        01/13/89        14453

  300011 bytes in     8 files
44707840 bytes remaining on drive
```

SELECT THE DATABASE FROM THE ABOVE LIST, TYPE "ESC" TO QUIT

*Figure 8-26 This menu lets the user select a database
from those available.*

Lines 36 through 70 are FIELDMSK.PRG plopped into LISTER.PRG. For readers wanting to learn programming as they learn dBASE IV, recognize that the programs we create in this book are built from programs we created earlier. There is nothing new under the sun, the sun simply hasn't yet shone on everything under it.

Lines 73 through 81 create another pop-up to offer choices regarding where to send the listing (figure 8-27). The methodology is identical to how other menus have been created.

SCREEN
FILE
PRINTER

SELECT A LIST TARGET FROM THE ABOVE OPTIONS

Figure 8-27 *This menu lets the user select a target for the output of LISTER.PRG.*

Lines 86 through 109 do something a little new. Careful readers will also see the solution to the earlier coding problem. We gave the user a choice of databases, a choice of fields in the database, and a choice of output targets. Now we want to give the user the ability to place conditions on the listing. Conditions can be placed in three ways. The user can directly enter the condition, activate an already existing query file, or create a new query file and make that active.

We ask if there are any conditions to place on the listing in line 83. If so, show all query files on line 90. This makes use of dBASE IV's ability to create a menu of available QBE (query-by-example) and QBO (compiled query) files. And here is another hint regarding the solution to our earlier coding problem: dBASE IV shows all available QBE and QBO files if *no* CATALOG is SET and ON; dBASE IV shows only QBE and QBO files linked to the selected database if a CATALOG is SET and ON. There is always the possibility that dBASE IV will show no QBE or QBO files.

dBASE III Plus users will have to learn that dBASE IV can use the SET FILTER TO FILE ? command, but only to use dBASE III Plus query files. The command will not show dBASE IV QBE or QBO files. This is a potential trouble spot for people bringing their III Plus applications into the dBASE IV arena. The dBASE IV command to use the new QBE and QBO files is SET VIEW TO ? or SET VIEW TO *filename.*

The precaution is found on line 89, ON ERROR DO NOTHING. It would be great if dBASE IV knew enough to DO NOTHING, but NOTHING is actually a program that does absolutely guess what.

Assume the SET VIEW TO ? command on line 90 accesses a QBE or QBO file. Does that query file have any effect on the database? This is checked in line 91. COUNT nonfiltered records to a variable, ALLRECS. Check if there is an equal number of nonfiltered records to total records in the database with our old friend RECCOUNT( ) on line 93.

If so, let the users know that the query file they selected had no choice (line 95) and create a pop-up to find out if they want to directly enter a condition on the database or design a new query form (lines 96 to 101).

At this point, we are ready to send the listing to the target. We SET the CONSOLE back ON (line 107), CLEAR it of all previous displays (line 108), then do the actual LIST command on line 109.

Look at that LIST command. LIST &FIELDNAMES &TARGET. The ampersands are used to create macro substitutions in the LIST command. This means dBASE IV sees &FIELDNAMES and instead reads the information that has been placed in the FIELDNAMES variable by GET-FIELD.PRG. dBASE IV sees &TARGET and reads what GETTARGET.PRG placed in the TARGET variable. Don't confuse macro substitutions with dBASE IV keyboard macros.

But make no mistakes—all the code we have described so far and all the called routines we have yet to discuss (GETDBF.PRG, GETFIELD.PRG, GETTARGET.PRG, NOTHING.PRG, and GETQUERY.PRG) lead up to line 109. Lines 110 through 112 simply reset the world to the way it was before we started LISTER.PRG.

Has anyone figured out the solution to our coding problem? Lines 11 and 30 are unnecessary if you remember that the DO WHILE...ENDDO loop on lines 21 through 30 can be recoded as a SCAN...ENDSCAN block. Further, lines 11 through 18 can be replaced by

```
USE ?
```

This lets the user select from any databases on the computer or network. You can even create a tighter option choice by using one of the following variations:

```
SET CATALOG TO ?
USE ?
```

or:

```
SET CATALOG TO catalog
USE ?
```

The first command pair gives the user the option of selecting both a Catalog file and a database from that catalog. The second command pair limits the user to selecting a database from the Catalog file you code into the program. Remember that either of these command forms places limits on which query files dBASE IV shows with the SET FILTER TO FILE ? command. Also, any query files you create are automatically appended to the current Catalog file and linked to the current database unless you SET CATALOG OFF or SET CATALOG TO before doing any query file work.

Now that we have explained the LISTER.PRG file, we can begin explaining how its ancillary files function. The first one encountered is GETDBF.PRG, listing 8-2. Be prepared for a fair degree of logical repetition in these files, by the way.

Listing 8-2

```
00001 : ** GETDBF.PRG
00002 : *
00003 : SET MESSAGE TO
00004 : GO BAR()
00005 : ENTRY = LEFT(ENTRY, AT([.], ENTRY) - 1)
00006 : USE &ENTRY
00007 : DEACTIVATE POPUP
00008 : *
00009 : ** EOF: GETDBF.PRG
```

The sole purpose of GETDBF.PRG is to place the selected database in USE. It also does some minor housekeeping, such as SET MESSAGE TO in line 3.

At this point, we are still using DIRTANK.DBF. DIRTANK.DBF contains useful database file data from record 3 to the third from the last record. We use the DEFINE BAR...SKIP command to make sure no non-database information is selected from the TANK pop-up. This means it is safe for us to GO BAR( ) in line 4, which causes dBASE IV to position the record pointer at a DIRTANK.DBF record that contains the name of a database as the first thing in the record.

Line 5 does something cutesy. We create a memory variable, ENTRY, and place the selected file name in that memory variable. How does this all work?

First, line 5 is not an equation. It has nothing to do with the mathematical concept of equality. Line 5 is computerese for "Do what is on the right of the equal sign and put the result in what is on the left of the equal sign." We use the LEFT( ) and AT( ) functions to accomplish this. Consider record #3 of DIRTANK.DBF:

EXOLD.DBF   12   01/26/89   1706

The important part of this line is everything to the left of the period, and I don't mean the five characters. If we had chosen the line

XYWORDS.DBF   0   01/26/89   66

we would still be interested in everything to the left of the period. The AT( ) function looks for the character or string you indicate in the string, field, or variable you indicate. Thus, AT([.], ENTRY) says "Look for the first occurrence of a period in the Entry field." The LEFT( ) function clips the string, field, or variable you give it at the character you state. Thus, LEFT(ENTRY, AT([.], ENTRY) − 1) says "Take the Entry field, find the first occurrence of a period (the AT( ) function), go left one character (the −1), and give me what is left." No pun intended, folks.

Line 6 is another macro substitution, as described in the LIST &FIELDNAMES &TARGET command in LISTER.PRG. We USE what is in the ENTRY memory variable.

Line 7 is a special type of housekeeping. dBASE IV would keep returning to the TANK pop-up unless we specifically DEACTIVATED or RELEASED that pop-up menu. The program would be in a blind, never-ending loop, constantly going from GETDBF.PRG to the TANK pop-up and back if DEACTIVATE POPUP wasn't on line 7.

Next we look at GETFIELD.PRG, listing 8-3.

Listing 8-3

```
00001 : ** GETFIELD.PRG
00002 : * THIS PROGRAM GETS FIELD NAMES AND BUILDS A FIELD LIST
00003 : *
00004 :    IF BAR() # 0
00005 :        FIELDNAMES = FIELDNAMES + ;
                   IIF(LEN(TRIM(FIELDNAMES)) # 0, [, ], []) ;
                   + FIELD(BAR())
00006 :    ENDIF
00007 : *
00008 : ** EOP: GETFIELD.PRG
```

Looks a lot like SETFIELD.PRG, doesn't it? That is what it was before we made some changes. Provided the user doesn't press [Esc] (BAR( ) # 0 on line 4), FIELDNAMES is built on the fields in the database, much as SETFIELD.PRG did in chapter 6. The difference in coding is because LIST needs commas between field names. Thus, take FIELDNAMES and determine if there is no information in it. This corresponds to FIELDNAMES = [ ], which corresponds to GETFIELD.PRG being accessed for the first time. IIF the LENGTH of the TRIMMED FIELDNAMES variable isn't 0, put a comma between it and the FIELD( ) corresponding to the BAR( ) menu option. IIF the LENGTH of the TRIMMED FIELDNAMES variable is 0, which means this is the first time we put information into FIELDNAMES, don't put a comma there.

And that is all there is to it. Next is GETTARGET.PRG, listing 8-4:

Listing 8-4

```
00001 : ** GETTARGET.PRG
00002 : *
00003 : DO CASE
00004 :    CASE BAR() < 2
00005 :         TARGET = []
00006 :    CASE BAR() = 2
00007 :         CLEAR
00008 :         FILENAME = SPACE(8)
00009 :         @ 10,0 SAY [WHAT IS THE OUTPUT FILE NAME? -> ] ;
                       GET FILENAME PICT "XXXXXXXX"
00010 :         READ
00011 :         TARGET = [TO FILE ] + FILENAME
00012 :    OTHERWISE
00013 :         TARGET = [TO PRINT]
00014 : *
00015 :         DO WHILE .NOT. PRINTSTATUS()
00016 :              CLEAR
00017 :              @ 10,0 SAY [THE PRINTER ISN'T READY. ] + ;
                          [TRY AGAIN? (Y/N) -> ] ;
                          GET TRUTH PICT "Y"
00018 :              READ
00019 : *
00020 :              IF .NOT. TRUTH
00021 :                   CANCEL
00022 :              ENDIF
00023 : *
00024 :         ENDDO
00025 : *
00026 : ENDCASE
00027 ı *
00028 : DEACTIVATE POPUP
00029 : *
00030 : ** EOF: GETTARGET.PRG
00031 :
```

GETTARGET.PRG has one function, to find out where the user wants the listing to go. The user has three options: screen, file, and printer. Something like this is best handled by a DO CASE...CASE...OTHERWISE... ENDCASE command block. Pressing the [Esc] key passes a BAR( ) value of 0 to GETTARGET.PRG. This is interpreted as a target of screen. Thus, the first CASE, on line 4, handles any BAR( ) value less than 2.

Lines 6 through 11 handle a request to send the output to a file. You can write some code to generate a file name in a variety of ways. This code asks the user for a file name. Notice that line 11 places the entered file name not only in TARGET, but also TO FILE. This is necessary so that dBASE IV knows that the &TARGET macro is more than just a misspelled field or variable name. In other words, we need TO FILE before the file name to make sure dBASE IV doesn't think it should look for a variable or field name like *Joseph*.

The only option left is to send the output to the printer, which is BAR( ) = 3. That is handled by OTHERWISE on lines 12 through 25. First we place TO PRINT into TARGET (line 13). Next we test to make sure the printer is attached and on with a DO WHILE...ENDDO loop (lines 15 through 24). The actual test is performed with the PRINTSTATUS( ) function. PRINTSTATUS( ) returns True if a printer is attached and on; False if a printer is neither attached nor on. As long as PRINTSTATUS( ) is .NOT. True, display an error message (line 17) and find out if the user wants to quit or correct the situation. If the user wants to quit (NOT. TRUTH), CANCEL the program and return to the DOS prompt. Note that CANCEL doesn't return you to the calling program. CANCEL stops all processing on all levels.

GETTARGET.PRG ends by DEACTIVATING the POPUP, which is done on line 28. We DEACTIVATE the POPUP because we don't want the user to return to the menu. We want the program to go to the next step.

The next program to investigate is NOTHING.PRG, listing 8-5. I won't attempt to explain it.

Listing 8-5

```
00001 : ** nothing.prg
00002 : ** eof: nothing.prg
```

And the last program necessary for LISTER.PRG is GET-QUERY.PRG, listing 8-6:

Listing 8-6

```
00001 : ** GETQUERY.PRG
00002 : * THIS PROGRAM LETS THE USER EITHER ENTER A ;
             CONDITION FOR THE
00003 : * LISTING OR DESIGN A NEW QUERY FILE
00004 : *
00005 : DO CASE
00006 :    CASE BAR() = 0
00007 :        CANCEL
00008 :    CASE BAR() = 1
00009 :        FILTNAME = SPACE(8)
00010 :        @ 14,0 SAY [WHAT IS THE NAME OF THE NEW ] + ;
                  [QUERY? -> ] ;
                  GET FILTNAME PICT "XXXXXXXX"
00011 :        READ
00012 :        CREATE QUERY &FILTNAME
00013 :        SET VIEW TO &FILTNAME
00014 :        SET EXACT OFF
```

```
00015 :    CASE BAR() = 2
00016 :       CLEAR
00017 :          PUBLIC CONDITION
00018 :          CONDITION = []
00019 :          SET CONSOLE ON
00020 :          DISPLAY STRUCTURE
00021 : *
00022 :          DO WHILE TYPE([&CONDITION]) = [U]
00023 :              @ 23,0
00024 :                 ACCEPT [WHAT IS THE CONDITION? -> ] ;
                              TO CONDITION
00025 :    ENDDO
00026 : *
00027 :          SET FILTER TO &CONDITION
00028 : *
00029 : ENDCASE
00030 : *
00031 : DEACTIVATE POPUP
00032 : *
00033 : ** EOF: GETQUERY.PRG
```

What do we do if there are no query files for SET FILTER TO FILE? We give the user the option of directly entering a condition for the listing or creating a new query file to use on this and subsequent listings. Giving the user these two options is what GETQUERY.PRG is all about, and it is best handled with a DO CASE...CASE...ENDCASE block.

The first CASE (line 6) handles the [Esc] key being pressed and CANCELs all programs (line 7). The second CASE (line 8) handles the user's request to design a new query form. The new query form must be given a name, so the user is prompted for a file name in lines 10 and 11. The query design system—which is discussed in more detail in the next chapter—is opened in line 12, and the query VIEW is SET on line 13. Note that we also SET EXACT OFF on line 14. This is necessary because dBASE IV assumes you want to be EXACT if you are using a query file. This might not be the case, especially if you are designing an inexact query.

Line 15 handles the user's request to directly enter a condition on the listing. Line 17 does something a little backwards, but intentionally so. We declare a PUBLIC variable, CONDITION. Declaring a variable as PUBLIC means it can be used by all levels of the program, not just levels beneath the current one. You may remember my saying that A can pass information to B, but B can't pass its own native information to A. Declaring a variable PUBLIC in B, however, lets dBASE IV know that this native information can be passed back up to A. We did not declare CONDITION in LISTER.PRG because we did not know if we would need it. Now we do, so we make sure the information can get back up to LISTER.PRG.

Lines 19 and 20 SET the CONSOLE back ON because we will DISPLAY the STRUCTURE of the current database there. We do this so that the user will have an idea of how to set up the CONDITION on the listing. The actual CONDITION is entered in line 24, which is nested in a DO WHILE...ENDDO loop (lines 22 through 25). Because we need to make sure a valid CONDITION will be used on the listing, we must test it somehow. The test is done with the TYPE( ) function on line 22.

TYPE( ) determines if something is character, numeric, date, float, logical, memo, or undefined data. You will note that the first six TYPEs are also dBASE IV database data types. You can also use TYPE( ) to determine if a variable makes sense in the current environment, which is what is done in line 22. We check if the entered CONDITION is logically True and a plausible entry for the current database (figure 8-28).

```
Structure for database: C:\4\EXERCISE.DBF
Number of data records:      19
Date of last update    : 01/26/89
Field  Field Name  Type       Width   Dec    Index
    1   EXERCISE    Character    20            Y
    2   DATE        Date          8            N
    3   TIME        Character     8            N
    4   SET_1_REPS  Numeric       3            N
    5   SET_1_WGT   Numeric       4            N
    6   SET_2_REPS  Numeric       3            N
    7   SET_2_WGT   Numeric       4            N
    8   SET_3_REPS  Numeric       3            N
    9   SET_3_WGT   Numeric       4            N
   10   SET_4_REPS  Numeric       3            N
   11   SET_4_WGT   Numeric       4            N
   12   SET_5_REPS  Numeric       3            N
   13   SET_5_WGT   Numeric       4            N
   14   SET_6_REPS  Numeric       3            N
   15   SET_6_WGT   Numeric       4            N
   16   TOTAL_WGT   Numeric       5            N
   17   COMMENT     Memo         10            N
WHAT IS THE CONDITION? -> EXERCISE = 'B'
```

Figure 8-28 GETQUERY.PRG places a structure listing on the screen when it prompts for a listing CONDITION.

If the TYPE of the CONDITION is undefined, continue asking for a valid CONDITION. (You might want to put an exit condition in the code here.) SET the FILTER TO the just entered CONDITION on line 27, DEACTIVATE the POPUP on line 31, and you are finished.

A lot of work? Perhaps, but think of what you have learned and the universality of the program.

Now, did we need to declare CONDITION PUBLIC in GETQUERY.PRG? No. Because the SET FILTER TO command that uses CONDITION is in GETQUERY.PRG, CONDITION does not have to be PUBLIC. You might want to make it so if you SET the FILTER in LISTER.PRG, however. Also, you can add a SET PROCEDURE TO GETFILES early in LISTER.PRG and gather all these ancillary files into a GETFILES.PRG PROCEDURE file, thus cleaning up the disk slightly and making dBASE IV run a tad quicker.

So much for quick and simple LISTs and DISPLAYs. This section gave a sparse introduction to the query system, the sole topic of the next chapter.

What dBASE IV Does With Your Report and Label Forms

I have mentioned that dBASE IV takes the report you lay out on the report form design system and creates an FRG file. This FRG file is a program that can be used to produce your report. Why is this necessary? dBASE III Plus users may be especially curious about this considering that dBASE III Plus creates a single and simple FRM file.

When you lay out your report form on the design system, it creates the FRM file, which is similar to the III Plus FRM file. You can't take an FRM file designed in dBASE IV and use it in III Plus. You can take a III Plus FRM file and use it in dBASE IV, but not until dBASE IV creates the related FRG and FRO files. After the report design is laid out, dBASE IV generates the FRG file. This is a text file that can be edited with the dBASE IV word processor or any standard text editor.

One of the few reasons (if not the only reason) to edit the FRG file is to change the program itself. The FRG file is more like a huge PROCEDURE file than anything else. Listing 8-7, for example, is the dBASE IV generated FRG file for EXBYDATE.FRM. This FRG file is explained so that you can have a better understanding of how programs work in dBASE IV and how to program your own dBASE IV code better.

Listing 8-7

```
001 : * Program............: C:exbydate.FRG
002 : * Date...............: 2-01-89
003 : * Versions...........: dBASE IV, Report 1
004 : *
005 : * Notes:
006 : * ------
007 : * Prior to running this procedure with the DO command,
008 : * it is necessary to use LOCATE because the CONTINUE
009 : * statement is in the main loop.
010 : *
011 : *-- Parameters
012 : PARAMETERS gl_noeject, gl_plain, gl_summary, gc_heading, gc_
       extra
013 : ** The first three parameters are of type Logical.
014 : ** The fourth parameter is a string.  The fifth is extra.
015 : PRIVATE _peject, _wrap
016 :
017 : *-- Test for no records found
018 : IF EOF() .OR. .NOT. FOUND()
```

Listing 8-7 (cont.)

```
019 :    RETURN
020 : ENDIF
021 :
022 : *-- turn word wrap mode off
023 : _wrap=.F.
024 :
025 : IF _plength < 13
026 :    SET DEVICE TO SCREEN
027 :    DEFINE WINDOW gw_report FROM 7,17 TO 11,62 DOUBLE
028 :    ACTIVATE WINDOW gw_report
029 :    @ 0,1 SAY "Increase the page length for this report."
030 :    @ 2,1 SAY "Press any key ..."
031 :    x=INKEY(0)
032 :    DEACTIVATE WINDOW gw_report
033 :    RELEASE WINDOW gw_report
034 :    RETURN
035 : ENDIF
036 :
037 : _plineno=0          && set lines to zero
038 : *-- NOEJECT parameter
039 : IF gl_noeject
040 :    IF _peject="BEFORE"
041 :       _peject="NONE"
042 :    ENDIF
043 :    IF _peject="BOTH"
044 :       _peject="AFTER"
045 :    ENDIF
046 : ENDIF
047 :
048 : *-- Set up environment
049 : ON ESCAPE DO prnabort
050 : IF SET("TALK")="ON"
051 :    SET TALK OFF
052 :    gc_talk="ON"
053 : ELSE
054 :    gc_talk="OFF"
055 : ENDIF
056 : gc_space=SET("SPACE")
057 : SET SPACE OFF
058 : gc_time=TIME()       && system time for predefined field
059 : gd_date=DATE()       && system date for predefined field
060 : gl_fandl=.F.         && first and last page flag
061 : gl_prntflg=.T.       && Continue printing flag
062 : gl_widow=.T.         && flag for checking widow bands
063 : gn_length=LEN(gc_heading)  && store length of the HEADING
064 : gn_level=2           && current band being processed
065 : gn_page=_pageno      && grab current page number
066 :
067 :
```

```
068 :
069 : *-- Set up procedure for page break
070 : IF _pspacing > 1
071 :    gn_atline=_plength - (4 * _pspacing + 1)
072 : ELSE
073 :    gn_atline=_plength - 5
074 : ENDIF
075 : ON PAGE AT LINE gn_atline EJECT PAGE
076 :
077 : *-- Print Report
078 :
079 : PRINTJOB
080 :
081 : *-- Initialize group break vars.
082 : r_mvar4=EXERCISE
083 :
084 : IF gl_plain
085 :    ON PAGE AT LINE gn_atline DO Pgplain
086 : ELSE
087 :    ON PAGE AT LINE gn_atline DO Pgfoot
088 : ENDIF
089 :
090 : DO Pghead
091 :
092 : gl_fandl=.T.          && first physical page started
093 :
094 : DO Rintro
095 :
096 : DO Grphead
097 :
098 : *-- File Loop
099 : DO WHILE FOUND() .AND. .NOT. EOF() .AND. gl_prntflg
100 :    DO CASE
101 :    CASE .NOT. (EXERCISE = r_mvar4)
102 :       gn_level=4
103 :    OTHERWISE
104 :       gn_level=0
105 :    ENDCASE
106 :    *-- test whether an expression didn't match
107 :    IF gn_level <> 0
108 :       DO Grpinit
109 :    ENDIF
110 :    *-- Repeat group intros
111 :    IF gn_level <> 0
112 :       DO Grphead
113 :    ENDIF
114 :    DO Upd_Vars
115 :    *-- Detail lines
116 :    IF .NOT. gl_summary
117 :       DO Detail
118 :    ENDIF
```

Listing 8-7 (cont.)

```
119 :     CONTINUE
120 : ENDDO
121 :
122 : IF gl_prntflg
123 :     gn_level=3
124 :     DO Rsumm
125 :     IF _plineno <= gn_atline
126 :        EJECT PAGE
127 :     ENDIF
128 : ELSE
129 :     gn_level=3
130 :     DO Rsumm
131 :     DO Reset
132 :     RETURN
133 : ENDIF
134 :
135 : ON PAGE
136 :
137 : ENDPRINTJOB
138 :
139 : DO Reset
140 : RETURN
141 : * EOP: C:exbydate.FRG
142 :
143 : *-- Update summary fields and/or calculated fields in the detail
        band.
144 : PROCEDURE Upd_Vars
145 : RETURN
146 : * EOP: Upd_Vars
147 :
148 : *-- Set flag to get out of DO WHILE loop when escape is pressed.
149 : PROCEDURE prnabort
150 : gl_prntflg=.F.
151 : RETURN
152 : * EOP: prnabort
153 :
154 : *-- Reset group break variables.  Reinit summary
155 : *-- fields with reset set to a particular group band.
156 : PROCEDURE Grpinit
157 : IF gn_level <= 4
158 :     r_mvar4=EXERCISE
159 : ENDIF
160 : RETURN
161 : * EOP: Grpinit
162 :
163 : *-- Process Group Intro bands during group breaks
164 : PROCEDURE Grphead
165 : IF EOF()
166 :     RETURN
```

```
167 : ENDIF
168 : gl_widow=.T.              && enable widow checking
169 : IF gn_level <= 4
170 :     DO Head4
171 : ENDIF
172 : gn_level=0
173 : RETURN
174 : * EOP: Grphead.PRG
175 :
176 : PROCEDURE Pghead
177 : IF _wrap
178 :     PRIVATE _wrap
179 :     _wrap = .F.
180 : ENDIF
181 : ?? "Exercise Progress Report" AT 42
182 : ?
183 : ?? "Carrabis, Page - " AT 42,
184 : ?? IIF(gl_plain,'',_pageno) PICTURE "999"
185 : ?
186 : *-- Print HEADING parameter, i.e. REPORT FORM <name> HEADING
      <expC>
187 : IF .NOT. gl_plain .AND. gn_length > 0
188 :     ?? gc_heading FUNCTION "I;V"+LTRIM(STR(_rmargin-lmargin))
189 :     ?
190 : ENDIF
191 : IF .NOT. gl_plain
192 :     ?? gd_date AT 42
193 :     ?
194 : ENDIF
195 : ?
196 : ?
197 : ?
198 : ?
199 : RETURN
200 : * EOP: Pghead
201 :
202 : PROCEDURE Rintro
203 : PRIVATE _indent, _lmargin, _rmargin, _tabs
204 : IF .NOT. _wrap
205 :     PRIVATE _wrap
206 :     _wrap = .T.
207 : ENDIF
208 : _indent=0
209 : _lmargin=0
210 : _pcolno=0
211 : _rmargin=65
212 : _tabs=;
213 : "8,16,24,32,40,48,56,64,72,80,88,96,104,112,120,128,136,144,152,
      160,168";
214 : + ",176,184,192,200,208,216,224,232,240";
215 :
```

Listing 8-7 (cont.)

```
216 : ?? "This report is based on an exercise format designed by
      Denise "
217 : ?? "Dargie of Gold's Gym in Amesbury, Massachusetts. The style
      of the "
218 : ?? "workout and intensity are changed over time, according to
      Ms. "
219 : ?? "Dargie's instructions; therefore, this report is broken down
       as "
220 : ?? "Exercise by Date, listing repetitions and weights. The goal
      of "
221 : ?? "this report format is to show the individual's progression
      over "
222 : ?? "time." ,
223 : ?
224 : _indent=0
225 : _lmargin=0
226 : _pcolno=0
227 : _rmargin=65
228 : _tabs=;
229 : "8,16,24,32,40,48,56,64,72,80,88,96,104,112,120,128,136,144,152,
      160,168";
230 : + ",176,184,192,200,208,216,224,232,240";
231 :
232 : ?
233 : _indent=0
234 : _lmargin=0
235 : _pcolno=0
236 : _rmargin=65
237 : _tabs=;
238 : "8,16,24,32,40,48,56,64,72,80,88,96,104,112,120,128,136,144,152,
      160,168";
239 : + ",176,184,192,200,208,216,224,232,240";
240 :
241 : ?? "Ms. Dargie is holder of several weight lifting and body
      building "
242 : ?? "titles in the Northeast and Eastern United States." ,
243 : ?
244 : _indent=0
245 : _lmargin=0
246 : _pcolno=0
247 : _rmargin=65
248 : _tabs=;
249 : "8,16,24,32,40,48,56,64,72,80,88,96,104,112,120,128,136,144,152,
      160,168";
250 : + ",176,184,192,200,208,216,224,232,240";
251 :
252 : ?
253 : _indent=0
254 : _lmargin=0
```

```
255 : _pcolno=0
256 : _rmargin=65
257 : _tabs=;
258 : "8,16,24,32,40,48,56,64,72,80,88,96,104,112,120,128,136,144,152,
      160,168";
259 : + ",176,184,192,200,208,216,224,232,240";
260 :
261 : ?
262 : ?
263 : RETURN
264 : * EOP: Rintro
265 :
266 : PROCEDURE Head4
267 : IF gn_level=1
268 :    RETURN
269 : ENDIF
270 : IF _wrap
271 :    PRIVATE _wrap
272 :    _wrap = .F.
273 : ENDIF
274 : IF 5 < _plength
275 :    IF (gl_widow .AND. _plineno+10 > gn_atline) ;
276 :    .OR. (gl_widow .AND. _plineno+4 > gn_atline)
277 :       EJECT PAGE
278 :    ENDIF
279 : ENDIF
280 : ?? "Exercise -> " AT 0,
281 : ?? EXERCISE FUNCTION "T"
282 : ?
283 : ?
284 : ?? "                    SETS                " AT 16
285 : ?
286 : ?? "  Date" AT 0,
287 : ?? " Reps/   1" AT 8,
288 : ?? "  2" AT 24,
289 : ?? "  3" AT 32,
290 : ?? "  4" AT 40,
291 : ?? "  5" AT 48,
292 : ?? "  6" AT 56
293 : ?
294 : ?? "Wgts" AT 10
295 : ?
296 : RETURN
297 :
298 : PROCEDURE Detail
299 : IF _wrap
300 :    PRIVATE _wrap
301 :    _wrap = .F.
302 : ENDIF
303 : IF 6 < _plength
304 :    IF gl_widow .AND. _plineno+5 > gn_atline
```

Listing 8-7 (cont.)

```
305 :      EJECT PAGE
306 :    ENDIF
307 : ENDIF
308 : ?? DATE AT 0,
309 : ?? SET_1_REPS PICTURE "999" AT 16,
310 : ?? SET_2_REPS PICTURE "999" AT 24,
311 : ?? SET_3_REPS PICTURE "999" AT 32,
312 : ?? SET_4_REPS PICTURE "999" AT 40,
313 : ?? SET_5_REPS PICTURE "999" AT 48,
314 : ?? SET_6_REPS PICTURE "999" AT 56
315 : ?
316 : ?? SET_1_WGT PICTURE "9999" AT 15,
317 : ?? SET_2_WGT PICTURE "9999" AT 23,
318 : ?? SET_3_WGT PICTURE "9999" AT 31,
319 : ?? SET_4_WGT PICTURE "9999" AT 39,
320 : ?? SET_5_WGT PICTURE "9999" AT 47,
321 : ?? SET_6_WGT PICTURE "9999" AT 55
322 : ?
323 : ?
324 : ?? "Total_Wgt ->  " AT 0,
325 : ?? TOTAL_WGT PICTURE "99999"
326 : ?
327 : ?
328 : ?
329 : RETURN
330 : * EOP: Detail
331 :
332 :
333 : PROCEDURE Rsumm
334 : PRIVATE _indent, _lmargin, _rmargin, _tabs
335 : IF .NOT. _wrap
336 :    PRIVATE _wrap
337 :    _wrap = .T.
338 : ENDIF
339 : _indent=0
340 : _lmargin=0
341 : _pcolno=0
342 : _rmargin=65
343 : _tabs=;
344 : "8,16,24,32,40,48,56,64,72,80,88,96,104,112,120,128,136,144,152,
       160,168";
345 : + ",176,184,192,200,208,216,224,232,240";
346 :
347 : ?? "Designing and laying out a report form can show previously "
348 : ?? "unnoticed flaws in the logic and flow of a database system.
       "
349 : ?? "Designing this report shows that we hardly ever use the
       COMMENT "
350 : ?? "field, but we do know that field is useful. " ,
```

```
351 : ?
352 : _indent=0
353 : _lmargin=0
354 : _pcolno=0
355 : _rmargin=65
356 : _tabs=;
357 : "8,16,24,32,40,48,56,64,72,80,88,96,104,112,120,128,136,144,152,
       160,168";
358 : + ",176,184,192,200,208,216,224,232,240";
359 :
360 : ?
361 : _indent=0
362 : _lmargin=0
363 : _pcolno=0
364 : _rmargin=65
365 : _tabs=;
366 : "8,16,24,32,40,48,56,64,72,80,88,96,104,112,120,128,136,144,152,
       160,168";
367 : + ",176,184,192,200,208,216,224,232,240";
368 :
369 : ?? "It would be useful to separate the EXERCISE database into
       two "
370 : ?? "separate databases. The first database, called EXERCISE,
       should "
371 : ?? "include the Date, Time, and Set_n fields. The second "
372 : ?? "database, called EXCOMMNT, should include the Date, Time,
       and "
373 : ?? "Comment fields. The Time field might prove unnecessary in
       both "
374 : ?? "cases, but we can keep it for now. The Date field is
       necessary "
375 : ?? "as a way to link the two databases. " ,
376 : ?
377 : _indent=0
378 : _lmargin=0
379 : _pcolno=0
380 : _rmargin=65
381 : _tabs=;
382 : "8,16,24,32,40,48,56,64,72,80,88,96,104,112,120,128,136,144,152,
       160,168";
383 : + ",176,184,192,200,208,216,224,232,240";
384 :
385 : ?
386 : _indent=0
387 : _lmargin=0
388 : _pcolno=0
389 : _rmargin=65
390 : _tabs=;
391 : "8,16,24,32,40,48,56,64,72,80,88,96,104,112,120,128,136,144,152,
       160,168";
392 : + ",176,184,192,200,208,216,224,232,240";
```

Listing 8-7 (cont.)

```
393 :
394 : ?? "Modifying the database in this way would mean reworking the
        screen "
395 : ?? "form and the report form (if we want to include the Comment
        "
396 : ?? "field from the EXCOMMNT.DBF file), but would also provide an
        "
397 : ?? "excellent opportunity for learning more about the workings
        of "
398 : ?? "dBASE IV." ,
399 : ?
400 : _indent=0
401 : _lmargin=0
402 : _pcolno-0
403 : _rmargin=65
404 : _tabs=;
405 : "8,16,24,32,40,48,56,64,72,80,88,96,104,112,120,128,136,144,152,
        160,168";
406 : + ",176,184,192,200,208,216,224,232,240";
407 :
408 : ?
409 : _indent=0
410 : _lmargin=0
411 : _pcolno=0
412 : _rmargin=65
413 : _tabs=;
414 : "8,16,24,32,40,48,56,64,72,80,88,96,104,112,120,128,136,144,152,
        160,168";
415 : + ",176,184,192,200,208,216,224,232,240";
416 :
417 : ?? "Let's do this in the next chapter." ,
418 : ?
419 : _indent=0
420 : _lmargin=0
421 : _pcolno=0
422 : _rmargin=65
423 : _tabs=;
424 : "8,16,24,32,40,48,56,64,72,80,88,96,104,112,120,128,136,144,152,
        160,168";
425 : + ",176,184,192,200,208,216,224,232,240";
426 :
427 : ?
428 : _indent=0
429 : _lmargin=0
430 : _pcolno=0
431 : _rmargin=65
432 : _tabs=;
433 : "8,16,24,32,40,48,56,64,72,80,88,96,104,112,120,128,136,144,152,
        160,168";
```

```
434 : + ",176,184,192,200,208,216,224,232,240";
435 :
436 : ?? "This report summary, by the way, should be considered as
        part of "
437 : ?? "the text of the book." ,
438 : ?
439 : _indent=0
440 : _lmargin=0
441 : _pcolno=0
442 : _rmargin=65
443 : _tabs=;
444 : "8,16,24,32,40,48,56,64,72,80,88,96,104,112,120,128,136,144,152,
        160,168";
445 : + ",176,184,192,200,208,216,224,232,240";
446 :
447 : ?
448 : _indent=0
449 : _lmargin=0
450 : _pcolno=0
451 : _rmargin=65
452 : _tabs=;
453 : "8,16,24,32,40,48,56,64,72,80,88,96,104,112,120,128,136,144,152,
        160,168";
454 : + ",176,184,192,200,208,216,224,232,240";
455 :
456 : ?? "            "
457 : gl_fandl=.F.          && last page finished
458 : ?
459 : RETURN
460 : * EOP: Rsumm
461 :
462 : PROCEDURE Pgfoot
463 : PRIVATE _box
464 : gl_widow=.F.          && disable widow checking
465 : ?
466 : IF .NOT. gl_plain
467 : IF _wrap
468 :    PRIVATE _wrap
469 :    _wrap = .F.
470 : ENDIF
471 : ?
472 : ?
473 : ?
474 : ENDIF
475 : EJECT PAGE
476 : *-- is the page number greater than the ending page
477 : IF _pageno > _pepage
478 :    GOTO BOTTOM
479 :    SKIP
480 :    gn_level=0
481 : ENDIF
```

Listing 8-7 (cont.)

```
482 : IF .NOT. gl_plain .AND. gl_fandl
483 :    DO Pghead
484 : ENDIF
485 : IF gn_level = 0 .AND. gl_fandl
486 :    gn_level=1
487 :    DO Grphead
488 : ENDIF
489 : gl_widow=.T.              && enable widow checking
490 : RETURN
491 : * EOP: Pgfoot
492 :
493 : *-- Process page break when PLAIN option is used.
494 : PROCEDURE Pgplain
495 : PRIVATE _box
496 : EJECT PAGE
497 : IF gn_level = 0 .AND. gl_fandl
498 :    gn_level=1
499 :    DO Grphead
500 : ENDIF
501 : RETURN
502 : * EOP: Pgplain
503 :
504 : *-- Reset dBASE environment prior to calling report
505 : PROCEDURE Reset
506 : SET SPACE &gc_space.
507 : SET TALK &gc_talk.
508 : ON ESCAPE
509 : ON PAGE
510 : RETURN
511 : * EOP: Reset
512 :
```

Look at the opening comments in this file and you will see that it is not intended to be run by itself. It requires some type of LOCATE command because there is a CONTINUE command in the file.

What are LOCATE and CONTINUE? LOCATE is one of three commands dBASE IV uses to find information in the database. These three commands are FIND, LOCATE, and SEEK. FIND and SEEK work with indexed databases because both FIND and SEEK can only find things in the key field or key expression. For example, we can FIND or SEEK the DB PRESS exercise in the Exercise field by getting to the dBASE prompt and typing either

```
FIND [DB PRESS]
```

or:

SEEK [DB PRESS]

These work when the controlling index uses the Exercise field as the first or only part of the index key. dBASE IV can retrieve information remarkably fast with FIND and SEEK, but remember that you have to look for information in the key field. What happens when you want to look for information that isn't in the key field? You use LOCATE.

You can LOCATE anything anywhere. You want to LOCATE 120 in Set_5_Wgt? Get to the dBASE prompt and type

```
LOCATE FOR SET_5_WGT = 120
```

This command searches the database—starting from the first record and moving to the last record—testing each record for the condition you entered in the command. There is a drawback to this: LOCATE starts with the first record and moves down to the last record. It does not matter how many times you LOCATE for the same condition, dBASE IV always starts with the first record in the database and searches until it LOCATEs the first record that matches the condition. You can have a 2000-record database and know that 100 records match your LOCATE condition. Each LOCATE command starts at the beginning of the file and goes to the first matching record. How do you get past that first matching record? You CONTINUE.

CONTINUE is the other side of LOCATE. You LOCATE the first occurrence of your match, then CONTINUE to the next match. What do you do after you reach the next match? You CONTINUE again, until you get to the end of the file. Remember: LOCATE the first one, then CONTINUE to the next one and until you reach the end of the file.

LOCATE and CONTINUE work on any database, whether or not the database is indexed. Because LOCATE goes to the first record in the file, it starts at the first record in the index if an index is active. CONTINUE picks up where LOCATE stops and goes through the rest of the database, again according to any index which might be active.

The exception to LOCATE starting at the first record and going through the database occurs when you place range-limiting qualifiers on the command. LOCATE's range-limiting qualifiers are REST, NEXT n, and WIIILE. REST and NEXT n start at the current record. REST starts at the current record position and goes until it reaches the end of the file. NEXT n starts at the current record position and goes until it has tried to LOCATE through the NEXT n records. You can LOCATE FOR SET_5_WGT = 120 through the NEXT 30 records with

```
LOCATE FOR SET_5_WGT = 120 NEXT 30
```

dBASE IV might encounter the end of the file before it scans through thirty records. If so, it simply stops the LOCATE operation. Also note that CONTINUE automatically uses whatever qualifiers you place on the preceding

LOCATE command. The preceding LOCATE command goes from the current record through the next thirty records. A subsequent CONTINUE would stop after thirty records were searched, counting from the record position when the LOCATE command was issued.

The WHILE qualifier implies that an index is active. It comes into use when you want to LOCATE something in a nonkey field, but you want a key field condition to be met during the LOCATE operation. For example, suppose you want a listing of all exercises where the Set_5_Wgt is 120, but only for 12 October 1988. First, make sure that the Date field is the key field in the current index. Next, FIND or SEEK the date you are looking for, 10/12/88 in this case. Then, enter the LOCATE command. The full sequence follows:

```
SET INDEX TO ndx file/mdx file order tag name
SEEK {10/12/88}
LOCATE FOR SET_5_WGT = 120 WHILE DATE = {10/12/88}
```

dBASE IV starts at the current record—the first record with a Date field matching 10/12/88—and searches until the Date field no longer contains 10/12/88. Remember that LOCATE searches for the first record where its search conditions are met. You must CONTINUE if you want to find other records that match the search conditions. Note that the CONTINUE command obeys the WHILE qualifier.

There is no LOCATE command in the EXBYDATE.FRG file. dBASE IV assumes you started a LOCATE outside the file. dBASE IV does not assume that you have tried to FIND or SEEK information.

The first executable command in EXBYDATE.FRG is line 12. This is also the first indication that dBASE IV thinks that EXBYDATE.FRG will be called from another routine. The PARAMETERS command was used in some of the programs in other chapters. A PARAMETER is a limitation that the calling program places on the called program. The PARAMETERS placed on EXBYDATE.FRG deal with whether to eject a page before printing the report, whether the report should be printed plain or styled, whether the report is a summary of the data it is working with, a report heading, and a miscellaneous variable in case one is needed. How do you read the variable names and know what they are for?

gl_noeject	global logical_do not *eject* a page
gl_plain	global logical_print a *plain* report
gl_summary	global logical_*summary* report
gc_heading	global character_report *heading*
gc_extra	global character_*extra* variable

Line 15 tells dBASE IV that two variables, _peject and _wrap, will have values unique to this program. Having values unique to this program does not mean these variables can't be used by other programs. The

PRIVATE command tells dBASE IV to set aside distinct variables and keep whatever values they may assume in this program solely for this program. Don't pass any values these variables assume in this routine to any program that calls this routine.

Both of these variables are also dBASE IV system memory variables. A system memory variable is one that dBASE IV creates when you first start work. Both _peject and _wrap have to do with how dBASE IV prints things. The first variable, _peject, tells dBASE IV whether it should eject a page of paper before any information is sent to the printer. The second variable, _wrap, tells dBASE IV whether text entries or long character and memo fields should be word wrapped when printed.

Lines 18 through 20 have to do with the LOCATE command, which this program assumes you have issued before this routine was called. Line 18 tries to determine if the LOCATE condition could find any matching information in the database. If no records were found with data to match the LOCATE condition, you are at the EOF( ) or the FOUND( ) function is False, hence .NOT. FOUND( ). The dBASE IV end-of-file function, EOF( ), returns .T. when you reach the physical end of a database file. FOUND( ) is used with SEEK, FIND, and LOCATE to determine if the sought after information or condition was found in the database.

Why use both EOF( ) and FOUND( )? EOF( ) is only True if dBASE IV has reached the physical end of file. This does not necessarily happen in an indexed database because the indexing scheme may place the logical end of file and physical end of file in different places. In other words, the index may place the last physical record before other records, for example: 4, 2, 3, 6, 7, 10, 1, 5, 9, 8. Thus, the physical end of the database is not the logical end of the database, and EOF( ) would be False. FOUND( ) does not care about the ordering of the records and concerns itself only with whether or not a requested item or condition can be found.

Line 19 works with the result of line 18 and cancels the report request if there is no information to print.

Lines 25 through 35 check that you have defined a page length long enough to hold your report. This is done with another dBASE IV system memory variable, _plength (_page length). If the currently defined page length is too small, display an error message (lines 26 to 30), wait for the user to acknowledge the message (line 31), get the error message from memory (lines 32 and 33), and end the report run.

How does dBASE IV know what _plength is? The value is passed to _plength when any print forms are created and executed.

Line 37 is another dBASE IV memory variable, _plineno. This variable is used to count the lines on a form as it is printed. Alternately, it can be used to tell dBASE IV where the printhead is on a piece of paper. Line 37 tells dBASE IV to act as if the printhead is at the top of the printer form.

Lines 39 through 46 take the global logical variable, gl_noeject, and determine how to set the private (to this routine, as shown in line 15) variable _peject. If the global variable is True and the private variable is BEFORE (as in eject a page BEFORE you print the report), set the private variable to NONE (as in don't eject a page before or after you print the report). However, if the global variable is False and the private variable is BOTH (as in eject a page BOTH before and after you print the report), set the private variable to AFTER (as in eject a page AFTER you print the report).

Line 49 provides an out in case you don't want to print the report. ON ESCAPE DO prnabort tells dBASE IV to watch for the [Esc] key. No matter what else dBASE IV is doing regarding the printing of this report, DO the prnabort routine when the [Esc] key is pressed. The prnabort routine starts on line 149. Take a look at this PROCEDURE now and you will see that it only sets a printer flag variable, gl_prntflg, to False. This stops any further printing.

Lines 50 through 65 actually set up the dBASE IV system for printing the report. Lines 50 through 55 test whether dBASE IV will be verbose. dBASE IV being verbose is determined by the status of the TALK parameter. SET TALK ON and dBASE IV tells you everything it is doing. SET TALK OFF and there is much less confusion for the user and on the screen. Lines 56 and 57 find out if an extra SPACE should be printed between database fields when the ? and ?? commands are used. The extra SPACE usually makes a clearer and more understandable printout. The ? and ?? commands tell dBASE IV to print on the next line and the current line, respectively. For example, you tell dBASE IV to print text on the next line with

```
? "Print this on the next line"
```

You tell dBASE IV to print on the current line with

```
?? "Print this on the current line"
```

Lines 58 through 65 are explained with their own notes. Lines 70 through 74 have the sole function of determining when dBASE IV should eject a page from the printer. The IF...ELSE...ENDIF block is not worth discussing because the logic is simple enough. What is interesting is the dBASE IV command in line 75. I mentioned that dBASE IV keeps track of where the printhead is on the page. This command is why that information is so useful. ON the PAGE, as it is printed, when you are AT LINE whatever, EJECT a PAGE. This is the type of control that makes dBASE IV slick. It is also an example of how much programming must be done in order to do the simplest thing.

Lines 79 through 137 contain the block of code that prints the report. The actual printing is handled through a variety of subroutines, all of which are listed starting at line 143. PRINTJOB...ENDPRINTJOB is another command set new to dBASE IV. This block tells dBASE IV that the commands in the block should be routed through the installed print driver.

Line 82 tells dBASE IV which field in the database is the primary grouping field for the report. Lines 84 through 88 determine if this report is plain (line 85) or has information to be printed at the bottom of each printed page (line 87). This is done with the ON PAGE AT LINE command discussed a few paragraphs back. You can have dBASE IV call a different procedure or external command file for each line on a page. This, by the way, might be a way to do some graphics.

The report starts printing at line 90, where the Pghead routine (lines 176 to 200) is called. Remember that we placed the report page heading to the right margin, without wrapping? PROCEDURE Pghead makes sure the heading doesn't wrap by creating its own PRIVATE _wrap variable (line 178) and making _wrap False (line 179).

Much of the rest of PROCEDURE Pghead uses the ? and ?? commands described previously. You can tell dBASE IV to print something on the current line with the ?? command and at a specific column by qualifying the ?? command with AT. This is demonstrated on lines 181, 183, and 192. Remember that the single ? means skip a line or print on the next line, depending on whether there is any information to print following the ? command. Line 184 shows another facet of the ?? command. Look at line 183 and you will see that a comma follows the command. The next line starts with ??. dBASE IV places the information on line 184 not only on the current line, but also at the current column. Lines 187 through 190 print the report heading, if one is given and the report is plain. Lines 191 through 194 print the system date if the report is not plain. Line 199 tells dBASE IV to return to the calling routine, line 90.

We have started the first page, so mark that flag True in line 92. Line 94 tells dBASE IV to call the routine that prints the report introduction. This routine spans lines 202 to 264. Much of how this routine works is evident from discussions of similar commands in other parts of the book. The report introduction is a text entry and we want it with a right margin and word wrap, so set word wrap True (lines 205 and 206). Consider how many times dBASE IV resets printing variables in this routine: each time a block of text is printed, including resetting the variables for printing a single blank line (line 232). dBASE IV does this principally because the imported text did not format properly and it was necessary to word wrap and insert a right margin for each paragraph separately.

The next line from PRINTJOB...ENDPRINTJOB is 96. This line calls the Grphead routine to print the group headings we defined in the report. PROCEDURE Grphead runs from line 164 to line 174. Grphead starts by checking to see if we have reached the end of the file. If so, RETURN to the calling program because there is nothing else to process. Otherwise, check how much room is left at the end of the page to ensure that there won't be any widows. (The terms *widow* and *orphan* describe the last few lines of a paragraph at the bottom of a page and the top of a page, respectively. It does not look too pleasing to see a single sentence on the last page of a report. It looks like you did not plan too well. dBASE IV checks to make sure your report looks good.)

The widow check occurs in PROCEDURE Head4 on line 275 and beyond. Head4 covers lines 266 to 296. Notice that Head4 only checks to ensure no widows exist, then prints the Group Intro 1 band. After that is done, back to Grphead and back to line 96.

Next, the program enters a DO WHILE...ENDDO loop from lines 99 to 120. A DO WHILE...ENDDO block contains a group of commands that are repeated under certain conditions. The conditions for this block include data being FOUND( ), the EOF( ) .NOT. being reached, and the gl_prntflg being True. Lines 100 to 105 are an example of DO CASE...CASE...OTHERWISE...ENDCASE. Note that this DO CASE...ENDCASE block primarily determines which part of the report we are printing at this point. That is the purpose of all the gn_level variables. And as long as we are not at a point where we are working with some part of the report (gn_level < > 0 in line 107), call the Grpinit routine. What does Grpinit do? From lines 156 to 160, Grpinit changes the value of the variable holding the Exercise field contents based on which part of the report we are working with.

The rest of the DO WHILE...ENDDO loop checks if another Grphead should be performed, updates the variables used in the report with the Upd_Vars routine on lines 144 and 145 (this is identical to nothing.prg—there are no variables to update in this report), and prints the report Detail band if we are not at a point to summarize. This is done with the Detail routine covering lines 298 through 330. The sole purpose of this routine is to print the information we placed in the Detail band of the report.

Back to PRINTJOB...ENDPRINTJOB. We encounter the other half of LOCATE, the CONTINUE command on line 119. Line 120 is the end of the DO WHILE...ENDDO loop. If there are no more records to process, dBASE IV prints the report summary information in the Rsumm procedure. This summarizing procedure runs from line 333 to line 460. It is identical to the Rintro routine described previously, except for the variations in the text. Note that Rsumm sets the last page flag to False in line 457, signifying the end of the report. Next is the Reset routine, lines 505 to 510, which returns the dBASE IV environment to its status before the report was run.

Quite a lot of code, especially if you are accustomed to the simple FMT files in dBASE III Plus. You can modify the code if you want, but my guess is that it would be simpler to change the report form through the MODIFY REPORT command. Quick changes that you might do through this program include changing the variables to alter the printing parameters, adding information to the report's intro and summary bands, and altering the spacing of information on the report.

Summary

This chapter has given you a solid introduction to creating your own report system through programming or the dBASE IV report form design system.

It also described the label form system, which is the report system in miniature.

The next step in working with data is filtering it. This is covered in chapter 9.

You can stop reading the book at this point and you will have a good understanding of the various dBASE IV interfaces, how they work, how to work with them, what problems you will encounter with them, and how to avoid those problems before they cost you precious work and the hours it took to complete the work.

The next section shows how to make modifications to what you have already done. This part of the book is best read only if you are comfortable with what you have learned about dBASE IV so far or if you have taken a few days to go over what has been presented in this section.

three

Making Things Work Better in dBASE IV

The last section gave you the fundamentals. Now we look at more advanced items. This section covers modifications you are likely to make to your database management system after you have been working with it for a while.

Why make modifications after you have designed the system? Because you are not an expert. For that matter, neither am I. The best definition of an expert is "I've been there before." The more someone has been to a particular place, the more likely he or she will be labeled an "expert." I think "they" gave me the label because I have been working with data systems for almost twenty years.

One thing I have noticed about database management systems, and this includes the best, is that the first few months of their lives they are mercurial, chameleonic, fluid, and lots of other words which basically mean quickly and radically changeable. You can be involved in data systems for twenty years and still find that things change from what you originally designed. The system designed so far in this book can benefit from modifications, as will most applications you develop. This section shows how to modify the system designed in this book, which will give you ideas and tips on how to make changes to your own database management system.

Working With Query Forms

You can ask the database any question you want. It will answer only questions that are correctly asked, and it might respond with no answer. No answer is a valid response; it means "I don't know."

Queries, normally built through the QBE (query-by-example) interface, are important in learning how to ask questions that dBASE IV can answer. Query files are used to place restrictions, called *filters*, on the database. You don't have to ask all your questions through the QBE interface, but it is the method novices will choose because the QBE interface handles all the programming for you.

We designed a programmatic reporting system in chapter 8 that made partial use of the QBE system. This chapter concentrates on the QBE interface; chapter 10 shows how query files affect report and label form output.

Things to Know Before You Start

You might expect this section to list helpful notes on navigation and such. Not the case here. Even though these warnings are premature—you don't know much about queries yet—they are necessary for readers who like to explore and investigate things on their own.

You lay out queries on the query design surface, shown in figure 9-1. After the queries are designed and you are comfortable that they work as intended, you can either remove the query from memory or save it to disk. There are several ways of saving a query to disk, and all of them have been described in previous parts of the book ([Alt-L] S, [Ctrl-Enter], [Ctrl-W], and [Alt-E] S are examples of standard methods of saving a file). Figure 9-2 shows the [Alt-L] S method of saving a file.

Any active Catalog file is updated when you save a query file to disk. Remembering that a query file is a filter on the database, dBASE III Plus users may try to use the SET FILTER TO FILE ? command to get a listing of ancillary query files. This won't work in dBASE IV unless dBASE III Plus query files exist on the default drive and path, whether or not the catalog is

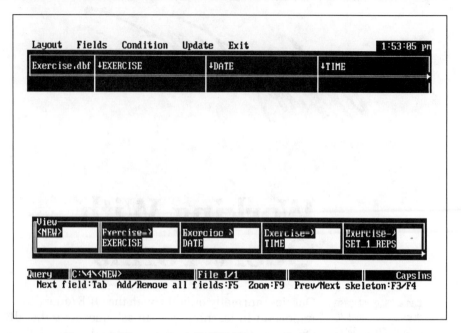

Figure 9-1 *The standard dBASE IV query design system screen.*

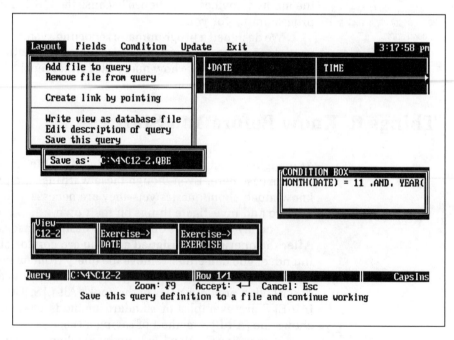

Figure 9-2 *dBASE IV does not prompt for confirmation when you are about to delete a condition box. Thus, you might inadvertently destroy a complex query condition. One way to safeguard against this happening is to save the file with the [Alt-L] S command.*

updated. What appears to happen is that the query file is placed in the catalog but dBASE IV does not make the link between the current database and the newly created or modified query file. You can use the SET FILTER TO FILE ? command but you will get the error messages shown in figures 9-3 and 9-4.

```
    No files of the requested type are cataloged.  Press any key to continue
*SET FILTER TO FILE ?
```

Figure 9-3 dBASE IV seems to have difficulty updating the current
Catalog file when query forms are created. Using the SET FILTER TO
FILE ? command produces the error messages shown in this figure
and in figure 9-4. SET FILTER TO FILE filename is a dBASE III
Plus command and is based on the difference between dBASE
III Plus view and query files. The correct dBASE IV
command is SET VIEW TO filename.

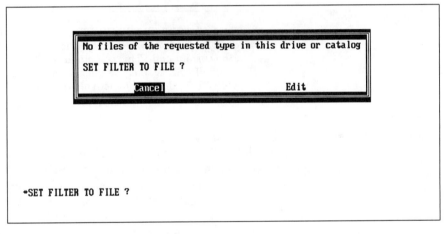

Figure 9-4 This is the second message (figure 9-3 is the first) dBASE IV
puts on the screen when you try using the SET FILTER TO FILE ?
command to get a listing of query files from the current catalog,
even when the query files are created or modified and the
Catalog file has been updated. This command worked in
dBASE III Plus. You must use SET VIEW TO filename
to activate a QBE file in dBASE IV.

Query files not showing up in the catalog is one problem. You can use the SET FILTER TO FILE command to interrogate dBASE IV for available dBASE III Plus query files even when a catalog is not active. This command form is the same as the one shown previously. dBASE IV will pop up a menu of available dBASE III Plus query files.

dBASE III Plus users should note that dBASE III Plus query files are recognized by the dBASE IV SET FILTER TO FILE command. This command does not recognize dBASE IV query files. You will get the message shown in figure 9-5, even though the requested query form is on disk and shows up in the directory directly under the error box.

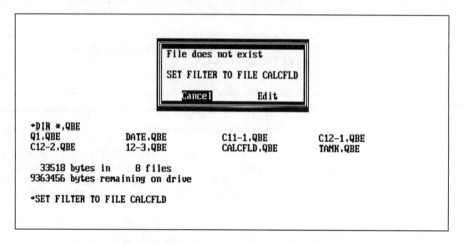

Figure 9-5 The SET FILTER TO FILE command often has trouble finding a QBE file even when that file is clearly on the current drive and in the current path. This command reads dBASE III Plus query files with dBASE IV, but you must then use the dBASE IV SET VIEW TO command to activate the dBASE IV modified dBASE III Plus query file.

dBASE III Plus and dBASE IV query files are not the same, and dBASE IV does not work with them in the same way.

The command that calls up dBASE IV QBE files is SET VIEW TO ?. Why would a VIEW command look for query files? Briefly, views and queries are the same animal. There are differences, but that is for more advanced books and even then you would be safe using the two interchangeably. The reason dBASE IV has both views and queries is for the benefit of dBASE III Plus users coming into the dBASE IV world. There were significant differences between views and queries in dBASE III Plus, not so much in dBASE IV.

You can use the SET VIEW TO ? command to locate query files both when there is no active catalog and when a catalog is active. This is shown in figures 9-6 and 9-7.

As always, I have a solution. And yes, it's not pretty. The SET FILTER TO FILE command is looking for dBASE III Plus query files. These III Plus query files have a QRY extension, not a QBE extension. You can't rename the QBE files to QRY files, because dBASE IV knows what a QRY file is supposed to look like and the QBE file does not fit the description. The end result of this is something that shows the difference between queries and views in III Plus and IV. dBASE IV understands III Plus queries as filters, but not as views. It does understand dBASE IV queries as both queries and views, making them interchangeable.

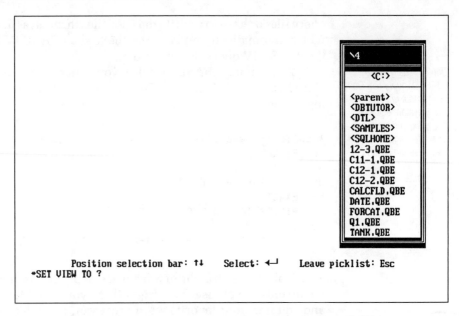

Figure 9-6 The SET VIEW TO ? command finds all available query files when there is no active catalog file.

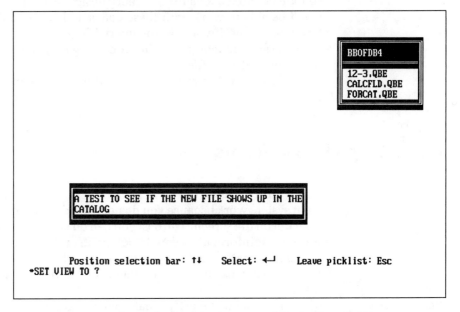

Figure 9-7 The SET VIEW TO ? command finds all available query files in the active catalog file, even if they are not linked to the current database.

People bringing their III Plus QRY files into dBASE IV have to become accustomed to using SET FILTER TO FILE to activate their III Plus query files or have to rewrite the QRY files through a SET VIEW command, which automatically updates the file to the dBASE IV format, or through the dBASE IV query design system.

Don't casually edit a dBASE IV query file. Doing so makes it unusable as a query system editable query file and causes error messages when you try to use the edited file with the SET VIEW TO command.

A last note. dBASE IV takes your queries and generates a file that looks like an ASCII text file. This is not entirely true. Consider the following listing:

```
* dBASE IV .QBE file
SET FIELDS TO
SELECT 1
USE EXERCISE.DBF AGAIN
SET EXACT ON
SET FILTER TO ((A->TOTAL_WGT> 2000))
GO TOP
SET FIELDS TO A->EXERCISE,A->TOTAL_WGT,A->DATE
```

This looks like a straightforward piece of programming, even if the actual commands are obtuse. You might think you could take this block of code and edit it in your favorite word processor, much like you could edit your FMT, FRG, and other files. Don't!

There is more to this file than meets the eye. In particular, this file contains hidden codes for the query design system. Your word processor won't be able to work with these codes and would either ignore them or throw them out. If you edit the query file, when you go back to the query design system to modify the file you will get the following error message: *Not a valid QUERY file.*

Okay, now that you know the bad news, we can get on with the good news.

Designing Query Forms

Query form design is different from most other facets of database management system work because you do not truly design a query form before you lay it out on the screen. The best you can do is decide what information you want, what information you do not want, and what information you want to change. That being the case, we will set down three queries for the EXERCISE database, then design them on the dBASE IV query form design system.

The cardinal rule of queries is: Know what you want to ask before you try to ask it.

First we must clarify what it means to say you do not truly design a query form before you lay it out on the screen. You can design the logic of the query form before you enter it into the computer, but it's better to just write simple English sentences of what you want the query to do, then write the query using query system operators. After you write the query using query system operators, check it against what you wrote in plain English. Your last step is to enter the query into the design system and check for errors. A strong suggestion is that you design some queries that you already know the answers to before you start working on queries that you need the answers to.

Our first query is: What exercises were done in January of 1989? The second query is: What exercises have we done that have a Total_Wgt over a ton? Both of these queries are in the category of "what information do we want/what information do we not want." How these queries produce filters that can be applied to full-screen editing commands (DISPLAY and LIST commands) and to our previously designed reports is covered in chapter 10. The actual queries are designed here, after which we explore more complex view queries.

View queries? Queries that tell us what we want to know or hide what we do not want to know are called *view queries* and are holdovers from dBASE III Plus days. These two queries answer questions we ask the database and are true filters of the database.

The other type of dBASE IV query is an *update query*. This query asks a what-if question and displays the results. For example, we notice that incorrect dates were entered for several records. We can manually edit these records, learn to live with the errors that might be produced from the incorrect data, or create an update query to change the incorrect data to correct information. The quickest method is the latter, especially if you have a large database. You might not want to make corrections to a file using the update query method. Your need for the update query might come from wanting to kick pay rates up ten percent across the board. It's up to you.

You can get to the dBASE IV query design system in a variety of ways. You can use the Assist system to highlight the ⟨create⟩ option in the Query column, then press [Enter]. dBASE IV displays the Layout menu's *Add file to query* option if no database is in use or the query work surface if a file is active. You can also enter the dBASE IV query design system by highlighting ⟨create⟩ in the Query column and pressing [Shift-F2].

What if you want to change an existing query? Highlight it and press [Enter] M to select the highlighted query file and modify it. Or simply highlight it and press [Shift-F2]. And, of course, there is always the standard method of using any of the following commands at the dBASE prompt:

```
MODIFY QUERY filename
CREATE QUERY filename
MODIFY VIEW filename
CREATE VIEW filename
```

If any of these commands can get you into the dBASE IV query design system, why do some say QUERY and others say VIEW? A worthy question without a good answer. There is no real difference between a dBASE IV VIEW and QUERY. The use of a VIEW command comes from dBASE III Plus, where a difference existed between a III Plus VIEW and QUERY.

III Plus users can best think of a dBASE IV application as a super version of a dBASE III Plus VIEW and can best think of the dBASE IV QUERY as a III Plus VIEW. The commands are interchangeable in dBASE IV and produce the same result. You won't see any real difference in the commands, although you might be fooled into thinking one exists if you inadvertently try to MODIFY or CREATE a QUERY or VIEW without placing a database in USE. dBASE IV opens the query design system but won't let you do anything until you place a database in use (figure 9-8). You select a file and dBASE IV responds with half the standard query screen, as shown in figure 9-9. The standard query screen is shown in figure 9-1.

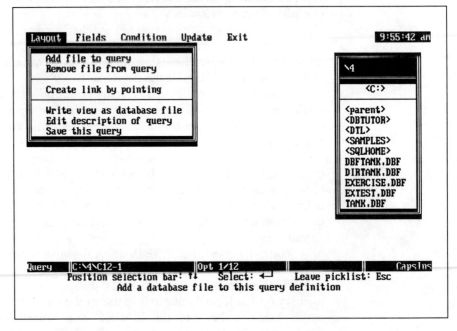

Figure 9-8 dBASE IV prompts you for a database file if you enter the query design system without a database active.

Note that you have to place some fields in the view area of the screen before dBASE IV will process the query. This operation is explained later in the chapter.

What if you want to create a query on the fly, for example, while you are in Browse or Edit mode and need to place some filter on the database you are working with? You can press [Alt-E] T to open the Exit menu and select the *Transfer to Query Design* option.

Views and queries are intimately linked. Views can generate queries and queries can generate views.

We will start the query design process by creating our first query from Browse mode. Make sure the correct database is in USE and type BROWSE [Alt-E] T. You can also type BROWSE [Shift-F2]. Both techniques will get you into the dBASE IV query design system shown in figure 9-1. Note that the screen is broken into two parts, top and bottom. The top part of the screen is the query area; the bottom is the view area. As you can see, these

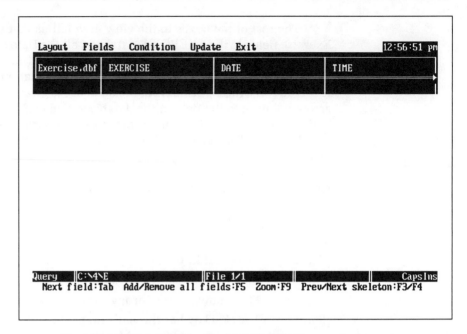

Figure 9-9 This is half the standard dBASE IV query design system screen. dBASE IV gives you this screen when you want to either MODIFY or CREATE a QUERY or VIEW but have not placed a database in USE outside the query design system.

two concepts—query and view—are intimately linked. What are these two sections telling you?

Looking at figure 9-1, notice that no information is under the field names in the query area. This means we have not placed any restraints on the database (EXERCISE, in this case). The top dark line in the query area (not the menu line), from left to right (and only describing what is on the screen), tells us that we are using the EXERCISE.DBF database, there are no constraints on the Exercise field, none on the Date field, and none on the Time field. You can see downward pointing arrows in the field label areas. These downward pointing arrows show you where to enter conditions for each field, should you want to do that. There is also a right pointing arrow on the right edge of the screen at the end of the double line that separates the field names from their condition areas. This arrow means more fields are in the database. You can scroll left to get to them with the cursor control keys and move from one field to the next with either the [Tab] key for right movement or [Shift-Tab] for left movement.

The fact that we have not placed any field restraints on the database is echoed on the bottom of the screen, where the view area shows us that all the fields in the database for this particular query/view will be displayed. The leftmost box tells us there is no name for this query/view. There is no name because we entered directly from Browse mode. dBASE IV will ask for a name when we save the file, if we do.

The rest of the boxes in the view area tell us that we will see all the Exercise fields in the EXERCISE database, all the Date fields in the EXERCISE database, all the Time fields in the EXERCISE database, and all Set_ 1_Reps fields in the EXERCISE database. The notation for this is similar to that in FMT files. The name of the database is given first, followed by an arrow pointing to the field in the database. You can also see a small right pointing arrow on the bottom of the screen under the Set_1_Reps view area field box. This arrow tells us that other fields in the database will be displayed.

Aside from cursor control keys, are there any other keys that have special functions in the query design system? Of course.

[F1]	Query help
[Shift-F1]	Condition builder
[F2]	Browse/Edit mode
[F3]	Move upwards through screen areas
[F4]	Move downwards through screen areas
[F5]	The [F5] key has three different functions, depending on where the cursor is when you press it. [F5] alternately removes or adds all information in the view area and hence all or any marked fields in that area when the cursor is in the query area and under the database name. It alternately removes or adds a particular field in the view area and hence in any filtering that might occur when the cursor is under a specific field in the query area. Last, [F5] removes the field under the cursor when the cursor is in the view area.
[F6]	Mark field or fields
[F7]	Move marked field or fields
[F9]	Zoom key. This opens the work surface so that the entire work surface becomes dedicated to whatever is currently under the cursor. This feature is useful when entering long, complicated expressions on fields or when linking conditions across databases.

Now, with all that explained, we need to enter a condition to our query file. The first query file will filter all records not dated in January of 1989 so that only records showing exercises in January of 1989 are displayed. How would you enter such a condition? I hope your first thought is that you would enter a date condition under the Date field. Yes, true enough.

But would you enter the condition directly into the Date field, or would you create an expression that applies to the Date field?

You have some options regarding this, and understanding these options will teach you a lot about the query system itself. First, you can create a condition and enter it directly into the Date field. Second, you can create a condition that applies to the Date field. Note that directly entering a condition into a field causes dBASE IV to display that field first when you go back to Browse or Edit mode. Both directly entering a condition into a field and creating a condition that applies to a field deal with what expressions can go in a query field that result in placing filters upon the data in the database as a whole, and this will take lots of explaining.

I suggest you take a break, because the QBE interface is not intuitively obvious to the casual observer. Most QBE interfaces are, but this one was specially designed for dBASE IV. This should correctly be interpreted as "We knew what we wanted, but we settled for what we got." This is not saying that dBASE IV's QBE interface is not powerful or that it does not do the job. I'm merely saying you should catch your breath before jumping in.

Back already? Okay, here we go.

You can place a filtering condition in any field in the query area, but you have to be careful how you enter that condition. For example, how would you list all leg press exercises in EXERCISE.DBF? You would move the cursor to the Exercise field, type *LEG PRESS*, and press [F2]. dBASE IV would go to Browse mode and display all leg press information. What if you wanted to display all exercises that begin with the letter L? Typing L won't work, but why?

Typing L to get all exercises that begin with L won't work because the query system is an exact search system, unless you tell it otherwise. Well, not exactly. Even when you tell it not to perform an inexact search, it will search for exactly what you told it to be inexact about. That is, it will search for an exact match to whatever you want to be inexact about. Ask the query system to search for L and it will tell you there are no exercises named L. Not surprising, eh?

How do you get a filtering of exercises that begin with L? You start by recognizing that you want a listing of exercises that look like L*. The asterisk is a wildcard character. Like a one-eyed jack or a deuce in some games of poker, the asterisk and the question mark are wildcard characters in dBASE IV's query design system. The L* tells the query system that we want anything, as long as it begins with the letter L.

As a matter of fact, the preceding paragraph contains the text you should place in the Exercise field. If you want something that looks *like* [L*], tell the query system

```
LIKE [L*]
```

This can be placed in any character field. The asterisk tells dBASE IV that you want to look for anything that begins with L and that you don't care how many characters come after it or what they are. Be careful, though. You might not want everything that begins with L. You might want only leg exercises and not lat exercises. Your entry would be

```
LIKE [LEG *]
```

Could you use LIKE [LEG]? You could if you had exercises that contained only the word *LEG* in the Exercise field. Why? Because the query system is inexact in an exact way. LIKE [LEG] tells the query system that you want to find exercises that match the pattern *LEG*. There are no wildcards to work with. No wildcards, no inexact matching. The LIKE may tell the query system that an inexact match is coming up, but you have asked for an inexact match on an exact item. Garbage in, garbage out.

What if you can't remember the exact spelling of what you are after? What if you know what something sounds like, but not the exact spelling? Think of what was just said. You know what something *sounds like.*

SOUNDS LIKE [LAIG]

I will bet you did not know that *LAIG* is really *LEG.* Well, it is to the SOUNDS LIKE function. Type *SOUNDS LIKE [LAIG]* into the Exercise field and the query system will pull up all records that deal with leg exercises. Did you notice that the SOUNDS LIKE function does not require any wildcards? Why should it? You can't be any more inexact than to say, "What I'm looking for sounds like . . ."

The fact that SOUNDS LIKE pulls up only exercises beginning with LEG is significant. SOUNDS LIKE should not be confused with "rhymes with" because a rhyme is not a sound-a-like. Typing *SOUNDS LIKE [KEG]* into the Exercise field produces no matching records (figure 9-10).

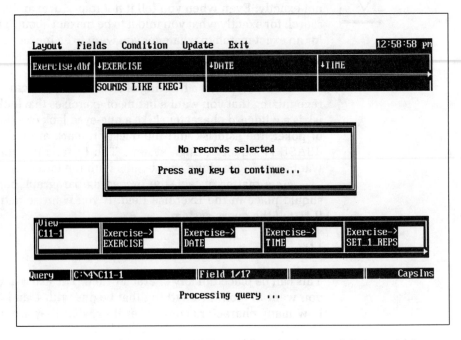

Figure 9-10 *The SOUNDS LIKE query function is not a "rhymes with"*
function. LAIG sounds like LEG, but KEG does not sound like either
LEG or LAIG and produces no results.

How far will SOUNDS LIKE let you go? Not very, unfortunately. It is excellent at what it does, looking for things very close to what you want. Very close. So close, in fact, that you might as well be able to spell them correctly, because the slightest variation will produce no good results.

What else can you do with the query system? Direct information searches have already been described. This is when you enter into a field exactly what you want. Remember that you have to enclose what you're looking for in either quotation marks or brackets ([ ]) when you are looking for character data. You don't have to use quotation marks or brackets when you are looking for numeric, floating, date, or logical data. What about memo fields? Sorry, memo fields can only be handled with condition boxes. These are covered later in this chapter.

What about direct searches in date, numeric, floating, and logical fields? Logical fields are easy. Logical fields are either True or False. How do you tell the query system that you are looking for a True or False entry? Go to the logical field and enter .T. for True or .F. for False. (You have to type the periods around the T and F.) Information can be entered into date fields by enclosing the request in braces ({}). Suppose that you want to know what was done on 8 October 1988? Go to the date field and type

```
{10/08/88}
```

Note that this assumes you are entering dates in the mm/dd/yy format. You can enter dates in any valid dBASE IV format, provided that is how you look for them in the query system. To query floating and numeric fields, enter the number you want for a direct search.

The query system provides a variety of operators to use for data searches. Two of these operators, LIKE and SOUNDS LIKE, have already been discussed. The others follow:

=   The equal sign tells the query system that you want to find exactly what you entered in the field. For example, if you want to find LEG EXTENSIONS, enter

```
= [LEG EXTENSIONS]
```

Note that this is a bit of a waste. You are asking for an exact match and don't need the equal sign to convince dBASE IV or the query system of this.

>   The greater than operator can be used in all fields except logical ones. It is easy to understand how the greater than operator works in numeric and floating fields; you simply type the greater than symbol followed by a base value. For example, to search for all numeric or floating values greater than 5000, type

```
> 5000
```

You can tell the query system to show the records for dates after 10/08/88 by typing the following in a date field:

> {10/08/88}

You can use > for character searches, but you have to understand the ASCII value system before doing so.

Characters can also be searched using the greater than symbol, but you have to know a little something about ASCII numbering to understand what is going on. All you really need to know is that *A* is less than *B*, *B* is less than *C*, and so on to *Z*. Also, *a* is less than *b*, *b* is less than *c*, and so on to *z*. You also need to know that *Z* is less than *a*. For example, *BOB* is less than *Bob*. How does this affect using the greater than operator in a query? You can search for everything greater than *BOB* and still get *Bob*. You can also search for everything greater than *B* and still get every record in which the required field starts with *B* but has other letters after it. The moral? Identify your search pattern as best you can before you go looking for anything.

<

Everything I said about the greater than symbol is true for the less than symbol. For example, you can search for numbers less than 5000 by entering

< 5000

You can search for records with dates before 10/08/88 by entering

< {10/08/88}

Note that in both this example and the greater than example braces are placed around the date to let dBASE IV know what it is working with.

The limits on using the less than operator with characters are identical to the limits described for the greater than operator. Typing < *[L]* tells the query system to display all records with data in the specified field that does not start with ASCII values less than the letter *L*. Records with fields containing *MOUSE* or even *MZZZZZZ* will come up on the screen. The query system will not return any records that start with any letter from *L* through *z*. Remember that.

>=

We covered greater than and equal to operators, now we combine the two with the greater than or equal to operator. You can search for numeric and floating values greater than or equal to 5000 with

>= 5000

Date fields can be searched for dates greater than or equal to 10/08/88 with

>= {10/08/88}

Character fields can also make use of the greater than or equal to operator. You can filter for character fields with data beginning with L or any ASCII character greater than L with

>= [L]

Don't forget that there is a difference between uppercase and lowercase letters when using operators. Filtering for >= [L] returns anything beginning with L through z. Filtering for >=[l] returns only those items beginning with l through z.

<=   Just as there is a greater than or equal to operator, so too there is a less than or equal to operator. You can search for numeric and floating values less than 5000 with

<= 5000

You can search for dates before or on 10/08/88 with

<= {10/08/88}

What was said about character fields and the greater than or equal to operator also applies to the less than or equal to operator. You can search for character entries that begin with any letter before L with

<= [L]

This will return character entries beginning with letters from A to entries that contain the single letter L. This means you will get *Abigail, Azzz, AZIMOV*, and so on, but not *LEG, LAIG,* or even "*L* ". You will get entries that contain the single letter L, without the space.

< > or #   These two operators serve as the not equal to operator. Both tell the query system that you want records that contain information that does not match what comes after the operator. For example, if you want data on numeric and floating values that don't equal 5000, enter

5000

The query system brings back records with values in the specified numeric or floating field of minus infinity to 4999.99999999999+ and 5000.00000000001− to infinity, but not 5000.

You can ask for dates that are not 10/08/88 with

{10/08/88}

This returns all records in which the designated date field does not contain 10/08/88.

The not equal to operator works in character fields, but it is another case of inexact exactness. If you enter # [L] you will get entries for *LAIG*, *LEG*, *Lazy*, *Lucy*, and so on, but you won't get any entries that contain the single letter *L*.

One other operator can be used in queries. This is the *can be found within* operator, $. What does "can be found within" mean?

Chances are a woman can find her purse in her pocketbook. Chances are a man can find his wallet in his pants pocket. These two statements would take the form (not a query form—this is only an example)

[purse] $ pocketbook

[wallet] $ pants pocket

The [purse] can be found within the pocketbook. The [wallet] can be found within the pants pocket. Suppose we had two character fields in the database, one with a field name of POCKETBOOK and the other with a field name of PANTSPOCKET. We want to search POCKETBOOK for *purse* and PANTSPOCKET for *wallet*. Those searches look like this:

[purse] $ POCKETBOOK

[wallet] $ PANTSPOCKET

Remember, we are using the *can be found within* operator. This means dBASE IV searches for the character string *purse* in each POCKETBOOK field in each record in the database. dBASE IV also searches for the character string *wallet* in each PANTSPOCKET field in each record of the database. These searches are front to back, left to right searches. It does not matter where *purse* or *wallet* is located in the respective fields; all that matters is that these collections of letters are located somewhere in those respective fields.

Transferring this search method to the query system, you would go to the POCKETBOOK field and enter

`$ [purse]`

You would go to the PANTSPOCKET field and enter

`$ [wallet]`

Note that you don't enter the name of the field. That is taken care of by entering the *can be found within* operator under a field name. This operator can only be used in character fields.

You can build complex queries using the operators we have described so far and others we have not yet discussed. Two operators, AND and OR, are not obvious because you don't explicitly place them in the query.

These operators take different forms depending on how you want things to be ANDed or ORed. Suppose that you want to locate numeric or floating values greater than 4000 AND less than 9000. You would go to the field in question and enter

```
> 4000, < 9000
```

You could search for dates after 11/01/88 AND before 12/01/88 by entering

```
> {11/01/88}, < {12/01/88}
```

And you can search for character data from L to l with

```
> [L], < [l]
```

This returns records in which the specified field contains the single letter L, any string that started with L, any string that started with letters from M to k, and the single letter l.

These are all ways of ANDing within a single field. What if you want to search for something in one field AND something in another field, both of which have equal importance? Suppose you are using the EXERCISE database and you want to find all LEG exercises performed on 10/12/88? This is handled by placing *LIKE [LEG *]* in the Exercise field and { *10/12/88*} in the Date field, as shown in figure 9-11.

You can AND as many fields as you want. Neither the query system nor dBASE IV restricts you regarding the AND condition when used in the preceding manner. You should be aware that the more you restrict a query, the fewer records will match the query condition. Further, you may inadvertently create a query condition so complex that you are no longer searching for what you want to find.

Can you AND as many conditions and fields as you want? Yes. Again using the EXERCISE database, suppose that you want to find all records with leg exercises done on 10/12/88 in which the Set_1_Wgt was greater than 20 but less than 120. This query is shown in figure 9-12. Note that the full query can't be seen because the Exercise field has scrolled off the screen. The query would read *All exercises beginning with LEG done on 12 October 1988 in which the Set_1_Wgt was between 20 and 120 pounds.*

What about ORing fields? Yes, you can OR fields, and you can even OR conditions within fields.

ANDing fields involved placing all your conditions on the same line under the fields. ORing fields involves placing your conditions on different lines. Figure 9-13 shows the condition EXERCISES LIKE [LEG *] OR DATE = {10/8/88}. It does not matter which of the two conditions is higher on the screen when you OR something. Both conditions have equal weight to the system.

You OR things by placing the field conditions on different lines on the query screen. This means you are limited to the number of lines available

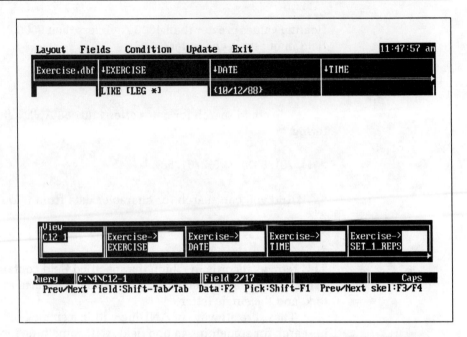

Figure 9-11 *You can create AND conditions between fields by placing the conditions in their respective fields. The actual AND comes from placing the condition on the same screen line. This figure shows the AND condition EXERCISE = [LEG *] AND DATE = {10/12/88}.*

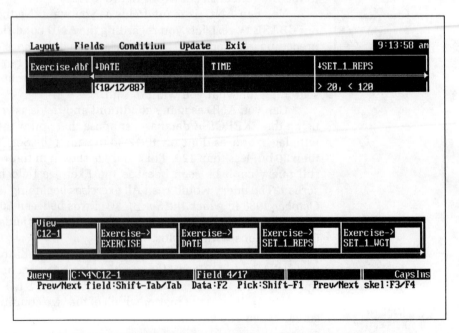

Figure 9-12 *This AND is more complex than that shown in figure 9-11 because we have added the condition 20 < SET_1_WGT < 120. Unfortunately, the Exercise field is scrolled off the screen.*

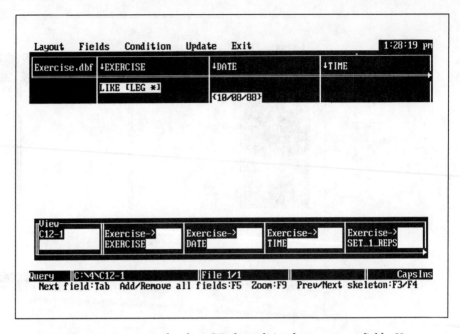

Figure 9-13 An example of an ORed condition between two fields. You can OR as many as twelve fields.

on the query screen, which is twelve. There is a possibility of going wild with power when you think about that, but I remind you that absolute power corrupts absolutely. I have suggested that you don't design a database with more than twenty-five fields. Twelve ORs on twenty-five fields will probably give you every record in the database even if you don't want them. There's also the risk of inadvertently ANDing something, as shown in figure 9-14.

Figure 9-14 shows the three-field condition (EXERCISE LIKE [LEG *] AND TIME = 09:00) OR DATE = 10/08/88. But the user meant to enter a three-field OR: EXERCISE LIKE [LEG *] OR DATE = 10/08/88 OR TIME =09:00. There is a greater risk of this when you work with twelve fields in your OR condition.

Can you OR conditions in a given field? Yes, if you are careful. You can tell the query system you want exercises in which the Set_1_Wgt is either 20 OR 40 as if you were entering an OR for different fields. You place the 20 on one line and the 40 on another, as shown in figure 9-15.

Designing Simple Queries

Simple queries are those first described in this chapter. A simple query might filter records for a specific date. This has already been demonstrated, but here we describe the steps involved.

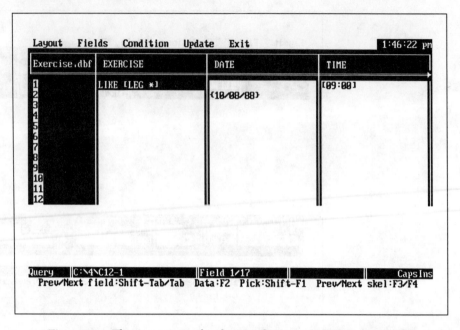

Figure 9-14 *This is an example of an inadvertent AND operation. The user meant to create the three-field OR: EXERCISE LIKE [LEG *] OR DATE = 10/08/88 OR TIME = 09:00 Instead, the user created (EXERCISE LIKE [LEG *] AND TIME = 09:00) OR DATE = 10/08/88.*

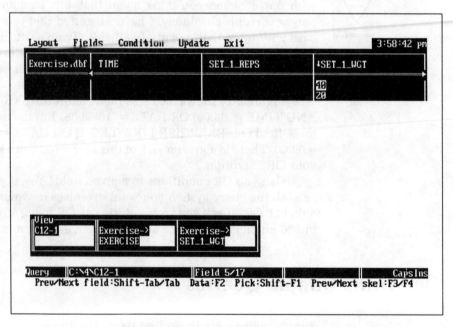

Figure 9-15 *You enter an OR for a single field in the same way you enter a multiple field OR. The first condition goes on one line; the second condition goes on another line.*

Our first query was: "What exercises were done in January of 1989?" We use the EXERCISE database to demonstrate how this query is built. Starting from the dBASE prompt with no current database will give us a more complete idea of how to handle query systems. You can activate the query design system by typing any of the MODIFY or CREATE commands listed previously in this chapter. You can also access the query design system through the Assist menu. Figure 9-8 shows you how dBASE IV responds if you don't have a database active. Figure 9-9 shows the query design screen without the view area, normally located at the bottom of the screen. You can tell dBASE IV to display all the fields in the database by placing the cursor under the name of the database at the top of the query design screen and pressing [F5].

In this query, however, we are not interested in the information in all the fields in the database. We are specifically interested in the exercises done in January, 1989. We don't want all the fields listed. If the fields are showing in the view area at the bottom of the screen, press [F5] again to remove them. Press [Tab] to get to the Exercise field, then press [F5]. dBASE IV responds as shown in figure 9-16.

It is a good idea to include a well-known and easily recognized field in a query, simply as a check to make sure things are working as you want them to.

Press [Tab] [F5] again and you have the Date field as part of the view. It is called a *view* because the bottom of the screen shows what you will view when the query is finished. We want to know what exercises were performed in January, 1989. The Date field is included to make sure the query system is performing the way it should.

"What?" you say. "He doesn't trust it?"

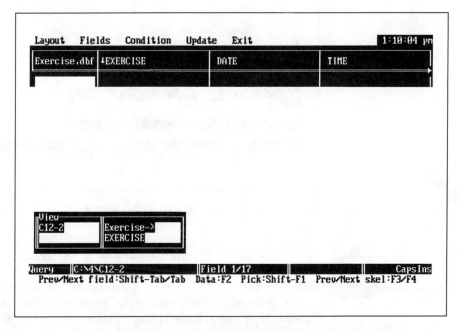

Figure 9-16 This figure demonstrates selecting fields for a query form using the [F5] key.

No way do I trust it. It is a computer running a program with information and queries designed by humans. You think I'm going to trust something with that many chances to go wrong? You want to buy a bridge? How about some land in Florida?

Because the Date field checks that dBASE IV is doing the job we have asked in the query, it might be nice if the Date field was before the Exercise field. We could scan the left column of Date data and quickly determine if something was wrong. (Obviously, this is not such a necessity when there are only two fields on display.)

One way to put the Date field before the Exercise field in the view area is to press either [F3] or [F4] to get down to the view area, then press [F5] twice to remove the fields from the view. This places you back up in the query area. Move to the Date field and press [F5] to place the Date field in the view area, then press [Shift-Tab] [F5] to move back to the Exercise field and place it in the view area. Your screen should look like the one in figure 9-17 if you are working along with this example.

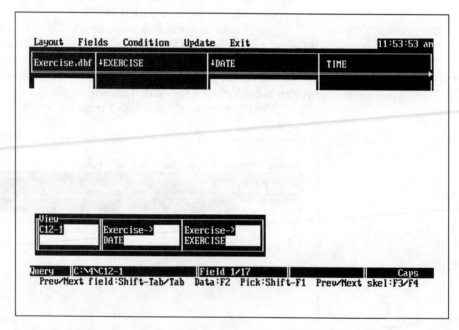

Figure 9-17 *This figure shows the Date field before the Exercise field.*

This method of getting fields where you want them in a view is not the best way. The best method is to press [F3] or [F4] to get to the view area. The first time you get to the view area you are on the first field in the view, which is Exercise in this example. Press [F6]. The Exercise field is highlighted. Now press [Enter] [Tab] [F7] [Enter]. This highlights only the Exercise field, moves the cursor to the Date field, moves the Exercise field after the Date field, and completes the move with [Enter]. This is much easier than the first method, especially when there are several fields to be rearranged in the view area. Note that your screen should look like figure 9-17.

Now that we have laid out the view the way we want it, how do we put in the condition? Press either [F3] or [F4] to get back up to the query area. You should return to the Date field, if you are following along with the example used here. We want only those exercises performed in January, 1989. There are two ways to enter that information. One method places the condition directly into the field; the other creates a condition. We start with the first method, as it was demonstrated earlier.

Type the following into the Date field:

> {12/31/88}, < {02/01/89}

This tells the query system that you want to see records in which the Date field contains a date after 31 December 1988 and before 1 February 1989. What does that leave? It leaves all the days in January, 1989. You may notice that this condition does not neatly fit under the Date field on the screen. You can press the [F9] key to Zoom the Date field condition, as shown in figure 9-18. This gives you room to enter complex conditions and see them on the screen. You don't have to use the [F9] (Zoom) feature to enter complex conditions; it just makes it easier to see them on the screen.

The second method of entering a condition deals with the condition box. Before we use the condition box, press [Ctrl-Y] to remove the condi-

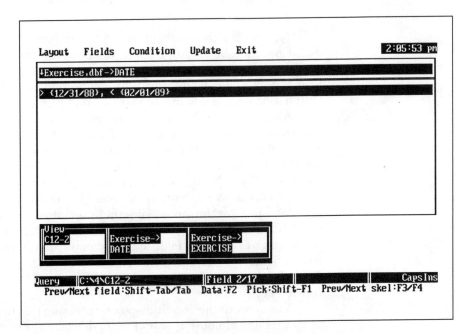

Figure 9-18 The [F9] (Zoom) key can be used to open
a field's condition area.

tion from the Date field itself. Now press [Alt-C]. The Condition box menu is opened, as shown in figure 9-19.

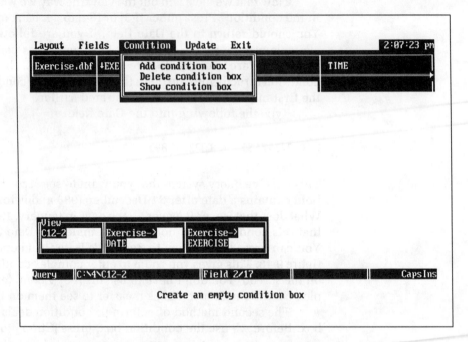

Figure 9-19 *The query design system's Condition box menu.*

Type A for *Add condition box*. A box is displayed, as shown in figure 9-20. Condition boxes can be used to enter different conditions than you can enter into fields. Mainly, you can use functions other than the query form functions when you work with a condition box. You can't use dBASE IV functions when you are entering a condition directly in a field.

An example of the differences between what you can do in a condition box and what you can do directly with a field is shown in figure 9-21. The condition we placed under the Date field produces an error when entered in the box. Why? The condition box works on all fields in all databases, if you have more than one active in a query (having more than one database active in a query is covered in the next chapter).

We can enter the same basic condition into the condition box by using dBASE IV functions. That is shown in figure 9-22. Remember that the condition box works on all fields in the database; therefore, we have to specify which fields we want to work with in the condition box. Also note that figure 9-22 uses the [F9] (Zoom) feature to expand the condition box to the full screen.

You can exit the condition box by pressing [F2] to get to a data screen or by pressing either [F3] or [F4]. Note that an active condition box causes dBASE IV to move from query area to view area to condition box back to query area when a condition box is active.

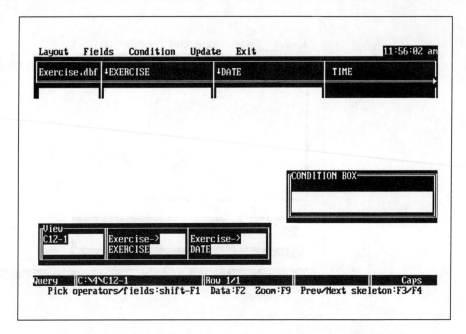

Figure 9-20 It does not matter what field you are in when you call the condition box because any conditions you enter there apply to the database as a whole, not only the single field you are in when you call the condition box.

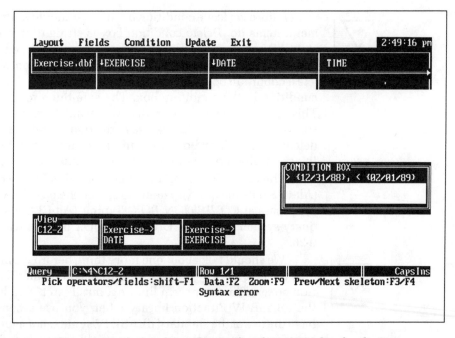

Figure 9-21 The condition that works when entered under the Date field produces an error message when entered in a condition box.

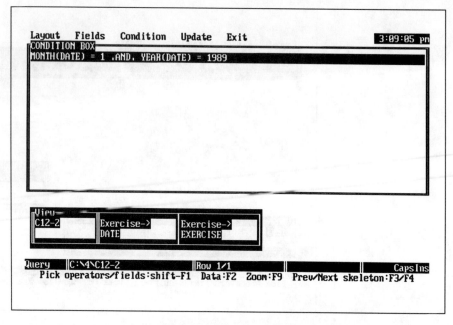

Figure 9-22 *This is identical to the condition shown in figure 9-18, but this condition is entered in the condition box and must specify which fields are used in the condition.*

 Before we leave condition boxes, you should know what the other two menu items do. *Delete condition box* is straightforward. When you press [Alt-C] D, whatever condition box is currently defined is removed from the query. dBASE IV does not prompt for confirmation when you want to delete a condition box, so be careful, especially if you have written a complex condition in the condition box. The safe thing to do is to press [Alt-L] S. This tells the query system that you want to save the current query, as shown in figure 9-2. You can save the query under a different name, then delete the condition box or modify it, as necessary. Your original query is intact on disk along with the complex condition box information.

The other Condition menu command is *Show condition box.* Typing [Alt-C] S tells the query system to replace the box shown in figure 9-20 with the message *CONDITION BOX.* Typing [Alt-C] S a second time tells the query system to toggle *CONDITION BOX* back to what is shown in figure 9-20.

 We should talk about one more thing before we move on to the second query. The only way to place conditions on memo fields is through condition boxes. This may seem limiting, but it isn't. You have all the power of the dBASE IV Function library when you use a condition box, and you have the use of the standard dBASE IV syntax, not a modified syntax necessary for the query system. A memo field can be searched or conditionally referenced with the $ function. For example, use the EXERCISE database and search its comment field for *this is a test* by opening a condition box and entering the following:

```
[this is a test] $ COMMENT
```

The condition box holds conditions for any and all databases that may be active in a query or view. This is important and is covered in more detail in chapter 10. Remember that you must use database identifiers when more than one database is active in a view, especially if the different databases contain fields with similar names. You can AND and OR in a condition box, but the AND and OR are now back to their logical forms of .AND. and .OR. An example of the logical .AND. form is shown in figure 9-22.

The second query deals with what exercises were performed with a Total_Wgt over a ton (2000 pounds). Get rid of the box by typing [Alt-C] D. Next, tab to the Total_Wgt field and type

```
> 2000
```

Because we might also want this field in our view, press [F5] to place the field in the view area. We have not removed any fields from the previous query design. Do we want Date there? Sure. This way we can see if our total weights for a given exercise have increased over time, while recognizing that we show only exercises for which the total weight was over a ton. We don't want the Date field first on the display, however, so press [F3] [F6] [Enter] [Tab] [Tab] [F7] [Enter]. Those keystrokes break down as follows:

[F3]	Move to the view area
[F6] [Enter]	Highlight the Date field
[Tab] [Tab]	Move to the Total_Wgt field
[F7] [Enter]	Move the Date field to the end of the view area

Now all we need to do is press [F2] to see our data displayed on the screen (figure 9-23).

Before going to the next section, you should be asking a question. You can get these great queries designed and see the results on the screen. Yippee. What good is that if you need to work with the data you have just listed with the query? Do you take a picture of it from the screen and use a red pen on the photograph? Do you gather everyone around your computer monitor and say, "See, that's what we're working with"?

Many times, you need to work on the data that results from your query. This resultant data can be thought of as a subset of the larger database. The concept of a masterbase was described and explained in chapter 7. Here the topic takes on importance again.

Think of the whole database as the masterbase and the results of the query as a database. You want to work with the subset of the masterbase. You can do this through the Browse and Edit modes, each of which is avail-

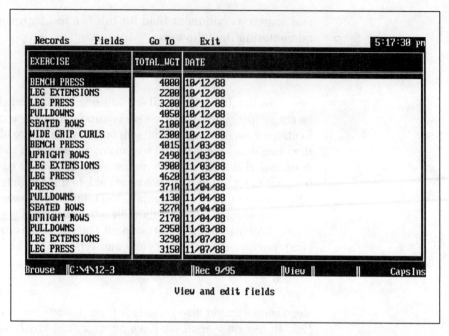

Figure 9-23 *This is the result of the query for TOTAL_WGT > 2000*
Notice that the data is not displayed in any particular order?
Ordering data is handled later in this chapter.

able from the query design surface with the [F2] (Data) key. What if you know there will be a lot of resultant data from your query or you just want a copy of the resultant data for use in another file?

You can get the resultant data in its own file through the query design surface or through a few commands at the dBASE prompt or in a program. First we explore the query design method.

Previously, we searched for all records pertaining to January, 1989. Now we want to gather just those records and work on them individually. Using EXERCISE.DBF as our example, get to the query design system and press [Alt-L] *W* to call up the Layout menu's *Write view as database file* command (figure 9-24). Note that dBASE IV defaults to giving the resultant database the same file name as your query form.

You can now work with the resultant database entirely on its own. You can do exactly what the query system did from the dBASE prompt, as well. The commands follow:

```
USE masterbase
SET VIEW TO query file
COPY TO new database name
USE new database
```

This command sequence is not difficult to fathom. We start by making the masterbase active. Next we SET the VIEW TO the query file that has the

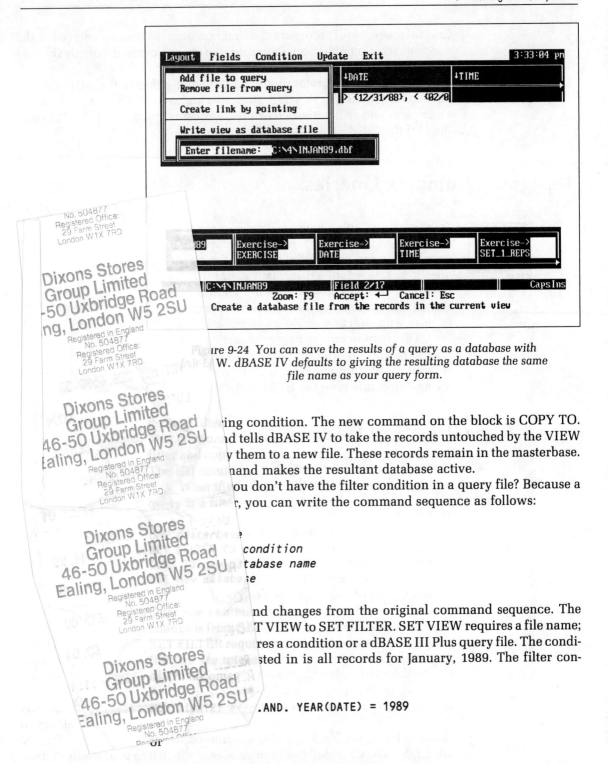

Figure 9-24 *You can save the results of a query as a database with W. dBASE IV defaults to giving the resulting database the same file name as your query form.*

...ing condition. The new command on the block is COPY TO. ...d tells dBASE IV to take the records untouched by the VIEW ...y them to a new file. These records remain in the masterbase. ...nand makes the resultant database active.

...ou don't have the filter condition in a query file? Because a ...r, you can write the command sequence as follows:

```
condition
tabase name
se
```

...nd changes from the original command sequence. The ...T VIEW to SET FILTER. SET VIEW requires a file name; ...res a condition or a dBASE III Plus query file. The condi- ...sted in is all records for January, 1989. The filter con-

.AND. YEAR(DATE) = 1989

or

DATE > {12/31/88} .AND. DATE < {02/01/89}

Careful readers will recognize the first condition as the one entered in the condition box and the second condition as the one entered directly into the Date field.

What about programming? You can enter either of the command sequences in the dBASE IV word processor and write them as PRG files. Be aware that you will get an error message using the SET VIEW TO command if the listed query file is not present.

Designing Complex Queries

So much for simple requests. How complicated can a query be? It can be elaborate, but it should not be too complex. Why? The more complex a query, the more chance for error in the query design. Remember those questions you would get in math class? They were something like "The pitcher is Tom, the island is in the Pacific, the electrician's wife is from Burma. What color is your lunch?" Those queries were nearly impossible to solve, and so will your query form be if it is equally complex.

This section covers using calculated fields, sorting, using summary operators, and variable and dependent relationships in queries. It does not cover the EVERY operator, which is used when linking files using query forms. Information on the EVERY operator is in chapter 10.

Using Calculated Fields in Query Forms

In one of the queries designed in the previous section, we were interested in Total_Wgt. We have already noted that the Total_Wgt field can be a calculated field, if that is your desire. Can we place a calculated field in a query? Yes.

We start with the query design system as described previously in this chapter (figure 9-1). Much as before, we are interested in only a few fields from the database: Exercise and Date. This time, we will create a calculated field to find the total weights for a given exercise. After we create the calculated field, we place the > 2000 condition on it.

The preceding section demonstrated how to remove the view area from the screen and select individual fields for the view. We want the fields to be viewed as Exercise, calculated total weight, and Date. Place the Exercise field in the view area as demonstrated previously. Now press [Alt-F] to call up the Fields menu (figure 9-25). The two top options, *Add field to view* and *Remove field from view*, behave identically to the [F5] (Fields) key. Type C to create a calculated field. This opens up another field list, usually placed in the middle of the screen (figure 9-26). You build your calculated fields in this area. Note that you are limited to twenty calculated fields, although each calculated field can be as complicated as your needs dictate.

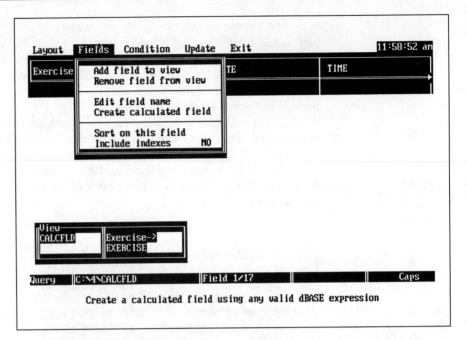

Figure 9-25 *The only way to create a calculated field for your query form is through the Fields menu Create calculated field option.*

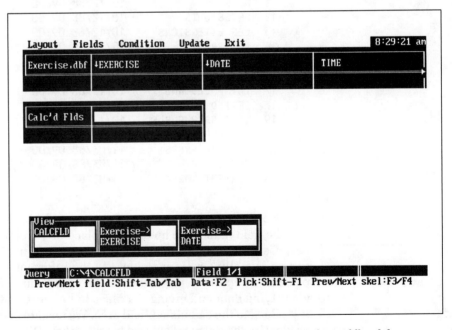

Figure 9-26 *The calculated fields area appears in the middle of the screen. You can build up to twenty calculated fields.*

The cursor shows up on the calculated fields area in a place where you would expect to find a field name. You have not given the calculated field a name yet, however. Don't rush in and type a name for your calculated field because the name does not go there. Consider the query area first and look at what is there. Yes, the top line of the query area contains field names. But what are field names?

Field names are placeholders. You can think of a dBASE IV database in much the same way as you would think of a spreadsheet. It is a series of rows and columns. The rows of the spreadsheet are the records in the database; the columns are the data. The field names run along the top of the data. This is very obvious when you look at a DISPLAY or LIST of the database, as follows:

Record#	EXERCISE	DATE	TIME	SET_1_REPS	SET_1_WGT
1	BENCH PRESS	10/08/88	09:00	10	45
2	INCLINE PRESS	10/08/88	09:00	10	15
3	DB PRESS	10/08/88	09:00	10	15
4	WIDE GRIP CURLS	10/08/88	09:00	10	25
5	PRESS OUTS	10/08/88	09:00	10	45
6	LEG EXTENSIONS	10/08/88	09:00	10	25
7	LEG CURLS	10/08/88	09:00	10	30
8	LAT PULLDOWNS	10/08/88	09:00	10	55
9	BENCH PRESS	10/12/88	09:00	10	45
10	INCLINE PRESS	10/12/88	09:00	10	15
11	DB PRESS	10/12/88	09:00	10	15
12	PRESS OUTS	10/12/88	09:00	10	20
13	LEG EXTENSIONS	10/12/88	09:00	10	20
14	LEG PRESS	10/12/88	09:00	10	50
15	LEG CURLS	10/12/88	09:00	10	20
16	SEATED CALVES	10/12/88	09:00	10	0
17	LAT PULLDOWNS	10/12/88	09:00	10	40
18	SEATED ROWS	10/12/88	09:00	10	50
19	WIDE GRIP CURLS	10/12/88	09:00	10	25
20	BENCH PRESS	11/03/88	09:00	10	45
21	INCLINE PRESS	11/03/88	09:00	10	20
22	PRESS	11/03/88	09:00	10	30
23	UPRIGHT ROWS	11/03/88	09:00	10	25

Now look at the view area of any query design screen and you will see that the field names are holding the place of the data you want to see. The purpose of this listing is to show you that a field name on the query design system is really a marker to identify the information located in a certain place in a record of the database. The field name is merely a means of identifying data and giving it a place to be represented in the view.

Back to the calculated field area. We need to create something to help us identify the data and act as a placemarker. What better thing to use as a placemarker than the calculation necessary for the calculated field? Sounds good to me.

But before we go into that, I want to emphasize the difference between the field name as a placemarker and a name assigned to a variable. I will emphasize it by asking you to press [Alt-F] *E*. This returns a screen similar to that shown in figure 9-27. Remember that we are working with a calculated field that will determine the total weight lifted for a given exercise. Enter a field name of TWEIGHT.

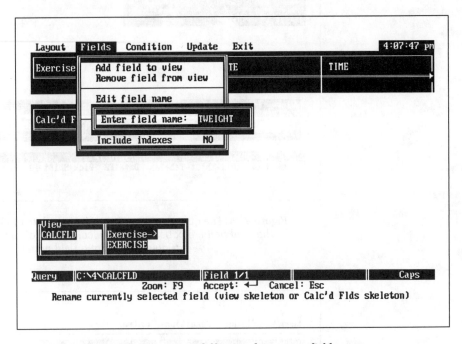

Figure 9-27 *There is a difference between a field name as a placemarker and a calculated field's name, which is actually a variable. This screen shows the Fields menu Edit field name option. You can only edit a calculated field's name, and this option is only available when working with a calculated field.*

Now look at figure 9-28 and see where the query system places the new name, and also note that the name is followed by an equal sign. We have created a variable, TWEIGHT, and told dBASE IV and the query system that we will equate it to something. What will we equate it to? The placemarker I mentioned earlier. This placemarker is the result of the equation of the sum of Set_n_Wgts times Set_n_Reps. Enter this in the calculated field with the [F9] (Zoom) key (figure 9-29).

You can bring the calculated field into the view area just as you would any field in the query area, using the [F5] (Fields) key.

It is important to note that you don't need an extensive knowledge of each field in the database and each function and arithmetic operator in dBASE IV to type in your condition for a calculated field or for the condition boxes. You can press [Shift-F1] and have dBASE IV pop up the pick list menu (figure 9-30). This gives you the opportunity to point and shoot to

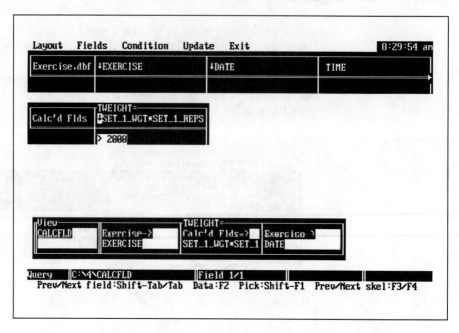

Figure 9-28 The query system places the calculated field's name above
the field name box because the calculated field's name is really a
variable name, not a field name.

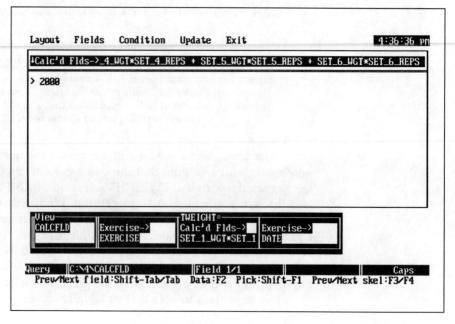

Figure 9-29 You can enter complex formulae for the calculated field
with the [F9] (Zoom) key.

build the calculated field as you go. This pop-up menu is identical to the [Shift-F1] menus shown in other chapters.

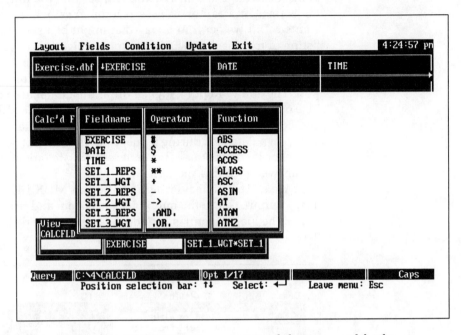

Figure 9-30 [Shift-F1] pops up a point-and-shoot menu of database fields, arithmetic operators, and dBASE IV functions. This pop-up menu is identical to the pop-up menus in the screen form design and report form design systems.

Good. We have the calculated field entered into the query system. But remember that we also wanted a condition on that total weight field? We wanted to look at records in which the total weight was over a ton. Placing a condition on a calculated field is no more difficult than placing a condition on any other field in the database. Get to the TWEIGHT=calculated field and press [Down-Arrow]. This puts the cursor into the area of the calculated fields region, where you can enter conditions. Now type

> 2000

All you need to do at this point is pull the Date field from the query area to the view area—go to the Date field with either the [F3] or [F4] key and press [F5]. The [F3] and [F4] keys begin to be useful as your query design grows more complex. The [F3] key moves up the screen. The [F4] key moves down the screen. Both keys cycle through the complete display as you continue to type them. Now, press [F2] and you are done.

Using Sorting Operators in Query Forms

Look back at figure 9-23 and you will see that the information is placed on the screen in a rather useless fashion. Yes, we got the information we wanted. Did we get it in a way that might be useful? Not really. We got a listing of exercises in which the total weight was over a ton. It would be nice to see the exercises ordered by name and date, so that we could see if the total weight for a given exercise went up as time went on.

The ability to put a logical order on a database is normally the province of index files. dBASE IV has two kinds of index files, NDX and MDX, and both were mentioned previously. Can we get an NDX or MDX file to act upon a database during a query operation? Is it possible to place some type of order on the query without resorting to index files? These questions are answered in this section.

We start by considering if NDX and MDX files can place order on query output. Get to the query design system and press [Alt-F]. At the bottom of the Fields menu is *Include indexes* and the default is *NO*. See figure 9-31.

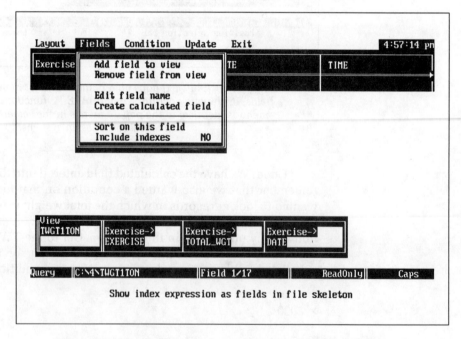

Figure 9-31 *The Fields menu has two options,* Include indexes *and* Sort on this field, *that can be used to place order on query output.*

Type *I* and look at the screen. (I'm assuming that you are following along with the EXERCISE.DBF example.) Notice some changes? There are several index expressions on the EXERCISE database. Two of these expressions are simply indices on the Exercise field and the Date field, independent of each other. Look at the Exercise field in the query area and you will see a pound symbol next to the field name. A similar mark is next to DATE in the query area's Date field box. Press [End] and you move to the last field in the database, right? That last field should be Comment, right? Not anymore. Now the last field is the index expression EXERCISE + DTOC (DATE). This is the index expression we labeled EXDATE when we designed the database and its MDX file. Press [Shift-Tab] a few times and you will see that all the MDX index expressions are now in the query area as fields. Simple index expressions such as Exercise and Date can be handled as fields, and the [F5] (Field) key can be used to place these expressions into the view. This is not the case with complex index expressions such as EXERCISE + DTOC(DATE).

But does placing a simple index expression into the view place any ordering on the database? Not likely. All it does is tell you and the query system that some fields have been indexed and, when the index expression is complex, that there are more fields to work with. How do you get order?

Press [Alt-F] again. This time type S to call up the Sort menu, shown in figure 9-32. This menu also shows the difference between ASCII sorting, mentioned previously, and dictionary sorting.

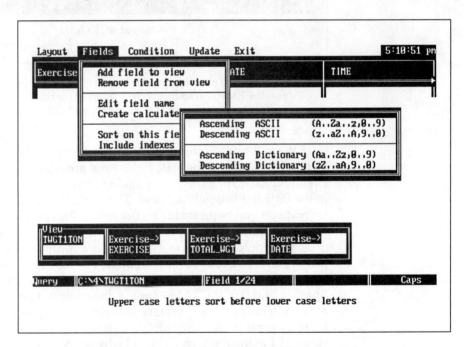

Figure 9-32 The query design system's Fields Sort submenu.

We are interested in a dictionary sort on the Exercise field. Highlight *Ascending Dictionary* and press [Enter]. You will see *ASCDICT1* in the condition box under the Exercise field. Now press [F2]. One screen of the data is shown in figure 9-33. What's wrong with it? The exercises are ordered alphabetically, which is what we wanted. But we also wanted the dates to be in order so we could see if our total weights went up over time.

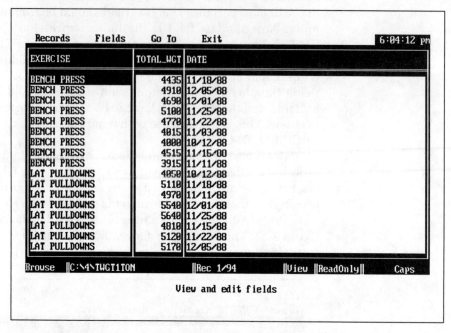

Figure 9-33 *This display is the result of an ascending dictionary sort on the Exercise field. It is close to what we want, records ordered by exercise name and date.*

Press [Shift-F2] to get back to the query design system, then press [Tab] until you are at the Date field. Now press [Alt-F] S for the Sort menu. Highlight *Ascending Dictionary* again and press [Enter]. Now *ASCDICT2* is in the Date field's condition area. The *2* is in *ASCDICT2* because this is the second sort you requested from the menu. Press [F2] again. A screenful of the result from this query is shown in figure 9-34. Bingo!

You could perhaps more easily type in the sort operators you want just as you type in any other condition. The four sorting operators are ASC (ascending ASCII), DESC (descending ASCII), ASCDICT (ascending dictionary), and DSCDICT (descending dictionary). The query system assigns a sort number to these operators each time one is placed in a field. The first sorting operator takes the value 1. This is why the ASCDICT operator has a suffix of 1 in the Exercise field and why the ASCDICT operator in the Date field has a suffix of 2. The query system won't assign the same numeric suffix to any two sort operators and gives you an error message if you do so while typing the sort operators into a field directly (figure 9-35).

Now go back to the query design system and press [Alt-F] I to remove the index expressions from the query area, then press [F2] again. Bingo again. What's the difference? Time, primarily. You may not notice any dif-

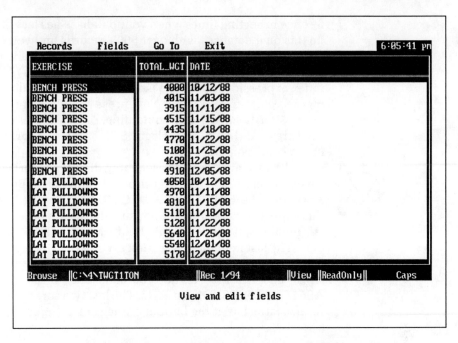

Figure 9-34 This display is the result of an ascending dictionary sort
on the Exercise field and a second ascending dictionary sort
on the Date field.

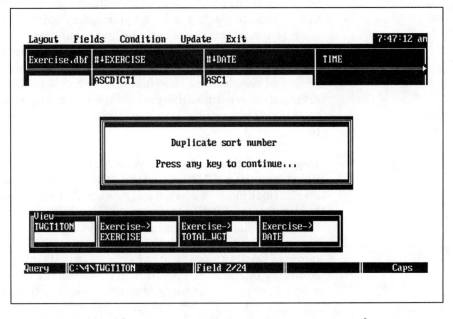

Figure 9-35 The query system gives you an error message when you
give two sort operators the same priority. This figure shows an
ascending dictionary first priority sort in the Exercise field and
an ascending ASCII first priority sort in the Date field.

ference in sorting times when your database has less than 200 records, but do this on a database with over 5000 records and you can get coffee, even on a 386. Can we speed things up for the dual index expressions used in figure 9-35? Go back to the query system and press [Alt-F] I to include the index expressions. Go to the Exercise and Date fields and remove the sorting operators with [Ctrl-Y]. Now press [End] to get to the EXDATE index expression field, the one containing EXERCISE + DTOC(DATE) in the field area. Use [Alt-F] S to select ASCII ascending sort or simply type *ASC1* in the condition area.

Bingo again. We used ascending dictionary sorts when we placed the sorting operators in the Exercise and Date fields. But we used ascending ASCII for the EXERCISE + DTOC(DATE) key field expression because this expression is a combination of database fields, arithmetic, and dBASE IV functions; it is not a single field from the database.

The last item for this section is knowing when you can edit the resulting Browse and Edit displays. You can edit the information from both ASCn and DSCn sorts, but you can't alter the information from either ASCDICTn or DSCDICTn sorts. The last two sorts place the ReadOnly flag in the status bar at the bottom of the screen (figure 9-35).

Using Summary, GROUP BY, and UNIQUE Operators in Query Forms

Sorting records by a field or fields, either alphabetically or numerically, is one method of placing order on your query output. Another type of order comes from selected summarizing and grouping of the information in your database. An example of grouping like items together is seen in both of the report forms designed previously. We grouped exercises by date in one form and weights and repetitions by exercise in the other. Summarizing information is a little different. Before explaining why summarizing information can be useful, I have to explain how dBASE IV summarizes a database.

There are five ways dBASE IV can gather information. These five ways are averaging (AVG or AVERAGE) either numeric or floating point fields, counting (CNT or COUNT) the number of entries in a given numeric, floating, character, date, or logical field or fields, determining the maximum (MAX) value in a numeric, floating point, character, or date field or fields, determining the minimum (MIN) value in a numeric, floating, character, or date field or fields, and summing (SUM) the values in a numeric or floating point field or fields. Note that you can't use more than one summary operator in a given field in any single query. The following list might help you better understand how each of these summarizing operators act on the different dBASE IV fields.

AVG or AVERAGE   Acts on only numeric and floating point fields
CNT or COUNT   Acts on all but memo fields

MAX	Acts on all but logical and memo fields
MIN	Acts on all but logical and memo fields
SUM	Acts on only numeric and floating point fields

No summary operators act on memo fields, only COUNT/CNT acts on logical fields, only MIN, MAX, and COUNT/CNT act on date and character fields, and all five operators act on numeric and floating point fields. Is there any logic to this? Most definitely. Memo fields are word processing files disguised as special fields in the database; therefore, there is nothing about a memo field to summarize. Logical fields can be either True or False; therefore, they have no minimum value, no maximum value, and no average, and cannot be summed. The only thing you can do with a logical field is COUNT for the number of True or False entries. Extending this logic, you can COUNT both date and character fields for specific entries. You can determine both minimum and maximum dates. Remembering that character data has values assigned to it through ASCII character values, we can determine a minimum and maximum character value by determining the minimum and maximum ASCII values, respectively. Both numeric and floating point fields are, of course, number data types. Numbers have maximum and minimum values and can be averaged, counted, and summed.

Now that you have read the book, see the movie. No, no. I mean now that you have learned what fields the operators act on, learn what the operators do.

AVG or AVERAGE: The AVG or AVERAGE operator determines the arithmetic mean or average for a given field. This operator is equivalent to determining the sum or total value for a field, then dividing the sum by the number of records counted to determine that sum. Arithmetically, the formula would have the form

average of field = total field value / number of records counted

We can take an average of all repetitions and all weights in the EXERCISE database by placing the AVG operator in each Set_n field in the query area (figure 9-36). Then we can view this information on the screen (figure 9-37).

Before going to the other summary operators, some caveats about what we just did. We performed a simple averaging of all Set_n data in all the records in the EXERCISE database. We did not perform any other ordering of the data. This means Set_n information about bench presses is mixed with Set_n information about lat pulldowns. It also means we asked for an average of the entire database, which is averaged into a single record as shown in figure 9-37.

Figure 9-37 also shows some other interesting facts about the results of our query. The status bar at the bottom of the screen shows ReadOnly towards the right. You can view this data—view is on the status bar immediately to the left of ReadOnly—but you can't edit it. Why? Because it is

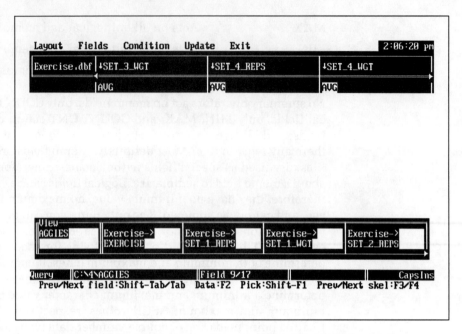

Figure 9-36 *The AVG operator in several Set␣n fields in the database.*
The resulting Browse screen is shown in figure 9-37.

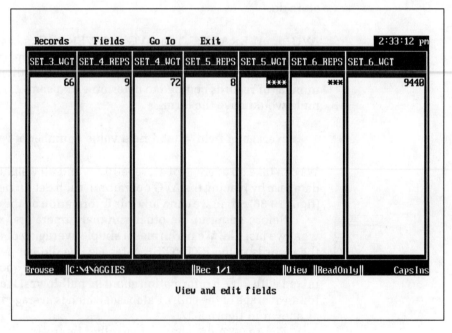

Figure 9-37 *The Browse mode resulting from placing the AVG operator*
in all Set␣n fields in the query area. This figure also shows that a
summary query form can be viewed but not edited. This Browse
display is read only, as shown on the right of the status bar.

summary data. You can't edit the sum because that would invalidate the original data.

Also note that figure 9-37 shows the summary fields Set_5_Wgt and Set_6_Reps with asterisks instead of values. Why did it do this? Part of the explanation is shown in figure 9-38.

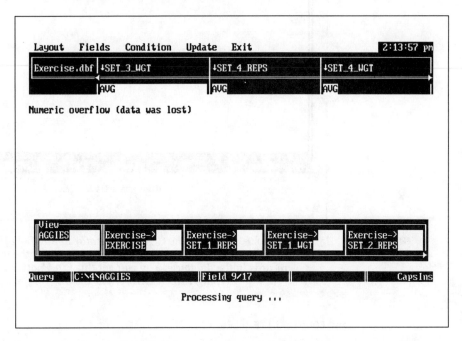

Figure 9-38 *dBASE IV's memory management problems once again show up. This time dBASE IV is having problems with summary query forms and can't process all the fields, as shown in figure 9-37.*

The average Set_5_Wgt is 67.11; the average Set_6_Reps is 8.24. (The values are rounded on the screen because the numeric fields do not have decimal digit areas.) These two fields simply got lost when dBASE IV did the calculations. The moral? Be careful and make sure there are no error messages when you process a summary query form. You can always write the summary information to a series of database files with the [Alt-W] command, then combine the different databases to produce the desired summary data.

CNT or COUNT: The CNT or COUNT operator counts the number of records that meet the conditions set in the query form. COUNT without any conditions on the fields merely tells you the total number of records in the database. Figure 9-39 tells us there are 192 records in the EXERCISE database.

You can group several requests together to produce a more interesting query. For example, typing

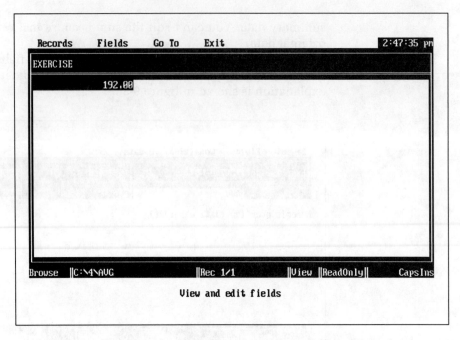

Figure 9-39 Putting the COUNT operator in any field in the database
without specifying any conditions merely returns the total number of
records in the database. You can get this information more easily by
typing ? RECCOUNT( ) at the dBASE prompt.


```
COUNT, LIKE [LEG *]
```

in the Exercise field tells the query system to find how many records in the
database contain data on exercises that begin with *LEG* (figure 9-40). There
are forty.

MAX: To determine the maximum value for a given field in the database,
use the MAX operator. For example, we are vain enough to want to know
the maximum weight used in each Set_n_Wgt field in the database. We
place MAX in each Set_n_Wgt field in the query area. We can also use the
[F5] key to select only the Set_n_Wgt fields for the view, because those are
the only fields we are interested in. Figure 9-41 also includes the Exercise
field. Notice that it is empty? Remember that we are still acting on all the
records in the database and not performing a more revealing summation
on the data.

MIN: The MIN operator is identical in operation to the MAX operator.
Figure 9-42 shows how this operator looks when entered in the query area.

SUM: SUM determines the arithmetic total of the specified records. Placing SUM in each of the Set_n fields tells the query system to determine the
total values for each of these fields, calculating the sum using each record

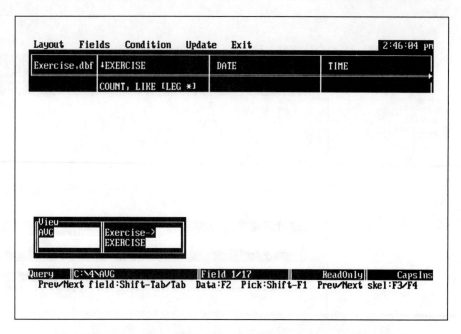

Figure 9-40 *You can combine the COUNT operator with other query form operators. This figure shows how to create a form that determines the number of records in the database with exercises that start with LEG.*

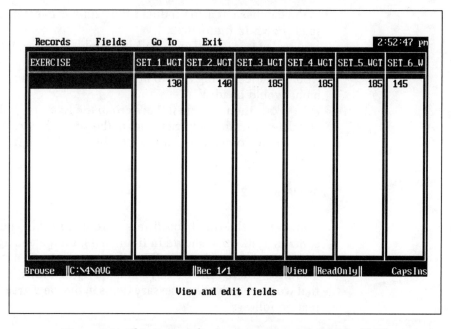

Figure 9-41 *This Browse display results from placing the MAX operator in each of the Set_n_Wgt fields. This figure also includes the Exercise field, which is empty because the entire database is being used in the summary operation to produce a single summary record.*

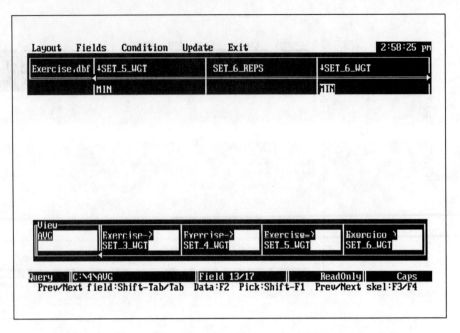

Figure 9-42 *This figure shows how to place the MIN operator in the query area. The MAX operator is placed in the query area in the same way.*

in the database. It also produces the *Numeric overflow (data was lost)* message shown in figure 9-38.

All of this is well and good, but could be better. It could be better if we had a way to collect similar data together. A type of grouping operation would be nice. Being able to take the exercise data and group by exercise name would be ideal.

Okay, then, let's do it. Let's group the Exercise field by exercise name and determine the average values of the Set_n fields. We placed AVG in the Set_n fields previously. Now get to the query design surface and tab to the Exercise field. Type

```
GROUP BY [F2]
```

Your data will no doubt be different from mine, but you should get a screen something like that shown in figure 9-43. I hope you agree that figure 9-43 shows more valuable data. How about getting a COUNT of the number of exercises GROUPED BY day? This query is shown in figure 9-44. Notice that we place only the necessary fields in the view area. The resulting information follows:

```
Record#   DATE             EXERCISE
      1   10/08/88             8.00
      2   10/12/88            11.00
```

3	11/03/88	9.00
4	11/04/88	8.00
5	11/07/88	7.00
6	11/08/88	8.00
7	11/10/88	7.00
8	11/11/88	8.00
9	11/14/88	7.00
10	11/15/88	9.00
11	11/17/88	5.00
12	11/18/88	8.00
13	11/21/88	7.00
14	11/22/88	8.00
15	11/25/88	8.00
16	11/28/88	6.00
17	12/01/88	8.00
18	12/02/88	7.00
19	12/05/88	8.00
20	12/08/88	7.00
21	12/09/88	8.00
22	12/15/88	2.00
23	12/19/88	7.00
24	12/20/88	8.00
25	12/22/88	5.00
26	12/23/88	8.00

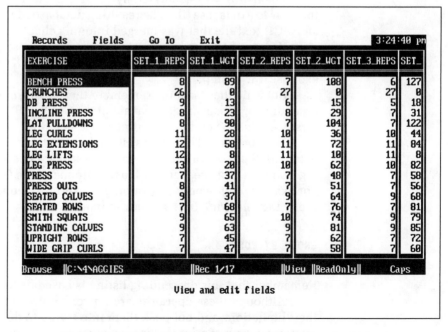

Figure 9-43 Using the GROUP BY operator adds order to your
summary query form. This Browse display is GROUPED BY
EXERCISE, and each of the Set_n fields is averaged.

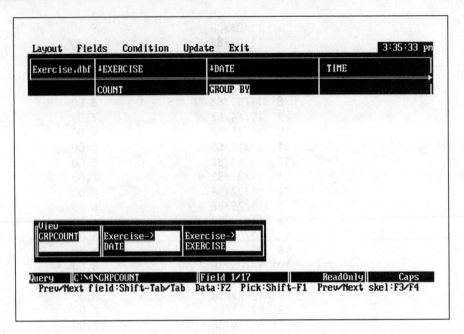

Figure 9-44 *An example of how to count the number of exercises performed on each date.*

The listing was generated by using the [Alt-L] W command to write the view to a database file. The resulting database file was then displayed to an ASCII text file that was merged into this chapter.

You can begin to appreciate the power of these operators. We could GROUP BY exercise name and determine the MAX weights used in each exercise, for example.

But wait, there's more. Remember that sorting operators can be either ascending or descending? What about the GROUP BY and summary operators? Can they be either ascending or descending?

Yes, they can. The query system defaults to an ascending grouping of data with these operators, but you can specify a descending order by adding a comma, a space, and DSC to the summary and GROUP BY operators. For example, a descending grouping of exercises would be obtained if you typed the following in the Exercise field:

```
GROUP BY, DSC
```

Remember that this descending listing is based on an ASCII text sort.

Although these operators are powerful, it is important to recognize their limitations and not push them into trying to do things they can't do. Suppose you want a descending list of maximum weights in a specific type of exercise, with dates showing the progression. A first look at the request seems to make it an ideal candidate for summary operators. But is it?

Would you GROUP BY EXERCISE, with MAX, DSC in the Total_Wgt field and maybe ASC1 in Date? I hope not.

Look at the request carefully and you will see that we want the maximum weights not for all exercises, but for specific exercises. We want a descending listing of total weights, because the total weights are the maximum weights for any given exercise on any given day. But we also want to show progression by days, so we need some kind of ordering on the Date field, too.

First we decide which exercise we want to see the progression in and enter it in the Exercise field. For example, enter [BENCH PRESS] into the Exercise field to see the progression in total weights in bench presses. Next, place ASC1 in the Date field because we want to see progression over time. This gives us a Date-based listing. Remove ASC1 from the Date field and type DSC1 in the Total_Wgt field to show the descending maximum weights, per the original request. The Exercise, Date, and Total_Wgt fields should be in the view area in both cases.

This is an indication that no one query can necessarily meet all requests. You can come close to the original request by typing DSC1 in the Total_Wgt field and ASC2 in the Date field. But remember that we did not use the summary operators to get our information. We can use the summary operators to determine the maximum weights for each exercise and the date on which those maximum weights were attained, but that isn't quite what we are looking for. That query starts with GROUP BY in the Exercise field and MAX, DSC in the Total_Wgt field. This time only the Exercise and Total_Wgt fields should be in the view area because the query system won't pick the specific dates on which the maximum total weights were attained for a given exercise (figure 9-45).

There is only one more thing to do before we leave this section. Sometimes you may want to scan the entire database or part of the database for individual occurrences of things. The EXERCISE database currently holds 216 records, for example. Many of those records contain duplicate exercise names. How many individual exercises do we do? This information can be seen in Browse mode using the last query we designed in figure 9-45, but you can place the following in the Exercise field to obtain the actual number of different exercises in the Exercise field:

```
CNT UNIQUE
```

This is interesting, but not terribly useful as is. How about determining not only the number of different exercises, but also the number of workouts since we started?

Sorry, this can't be done. If you type CNT UNIQUE in both the Exercise and Date fields, an error message tells you that you can only use UNIQUE if no other fields contain summary operators.

But we can get some sophisticated information using combinations of summary operators and other operators. We can find out how many work-

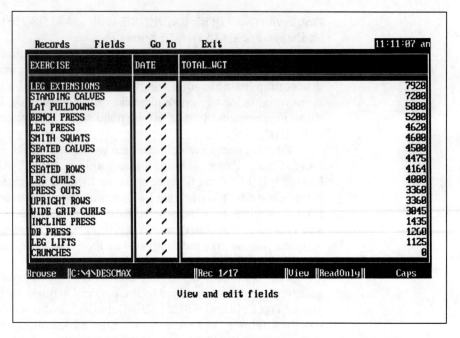

```
  Records     Fields     Go To     Exit                      11:11:07 am
 ┌─────────────────┬────────┬──────────────────────────────────────────┐
 │ EXERCISE        │ DATE   │ TOTAL_WGT                                  │
 ├─────────────────┼────────┼──────────────────────────────────────────┤
 │ LEG EXTENSIONS  │ ⁄   ⁄  │                                      7920 │
 │ STANDING CALVES │ ⁄   ⁄  │                                      7200 │
 │ LAT PULLDOWNS   │ ⁄   ⁄  │                                      5880 │
 │ BENCH PRESS     │ ⁄   ⁄  │                                      5200 │
 │ LEG PRESS       │ ⁄   ⁄  │                                      4620 │
 │ SMITH SQUATS    │ ⁄   ⁄  │                                      4600 │
 │ SEATED CALVES   │ ⁄   ⁄  │                                      4500 │
 │ PRESS           │ ⁄   ⁄  │                                      4475 │
 │ SEATED ROWS     │ ⁄   ⁄  │                                      4164 │
 │ LEG CURLS       │ ⁄   ⁄  │                                      4000 │
 │ PRESS OUTS      │ ⁄   ⁄  │                                      3360 │
 │ UPRIGHT ROWS    │ ⁄   ⁄  │                                      3360 │
 │ WIDE GRIP CURLS │ ⁄   ⁄  │                                      3045 │
 │ INCLINE PRESS   │ ⁄   ⁄  │                                      1435 │
 │ DB PRESS        │ ⁄   ⁄  │                                      1200 │
 │ LEG LIFTS       │ ⁄   ⁄  │                                      1125 │
 │ CRUNCHES        │ ⁄   ⁄  │                                         0 │
 ├─────────────────┴────────┴──────────────────────────────────────────┤
 │ Browse   ‖C:\4\DESCMAX      ‖Rec 1/17      ‖View ‖ReadOnly‖     Caps  │
 └──────────────────────────────────────────────────────────────────────┘
                         View and edit fields
```

Figure 9-45 *The query system can determine the maximum total weight for a given exercise, but can't list the dates on which these maximum weights were attained. This is a limit to the query design system. Using the GROUP BY operator in the Exercise field shows that only seventeen different exercises are in the regimen.*

out sessions we had in November, 1988 by typing the following into the Date field:

```
> {10/31/88}, < {12/01/88}, CNT UNIQUE
```

The UNIQUE summary qualifier works with the AVG, CNT, and SUM summary operators only. Typing AVG UNIQUE in a field tells the query system to determine the average of unique values only. CNT UNIQUE tells the query system to count only unique values in the given field. SUM UNIQUE tells the query system to determine the arithmetic sum of values in a field but use only unique values to determine the sum.

Now you can go wild making queries with these interesting operators, right? No, not until you learn their order of precedence.

Order of precedence? How's My Dear Aunt Sally? You don't know about her? The order of precedence of arithmetic operations is Multiplication, Division, Addition, and Subtraction, which is also known as My Dear Aunt Sally. If you work with a math expression, you must perform multiplication, division, addition, and subtraction operations in that order. At least you should unless you want to be shipped to a remedial math farm.

There is also an order of precedence in the use of the operators listed in this section. This order of precedence is GROUP BY, summary, then the sorting operators ASCn/ASCDICTn/DSCn/DSCDICTn. Remember that sorting operators have their own precedence system involving their numbering scheme. Place any query on the screen and include summary operators, the GROUP BY operator, then sorting operators and dBASE IV will perform the grouping first, summarizing second, then any sorting. It does not matter if you switch the order of the fields in the view area; dBASE IV works by its own rules on this one.

Using Variable and Dependent Requests in Query Forms

That's a heck of a title for a section. Does anybody know what it means? The dBASE IV documentation lists what I will talk about as using algebraic notation in query forms. What they say is accurate enough, unless we have some mathematicians out there reading this book and the dBASE IV documentation, so I will go along with the documentation's concept and expand on it a bit.

Basically, this section talks about the capability of the dBASE IV query system to perform comparisons and evaluations between fields of the same data type. This is done by declaring one field as a variable and creating a dependency to that field in another field. If this was a mathematics text, the preceding sentence would look like this:

$$y = f(x)$$

The *y* in the equation is dependent on the variable *x*. The dependency takes the form of some function, *f(x)*.

This becomes more concrete when you enter something using field names instead of *y* and *x*. Suppose we want to see when the Set_2_Wgts are twenty pounds heavier than the Set_1_Wgts. This would take the following mathematical form:

```
SET_2_WGT = f(SET_1_WGT)
```

The *f(x)* in this particular relationship is

```
SET_2_WGT = SET_1_WGT + 20
```

Note that we are not updating any data in the database. We are not telling the query system to add twenty to each value in the Set_1_Wgt fields and place that new value in the Set_2_Wgt fields. We are only asking for a listing of exercises in which the Set_2_Wgt is twenty pounds heavier than the Set_1_Wgt. Figures 9-46 and 9-47 show the query form and the result-

ing Browse display, respectively. We have activated the index expressions
and are using the ASC1 sorting operator in the EXERCISE +DTOC(DATE)
expression field to place some order on the Browse display.

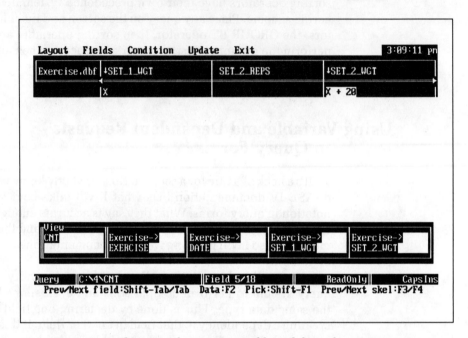

Figure 9-46 *This query form uses variable and dependent operators to
determine which exercises had an increase of twenty pounds from
Set_1_Wgt to Set_2_Wgt. The result of this query is shown
in figure 9-47.*

Our EXERCISE database lends itself to this type of analysis quite
nicely. And once again, complexity becomes an issue. Suppose we want a
listing of all exercises in which Set_3_Wgt is twenty pounds heavier than
Set_2_Wgt and Set_2_Wgt is twenty pounds heavier than Set_1_Wgt.
What does this query look like? Like this:

```
(SET_1_WGT + 20 = SET_2_WGT) AND (SET_2_WGT + 20 = SET_3_WGT)
```

What does that look like on the query screen? Like figure 9-48. The expression in the Set_1_Wgt condition area has not changed from that shown in
figure 9-46. It is still the single variable, X. The result of the query is shown
in figure 9-49.

Compare figures 9-48 and 9-49 with the query and resulting Browse
display in figures 9-50 and 9-51, respectively. Figure 9-48 shows the standard method of ANDing two conditions. The only difference between this
AND and those shown previously is that this AND uses variable and de-

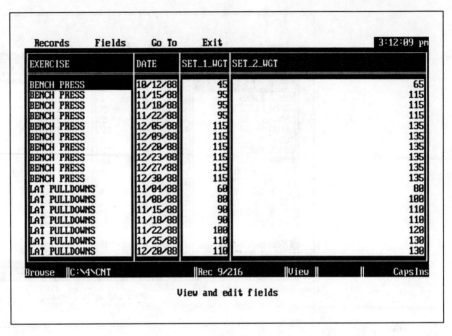

Figure 9-47 This Browse display is the result of the query
in figure 9-46.

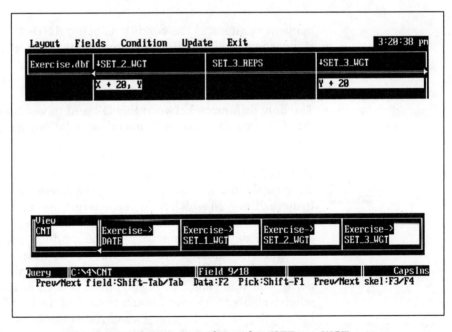

Figure 9-48 This query can be read as (SET_1_WGT + 20 =
SET_2_WGT) AND (SET_2_WGT + 20 = SET_3_WGT).
The result of this query is shown in figure 9-49.

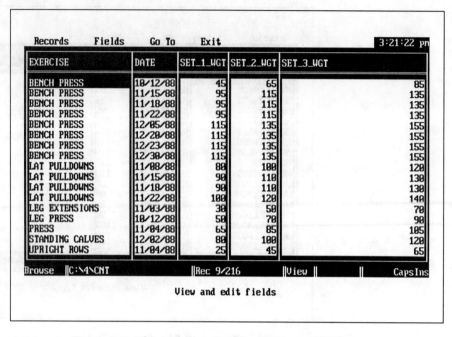

Figure 9-49 *This is the result of the (SET_1_WGT + 20 =*
SET_2_WGT) AND (SET_2_WGT + 20 = SET_3_WGT)
query in figure 9-48.

pendent relations as the conditions being ANDed. Figure 9-50 shows the standard method of ORing two conditions. The OR query looks like this:

```
(SET_1_WGT + 20 = SET_2_WGT) OR (SET_2_WGT + 20 = SET_3_WGT)
```

The only difference between this OR and those shown previously is that this OR uses variable and dependent relations as the conditions being ORed.

One last note on figure 9-51, for readers who are analyzing it and saying dBASE IV failed in my request. No, dBASE IV did not fail. I asked for records that met the condition. The query system responded with a Browse display in which some records met the condition on the left side of the OR, some records met the condition on the right side of the OR, and some records just happened to meet the conditions on both sides of the OR.

So, how complex can these variable and dependent relationships be when used as conditions? We can check for records in which the weights performed the weight lifting pyramid (a weight lifting pyramid occurs when weights go up a set amount in each of the first five sets and return to the starting weight for the last set. An example would be starting at 100, going through 110, 120, 130, 140, and returning to 100 for the last set) and repetitions were consistent. Using *X*'s and *Y*'s for a query this complex could get confusing, so we will use variable names. The field names and their variable counterparts follow:

```
 Layout   Fields   Condition   Update   Exit            3:22:02 pm
┌─────────────┬────────────────┬───────────────┬─────────────────┐
│Exercise.dbf │↓SET_2_WGT      │ SET_3_REPS    │↓SET_3_WGT       │
│             ◄────────────────┼───────────────┼─────────────────►
├─────────────┼────────────────┼───────────────┼─────────────────┤
│             │X + 20          │               │                 │
│             │Y               │               │Y + 20           │
└─────────────┴────────────────┴───────────────┴─────────────────┘



┌─View──────┬────────────┬────────────┬────────────┬────────────┐
│ CNT       │ Exercise-> │ Exercise-> │ Exercise-> │ Exercise-> │
│           │ DATE       │ SET_1_WGT  │ SET_2_WGT  │ SET_3_WGT  │
└───────────┴────────────┴────────────┴────────────┴────────────┘
 Query    C:\4\CNT            Field 7/18                  Caps Ins
    Prev/Next field:Shift-Tab/Tab   Data:F2  Pick:Shift-F1  Prev/Next skel:F3/F4
```

Figure 9-50 This query can be read as (SET_1_WGT + 20 = SET_2_WGT) OR (SET_2_WGT + 20 = SET_3_WGT). This is an ORed query; the query in figure 9-48 is ANDed. The result of this query is shown in figure 9-51.

```
 Records      Fields     Go To     Exit            3:23:48 pm
┌──────────────┬────────┬─────────┬─────────┬─────────┐
│ EXERCISE     │ DATE   │SET_1_WGT│SET_2_WGT│SET_3_WGT│
├──────────────┼────────┼─────────┼─────────┼─────────┤
│ BENCH PRESS  │10/12/88│      45 │      65 │      85 │
│ BENCH PRESS  │11/03/88│      45 │      85 │     105 │
│ BENCH PRESS  │11/11/88│      85 │      95 │     115 │
│ BENCH PRESS  │11/15/88│      95 │     115 │     135 │
│ BENCH PRESS  │11/18/88│      95 │     115 │     135 │
│ BENCH PRESS  │11/22/88│      95 │     115 │     135 │
│ BENCH PRESS  │12/01/88│      95 │     135 │     155 │
│ BENCH PRESS  │12/05/88│     115 │     135 │     155 │
│ BENCH PRESS  │12/09/88│     115 │     135 │     185 │
│ BENCH PRESS  │12/20/88│     115 │     135 │     155 │
│ BENCH PRESS  │12/23/88│     115 │     135 │     155 │
│ BENCH PRESS  │12/27/88│     115 │     135 │     135 │
│ BENCH PRESS  │12/30/88│     115 │     135 │     155 │
│ LAT PULLDOWNS│11/04/88│      60 │      80 │     120 │
│ LAT PULLDOWNS│11/08/88│      80 │     100 │     120 │
│ LAT PULLDOWNS│11/15/88│      90 │     110 │     130 │
│ LAT PULLDOWNS│11/18/88│      90 │     110 │     130 │
└──────────────┴────────┴─────────┴─────────┴─────────┘
 Browse    C:\4\CNT           Rec 9/216        View         Caps Ins
                      View and edit fields
```

Figure 9-51 This is the result of the (SET_1_WGT + 20 = SET_2_WGT) OR (SET_2_WGT + 20 = SET_3_WGT) query in figure 9-50.

Field Name	Variable Name
SET_1_REPS	REP1
SET_1_WGT	WGT1
SET_2_REPS	REP2
SET_2_WGT	WGT2
SET_3_REPS	REP3
SET_3_WGT	WGT3
SET_4_REPS	REP4
SET_4_WGT	WGT4
SET_5_REPS	REP5
SET_5_WGT	WGT5
SET_6_REPS	REP6
SET_6_WGT	WGT6

The relations are as follows:

$$REP1 = REP2 = REP3 = REP4 = REP5 = REP6$$
$$WGT2 = WGT1 + 10$$
$$WGT3 = WGT2 + 10$$
$$WGT4 = WGT3 + 10$$
$$WGT5 = WGT4 + 10$$
$$WGT6 = WGT1$$

These relations can be typed into the condition boxes under the necessary fields in the query area. No figure will show all of this, but the following list indicates how complex this can be:

Field Name	Condition
SET_1_REPS	REP1
SET_1_WGT	WGT1
SET_2_REPS	REP2, = REP1
SET_2_WGT	WGT2, WGT1 + 10
SET_3_REPS	REP3, = REP2
SET_3_WGT	WGT3, WGT2 + 10
SET_4_REPS	REP4, = REP3
SET_4_WGT	WGT4, WGT3 + 10
SET_5_REPS	REP5, = REP4
SET_5_WGT	WGT5, WGT4 + 10
SET_6_REPS	REP6, = REP1
SET_6_WGT	WGT6, = WGT1

I hope someone out there sees that this is overkill. Think about what you are asking and you will see that the preceding list can be simplified greatly. The query will work if this list is entered into the condition lines of the query area, but all those variables are not really necessary and will slow dBASE IV down. That's the last thing you want.

The relations can be rewritten as follows:

REP1 = REP2 = REP3 = REP4 = REP5 = REP6

WGT2 = WGT1 + 10

WGT3 = WGT1 + 20

WGT4 = WGT1 + 30

WGT5 = WGT1 + 40

WGT6 = WGT1

And now the listing is

Field Name	Condition
SET_1_REPS	REP1
SET_1_WGT	WGT1
SET_2_REPS	= REP1
SET_2_WGT	WGT1 + 10
SET_3_REPS	= REP1
SET_3_WGT	WGT1 + 20
SET_4_REPS	= REP3
SET_4_WGT	WGT1 + 30
SET_5_REPS	= REP4
SET_5_WGT	WGT1 + 40
SET_6_REPS	= REP1
SET_6_WGT	= WGT1

Only two records in the entire database meet those conditions. Those two records were written to a database file, VARDEP, and DISPLAYed TO an ASCII FILE, which is included here.

```
Record#      195              100
EXERCISE     LEG EXTENSIONS   STANDING CALVES
DATE         12/27/88         11/21/88
TIME         09:00            09:00
SET_1_REPS   10               10
SET_1_WGT    90               50
SET_2_REPS   10               10
SET_2_WGT    100              60
```

SET_3_REPS	10	10
SET_3_WGT	110	70
SET_4_REPS	10	10
SET_4_WGT	120	80
SET_5_REPS	10	10
SET_5_WGT	130	90
SET_6_REPS	10	10
SET_6_WGT	90	50
TOTAL_WGT	6400	4000

If nothing else, we see that my workouts are not following the ideal paradigm of weight training. Only 2 records out of 216 matched the query conditions we entered.

All this talk of variables and dependent relations should bring another topic to our attention. The topic is *reserved words*. A reserved word is something that is used by the software and hence cannot be used by the user. I have demonstrated that you can use variable names when you create dependent conditions in the query form. Do you think you can use AVG as a variable name? I hope you don't. The query system will assume you want to average the field in which you type AVG because AVG is a *word* dBASE IV's query system *reserves* all for itself. The reserved words are AVERAGE, AVG, CNT, COUNT, EVERY, LIKE, MAX, MIN, SUM, SOUNDS, UNIQUE, and WITH. Noticeably missing from this listing is GROUP BY. How come? For the same reason SOUNDS LIKE is not listed. You can't create variable names that are more than one word long. What about the ASCDICT, DSCDICT, ASC, and DSC sorting operators? They don't count as reserved words if you enter them as shown because the actual sort operators include numbers. These numbers indicate the order in which the sorting will occur. There are other operators, called LINKn. The actual operator can be LINK1, LINK2, and so on through as many LINKs (connections between databases) that you want to make. You can use LINK. You can't use LINK and a number.

Designing Update Queries

The preceding section did not quite exhaust all the possibilities of view queries (although it did come close). In the next chapter, we do some more work with complex queries, specifically making links between files. Right now we will investigate the other query form, the update query.

Update queries don't answer direct questions so much as they demonstrate what-ifs. You can use update queries to see what would happen if certain things changed by some percentage, how data would be skewed if some field were altered to match other fields, and so on. The beauty of update queries is that you can confirm changes before they become permanent. This is not exactly true and requires some explanation.

You can see changes to the database on the screen. This is true. We can specify an update procedure, such as *Mark records for deletion* from the Update menu (figure 9-52). You can press [F2] to get to Browse and Edit modes with no changes in place. Press [Alt-U] *P* to tell the query system to perform the update, however, and all heck breaks loose (figure 9-53). Note that marking records for deletion without specifying a condition tells the query system to delete all the records in the database. You can press [F2] and dBASE IV will respond with: *No records selected. Press any key to continue.*

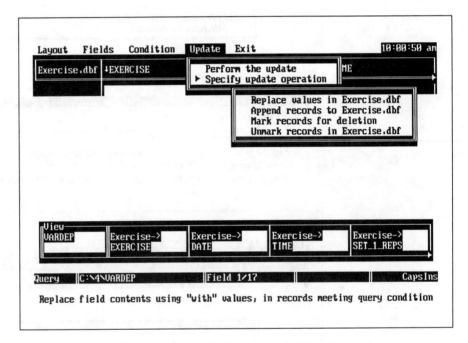

Figure 9-52 *The query system's Update menu. The main update menu has two options,* Perform the update *and* Specify the update. *The secondary menu branches from Specify and lets you replace existing information with new information, append records to the database, and delete (mark) and undelete (unmark) records in the file.*

You can write a view query and change it to an update query by selecting an update option from the Specify update operation menu or by typing the update operation directly into the condition box under the file name. You will notice that specifying an update operation from the menu causes one or two things to happen. Two things happen if you are designing your update query from a view query. One thing happens if you are directly creating an update query.

Starting with a view query, dBASE IV tells you that changing from a view to an update query will cause you to lose your view area information (figure 9-54). This is no great loss because you don't care about viewing

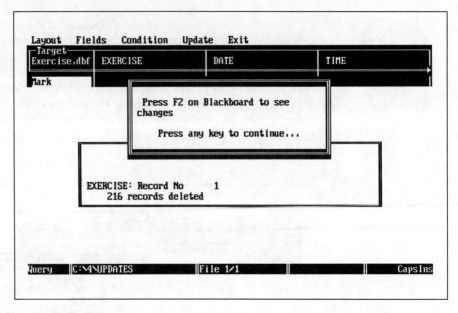

Figure 9-53 *Query system messages during a typical Mark records for deletion update. The top box shows up on all updates. Variations of the bottom box depend on what update operation you have requested.*

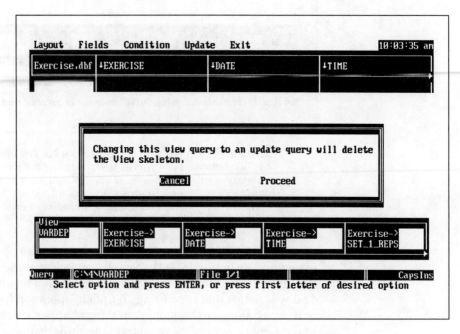

Figure 9-54 *The query system warns you that you will lose your view area information if you change a view query to an update query. You can save your current query with the [Alt-S] command if this is a concern.*

fields; all you care about is updating the database. Note that update queries show all fields when the Browse display is presented.

Two update procedures, mark and unmark records for deletion, are straightforward. You select these options and place a condition somewhere in the query area. Then the query system marks or unmarks the records that meet the specified condition. The query system tells you the status of your update operation by marking the file name in the query area with two tags (figure 9-55). One tag is a one-word description of the update operation located in the condition area under the file name. The second tag is the word *Target* located above the file name in the query area.

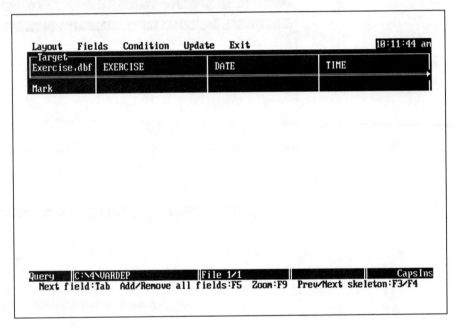

Figure 9-55 *This figure demonstrates how update operations show themselves on the query design surface. Note the words* Mark *under the file name and* Target *above the file name. This update marks records for deletion that met a specified condition.*

The Append records option is discussed in more detail in the next chapter. Basically, *Append records* gives you the option of getting data from one database and adding it to another database. This chapter includes a simplified example. The next chapter shows how to split a database using the append update query.

This leaves us with the replace update query. The replace query lets us change existing data. Suppose we noticed that incorrect dates were entered for several records—the Date field data was entered as 01/04/88 when we wanted the date as 01/04/89.

First we get to the query design surface and press [Alt-U] S R to call up the Update menu's *Specify update condition, Replace values* option (figure

9-52). dBASE IV returns to the query area, and you see *Replace* under the file name and *Target* above the file name. Tab over to the Date field and enter the erroneous data and the correction as shown in the following and in figure 9-56.

{01/04/88}, WITH {01/04/89}

```
 Layout   Fields   Condition   Update   Exit                     10:11:16 am
┌────────────────────────────────────────────────────────────────────────┐
│ Exercise.dbf->DATE                                                       │
├────────────────────────────────────────────────────────────────────────┤
│ {01/04/89}, WITH {01/04/88}                                              │
│                                                                          │
│                                                                          │
│                                                                          │
│                                                                          │
│                                                                          │
│                                                                          │
│                                                                          │
│                                                                          │
│                                                                          │
│                                                                          │
│                                                                          │
└────────────────────────────────────────────────────────────────────────┘
 Query   C:\4\REPL              Field 2/18                          Caps
       Prev/Next field:Shift-Tab/Tab  Data:F2  Pick:Shift-F1  Prev/Next skel:F3/F4
```

Figure 9-56 *This figure uses the [F9] (Zoom) option to show the Replace condition in full. We want to correct the Date field for entries dated 01/04/88.*

Remember that dBASE IV does not recognize information as date type data unless the information is surrounded by braces. Note the syntax of the command. The data to be replaced is listed first. It is separated from the rest of the expression by a comma, then the new data is listed. This serves the same purpose as creating a condition for the REPLACE operation. The condition is "Only make replacements in records in which the Date field is 01/04/88." The dBASE prompt form of this command is

REPLACE DATE WITH {01/04/89} FOR DATE = {01/04/88}

 Slightly more advanced or more adventuresome readers might see an alternative that uses active index expressions. Be careful when using index expressions to speed up REPLACE operations. The mistake is to use the EXERCISE.MDX file's DATE index expression (in this example) to speed up the preceding REPLACE operation:

```
SET ORDER TO DATE
SEEK {01/04/88}
REPLACE DATE WITH {01/04/89} WHILE DATE = {01/04/88}
```

What is wrong with this? You can SET ORDER TO DATE. This tells dBASE IV to place EXERCISE.DBF in DATE indexed order. You can then SEEK the specific date, and dBASE IV will place you at the first record in which the specified date occurs. No problem so far.

The REPLACE command is where things go wrong. dBASE IV sees the REPLACE command and makes the change to the first record that meets the condition. Immediately upon making the change to the data, the first record that meets the condition is no longer located in the same place in the Date index. That record, which had a date of 01/04/88, now has a date of 01/04/89. The record pointer stays on that record while it is given a new position in the index. dBASE IV then goes to the next record in the index. The next record in the index, however, does not have a date of 01/04/88. At best, there is no next record. At worst, the next record has a date sometime in 1989. In either case, dBASE IV can no longer satisfy the WHILE qualifier on the REPLACE command and stops the REPLACE operation. The net result is that only one record is changed.

You can perform a replace update query on any field except memo fields. You can replace all data in a numeric field with the value 10 by typing the following line in the condition area under the specified numeric or floating field:

```
WITH 10
```

What if you want to increase the value in the numeric or floating field by 10? Using the Set_1_Reps field as an example, that command looks like this

```
WITH SET_1_REPS + 10
```

Replacements to character fields follow the same form. You can replace a given character field in all records with the name FRED with the following command:

```
WITH [FRED]
```

Logical fields can also be replaced. A given logical field can be made True for all records with

```
WITH .T.
```

Unfortunately, no replacements can be made to memo fields.

The REPLACE command we used in the Date example showed how to set a condition as well as perform a replacement. You could do the same thing with logical fields, although it would be a worthless exercise. Suppose you want to change all False field values to True. Because a logical field can only be True or False, nothing in between, the preceding command works fine. You could create more work for yourself by entering

```
.F., WITH .T.
```

A conditional replacement of numeric values is something to consider, however. We can locate each Set_1_Reps with a current value of 10 and change it to 12. This replacement would not affect any records in which the Set_1_Reps value was anything other than 10. The command looks like the following:

```
10, WITH 12
```

How about conditional replacement of a character field? Yes, this is possible. We could change every occurrence of BENCH PRESS in the Exercise field with 100 METER ELECTRIC LOW HURDLES by placing the following command in the condition area under the Exercise field:

```
[BENCH PRESS], WITH [100 METER ELECTRIC LOW HURDLES]
```

Careful readers might also see that this replace update is a way to determine the Total_Wgt field value. You would issue the [Alt-U] S R command, [Shift-Tab] to the Total_Wgt field, and enter

```
WITH SET_1_REPS*SET_1_WGT + SET_2_REPS*SET_2_WGT +;
     SET_3_REPS*SET_3_WGT + SET_4_REPS*SET_4_WGT +;
     SET_5_REPS*SET_5_WGT + SET_6_REPS*SET_6_WGT
```

Note that this request can be entered directly into the condition area under Total_Wgt or with the [F9] (Zoom) key. The command includes semicolons so that it will fit in the margins of this book. (dBASE IV accepts semicolons to demarcate a command as continuing on the next line.) This command does not need to be entered in the query design system as such, though.

Pressing [Alt-U] P tells the query system to perform the update. Be prepared, however, to wait a while for dBASE IV to come back to you, even if you are using a 386. This is a long request to make, especially if your database contains more than a thousand records.

We have covered conditional replacements within a given field. What about replacing data in fields when conditions are placed on other fields? We can do that, too.

Suppose we want to replace Set_1_Wgt with 200 for each LEG

PRESS exercise. Type *[LEG PRESS]* in the Exercise field condition area, tab over to the Set_1_Wgt condition area, and type *WITH 200*. Now press [Alt-U] *P* and dBASE IV makes the changes to the Set_1_Wgt field, but only for records in which the Exercise field is LEG PRESS.

You can enter as many replacements in the query area as you want. However, a condition on any one field affects all replacements. You can enter a conditional Date field change, a conditional Set_1_Reps change, and a conditional Set_1_Wgt change for the same update. For example, suppose we place the following three conditional replacements into the listed fields:

```
DATE           {10/08/88}, WITH {10/20/88}
SET_1_REPS     15, WITH 20
SET_1_WGT      20, WITH 35
```

The query system reads this as "Search for records in which the Date field is 10/08/88, the Set_1_Reps field is 15, and the Set_1_Wgt field is 20. When a record is found in which these three conditions are met, change the Date data to 10/20/88, the Set_1_Reps field to 20, and the Set_1_Wgt field to 35."

A dBASE IV command to perform the same function looks like this:

```
REPLACE DATE WITH {10/20/88}, SET_1_REPS WITH 20,;
    SET_1_WGT WITH 35 FOR (DATE = {10/08/88} .AND.;
    SET_1_REPS = 15 .AND. SET_1_WGT = 35)
```

As before, semicolons divide the command so that it will fit in the margins of the book. The command form clearly shows that there is a triple AND condition on this replacement. Sometimes these conditions gang up on each other and nothing that we want to replace is updated. Be careful when you try to update things through the query system.

File-Level Query Commands

It should not surprise you that much of what you can do through the query system menus can also be done through direct command entry. You can APPEND, MARK, REPLACE, and UNMARK records by typing those commands under the file name in the query area. The query system recognizes those words as commands and, should any view information be on the screen, tells you that you will lose the view area information if you proceed (figure 9-54). You can type in these commands and the query system will behave as if they were entered from a menu. All caveats listed in previous sections apply.

Two file-level commands, FIND and UNIQUE, have not been mentioned in this chapter. UNIQUE was mentioned as a qualifier for the summary operators, but that isn't the same UNIQUE mentioned here. UNIQUE can also simulate a unique indexing of data.

A unique indexing of data is when you index a file on a field, a combination of fields, fields and expressions, and so on, but look at only the entries that are distinctly different from all other entries. For example, 236 records are currently in the EXERCISE database. And 17 different and distinct exercises are in the 236 records:

```
Record#  Exercise
      1  BENCH PRESS
     42  CRUNCHES
      3  DB PRESS
      2  INCLINE PRESS
      8  LAT PULLDOWNS
      7  LEG CURLS
      6  LEG EXTENSIONS
     43  LEG LIFTS
     14  LEG PRESS
     22  PRESS
      5  PRESS OUTS
     16  SEATED CALVES
     18  SEATED ROWS
     97  SMITH SQUATS
     41  STANDING CALVES
     23  UPRIGHT ROWS
      4  WIDE GRIP CURLS
```

This an example of a unique exercise listing. The question is, how unique is unique? Type UNIQUE in the condition area under the file name in the query area. We are going to have some fun.

The fun starts when you realize that the query system only simulates a unique indexing of data on the fields in the view area. For example, figure 9-57 shows the UNIQUE operator under the file name and Exercise as the only field in the database listed in the view area. What happens to the Browse display? Not much, except only unique exercise names are listed. The 236 records become 17 separate entries, the unique exercise names without duplicates (figure 9-58).

Now we go back to the query design surface. Press [F5] to remove Exercise from the view area, tab to the Date field, press [F5] to include the Date field in the view area, and press [F2] to go to Browse mode. Now there are 31 records listed, indicating that we have entered data for 31 different days of exercising.

Okay, okay. Where does the fun come in? Get back to the query design surface and place both Exercise and Date in the view area. Now press [F2] to go to Browse mode. Every record is listed (assuming your database is like mine). Why would the query system, when specifically asked to list only those unique records, return every record in the database? Because we

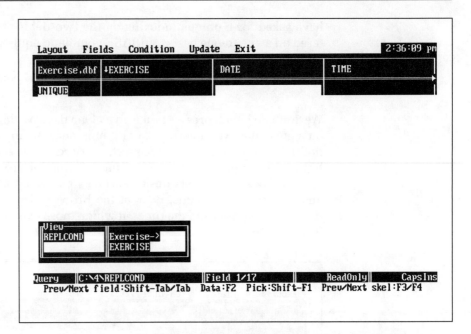

Figure 9-57 *The UNIQUE operator is under the file name and only the Exercise field is in the view area. The query system will produce a Browse display that lists only unique exercise names.*

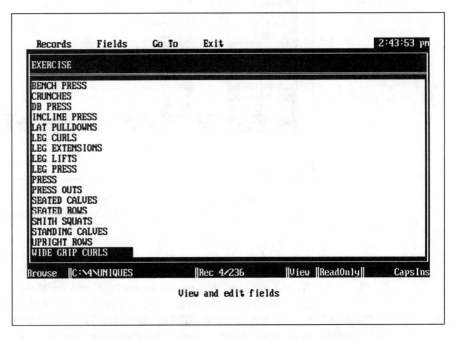

Figure 9-58 *The Browse display resulting from the query in figure 9-57 Because the only field in the view area in figure 9-57 is Exercise, the query system performs a unique indexing of only that field.*

have asked for a unique indexing on the two fields that we know are entered on a one-to-one basis. A dBASE command equivalent of this query is

```
INDEX ON EXERCISE + DTOC(DATE) TAG EXDATE OF EXERCISE UNIQUE
```

We don't do bench presses twice on a given day. We don't do leg lifts twice
on a given day. We do each exercise only once on any given day. Because
nothing is unique about this request, every record is returned. You should
begin to see a pattern in the resulting information from this request.

Go back to the query design surface, remove Date from the view area,
and replace it with Time. Back at the Browse display we have a unique
listing of exercises and the times at which those exercises were performed
(figure 9-59).

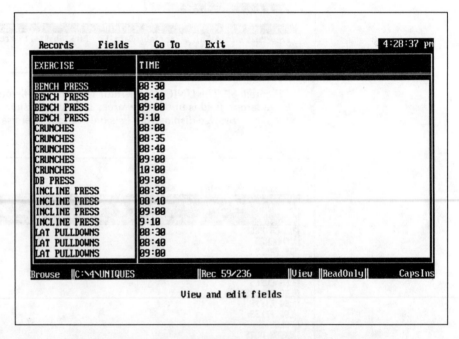

Figure 9-59 *This Browse display is the result of asking the query
system for a UNIQUE listing of Exercises and Times.*

There are 67 unique Exercise and Time combinations. How about
Exercise and Time and Set_1_Reps? You know how to build that, so do it.
What happens? The query system returns a listing of records in which the
combination of Exercise, Time, and Set_1_Reps are not duplicated.

What you should begin to notice is that the query system decides what
is unique based on what fields are in the view area. If you place all the
database fields in the view area and ask for a unique query, you will see
only those records in which each field is unique from all others. If your

database is comprised of widely varying data, you will probably see every record listed in Browse mode. The key to UNIQUE is to remember that the unique listings are built based on the fields included in the view area. The more fields placed in the view area, the more likely that the Browse displays will be less and less unique.

You should know one other thing about UNIQUE before going to the next topic. Entering UNIQUE under the file name tells the query system to list only the *first* occurrence of whatever is in your view area. Ask for a UNIQUE listing with only the Exercise field in the view area and the query system returns the first records in which a new exercise name appears. Suppose that bench presses are in records 5, 12, 23, 54, 256, and 300. UNIQUE will return record 5 and hide the rest. The next item listed will be whatever alphabetically follows [BENCH PRESS] in the database.

This brings up an interesting point: how did the query system know to produce the alphabetized listings in figures 9-58 and 9-59 when we did not specify any sorting operators, any included indices, and so on? Look at figure 9-60, and you will notice that not only are exercises alphabetically listed, but the Set_1_Reps are in numerical order as well.

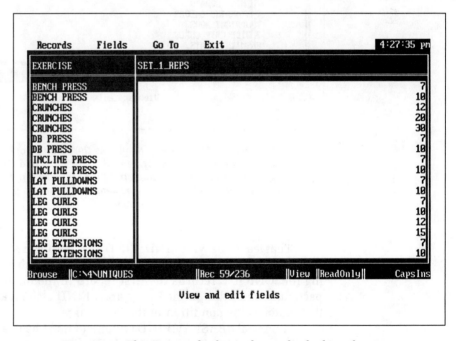

Figure 9-60 This Browse display is the result of asking the query system for a UNIQUE listing of Exercises and Set_1_Reps. Note that the exercises are listed alphabetically and the Set_1_Reps are listed numerically.

"Curiouser and curiouser," said Alice.

Well, as long as we are growing curious, let's up the ante. What happens if you switch the view information on the query that creates figure 9-60 so that Set_1_Reps is before Exercise? You get the Browse display in figure 9-61. The UNIQUE command tells the query system to list only records that have information unique to the combination of fields in the view area. In addition, the order of fields in the view area greatly affects how the UNIQUE command generates the view.

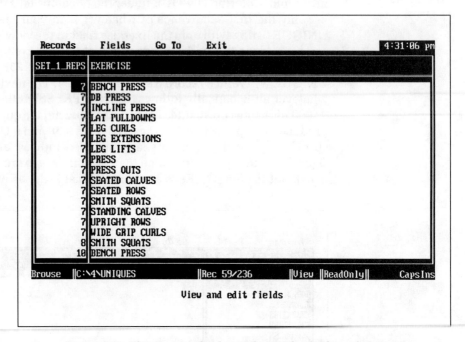

Figure 9-61 This Browse display is the result of asking the query system for a UNIQUE listing of Set_1_Reps and Exercises. This figure and figure 9-60 demonstrate that the order of the fields in the view area tells the query system how to set up the UNIQUE Browse display.

That leaves us with FIND. FIND and UNIQUE share some attributes. In particular, both return the first record that matches what they are looking for. UNIQUE returns the first record in the database that matches a particular condition in the query area. FIND also locates the first record that matches the condition in the query area.

A normal dBASE IV FIND command must be used with active index expressions, either in an NDX or MDX file. Not so with the query form FIND. You don't need to include the index expressions with the [Alt-F] *I* command in order for the query system to find the first record that matches the conditions entered in the query area. dBASE IV can find the first record that matches those conditions quicker if you are interested in finding something that is part of a key field in an index file, but that particular index file must be active in order to do so.

Of course, there's a rub. A normal dBASE IV FIND command, because it is used with an index file, drops you at the first record that matches the FIND condition. And, normally, each record following the first match will also match, or come close (more adventuresome readers may want to experiment with the SET NEAR ON/off command regarding close matches to a FIND command). Using FIND in a query does not produce an order the way it does when using FIND from the dBASE prompt. The query system drops you at the first record that matches the condition. Other records may match the condition, but they are not placed immediately following the first matching record, unless you activate sorting operators along with the FIND command.

An example of this is shown in figure 9-62. We asked the query system to FIND "LEG LIFTS" in the Exercise field. It drops us at the first record that matches the condition, but the listing is not in any particular order.

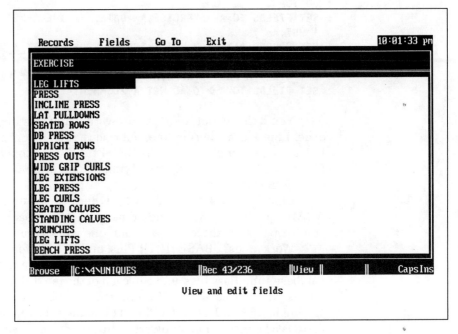

Figure 9-62 *The FIND command brings you to the first record that matches the condition set in the query area, but it does not create the ordered listing you would see with the normal dBASE IV FIND command when used with an index file.*

Looking at the QBE File

This is the last section in the chapter, and it is well saved until the end. We will look at how the query system interprets our requests and creates command files from them.

I mentioned that the query system creates QBE files with hidden characters. This means you can't directly edit and save a QBE file and expect dBASE IV to use it. You can directly edit a QBE file and save it under a different name, however. This preserves the integrity of your original QBE file and lets you put what the query system creates into your own program files.

We start with the bench press query, listing 9-1:

Listing 9-1

```
 1 : * dBASE IV .QBE file
 2 : SET FIELDS TO
 3 : SELECT 1
 4 : USE EXERCISE.DBF AGAIN
 5 : SET EXACT ON
 6 : SET FILTER TO ((A->EXERCISE=[BENCH PRESS]))
 7 : GO TOP
 8 : SET FIELDS TO A->EXERCISE,A->DATE,A->TIME,A->SET_1_REPS,A->SET_
     1_WGT,A->;
 9 : SET_2_REPS,A->SET_2_WGT,A->SET_3_REPS,A->SET_3_WGT,A->SET_4_
     REPS,A->;
10 : SET_4_WGT,A->SET_5_REPS,A->SET_5_WGT,A->SET_6_REPS,A->SET_6_WGT
11 : SET FIELDS TO A->TOTAL_WGT,A->COMMENT
```

You'd throw out line 1 if you were using this in your own program code. Line 2 is a filtering line, but one that shuts off any active filtering. Filters are set in place with the SET FILTER TO *condition* (or dBASE III Plus query file) command. Specifying no condition tells dBASE IV to shut off any filtering that may be active.

Lines 3 and 4 tell dBASE IV where to set up housekeeping. The AGAIN qualifier in line 4 should be used with great discretion. It allows you to open a database in more than one work area.

Work areas? dBASE III, III Plus, and IV have ten separate work areas when the programs are active. You can have a separate database and that database's ancillary files active in each of the ten different work areas. This means you can have ten different databases active during a given work session in dBASE III and III Plus. This same rule applies to dBASE IV, but there is a significant and powerful difference between the dBASE IV program and the dBASE III and III Plus programs.

In dBASE III and III Plus, you can use a given database in only one of the ten available work areas. This means you can have up to ten different databases available for referencing at any given moment. What you can't have with dBASE III and III Plus is the same database open in more than a single work area. dBASE IV lets you do that, but you have to be careful. Using a database AGAIN can cause problems when one work area changes the database, when you try to close the files with the CLOSE DATABASES command, and so on. The other big reason to shy away from the AGAIN qualifier is that there is no guarantee it will be around in the next incarnation of dBASE.

Why does the query system start with SELECT 1? These queries were designed in work area 1, also known as work area A (the ten work areas have numeric references 1 through 10 and alphabetic references A through J). We USE a database AGAIN because the query system is looking ahead to a time when you might have the selected database already open in another work area. The next chapter shows how the query system modifies the query design surface when it knows a database is open in different work areas simultaneously.

Line 5 tells dBASE IV that we want only records that meet our specified condition. Line 6 tells dBASE IV what condition we want, but the condition is not set until the record pointer is moved. Line 7 is the line that actually activates the condition set in line 6. GO TOP moves the record pointer. Note that GO TOP works on both indexed and unindexed files.

The rest of the code tells dBASE IV which fields to place on the Browse display. Note that the field names are preceded by A->. This tells dBASE IV to list the fields from the first work area (work area 1), which was SELECTed in line 3.

The next QBE file we investigate is TWGT1TON.QBE, listing 9-2. This file is used to list only those records in which the Total_Wgt field is greater than one ton.

Listing 9-2

```
00001 : * dBASE IV .QBE file
00002 : SET FIELDS TO
00003 : SELECT 1
00004 : USE EXERCISE.DBF AGAIN
00005 : SET EXACT ON
00006 : SET FILTER TO ((A->TOTAL_WGT> 2000))
00007 : GO TOP
00008 : SET FIELDS TO A->EXERCISE,A->TOTAL_WGT,A->DATE
```

Again, you would throw out line 1. This code is similar to listing 9-1. The only differences are in the condition and the fields that are displayed. How about something a little more interesting, like the calculated field query in listing 9-3, CALCFLD.QBE:

Listing 9-3

```
1 : * dBASE IV .QBE file
2 : SET FIELDS TO
3 : SELECT 1
4 : USE EXERCISE.DBF AGAIN
5 : SET EXACT ON
6 : SET FILTER TO;
7 : (((A->SET_1_WGT*A->SET_1_REPS +;
    A->SET_2_WGT*A->SET_2_REPS +;
    A->SET_3_WGT*A->SET_3_REPS +;
    A->SET_4_WGT*A->SET_4_REPS +;
    A->SET_5_WGT*A->SET_5_REPS +;
```

Listing 9-3 (cont.)

```
         A->SET_6_WGT*A->SET_6_REPS);
 8 :  > 2000))
 9 :  GO TOP
10 :  SET FIELDS TO A->EXERCISE,; TWEIGHT=(
11 :  A->SET_1_WGT*A->SET_1_REPS +;
         A->SET_2_WGT*A->SET_2_REPS +;
         A->SET_3_WGT*A->SET_3_REPS +;
         A->SET_4_WGT*A->SET_4_REPS +;
         A->SET_5_WGT*A->SET_5_REPS +;
         A->SET_6_WGT*A->SET_6_REPS;
12 :  )
13 :  SET FIELDS TO A->DATE
```

This looks like a mess because of the word wrapping to fit the page. The filter condition spans lines 7 and 8, and basically results in calculating if the sum of the Set_n_Reps times the Set_n_Wgts is greater than 2000. The fields listed on lines 10 through 13 are displayed for any records meeting this condition. Note that line 11 builds the calculated field a second time.

Summary

By now you should be getting the idea. You have seen how to design dBASE IV queries from the sublime to the ridiculous. You have also seen how dBASE IV builds your queries into command files that you can edit and include in your own code.

The next chapter goes a little further with query files. It shows you how to work with more than one database file at a time, how to link files, how to append from one database to the other, as well as how to make useful and logical modifications to the database, format files, screen files, and so on.

The next chapter follows the pattern of learning as you go. You designed what you thought you wanted. But after working with what you designed, you know how it really should work. Putting in the changes is what happens in the next chapter.

Right now, work a little with query files on your own. Experiment a bit, and I will meet you in the next chapter.

Redesigning and Modifying

This chapter will show how to correct our original ideas that went wrong. Much of what is presented will answer questions that may have arisen since we originally designed and used the system.

The first part of this chapter talks about redesigning the database without losing information currently located there. In particular, we divide the EXERCISE.DBF file into two separate files. One file contains much of the exercise information; the other file is our Comment file. The two files are linked only by the Date field.

Next, we remove the Time field from the EXERCISE.DBF file because we have not made use of it so far and probably never will.

After redesigning our database, we modify the screen form to use both databases. The redesigned screen form is then broken into its program form for readers who want to use the FMT file as demonstrated earlier.

Modifying the databases also means we have to modify our report forms to handle two database files at once. This is the subject of the next section. We also design a report to scan the Comment field for the word *PROBLEM*. This gives us a listing of which days we had problems and what the problems were.

The last part of this chapter deals with designing the query forms to handle two files at once, linking the files, and appending data from one file to the other.

I want to point out before actually starting this chapter that you might want to play with dBASE IV a little before you read what is discussed here. There is no doubt in my mind that you can handle this chapter. This is not a "Remember, kids, these people are highly trained professionals. Do not try these things at home," type of situation. I merely suggest you gauge your comfort with the dBASE IV system before you start working with the level of modifications presented in this chapter.

Enough said? Here we go.

Getting Two Databases From One

One of the things we have noticed about the Exercise database is that the original design is not flexible in regards to queries, reports, and so on. In particular, we want to divide the original database into two or more manageable databases. The Exercise database lends itself to being separated into two databases. One of the databases is the EXERCISE.DBF file minus the Comment and Time fields. The other database is EXERCISE.DBF's Comment and Date fields.

There are lots of ways to split a database into different parts. Remember, we are not talking about taking a database with several thousand records and making smaller databases from it. Splitting a database with lots of records into smaller databases goes back to the concept of masterbase and database. Here we are talking about putting some fields from one database in another database.

The first method of splitting a database into its component fields is the bigger hammer method. We start with the Assist menu, shown in figure 10-1. Your Assist system may vary greatly from mine. Don't worry. What I will show you will work on any database.

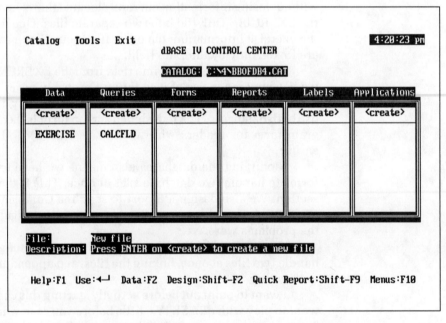

Figure 10-1 *The Assist system is one place to start the process of breaking an existing database into its components.*

You must first make sure that the database you intend to fracture is not currently active. We will use the Assist menu's *Tools, Dos utilities* option to copy the source file. The operating system will have a fit if the file is active and a second call is made on it.

Did some of the terms in the preceding give you a fit? *Source file,* for example? When you make a copy of a file, the original file is the source of the copy. The file you are copying the source to is the *target file.* Sometimes the target file is called the *destination file.* You should know what an *active file* is by now, but for those who read from the back of the book to the front, an active file is one that is being used by the computer. It does not matter if nothing is happening to the file. The fact that the computer opens a file means it thinks something is going to happen to the file.

What you might not know is the term *call.* dBASE IV calls and opens the database file when you place the database in use, either through the Assist system, by SETting a VIEW or QUERY file, or by the dBASE prompt USE command. DOS only allows one call on a file at a time in a single-user system. Actually, DOS only allows one call on a file at a time in a multiuser and network system as well, but the multiuser or networking software tell DOS to shut up and live with it.

The important thing to note is that you would be ill advised to keep a database open and active if you plan on doing some DOS-level work (such as COPY, DEL, ERASE, or TYPE) on the file.

You want the Tools menu, so press [Alt-T] *D* to open the Tools menu *DOS utilities* option (figure 10-2). The first thing the DOS utilities do is read the current directory. You are then presented with an alphabetized directory listing, as shown in figure 10-3.

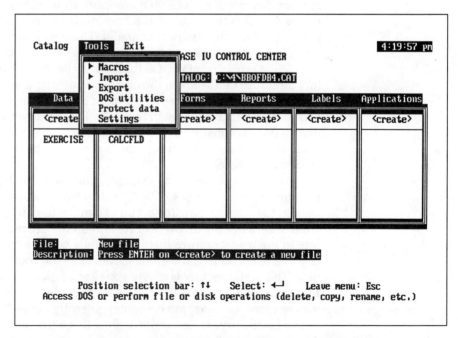

Figure 10-2 The Tools menu DOS utilities option is where you can make a copy of the database with menu options.

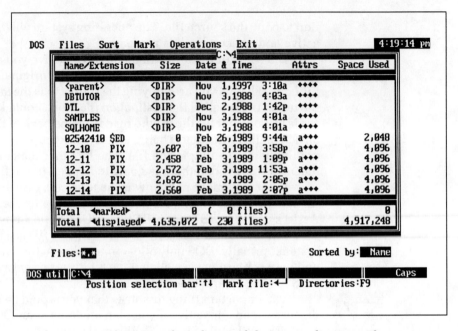

Figure 10-3 The DOS utilities first read the current directory. Then you are presented with an alphabetized file listing.

The directory listing is telling you quite a bit about the files in the current directory, so let's take a minute to investigate it. The top of the listing contains the name of the current drive and path (C:\4 on the computer on which the figure was made). The next line contains the titles for the columns that make up the actual directory listing.

What is a ⟨parent⟩? DOS thinks of a ⟨parent⟩ as the part of the directory structure that leads to the current directory. This is clearly shown on what is called the tree structure of the disk. The tree structure for the hard disk in figure 10-3 is shown in figure 10-4. You can get a tree listing for your disk (it does not matter if you are working with a hard disk or a floppy or some other removable media, for that matter) by pressing [F9] from the DOS utilities screen.

Using figure 10-4 as an example, the arrow and highlight tell you that the current directory is 4. The tree structure always starts with the highlight in the current directory. You can move the highlight with the cursor control keys but the arrow will remain on the current directory. The first line in the tree structure display box tells you the current drive. Beneath that is a backslash. The backslash indicates the root directory of the hard disk. The root directory is where your hard disk starts looking for information each time you start the computer, provided you do not place a floppy disk in drive A to start the computer. Directly beneath the backslash is the current directory, 4. This is due to how this hard disk is set up, not because 4 is the current directory.

The parent of the \4 directory is the root directory. Directory 4 is

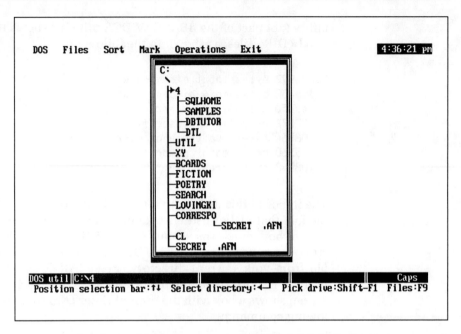

```
    DOS   Files   Sort   Mark   Operations   Exit                    4:36:21 pm

                        C:
                        \
                        ▶4
                              ┌─SQLHOME
                              ├─SAMPLES
                              ├─DBTUTOR
                              └─DTL
                        ┤UTIL
                        ┤XY
                        ┤BCARDS
                        ┤FICTION
                        ┤POETRY
                        ┤SEARCH
                        ┤LOVINGKI
                        ┤CORRESPO
                                    └─SECRET   .AFN
                        ┤CL
                        └─SECRET   .AFN

DOS util C:\4                                                          Caps
    Position selection bar:↑↓  Select directory:◀┘  Pick drive:Shift-F1  Files:F9
```

Figure 10-4 The tree structure of the hard disk in figure 10-3.

linked to the root directory by a vertical line. Several other directories (4, UTIL, XY, BCARDS, FICTION, POETRY, SEARCH, LOVINKI, COR-RESPO, CL, and SECRET.AFN) are listed underneath directory 4, all of which are attached to the same vertical line that directory 4 is attached to. This vertical line links all first-level directories to the root directory. The root directory is the parent to each of these directories, as well.

Four directories (SQLHOME, SAMPLES, DBTUTOR, and DTL) are attached to a vertical line that leads to directory 4. These directories comprise a second-level directory listing and are subdirectories of 4, making 4 their parent. Similarly, you can say that the first-level directory listings are subdirectories of the root directory. DOS uses the 〈parent〉information much as Theseus used a ball of string to find his way out of Minos's labyrinth after he slew the Minotaur.

Highlight the 〈parent〉 listing, press [Enter], and the DOS utilities send you to the root directory. Highlight any of 4's subdirectories, press [Enter], and the DOS utilities move to the selected directory. Guess what you will find there. A similar listing, complete with the 〈parent〉 directory entry. Highlight 〈parent〉in a subdirectory, press [Enter], and you are back at the dBASE IV directory.

You can get back to the type of listing in figure 10-3 by pressing [F9]. Look at figures 10-3 and 10-4 and you will notice that what figure 10-4 shows as directory 4's subdirectories are shown as 〈DIR〉files in figure 10-3.

The size of each file is shown to the right of the file. The 〈parent〉 directory and subdirectories don't show a size. Don't be fooled into thinking a 〈DIR〉 listing does not take up any space on a disk. The DOS CHKDSK utility (not part of the dBASE IV DOS utilities) shows the truth of the un-sized ⟨DIR⟩ files, as shown in the following:

```
21204992 bytes total disk space
  358400 bytes in 4 hidden files
   45056 bytes in 16 directories
11292672 bytes in 716 user files
 9508864 bytes available on disk
  655360 bytes total memory
  108048 bytes free
```

The italics in this listing are mine and are there to draw your attention to the fact that ⟨DIR⟩ listings take up space on a hard disk. You can get an idea of how much space your ⟨DIR⟩ listings use with the following key-strokes, provided the DOS CHKDSK.COM or CHKDSK.EXE file is accessi-ble from your current directory. Press [Alt-D] P. This opens the DOS utilities *Perform DOS command* option (figure 10-5). The middle of the screen shows a box with the prompt *Enter DOS command.* Type in the fol-lowing command:

```
CHKDSK /F [Enter]
```

The /F is a useful part of the CHKDSK utility; it tells CHKDSK to write

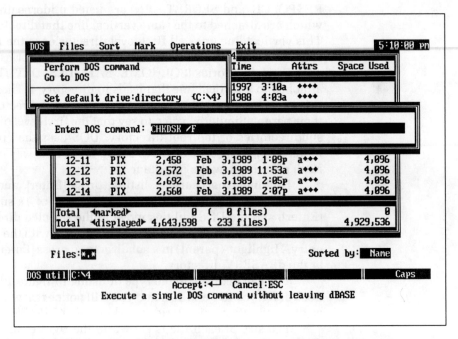

Figure 10-5 The DOS utilities Perform DOS command option lets you enter any DOS-level command without exiting the dBASE IV system.

as files any parts of the disk with lost data parts. Most often, this lost data consists of files left open or called when they should not have been, such as when the power suddenly goes out or when more than one application tries to call and open a file at a given time. DOS gets nervous in situations like this and basically throws the file on the floor, saying, "I can't handle this. I'm sorry."

It is up to you to clean up the mess, and CHKDSK /F is one way to do it. CHKDSK prompts you if it finds any irregularities and asks if it should write the lost data as files. Press Y for yes if this happens. If nothing else, you can delete the files CHKDSK writes—all of which have file names like FILE????.CHK (the ???? can be any number from 0000 to 9999)—and free up disk space for real work. Usually you can use an editor to pick through these files and recover otherwise hopelessly lost information. Nice.

Back to the directory listing in figure 10-3. Do you see the 02542410.$ED file directly beneath the ⟨DIR⟩ files? There is a good chance you have one or more of these *.$?? files on your hard disk, especially if you have been using dBASE IV right along with this book. These are dBASE IV's temporary files. Sometimes dBASE IV erases these files from the disk when you leave dBASE IV for another application. More often than not dBASE IV forgets to erase these files. You might also see files that look like F?????AA.MLF, *.W44, and other oddities. These are also dBASE IV temporary work files. Feel free to remove these files from your disk *after you have exited dBASE IV completely.* Do not erase any of dBASE IV's temporary files if you have made a temporary exit to DOS or with the DOS utilities system. Your computer will hang or worse because dBASE IV uses many of these temporary files to keep track of what it is doing, where it has been, and where it is going, especially when you make a temporary exit to DOS or another application.

To the right of the sizes are the dates and times of the last update to the listed files. Readers paying close attention to figure 10-3 will see that I'm capable of pantemporal work. ("Who can do that?" "Yes, he can." Free pizza for any readers who know what I'd be driving if I was the object of the preceding quotes!) The last update for many files is the date and time these files were created at the factory.

Attrs is to the right of Date & Time, and it means attributes, as in file attributes. There are four file attributes: *archive, hidden, read only,* and *system.* An archived file is one that shows up in the directory, can be read, can be written to, and can be backed up in a special way. All of these four file types can be backed up. An archive file is special because it has an archive flag that tells backup software (such as BACKIT, BACKUP, DS BACKUP, and FASTBACK) that the file has been changed since it was last backed up. This is useful because, with backup software, you have the option of backing up only files that have been changed since the last backup. How does the software know which files have been changed? It checks the archive bit. A hidden file is one that does not show up in a standard DIR listing. Read only files are just that. You can read them but you can't write to them. System files are special files that DOS uses to run the computer.

The rightmost column of figure 10-3 is Space Used. Pay attention, class, and you will see that the size of the file (from the second column in the listing) and the space used by the file (from the rightmost column in the listing) differ a tad.

The numbers in the Space Used column are integer multiples of 1024. The smallest amount of space my computer will give a file is 2048 bytes. That is why the 02542410.$ED file, which is 0 bytes in size, takes up 2048 bytes of file space. Any file from 0 to 2048 bytes takes up 2048 bytes. Any file from 2049 to 4096 bytes takes up 4096 bytes. This goes on—each file is given some multiple of 2048 bytes (on my computer) in which to live, regardless of how efficiently the file makes use of the space it is given.

Copying Files Through Menus

Okay, you have learned a lot about files and something about DOS, but we came to this work surface to make a copy of the EXERCISE.DBF file. There are several ways to accomplish this. Some methods are completely menu driven, others require a little knowledge of what DOS can do. We will cover most of the possible methods in this section.

The first method of copying a file is the menu method. This method starts by marking the files we want to copy. The directory listing is partially shown in figure 10-3. Cursor through it until you see the files you want to mark. Highlight the file or files you want to copy and press [Enter] to mark them. You can tell they have been marked because the DOS utilities system places a right pointing arrow to the left of the file name.

Now, before we go any further, let's take a step back and look at what we are doing. We are copying the EXERCISE.DBF file to some other file that we can then alter to contain only the Date and Comment fields. But no file is an island, and EXERCISE.DBF has other files associated with it. I am not talking about report, screen, query, label, and similar files. I am talking about memo field and MDX files. Should you mark these files for the copy as well?

This question can best be answered when you know a little bit more about how dBASE IV tags DBT (memo field) and MDX files to their respective databases. dBASE IV knows that a given DBF file has an associated DBT file because the DBF file says, "I have a DBT file. Go find it." The DBF file says this with a flag located in the file header (DBF file headers and their flags were discussed in chapter 7). The only other information dBASE IV needs to find the DBT file is the name of the DBF file, which it already knows because you have just asked it for a specific DBF file.

dBASE IV knows about MDX files in much the same way. A flag in the file header says that a production MDX file exists. Remember, dBASE IV makes production MDX files when you first create or modify a database and ask for fields or expressions to be used as index expressions. dBASE IV knows production MDX files exist because of the flag and looks for them using the *name of the DBF file under which they were created*. This is radically different than how it finds a DBF's associated DBT file. The MDX flag located in the DBF file header knows the name of the MDX file. Change the name of the DBF, DBT, and MDX files and dBASE IV will find the DBT file but not the MDX file.

What does all this have to do with copying the file? It has to do with copying only what dBASE IV will make use of and not something it will eventually forget about. Figure 10-6 shows the EXERCISE.DBF and EXER-CISE.DBT files marked. At the bottom of the directory listing is the EXER-CISE.MDX file, which is not marked. You could mark this file for copying along with the DBF and DBT files, copy it, and then try to use the copied files. dBASE IV tells you there is no MDX file for the new database, even though you copied it. You can't directly copy a production MDX file as part of a three-file set (associated DBF, DBT, and production MDX files) because dBASE IV won't recognize the newly named MDX file as being associated to the newly named DBF file. This is also true if you are copying only a DBF and production MDX file pair.

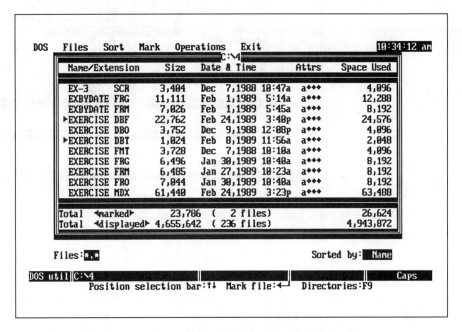

Figure 10-6 You can mark files for a variety of DOS-level operations by highlighting them and pressing [Enter].

The problem of dBASE IV not being able to find newly named MDX files occurs only when you attempt to copy a production MDX file. Also, it does not matter if the DBF file has an associated DBT file. The problem is local to the MDX file. What is important is that dBASE IV hears the DBF file asking for a production MDX file, does not believe one exists, and con-vinces the DBF file that one does not exist. You then have to go back through the database design interface and create another production MDX file, if you do indeed want one. Also remember that you can tell dBASE IV to link any valid MDX file, production or not, to a given database with the SET INDEX TO command.

So, figure 10-6 shows only the DBF and DBT files marked for copying. You perform the copy with menus. Press [Alt-O] *C M*. This is the Operations menu *Copy, Marked Files* option (figure 10-7). You have to mark the files before you attempt to copy them. If you don't, dBASE IV tells you that things won't work as you hoped: *There are no marked files in the current directory. Press any key...*

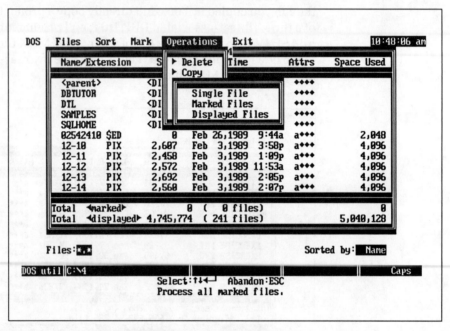

Figure 10-7 The DOS utilities system's Operations menu lets you perform DOS-level operations with menu options.

Now you have to tell dBASE IV the file name you want to copy the marked files to. Be careful. Remember, you are using a type of wildcard copy here. An equivalent DOS-level command is

```
COPY EXERCISE.DB? EXNEW.*
```

This tells DOS to copy the EXERCISE.DBF file to EXNEW.DBF and the EXERCISE.DBT file to EXNEW.DBT. Note that it would also copy EXERCISE.DBO to EXNEW.DBO. The DOS utilities system won't do that, however, unless you mark EXERCISE.DBO for copying.

You tell dBASE IV the new file name on the screen shown in figure 10-8. You can tell the DOS utilities system to copy the marked files to another directory by changing the Drive:Directory information. Because we want to copy the files to the current directory, press [Enter] to get to the Filename area and type in the new file names. Remember this command's wildcard structure and type in the target file's name as shown in figure 10-8. You tell dBASE IV to copy the marked files with [Ctrl-Enter]. dBASE IV will prompt you for confirmation if you are about to write over existing files.

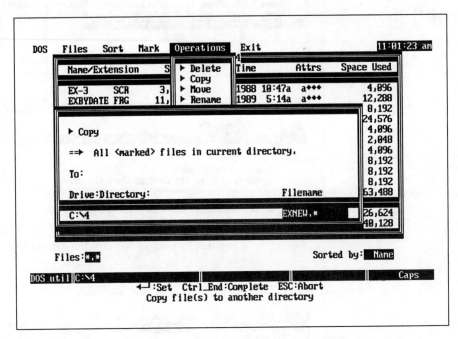

Figure 10-8 *The DOS utilities Operations* Copy, Marked Files *screen.*

You can now exit from the DOS utilities system by pressing [Alt-E]. This gets you back to the Assist system. From there you can either exit to the dBASE prompt to USE the newly copied database or you can add it to the current Catalog with the [Alt-C] A command, as shown in figure 10-9. Select the actual file by highlighting it and pressing [Enter].

Okay, we have covered copying the database through the menu system. What are the other methods? One was demonstrated when we talked about the DOS CHKDSK command in this chapter. The other method is also based on the DOS utilities DOS menu. From the DOS utilities system, press [Alt-D] to open the DOS menu. The two options that can help us are *Perform DOS command* and *Go to DOS.*

The *Perform DOS command* method works identically to the CHKDSK example given previously, except the command you place on the prompt line is the COPY command. See figure 10-10. Remember that this command copies any files that match the pattern EXERCISE.DB?, and this includes the EXERCISE.DBO file. Because this is a DOS-level command, you won't be prompted for confirmation if you are about to write over existing files.

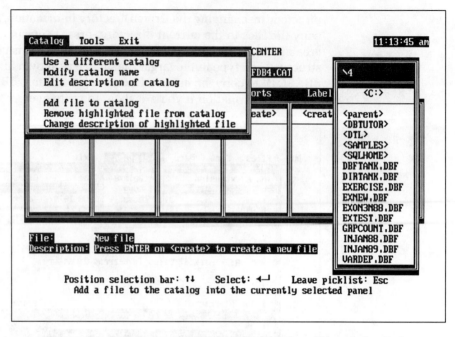

Figure 10-9 *You can use the newly copied database through the Assist system by first adding it to the current Catalog.*

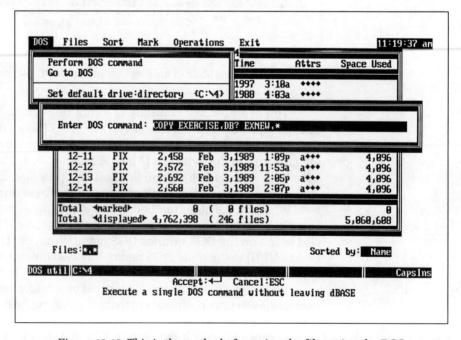

Figure 10-10 *This is the method of copying the files using the DOS menu's Perform DOS command option.*

The last method is to use the [Alt-D] *G* command. This tells dBASE IV to open the DOS menu and *Go to DOS*. dBASE IV sends you out to DOS, where you can do lots of things, such as entering the COPY command directly as shown in figure 10-11. As with the *Perform DOS command* option, you won't be prompted for confirmation if you are about to write over existing files.

```
MS-DOS(R) Version 3.30
        (C) Copyright Toshiba   Corporation 1983, 1988
        (C) Copyright Microsoft Corporation 1981, 1987


dBASE DOS Window                          Type "EXIT↵" to return to dBASE.

C:\4>COPY EXERCISE.DB? EXNEW.*
EXERCISE.DBO
EXERCISE.DBF
EXERCISE.DBT
        3 File(s) copied

dBASE DOS Window                          Type "EXIT↵" to return to dBASE.

C:\4>
```

Figure 10-11 The DOS menu's Go to DOS option drops you out to DOS, where you can use the DOS-level COPY command directly.

Copying Files at the dBASE Prompt

So much for menus. Are there other methods? There are four, and all start at the dBASE prompt. The first method is with the dBASE IV COPY FILE command. Do not confuse the COPY FILE command with the COPY command. COPY FILE is the dBASE IV version of the DOS COPY command with the exception that dBASE IV's COPY FILE command does not accept wildcards. Thus, you would have to enter the following commands to copy a DBF file and its associated DBT file, if the latter existed and you wanted it copied.

```
COPY FILE EXERCISE.DBF TO EXNEW.DBF
COPY FILE EXERCISE.DBT TO EXNEW.DBT
```

Again note that no attempt is made to copy the production MDX file. Also, with the COPY FILE command, the source file should not be open or in use or active in any other way. Try to COPY an open FILE and you will only get headaches. Careful readers should also note that I have stopped saying database and started saying file. Yes, the COPY FILE command works on any DOS file, not just databases.

Option two is with the dBASE IV COPY command. This is the better method of copying a database to a new file because dBASE IV has a much better idea of what is going on and what to do. The difference between COPY and COPY FILE is that when you use COPY the file must be currently active. The command sequence would be

```
USE EXERCISE
COPY TO EXNEW
```

The big news is that the COPY command knows enough to COPY the DBT file when it copies the DBF file. You don't have to use a separate command to make sure the DBF file's DBT file goes along with it. However, dBASE IV still won't automatically copy the production MDX file.

The next method is the dBASE prompt version of the DOS menu *Perform DOS command* option. Type the following at the dBASE prompt:

```
! COPY EXERCISE.DB? EXNEW.*
```

The exclamation mark tells dBASE IV that the rest of the line should be sent directly to DOS. This technique can be used to get anything from DOS. The only problem might be dBASE IV hogging memory. dBASE IV's kernel—the minimum amount of itself dBASE IV needs to operate—is 457K, and the extended/expanded memory driver does not work as this book is being written. This means dBASE IV will give up only 183K of memory on a 640K machine, and only if there are no files open in the dBASE IV system. A 512K computer would only get 55K of memory back. How many applications or DOS-level commands do you know that can work in 55K? Some applications can run in 183K, but not too many that I know of.

The last option is to completely exit to DOS by typing

```
RUN COMMAND
```

This is the dBASE prompt equivalent of the DOS menu *Go to DOS* option.

Modifying the Databases

Hey, great, we have finally copied that database. The second database will be the Comment field file, so let's call that database EXCOMMENT.

Nothing we have done seems to have gotten over the MDX file problem, however. Don't worry. We will modify the query files to take care of this problem.

Now we must modify the two newly created databases. Start with the Exercise file at the database design screen, shown in figure 10-12.

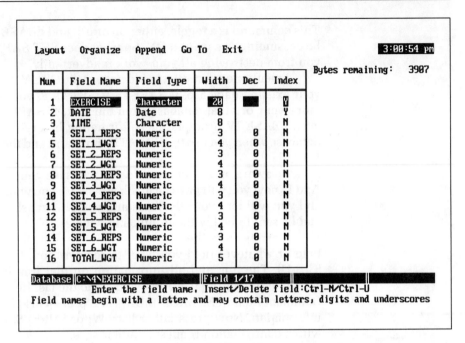

Figure 10-12 *The database design work surface.*

There are lots of ways to get to the database design surface. You can go through the Assist menu system or you can use the MODIFY STRUCTURE command from the dBASE prompt. What you cannot do is use the CREATE command at the dBASE prompt. Why not? Because there is a very good chance you will destroy the existing database. Why would that happen?

dBASE IV comes with a file called CONFIG.DB. This file tells dBASE IV what kind of computer it is working with, what kind of monitor you have, what kind of printer you have, how that printer is attached to your computer, whether or not you are working on a network, whether or not you have extended or expanded memory in your computer—lots of information about how you (or whoever set up dBASE IV for you) want dBASE to behave when you start your database management system work. One of the things that might be in your CONFIG.DB file is

```
SAFETY = OFF
```

Whoever put this command in the CONFIG.DB file is terribly sure of himself or herself, but probably does not know a thing about you or your work habits. This command is the CONFIG.DB version of the dBASE IV command

```
SET SAFETY OFF
```

This command is a toggle, either on or off, and dBASE IV comes out of the box assuming you want it ON. So what does SET SAFETY do? It prevents you from destroying all your work inadvertently.

I mentioned that you should not use the CREATE command to modify your existing database. If SAFETY is SET OFF, you will permanently remove your original database from the disk. If SAFETY is SET ON, however, dBASE IV prompts for confirmation before destroying an existing database when you use the CREATE command and the name of an existing DBF file.

Be aware of this danger and you will save yourself lots of headaches. And I know you will have headaches because you won't back up your work and you will lose your database and you will gnash your teeth and curse and be sent to bed without milk and cookies.

Starting from the database design work surface, cursor to the Time field or whatever field you want to remove from the database and press [Ctrl-U]. The line and all information on that line is removed from the screen. Press [PgDn] [Up-Arrow] to get to the last field in the database (the Comment field in EXERCISE.DBF) and press [Ctrl-U] to remove this line's information. Now press either [Ctrl-W] or [Alt-E] S. dBASE IV responds with a confirmation request in either case.

Now make the EXCOMMENT.DBF file active and MODIFY its STRUCTURE. This time we only want to keep the Date and Comment fields. Use the [Ctrl-U] keystroke combination to remove all but those two fields from the EXCOMMENT database, then press [Alt-E] S Y to save this new structure to disk.

These two databases now have the same number of records. They also share one field in common, Date. A problem with this arrangement may not be obvious. We don't need a separate record for each exercise anymore. Now we only want a separate record for each day we exercised. The purpose of this operation was to get a single Comment field for each day of exercising, thereby simplifying our database needs, remember?

So how do we get all the Comment field entries into a single Comment field entry? We do it with a program, of course.

Listing 10-1

```
00001 : ** A TINY PROGRAM TO TAKE ALL COMMENT FIELDS FOR A;
                GIVEN DATE AND
00002 : * COMBINE THEM INTO A SINGLE COMMENT FIELD
00003 : *
00004 : SCAN
00005 :    THISDATE = DATE
00006 :    FIRSTREC = .T.
00007 : *
00008 :    DO WHILE DATE = THISDATE
00009 : *
00010 :        IF FIRSTREC
00011 :            COPY MEMO COMMENT TO TANK
00012 :            FIRSTREC = .F.
```

```
00013 :          ELSE
00014 :              *REPLACE COMMENT WITH STUFF(COMMENT, 0,;
                         0, CHR(13) + CHR(10) + CHR(9))
00015 :              COPY MEMO COMMENT TO TANK ADDITIVE
00016 :          ENDIF
00017 : *
00018 :          DELETE
00019 :          SKIP
00020 :     ENDDO
00021 : *
00022 :     SKIP -1
00023 :     RECALL
00024 :     APPEND MEMO COMMENT FROM TANK OVERWRITE
00025 :     SKIP
00026 : ENDSCAN
00027 : *
00028 : PACK
00029 : *
00030 : ** EOP
```

This program assumes that the EXCOMMENT.DBF file is open and currently active. We start SCANning the database on line 4. Remember that SCAN...ENDSCAN starts at the first record of the database and goes until the end, unless you tell it otherwise. We want to combine records so that the Date entries are unique, with all Comment field entries for a given date collected in a single Comment field. This process is started by creating a variable, THISDATE, which keeps track of all unique dates while SCANning the database. FIRSTREC (line 6) is a logical variable that tells the COPY MEMO command whether to create the TANK.TXT file and add data to the new file (line 11) or to simply add data to the existing file (line 15). Because the only time we want to create a new TANK.TXT file is when we start reading records for a new date, we should turn FIRSTREC off (line 12) to make sure we don't repeatedly create a TANK.TXT file for each record, even when date entries are repeated.

DELETE the current record (line 18) and SKIP to the next record (line 19), then go back through the DO WHILE...ENDDO loop to check for records with the same date. What if we run out of records with the same date? SKIP -1 to go back to the last record with a similar date (line 22), RECALL it (line 23) because it was DELETEd in the DO WHILE...ENDDO loop, and APPEND the MEMO field COMMENT FROM the TANK.TXT file and OVERWRITE any information currently in that memo field (line 24).

Now SKIP to the next record (line 25) and go back to SCAN...ENDSCAN again. This continues until we reach the end of the file, at which point dBASE IV leaves the SCAN...ENDSCAN loop. The database is now comprised of lots of deleted records and some recalled records that contain all the memo field information. We need to PACK the database to get rid of the deleted records (line 28).

Why is line 14 in there if it is never used? (The asterisk in front of the line prevents dBASE IV from processing it.) The dBASE IV documentation is confusing regarding the STUFF( ) function's ability to work with a memo field. It alternately says it can and can't. If later versions of dBASE IV have a STUFF( ) function that can work with memo fields, this command can be used to make each record's Comment field appear as a separate paragraph in the final memo field. This would normally be done by REPLACEing each non-FIRSTREC record's Comment field with a new line and tab at the top of the Comment field, followed by the Comment field's text.

As another point of interest, listing 10-1 assumes that the data was entered consecutively. If this is not the case, you would SET some INDEX expression TO either an NDX file or some MDX tag to place an order on the file.

So, you have successfully modified a database design form without sacrificing any data. We have paved the way for the eventual linking of the databases by keeping the Date field in both. Our next step is to modify the screen form originally developed in chapter 6 to handle two databases.

Modifying Screen Forms

Our original database is now two databases. Can we modify the screen form to handle input to two databases on a single screen? Of course we can, and this section shows you how to do it. You can modify the techniques shown in this section to create screen forms that allow input to any number of databases.

You can get to the screen design work surface using whatever method you choose, but some interesting things might happen depending on how you call up the screen form. For example, you can go through the Assist system, but you first have to call up a database. The two databases we are working with are EXERCISE and EXCOMMENT. Call up the chapter 6 screen form with EXCOMMENT and you will be told that several of the screen form's fields don't exist in the database (figure 10-13). The same is true if you call up the C9.SCR file with EXERCISE.DBF active, but now you are told there are only two fields missing. Our original screen form is shown in chapter 6.

There is no reason to change the layout as it appears on the screen, except for removing the Time field from the screen and possibly reshaping the line that contained the Time field. We also need to tell the design system that the Comment field can now be found in another database. Cursor to the screen form's Comment field and press [Alt-L] *U* to tell dBASE IV you want to use the Layout menu's *Use different database file or view* option (figure 10-14). Select the appropriate database, not a view or query file, by highlighting it and pressing [Enter]. dBASE IV tells you that the newly selected database is missing some necessary fields (as it did in figure 10-13). Press [Spacebar] to go through the list of missing fields. When these steps are completed, dBASE IV will link the Comment field to the EXCOMMENT database, provided you are working along with the example in this book.

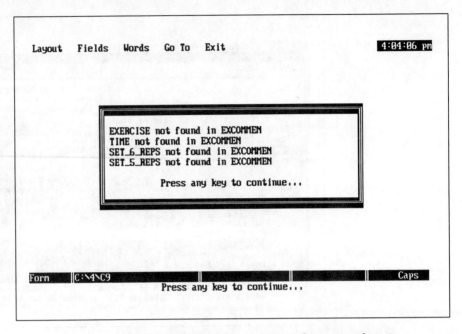

Figure 10-13 The old C9.SCR file contains information about its associated database file that is no longer valid. This figure shows the C9.SCR file called for modification when the EXCOMMENT.DBF file is active. dBASE IV tells you that several of the fields mentioned in C9.SCR are not in the database.

You can tell that dBASE IV has accepted the EXCOMMENT Comment field by looking at the bottom of the screen (figure 10-15). You will see the field name as EXCOMMEN->COMMENT. Just for amusement, cursor up to the Date field. Place the cursor directly on the Date field, not on the DATE label. Look at the bottom of the screen and you will see that the Comment field is not the only thing that was changed when you called up the EXCOMMENT.DBF file. The Date field, as listed at the bottom of the screen, is also being called from the EXCOMMENT.DBF file.

You do not need to change the Date field back to EXERCISE->DATE immediately, unless you intend to use the generated FMT file as is, with APPEND, EDIT, or other full-screen editing commands. If that is the case, keep the cursor on the Date field and press [Alt-L] U again, highlight the EXERCISE.DBF file when the file list is presented, and press [Enter]. The Date field is once again associated with the EXERCISE.DBF file.

Why do we need to make sure the screen form's Date field is associated with the EXERCISE.DBF file and not the EXCOMMENT.DBF file? There will probably be several Exercise records added for any given day, but only one EXCOMMENT field, if any, added for a given day. We can easily send the

EXERCISE->DATE

413

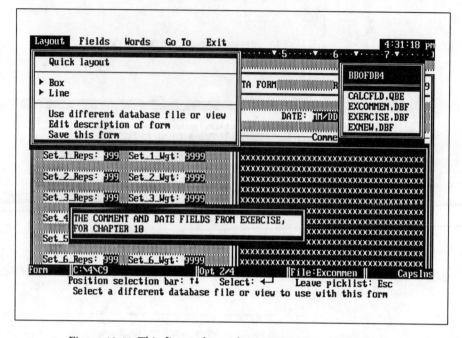

Figure 10-14 *This figure shows the C9.SCR file called with the EXERCISE.DBF file active. This EXERCISE.DBF file was modified in the last section and no longer contains the Time or Comment fields. The Time field is easily removed from the screen by backspacing over it or by using the [Del] key. You then need to tell the C9.SCR form that the Comment field is in the EXCOMMENT database, as shown in this figure.*

data to the EXCOMMENT–>DATE field when we enter the Comment field information, but that will be done when we have completed data entry for a full day's workout.

Bonus points for readers who have recognized that some programming is inevitable, even if you plan on using only FMT files. We will let the screen design system write our new form. Make sure you give the file a new name with the [Alt-L] S command. I will call the new screen form C13. The newly generated FMT file is shown in listing 10-2.

Listing 10-2

```
001 : ************************************************************
002 : *-- Name....: C13.FMT
003 : *-- Date....: 2-27-89
004 : *-- Version.: dBASE IV, Format 1.0
005 : *-- Notes...: Format files use "" as delimiters!
006 : ************************************************************
007 :
008 : *-- Format file initialization code ------------------------
009 :
010 : IF SET("TALK")="ON"
```

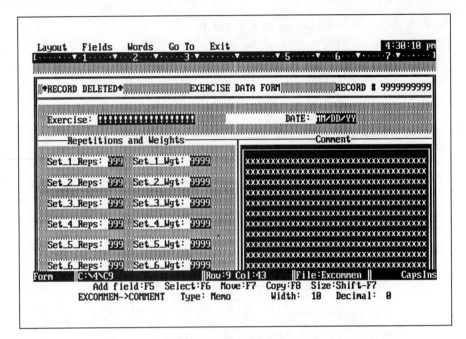

Figure 10-15 *You can tell dBASE IV has accepted the Comment field
from the EXCOMMENT.DBF file by the field name listing
at the bottom of the screen. It now lists the field
as EXCOMMEN-> COMMENT.*

```
011 :    SET TALK OFF
012 :       lc_talk="ON"
013 : ELSE
014 :       lc_talk="OFF"
015 : ENDIF
016 :
017 : *-- This form was created in COLOR mode
018 : SET DISPLAY TO COLOR
019 :
020 : lc_status=SET("STATUS")
021 : *-- SET STATUS was OFF when you went to the Forms Designer
022 : IF lc_status = "ON"
023 :    SET STATUS OFF
024 : ENDIF
025 :
026 : *-- Window for memo field comment.
027 : DEFINE WINDOW Wndow1 FROM 8,41 TO 23,78
028 :
029 : lc_carry = SET("CARRY")
030 : *-- Fields to carry forward during APPEND.
031 : SET CARRY TO date, set_1_reps, set_2_reps, set_3_reps;
032 :   set_4_reps,set_5_reps,set_6_reps ADDITIVE
033 :
034 : *-- @ SAY GETS Processing. --------------------------------
```

Listing 10-2 (cont.)

```
035 :
036 : *--  Format Page: 1
037 :
038 : @ 1,0 TO 24,79 DOUBLE
039 : @ 2,2 SAY CHR(6)
040 : @ 2,3 SAY "RECORD DELETED"
041 : @ 2,17 SAY CHR(6)
042 : @ 2,31 SAY "EXERCISE DATA FORM"
043 : @ 2,60 SAY "RECORD # 9999999999"
044 : @ 3,1 SAY "═══════════════════════════════════════
         ═════════════════════"
045 : @ 5,3 SAY "Exercise: "
046 : @ 5,13 GET exercise PICTURE "!!!!!!!!!!!!!!!!!!!!!" ;
047 :     MESSAGE "╙═══════════════════Enter the name of the exercise
         here═══════════════════╜"
048 : @ 5,38 SAY "           Date: "
049 : @ 5,57 GET date ;
050 :     VALID DATE < DATE() + 1 ;
051 :     ERROR "You can't enter data for future workouts!" ;
052 :     DEFAULT {01/01/89} ;
053 :     MESSAGE "Enter the date you exercised here."
054 : @ 7,1 SAY "══════Repetitions and ;+ Weights══════════┬
         ════════Comment══════════════════"
055 : @ 8,40 SAY "|"
056 : @ 8,41 GET comment OPEN WINDOW Wndow1 ;
057 :     MESSAGE "Enter any comments about this exercise set here"
058 : @ 9,3 SAY "Set_1_Reps: "
059 : @ 9,15 GET set_1_reps PICTURE "@Z 999" ;
060 :     DEFAULT 0 ;
061 :     MESSAGE "Enter the number of repetitions you performed for
         your first set here."
062 : @ 9,20 SAY "Set_1_Wgt: "
063 : @ 9,31 GET set_1_wgt PICTURE "@Z 9999" ;
064 :     WHEN SET_1_REPS # 0 ;
065 :     DEFAULT 0 ;
066 :     MESSAGE "Enter the amount of weight used for your first set
         here."
067 : @ 9,40 SAY "|"
068 : @ 10,40 SAY "|"
069 : @ 11,3 SAY "Set_2_Reps: "
070 : @ 11,15 GET set_2_reps PICTURE "@Z 999" ;
071 :     DEFAULT 0 ;
072 :     MESSAGE "Enter the number of repetitions you performed for
         your second set here."
073 : @ 11,20 SAY "Set_2_Wgt: "
074 : @ 11,31 GET set_2_wgt PICTURE "@Z 9999" ;
075 :     WHEN SET_2_REPS # 0 ;
076 :     DEFAULT 0 ;
```

```
077 :    MESSAGE "Enter the amount of weight you used for your second
         set here."
078 : @ 11,40 SAY "|"
079 : @ 12,40 SAY "|"
080 : @ 13,3 SAY "Set_3_Reps: "
081 : @ 13,15 GET set_3_reps PICTURE "@Z 999" ;
082 :    DEFAULT 0 ;
083 :    MESSAGE "Enter the number of repetitions you performed for
         your third set here."
084 : @ 13,20 SAY "Set_3_Wgt: "
085 : @ 13,31 GET set_3_wgt PICTURE "@Z 9999" ;
086 :    WHEN SET_3_REPS # 0 ;
087 :    DEFAULT 0 ;
088 :    MESSAGE "Enter the amount of weight used for your third set
         here."
089 : @ 13,40 SAY "|"
090 : @ 14,40 SAY "|"
091 : @ 15,3 SAY "Set_4_Reps: "
092 : @ 15,15 GET set_4_reps PICTURE "@Z 999" ;
093 :    DEFAULT 0 ;
094 :    MESSAGE "Enter the number of repetitions you performed for
         your fourth set here."
095 : @ 15,20 SAY "Set_4_Wgt: "
096 : @ 15,31 GET set_4_wgt PICTURE "@Z 9999" ;
097 :    WHEN SET_4_REPS # 0 ;
098 :    DEFAULT 0 ;
099 :    MESSAGE "Enter the amount of weight you used for your fourth
         set here."
100 : @ 15,40 SAY "|"
101 : @ 16,40 SAY "|"
102 : @ 17,3 SAY "Set_5_Reps: "
103 : @ 17,15 GET set_5_reps PICTURE "@Z 999" ;
104 :    DEFAULT 0 ;
105 :    MESSAGE "Enter the number of repetitions you performed for
         your fifth set here."
106 : @ 17,20 SAY "Set_5_Wgt: "
107 : @ 17,31 GET set_5_wgt PICTURE "@Z 9999" ;
108 :    WHEN SET_5_REPS # 0 ;
109 :    DEFAULT 0 ;
110 :    MESSAGE "Enter the amount of weight you used for your fifth
         set here."
111 : @ 17,40 SAY "|"
112 : @ 18,40 SAY "|"
113 : @ 19,3 SAY "Set_6_Reps: "
114 : @ 19,15 GET set_6_reps PICTURE "@Z 999" ;
115 :    DEFAULT 0 ;
116 :    MESSAGE "Enter the number of repetitions you performed for
         your sixth set here."
117 : @ 19,20 SAY "Set_6_Wgt: "
118 : @ 19,31 GET set_6_wgt PICTURE "@Z 9999" ;
119 :    WHEN SET_6_REPS # 0 ;
```

Listing 10-2 (cont.)

```
120 :     DEFAULT 0 ;
121 :     MESSAGE "Enter the amount of weight used for your first set
          here."
122 : a 19,40 SAY "|"
123 : a 20,40 SAY "|"
124 : a 21,10 SAY "Total_Wgt: "
125 : a 21,21 SAY total_wgt PICTURE "aZ 99999"
126 : a 21,40 SAY "|"
127 : a 22,40 SAY "|"
128 : a 23,40 SAY "|"
129 : a 24,40 SAY "±"
130 :
131 : *-- Format file exit code ----------------------------------
132 :
133 : *-- SET STATUS was OFF when you went to the Forms Designer
134 : IF lc_status = "ON"   && Entered form with status on
135 :     SET STATUS ON      && Turn STATUS "ON" on the way out
136 : ENDIF
137 :
138 : IF lc_carry = "OFF"
139 :    SET CARRY OFF
140 : ENDIF
141 :
142 : RELEASE WINDOWS Wndow1
143 :
144 : IF lc_talk="ON"
145 :     SET TALK ON
146 : ENDIF
147 :
148 : RELEASE lc_carry,lc_talk,lc_fields,lc_status
149 : *-- EOP: C13.FMT
```

Careful readers will see that listing 10-2 is not radically different from the listing in chapter 6. You could perhaps more easily have used the C9.FMT file, deleting the line that referenced the Time field and altering the line that referenced the Comment field so that dBASE IV knows it should look in the EXCOMMENT.DBF file to find it. This last item is one that needs to be done to listing 10-2, as well.

What needs to be changed, then, is the code that generates the screen form. If you are going to use listing 10-2 with full-screen editing commands, you will have to use the following code.

Listing 10-3

```
01 : ** C13-1.PRG, A SHORT FILE TO DEMONSTRATE THE USE OF
02 : * FMT FILES WHEN WORKING WITH NON-CONTIGUOUS DBF FILES
03 : *
04 : GOON = .T.
05 : DEFINE WINDOW Wndow1 FROM 8,41 TO 23,78
```

```
06 : SELECT 2
07 : USE EXCOMMENT
08 : SELECT 1
09 : USE EXERCISE
10 : *
11 : DO WHILE GOON
12 :      SET FORMAT TO EXERONLY
13 :      APPEND
14 :      CLOSE FORMAT
15 :      DO EXERSAY
16 :      DO EXERGET
17 :      CLEAR GETS
18 :      a 0,0 SAY [DO YOU WANT TO ENTER A COMMENT FOR THIS EXERCISE
     SET (Y/N)? -> ] GET GOON
19 :      READ
20 :      a 0,0 SAY SPACE(80)
21 : *
22 :      IF GOON
23 :          SELECT 2
24 :          APPEND BLANK
25 :          REPLACE DATE WITH A->DATE
26 :          a 8,41 GET comment OPEN WINDOW Wndow1 ;
27 :              MESSAGE "Enter any comments about this exercise
     or set here"
28 :          READ
29 :          SELECT 1
30 :      ENDIF
31 : *
32 :      a 0,0 SAY;
         [DO YOU WANT TO ENTER MORE DATA (Y/N)? -> ] GET GOON
33 :      READ
34 :      a 0,0 SAY SPACE(80)
35 : *
36 : ENDDO
37 : *
38 : ** EOP
```

Listing 10-3 is designed for adding information to two linked databases that do not have one-for-one record entry. In other words, there will be one record added to EXCOMMENT.DBF for each set of daily records added to the EXERCISE database.

We start by declaring a logical variable, GOON, in line 4. The variable should not be read as a nightmarish creature, but as GO ON. Line 5 is lifted directly from listing 10-2 (line 27) to create the window box needed for the EXCOMMENT.DBF Comment field. Lines 6 through 9 open the two databases in work areas 2 and 1.

Lines 11 through 36 are the principal data entry loop. Data is added to the databases while GOON is TRUE, which is why we initialize the variable to True in line 4. The first database we will add data to is EXERCISE, and we will use the SET FORMAT TO and APPEND commands to do it. (In terms of programming, this is a waste of time. A cleaner method will be shown momentarily.) Remember that we do not want to open an area for a Comment field with this SET FORMAT TO command because there is no longer a Comment field in EXERCISE.DBF. We take listing 10-2 and remove lines 26, 27, 56, and 57. These are the lines directly addressing the Comment field. Lines 56 and 57 in listing 10-2 are moved to lines 26 and 27 of listing 10-3.

What is left of listing 10-2 becomes EXERONLY.FMT and is SET in line 12. Line 13 tells dBASE IV to APPEND records and allow data entry to EXERCISE. Remember that the APPEND command keeps adding records to the active database until you press [Enter] when the cursor is in the first field in a totally blank record. This means dBASE IV stays at line 13 of listing 10-3 until you exit APPEND's full-screen editing mode. Line 14 CLOSEs the FORMAT file. This command, which is equivalent to SET FORMAT TO with no file name, essentially removes the FMT file from memory. We do this because of the READ command in line 19. READ is another full-screen editing command. Not removing the FMT file from memory would cause dBASE IV to READ from the first field in the FMT file, instead of from the question on line 18.

This brings us to lines 15 and 16, and why using an FMT file for this type of data entry—two noncontiguous databases—is not the best method. We broke C9.FMT into its GET and SAY commands and stored them in PROCEDURES EXERGET and EXERSAY, respectively. These types of procedures are called again in listing 10-3 to paint the screen.

Paint the screen? Yes, as in keeping the image of EXERONLY.FMT on the screen even if we do not want it active. Exiting the full-screen editing APPEND command in line 13 clears the screen of the EXERONLY.FMT image. This means the user is left with a blank screen and only the query in line 18 when the READ command in line 19 is executed. Not very pretty, and possibly confusing. Thus, we paint the screen with EXERSAY and EXERGET information, then CLEAR the GETS in line 17 to make sure the READ in line 19 does not perform the same error it would have if we did not CLOSE the FORMAT file in line 14.

This brings us to the query in line 18, where listing 10-3 finds out if you want to add a record to EXCOMMENT.DBF. Your answer is stored in GOON. Line 20 does the simple housekeeping of clearing the query in line 18 from the screen.

Lines 22 through 30 act upon your answer to the query in line 18. If you wanted to add a comment, make the EXCOMMENT.DBF file active in line 23 and APPEND a BLANK record in line 24. Note that we do not simply APPEND to EXCOMMENT. Because we do not want full-screen editing here (we want to retain all control), we create a BLANK record and then work with it.

The APPEND command in line 13 leaves EXERCISE.DBF's record pointer on the last entered record. This last entered record contains a valid Date entry, and line 25 REPLACES EXCOMMENT's empty Date field with EXERCISE's Date entry. Then lines 26 through 28 GET the data you want to add to the Comment field. Line 29 returns us to work area 1.

Lines 32 through 34 serve the same basic purpose as lines 18 through 20. This time we are not finding out if we want to add a comment; we are finding out if we want to add more data to EXERCISE.

And that's it. Not bad, actually. A nice, tidy, little bit of code that lets us add data to two noncontiguous databases using one simple system. Remember that we modified the C9.FMT file to handle the Total_Wgt field and some other minor details. Those changes were placed in the EX-PROC.PRG file and should be echoed in EXERONLY.FMT and listing 10-2. The only other item I could bring to your attention is what might happen if you do not have enough memory in your computer to handle everything that is being requested. The problem arises when you try to edit the Comment field. dBASE IV displays *Insufficient memory*. This is due to the number of files opened by listing 10-3 and dBASE IV's severe memory requirement restrictions.

This is a serious problem that won't cause you to lose data, but will inhibit your ability to add data to EXCOMMENT.DBF. Suggested solutions are to remove any TSRs (such as SideKick) that you might have loaded. When it comes to memory, dBASE IV is an unyielding beast.

I mentioned solutions to the problems brought on by the FMT file in listing 10-3. These solutions are identical to those used in chapter 6. Listing 10-2 is broken into its component parts and gathered into a PROCEDURE file. Listing 10-3 file can be rewritten as follows:

Listing 10-4

```
01 : ** C13-2.PRG, A SHORT FILE TO DEMONSTRATE AN ALTERNATIVE TO
02 : *    FMT FILES WHEN WORKING WITH NONCONTIGUOUS DBF FILES
03 : *
04 : GOON = .T.
05 : DEFINE WINDOW Wndow1 FROM 8,41 TO 23,78
06 : SELECT 2
07 : USE EXCOMMENT
08 : SELECT 1
09 : USE EXERCISE
10 : COPY STRUCTURE TO TANK
11 : USE TANK
12 : SET PROCEDURE TO EXPROC
13 : DO EXERSAY
14 : *
15 : DO WHILE GOON
16 : *
17 :     DO WHILE .T.
18 :         APPEND BLANK
19 :         DO EXERGET
20 :         READ
21 : *
22 :         IF LEN(TRIM(EXERCISE)) = 0
23 :             DELETE
24 :         ENDIF
```

Listing 10-4 (cont.)

```
25 : *
26 :     ENDDO
27 : *
28 :     SKIP -1
29 :     DO EXERGET
30 :     CLEAR GETS
31 :     @ 0,0 SAY;
    [DO YOU WANT TO ENTER A COMMENT FOR THIS EXERCISE SET (Y/N)?
    -> ] GET GOON
32 :     READ
33 :     @ 0,0 SAY SPACE(80)
34 : *
35 :     IF GOON
36 :         SELECT 2
37 :         APPEND BLANK
38 :         REPLACE DATE WITH A->DATE
39 :         @ 8,41 GET comment OPEN WINDOW Wndow1 ;
40 :             MESSAGE "Enter any comments about this exercise
    or set here"
41 :         READ
42 :         SELECT 1
43 :     ENDIF
44 : *
45 :     @ 0,0 SAY;
    [DO YOU WANT TO ENTER MORE DATA (Y/N)? -> ] GET GOON
46 :     READ
47 :     @ 0,0 SAY SPACE(80)
48 : *
49 : ENDDO
50 : *
51 : USE EXERCISE
52 : APPEND FROM TANK
53 : ERASE TANK.DBF
54 : *
55 : ** EOP
```

This code is similar to listing 10-3. What is different? We COPY the STRUCTURE of EXERCISE.DBF to a temporary TANK file in line 10, then USE the TANK file (line 11) and SET the PROCEDURE file to EXPROC in line 12. Note that this EXPROC file does not reference Time or Comment fields, as does EXPROC.PRG in chapter 6.

We DO the @ SAY expressions from listing 10-2 on line 13. Listing 10-4 then goes into the DO WHILE...ENDDO loop presented in listing 10-3. Lines 17 to 26 present an interesting addition, however. We APPEND a BLANK record to TANK, then DO the @ GET expressions from listing 10-2 and READ any data from lines 18 through 20. Lines 22 through 24 insure that our EXERCISE.DBF file does not get cluttered with BLANK records when the data from TANK.DBF is APPENDED to EXERCISE.DBF in line 52. From lines 28 through the end, listing 10-4 follows the logic of listing 10-3.

Modifying Report Forms to Handle More Than One Database

The reports designed previously are still useful, but now we want to modify one of them, DATEBYEX.FRM, to handle information in the EXCOMMENT.DBF Comment field. Before we do that, we have to make sure that information entered into EXERCISE and EXCOMMENT tracks congruently. Although there is not a one-to-one relationship between the records in EXERCISE and EXCOMMENT, there is a date-by-date relationship. Therefore, we must link the two databases by their Date fields.

We link two databases by fields with indices and the SET RELATION TO command. We know that EXERCISE.DBF is indexed on the Date field; all we need to do is create a similar index for the EXCOMMENT.DBF file. This is done with the following command:

```
INDEX ON DATE TAG DATE OF EXCOMMENT
```

You should realize that this won't create a production MDX file. It will produce an MDX file, but one that you will constantly need to specify in the USE command, as in

```
USE EXCOMMENT ORDER DATE
```

dBASE IV knows to look for the EXCOMMENT.MDX file; all it needs to be told is to place the Date index expression in action. The alternative to this is going to the database design system with EXCOMMENT.DBF active and using the [Alt-O] *C* command to create a new index expression. You still need to call the EXCOMMENT.MDX file in the USE command, as shown.

The actual relation between the two databases is done with the following commands:

```
SELECT 2
USE EXCOMMENT ORDER DATE
SELECT 1
USE EXERCISE ORDER DATE
SET RELATIONSHIP TO DATE INTO B
```

Now EXCOMMENT, although it has significantly fewer records than EXERCISE, tracks the latter database as the report form is run.

The next step is to modify the report form. Get to the report form design system and make the DATEBYEX form active. A slight change has to be made to accommodate the EXCOMMENT.DBF Comment field. Place the cursor in the Group 1 Summary Band, a few lines underneath the *Total number of exercises performed on MM/DD/YY –> 99* line and on the left margin. Type *Comments:* and a space, then press [Alt-L] *U* to call up a listing of the other databases on the disk. You have to do this because EXER-CISE.DBF does not contain the Comment field and you have to make the EXCOMMENT.DBF file active. dBASE IV tells you that it does not have all the fields necessary for the report form.

Simply press [Spacebar] to pass over these messages. Now press [Alt-F] A to place a title on the report and open the Fields menu. Highlight *Comment* and press [Enter]. You are presented with the Fields Template and Picture function menu. Note that dBASE IV has entered the V Picture function for you. This is the *Vertical stretch* function (figure 10-16), and it means dBASE IV will add lines as needed to the finished report to fit the Comment field in the form. Don't forget to put a few blank lines under the Comment field entry. This will insure that the report leaves some space between the Group 1 Summary Band and the Report Summary Band (figure 10-17).

The report form design system generates the FRM, FRG, and FRO files from this. Unfortunately, you have to edit the FRG file before you can use this report because the FRG file still does not know where the Comment field is. How come? Didn't we just call up the EXCOMMENT.DBF file to place Comment on the report form?

Yes, but that was inside the design system. It is ancient history. We need the SELECT...USE...SET RELATION command sequence, shown previously, to get this report form to work correctly. The last command in the sequence should be

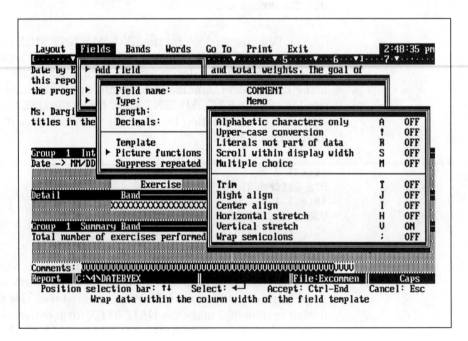

Figure 10-16 The Vertical stretch *Picture function tells dBASE IV to make room on the finished report for the Comment field, no matter how many lines of text the Comment field contains.*

REPORT FORM DATEBYEX

The result is a blow out, as shown in figure 10-18. Fortunately, dBASE IV tells you where the problem occurs (figure 10-19).

Changing line 127 from *r_foot2=COMMENT* to *r_foot2= B–>COMMENT* solves the problem. This tells dBASE IV that the Comment field is in the second work area. An example of the report output follows:

```
                                    Date by Exercise Report
                                    Carrabis, Page -   1
                                    03/03/89
```

```
This report is based on an exercise format designed by Denise
Dargie.  The style of the workout and intensity are changed over
time, according to Ms. Dargie's instructions; therefore, this
report is broken down as Date by Exercise, listing exercises and
total weights. The goal of this report format is to show the
individual's daily regimen and the progress in that regimen.

Ms. Dargie is holder of several weight lifting and body building
titles in the Northeast and Eastern United States.
```

```
Date -> 10/08/88

                        Exercise                Total_Wgt
                        BENCH PRESS                 450
                        INCLINE PRESS               350
                        DB PRESS                    150
                        WIDE GRIP CURLS             250
                        PRESS OUTS                  450
                        LEG EXTENSIONS              250
                        LEG CURLS                   300
                        LAT PULLDOWNS               550

Total number of exercises performed on 10/08/88 -> 8


Comments: First training session at FPC. Went over
          stretching and warm up. Showed proper lifting
          technique. Went over exercises to start on
          Monday.
```

```
  Layout  Fields  Bands  Words  Go To  Print  Exit          3:32:53 pm
  [········▼··1···▼··2··▼··3·▼·······▼·····5··▼···6··▼]··7·▼·······

  Group 1 Intro  Band───────────────────────────────────────────
  Date -> MM/DD/YY

                      Exercise                  Total_Wgt
  Detail          Band
                  XXXXXXXXXXXXXXXXXXX             99999

  Group 1 Summary Band───────────────────────────────────────────
  Total number of exercises performed on MM/DD/YY -> 99


  Comments: UUUUUUUUUUUUUUUUUUUUUUUUUUUUUUUUUUUUUUUUUUUUUUUUUU


  Report    Summary Band───────────────────────────────────────
  Page      Footer  Band───────────────────────────────────────


  CodeGen │C:\4\REPORT.GEN        │Lines: 30        │DATEBYEX
         Add field:F5  Select:F6  Move:F7  Copy:F8  Size:Shift-F7
                    Opening file [C:\4\DATEBYEX.FRG]
```

Figure 10-17 Make sure you place a few extra lines underneath the Comment field to leave room between the Group 1 Summary Band and the Report Summary Band.

```
                                    Carrabis, Page -   1
                                    03/03/89




  This report is based on an exercise format designed by Denise
  Dargie of Gold's Gym in Amesbury, Massachusetts. The style of the
  workout and intensity are changed over time, according to Ms.
  Dargie's instructions, the┌──────────────────────┐n down as
  Date by Exercise, listing  │ Variable not found   │. The goal
  of this report format is t │                      │ly regimen
  and the progress in that r │ r_foot2=COMMENT      │

  Ms. Dargie is holder of se │ [Cancel] Ignore Suspend│dy building
  titles in the Northeast an └──────────────────────┘




  Date -> 10/08/88

                      Exercise                  Total_Wgt
              BENCH PRESS                          450
```

Figure 10-18 The DATEBYEX.FRG file won't find EXCOMMENT's Comment field by using the commands that the report design system used when it wrote the FRG file. Fortunately, dBASE IV tells you where the problem occurs (figure 10-19).

```
Dargie of Gold's Gym in Amesbury, Massachusetts. The style of the
workout and intensity are changed over time, according to Ms.
Dargie's instructions, therefore this report is broken down as
Date by Exercise, listing exercises and total weights. The goal
of this report format is to show the individual's daily regimen
and the progress in that regimen.

Ms. Dargie is holder of several weight lifting and body building
titles in the Northeast and Eastern United States.




Date -> 10/08/88

                         Exercise                 Total_Wgt
               BENCH PRESS                            450




Variable not found
r_foot2=COMMENT
** At    line  127 in file datebyex.frg, procedure DATEBYEX
   from dot prompt
Cancel
♦
```

*Figure 10-19 dBASE IV tells you where the problem occurs in the FRG
file. This makes it easy to edit using any text editor.*

Previously in this chapter, I mentioned designing a report that
scanned for the word *PROBLEM* in the Comment field and printed information on the problem and what happened that day regarding exercises. It
might have sounded involved when you first read it, but you should be
aware that it is not an involved process. You can do it in two ways.

The first method is to use the SET FILTER TO command and a modified EXBYDATE report form. The dBASE prompt commands to get everything rolling follow:

```
SELECT 1
USE EXCOMMENT ORDER DATE
SET FILTER TO [PROBLEM] $ COMMENT
SELECT 2
USE EXERCISE ORDER DATE
SET RELATION TO DATE INTO A
REPORT FORM PROBLEMS
```

The first three commands set up the EXCOMMENT database in work area
1 and SET a FILTER on EXCOMMENT's Comment field. The second three
commands open the Exercise file in work area 2 and SET a RELATION

between the Date fields in both databases. The last command generates our report. All that is left is to show the new report form.

We start with the old EXBYDATE report form, described in chapter 8 and shown in both figures 10-20 and 10-21 and the following listing.

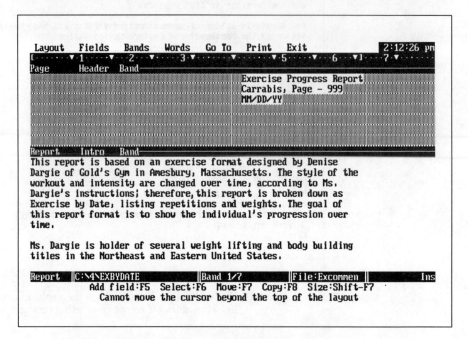

Figure 10-20 *The old EXBYDATE.FRM file as shown on the report form design surface. This is the top of the report form. The bottom is shown in figure 10-21.*

```
                                    Exercise Progress Report
                                    Carrabis, Page -    1
                                    03/04/89
```

```
This report is based on an exercise format designed by Denise
Dargie. The style of the workout and intensity are changed over
time, according to Ms. Dargie's instructions; therefore, this
report is broken down as Exercise by Date, listing repetitions
and weights. The goal of this report format is to show the
individual's progression over time.

Ms. Dargie is holder of several weight lifting and body building
titles in the Northeast and Eastern United States.
```

Exercise -> BENCH PRESS

Date	Reps/ Wgts	SETS					
		1	2	3	4	5	6
10/08/88		10	0	0	0	0	0
		45	0	0	0	0	0
Total_Wgt ->		450					
10/12/88		10	10	10	10	10	10
		45	65	85	95	65	45
Total_Wgt ->		4000					
11/03/88		10	10	7	7	7	10
		45	85	105	95	95	65
Total_Wgt ->		4015					
11/11/88		7	7	7	5	4	7
		85	95	115	135	145	85
Total_Wgt ->		3915					
11/15/88		7	7	5	5	6	7
		95	115	135	155	155	95
Total_Wgt ->		4515					
11/18/88		7	7	6	4	5	8
		95	115	135	155	155	95
Total_Wgt ->		4435					
11/22/88		7	7	7	4	6	7
		95	115	135	155	155	115
Total_Wgt ->		4770					
11/25/88		7	7	7	5	5	7
		95	135	135	155	165	135
Total_Wgt ->		5100					

12/01/88	7	7	5	4	4	7
	95	135	155	165	175	135

Total_Wgt -> 4690

12/05/88	7	7	5	4	4	7
	115	135	155	175	185	135

Total_Wgt -> 4910

12/09/88	7	7	4	4	6	7
	115	135	185	185	155	115

Total_Wgt -> 4965

12/20/88	7	7	5	4	5	7
	115	135	155	175	155	115

Total_Wgt -> 4805

12/23/88	7	7	6	4	5	7
	115	135	155	175	175	135

Total_Wgt -> 5200

12/27/88	7	7	7	7	7	7
	115	135	135	115	115	115

Total_Wgt -> 5110

12/30/88	7	7	6	4	4	6
	115	135	155	175	175	135

Total_Wgt -> 4890

01/05/89	7	7	7	4	7	6
	115	135	155	165	135	135

Total_Wgt -> 5250

The exercises are listed alphabetically and then by date. Nice and what we wanted. Not what we want now, however.

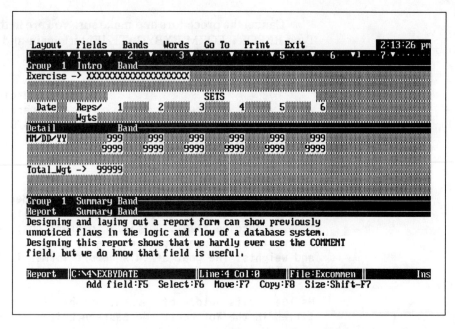

Figure 10-21 *This is the bottom of the EXBYDATE.FRM file as shown on the report form design surface. The top of the form is shown in figure 10-20.*

Before we get into what we want now, we should take a moment to see what happens when you are not careful. This is where I get to show you what happens when you forget what you are doing and why you should always send output to the screen before you commit it to a file or to disk. The preceding listing is the correct EXBYDATE output, but you should be aware of what can happen if you are not careful.

First, what happens if you have the wrong database currently active? The EXBYDATE.FRM file was written to use the old EXERCISE database. Make the currently active database EXCOMMENT in work area 1, and the first thing you will get if you enter REPORT FORM EXBYDATE [Enter] is shown in figure 10-22.

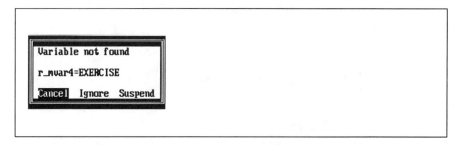

Figure 10-22 *You can't run the REPORT FORM EXBYDATE command correctly if you previously entered the seven dBASE prompt commands shown in this section. The wrong database would be active.*

Cancel the procedure and make sure you are in the correct work area. Type REPORT FORM EXBYDATE [Enter] again and you will get the following output:

```
                                       Exercise Progress Report
                                       Carrabis, Page -    1
                                       03/04/89
```

This report is based on an exercise format designed by Denise Dargie. The style of the workout and intensity are changed over time, according to Ms. Dargie's instructions; therefore, this report is broken down as Exercise by Date, listing repetitions and weights. The goal of this report format is to show the individual's progression over time.

Ms. Dargie is holder of several weight lifting and body building titles in the Northeast and Eastern United States.

Exercise -> BENCH PRESS

Date	Reps/ Wgts	1	2	3	4	5	6
				SETS			
10/08/88		10	0	0	0	0	0
		45	0	0	0	0	0

Total_Wgt ->   450

Exercise -> INCLINE PRESS

Date	Reps/ Wgts	1	2	3	4	5	6
				SETS			
10/08/88		10	10	0	0	0	0
		15	20	0	0	0	0

Total_Wgt ->   350

Exercise -> DB PRESS

Date	Reps/ Wgts	1	2	3	4	5	6
				SETS			

```
10/08/88        10      0       0       0       0       0
                15      0       0       0       0       0

Total_Wgt ->    150
```

Exercise -> WIDE GRIP CURLS

				SETS			
Date	Reps/ Wgts	1	2	3	4	5	6
10/08/88		10	0	0	0	0	0
		25	0	0	0	0	0

```
Total_Wgt ->    250
```

Exercise -> PRESS OUTS

				SETS			
Date	Reps/ Wgts	1	2	3	4	5	6
10/08/88		10	0	0	0	0	0
		45	0	0	0	0	0

```
Total_Wgt ->    450
```

Exercise -> LEG EXTENSIONS

				SETS			
Date	Reps/ Wgts	1	2	3	4	5	6
10/08/88		10	0	0	0	0	0
		25	0	0	0	0	0

```
Total_Wgt ->    250
```

Exercise -> LEG CURLS

				SETS			
Date	Reps/ Wgts	1	2	3	4	5	6
10/08/88		10	0	0	0	0	0
		30	0	0	0	0	0

```
Total_Wgt ->    300
```

Exercise -> LAT PULLDOWNS

				SETS			
Date	Reps/	1	2	3	4	5	6
	Wgts						
10/08/88		10	0	0	0	0	0
		55	0	0	0	0	0

```
Total_Wgt ->    550
```

What went wrong? We had the database ORDERED by Date, not Exercise. The moral? Send the output to the screen and check it before you print it or send it to disk and give the printout or the text file output to your peers or, even worse, your boss.

Back to correcting the report form to what we really want. We want to list only days on which there were problems. Good. We probably want to see the problem comment first, then see a listing of what went wrong. Start the process with

```
MODIFY REPORT EXBYDATE [Enter]
```

The Page Header Band should be changed from Exercise Progress Report to Exercise Problem Report. No other changes are necessary there. The Report Intro Band should be changed to the following paragraph:

```
This report is designed to find the word [PROBLEM] in the
EXCOMMENT database and list both the COMMENT and the exercises
for the day the problem occurred.
```

You can enter this directly; or you can use a text editor to write this as a file, then use the [Alt-W] W R command to copy the file into the Report Intro Band; or you can simply cursor to the band and enter the text. How do you get rid of the other text? You use the [F6] (Select) key and the cursor keys to highlight the offending words, then press [Enter] [Del] Y to remove the text from the Report Intro Band.

We now need to place our new Group Band on the report. Place the cursor directly above the Group 1 Intro Band's header line and press [Alt-B] [Alt-F] to add a group band based on a field value. You will be shown EX-COMMENT's field list. Select DATE (figure 10-23). The report form screen changes as shown in figure 10-24.

We need some labels and data fields for the new Group 1 Intro Band. The labels are for the Date and Comment fields and are entered through the [F5] (Add field) key as shown in figure 10-25. Note that figure 10-17 shows the Comment field in the vertical stretch mode described in this section. Also note that we did not give the Comment field a title because the entire purpose of this report form is to list problem days.

Move the cursor into the Group 2 Intro Band, and you will see some editing needs to be done. We no longer need the Date title in this area, so

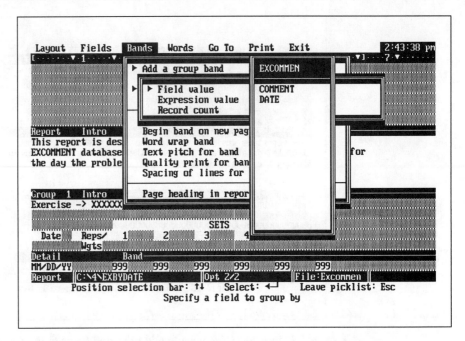

Figure 10-23 We need to create a new group band for the PROBLEMS.FRM report form file. Press [Alt-B] [Alt-F] to open the field list for EXCOMMENT.DBF, then select the DATE field.

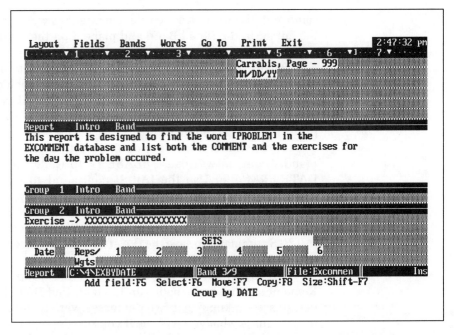

Figure 10-24 The report form design system places the new group band at the cursor.

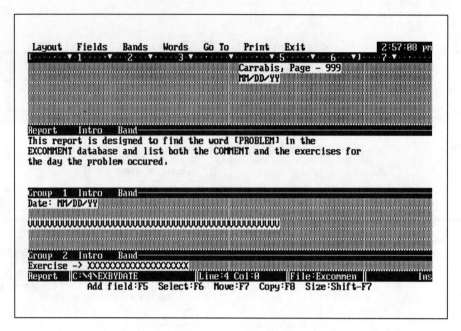

Figure 10-25 We need to add titles and fields to the new group band, as shown in this figure. We enter a title for the Date field, but not for the Comment field because the purpose of this report form is to list problem days.

remove it. If we remove the title, we might as well remove the field. Move the cursor to the Detail Band and place it on the Date field. Press [Del] to remove the field from the report.

There is no Group 2 or Group 1 Summary information, so you can close those two bands by placing the cursor on each of the band's header bars and pressing [Enter]. Likewise, we don't need the information in the Report Summary Band. Use the [F6] key to highlight all the text, then press [Enter] [Del] Y to remove it.

Now, whatever you do, don't save this file with the [Alt-E] S command. Doing so will cause dBASE IV to write over the existing EXBY-DATE.FRM file. Use the [Alt-S] command to save the file with the PROBLEM file name. You might run into memory problems, and dBASE IV won't be able to save the file using this method. Don't worry. The primary concern at this point is to give the file a new name. You can use the [Alt-E] S command to save the file after you have used the [Alt-S] command to give it a new name.

Do you think you will be able to run the report without problems? Remember what happened with the modified DATEBYEX.FRM file? The design system knew that two databases were being used, but the FRG file didn't. Guess what you will see if you run the report? You will get an error message like that shown in the previous report form.

What we need to do is get our handy word processor and change each field reference (as opposed to text or label reference) of COMMENT to A->COMMENT. The finished output follows:

```
                                    Exercise Problem Report
                                    Carrabis, Page -   1
                                    03/04/89
```

This report uses two databases, EXERCISE and EXCOMMENT, to list days in which problems occurred during the workout, along with the exercise sets which may have caused the problems.

Date: 11/03/88

PROBLEM: Had to leave, workout too long. Getting too exhausted to get stronger on 2nd part of workout. Go to 4 days, cut routine time down.

Exercise -> BENCH PRESS

			SETS			
Reps/ Wgts	1	2	3	4	5	6
	10	10	7	7	7	10
	45	85	105	95	95	65

Total_Wgt ->   4015

Exercise -> INCLINE PRESS

			SETS			
Reps/ Wgts	1	2	3	4	5	6
	10	10	10	10	7	10
	20	25	25	25	30	25

Total_Wgt ->   1410

Exercise -> PRESS

			SETS			
Reps/	1	2	3	4	5	6

```
                         Wgts
                               10        10         7         7         7        10
                               30        30        30        20        20        10

        Total_Wgt ->     1190
```

```
        Exercise -> UPRIGHT ROWS


                                              SETS
                         Reps/    1         2         3         4         5         6
                         Wgts
                               10        10        10         8        10        10
                               25        35        45        55        55        45

        Total_Wgt ->     2490


        Exercise -> PRESS OUTS


                                              SETS
                         Reps/    1         2         3         4         5         6
                         Wgts
                               10        10        10        10         7        10
                               10        20        30        30        40        20

        Total_Wgt ->     1380


        Exercise -> LEG EXTENSIONS


                                              SETS
                         Reps/    1         2         3         4         5         6
                         Wgts
                               10        10        10        10        10        10
                               30        50        70        90       100        50

        Total_Wgt ->     3900


        Exercise -> LEG PRESS


                                              SETS
                         Reps/    1         2         3         4         5         6
```

Wgts

| 10 | 10 | 8 | 10 | 10 | 10 |
| 50 | 140 | 140 | 110 | 50 | 0 |

Total_Wgt -> 4620

Exercise -> LEG CURLS

			SETS			
Reps/	1	2	3	4	5	6
Wgts						
	10	10	10	10	10	0
	20	30	40	50	20	0

Total_Wgt -> 1600

Exercise Problem Report
Carrabis, Page -   3
03/04/89

Exercise -> LAT PULLDOWNS

			SETS			
Reps/	1	2	3	4	5	6
Wgts						
	10	10	10	10	0	0
	40	70	115	70	0	0

Total_Wgt -> 2950

Date: 11/07/88

PROBLEM: Energy level could be better. He didn't
eat; other than that, workout level good.

Exercise -> LEG EXTENSIONS

			SETS			
Reps/	1	2	3	4	5	6
Wgts						
	7	7	7	7	7	7

```
                          40        70        90       110        90        70

Total_Wgt ->    3290


Exercise -> LEG PRESS

                                              SETS
                   Reps/    1         2         3         4         5         6
                   Wgts
                           15        15        15        15        15         0
                            0        50        90        70         0         0

Total_Wgt ->    3150


Exercise -> LEG CURLS

                                              SETS
                   Reps/    1         2         3         4         5         6
                   Wgts
                           12        12        12        12        15        15
                           20        30        40        40        30        30

Total_Wgt ->    2460
```

```
                                        Exercise Problem Report
                                        Carrabis, Page -    4
                                        03/04/89
```

```
Exercise -> SEATED CALVES

                                              SETS
                   Reps/    1         2         3         4         5         6
                   Wgts
                           10         7         7         7         7         7
                           25        45        35        45        25        25

Total_Wgt ->    1475


Exercise -> STANDING CALVES

                                              SETS
                   Reps/    1         2         3         4         5         6
                   Wgts
                            7         7         7         7         7         7
```

	20	70	50	50	40	40

Total_Wgt -> 1890

Exercise -> CRUNCHES

			SETS			
Reps/ Wgts	1	2	3	4	5	6
	12	12	15	20	20	20
	0	0	0	0	0	0

Total_Wgt -> 0

Exercise -> LEG LIFTS

			SETS			
Reps/ Wgts	1	2	3	4	5	6
	7	10	12	15	0	0
	0	0	0	0	0	0

Total_Wgt -> 0

Modifying Query Forms to Handle More Than One Database

The only thing we have left to do is change our query forms to handle more than one field from more than one database. This is not difficult, but pay attention. What we will do is so simple it may pass you by.

Keep the databases open and active as we did previously: go to the dBASE prompt and type in the SELECT...USE...SET RELATION command sequence we entered in the last section. Now, still at the dBASE prompt, type CREATE VIEW C13-1, CREATE QUERY C13-1, MODIFY VIEW C13-1, or MODIFY QUERY C13-1. The command form does not matter. You are presented with a screen as shown in figure 10-26.

And your work is done. The query system automatically links the two files by the Date field. It did so by reading the SET RELATION TO DATE INTO B information from memory. It also read which databases were open from memory. Further, it read that we wanted EVERY record in EXERCISE listed, but only the FIRST matching record in EXCOMMENT listed. Don't worry that the query system read EXCOMMENT's indexing information and came up with FIRST. It merely signifies that there is only a single EXCOMMENT record for several EXERCISE records. Remember that you

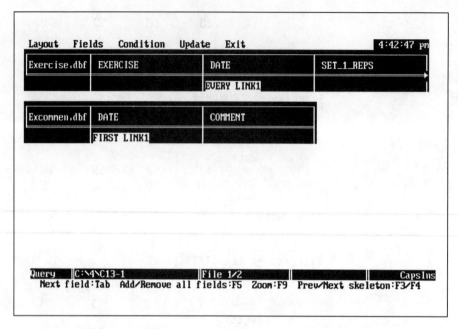

Figure 10-26 *The CREATE VIEW, MODIFY VIEW, CREATE QUERY, and MODIFY QUERY commands read the information in dBASE IV regarding which databases are in USE and any RELATIONS SET between them when designing new query files.*

must place some fields into the VIEW area before you can go to either Browse or Edit mode.

Now, could we create this type of query working strictly from the query system's menus? Yes, we could, but the preceding method certainly is easier. You should also note that you could not easily design this type of query from the Assist system because it only allows one active database at a time. You can bypass this problem by opening up other databases through the query system menus.

This leads us to designing the query from the menus. Make sure you CLOSE ALL files at the dBASE prompt if you plan on following along with the next section.

Starting with a blank query design screen, press [Alt-L] A to add a file to the query. The first file you want is EXERCISE.DBF, so highlight it and press [Enter]. Now you must add the EXCOMMENT.DBF file to the query, so press [Alt-L] A again. This time highlight EXCOMMENT.DBF and press [Enter]. We want to create a link between the two databases using each file's Date field. The cursor should be under the EXCOMMENT.DBF file name. Tab to the EXCOMMENT Date field and type in *FIRST LINK1*. Now press [F4], tab to the EXERCISE Date field, and type *EVERY LINK1*. The query is complete, and you have created a link between two files.

What is so special about a LINK? LINKs are the query form's answer to SET RELATION TO. You can only LINK files through fields with identical data types or index expressions. This example shows files linked by the Date field. You can link databases with character fields, numeric or floating fields, or date fields. You cannot link files with logical or memo fields. Why?

You cannot make a link between files using logical fields because logical fields have only two values. What is the point of linking two databases, each with several thousand records, on a field with only two values? Not much order would be imposed by this linking. You cannot make a link between files using memo fields because the DBF file's memo field is simply a pointer to a location in the DBT file; hence, linking through the memo field is an invalid operation.

Can file linking make things work faster? The whole point of file linking is to show static references between two files. It cannot run faster simply by linking, but you can make things run faster by activating index files and expressions as part of your queries.

Remember that the true SET RELATION TO command needs index files active in both work areas? What you may not have noticed is that identical index expressions are active on both databases. This is important. The SET RELATION TO command works only two ways. One method is to match files by index expressions; the other is to match files by record number. The command forms are

```
SET RELATION TO fieldname INTO work area/filename/alias
```

and

```
SET RELATION TO RECNO() INTO work area/filename/alias
```

The first command form uses a field name from the current work area as the basis for linking INTO another work area. You can reference the other work area by letter (A-1, B-2, C-3, D-4, E-5, F-6, G-7, H-8, I-9, J-10), by the name of the file active in the work area, or by the alias name you have assigned the database in the work area. Of all the terms mentioned here, the only one that might be confusing is *alias*. In dBASE III Plus and dBASE IV, you can give a database a new name when you open it in a work area. The command form is

```
USE filename ALIAS other name
```

An example that applies to our work follows:

```
USE EXERCISE ALIAS WORKOUT
SELECT 2
USE EXCOMMENT ALIAS COMMENTS
```

One reason to give a file an alias is to avoid confusion. We have already seen that dBASE IV lets you use a database in more than one work area at a time. You might want to reference the different work areas by names instead of letter references (A through J), as follows:

```
USE EXERCISE ALIAS FIRST
SELECT 2
USE EXERCISE AGAIN ALIAS SECOND
```

Back to speeding up linked files. The SET RELATION TO command requires either identical index expressions to be active on the files it wants to link or files linked by record numbers. Note that the files do not need the same number of records for this latter method to be used. The query forms do not require open and active index expressions to link files, but you can speed up information processing if you use the [Alt-F] *I* command to activate index expressions and then use those expressions for your links.

When you are linking files, you can place anything in the view area, provided it is part of the files in the query area or a calculated field you have designed in the calculated field area.

Suppose you place something in the view area. What do you expect to see, especially when one of the databases has significantly fewer records than the other database? The report form from the last section used this variance in total record number to create a report that listed several records worth of information from EXERCISE.DBF for each one record in EXCOMMENT.DBF. You might expect to see a Browse display in which a single EXCOMMENT Comment field is listed beside several Exercise fields. This does not happen, as figure 10-27 shows. Instead, dBASE IV repeats the single EXCOMMENT record several times for each set of Exercise records.

Notice anything else new and different in the Browse display in figure 10-27? What you should notice is that you have never seen the name of one of the fields in the Browse display. Even though the data under the name, CMNTDATE, looks like DATE field data, where did it come from?

The answer is shown in figure 10-28. We have already placed the EXERCISE Date field into the view area, and the view area dictates what is in the Browse display. dBASE IV won't allow you to place two fields with the same name in the view area. How do you get around this? You give one of the fields a different name. dBASE IV forces you to do this by presenting a calculated field name box in which to enter a new name for the field. You can see the new name presented as a calculated field name in the view area of figure 10-28.

All this is interesting, but what does it really get you? You can design linked queries through the query design work surface or you can create the query environment with dBASE commands as we did previously, then enter the query design surface and work with the query as you go.

One option we have not discussed is creating the view from the envi-

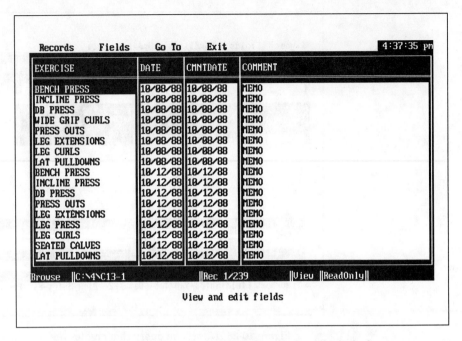

Figure 10-27 *This Browse display is the result of the linked query based on the USE...SELECT....SET RELATION command sequence shown in this chapter.*

ronment. This goes one step beyond entering commands and using the CREATE QUERY, MODIFY QUERY, CREATE VIEW, and MODIFY VIEW commands to pull information from dBASE IV's memory and put it in the query design work surface. The command is

`CREATE VIEW FROM ENVIRONMENT`

This command creates a VUE file, not a QBE file. The VUE file does much more than set a filtering condition on your databases. It reads all information, except variables and such, currently in dBASE IV's memory. This includes all information regarding which databases are active in which work areas, which format files are active in which work areas, index files and master index expressions for each database, relations set between files, which fields are open for editing in each work area, and so on. This is more than the query files give you; query files determine only which files are open and any links that are active between the files.

There is only one other topic to cover in this chapter: appending files through the query system. We will demonstrate an alternative method to moving data from one database to the other. This method works, but it requires lots of time to make it work properly for our purposes.

First we need to get back to a point where we have two databases, one filled with data and the other simply a structure, then get information from

445

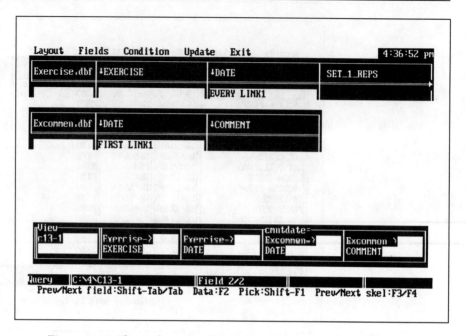

Figure 10-28 *This is the query that creates the Browse shown in figure 10-27. The EXCOMMENT Date field must be renamed as a calculated field to be used in the view area because you can't have two fields with the same name in the view area, even though the two fields come from different databases.*

one to the other. We need EXCOMMENT.DBF as an empty file and EXERCISE.DBF with a Comment field. We are not interested in EXERCISE.DBF having a Time field, but we do want the Comment field to be there.

No problem. MODIFY EXERCISE.DBF's STRUCTURE so that it contains a Comment field. Make sure the Comment field is a memo field. dBASE IV asks for confirmation that you want these changes. Press Y for yes. dBASE IV then creates a Comment field for each of the records in the EXERCISE.DBF file. Now we want to move the data from EXCOMMENT.DBF's Comment field to the EXERCISE Comment field. But remember, we do not want the Comment field scattered throughout the EXERCISE database. We want the Comment data to be in only those records in EXERCISE.DBF that contain the same date as the records in EXCOMMENT.DBF. This is essentially the reverse of what we demonstrated before, but this time we build it through the query system instead of the dBASE prompt. We start at the query system design surface and call up the two files of interest, EXERCISE.DBF and EXCOMMENT.DBF.

Now I want you to think about what we are doing. We are not APPENDing new data to the EXERCISE.DBF file; we are REPLACEing EXERCISE.DBF data with EXCOMMENT.DBF data. Your screen should look like figures 10-29 and 10-30.

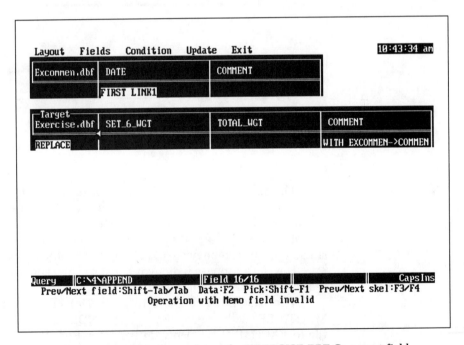

```
 Layout  Fields  Condition  Update  Exit              10:39:08 am

 Exconmen.dbf  DATE              COMMENT
               FIRST LINK1


 Exercise.dbf  EXERCISE          DATE              SET_1_REPS
 REPLACE                         EVERY LINK1









 Query  C:\4\APPEND        File 2/2                         Caps
     Next field:Tab  Add/Remove all fields:F5  Zoom:F9  Prev/Next skeleton:F3/F4
                     Operation with Memo field invalid
```

Figure 10-29 This figure shows the linking between the files and the REPLACE command in the EXERCISE.DBF file command area.

```
 Layout  Fields  Condition  Update  Exit              10:43:34 am

 Exconmen.dbf  DATE              COMMENT
               FIRST LINK1

 ┌Target┐
 Exercise.dbf  SET_6_WGT         TOTAL_WGT         COMMENT
 REPLACE                                           WITH EXCOMMEN->COMMEN









 Query  C:\4\APPEND        Field 16/16                     CapsIns
     Prev/Next field:Shift-Tab/Tab  Data:F2  Pick:Shift-F1  Prev/Next skel:F3/F4
                     Operation with Memo field invalid
```

Figure 10-30 This figure shows the EXERCISE.DBF Comment field with the update condition EXCOMMENT->COMMENT.

Figure 10-29 shows the linking between the files and the REPLACE command in the EXERCISE.DBF file command area. In figure 10-30, you can see the EXERCISE.DBF Comment field with the update condition EX-COMMENT-> COMMENT.

This is where I pretend I am the robot on the old "Lost in Space" TV show. I am going to throw up my hands and spin around and say, "Warning! Warning! Bad Software approaching." Did you ever wonder how an earth designed robot knew what was alien and what wasn't? It is much easier for us. All we have to do is look at the screen (figure 10-31).

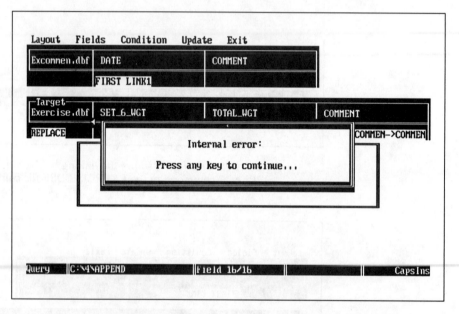

Figure 10-31 The REPLACE query operation will cause dBASE IV headaches, even though it is a perfectly acceptable operation. This bug should be cleared up in later editions of dBASE IV.

The end result of the internal error in figure 10-31 is that no records are updated. Please note that this is a bug that should be fixed in later editions of dBASE IV. If you try this command query sequence on your computer, it may work. We have tried it on four different computers, some single-user and some networked, and the problem always occurs.

Hey, let's suppose it did work, just so I can show you how to APPEND records through the query system.

The first thing to do is to get rid of all records in the EXCOM-MENT.DBF file because we will APPEND data from the EXERCISE.DBF file to EXCOMMENT. How do we get rid of all records in the EXCOM-MENT.DBF file?

No problem, ZAP the current EXCOMMENT.DBF file.

ZAP is a dBASE IV prompt command that tells dBASE IV to totally and irrevocably remove all records from the database. You are prompted for confirmation if you have SET SAFETY ON, but otherwise you are simply dropped back at the dBASE prompt. The moral of ZAP? Do not ZAP the database just yet. For that matter, do not ZAP any database just yet. Use the following commands first:

```
USE
COPY FILE filename.DBF TO filename.SVF
COPY FILE filename.DBT TO filename.SVT
ZAP
```

Note that *filename* denotes whatever database file you want to ZAP. We COPY the database FILE TO a storage file, using the SVF (save dbf) extension to signify that we should not erase this file from the disk when we are through with the exercise. This same command form is used to copy the DBT file to a storage SVT file. The last step is to ZAP. This command sequence insures that data is still stored somewhere, this time in the filename.SV? files, before it is forever removed from the source files.

Can anybody hazard a guess as to why we did not simply USE the database and COPY TO the storage file? Our database in this exercise has an associated DBT file. We would use the following command sequence to COPY active files to storage files:

```
USE filename
COPY TO filename.SVF
```

The problem is that there is no provision to create a new DBT file with the extension SVT. In other words, dBASE IV is perfectly willing to copy the DBF file to an SVF file, but it will still try to copy the DBT file to a DBT file. It can't do that because the filename.DBT file is already open, as shown in figure 10-32. The error message posts the database file, but the real problem is with the DBT file.

Also remember that you don't want to copy the MDX file in any way. It will only confuse dBASE IV and possibly you if you try to use the MDX file after you have copied the DBF and DBT files.

Okay, we are back to having the EXERCISE.DBF file with lots of information and the EXCOMMENT.DBF file with no information. We need to copy all Date fields and all Comment fields from EXERCISE to insure that we get all Comment data into EXCOMMENT.

We want to create a one-to-one link between EXERCISE and EXCOMMENT on the Date field, and we want to APPEND to EXCOMMENT.DBF. The query design screen should look like figure 10-33.

There is no information in any other field in the EXERCISE.DBF query area. Press [Alt-U] P and dBASE IV will do its stuff, but don't expect any messages to clue you in to what is happening (figure 10-34). You will see the disks spin and lights blink, but you won't be told what is happening.

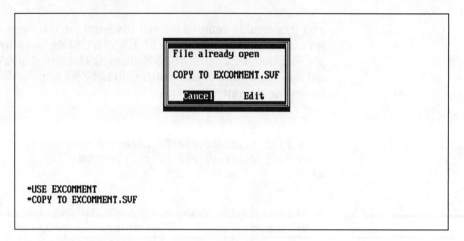

Figure 10-32 *You can't COPY TO new files with the same file name when the source file has an associated DBT file. You will get an error, shown in this figure, even though the error does not directly reference the memo field file.*

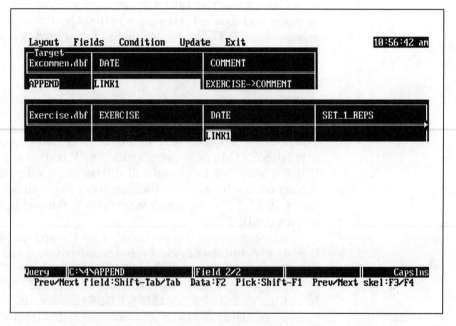

Figure 10-33 *We want to create a one-to-one link between EXERCISE and EXCOMMENT on the Date field, and we want to APPEND to EXCOMMENT.DBF.*

Rest assured, something is happening, and it is not an internal error and you will get the results you want (figure 10-35).

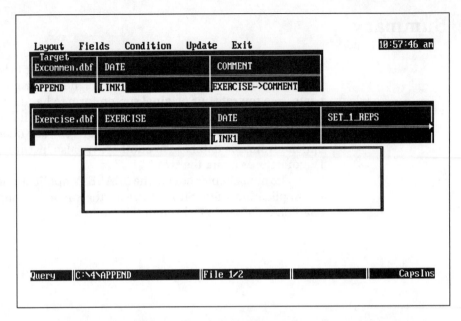

Figure 10-34 dBASE IV likes to be secretive about what is happening during an APPEND update query. Do not be alarmed. Good things are going on . . . somewhere in the world.

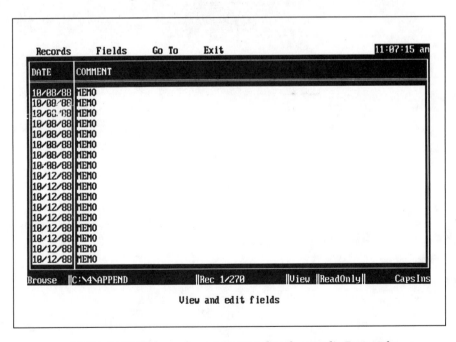

Figure 10-35 The query system copied each record's Date and Comment fields from EXERCISE.DBF to EXCOMMENT.DBF. The memo fields are in uppercase because each field has data. You can use the program in this chapter to remove repeated entries and gather all the memo fields into a single record for each day.

Summary

This chapter has shown you ways to improve your original dBASE IV designs and make things work better. We made our original database designs neater, we rewrote our original screen form to handle more than one database at a time, we rewrote our report form to get information from more than one database at a time, and we rewrote our queries to replace and append from one database to another. We also learned about other dBASE IV commands along the way.

The next chapter covers the dBASE IV applications generator. We use the applications generator to create the same system we created in this chapter, only we do it through the menu system.

Using the dBASE IV Applications Generator

We have covered every major topic in the dBASE IV system except using the Applications Generator, shown in figure 11-1. The Assist system's Applications ⟨create⟩ command lets you design dBASE IV programs or full applications. What is the difference?

A dBASE program is one of those things we have been developing all along in this book. The Assist system's Applications Generator is kind enough to assume that you know what you are doing when you want to

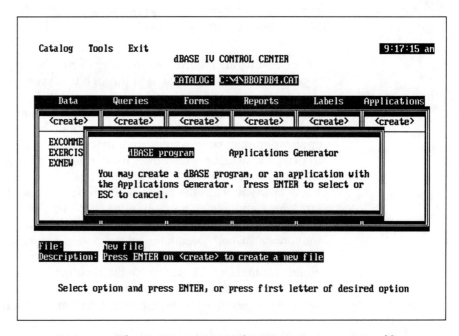

Figure 11-1 The Assist system's Applications ⟨create⟩ command lets you design dBASE programs or full applications.

write a program; thus, it drops into the dBASE IV text editor (discussed in chapters 4 and 8). The dBASE IV text editor/word processor is a rudimentary word processor and can be used to create or edit any text files, not just program files, with the dBASE prompt commands

```
MODIFY COMMAND filename
MODIFY FILE filename
```

MODIFY COMMAND assumes the file has a PRG extension. You need to enter something other than the PRG extension if you are not working with a dBASE IV PRG file. You always need to enter the complete file name when using the MODIFY FILE command.

The Assist system's Applications Generator creates a total dBASE IV environment that links databases, index files, format files, report forms, label forms, query files, and so forth. There are two things to know about the Applications Generator before you use it, and what you need to know is something I have hammered into you all through this book.

First, the Applications Generator is the most memory hoggish aspect of dBASE IV. You need a 640K computer just to start it through the Assist system. Attempting to run the Assist system's Applications Generator without 640K of memory might cause problems, depending on what software you have already loaded into memory. You can always start the Applications Generator with either of the dBASE prompt commands

```
CREATE APPLICATION application name
MODIFY APPLICATION application name
```

These commands require less memory to run the Applications Generator because you are not accessing it through the Assist system.

There is nothing difficult in creating an application. Just break the application into small pieces, then link the pieces together.

Second, you need to design your application before you begin creating it. The design phase of application development is not as involved as many people think. The basic process is done by recognizing that all big applications can be broken down into lots of little applications. It is easier to design a steering wheel than it is to design a whole car. That is how application development is best done. You know you want a car, and you know how you want the car to look and ride. Good. Keep that picture in your head and design an engine for that car, a braking system, a power train, an interior, and so on. You have the picture in your head of an engine for your car? Good. Design the intake system, the exhaust system, the cooling system, and so on. You have the picture of an intake system for the engine for that car? Good. Design the air filter, the carburetor, the gas line, the accelerator linkage, and so on. You have the picture of the carburetor for the intake system for the engine for that car? Good. Design the ventures
. . .

You get the idea.

This chapter first shows how to develop an Exercise maintenance system using the Applications Generator. The second section describes using the dBASE IV word processor/text editor to modify the Exercise system.

All through this book I have been telling you to think before you act. This is good advice for lots of things, not just working with databases. The dBASE IV Applications Generator helps you think things through logically, which is good. But do not go into it blind. A little forethought can save lots of questions later in the game.

Our project is to design a complete, menu-driven Exercise system. So far we have the databases (EXERCISE and EXCOMMENT), the input forms (either EXERSAY and EXERGET or the FMT files), the report forms (EXBYDATE, DATEBYEX, and PROBLEMS), and lots of queries. There are no labels in this system.

And this is where I get to explain the terribly confusing term *objects*. The Applications documentation uses that word all over the place. What does it mean?

The databases, the screen forms, the report forms, the queries, the index files, and any labels are objects in the completed application. They are objects because they are parts of the completed application. I mentioned that you design complete systems by designing small parts and linking them together to make the complete system. Each of these small pieces of the complete system is an object. The application developer links these objects together along with other objects that are actual program code. Some of the program code might be menus; other code might be operations that occur behind the scenes and are unknown to the user.

These "behind the scenes" operations are called batch operations and are what most dBASE III Plus programmers remember as *code*. It is useful to think of all that was previously designed in this book along with menus as objects and to think of batch processes as the commands that link these objects together and manipulate them to make work easier for the user. The LISTER.PRG program developed in chapter 8 is an example of batch processing that manipulates various dBASE IV objects.

We have most of the objects for the Exercise menu system already developed. We now need the menus and batch processes to link all these objects. We start with the menus.

Designing Menus

From the Main menu, the user should be able to edit/browse individual records, run reports, run queries, access some dBASE IV utilities such as packing, reindexing, and making backups of the database, and perhaps access DOS. And we must not forget a Quit option for those few unreasonable people who would rather not use our system. We can map out the Main menu as follows

```
EDIT   REPORTS   QUERIES   UTILITIES   DOS   QUIT
```

The Edit menu will have different options depending on whether we are browsing the data or using Edit mode. Browse mode handles itself; Edit mode needs the following options:

```
EDIT   BACKUP   SKIP      GOTO      KILL    RECALL   QUIT
FIND   LOCATE   CONTINUE  DISPLAY   COPY    ADD      UPDATE
```

Some of these terms might need explaining. Backup means SKIP -1 (backup is more likely to be understood than SKIP -1). Kill means DELETE. (We cannot have two menu options starting with the same letter if we want dBASE IV to design the system so that the first letter of the option activates the code assigned to that option.) Update performs replacements.

The Reports option on the Main menu should include target settings (Screen, File, and Printer) and report form names. The Queries option should list queries we have designed for the system. Utilities might be broken into two subsystems, computer system utilities and application-specific utilities. System utilities might include options for specifying backup and restore utilities, changing the date format, setting the default drive and path, and in more advanced systems, setting printer drivers. Application-specific utilities might include options to pack the files, reindex the files, run the backup, and restore utilities. The DOS and Quit options are simple enough.

We have designed a menu tree.

Creating Menus

Now we can create the next set of objects for our Exercise system, which are the menus. dBASE IV starts the Applications Generator with a definition screen (figure 11-2). The only things that we have not already thought of that the Applications Generator wants to know immediately are the Main menu type, the database or view name, the index file name, and the index expression order.

There are three types of menus in the Applications Generator: bar, pop-up, and batch. Bar and pop-up menus have been shown throughout this book. The bar menu is always on the screen and uses a highlight to select items. The pop-up menu is similar to the bar, but is only on the screen when called for. What is a batch menu?

A batch menu is nothing special. You can create options, enter program lines, and so on just like any other menu. The difference is noted purely for dBASE IV's sake. The batch menu option tells dBASE IV that whatever is on the menu is something that will run behind the scenes, with no messages to the user and precious little input from the user. This option simply tells dBASE IV to set up commands to be run in background mode. As mentioned earlier in this chapter, batch processes are the ones that do the real work of the system.

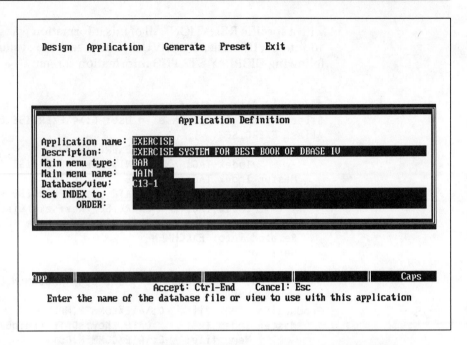

Figure 11-2 The Applications Generator wants to know something
about the entire system before it lets you create any of it.

What do we want to set the database/view to? This is best answered
with two examples, one of which forces us to jump ahead to the mail list
system developed in Appendix A. We know we want to develop a mail list
generator, so we can name the database MAIL. The index file name is also
MAIL because we will use a production MDX file. What about the index
expression order?

A mail list generator, whether it is a file card system or a bulk mail
system, needs to be indexed. The file card system can live happily with
index expressions on the name, company, and possibly subject of who or
what you are looking up. The bulk mailing system would be happier if it
knew the mail ID (the original code assigned to each record), the zip code,
and possibly the last name of who or what you are looking up. Because the
two things these systems have in common is name, last or otherwise, we
can set the index expression order to LASTNAME.

Note that you can always use [Shift-F1] to ask dBASE IV for a file pick
list, identical to those shown in other work surfaces, for both database and
index files. You can also group index files, both MDX and NDX, by entering their names on the SET INDEX TO line. Each MDX and NDX file
should be separated from others by a comma.

You tell dBASE IV you are finished filling out the application definition screen by pressing [Ctrl-End].

Back to the Exercise system example. The Exercise system uses two
different databases, each with their own MDX files, and links the two files

with a specific RELATION. All of this information was gathered in chapter 10 into a VIEW file, C13-1.VUE, which sets the system as shown in the following DISPLAY STATUS information screen:

```
Currently Selected Database:
Select area:  1, Database in Use: C:\4\EXERCISE.DBF
Alias: EXERCISE
Production   MDX file:  C:\4\EXERCISE.MDX
            Index TAG:      EXUNIQ  Key: EXERCISE (Unique)
    Master Index TAG:   DATE  Key: DATE
            Index TAG:      EXDATE  Key: EXERCISE + DTOC(DATE)
            Index TAG:      EXERCISE  Key: exercise
            Index TAG:      DATEUNIQ  Key: date (Unique)
    Related into: EXCOMMEN
    Relation: date

Select area:  2, Database in Use: C:\4\EXCOMMEN.DBF
Alias: EXCOMMEN
Production   MDX file:  C:\4\EXCOMMEN.MDX
    Master Index TAG:       DATE  Key: DATE (Unique)
          Memo file:    C:\4\EXCOMMEN.DBT
```

We can use the C13-1.VUE object to handle the Exercise system's requests for Database/view, Set INDEX to, and ORDER (see figure 11-2).

The next thing dBASE IV wants you to do is design your logo. Although this should be the last thing you do, let's do it now because it won't take long. Start with the screen shown in figure 11-3. Your logo does not have to look like mine (figure 11-4).

The idea you should be getting is that the box dBASE IV gives you is too small. But don't worry, we can correct that.

First, I merely typed over the existing information in the box to enter my own information. Information that I did not directly type over I removed from the screen with [Ctrl-Y] or [Ctrl-T]. [Ctrl-Y] removes complete lines from the screen; [Ctrl-T] removes words to the right of the cursor, one word at a time. I stretched the box by pressing [Shift-F7]. Then I used the cursor keys to stretch the box down an extra line and pressed [Enter] to let dBASE IV know that I had finished modifying the box. Note that this part of the system does not provide any word formatting commands. It is up to you to make sure you have centered text on the screen, if that is what you want.

Now that you have designed a sign-on screen, it might be nice to make sure dBASE IV uses it when your application is run. Press [Alt-A] to pop up the Application menu (figure 11-5). The option of interest is *Display sign-on banner.* You are presented with another menu asking whether or not to display the object you have just created when your application is run. Type Y because you are vain and you know it.

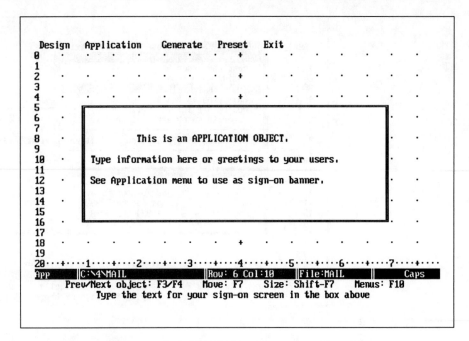

Figure 11-3 This is what dBASE IV presents as its idea of your sign-on
or logo screen.

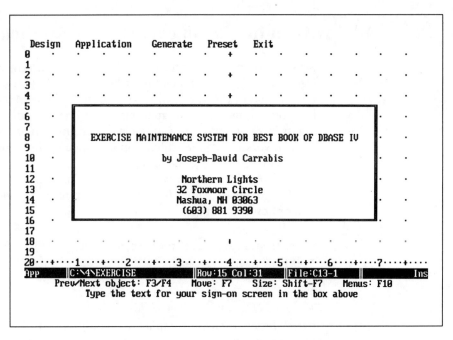

Figure 11-4 This is a more egocentric sign-on or logo screen. You can
stretch the box to fit your logo with the [Shift-F7]
and cursor control keys.

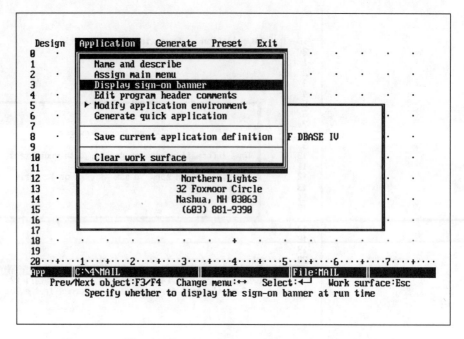

Figure 11-5 The Application menu contains options to change the screen shown in figure 11-2.

Adding Opening Comments to Your Application Code

Several other options on the Application menu reference items shown in figure 11-2. The *Name and describe* option lets you change the name and description of the application, as shown in figure 11-2. *Assign main menu* lets you change the Main menu type and name. *Edit program header comments* lets you enter your name, a copyright notice, and a reference to the dBASE version under which you are developing your application (figure 11-6). You can change the information dBASE IV provides to whatever you want. dBASE IV normally uses the first four lines of a generated FRG file for this purpose. Those four lines, which follow, give you an idea of what this option is looking for:

```
* Program.............: C:exbydate.FRG
* Date................: 2-01-89
* Versions............: dBASE IV, Report 1
*
```

The *Save current application definition* option stores your work in progress but does not allow you to change the application name when you save it. Don't confuse this option with the [Alt-S] option found on many other dBASE IV design surface menus. The *Clear work surface* option removes items from the screen, one at a time. Each time something is re-

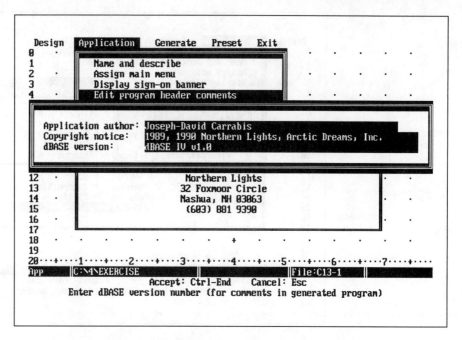

Figure 11-6 With the Edit program header comments *option, you can change what normally appears as the first four lines of comments in a generated PRG file to something more to your liking.*

moved from the screen, you will be prompted for confirmation. *Generate quick application* is covered later. This leaves us with *Modify application environment.*

Changing the Development Environment

There are four options on the *Modify application environment* submenu (figure 11-7). The first option, *Display options*, has its own submenu. The first display option that you can change is the *Object border style*.

This part of the chapter deals with the sign-on screen as an object; therefore, the *Object border style* is for the sign-on screen object. You can toggle from *Double* (as in a box defined by double lines), *Single* (as in a box defined by a single line), *Panel* (as in a background color and foreground color window), and *None*. Most applications are attractive enough with double and single bars around boxes and windows, but play around to decide what you like best.

The rest of this submenu deals with screen colors for the current object (figure 11-8). You can choose the colors for the foreground and background of your object. The foreground is the actual text. The background is the color that surrounds the text. Each of this submenu's options, *Standard—All, Normal text, Messages, Titles, Enhanced—All, Highlight, Boxes, Information,* and *Fields,* show the same menu as shown in figure 11-8.

461

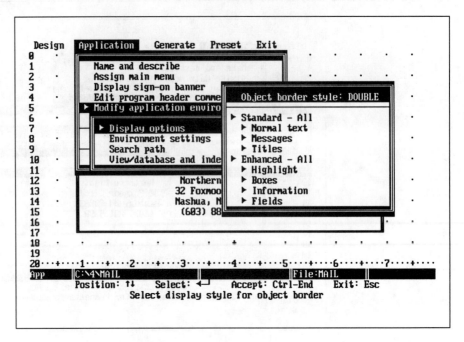

Figure 11-7 The Application menu's Modify application environment
option has its own submenu. This submenu controls the general
appearance of the finished code's menus and screen forms.

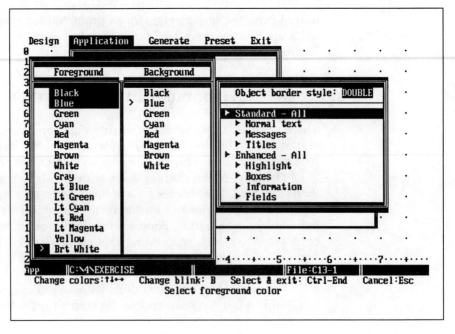

Figure 11-8 The Modify application environment option's submenu
lets you set the foreground and background colors
for your entire application.

dBASE IV places a right pointing arrow next to the currently selected colors.

The *Environment settings* option in the Modify application environment submenu handles how dBASE IV communicates with your application's end user. This menu (figure 11-9) lets you ding the user by SETting the BELL ON and SETting the BELL frequency and duration. Frequency and duration?

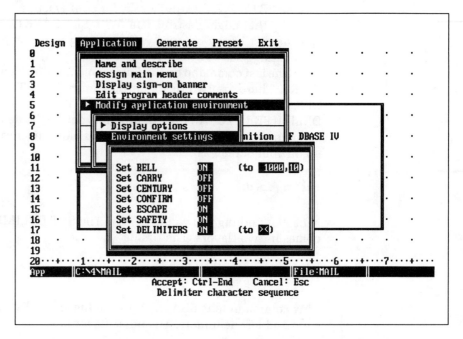

Figure 11-9 *The* Environment settings *options lets you indicate how you want your application to interact with the user.*

The frequency of the bell is the actual tone of the bell. PCs can produce a variety of sounds from their tiny speakers, and this is dBASE IV's way of letting you in on the fun. Remember that you should not make the bell ding too long. Anything over two seconds can become annoying.

The CARRY command was discussed in chapter 6. You SET CARRY ON to tell dBASE IV to bring information from the last record to the next record. This is useful when there is repetitive data entry in a work session. The CENTURY command toggles whether or not the year is 1989 or simply 89. SET CENTURY ON and you are in the present. SET CENTURY OFF and you are back in the days when Rome was grand, if you went for that kind of thing, that is.

CONFIRM has to do with how dBASE IV decides if you are ready to go to the next field during data entry and editing. If you SET CONFIRM ON, dBASE IV won't leave a field until you press [Enter]. If you SET CON-

FIRM OFF, dBASE IV leaves a field or variable when you press [Enter] or when the field is filled.

All software should have an ESCAPE hatch, something that allows the user to bail out with the minimum damage to the system you have developed. With SET ESCAPE ON, your user can bail out of your application by pressing [Esc]. If you SET ESCAPE OFF, users are along for the duration, whether they want to be or not.

The SET SAFETY toggle was discussed in chapters 5, 8, and 10. With SET SAFETY ON, dBASE IV asks for confirmation before doing much of anything that might destroy data. With SET SAFETY OFF, you will make your dentist happy because you are going to gnash your teeth into little enamel nuggets.

The last command on the *Environment settings* screen is SET DELIMITERS. There are two fields for data entry here. The first field is ON or OFF, as in SET DELIMITERS ON or OFF. The second field is *to*, as in SET DELIMITERS TO. All dBASE products define the default delimiter as the colon for both right and left of the data field. This means your data shows up on your screen as

`:data field:`

Nice, but nothing you would die for. The SET DELIMITER TO command comes in two flavors. The first is

`SET DELIMITER TO character`

This command tells dBASE IV to use the single listed character for both right and left delimiters. The other flavor is

`SET DELIMITER TO left character right character`

There is no separation between the two characters in the preceding command. For example, you would tell dBASE IV to use the greater than and less than symbols for left and right delimiters with the following command

`SET DELIMITER TO ><`

Your data would look like the following

`>data field<`

Not much, but better than colons.

The next option on the Modify application environment submenu is *Search path*. This is an important option that many beginning developers overlook. The search path is where your application defaults to looking for its data and program files. The default drive for most systems is C. The default path is anyone's guess. For example, systems written by Northern Lights create and load themselves into the following directories

```
BCARDS
CABLE
DMASTER
EYES
LIBRARY
LABELER
MAILMAN
WFAL
WORDSMTH
```

This means each of the preceding creates a default directory for its own application. The application then assumes all necessary files will be found on the default drive in the particular directory. This holds true unless the user specifically changes the default drive and directory information at some point.

The last option on the Modify application environment submenu is *View/database and index*. This option lets you change the database/view, set index to, and order information located in figure 11-2.

Okay, we have a pretty sign-on screen. Can we get on with the actual menu generation? Yes, but there are a few other things I want to show you first.

The Application menu has many things in common with the Preset menu. The Preset menu's *Sign-on defaults* holds the dBASE IV defaults for what the Application menu calls *Edit program header comments*. The *Display* options in the Preset menu are identical to *Display options* in the Application menu's Modify application environment submenu. The *Environment* settings in the Preset menu are those found on *Environment settings* in the Application menu's Modify application environment submenu. The *Application drive/path* option in the Preset menu is identical to the *Search path* option in the Application menu's Modify application environment submenu.

What's going on? The operative word in the preceding paragraph is the name of the menu, Preset. These are things that dBASE IV assumes it should bring to the picnic. Specifically, these are things dBASE IV thinks you want it to bring to every picnic. In this case, the picnic is the Applications Generator. If you don't change anything, dBASE IV puts the Preset menu defaults on each application that you create. Go through the Preset menu options and you will see that dBASE IV is at times naive and at other times more egocentric than you could ever be when it comes to bringing things to the picnic.

Main Menu Generation

Next we design our Main menu. Press [Alt-D] to open the Design menu and select *Horizontal bar menu*. Because no menus are currently defined (figure 11-10), the Applications Generator assumes you want to create one. You are prompted for information regarding the Main menu. The only item you don't need to fill out is the *Message line prompt*. Each item on the Main menu will have its own prompt.

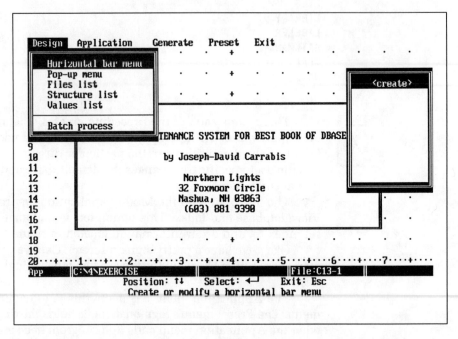

Figure 11-10 *Because no horizontal bar menus are currently defined, dBASE IV assumes you want to create a new one.*

The menu itself is placed at the top of the screen by the Applications Generator (figure 11-11). You fill in your menu options by pressing [F5], typing your option, then pressing [F5] again to indicate you have completed entering the option. One thing you must remember is that your menus will be both cursor and key letter driven. This means you can select an option either by highlighting the option and pressing [Enter] or by typing the first letter of the option and pressing [Enter]. Therefore, make sure your menus have options with unique first letters. You cannot have the Main menu with any of the following option lists:

EDIT REPORTS QUERIES UTILITIES DOS QUIT   Repeated *Q*

EDIT REPORTS QUERIES UTILITIES DOS EXIT   Repeated *E*

EDIT REPORTS QUERIES UTILITIES DOS RETURN *·* Repeated *R*

Note that if you SET CONFIRM OFF, you need to type only the first letter of an option.

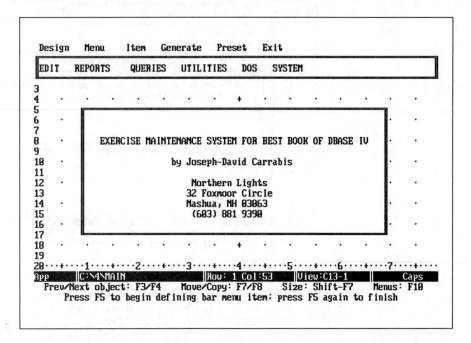

Figure 11-11 *The Applications Generator automatically places your horizontal bar menu across the top of the screen.*

Our Main menu is finished. Now we are going to assign our second-level menus. The second-level menus will be pull-down menus. Press [Alt-M] to open the Menu menu and select the *Attach pull-down menus* option (figure 11-12). You are asked if you want dBASE IV to automatically assign colors to the pull-down menus based on what you have already selected for other menus. Type *Y* for now. You can be creative later.

You should have noticed some changes to the screen between figures 11-10 and 11-11. The options at the top of the screen changed—from Design, Application, Generate, Preset, and Exit to Design, Menu, Item, Generate, Preset, and Exit. We lost Application and gained Menu and Item. The next sentence will win an award from the Redundancy Department. The Menu menu options are to your menus what the Application menu options are to your applications.

That is really not as bad as I thought it would be. With the *Menu* option shown in figure 11-12, you can change the name and description of the currently defined menu, modify the display options associated with the menu, save the current menu without removing it from the screen or changing the menu's name, put away the current menu by saving it to disk and removing it from the screen, or clear the work surface of the last worked upon object (the current menu, in this case) but continue working.

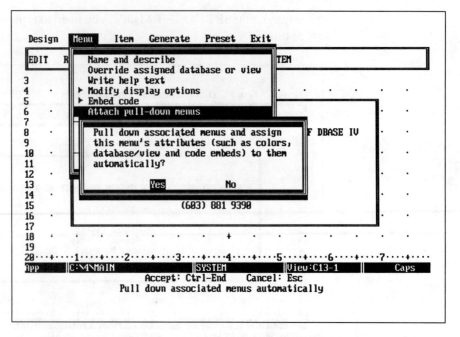

Figure 11-12 *The Menu menu options let you modify your menus in much the same way the Application menu lets you modify your applications. This figure shows you how to tell the Applications Generator that you want to link some pull-down menus to the current menu.*

Note that this last option does not destroy the last worked upon item; it merely removes it from the work surface.

Other options on the Menu menu are important, although we won't be using them. The *Override assigned database or view* option is shown in figure 11-13. Remember that we told the Applications Generator which database/view to use in figure 11-2. This option lets you change the database and associated files for the current menu. The word *ABOVE* in figure 11-13 toggles to *ENTERED BELOW* and *IN EFFECT AT RUN TIME* as you press [Spacebar]. *ABOVE* refers to the files you told the Applications Generator to use when you first entered the system. *ENTERED BELOW* lets you specify files for the menu you are currently working on. *IN EFFECT AT RUN TIME* puts a lot of burden on your shoulders as a developer. It makes you responsible for knowing which files will be active before any user starts your system. Unless you plan on handcuffing your users, I strongly recommend that you don't use this option.

Another Menu option is *Write help text*. Help text could be useful for people using our system, so let's add some. Note that the help text we enter here will be associated with our application's Main menu and will be accessed through the standard dBASE [F1] (Help) key.

dBASE IV presents you with a blank, nineteen-line screen in which to write your help messages (figure 11-14). Note that you cannot use double

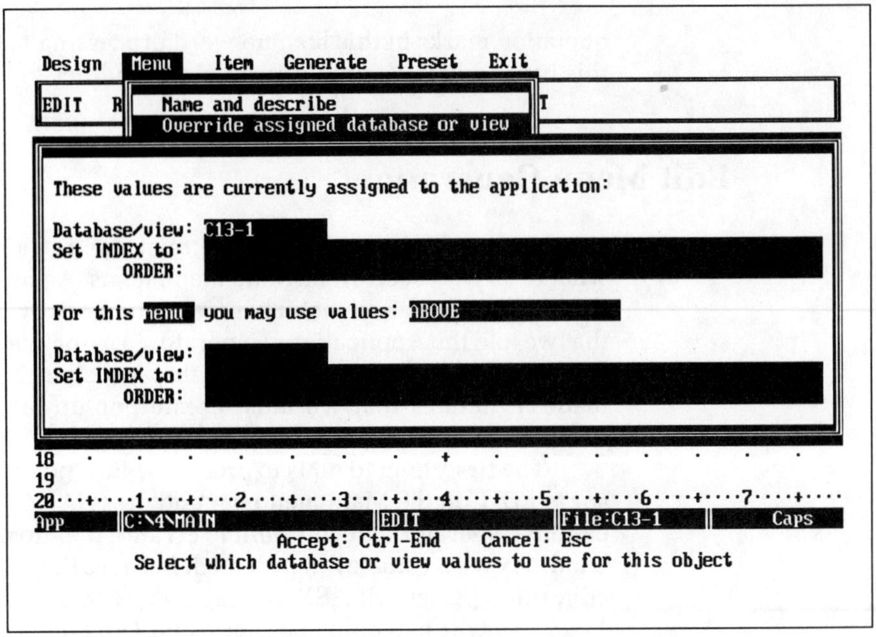

```
Design  Menu   Item   Generate   Preset   Exit

EDIT  R    Name and describe                          T
            Override assigned database or view

    These values are currently assigned to the application:

    Database/view: C13-1
    Set INDEX to:
        ORDER:

    For this menu you may use values: ABOVE

    Database/view:
    Set INDEX to:
        ORDER:

18  .   .   .   .   .   .   .   +   .   .   .   .
19
20 ···+····1····+····2····+····3····+····4····+····5····+····6····+····7····+····
App    C:\4\MAIN              EDIT          File:C13-1          Caps
                    Accept: Ctrl-End    Cancel: Esc
            Select which database or view values to use for this object
```

Figure 11-13 *The Override assigned database or view Menu option
lets you change the database and associated files
for a given menu option.*

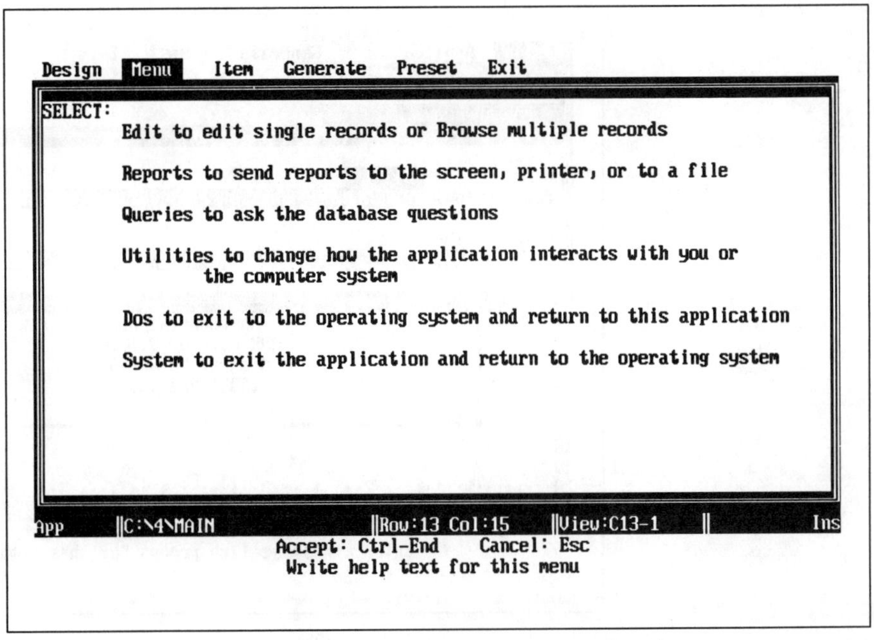

```
Design  Menu   Item   Generate   Preset   Exit

SELECT:
        Edit to edit single records or Browse multiple records

        Reports to send reports to the screen, printer, or to a file

        Queries to ask the database questions

        Utilities to change how the application interacts with you or
                the computer system

        Dos to exit to the operating system and return to this application

        System to exit the application and return to the operating system

App    C:\4\MAIN              Row:13 Col:15   View:C13-1          Ins
                    Accept: Ctrl-End    Cancel: Esc
                    Write help text for this menu
```

Figure 11-14 *You can write help text for the current menu by selecting
Write help text from the Menu options.*

quotation marks in this box, no word processing features are available for this box, and you cannot exceed nineteen lines of text.

Edit Menu Generation

We have our Main menu on the screen. Next, we need to tell dBASE IV what to do with each of the Main menu items. Again, no problem. We know that the first-level Edit menu has two options, Browse and Edit. Remember that we told the Applications Generator to associate pull-down menus with the Main menu. You can change that selection if you want, but having made it dictates that we must create pop-up menus for our first-level menus.

The first thing to do is to create the Edit pop-up menu. Move the cursor to *EDIT* on the Main menu bar and press [Alt-D] P. This tells the Applications Generator that you want to create a pop-up menu. You are shown a blank box with 〈create〉 highlighted. Because there are no pop-up menus to edit, press [Enter]. dBASE IV responds with a screen as shown in figure 11-15. We will name this pop-up menu *EDIT-1* because it is the first-level edit menu. The description is for anyone needing to edit our system after we have developed it, and the message line prompt is for the user at runtime. The next thing to do is to create the menu itself (figure 11-16).

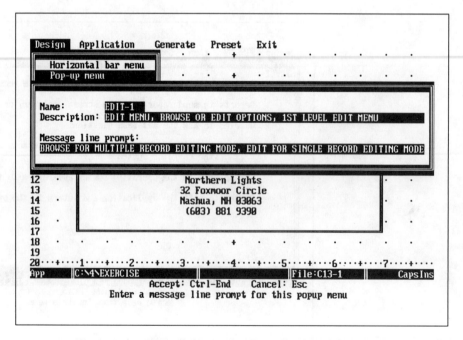

Figure 11-15 You tell the Applications Generator the name, description, and any message line prompts for the pop-up menu on a screen identical to that used for the bar menus.

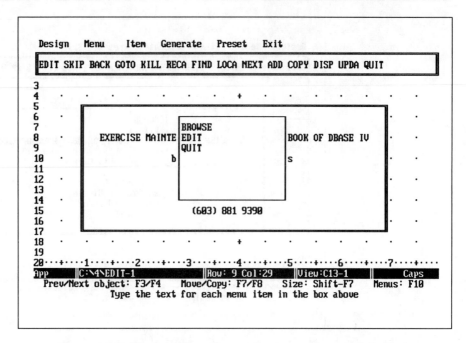

Figure 11-16 *The second step in creating a pop-up menu is laying it out on the screen. dBASE IV gives you much more room than you need and leaves it to you to size the pop-up menu accordingly.*

Did you notice that figure 11-16 includes a Quit option even though we did not specify one earlier? Many developers will not bother including a specific Quit option on their menus. Instead, they make use of dBASE IV's ON ESCAPE command to use the [Esc] key as a standard means of backing up through menus. This is pretty much an industry standard. You can decide to do so, if you want. My experience is not to do so because dBASE IV prefers to use the [Esc] key for other things and it removes one more item of control from you, the developer. You might also notice problems with dBASE IV's desire to wrestle control from you or the user if you try to run your application and use the [Esc] key to back up through things.

You can size the pop-up menu by pressing [Shift-F7] and using the cursor keys to change the borders. Pressing [Enter] tells dBASE IV you have completed sizing the menu.

What to do with this new menu, eh? The first thing to do is move it to where it will appear on the screen. The cursor should still be inside the Edit-1 pop-up menu. Press [F7]. You are asked if you want to move the entire frame or the single highlighted item in the frame. You will notice that the original menu stays where the Applications Generator originally placed it as you move another box around the screen (figure 11-17). Press [Enter] when you have the menu placed where you want it.

We know that the Browse option will simply allow browsing; we should tell the Applications Generator that. Place the cursor on the Browse option in your menu and press [Alt-I] *C B*. This opens the Item menu's

471

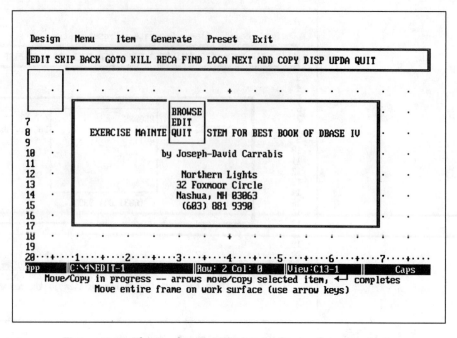

Figure 11-17 *The Applications Generator leaves the menu in its original location as you move another box to where you want the menu to be placed.*

Change action option and tells the Applications Generator to select the *Browse* option. Next, the Applications Generator asks for information regarding how you want the user to Browse through the database (figure 11-18).

Notice that we do not have any *Fields* or *Filter* information in figure 11-18. There is no need because the fields are defined in the C13-1.VUE file. We do not want any filters for the database, so we pass that option as well. Make as many changes to the Browse options as you want.

What about the first-level Edit option? We want something more for that than simple editing of single records. That option should open another bar menu, Editor.

Tell the Applications Generator that you want to leave the *Open menu* option by pressing [Ctrl-End]. Cursor over to *design* and select the *Horizontal bar menu* option. Name the new menu *EDITOR*, give it a general description of *General-purpose editing menu for single-record editing* and leave the message line prompt blank. The options for the Editor bar menu are

```
ADD    BACKUP   CONTINUE  COPY  DISPLAY  EDIT  FIND
GOTO   KILL     LOCATE    QUIT  RECALL   SKIP  UPDATE
```

This is a good alphabetized order for the options, but doesn't make sense

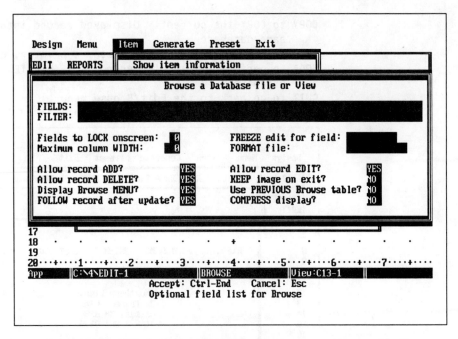

Design   Menu   **Item**   Generate   Preset   Exit

| EDIT | REPORTS | Show item information |

Browse a Database file or View

FIELDS:
FILTER:

Fields to LOCK onscreen: `0`   FREEZE edit for field:
Maximum column WIDTH: `0`   FORMAT file:

Allow record ADD?   YES   Allow record EDIT?   YES
Allow record DELETE?   YES   KEEP image on exit?   NO
Display Browse MENU?   YES   Use PREVIOUS Browse table?   NO
FOLLOW record after update? YES   COMPRESS display?   NO

```
17
18   .      .      .      .      .      +      .      .      .      .      .      .
19
20 ··+····1····+····2····+····3····+····4····+····5····+····6····+····7····+····
```
App   C:\4\EDIT-1   BROWSE   View:C13-1

Accept: Ctrl-End   Cancel: Esc
Optional field list for Browse

*Figure 11-18 With the Item menu's Change, Browse option, you decide
how much of the dBASE IV BROWSE command's abilities the user
can have in your application.*

when you know what the menu options do. A better listing is shown in
figure 11-19.

It might be a good idea to save your work so far by pressing [Ctrl-End].
This stores all your files without writing the actual programs associated
with them. [Ctrl-End] sends you back whence you came, to either the Assist
system or the dBASE prompt.

Start up the Applications Generator again and get back to the Editor
menu by pressing [Alt-D] H. You are presented with a box as shown in
figure 11-20. We placed a lot of options on that menu; chances are the user
will need a help screen to understand them all. The help text entered is

```
SELECT:
EDIT to make changes to the currently displayed record
SKIP to go to the next record in the database
BACK to go to the previous record in the database
GOTO to specify a record to display on the screen
KILL to delete the currently displayed record
RECA to undelete (RECALL) the currently displayed
     record
FIND to move to a record using an INDEX expression
LOCA to LOCATE a record using an unINDEXed expression
NEXT to CONTINUE the last LOCATE
ADD  to APPEND data to the database
```

```
COPY to COPY the currently displayed record into the
     same database
DISP to DISPLAY data to the screen, a printer, or a file
UPDA to perform a multiple-record edit (UPDATE) of the
     database
QUIT to go back to the Edit/Browse menu
```

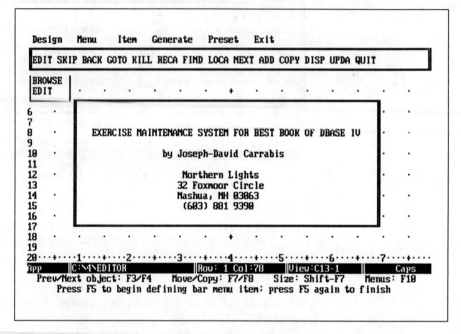

Figure 11-19 *This figure shows a more logical Editor menu, one which puts frequently used commands to the front of the menu.*

Reports Menu Generation

The next menu to develop is the Reports pop-up menu. This menu does two things. First, it lets the user select whether the report target is the screen, a printer, or a file. Second, the menu must let users decide which report form they want to use. Our menu options are therefore *Reports, File, Printer,* and *Screen.* Press [Alt-D] *P* to design a pop-up menu. Enter the name as *RE-PORT-1,* to be consistent with our Edit-1 menu, but fill in the rest of the information as you want. You might want to leave a blank line between *REPORTS* and *FILE* in the menu design, as shown in figure 11-21.

Figure 11-21 shows the Report-1 pop-up menu positioned under the Main menu. Readers coming into the Applications Generator at the middle of an application might wonder how we got the Main menu on the screen when we were designing the Report-1 menu. It was done by pressing [Alt-D] *H,* selecting the MAIN menu from the list provided, then using the [F3]

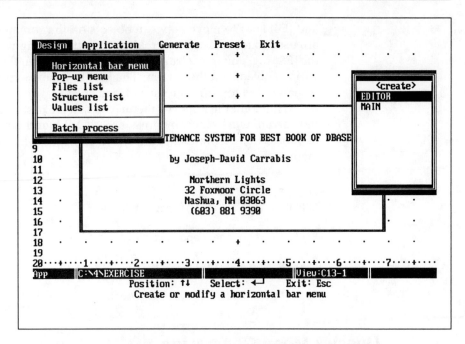

Figure 11-20 *You can edit any menu you have created by calling it up on the Applications Generator's Design menu.*

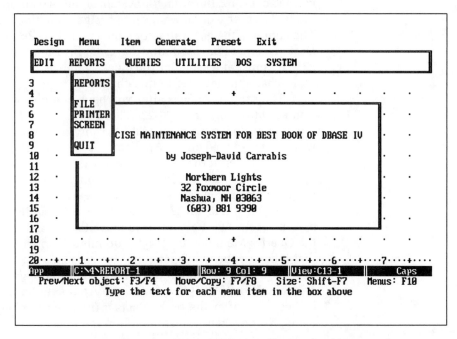

Figure 11-21 *The Reports pop-up menu is designed to list report forms and select a report target (file, printer, or screen).*

and [F4] keys to move between objects on the screen, much as these keys are used to move between areas on the query design surface. As you press the [F3] key, you move from the top of the screen to the bottom through the various objects on the screen. The [F4] key moves from the bottom of the screen to the top through the various objects.

Highlight the Report-1 menu (you can make sure the Report-1 menu is the current work object by pressing [Alt-M] N and seeing where the Applications Generator thinks you are) and enter the following help text for this menu:

```
SELECT:
REPORTS for a list of report forms

FILE to send the report to a disk file
PRINTER to send the report to a printer
SCREEN to send the report to the screen

QUIT to go back to the Main menu
```

Queries Menu Generation

The next Main menu item is *Queries*. This will require a file list so the user can select a QBE file; then the system should go automatically into Browse mode. In other words, we need to assign an action directly to this option. The action is the generation of a query file list. Press [Alt-D] F to open the Design menu's *Files list* option and enter information as shown in figure 11-22. You must at least enter the object name as *QBEFILES* for consistency with what appears later in this chapter.

The screen changes after you have completed entering the information as shown in figure 11-22. There is a new menu option, *List*. We are creating a file list, so press [Alt-L]. Many of these options are identical to what was provided on the Applications Generator's Menu and Application menus and therefore won't be discussed here. The item of interest is *Identify files in list*. Enter *.QBE at the prompt shown in figure 11-23. Do not forget to finish your selection with [Ctrl-End].

We have told dBASE IV to create a QBE file list when the *Queries* option is selected. Remember to move the file list so that it appears under the *Queries* Main menu option. You might also want to expand the box so that it covers the whole length of the screen.

Now we have to tell dBASE IV what to do after one of those files is selected. Press [Alt-I] E A to tell the Applications Generator you want to embed code after the user selects a file from the list. What code do you want? Nothing fancy, just the following lines:

```
BROWSE LOCK 1 NOEDIT
SET VIEW TO C13-1
```

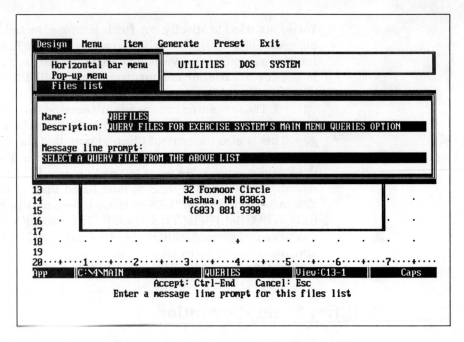

Figure 11-22 The Main menu's Queries option needs to generate a QBE file list. This is done with the [Alt-D] F option.

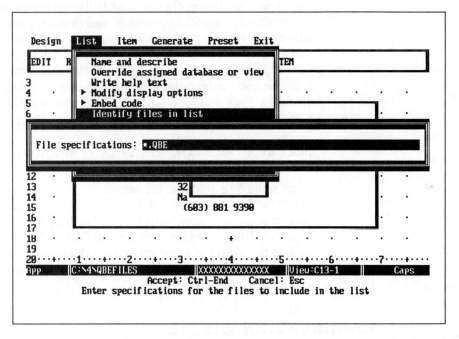

Figure 11-23 Because you want the user to have a list of query files, enter *.QBE at the prompt.

We do not need to specify any fields because the fields are defined in the different QBE files. We LOCK 1 to make sure the first field on the screen remains as a reference. We use NOEDIT because we are nasty and want to force people to use our Edit menu options. We SET the VIEW back to C13-1 because some of the query files might open databases that we don't want opened. The preceding commands are entered into the dBASE IV text editor, but without any of the text editor's menus to help you.

This is also the perfect place to note that the *Reports* option on the Report-1 pop-up menu needs a list of report forms. Press [Alt-D] *F* to open the *Files list* option. We want to create a new file list, but notice that the recently created QBEFILES is now listed under ⟨create⟩. This file list should be named FRMFILES and have a message line prompt of *SELECT A REPORT FORM FROM THE ABOVE LIST*. Press [Ctrl-End] to accept what you have just done, highlight the Applications Generator menu's *List* option, and select *Identify files in list*. This time you want to enter *.FRM to specify report form files.

Utilities Menu Generation

Onto Utilities. Note that many of the keystrokes involved in designing the rest of these menus repeat what was described earlier. Remember that the menus are not saved until you use the [Alt-M] *S* or [Alt-M] *P S* option.

There are two options for the Utilities pop-up menu, *Exercise* (which we previously named *Application*) and *System*. I won't go through the details of designing a pop-up menu again, but I will remind you to name this pop-up *UTIL-1*.

The next step is designing the bar menus associated with Util-1. The Exercise options include indexing, packing, backing up, and restoring the database. This will be a horizontal bar menu called *UTIL-2A*. Enter the menu options as

```
INDEX DATA   PACK DATA   BACKUP DATA   RESTORE DATA   QUIT
```

Write some help text for this menu.

The System submenu has the following options: *Backup* (select backup utility), *Restore* (select restore utility), *Change Date Format, Drive, Path, LPT Driver*, and the ever popular *Quit*. As you can see, you sometimes have to be careful to make sure first letters are not repeated in your menu options. This will be another bar menu, one named *UTIL-2B*. This menu also requires help text.

Creating a DOS Window

The DOS Main menu option is another easy menu item to place in our system. Highlight DOS on the Main menu bar and press [Alt-I] *C R R* (figure

11-24). You are prompted for the file name you want to RUN. Because we want a general exit to DOS, not a specific program, enter COM-MAND.COM. This PC-DOS file automatically loads when you start your computer and puts you at the DOS prompt. Do not enter any parameters. You would enter parameters if you wanted to pass a file name to the program you want to RUN, such as a word processor. For example, we could load XyWrite III Plus and tell XyWrite III Plus to load a file called EXER-CISE.DOC by placing EXERCISE.DOC on the parameters line in the prompt shown in figure 11-25.

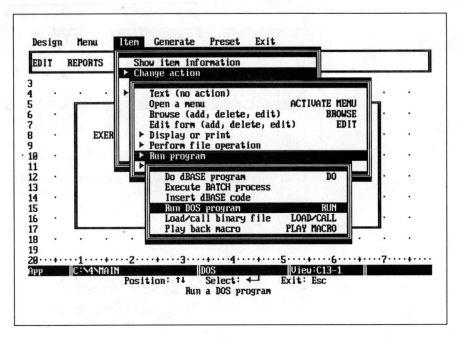

Figure 11-24 With the [Alt-I] C R R option, you can assign a DOS program to a menu item.

Quitting to DOS

The last option on the Main menu is *System*, which really is a QUIT back to DOS; it closes all open files and leaves the dBASE IV framework. Highlight *System* and press [Alt-I] C Q Q (figure 11-26) to tell the Applications Generator that the Main menu *System* option should be equated with QUITting to DOS. Press [Ctrl-End] to let the Applications Generator know you really want the Main menu *System* option to QUIT to DOS.

We need to design one other menu, a pop-up for the LPT TARGET on the System menu. The LPT TARGET could offer options that range from different printer ports to different computers on a network to a disk file. We will go the easy route by offering the user a selection of *LPT1*, *LPT2*, *LPT3*, *COM1*, *COM2*, and *FILE*. This is an example where we cannot get

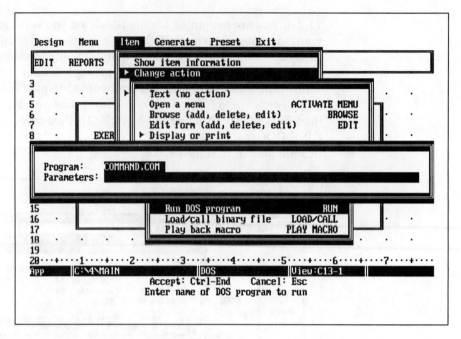

Figure 11-25 The Exercise system lets you exit to DOS for temporary
DOS-level work. This means you need to tell dBASE IV to RUN
COMMAND.COM, the DOS-level command processor.

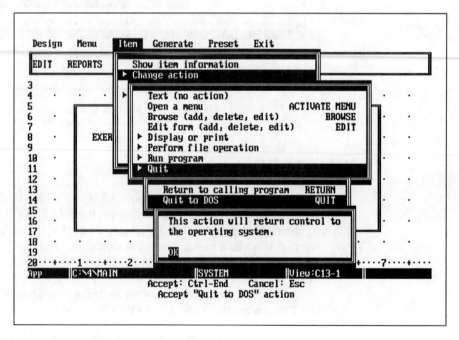

Figure 11-26 You must confirm that you want the Main menu System
option to QUIT to DOS before dBASE IV will accept your request.

away from repeated first letters on our menu options. Sorry about that. You will notice that this menu has no quit option—it is an example of "choose it or lose it" (figure 11-27).

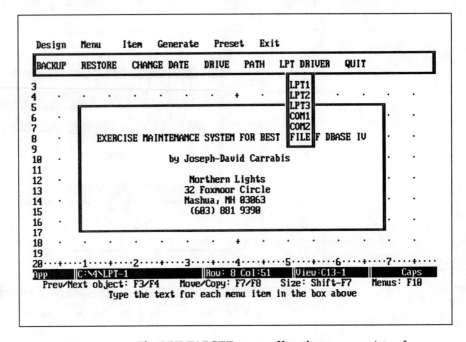

Figure 11-27 The LPT TARGET menu offers the user a variety of printer destinations.

Time for another controlled save of our work. Press [Alt-E] S, get back to either the dBASE prompt or the Assist system, and get a coffee. Our next task is to link the menus.

Linking Menus

So far we have not linked our menus. The last section showed only how to design objects, and the only objects we have designed through the Applications Generator are the menus themselves. The next thing to do is to tell dBASE IV which menus go with which options.

Get back to the Applications Generator and press [Alt-D] H. Select the Main menu and highlight the *Edit* option. Press [Alt-I] *C O* to specify that the Main menu's *Edit* option will open a menu. You are presented with a bar menu type and no menu name. The cursor is in the *Menu type* field, and pressing [Spacebar] toggles through *Bar, Pop-Up, Files, Structure, Values,* and back to *Bar.*

We want to link the Edit-1 pop-up menu to the Main menu *Edit* option,

so toggle to *Pop-Up* and press [Enter]. Because we have previously attached
a pop-up menu to *Edit* with the [Alt-M] *A* menu option, dBASE IV offers us
one (figure 11-28). Press [Ctrl-End] when you are done. Check your work by
typing *S* to open the *Show item information* option (figure 11-29).

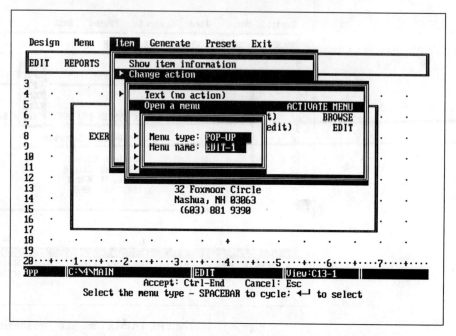

Figure 11-28 *You must attach actions to your menu options or the
Applications Generator won't do anything when your menu options
are selected by the user.*

Next, link the Report-1 pop-up menu to the *Reports* Main menu option. What are we going to do for the *Queries* option? That Main menu
option activated a file list, not a menu. Use the [Alt-I] *C O* command as
before. This time toggle to *Files* in the *Menu type* field. Press [Enter] and
type in *QBEFILES* in the *Menu name* field. The Util-1 pop-up should be
linked to the *Utilities* Main menu option.

We have already entered actions for the *DOS* and *System* Main menu
options, so we are done linking first-level menus to our Main menu option.
Save the links you have just made to the Main menu by pressing [Alt-M] *P S*.
This also clears the work surface for our next step, working with the first-
level menus.

Our first level one menu is Edit-1. We have already assigned an action
to the *Browse* option, but you can check that it is there by pressing [Alt-I] *S*,
as we did earlier. Press [Esc] to remove the Applications Generator's Items
menu and highlight the *Edit* option on the Edit-1 pop-up menu. Press [Alt-I]
C O.

This time we want to link a bar menu, named *Editor*, to the Edit-1

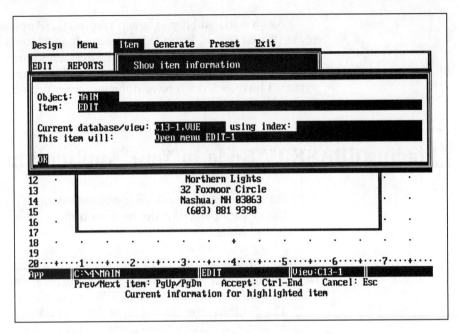

Figure 11-29 *You can check your option action handiwork by highlighting a menu option and pressing [Alt-I] S.*

menu's *Edit* option. Press [Ctrl-End] when you have entered the *Bar* and *Editor* options correctly, then [Esc] to get back to the Edit-1 pop-up. Highlight *Quit* and press [Alt-I] *C Q R* to tell the Applications Generator that this quit merely goes back to the previous menu (you can see this option in figure 11-26). The Applications Generator asks for confirmation. Press [Ctrl-End] [Left-Arrow] *P S* to confirm the Applications Generator's suspicions, move to the Menu menu and save the changes to the Edit-1 menu.

Press [Alt-D] *P* to get another list of pop-up menus and select the Report-1 pop-up. Highlight *Reports*. We need to tell the Applications Generator that this option links to the list of report forms we designed in the previous section. This is identical to linking the QBEFILES list to the Main menu's *Queries* options. Type [Alt-I] *C O*. Toggle to *Files* on the *Menu type* line, then enter *FRMFILES* on the *Menu name* line. Press [Ctrl-End] to accept your work.

The next step is the *Quit* option. You can tell the Applications Generator that this quit goes back to the Main menu, as we did with the Edit-1 *Quit* option. We will bypass the *File, Printer,* and *Screen* options for now; we will hard code those items later.

Link the Utilities menu's *System* option to Util-2B and the *Exercise* option to Util-A. The *Quit* option is handled as we did before. Don't forget to link the LPT driver menu to the *LPT Driver* option on the System menu.

Okay, enough of linking menus to each other. Press [Alt-E] S. Next we put as much code into our system as the Applications Generator menu options allow us.

As an aside and if you haven't exited the Applications Generator yet, press [Alt-G] *D Y B*. Provided you have loaded the MENU.GEN template (the dBASE IV default), the Applications Generator will begin writing the code for what we have done so far. If you have been developing the same system I have, what we have done so far comes out at a whopping 1,860 lines of code.

Placing dBASE IV Code in Your Application

This is the part of the book where some people get sweaty palms. Don't. Save the sweaty palms for the next section.

Just kidding.

This is where we start entering code, vital code, into our application. Fortunately, we let dBASE IV and the Applications Generator do most of this coding for us through the Applications Generator's menus. We start with the Exercise system's Utilities Exercise menu.

The Utilities Exercise menu had five options: *Pack, Reindex, Backup, Restore,* and *Quit.* Call up this menu by pressing [Alt-D] *H,* then select the Util-2A menu from the files listed. The cursor automatically appears on the *Index Data* option. Press [Alt-I] *C P R.* This command tells the Applications Generator to assign a REINDEX command to the current menu option, *Index Data* (figure 11-30). The Applications Generator asks for confirmation. Press [Ctrl-End]. Note that this option doesn't let users create new index keys; it only allows them to reindex existing index files or tags. Also note that we will need to make sure that the Applications Generator reindexes both databases, not just one or the other.

Press [Esc] to get the cursor back on the Exercise menu. Highlight *Pack Data* and press [Alt-I] *C P D.* This activates the *Pack* option. Confirm this selection by pressing [Ctrl-End].

The *Backup Data* option will be a little different. We don't know if the user has installed a backup program. We will use the dBASE IV COPY TO command and worry about checking for existing files later. Press [Alt-I] *C P C.* You are presented with a screen requesting lots of information about your target file (figure 11-31).

Enter the name of the target file in the *Copy records TO file/array* field. You can toggle between file types by placing the cursor in the *Of TYPE* field and pressing [Spacebar].

The *Restore Data* option isn't quite so easy to work with, however. The *Restore Data* option needs to CLOSE ALL the databases, get the backed-up databases and name them so that they will be recognized by the system, then SET the VIEW TO C13-1 again. This requires some real coding, as in we have to type it ourselves. The last thing we can do on the Util-2A menu is assign to the *Quit* option the capability to go back to the Util-1 menu. We must stop working on the Exercise menu at this point.

Are there any other menus we can work with at present? We can

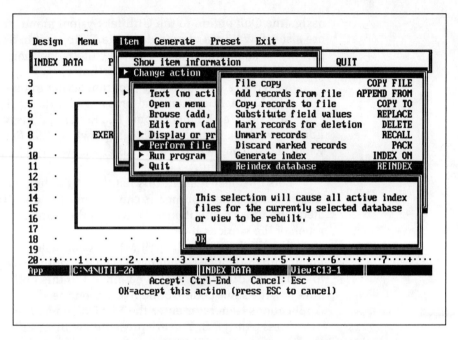

Figure 11-30 Many dBASE IV commands can be assigned to menu
items directly through the Applications Generator menu system.

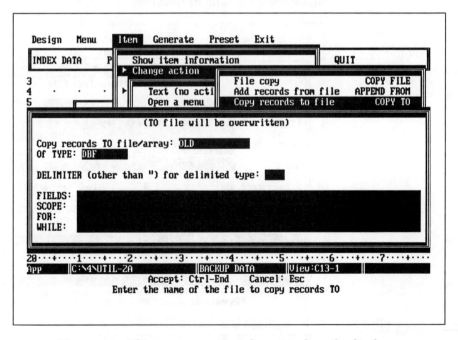

Figure 11-31 This screen requests information from the developer
regarding target file specifications for the Exercise menu's
Backup Data option.

assign the *Quit* option to the Utilities System menu, called Util-2B. There are also a few things we can do to the Editor menu. Save Util-2A with the [Alt-M] *P S* command and call up the Util-2B command by pressing [Alt-D] *H*, highlighting *Util-2B*, and pressing [Enter].

Assign a return to calling program action to the System menu's *Quit* option by highlighting *Quit* and pressing [Alt-I] *C Q R* [Ctrl-End].

Now onto the *Editor* options. The *Editor* options we can work with are *Edit* (somewhat), *Back*, *Skip*, *Goto* (somewhat), *Kill*, *Reca*, *Quit*, *Find* (somewhat), *Loca* (somewhat), *Next*, *Add* (somewhat), *Copy* (somewhat), *Disp* (somewhat), and *Quit*.

Lots of *somewhat's* in this list. What do they mean? They mean the Applications Generator menus can do some but not all of the work associated with those menu items. We will let the Applications Generator do as much of the work as it can.

Save Util-2B with the [Alt-M] *P S* command, then call up the Editor menu with the [Alt-D] *H* command. The *Edit* option is highlighted. We want to assign the dBASE IV EDIT command to this option, although we will have to write some code around it to suit our needs. We can at least have the Applications Generator enter the EDIT command for us.

Press [Alt-I] *P E*. You are presented with an Edit information screen, shown in figure 11-32. We are not using a format file; we want Edit mode (you can toggle from Edit to Append); we want to be able to edit the REST of the database, if necessary, from the first edited record; and we will not allow record adding or deleting.

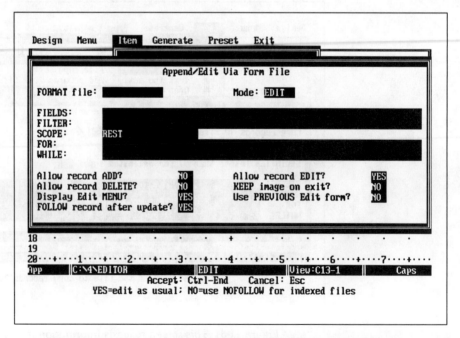

Figure 11-32 *This is the [Alt-I] P E information screen. We want to let the user edit records, but not go wild with that power.*

The *Skip* option is easy. Highlight *Skip* and press [Alt-I] *C R I*. Type *SKIP*, press [Enter], type *DO EXERGET* and press [Ctrl-End] on the text editing screen. You're done. *Back* is similar, but type *SKIP -1* instead of *SKIP* on the text editing screen.

The *Goto* option is handled by a unique Applications Generator menu generator. Highlight *Goto* and press [Alt-I] *P*. You will see a screen such as that shown in figure 11-33. Although there is a *Goto* option, we want the Applications Generator to *Display a POSITIONING MENU at RUN TIME*. Toggle to *Yes* for that option and press [Ctrl-End].

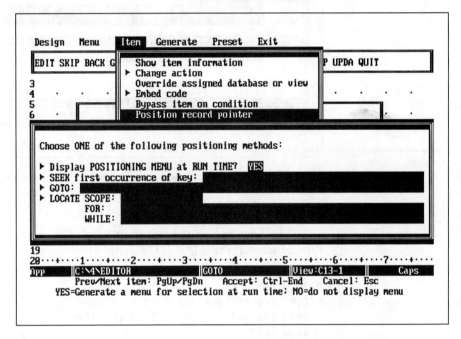

Figure 11-33 *The Applications Generator offers an excellent option for coding the* Goto *option for us.*

The *Kill* and *Reca* options are both handled through [Alt-I] *C P*. *Kill* is option *M*; *Reca* is option *U*. Neither of these options requires any additional information in the *Scope, For,* or *While* fields (figure 11-34).

The *Find* option is entered with [Alt-I] *C R I*. Type the following code on the screen:

```
FINDTHIS = "  /  /  "
@ 22,0 CLEA
@ 22,0 SAY [WHAT DATE DO YOU WANT TO FIND? -> ] GET
FINDTHIS
READ
SEEK {FINDTHIS}
@ 22,0 CLEA
DO EXERGET
```

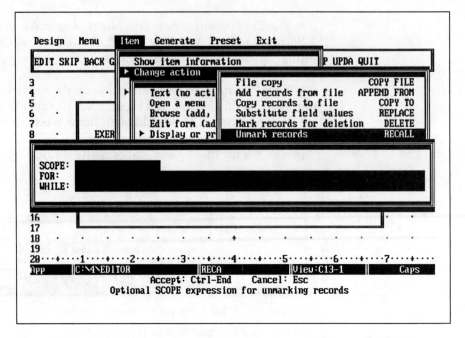

Figure 11-34 *This menu is displayed when you want to use the [Alt-I]
C P M (Delete) or U (Recall) options.*

The *Loca* option is entered in much the same way and on the same
type of screen. Press [Alt-I] *C R I* and enter

```
@ 22,0 CLEA
ACCEPT [LOCATE WHAT -> ] TO LOCATEWHAT
ACCEPT [IN WHAT FIELD -> ] TO LOCATEWHERE
@ 22,0 CLEA
LOCA FOR &LOCATEWHAT = &LOCATEWHERE
```

The *Next* option is entered with the same commands. The actual command you want is CONTINUE. The *Add* option is done with [Alt-I] *C E*.
This calls up the menu shown in figure 11-32. We want Append mode; we
want adding and editing of records; we want the Edit menu on the screen;
and we want records to be followed after they are entered in the database.
Note that we are providing the basic code structure; we are not developing
a beautiful finished product. That comes later as you get more comfortable
editing code.

The *Copy* option is handled with [Alt-I] *C P C*. The Applications Generator returns the screen shown in figure 11-31. The target file is TANK, of
TYPE DBF, and the SCOPE is NEXT 1. Now press [Alt-I] *E A* and enter
APPEND FROM TANK. This tells dBASE IV to take the record you just
copied to the temporary file and add it to the working file. You might also
want to include code to erase the TANK.DBF file.

The *Disp* option is handled with [Alt-I] *C D D*. This opens the menu shown in figure 11-35. Fill in the blanks as you see them in that figure. This is another option that requires some coding later on if you want to finesse things.

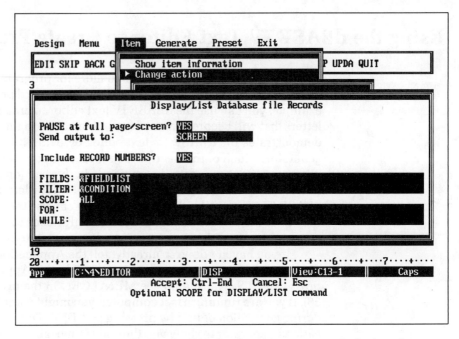

Figure 11-35 The Display/List database menu creates the basic code needed for the Editor Disp option.

The last option to concern ourselves with is *Upda*. This is the RE-PLACE command in disguise. The REPLACE command can be thought of as a *Loca* that does something. This is also my way of telling you that you can use the *Loca* code presented previously, with a few modifications. Press [Alt-I] *C R I* and enter

```
@ 22,0 CLEA
ACCEPT [REPLACE WHAT FIELD -> ] TO REPLACEWHAT
ACCEPT [WITH WHAT -> ] TO REPLACEWITH
@ 22,0 CLEA
REPL ALL &REPLACEWHAT WITH &REPLACEWITH
```

The *Quit* option is handled just like before.

We are finished with this part of the project. Next, we have the untidy task of entering code that the Applications Generator couldn't easily handle. (We could have used the [Alt-I] *E A* and [Alt-I] *E B* commands to open the text editor and enter the necessary code, but that wouldn't have given us the chance to explore the dBASE IV text editor itself.) Save your work with the [Alt-E] *S* command.

The modifications we made in this section now bring the code created by the Applications Generator to 2035 lines. Not much of a jump in code size, which is proof that the front end of a system is usually far larger in code than what runs in the background.

Using the dBASE IV Text Editor to Create Programs

The dBASE IV text editor is designed more for programming than for letter writing, although you can use it for elementary word processing needs. For example, you can use the dBASE IV text editor to create, format, and print letters that will become parts of reports or stand on their own. This section demonstrates the dBASE IV text editor by using it to develop a mail list generator. Much of this section also discusses some theories of dBASE IV programming. Note that all commands in this section are dBASE IV four-letter abbreviations. (Appendix C lists the four-letter abbreviations for dBASE IV commands and functions.) You can use these abbreviations as if they were the full command; dBASE IV only needs the first four letters of a command or function to recognize what you are telling it.

If you haven't done so already, tell the Applications Generator to create the code from our objects. From inside the Applications Generator, press [Alt-G] S. You should see MENU.GEN in the prompt box (figure 11-36). If you are running a fast computer, you might want to select the *Display during generation* option by pressing [Alt-D] Y. This option tells the Applications Generator to show you the code as it begins generating it. I strongly suggest you don't ask to see the code as it is being generated because sending this information to the screen slows down the generation of the code incredibly. Finally, press B to begin creating the code.

We will start with a simple task, adding *Restore Data* to the Utilities Exercise menu. Getting the necessary code into the correct place, however, takes some work. The Applications Generator takes our objects and writes two huge PRG files, EXERCISE and MAIN. We need to find what we are looking for in these two files.

Start the dBASE IV word processor through the Assist system or with the MODIFY COMMAND dBASE prompt command. The latter command should be entered as

```
MODIFY COMMAND EXERCISE
```

You can edit EXERCISE.PRG through the Assist system in one of two ways, depending on whether or not the Assist system knows EXERCISE.PRG exists. If it doesn't, highlight ⟨create⟩ under Applications, then select the dBASE program. The program drops into the dBASE IV text editor. Press [Alt-W] W R, enter *EXERCISE.PRG* and press [Enter] to load in the EXERCISE.PRG file created by the Applications Generator. This might take a moment because we are working with a huge file. The first thing you

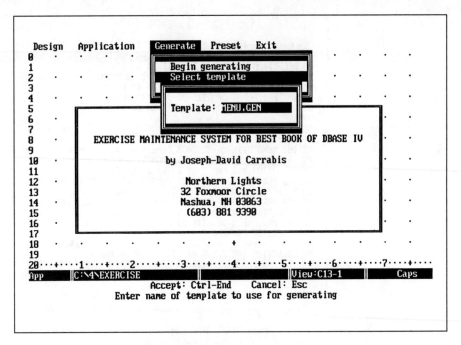

Figure 11-36 You must specify which template you want to use when
you tell the Applications Generator to create your PRG files.

will notice is that the dBASE IV text editor drops to the bottom of the file,
and the file doesn't say EXERCISE.PRG. The cursor is on *— EOP:
1HELP1. You will also see that the status bar at the bottom of the screen
still thinks you are working with a ⟨NEW⟩ file.

The first thing you might want to do is press [Alt-L] S and enter *EXER-
CISE.PRG* when prompted. The status bar now lists the file name as EXER-
CISE. Press [Alt-G] *B* and enter *RESTORE DATA* at the prompt. You are
asking the text editor to perform a backward search (you are at the end of
the file, so you need to search from the end to the beginning) for the *Restore
Data* menu item. The text editor stops at line 693, column 37 (figure 11-37).

If the Assist system does know EXERCISE.PRG exists, or if you are
working with the MODIFY COMMAND dBASE prompt command, simply
highlight that file name under Applications, press [Enter], then press M for
Modify. You will be at the top of the file. Press [Alt-G] *F* to perform a forward search, and enter *RESTORE DATA* at the prompt. The program stops
at line 693, as before.

Good. Now to work. Roll up your sleeves and get the coffee brewing,
strong and hot.

We used *Restore Data* as a marker to find what we really need to
know, which is what dBASE IV will do when we want to restore data. Right
now we have no idea what the Applications Generator told dBASE IV to do
when we asked for *Restore Data*. Look at line 694 and you will see that
dBASE IV will jump to something called ACT08.

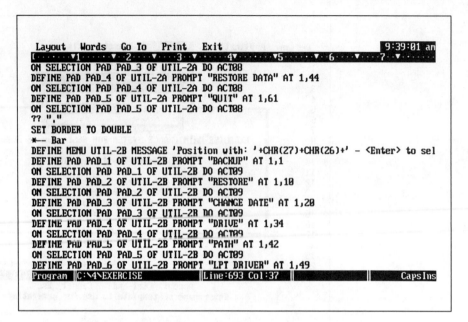

```
 Layout   Words   Go To   Print   Exit                        9:39:01 am
[······▼1·····▼·2·····▼····3·▼····4▼····▼5····▼·6···▼···7·▼···
ON SELECTION PAD PAD_3 OF UTIL-2A DO ACT08
DEFINE PAD PAD_4 OF UTIL-2A PROMPT "RESTORE DATA" AT 1,44
ON SELECTION PAD PAD_4 OF UTIL-2A DO ACT08
DEFINE PAD PAD_5 OF UTIL-2A PROMPT "QUIT" AT 1,61
ON SELECTION PAD PAD_5 OF UTIL-2A DO ACT08
?? ","
SET BORDER TO DOUBLE
*-- Bar
DEFINE MENU UTIL-2B MESSAGE 'Position with: '+CHR(27)+CHR(26)+' - <Enter> to sel
DEFINE PAD PAD_1 OF UTIL-2B PROMPT "BACKUP" AT 1,1
ON SELECTION PAD PAD_1 OF UTIL-2B DO ACT09
DEFINE PAD PAD_2 OF UTIL-2B PROMPT "RESTORE" AT 1,10
ON SELECTION PAD PAD_2 OF UTIL-2B DO ACT09
DEFINE PAD PAD_3 OF UTIL-2B PROMPT "CHANGE DATE" AT 1,20
ON SELECTION PAD PAD_3 OF UTIL-2B DO ACT09
DEFINE PAD PAD_4 OF UTIL-2B PROMPT "DRIVE" AT 1,34
ON SELECTION PAD PAD_4 OF UTIL-2B DO ACT09
DEFINE PAD PAD_5 OF UTIL-2B PROMPT "PATH" AT 1,42
ON SELECTION PAD PAD_5 OF UTIL-2B DO ACT09
DEFINE PAD PAD_6 OF UTIL-2B PROMPT "LPT DRIVER" AT 1,49
Program ║C:\4\EXERCISE          ║Line:693 Col:37 ║         ║   CapsIns
```

Figure 11-37 You can use the [Alt-G] B menu option to perform a backward search of the file for Restore Data.

Onto ACT08. Move the cursor to line 697. This places the cursor after the point where ACT08 is part of any immediate command lines. Now press [Alt-G] *F* and enter *ACT08* at the prompt. The text editor drops to line 688, column 38. This indicates that ACT08 isn't defined as a PROCEDURE in EXERCISE.PRG.

We have to look in MAIN.PRG. Because we didn't change EXER-CISE.PRG, press [Alt-E] *A* to exit and get MAIN.PRG on the screen. Press [Alt-G] *F* and search for ACT08. You will find it on line 912. Move the cursor down to line 978, where PAD_3 (the *Backup* option) is defined. *Restore Data* was PAD_4. We will copy the PAD_3 commands and edit them to work for PAD_4.

Place the cursor on the margin in line 978, press [F6], and move the cursor to the end of line 996, which is the end of the PAD_3 commands. Press [Enter] to tell dBASE IV you have finished marking off the text. Place the cursor at the beginning of the next line and press [F8] to copy the blocked text. Press [Esc] to release the blocked text.

Edit PAD_3 to *PAD_4*. The lc_say variable should be edited to read *Restoring records from OLD*. The descriptive note can be changed if you want. The line COPY TO OLD should be changed, but in an unapparent way. Remember that we are working with two databases, not one. Replace COPY TO OLD with the following code:

```
CLOSE DATA
RENA EXERCISE.DBF TO EXTANK.DBF
RENA EXOLD.DBF TO EXERCISE.DBF
```

```
RENA EXTANK.DBF TO EXOLD.DBF
USE EXERCISE ORDE DATE
REIN
USE
RENA EXCOMMENT.DBF TO COMMTANK.DBF
RENA EXCOMMENT.DBT TO COMMTANK.DBT
RENA COMMOLD.DBF TO EXCOMMENT.DBF
RENA COMMOLD.DBT TO EXCOMMENT.DBT
RENA COMMTANK.DBF TO COMMOLD.DBF
RENA COMMTANK.DBF TO COMMOLD.DBT
USE EXCOMMENT ORDE DATE
REIN
SET VIEW TO C13-1
```

This is also an indication that we need to make some changes to the *Backup* option on PAD_3. Move up to line 990, which contains PAD_3's COPY TO OLD command. Rewrite that command as follows:

```
COPY TO EXOLD
SELE 2
COPY TO COMMOLD
SELE 1
```

So much for the little bit of editing necessary for the Exercise menu; now we need to change the Util-2B System menu. A quick look at the EXERCISE.PRG file tells us that all Util-2B options activate ACT09, which now starts on line 1141 of MAIN.PRG. Line 1141 isn't where it started before, but remember that we edited MAIN.PRG and added lines.

The first item to add to ACT09 is the *Backup* file selection. In the previous paragraphs, we told dBASE IV what to do when we wanted files backed up. The following few paragraphs deal with adding an external backup utility to your dBASE IV system. You can decide where to place these items on the screen; the following code is just an example.

```
CASE "PAD_1" = PAD()
a 20,0 SAY [ENTER THE NAME OF THE BACKUP PROGRAM BELOW] +;
    [(drive:\path{\path\}filename)]
a 22,0 SAY [CURRENT BACKUP PROGRAM ] + BACKPROG
a 23,0
ACCE TO BACKPROG
a 20,0 CLEA
```

We also need to add code for installing RESTORE software. That code follows.

```
CASE "PAD_2" = PAD()
a 20,0 SAY [ENTER THE NAME OF THE RESTORE PROGRAM BELOW] +;
    [(drive:\path{\path\}filename)]
```

```
@ 22,0 SAY [CURRENT RESTORE PROGRAM ] + RESTPROG
@ 23,0
ACCE TO RESTPROG
@ 20,0 CLEA
```

We also need to add code to change the data format and set default drives and paths. The drive and path code follows.

```
CASE "PAD_4" = PAD()
     @ 21,0 SAY "Current default drive is " + CDRIVE
     @ 22,0 SAY "New default drive is -> " ;
          GET CDRIVE PICT "A"
     READ
     SET DEFA TO &CDRIVE
     @ 21,0 CLEA
CASE "PAD_5" = PAD()
     @ 21,0 SAY "Current default path is " + CPATH
     CPATH = CPATH + SPACE(30)
     @ 22,0 SAY "New default path is -> " GET CPATH
     READ
     CPATH = TRIM(CPATH)
     SET PATH TO &CPATH
     @ 21,0 CLEA
```

What about changing the date format? You can do that through another menu, one which lists all the dBASE IV SET DATE TO options, or you can offer the user a toggle of one date to another. A menu to change the date is created like any other menu. The code behind each menu selection parallels the following code, which is for a simple date format toggle:

```
IF SETDATE = 1
     SETDATE = 2
     SET DATE BRIT
ELSE
     SETDATE = 1
     SET DATE AMER
ENDIF
```

This code uses the IF...ELSE...ENDIF command block to toggle between MM/DD/YY format and DD/MM/YY format. You can extend this to several date formats with a DO CASE...CASE...OTHERWISE...ENDCASE block, much like what follows.

```
DO CASE
     CASE datepad_1 = PAD()
          SET DATE AMER
     CASE datepad_2 = PAD()
          SET DATE BRIT
```

```
    .
    .
    .
ENDCASE
```

Note that in this code, we assume that a menu is passing information to the ACT09 PROCEDURE in the form of datepad_n data.

The preceding DO CASE...CASE...OTHERWISE...ENDCASE block is also how we select a printer target device. We want to let the user decide which DOS device to send the file to. Each CASE option should include the appropriate SET PRINT TO device command and nothing more. Interested readers can open the EXERCISE.PRG file and perform a forward search for PrintSet. Much of the code you need is there and can be edited easily to suit your particular computer environment.

So what are SETDATE, CDRIVE, CPATH, and other variable names that keep appearing? They are where your code stores information it needs at startup to set up the dBASE IV system the way you or the user wants. Thus, these variables have to be stored where dBASE IV can get them when it starts working. We will store them in a memory variable file, EXERCISE.MEM. When will we do this? When we finish working with the Exercise system. When will we read from this file? When we start the Exercise system.

We need to place RESTORE FROM EXERCISE in EXERCISE, probably at line 30. This means you can remove lines 31 to 63 by blocking them off with the [F6] key and pressing [Enter] [Del] Y. The variables are saved to a memory file by placing SAVE TO EXERCISE after line 133. This means you can block delete lines 111 to 122, unless you want dBASE IV to recreate its environment prior to starting your application.

The next easiest thing to do is to check what dBASE IV does when the user selects a query file. This is handled by ACT04. Find ACT04 with the [Alt-G] F command. One of the commands in PROCEDURE ACT04 is listval=PROMPT( ). This command determines which QBE file the user selected. We need to enter the following command after listval=PROMPT( ):

```
SET QUERY TO &LISTVAL
```

All is easy so far. The preceding methodology works for selecting a report file. Report files are handled by ACT03. We need to add

```
listval= ' '
```

immediately before the DO CASE command because we need that variable passed back to us from the actual report menu, handled by ACT07. Next, we add code to ACT03 as follows:

```
CASE BAR() = 3
    REPORT FORM &LISTVAL TO FILE REPORT
```

```
CASE BAR() = 4
     REPORT FORM &LISTVAL TO PRINT
CASE BAR() = 5
     REPORT FORM &LISTVAL
```

Summary

And there you have it. The code developed in this chapter should work on your computer, but I hasten to warn you about dBASE IV's constant and unnerving memory problems. The code will work, but you will probably have to remove any TSRs in memory. Even so, you might encounter one of dBASE IV's internal errors. If this occurs, don't worry. You won't lose any information, although you might have to get back out to DOS and start your application again.

Be that as it may, you have tasted everything the dBASE IV system has to offer nondeveloper users, even though I spoke of you as developers in this last chapter. There are differences between the Developer's edition and the regular edition of dBASE IV, but nothing necessary to new and intermediate users of the product.

You are now capable of working with the full dBASE IV system. This book hasn't covered certain aspects of dBASE IV that are available only in the Developer's edition; doing so would confuse more than clarify things. What you need to remember is that the dBASE IV product is a worthy tool for beginning database management explorations.

Appendices

Appendices

A Simple Mail List Generator

Before writing code for this appendix, we have to decide exactly what kind of mail system we want. Do we want to develop a simple file card type of system or do we want something that can be used for bulk mailing applications? Well, a bulk mailing system is a superset of the file card system, so let's start small and work our way up.

We have decided on a system, now what? Next we think about what we want our system to do. Well, a file card system can be used for a lot more than just generating mailing lists. (For example, you can use a file card system to get phone numbers.) We want the ability to quickly find records. We also want to edit the records and generate labels. We should include utilities for users with different computers than the one we design the system on. We also want an easy method for getting rid of records that are no longer valid. Anything else? It would be nice if we could quit back to DOS. Somewhere along the way we might want to add a feature to copy address information to a text file for use in individual letters.

What we have just laid out is our main menu. The next thing to do is map it on the Applications Generator. The important thing to remember about program development is to use all the tools you are given. You don't need the complete Applications Generator package to develop the mail list manager from a programming point of view, but you can use parts of it to make life easier. Generating menus is an example of using the Applications Generator to save lots of time. If you use the Applications Generator to create the front end of the program (what the user actually sees and uses), you are freed up to work on the back end of the program, where the real work of the program takes place.

The following dBASE III Plus code—which will also work in dBASE IV—can be used to generate mail lists. It is modifiable and will work with any database or label form, provided the necessary fields are located in both database and label form.

Listing A-1

```
** MAIL.PRG
*
USE database INDE ndx file list or mdx file
TARGET = [SCREEN]
CONDITION = SPACE(65)
ANSWER = 'X'
*
DO WHIL .T.
    CLEA
    @ 1,0 TO 15,79 DOUB
    @ 3,1 TO 3,78 DOUB
    @ 2,25 SAY [L A B E L   G E N E R A T O R]
    @ 2,60 SAY IIF(CONDITION # SPACE(65),;
        [CONDITION EXITS], SPACE(16))
      @ 6,32 SAY [CREATE CONDITION]
    @ 7,32 SAY [SET LABEL TARGET (&TARGET)]
    @ 8,32 SAY [PRINT LABELS]
    @ 11,32 SAY [QUIT]
    SET CONS OFF
    @ 20,0 GET ANSWER
*
    DO CASE
        CASE ANSWER = [Q]
            RETU
        CASE ANSWER = [C]
*
            IF CONDITION # SPACE(65)
                SET FILT TO
                CONDITION = SPACE(65)
            ELSE
            CLEA
            DO SAYER
            DO GETTER
            CLEA GETS
            @ 23,0 SAY [CONDITION  ] GET CONDITION
            READ
*
            IF LEN(TRIM(CONDITION)) = 0
                CONDITION = SPACE(65)
                SET FILT TO
            ELSE
                SET FILT TO &CONDITION
            ENDI
*
        ENDI
*
        LOOP
    CASE ANSWER = 2
        @ 20,0 SAY [SEND LABELS TO P(rinter), F(ile), ] +;
```

```
                              [or S(creen) (P/F/S) ->] GET TARGET PICT "!"
                 READ
    *
                 DO CASE
                     CASE TARGET = [F]
    *
                             IF CONDITION = SPAC(65)
                                  TARGET = [ADDRESSES]
                             ELSE
                                  TARGET = RIGHT(TRIM(CONDITION),;
                                      LEN(TRIM(CONDITION)) -;
                                      RAT([ ], TRIM(CONDITION)))
                             ENDI
    *
                     CASE TARGET = [P]
                             TARGET = [PRINT]
                     OTHE
                             TARGET = [SCREEN]
                 ENDC
    *
             CASE ANSWER = 3
                 TRUTH = .T.
    *
                 IF TARGET = [PRINT]
                     @ 24,0 SAY [DO YOU WANT TO START WITH ] +;
                         [SAMPLES? (Y/N)  ] GET TRUTH
                     READ
                     CLEA
                     SET COLO TO W*+
                 ELSE
                     TRUTH = .F.
                 ENDI
    *
                 @ 20,0 CLEA
                 @ 20,0 SAY [PRINTING LABELS. DO NOT DISTURB.]
                 SET COLO TO
    *
                 DO CASE
                     CASE TRUTH
                             SET CONS OFF
                             LABEL FORM ADDRESS SAMP TO PRINT
                     CASE TRUTH .AND. TARGET = [PRINT]
                             SET CONS OFF
                             LABE FORM ADDRESS TO PRINT
                     CASE TARGET = [SCREEN]
                             CLEA
                             LABE FORM ADDRESS
                     OTHE
                             SET CONS OFF
                             LABE FORM ADDRESS TO FILE &TARGET
                 ENDC
```

Listing A-1 (cont.)

```
*
                ERRMESS = []
                DO ATTENTION
                SET CONS ON
      ENDC
*
ENDD
*
** EOF: LABELS.PRG
```

Listing A-1 uses three subroutines. The first is SAYER. The SAYER file is nothing more than a collection of the @ SAY commands from the format file designed for your database. An example of a SAYER file is the EXERSAY PROCEDURE in EXPROC.PRG. Similar logic holds for the GETTER file. The last subroutine is ATTENTION. The purpose of ATTENTION is to alert the user to something. The ATTENTION file follows:

```
** ATTENTION.PRG
*
@ 0,0 SAY ERRMESS
SET BELL TO 100,1
SET CONS OFF
? CHR(7)
SET BELL TO 900,2
? CHR(7)
SET CONS ON
@ 0,0 SAY SPAC(80)
*
** EOP: ATTENTION.PRG
```

The dBASE IV version of MAIL.PRG would look similar to the dBASE II Plus version. We can create the menu as a bar menu using the Applications Generator, which produces some 750 lines of code just for the menu. Then we can weed through what dBASE IV produces to find what we need.

What we need is

```
DEFINE MENU MAIN MESSAGE "SELECT AN OPTION FROM THOSE LISTED
ABOVE"
DEFINE PAD PAD_1 OF MAILMAIN PROMPT "CREATE CONDITION" AT 1,1
ON SELECTION PAD PAD_1 OF MAILMAIN DO ACT01
DEFINE PAD PAD_2 OF MAILMAIN PROMPT "SET LABEL TARGET" AT 1,22
ON SELECTION PAD PAD_2 OF MAILMAIN DO ACT01
DEFINE PAD PAD_3 OF MAILMAIN PROMPT "PRINT LABELS" AT 1,43
ON SELECTION PAD PAD_3 OF MAILMAIN DO ACT01
DEFINE PAD PAD_4 OF MAILMAIN PROMPT "QUIT" AT 1,60
ON SELECTION PAD PAD_4 OF MAILMAIN DO ACT01
```

Instead of DO ACT01 at the end of four of these lines, we can enter ANSWER = n, where *n* is the number of the selection. Thus the preceding becomes

```
DEFINE MENU MAIN MESSAGE "SELECT AN OPTION FROM THOSE LISTED
ABOVE"
DEFINE PAD PAD_1 OF MAILMAIN PROMPT "CREATE CONDITION" AT 1,1
ON SELECTION PAD PAD_1 OF MAILMAIN ANSWER = 1
DEFINE PAD PAD_2 OF MAILMAIN PROMPT "SET LABEL TARGET" AT 1,22
ON SELECTION PAD PAD_2 OF MAILMAIN ANSWER = 2
DEFINE PAD PAD_3 OF MAILMAIN PROMPT "PRINT LABELS" AT 1,43
ON SELECTION PAD PAD_3 OF MAILMAIN ANSWER = 3
DEFINE PAD PAD_4 OF MAILMAIN PROMPT "QUIT" AT 1,60
ON SELECTION PAD PAD_4 OF MAILMAIN ANSWER = 4
```

This block of code is entered above our MAIL.PRG's main DO WHILE...ENDDO loop. The menu itself is called with ACTIVATE MENU MAIN. This command takes the place of our original menu definition in the III Plus code. The separate CASEs in the DO CASE...CASE...ENDCASE block are rewritten only so that each option corresponds to the numeric ANSWER value and not the character ANSWER value originally used in the III Plus code.

Using SQL

We will start exploring SQL database applications by using SQL interactively. Suppose that you are an occasional user of your corporation's databases. How would you go about using SQL to solve a problem? The example we will use is finding all unpaid invoices for a specific customer so that you can do further analysis (such as the total amount owed, the amount each customer owes, and the average amount owed).

There is more than one way to approach the problem. In this example we would expect to find two tables, CUSTOMER and ORDERS, with the structure shown in figure B-1.

The key stages in solving this kind of problem using highly interactive tools are as follows:

1. Learn the organization of the data.

2. Work out the correct data selection criteria.

3. Manipulate the output from the data selection to get the required format.

First, you need to establish which database to look in. Second, consider the structure of the database. Specifically, you must know the names of the tables and the relationships between them. Finally, you need to know the names of the required fields.

At the heart of SQL is the SELECT statement. The SELECT statement, as its name suggests, specifies what data will be selected for output. After you work out the correct SELECT statement, you can put it directly into a report or 3GL/4GL program.

The syntax for the basic SELECT statement is very simple:

```
SELECT field(s)
FROM table(s)
```

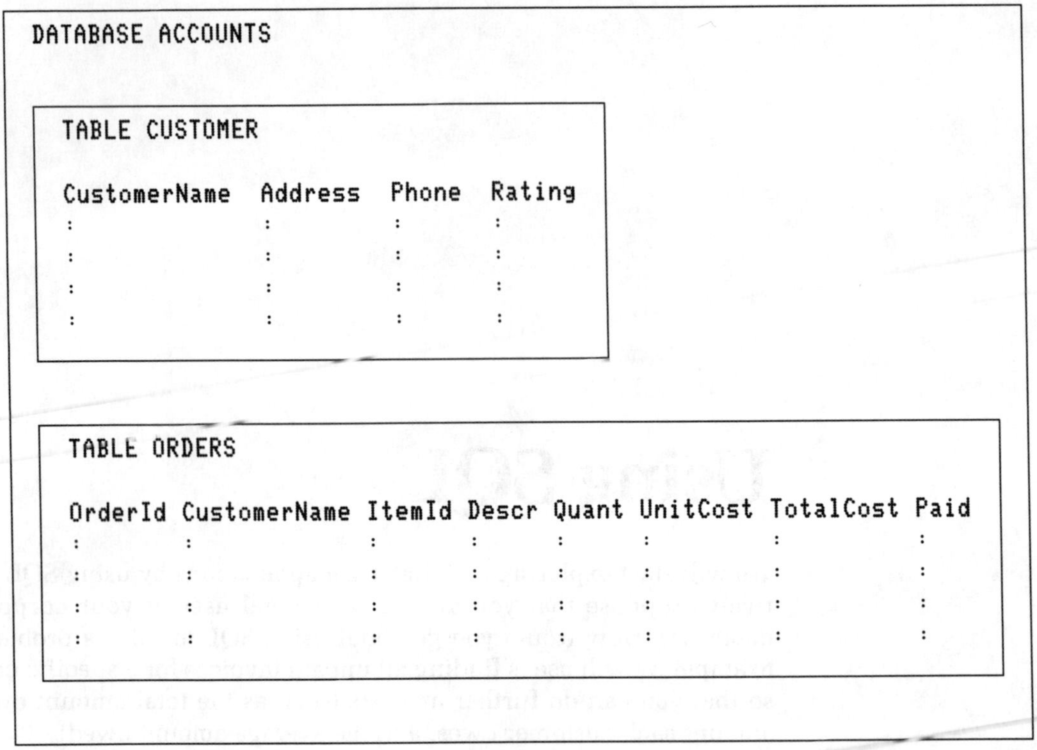

```
┌─────────────────────────────────────────────────────────────────────┐
│  DATABASE ACCOUNTS                                                     │
│                                                                       │
│  ┌──────────────────────────────────────────────┐                     │
│  │ TABLE CUSTOMER                                 │                     │
│  │                                                │                     │
│  │ CustomerName  Address   Phone    Rating        │                     │
│  │     :            :        :         :          │                     │
│  │     :            :        :         :          │                     │
│  │     :            :        :         :          │                     │
│  │     :            :        :         :          │                     │
│  └──────────────────────────────────────────────┘                     │
│                                                                       │
│  ┌─────────────────────────────────────────────────────────────────┐ │
│  │ TABLE ORDERS                                                      │ │
│  │                                                                   │ │
│  │ OrderId CustomerName ItemId Descr Quant UnitCost TotalCost Paid   │ │
│  │    :        :          :      :     :      :         :       :    │ │
│  │    :        :          :      :     :      :         :       :    │ │
│  │    :        :          :      :     :      :         :       :    │ │
│  │    :        :          :      :     :      :         :       :    │ │
│  └─────────────────────────────────────────────────────────────────┘ │
└─────────────────────────────────────────────────────────────────────┘
```

Figure B-1.

```
<WHERE condition(s)>
<ORDER BY sort_order>
```

Each clause starts on a new line for easier reading; you can put the whole statement on a single line, if you want. You can either identify the fields you want to see, or use * as a wildcard to view all the fields in the given table. The WHERE clause is optional; if WHERE is not used, you will see all data in the table.

An example of the simplest SELECT is

```
SELECT *
FROM CUSTOMERS
```

This results in the following output:

```
CustomerName        Address         Phone        Rating
SPB                 Nashua          603-555-1234    AA
BTS                 Manchester      603-555-4321    AAA
```

You use the WHERE clause to restrict the set of data you want to look at. For example, you would enter the following to find all customers with a high credit rating:

```
SELECT CustomerName, Phone
FROM CUSTOMER
WHERE Rating = 'AAA'
```

This results in the following output:

```
CustomerName        Phone
BTS                 603-555-4321
```

Another example, close to what we need, is to find all customers with unpaid orders:

```
SELECT CustomerName, OrderId, TotalCost, Paid
FROM CUSTOMER, ORDERS
WHERE CUSTOMER.CustomerName = ORDERS.CustomerName AND
TotalCost > Paid
ORDER BY TotalCost DESC
```

This produces the following output:

CustomerName	OrderId	TotalCost	Paid
SPB	04587	4801.03	3454.00
BTS	47688	3487.00	3240.00
BTS	33241	2492.33	2467.33
SPB	01138	2488.21	2106.76

In this case, the CUSTOMER and ORDERS tables are joined by the CustomerName field. Customer name is the common information, or column, that relates the two tables. Make sure that the tables are joined by the correct fields. Generally, fields from different tables have similar names and the relationship will be self-evident.

The other point to note is the use of the ORDER BY clause. There is no "natural order" for data stored in an SQL database; data is returned in random order unless you use the ORDER BY clause. The DESC keyword requests output to be in descending order: in this case, you get the largest unpaid orders first.

The previous description of ORDER BY is intended to help you identify the correct selection criteria, as if you were using an indexed dBASE file. Look closely at which records are output, to ensure that the right set of data is reported. Very simple queries like the ones shown here are not likely to be wrong, but more complex WHERE clauses can have unexpected results.

After you have mastered using interactive SQL tools, you need to look at how you can save frequently used queries and elaborate upon them to get the desired output format. Interactive SQL generally has some facility for storing those queries—but there are often severe limitations on the queries you can create, such as limits on the use of parameters and the format of the output.

The rest of this section describes one of the different approaches you can use to create your own set of reports. Which option you choose will depend upon which tools you have available, your level of skill, the time available to make these programs, and the required performance.

The best tool to begin with is a report writer because it requires the least time and skill to learn. The report writer demonstrates the power of SQL to generate complex reports in very few lines of code. The key components of a report are a SELECT statement, defining the required data to be reported on, and the output format definition.

The general format of the generated report program is shown in figure B-2. The DATABASE...END statement tells SQL in which database application the tables for the report can be found. The SELECT...END statement tells SQL which fields in all rows of which tables will be used in the report. The FORMAT...END section tells SQL which fields from which rows of the table (EVERY ROW, in this case) will be listed in the output.

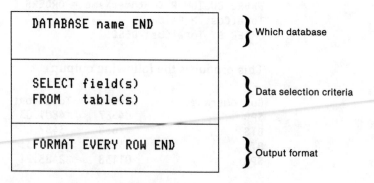

Figure B-2.

A sample report that produces the desired results and demonstrates all the key components of a typical report writer is

```
DATABASE
    ACCOUNTS
END

SELECT      *
    FROM    CUSTOMER, ORDERS
    WHERE   CUSTOMER.CustomerName = ORDERS.CustomerName
        AND TotalCost > Paid
    ORDER BY CustomerName
END

FORMAT
    PAGE HEADER "Overdue Accounts for Fiscal September, 1988"
```

```
BEFORE GROUP OF CustomerName
   SKIP TO TOP OF PAGE
   PRINT COLUMN 20, "Customer: ", CustomerName
   SKIP 2 LINES
   PRINT "Order#", COLUMN 20, "Overdue amount"
   SKIP 1 LINE
ON EVERY ROW
   PRINT OrderId, COLUMN 20, (TotalCost - Paid)
AFTER  GROUP OF CustomerName
   SKIP 1 LINE
   PRINT "Total Due:", GROUP TOTAL OF (TotalCost-Paid)
ON LAST ROW
   SKIP TO TOP OF PAGE
   PRINT SKIP 3,"Number of Accounts:", COUNT CustomerName
   PRINT SKIP 1,"Report Total     :", TOTAL   OF (TotalCost-
Paid)
   PRINT SKIP 1,"Average amount due:", AVERAGE OF (TotalCost-
Paid)
END
```

The FORMAT section can be broken down as follows:

PAGE HEADER clause	Defines a heading for each page of the report.
BEFORE GROUP OF clause	Defines a heading for each customer in the report.
ON EVERY ROW clause	Defines the report's detail lines, or what information will be taken from each individual row of the table and placed on each individual row of the report. In this example, the order number and the amount owed for each order selected is reported from the table.
AFTER GROUP OF clause	Generates the required summary for each customer—the total amount owed for all records with the same CustomerName. For this report to work properly, the SELECT statement must have the ORDER BY clause to ensure that the data is sorted by CustomerName.
ON LAST ROW clause	Generates the report summary: the number of customers in the report, the total amount owed, and the average amount owed. This is similar to the AFTER GROUP OF clause, except it operates on all records found by the SELECT statement.

This report produces the output shown in figure B-3.

```
Overdue Accounts for Fiscal September, 1988

Customer: BTS

Order#              Overdue amount

33241              $  23.00
47688              $ 247.00

Total Due:         $ 270.00
                                                    Page 1
```

```
Overdue Accounts for Fiscal September, 1988

Customer: SPB

Order#              Overdue amount

01138              $ 381.45
04587              $1347.03

Total Due:         $1728.48
                                                    Page 2
```

```
Overdue Accounts for Fiscal September, 1988

Number of Accounts: 2

Report Total      : $1998.48

Average amount due: $ 999.24
                                                    Page 3
```

Figure B-3.

Early attempts at relational databases resulted in the development of special programming languages. These languages generally offered most of the following:

1. A proprietary query language, often more set oriented and based on the entity-relationship model. (If you don't know what this means, don't worry. Most people are better off not knowing what model their database management system uses.)

2. Limited general computing functions.

3. An integrated dictionary. This means the program can directly access by name the tables and fields defined in the dictionary and get their attributes (such as size and type).

4. Report writers for formatted output.

5. Forms packages for adding and editing data.

Some implementations, such as dBASE SQL, are directly based on SQL. The addition of SQL to dBSAE IV presents a very sophisticated database management system. The range of tools available in traditional languages and the runtime efficiency of dBASE IV make this approach attractive, particularly for complex input and update. However, these types of languages are not recommended for the output and report side of things: it is generally accepted that report writers and 4GLs are much easier to use and require much less development time.

Large corporations are under great pressure to capture more information about their enterprises in databases and produce very accurate and up-to-date analysis at short notice. The ability to formulate ad hoc queries without going through the traditional program development cycle is a major attraction of SQL. Thus, a working knowledge of SQL is a valuable skill for many business professionals. This appendix can't cover the entirety of SQL, but I hope it demonstrates that the basic concepts are easy to understand and shows that the basic simplicity of the tools available do not demand traditional programming skills.

dBASE IV Command and Function Abbreviations

All commands and functions in dBASE IV can be rewritten as four-letter commands and functions. This is a shorthand that provides for somewhat faster compiling and processing of your program files. You can use these four-letter command and function equivalents at the dBASE prompt, although you will never notice the difference in execution times. The commands and functions are listed alphabetically. Note that some commands and functions, such as ABS( ) and GOTO, can't be abbreviated.

Command/ Function	Abbreviation	Command/ Function	Abbreviation
ABS	ABS	ATN2	ATN2
ACCEPT	ACCE	AUTOSAVE	AUTO
ACOS	ACOS	AVERAGE	AVER
ACTIVATE	ACTI	AVG	AVG
ALIAS	ALIA	BAR	BAR
ALL	ALL	BEFORE	BEFO
ALTERNATE	ALTE	BEGIN	BEGI
APPEND	APPE	BELL	BELL
APPLICATION	APPL	BLANK	BLAN
ARRAY	ARRA	BLOCKSIZE	BLOC
ASC	ASC	BOF	BOF
ASIN	ASIN	BOTTOM	BOTT
ASSIST	ASSI	BOX	BOX
AT	AT	BROWSE	BROW
ATAN	ATAN	CALL	CALL

CANCEL	CANC	DEVICE	DEVI
CARRIAGE	CARR	DIFFERENCE	DIFF
CASE	CASE	DIRECTORY	DIRE
CATALOG	CATA	DISKSPACE	DISK
CDOW	CDOW	DISPLAY	DISP
CEILING	CEIL	DMY	DMY
CENTURY	CENT	DO	DO
CHANGE	CHAN	DOHISTORY	DOHI
CHR	CHR	DOS	DOS
CLEAR	CLEA	DOUBLE	DOUB
CLOSE	CLOS	DOW	DOW
CMONTH	CMON	DROP	DROP
COL	COL	DTOC	DTOC
COLOR	COLO	DTOR	DTOR
COMMAND	COMM	DTOS	DTOS
COMPILE	COMP	ECHO	ECHO
CONTINUE	CONT	EDIT	EDIT
CONVERT	CONV	EGA2	EGA2
COPY	COPY	EGA4	EGA4
COS	COS	EJECT	EJECT
COUNT	COUN	ELSE	ELSE
CREATE	CREA	ENCRYPTION	ENCR
CTOD	CTOD	END	END
DATA	DATA	ENDCASE	ENDC
DATE	DATE	ENDDO	ENDD
DAY	DAY	ENDIF	ENDI
DBCHECK	DBCH	ENDPRINTJOB	ENDP
DBDEFINE	DBDE	ENDSCAN	ENDS
DBF	DBF	ENDTEXT	ENDT
DEACTIVATE	DEAC	ENVIRONMENT	ENVI
DEBUG	DEBU	EOF	EOF
DECIMALS	DECI	ERASE	ERAS
DECLARE	DECL	ERROR	ERRO
DEFAULT	DEFA	ESCAPE	ESCA
DEFINE	DEFI	EXACT	EXAC
DELETE	DELE	EXCLUSIVE	EXCL
DELIMITERS	DELI	EXIT	EXIT

EXP	EXP	INKEY	INKE
EXPORT	EXPO	INPUT	INPU
EXTERNAL	EXTE	INSERT	INSE
FETCH	FETC	INSTRUCTION	INST
FIELD	FIEL	INT	INT
FILE	FILE	INTEGER	INTE
FILL	FILL	INTO	INTO
FILTER	FILT	ISALPHA	INSA
FIND	FIND	ISCOLOR	INSO
FIXED	FIXE	ISLOWER	ISLO
FKLABEL	FKLA	ISMARKED	ISMA
FKMAX	FKMA	ISUPPER	ISUP
FLOAT	FLOA	JOIN	JOIN
FLOCK	FLOC	KEY	KEY
FLOOR	FLOO	LABEL	LABE
FOR	FOR	LASTKEY	LAST
FOUND	FOUN	LEFT	LEFT
FREE	FREE	LEN	LEN
FROM	FROM	LIKE	LIKE
FULL	FULL	LINENO	LINE
FUNCTION	FUNC	LIST	LIST
FV	FV	LKSYS	LKSY
FRAMEWORK2	FW2	LOAD	LOAD
GETENV	GETE	LOCATE	LOCA
GETS	GETS	LOCK	LOCK
GO	GO	LOG	LOG
GOTO	GOTO	LOGOUT	LOGO
GRANT	GRAN	LOOKUP	LOOK
HEADER	HEAD	LOOP	LOOP
HEIGHT	HEIG	LOWER	LOWE
HELP	HELP	LTRIM	LTRI
HISTORY	HIST	LUPDATE	LUDA
HOUR	HOUR	MACRO	MACRO
IF	IF	MARGIN	MARG
IIF	IIF	MARK	MARK
IMPORT	IMPO	MASTER	MAST
INDEX	INDE	MAX	MAX

MDX	MDX	PRECISION	PREC
MDY	MDY	PRINTER	PRIN
MEMLINES	MEML	PRIVATE	PRIV
MEMORY	MEMO	PROCEDURE	PROC
MENU	MENU	PROMPT	PROM
MESSAGE	MESS	PROTECT	PROT
MIN	MIN	PROW	PROW
MLINE	MLIN	PUBLIC	PUBL
MOD	MOD	PV	PV
MODIFY	MODI	QUERY	QUER
MONOCHROME	MONO	QUIT	QUIT
MONTH	MONT	RAND	RAND
MOVE	MOVE	RANGE	RANG
NDX	NDX	READ	READ
NEAR	NEAR	RECALL	RECA
NETWORK	NETW	RECCOUNT	RECC
NOMENU	NOME	RECNO	RECN
NOTE	NOTE	RECORD	RECO
ODOMETER	ODOM	RECSIZE	RECS
OFF	OFF	REDO	REDO
ON	ON	REFRESH	REFR
ORDER	ORDE	REINDEX	REIN
OS	OS	RELATION	RELA
OTHERWISE	OTHE	RELEASE	RELE
PACK	PACK	RENAME	RENA
PAD	PAD	REPLACE	REPL
PAGE	PAGE	REPORT	REPO
PARAMETERS	PARA	REPROCESS	REPR
PATH	PATH	RESET	RESE
PAUSE	PAUS	RESTORE	REST
PAYMENT	PAYM	RESUME	RESU
PCOL	PCOL	RETRY	RETR
PFS	PFS	RETURN	RETU
PI	PI	REVOKE	REVOKE
PICTURE	PICT	RIGHT	RIGH
POINT	POIN	RLOCK	RLOC
POPUP	POPU	ROLLBACK	ROLL

ROW	ROW	TABLE	TABL
RPD	RPD	TAG	TAG
RTOD	RTOD	TALK	TALK
RTRIM	RTRI	TAN	TAN
RUN	RUN	TEXT	TEXT
RUNSTATUS	RUNS	TIME	TIME
SAFETY	SAFE	TITLE	TITL
SAVE	SAVE	TO	TO
SCAN	SCAN	TOP	TOP
SCOREBOARD	SCOR	TOTAL	TOTA
SCREEN	SCRE	TRANSFORM	TRAN
SDF	SDF	TRAP	TRAP
SEEK	SEEK	TRIM	TRIM
SELECT	SELE	TYPE	TYPE
SEPARATOR	SEPA	UNIQUE	UNIQ
SET	SET	UNLOCK	UNLO
SHOW	SHOW	UPDATE	UPDA
SIGN	SIGN	UPPER	UPPE
SIN	SIN	USE	USE
SKIP	SKIP	USER	USER
SORT	SORT	VAL	VAL
SOUNDEX	SOUN	VARREAD	VARR
SPACE	SPAC	VERSION	VERS
SQL	SQL	VIEW	VIEW
SQRT	SQRT	WAIT	WAIT
START	STAR	WHILE	WHIL
STATUS	STAT	WIDTH	WIDT
STEP	STEP	WINDOW	WINDOW
STOP	STOP	WITH	WITH
STORE	STOR	WK1	WK1
STR	STR	YEAR	YEAR
STRUCTURE	STRU	ZAP	ZAP
STUFF	STUF		
SUBSTR	SUBS		
SUM	SUM		
SUSPEND	SUSP		
SYNONYM	SYNO		

Menu Maps

This appendix is a guide to users who want to dispense with the menu system and directly enter commands at the dBASE prompt. Note that not all menu items have command equivalents, and some menu options must be entered as strings of commands and not as a single command.

Assist Menu Map

Catalog

Use a different catalog	`SET CATALOG TO ?`
⟨create⟩	`SET CATALOG TO new filename`
Modify catalog name	`RENAME old filename TO new filename`

Edit description of catalog	`** command string`
	`USE CATALOG.CAT`
	`LOCATE filename`
	`EDIT`
	`** end command string`

Add file to catalog	`SET CATALOG TO filename`
	`USE/CREATE database`
	`MODIFY STRUCTURE`
	`MODIFY COMMAND`
	`MODIFY/CREATE query`
	`MODIFY/CREATE report`
	`MODIFY/CREATE label`

| | MODIFY/CREATE *screen* |
| | MODIFY/CREATE *application* |

Remove highlighted file	** command string
	SET CATALOG TO *filename*
	LOCATE *filename*
	DELETE
	PACK
	** end command string

Change description of	** command string
highlighted file	SET CATALOG TO *filename*
	LOCATE *filename*
	EDIT

Tools

Macros

Begin recording	[Shift-F10] B
End recording	Cancel: [Shift-F10] C
	End: [Shift-F10] E
Append to macro	No equivalent command
Insert user-input break	[Shift-F10] I
Modify	No equivalent command
Name	No equivalent command
Copy	No equivalent command
Play	No equivalent command
Talk	No equivalent command
Load library	RESTORE MACROS FROM *filename*
Save library	SAVE MACROS TO *filename*

Import

Rapidfile	IMPORT FROM *filename* RPD
dBASE II	IMPORT FROM *filename* dBASEII
Framework II	IMPORT FROM *filename* FW2
Lotus 1-2-3	IMPORT FROM *filename* WK1
PFS:FILE	IMPORT FROM *filename* PFS

Export

Rapidfile	EXPORT TO *filename* RPD
	COPY TO *filename* RPD
dBASE II	EXPORT TO *filename* dBASEII
	COPY TO *filename* dBASEII
Framework II	EXPORT TO *filename* FW2
	COPY TO *filename* FW2
Lotus 1-2-3	EXPORT TO *filename* WK1
	COPY TO *filename* WKS

VisiCalc	`COPY TO` *filename* `DIF`
PFS:FILE	`EXPORT TO` *filename* `PFS`
Multiplan	`COPY TO` *filename* `SYLK`
Text fixed-length fields	`COPY TO` *filename* `SDF`
Blank delimited	`COPY TO` *filename* `DELIMITED WITH BLANK`
Character delimited	`COPY TO` *filename* `DELIMITED WITH` *character*
	`COPY TO` *filename* `DELIMITED`

DOS Utilities	*See DOS Utilities Menu listings*
Protect Data	*No command equivalents*
Settings	*See Settings Menu listings*

Exit

Exit to dot prompt	*No equivalent command*
Quit to DOS	`QUIT`

Data Column Options

⟨create⟩	`CREATE` *database*
Use file	`USE` *database*
Modify structure/order	`MODIFY STRUCTURE`
Display data	`DISPLAY ALL`
Close file	`USE` `CLOSE DATABASE`

Queries Column create	`CREATE/MODIFY` *query* `CREATE/MODIFY` *view*
Forms Column create	`CREATE/MODIFY` *screen*
Reports Column create	`CREATE/MODIFY` *report*
Labels Column create	`CREATE/MODIFY` *label*

Applications Column create

dBASE program	`MODIFY COMMAND`

MODIFY FILE *filename*

Applications Generator   **CREATE/MODIFY** *application*

Database Menu Map

Layout

    Print database structure   `DISPLAY STRUCTURE TO PRINT`
                                       `LIST STRUCTURE TO PRINT`

    Edit database description   `** command sequence,`
                                       `** assumes active catalog`
                                       `** file`
                                       `SELECT 10`
                                       `LOCATE FOR FILENAME = `*filename*
                                       `EDIT TITLE`
                                       `SELECT `*previous work area*
                                       `** end of commands`

    Save this database file structure `[Ctrl-W]`
                                         `[Ctrl-End]`
                                         `[Ctrl-Return]`

Organize

    Create new index   `INDEX ON `*expression*` TAG `*tag name*
                                                 `OF `*mdx file*
                                       `INDEX ON `*expression*` TO `*ndx file*

    Modify existing index   `INDEX ON `*expression*` TAG `*tag name*
                                                 `OF `*mdx file*
                                       `INDEX ON `*expression*` TO `*ndx file*

    Order records by index   `SET ORDER TO TAG `*tag name*` OF `*mdx*
                                                 file
                                       `SET ORDER TO `*ndx file*
                                       `SET INDEX TO TAG `*tag name*` OF `*mdx*
                                                 file
                                       `SET INDEX TO `*ndx file*

    Activate .NDX index file   `SET INDEX TO `*ndx file*

    Include .NDX index file   `SET INDEX TO ORDER `*ndx file*

    Remove unwanted index tag   `DELETE TAG `*tag name*` OF `*mdx file*
                                       `DELETE TAG `*ndx file*

    Sort database on field list   `SORT ON `*field list*` TO `*target*

Unmark all records	`RECALL ALL`
Erase marked records	`PACK`

Append

Enter records from keyboard	`APPEND`
Append records from dBASE file	`APPEND FROM` *filename*

Copy records from non-dBASE file

Rapidfile	`APPEND FROM` *filename* `RPD`
dBASE II	`APPEND FROM` *filename* `dBASEII`
Framework II	`APPEND FROM` *filename* `FW2`
Lotus 1-2-3	`APPEND FROM` *filename* `WK1`
VisiCalc	`APPEND FROM` *filename* `DIF`
Multiplan	`APPEND FROM` *filename* `SYLK`
Text fixed-length fields	`APPEND FROM` *filename* `SDF`
Blank delimited	`APPEND FROM` *filename* `DELIMITED WITH BLANK`
Character delimited	`APPEND FROM` *filename* `DELIMITED WITH` *character*

Goto — No command equivalents

Exit

Save changes and exit	[Ctrl-W] [Ctrl-End] [Ctrl-Return]
Abandon changes and exit	[Ctrl-Q] [Esc]

Query Menu Map

Layout

Add file to query	`** command sequence`
	`USE database`
	`SET FILTER TO condition`
	`** end command sequence`

Remove file from query	No command equivalent
Create link by pointing	`SET RELATION TO field INTO alias`

Write view as database file	`** command sequence`
	`USE database`
	`SET FILTER TO condition`
	`COPY TO new file`
	`** end command sequence`

Edit description of query	`** command sequence,`
	`** assumes active catalog`
	`** file`
	`SELECT 10`
	`LOCATE FOR alias = filename`
	`EDIT TITLE`
	`SELECT original work area`
	`** end command sequence`

Save this query	`[Ctrl-Enter]`
	`[Ctrl-End]`
	`[Ctrl-W]`

Fields

Add field to view	No command equivalent
Remove field from view	No command equivalent
Edit field name	No command equivalent
Create calculated field	No command equivalent

Sort on this field	`INDEX ON field TAG tag name OF mdx`
	`          file`
	`INDEX ON field TO ndx file`
	`SORT ON field TO new file`

Include indexes	SET INDEX TO ORDER *tag name* OF *mdx file* SET INDEX TO *ndx file*

Condition

Add condition box	SET FILTER TO *condition*
Delete condition box	SET FILTER TO
Show condition box	No command equivalent

Update

Perform the update	REPLACE *field1* WITH *expression1*, *field2* WITH *condition2,...* UPDATE ON *keyfield* FROM *alias* REPLACE *field1* WITH *condition1*, *field2* WITH *condition2,...*
Specify update operation	
Replace values in database	REPLACE *field1* WITH *condition1*, *field2* WITH *condition2,...* FOR *condition*
Append records to database	APPEND FROM *file* FOR *condition*
Mark records for deletion	DELETE FOR *condition*
Unmark records in database	RECALL FOR *condition*

Exit

Save changes and exit	[Ctrl-W] [Ctrl-Enter] [Ctrl-End]
Abandon changes and exit	[Ctrl-Q] [Esc]

Screen Forms Menu Map

Layout

Quick layout	`EDIT`

Box
- Single line   `@ x,y TO z,t`
- Double line   `@ x,y TO z,t DOUBLE`
- Using specified character   `@ x,y TO z,t PANEL character`

Line
- Single line   `@ x,y TO z,t`
- Double line   `@ x,y TO z,t DOUBLE`
- Using specified character   `@ x,y TO z,t PANEL character`

Use different database file or view   `USE database`

Edit description of form

```
** command sequence,
** assumes active catalog
** file
SELECT 10
LOCATE FOR FILE_NAME = filename
EDIT TITLE
SELECT 1
** end command sequence
```

Save this form

```
[Ctrl-Enter]
[Ctrl-End]
[Ctrl-W]
```

Fields

Add field

```
@ x,y GET field name PICTURE
      expression RANGE low,
      high VALID condition
      ERROR message WHEN
      condition DEFAULT
      expression MESSAGE
      expression
```

⟨create⟩

```
** command sequence
memory variable = expression
@ x,y GET memory variable PICTURE
      expression RANGE low,
```

527

	high **VALID** *condition* **ERROR** *message* **WHEN** *condition* **DEFAULT** *expression* **MESSAGE** *expression* ****** end command sequence
Remove field	No command equivalent
Modify field	@ *x,y* **GET** *field name* **PICTURE** *expression* **RANGE** *low,* *high* **VALID** *condition* **ERROR** *message* **WHEN** *condition* **DEFAULT** *expression* **MESSAGE** *expression*
Insert memory variable	@ *x,y* **GET** *memory variable* **PICTURE** *expression* **RANGE** *low,* *high* **VALID** *condition* **ERROR** *message* **WHEN** *condition* **DEFAULT** *expression* **MESSAGE** *expression*
Words	
Style	No command equivalents
Display	**SET COLOR OF FIELDS TO** *color code* **SET COLOR TO** *standard color code, color code, background color code*
Position	No command equivalents
Modify ruler	No command equivalents
Hide ruler	No command equivalents
Enable automatic indent	No command equivalents
Add line	No command equivalents
Remove line	No command equivalents
Insert page break	No command equivalents

Write/Read text file   No command equivalents

Goto   No command equivalents

Exit

Save changes and exit   [Ctrl-W]
                                 [Ctrl-End]
                                 [Ctrl-Enter]

Abandon changes and exit   [Ctrl-Q]
                                 [Esc]

Report Forms Menu Map

Layout

Quick layouts
Column layout — `LIST`

Form layout —
```
** command sequence,
** READ statements must
** not be in the format
** file when this code
** is executed.
SET DEVICE TO PRINT
*
SCAN
 DO format file
 EJECT
ENDSCAN
** end command sequence
```

Mailmerge layout — No command equivalent

Box
Single line — `@ x,y TO z,t`
Double line — `@ x,y TO z,t DOUBLE`
Using specified character — `@ x,y TO z,t PANEL character`

Line
Single line — `@ x,y TO z,t`
Double line — `@ x,y TO z,t DOUBLE`
Using specified character — `@ x,y TO z,t PANEL character`

Use different database file or view — `USE database`

Edit description of report —
```
** command sequence,
** assumes active catalog
** file
SELECT 10
LOCATE FOR FILE_NAME = filename
EDIT TITLE
SELECT 1
** end command sequence
```

Save this report —
```
[Ctrl-Enter]
[Ctrl-End]
[Ctrl-W]
```

Fields	No command equivalents
Bands	
Add a group band	No command equivalents
Remove group	No command equivalents
Modify group	No command equivalents
Group intro on each page	No command equivalents
Open all bands	No command equivalents
Begin band on new page	No command equivalents
Word wrap band	_WRAP = *condition*
Text pitch for band	_PPITCH = *expression*
Quality print for band	_PQUALITY = *condition*
Spacing of lines for band	_PSPACING = *expression*
Page heading in report intro	No command equivalents
Words	
Style	No command equivalents
Display	SET COLOR OF FIELDS TO *color code* SET COLOR TO *standard color code,* *color code, background* *color code*
Position	No command equivalents
Modify ruler	No command equivalents
Hide ruler	No command equivalents
Enable automatic indent	No command equivalents
Add line	No command equivalents
Remove line	No command equivalents

Insert page break	No command equivalents
Write/Read text file	No command equivalents
Goto	No command equivalents
Print	
Begin printing	*command* TO PRINT
Eject page now	EJECT
View report on screen	REPORT FORM *filename*
Use print form	_PFORM = *filename*
Save settings to print form	No command equivalents
Destination	
Write to printer	*command* TO PRINT
	SET PRINTER TO PRN
Write to DOS file	*command* TO FILE *filename*
	SET PRINTER TO FILE *filename*
Name of DOS file	*command* TO FILE *filename*
	SET PRINTER TO FILE *filename*
Printer model	_PDRIVER = *filename*
Echo to screen	SET ECHO OFF
Control of printer	
Text pitch	_PPITCH = "*expression*"
Quality print	_PQUALITY = "*expression*"
New page	_PEJECT = "*expression*"
Wait between pages	_PWAIT = *condition*
Advance page using	_PADVANCE = "*expression*"
Starting control codes	_PSCODE = *expression*
Ending control codes	_PECODE = *expression*
Output options	
Begin on page	_PAGENO = *expression*
End after page	_PEPAGE = *expression*
First page number	_PBPAGE = *expression*
Number of copies	_PCOPIES = *expression*
Page dimensions	
Length of page	_PLENGTH = *expression*
Offset from left	_PLOFFSET = *expression*
Spacing of lines	_PSPACING = *expression*

Exit

Save changes and exit	[Ctrl-W] [Ctrl-End] [Ctrl-Enter]
Abandon changes and exit	[Ctrl-Q] [Esc]

Labels Menu Map

Layout

    Use different database file or view

    `USE database`

    Edit description of report

```
** command sequence,
** assumes active catalog
** file
SELECT 10
LOCATE FOR FILE_NAME = filename
EDIT TITLE
SELECT 1
** end command sequence
```

    Save this label design

    [Ctrl-Enter]
    [Ctrl-End]
    [Ctrl-W]

Dimensions

    No command equivalents

Fields

    No command equivalents

Words

    Style

    No command equivalents

    Display

```
SET COLOR OF FIELDS TO color code
SET COLOR TO standard color code,
            color code, background
            color code
```

    Position

    No command equivalents

    Modify ruler

    No command equivalents

    Hide ruler

    No command equivalents

    Enable automatic indent

    No command equivalents

    Add line

    No command equivalents

    Remove line

    No command equivalents

    Insert page break

    No command equivalents

Write/Read text file	No command equivalents
Goto	No command equivalents
Print	
Begin printing	*command* TO PRINT
Eject page now	EJECT
View report on screen	REPORT FORM *filename*
Use print form	_PFORM = *filename*
Save settings to print form	No command equivalents
Destination	
Write to printer	*command* TO PRINT
	SET PRINTER TO PRN
Write to DOS file	*command* TO FILE *filename*
	SET PRINTER TO FILE *filename*
Name of DOS file	*command* TO FILE *filename*
	SET PRINTER TO FILE *filename*
Printer model	_PDRIVER = *filename*
Echo to screen	SET ECHO OFF
Control of printer	
Text pitch	_PPITCH = "*expression*"
Quality print	_PQUALITY = "*expression*"
New page	_PEJECT = "*expression*"
Wait between pages	_PWAIT = *condition*
Advance page using	_PADVANCE = "*expression*"
Starting control codes	_PSCODE = *expression*
Ending control codes	_PECODE = *expression*
Output options	
Begin on page	_PAGENO = *expression*
End after page	_PEPAGE = *expression*
First page number	_PBPAGE = *expression*
Number of copies	_PCOPIES = *expression*
Page dimensions	
Length of page	_PLENGTH = *expression*
Offset from left	_PLOFFSET = *expression*
Spacing of lines	_PSPACING = *expression*

Exit

Save changes and exit	[Ctrl-W] [Ctrl-End] [Ctrl-Enter]
Abandon changes and exit	[Ctrl-Q] [Esc]

Applications Menu Map

dBASE program	*See Editor Menu Map*
Applications Generator	No command equivalents

DOS Utilities Menu Map

DOS

Perform DOS command	`! `*`command`*
Go to DOS	`! `*`command`*
Set default drive:directory	`SET DEFAULT TO `*`drive`* `! CD\`*`directory`*

Files

Change drive:directory	`SET DEFAULT TO `*`drive`* `SET PATH TO `*`path`*
Display only	`! DIR `*`file skeleton`* `DIR ON `*`drive`*` LIKE `*`path\file`* *`skeleton`*

Sort
  Name   No command equivalent
  Extension   No command equivalent
  Date and time   No command equivalent
  Size   No command equivalent

Mark
  Mark all   No command equivalent
  Unmark all   No command equivalent
  Reverse marks   No command equivalent

Delete
  Single file   `DELETE FILE `*`filename`*
                      `ERASE `*`filename`*
  Marked files   No command equivalent
  Displayed files   No command equivalent

Copy
  Single file   `COPY FILE `*`source`*` TO `*`target`*
                      `! COPY `*`source target`*
                      `COPY TO `*`target`*
                      `USE `*`database`*
  Marked files   No command equivalent
  Displayed files   No command equivalent

Move
    Single file   No command equivalent
    Marked files   No command equivalent
    Displayed files   No command equivalent

Rename
    Single file   **RENAME** *old name* **TO** *new name*
                            ! REN *old name new name*

    Marked files   No command equivalent
    Displayed files   No command equivalent

View   **TYPE** *filename*
                            ! TYPE *filename*

Edit   See *Editor Menu command*

Exit   No command equivalents

Settings Menu Map

Options

Bell	SET BELL OFF/on
Carry	SET CARRY OFF/on
Century	SET CENTURY OFF/on
Confirm	SET CONFIRM OFF/ON
Date order	SET DATE *convention*
Date separator	SET MARK TO *character*
Decimal places	SET DECIMALS TO *n* SET FIXED TO *n*
Deleted	SET DELETED OFF/on
Exact	SET EXACT OFF/on
Exclusive	SET EXCLUSIVE OFF/on
Instruct	SET INSTRUCT off/ON
Margin	SET MARGIN TO *n*
Memo width	SET MEMOWIDTH TO *n*
Safety	SET SAFETY off/ON
Talk	SET TALK off/ON
Trap	SET TRAP OFF/on

Display

Display mode	SET DISPLAY TO *monitor type*
Standard	
All	SET COLOR TO *color code*
Normal text	SET COLOR OF NORMAL TO *color codes*
Messages	SET COLOR OF MESSAGES TO *color codes*

Titles	SET COLOR OF TITLES TO *color codes*
Enhanced	
All	SET COLOR TO *standard, color code*
Highlight	SET COLOR OF HIGHLIGHT TO *color codes*
Boxes	SET COLOR OF BOXES TO *color codes*
Information	SET COLOR OF INFORMATION TO *color codes*
Fields	SET COLOR OF FIELDS TO *color codes*
Perimeter of Screen	SET COLOR TO *standard, enhanced, color code*
Exit	No command equivalent

Editor Menu Map

Layout

    Modify a different file

        `MODIFY FILE filename`
        `MODIFY COMMAND command filename`

    Save this file

        [Ctrl-End]
        [Ctrl-W]
        [Ctrl-Return]

Words

    Style   No command equivalents

    Display   `SET COLOR OF FIELDS TO color code`
        `SET COLOR TO standard color code,`
                `color code, background`
                `color code`

    Position   No command equivalents

    Modify ruler   No command equivalents

    Hide ruler   No command equivalents

    Enable automatic indent   No command equivalents

    Add line   No command equivalents

    Remove line   No command equivalents

    Insert page break   No command equivalents

    Write/Read text file   No command equivalents

Goto   No command equivalents

Print

    Begin printing   No command equivalent

    Eject page now   `EJECT`
        `_PEJECT =`
             `"expression"`

Line numbers	No command equivalent
Use print form	`_PFORM = `*filename*
Save settings to print form	No command equivalent
Destination	
Write to printer	*command* `TO PRINT` `SET PRINTER TO PRN`
Write to DOS file	*command* `TO FILE `*filename* `SET PRINTER TO FILE `*filename*
Name of DOS file	*command* `TO FILE `*filename* `SET PRINTER TO FILE `*filename*
Printer model	`_PDRIVER = `*filename*
Echo to screen	`SET ECHO OFF`
Control of printer	
Text pitch	`_PPITCH = "`*expression*`"`
Quality print	`_PQUALITY = "`*expression*`"`
New page	`_PEJECT = "`*expression*`"`
Wait between pages	`_PWAIT = `*condition*
Advance page using	`_PADVANCE = "`*expression*`"`
Starting control codes	`_PSCODE = `*expression*
Ending control codes	`_PECODE = `*expression*
Output options	
Begin on page	`_PAGENO = `*expression*
End after page	`_PEPAGE = `*expression*
First page number	`_PBPAGE = `*expression*
Number of copies	`_PCOPIES = `*expression*
Page dimensions	
Length of page	`_PLENGTH = `*expression*
Offset from left	`_PLOFFSET = `*expression*
Spacing of lines	`_PSPACING = `*expression*
Exit	
Save changes and exit	[Ctrl-W] [Ctrl-End] [Ctrl-Enter]
Abandon changes and exit	[Ctrl-Q] [Esc]

Index

80386 (supermicro) computer
architecture, 12
dBASE IV use on, 17
@ before Picture function to
introduce actions, 166
& to create macro substitutions,
292
⟨create⟩
for calculated field, 162–63
command in Assist system to
design full applications, 453
as default in Data column, 70,
86
from Design menu to create a
pop-up menu, 470
from Forms column to access
screen design work space,
126, 128
Query column option, 327

A

Accounting as a "fixed digit
application," 97
Append mode, entering, 199
Applications created with the
Applications Generator
Browse capability for users
selected for, 471–73
dBASE IV code added to,
484–90
dBASE IV text editor to create
programs for, 490–96
DOS window created for,
478–79

Applications created with the
Applications Generator—cont
Edit menu generation for,
470–74
help text for, 468–70
linking menus for, 481–84
mail list, 499–503
Main menu generation for,
466–70
menu creation for, 455–60
menu design for, 455–56
opening comments for, 460–61
Queries menu generation for,
476–78
quitting to DOS from, 479–81
Reports menu generation for,
474–76
Utilities menu generation for,
478
Applications, dBASE IV
automatic generation with
Applications Generator of,
453–96
linked with library routines, 30
speeding up execution of,
443–44
Applications Generator, 453–96
code generation by the, 484
designing the application before
you use the, 454
mail list generator created by
the, 499–503
memory consumption by the,
454

Applications Generator—cont
modifying the development
environment with the,
461–65
problems of code created with
the, 55
three types of menus in the, 456
Archive flag, 401
Arithmetic mean, 361–63
ASCII character set displayed in
dBASE IV, 141
ASCII text
printing, 113
word processors read database
data in reports created with
LIST as, 282
Assist system. See Applications
Generator and Menus and
submenus, dBASE IV
AUTOEXEC.BAT file, starting
dBASE IV from the, 28
AUTOSAVE to commit a record
after changes, 197, 287
Average, calculating an, 361–63

B

Bar menus, 456, 466–67, 482–83
BASIC, 12
Batch menus, 456
Batch operations, 455–56
Bell frequency (tone) and duration
(length), 463
Box
to enclose memo field, 163–64
as form border, 136–37